THE MODERN AFRICAN AMERICAN POLITICAL THOUGHT READER

The Modern African American Political Thought Reader compiles the work of great African American political thinkers throughout the twentieth century and up through today to show the development of black political thought and trace the interconnectedness of each person's ideas through their own words. From abolition, through civil rights, Black nationalism, radical feminism, neo-conservativism, and the new Black Moderate, Angela Jones has collected the key readings of the most important figures in black political history.

Each chapter includes an introduction to the themes of the chapter, a biographical sketch of the person profiled, and some of their greatest works, chosen to show the range of political subjects of interest to African Americans. From Radicals like Angela Y. Davis to Conservatives such as Michael Steele, this anthology showcases the diversity of political thought within the African American community. It is a must for anyone interested in African American history and politics.

Cutting through the "noise" of a new class of mainstream media pundits, *The Modern African American Political Thought Reader* provides a great social and intellectual service by connecting an illustrious past and present of African American thought production. The discourse, and the actions this discourse inspires, is an invaluable contribution to a much-needed delineation of the nuances within black historical and contemporary political thought. Most importantly, *The Modern African American Political Thought Reader* necessarily troubles our conception of "the" black community as a singular, unified entity. Instead, Jones' volume reveals the plurality and collisions of intellectual debate that are crucial to shaping a vital vision of African Americans with a linked destiny, but disparate strategies for achieving social justice.

Kimberly Springer, author of *Living for the Revolution: Black Feminist Organizations, 1968–1980*

Angela Jones is Assistant Professor of Sociology at Farmingdale State College, State University of New York.

D1518691

THE MODERN AFRICAN AMERICAN POLITICAL THOUGHT READER

FROM DAVID WALKER TO BARACK OBAMA

Edited by

ANGELA JONES

Routledge
Taylor & Francis Group

NEW YORK AND LONDON

First published 2013
by Routledge
711 Third Avenue, New York, NY 10017

Simultaneously published in the UK
by Routledge
2 Park Square, Milton Park, Abingdon, Oxon OX14 4RN

Routledge is an imprint of the Taylor & Francis Group, an informa business

© 2013 Taylor & Francis

Library of Congress Cataloging in Publication Data
Jones, Angela, 1978–
The modern African American political thought reader : from David Walker to Barack Obama / Angela Jones.
    p. cm.
    "Simultaneously published in the UK"—T.p. verso.
    Includes bibliographical references and index.
    ISBN: 978-0-415-89570-5 (hbk. : acid-free paper)—
    ISBN: 978-0-415-89573-6 (pbk. : acid-free paper)
    1. African Americans—Politics and government. 2. African Americans—Politics and government—Sources. 3. Political science—United States—History. 4. Political science—United States—History—Sources. I. Title.
    E185.J648 2012
    323.1196'073—dc23

ISBN: 978-0-415-89570-5 (hbk)
ISBN: 978-0-415-89573-6 (pbk)

Typeset in Minion
by Wearset Ltd, Boldon, Tyne and Wear

SFI Certified Sourcing
www.sfiprogram.org
SFI-00453

Printed and bound in the United States of America
by Edwards Brothers, Inc.

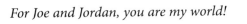
For Joe and Jordan, you are my world!

CONTENTS

INTRODUCTION

One does not learn, nor does one assist in the struggle, by standing on the sidelines, constantly complaining and criticizing. One learns by participating in the situation—listening, observing and then acting.

Shirley Chisholm

Praxis- n. related to action; in practice; the implementation of social theory.

The Modern African American Political Thought Reader is a comprehensive anthology of the speeches and writings of African American political leaders who have actively involved themselves in bringing about social change. All of the African American political thinkers included in the volume have at least held high rank within African American political organizations, if not been their founder, and in many cases have held or at least run (even if unsuccessfully) for political office. It is important that one distinction is clear from the outset. Most previously published anthologies of Black political thought focus on Black public intellectuals; this book takes a different approach.

The ideas of Black public intellectuals, most notably academics, are incredibly important for understanding Black experience. However, the production of discourse does not necessarily translate into political leadership. For example, if accustomed to the dominant approach to African American political thought, readers may be disappointed when reading about Black feminism to not find the writings of Patricia Hill Collins or bell hooks. In contemporary sections, others might be hoping to see Cornell West. While these brilliant intellectuals have adroitly helped us better understand Black experience, this book is about people who author ideas and are actively involved in praxis, in the implementation of the very ideas they espouse. As much as readers might love to read the polemical diatribes of Bill Cosby as exemplified in his famous "pound-cake speech"[1] in the section on conservative thought, this book is not just about ideas; it is about leadership. While many African American intellectuals, including individuals in this anthology, have made intriguing arguments about ontology and metaphysics, this is not a book about social theory; it is about political theory. *The Modern African American Political Thought Reader* focuses on African American political thought in praxis—that is to say, it examines political thought as it was utilized and continues to be utilized by various African Americans to improve the overall condition of life for Black folk.

The Modern African American Political Thought Reader has three basic objectives. First, its most modest aim is to present a comprehensive portrait of African American political thought and leadership from the nineteenth to twenty-first centuries through the presentation of primary source materials. The canon's treatment of African American leadership has been flippant at best. Scholarship on African American political leadership and popular discourse on Black leadership suffers from what I have previously conceptualized as *spotlight syndrome.*[2] We tend to celebrate the most charismatic figures in American history. In addition, as this book highlights, we tend to commemorate leaders who best adhered to cultural conservatism and advocated the policing of Black bodies through rigid moral codes.

Finally, patriarchy has marginalized women from the canon's presentation of African American political thought. This has interesting implications given that after extensive historical analysis this book posits that Black radical feminists have articulated incredibly radical positions in comparison to many of their more moderate counterparts. The marginalization of Black radical feminists can be explained when we consider that Black leaders who have maintained the most conservative to moderate political positions gained the most positive media attention and those that have articulated the most radical positions have either been publicly demonized or in the case of radical Black women, bastardized.

Most anthologies generally reduce nineteenth-century Black political thought to Frederick Douglass, at the expense of public figures such as Maria Stewart. Most reduce twentieth-century political thought to Booker T. Washington, W.E.B. Du Bois, Marcus Garvey, and Martin Luther King Jr. While these important figures are paid homage in this text readers also benefit from reading less celebrated figures such as: William Monroe Trotter, Bayard Rustin, Flo Kennedy, and Stokley Carmichael, just to name a few. Finally, the inclusion of Barack Obama allows readers to think about the development of African American political thought and leadership in the twenty-first century. Although the book covers many epochs of history readers are given the opportunity to chart the interconnectedness of the ideas espoused by all these leaders.

An additional aim of *The Modern African American Political Thought Reader* is to deconstruct the traditional linear portrait of African American political thought presented in most scholarly texts. Many volumes are limited in scope because they only focus on one particular framework or political paradigm such as civil rights or Black Nationalism, or Black Feminism. Others are problematic because while they present a longer timeline and more genres of thought they present them in a linear fashion. The linear portrait presented in most texts begins at the turn of twentieth century and promulgate that we witnessed the rise of conservative leadership under Booker T. Washington. Then the rise of W.E.B. Du Bois, followed by later civil rights advocates such as Martin Luther King ushered in a more radical platform. And finally these volumes generally culminate with a discussion of Black Power, as articulated by groups such as the Black Panther Party who exposed the moderate stance of the civil rights era and stood out as the most radical of Black leadership. The analyses presented in these texts, if available, merely compare genres or epochs. Many scholars offer the conclusion that Black Power was more radical than other previous eras. That approach seems

counterintuitive; each historical period came with different sets of structural opportunities that either thwarted or enhanced their ability to publicly articulate their ideas
and mobilize action. The goal of this book is to avoid this pitfall not surmounted by
most volumes on African American political thought. As Michael C. Dawson astutely
noted:

> It is ... critical to focus on the dynamic properties in the development of black political thought.
> For example, it is a mistake to try to understand the work of activists such as Du Bois and King
> as temporally coherent; we cannot assume that their ... work fits into the same philosophical
> framework. ... Consequently, historical specificity and nuance are important factors to account
> for when modeling contemporary black ideologies.[3]

Here, readers will find a more dynamic and fluid presentation of African American
political thought. This text covers abolitionist ideology, civil rights discourse, Black
Nationalism, Black radical feminism, Modern Black Conservatism, and the rise of
Black Moderatism in the twenty-first century. The unique goal of this text is to expose
the limitedness of a linear portrait of these schools of thought. There are conservatives, moderates, and radicals within each genre.

Finally, *The Modern African American Political Thought Reader* posits that in general
African American political thought has been far more conservative than the canon
chooses to acknowledge. In particular, readers will find cultural conservatism running
through every school of thought presented in this text, except Black radical feminism.
There are leaders from every other genre that spend copious time policing behavior
and attempting to refine Black behavior and sensibilities according to White bourgeois
standards—most often under the guise that this was the way a good Christian would
behave. Individual moral transformation and the building of good character will
demonstrate that you are worthy of rights. Because various leaders' political philosophies, views on capitalism or race have been radical we tend to gloss over the culturally
conservative ideology that runs through much of Black political thought. There is an
incredibly puritan and Victorian moral ethos that runs through a substantial portion
of their ideas.

African American political thought and Black leaders have consistently, with a few
exceptions (namely, Black Power activists and Black radical feminists) adhered to
what Evelyn Brooks Higginbotham called the *politics of respectability*. In *Righteous
Discontent: The Women's Movement in the Black Baptist Church, 1880–1920* (1993)
Higginbotham astutely analyzed the role that Black Baptist women played in early
struggles for Black liberation and women's rights. One of her main contentions was
that these women's strategic approach to gaining equality was actually quite conservative because they advanced the idea that in order to gain equality Black people
needed to adhere to Victorian, middle-class White cultural values. These church-
women, while empowered, denounced patronizing dance halls and the consumption
of jazz music. They told women to refrain from wearing newer more revealing fash-
ions and to adopt a conservative aesthetic. Through moral reform, cultural reform,
and a refinement of aesthetics Black people would demonstrate to White American
society that they were worthy of rights. This book draws heavily from Higginbotham's

ideas. Because Black leadership at large has adhered to the politics of respectability, African American political thought, generally speaking, has been far more conservative than commonly acknowledged.

People tend to see the rise of the "Black Neo-Cons" as a recent phenomenon. However, this argument is ahistorical. It neglects to understand that from Abolition to integration to Black Nationalism there have been conservative ideas running through much if not all of African American political thought. Alan Keyes, Michael Steele, and Clarence Thomas were not the first Black people to see large social welfare programs and race-based policies as crutches. They are not the first to argue for self-help. When scholars note the early presence of conservatism in Black political thought, it is generally acknowledged only in Booker T. Washington.

African American political thought has been far more in line with American liberalism than is commonly noted. Conservatives tend to adhere to traditional American liberalism, the classic Horatio Alger[4] tale that tells us that individuals make their own destiny. Conservatives have long since been telling us that poverty is caused by individual pathology and that adherence to the Protestant work ethic leads to success. American liberalism tells us that government intervention is not necessary. With self-sufficiency, independence, thrift, and hard work anyone can succeed in the American land of opportunity. We will see very clearly that this is what many African American leaders, from abolitionists to Black Nationalists, have been saying for years. The idea that the "Black Neo-Cons" have just made an appearance in the public sphere reveals a flippant account of African American political thought. The notable difference is that conservative ideas within the African American community and its leadership are as old as the Black public sphere; we are only more cognizant of them now because expanding media technologies have resulted in Black conservatives receiving more public attention. In addition, they also have risen to prominent positions in government and public life, which has given them more public exposure. African American political thought may have far more in common with the ideology championed by predominately White conservatives than we like to acknowledge.

Throughout this text you will find differences between the leader's ideological paradigms, which includes their articulation of the quagmires in need of remedy, strategic plans for resolution of these problems, views on White intervention in Black struggle, and their views on government intervention in Black liberation. The problems impacting Black folk have been born out of the specific historical period in which the leaders lived. Therefore, while battling racism broadly speaking was a primary focus of all the thinkers in this volume the mechanisms that buttress racism have changed, as did the strategies they adopted to fight racism. In addition, various Black leaders have labored arduously to demonstrate the interconnectedness of race, class, and gender in conditioning oppression. Despite their differences, all of the leaders in this book have an Afrocentric aim. All of the thinkers (even the ones flippantly reduced to privileged "Uncle Toms") speak from the standpoint of an African American in American society. And while this standpoint was certainly also conditioned by class, gender, and sexual orientation, the common thread between all these leaders and all these genres of thought is that they are the result of lived racial experience and a sincere desire to uplift Black people.

Part I: The Antebellum Era: The Rise of Abolitionism

In this first section readers are introduced to the ideas and works of David Walker, Maria Stewart, Frederick Douglass, and Anna Julia Cooper. These extraordinary political figures fought endlessly to bring an end to the genocide and horrific circumstances imposed upon Africans in the United States during the antebellum era. In addition, in all, we find spokespeople for the rights of women and other oppressed ethnic groups in the United States. Readers are encouraged to approach the reading of their work analytically. Each leader's ideas should be read in relation to other ideas of the period; their work should be read comparatively. Again, rather than comparing abolitionists to civil rights leaders, here, it is suggested that we compare the leaders within each genre itself. For example, while the most acclaimed leader in this chapter, Douglass, advocated democratic reform, David Walker was more radical by calling for revolt.

From one perspective all these abolitionists were radicals. Publicly demanding an end to slavery, one of the most oppressive and horrific institutions ever created, was certainly a radical act. However, when we consider the strategies offered for bringing about these ends we may want to consider that these leaders were far more conservative than they appeared at first judgment. All leaders in this section articulated varying degrees of cultural conservatism by urging self-help and moral transformation. All argued that religion should play a role in the struggle for emancipation. Maria Stewart probably argued the most vocally for utilizing religion as a means by which to acquire emancipation. By appealing to morality and Christian values, Whites could be convinced that the abolition of slavery was the only moral path for the future. Anna Julia Cooper fought for the rights of both Black people and women. Cooper was a pioneering feminist. However, she too utilized a conservative logic to buttress her arguments. She argued that women were inherently virtuous and morally superior and therefore could teach the nation about how it should proceed.

Was publicly demanding an end to slavery radical? Absolutely. However, with the exception of Walker, the strategic means offered to achieve these goals were quite conservative. It might be hasty to deem abolitionists radicals or conservatives. Instead, you will find that the ideas of abolitionists ranged from radical to moderate to conservative. For example, Walker might be categorized as a radical, Douglass a moderate, and Cooper conservative.

Part II: Reconstruction and Beyond: Debates over the Negro Problem and the Creation of Civil Rights Discourse

After Emancipation, the Black public sphere became inundated with debate and dialogue over what to do about the "Negro Problem," or the millions of newly freed slaves who were still persecuted and marginalized from the economic, political, and social spheres of life. As abolitionists had obviously primarily focused their objective goals on ending slavery, after Emancipation these goals had to change and debates surrounding civil rights emerged profoundly in the Black public sphere. This section chronicles the development of civil rights discourse and the ideas proposed as part of these public debates over the future and progress of African Americans. It includes: Alexander Crummell, Booker T. Washington, Ida B. Wells-Barnett, William Monroe Trotter, W.E.B. Du Bois, A. Philip Randolph, Bayard Rustin, Mary McLeod Bethune, and Martin Luther King Jr.

Interestingly, this section starts with the work and ideas of Alexander Crummell whose self-help ideology and gradualist approach came to influence Booker T. Washington, who most commonly receives the credit for authoring these ideas. Washington is probably one of the most poorly represented figures in African American history. He has been typecast as an Uncle Tom, an apologist for segregation, and a sycophant. Washington's ideas are generally juxtaposed with W.E.B. Du Bois's ideas and as a result classified as a conservative. Both leaders were far more moderate than generally noted. As Cary D. Wintz noted, "the differences between Du Bois and Washington, though substantial, were differences in degree rather than substance, differences in means rather than ends. Both men were committed to uplifting their race, instilling racial pride, and securing political and civil rights."[5] Let us be clear, Washington did not argue that segregation was permissible or ideal or that political and civil rights were not needed. The strategic plan he suggested was one of gradualism. He argued that once economic uplift was secured then African Americans would have the power to lay claim to civil rights.

All leaders in this chapter argued that African Americans required equal access to basic social institutions such as: the economy, education, housing, healthcare, and government. All saw education as pivotal to advancement. All agreed that integration was vital; disagreement lay in when integration should take place and within which institutions. However, the primary difference between these leaders lay in the strategies offered to acquire equal access to these institutions. The key point of contention between them was also in the role of the government in this goal. They debated strategy, specifically whether social change was best realized through self-help, democratic reform, and political agitation, direct action protest, or some combination of the above.

Interestingly, the most celebrated figures were the most culturally conservative figures and placed huge emphasis on cultural refinement and moral transformation, whereas the most neglected figures such as Trotter, Wells-Barnett, and Randolph reserved their attacks for structural quagmires such as poverty and saw government intervention and not self-help as the primary solution to the horrific problems facing African Americans. Bayard Rustin, who was an openly gay man, was one of the architects of the mid-twentieth century phase of the Civil Rights Movement. However, King was seen as a far better spokesman for the movement because the preacher was deemed more respectable. Figures such as Rustin stand out because of his attacks against homophobia, which given the historical era were radical. Again, readers will find conservatives, moderates, and radicals within this section. For example, William Monroe Trotter was a radical compared to Crummell. W.E.B. Du Bois, who is generally compared with Washington, is commonly seen as a radical, however, when placed in a wider context, he is best characterized as a moderate. Martin Luther King Jr, too, when compared with Bayard Rustin and A. Philip Randolph, was also far more moderate than popular discourse may note.

While the majority of the leaders in this section were politically moderate, there were still leaders that attempted to add a more radical perspective to the dominant political paradigm.

Part III: Black Nationalism: Its Roots and Development

This section chronicles the development of Black Nationalism. Unfortunately, Black Nationalism, too, has been reduced to a couple of key figures. Many students of African American history are generally led to believe that Black Nationalism began with Marcus Garvey and was most profoundly reshaped by Malcolm X. This section, while admittedly still not a complete portrait of every noteworthy Black Nationalist, gives a more comprehensive portrait of Black Nationalism. It spans two centuries and includes: Martin Delany, Henry McNeal Turner, Marcus Garvey, Malcolm X, Stokley Carmichael/Kwame Toure, and The Black Panthers, primarily its founders Huey P. Newton and Bobby Seale.

Black Nationalism is the general term given to a strand of Black political thought that stresses the importance of placing Afrocentrism at the center of the program for Black liberation. It is generally comprised of three branches: political nationalism, economic nationalism, and cultural nationalism.

Political nationalism originated as the ideology that African Americans require their own homeland or nation. Originally Black Nationalists such as Martin Delany and Henry McNeal Turner posited that it was essential to return to Africa and other nations in South and Central America where Black people could create an autonomous Black nation free from White colonialism and oppression. Political nationalism entailed separation. While most of the leaders in the previous section championed integration as the primary solution to the supposed Negro Problem, Black nationalists advocated separatism. This separation was twofold. First, it entailed a separate Black nation; this meant organizing and maintaining a separate Black state and government and other basic institutions such as businesses, housing, education, etc. It entailed the creation and maintenance of an independent Black public sphere. Second, political nationalism also meant social segregation; for leaders such as Marcus Garvey political nationalism also necessitated strong resistance against miscegenation and integrated race relations in the private sphere. Readers should note the contentious debates that emerged amongst these leaders over time over social separatism and the role that Whites might play in Black liberation. For example, Delany was skeptical of White involvement. In fact, this is why he opposed the emigration to Liberia. He posited that this idea originated in the American Colonization Society and with racist Whites who wanted to expel Blacks from the United States. Again, Black Nationalists such as Garvey staunchly opposed social integration. However, later, this was an issue that Malcolm X would waver on. In addition, the Black Panthers, while having no White members, were not opposed to working with White radical organizations such as the Weather Underground.[6]

Cultural nationalism suggests that African Americans need to become educated about, embrace, and celebrate their African heritage. Slavery stripped Black people of their culture; this was done to dehumanize Africans and thwart the solidarity fostered by cultural ties that might lead to insurrection. Reaffirming one's African identity and rekindling African cultural practices would foster unity and pride or *negritude*. It is interesting to note that while Black Nationalists such as Amiri Baraka, founder of the Black Arts Repertory Theatre and School, saw the development of a distinct Black aesthetic as important for fostering cultural pride within the Black community, members of the Black Panther Party such as Huey P. Newton called this "pork chop" nationalism. Consuming Black art, wearing a dashiki and/or eating so-called soul food would not lead to political liberation.

Cultural nationalism often included Pan-Africanism; this meant that the struggle of Black people in the United States should not be separated from the struggle of Black people globally. It is paramount that we note that Pan-Africanism was not just particular to Black Nationalists. Many Black leaders from David Walker to W.E.B. Du Bois to Claudia Jones emphasized the importance of a global struggle of Black people to overthrow colonialism and imperialist powers, oppressing Black people globally.

Economic nationalism suggests that Black people need to own and control the means of production, independent from White people. Black Nationalists encouraged Black owned businesses and put emphasis on cultivating black entrepreneurship and Black business networks. Black Nationalists have always posited that self-sufficiency and independence was important. Surprisingly, this idea is similar to the conservative ideology espoused by traditional American liberalism and which has become the benchmark of modern neo-liberal talking points. This means that if poverty is crushing the Black community, then the Black community needs to build itself up through economic and political self-sufficiency.

In fact, popular discourse, particularly as advanced by the media, has portrayed Malcolm X as one of the most radical revolutionary Black figures in American history. However, ideologically Malcolm was far more conservative than many realize. What his unapologetic racially charged diatribes may have masked is that Brother Malcolm advocated the curtailment of vices such as smoking, sex outside of marriage, drinking alcohol, etc. He advocated moral transformation and reform of the individual pathologies plaguing the Black community. This sentiment is quite conservative. In addition, the argument made by most Black Nationalists that change within the Black community needed to be fostered within the Black community and not by the government, was again a politically conservative ideal.

All Black Nationalists are not created equal; there is huge variation amongst Black Nationalists. Leaders of the Black Power movement moved away from these more conservative ideals by placing more emphasis on the need for structural transformation, particularly within the economy. For example, the Black Panthers were concerned with atrocities such as crime, mass incarceration, and drugs that plagued Black communities and were caused by the inevitable poverty that was the byproduct of capitalism. Many Black Power advocates ingeniously incorporated Black Marxism[7] into the Black Nationalist platform. They transformed economic nationalism by attacking the bourgeoisie's[8] control of the means of production and the alienation of all workers globally; although the bourgeoisie was almost all White, not all White people were part of the bourgeoisie. Therefore, the solution lied in a workers' revolution, a true proletariat[9] revolution to overthrow the bourgeoisie, not just a revolution compromised of Black people. However, because Black people constituted such a large portion of the lumpen-proletariat,[10] or the so-called "underclass," they would play the most revolutionary part in the revolution.

Black Nationalists all called for revolutionary methods to bring about social change. Democratic reform and political agitation had proved to be futile. Racism de facto still persisted despite civil rights legislation. Problems related to poverty, crime, drugs, inadequate housing, poor education, and poor access to healthcare all still plagued large numbers of Black people. In particular, these quagmires had the most profound impact on the Black urban poor. The Black Nationalist program shifted to address these conditions and Black Nationalists began to make valiant efforts to reach out to the urban poor. Therefore, by the 1960s many Black Nationalists had parted ways with former Black Nationalists such as Garvey, in that the political nationalism he advocated, the utopian back-to-Africa approach, obviously did not address the every-day struggles affecting Black people. Despite the shifts in strategy, Black Nationalists remained a revolutionary vanguard always feverishly demanding and fighting for the rights of Black people.

Part IV: Black Radical Feminism

Black radical feminists successfully incorporated the issue of gender inequality into the Black Liberation movement and political struggle. In many ways these women rose to prominence in the face of exclusion, either from the already burgeoning middle class White dominated second wave of the women's movement, from the male dominated Black Power movement, and from a White male dominated political arena. For these radical women the widespread neglect of issues that impacted women of color by already existing organizations and power structures was inexcusable. This section examines the works and ideas of: Claudia Jones, Florynce "Flo" Kennedy, Shirley Chisholm, and Angela Y. Davis and their resolute struggles to demonstrate the interconnectedness of race and gender in conditioning oppression. In addition, as Communists, Angela Davis and Claudia Jones worked hard to show how class also buttressed oppression and was part of this matrix of oppression. Flo Kennedy also exposed the ways in which sexual orientation, too, conditioned a woman's experience of oppression.

Black radical feminism represented an apex in radical African American political thought. Again, the leadership in this section, too, differed in their ideas related to strategy which rendered some more radical than others. However, this genre by far represented the most radical genre of African American political thought; it is free from conservative ideology. However, it was the most short-lived and poorly supported. It is interesting that Black radical feminism may represent the most radical genre of African American political thought; these women may have been several of the most radical Black leaders we have seen in our history. This is interesting because it goes a long way to explain their marginalization from public discourse, memory, and the academic canon. People still champion Du Bois and idolize King and while it is right that they do, their politics were comfortable; they adhered to the politics of respectability. They toed the American cultural line. I suppose for many the "foul-mouthed" Flo Kennedy and her Hooker's rights were more than most culturally conservative Americans, Black and White, could handle.

Claudia Jones and Angela Davis shared in common a background as activists in the Communist Party. Both Marxist revolutionaries, they saw capitalism as a large part of the problem facing Black people in the United States. However, like many Black Marxists, they attempted to reconcile classic Marxism with American racism. Their contribution was to also address gender inequality in the capitalist state.

All the women in this section were outspoken advocates of women's reproductive freedom. Davis, Jones, Chisholm, and Kennedy worked hard to demonstrate how this issue impacted poor women of color the hardest. Chisholm, a candidate for president, and the first African American woman to hold a seat in the United States Congress, was a staunch advocate for the rights of immigrants, the poor, Black Americans, and women. However, her official position in government may have stifled her ability to pursue a more radical agenda while in office unlike the other Black radical feminists in this section.

All had their own special projects and movements. Davis became one of the leaders of the prisoners' rights movement and today continues to be one of the most candid critics of the prison industrial complex. Kennedy was an advocate for the rights of sex workers. Chisholm worked endlessly for nationalized day care and Claudia Jones continued to speak out unequivocally against imperialism, fascism, and fought for the emergence of socialism.

Part V: Modern Black Conservatives: Why Black "Neo-Cons" Matter

The section on conservatism focuses on late twentieth-century conservatives. Having read the previous sections in the book, it is the author's hope that readers will clearly see no novelty in the ideas espoused in this section. While new problems have emerged in the Black community, the solutions proffered by the thinkers in this section are drawn from the same logic offered by various abolitionists, civil rights leaders, and Black Nationalists. Again, to see modern Black conservatives as a new rising cohort may be a reflection of facetious accounts of African American political thought. These are old ideas; what has changed is that the Black politicians and leaders who articulate these ideas have been elevated to high positions in electoral politics and are more publicly visible. This section includes several modern Black conservatives: Clarence Thomas, Alan Keyes, Michael Steele, and Star Parker.

Many scholars of African American political thought and leadership have been flippant in their treatment of Black conservatives. While the overwhelming majority of African American political thought is politically leftist, why does that render Black conservatives unimportant? The canon has marginalized these Black leaders because of its own disdain for the ideologies they espouse. The liberal academic canon has allowed its own biases to cast a nebulous cloud over a crucial part of African American history.

It has discursively rendered Black conservatives invisible and insignificant. A primary objective here is to make a case for why the so-called "Black Neo-Cons" matter.

According to the Joint Center for Political and Economic Studies, while 43.6 percent of Black individuals in the United States identify as liberal, 24.4 percent identify as moderate and another 31.3 percent identify as conservative.[11] If at least one-third of Black folk identify as conservative is there a legitimate reason the leaders who speak to these Black people have been rendered invisible and deemed irrelevant by the canon?

It may be that many people are misled to think that all Black people are liberals, particularly as measured by participation in the Democratic Party. It is accurate that currently 73 percent of Black voters identify as Democrats and only 4 percent as Republicans. However, historically Black people have supported Republican candidates. For example, Oscar DePriest, a Republican from Chicago, was not only the first Black congressman to be elected from the windy city but also was put into office by an overwhelmingly Black working class constituency. Also in Chicago was the country's most powerful Black newspaper—the Chicago *Defender*. It is noteworthy that the incredibly wealthy and elite Abbot family, who were staunchly conservative and Republican supporters, published the *Defender*. The family behind the loudest mouthpiece in the Black public sphere was conservative.[12] In 1960, Richard Nixon received 32 percent of the Black vote. In 2004 the number of votes cast for George W. Bush by Black constituents doubled. Bush garnered 11 percent of Black votes; he received 8 percent in 2000.[13] Black voters constituted approximately 13.2 million votes cast in 2004; this means approximately 1.45 million Black people voted for Bush, a conservative Republican. How do you justify Black academia's marginalization of the Black leaders who speak to millions of Black Americans? In addition, this data does not reflect the views of Black conservatives who did not vote. Utilizing participation in electoral politics to measure political attitudes amongst African Americans is problematic given that the majority of African Americans do not vote.[14] Moreover, to assume that all those Black people who do not vote would vote for Democrats or other liberal and progressive parties is presumptuous. This volume aims to present a comprehensive and well-rounded presentation of Black political thought, which is complex and multi-faceted. We cannot continue to only study those leaders who speak to our own political predilections.

According to the previous poll from the Joint Center for Political and Economic Studies, of those individuals who identified as conservative (31.3 percent), 78.3 percent said they were Christian conservative. For over two and half centuries the Black church has continued to be a primary institutional hub in the African American community with unparalleled influence over its members.[15] Studies continue to demonstrate that as many 97 percent of African Americans identify as Christian.[16] While many African Americans may feel apprehensive about joining the Republican Party there is no reason to think that African Americans, most of whom are guided by Christian dogma, do not often agree ideologically with conservatives. It is reasonable to suggest that this level of religious sentiment may cause a large portion of African Americans to side with conservatives on hot button political issues. This is a fact that should not be overlooked.

Political party membership cannot be the only measure we utilize to understand the political attitudes of Black people in the United States. When we examine attitudinal studies gauging political sentiment we begin to see a different picture unfold. Linda Lopez and Adrian D. Pantoja conducted a quantitative study examining American attitudes toward race-conscious policies such as government-sponsored job training, educational assistance, and affirmative action. Unlike other studies that primarily focus on Whites' attitudes toward programs such as affirmative action they compared the preferences of Whites, Blacks, Hispanics, and Asians. Their primary findings may not seem altogether shocking: "African Americans [of both lower class and upper class] display the strongest support for both policies [opportunity enhancing-education assistance and job training and outcome-directed programs—affirmative action] while whites display the lowest support."[17] The authors focused on how much more likely it was for Blacks to support what we colloquially call liberal policies than Whites; they did not highlight what seemed like an even more interesting finding. Of the 1,103 African American participants in their sample, 57.8 percent favored opportunity enhancing governmental policies (self-help programs) and 39.8 percent favored outcome-directed programs which would create preferences in hiring and promotion in order to address past and current racial discrimination. Of the White participants, 46.3 percent favored the self-help type programs initiated in opportunity enhancing programs and only 15.4 percent supported outcome-directed programs more frequently called affirmative action. Again, these findings are not surprising. What is terribly interesting is that while more African Americans support liberal policies than Whites, or Hispanics and Asians for that matter, the majority (almost 60 percent) of African Americans in this sample opposed affirmative action and 42.2 percent opposed opportunity enhancing programs. Before readers of this section jump to call Clarence Thomas an "Uncle Tom" for his vitriolic diatribes against affirmative action, maybe Thomas is speaking to, and supported ideologically by, far more African Americans than many would care to admit.

While anecdotal and certainly not functioning as scientific evidence, I am compelled to note that for years when I have taught undergraduates about poverty, I am always moved by the number of students who rebuke sociological arguments that poverty primarily stems from structural deficiencies such as: lack of access to jobs, poor housing, under-funded educational institutions, etc. in favor of arguments derived from cultural pathology. In many of my courses, my African American students have argued that Charles Murray and Oscar Lewis were accurate, in that they grew up first-hand witnessing cyclical welfare dependency, an inability to delay gratification, laziness, and readily provide anecdotes of the welfare queen they knew. This is just to suggest that to not acknowledge the prevalence of fundamentally conservative ideas within the black community is downright naïve.

The dismissal of Black conservatives has consequences. For those passionate about history, specifically the history of ideas, thus far we have not received an accurate portrait of African American political thought. It is interesting that Black conservatives have largely been deemed Uncle Toms, "as good as being White," and a bunch of

House Negroes aligned more with their masters than with the plight of "their" people. Within this volume, I think readers will clearly see that the Black conservatives in this volume care about Black people and radically push their parties and organizations to reach out and speak to the needs of Black people. The only difference lies in the solutions they offer. Their solutions push for cultural reform and not structural reform; Black conservatives focus on individual and cultural pathology, which is dismissed by Black public intellectuals not because these conservatives' arguments are not sound but because they do not agree. We academics have the power to discursively legitimatize knowledge and should be careful of marginalizing Black leaders just because their ideas differ from our own.

Crucially, for those interested in modern politics this marginalization may have even greater consequences. When charting the recent conservative turn in the United States, we may have underestimated the role Black political figures have played in giving legitimacy and support to the burgeoning neo-liberal agenda. As we have witnessed the almost complete repeal of the Great Society, have we considered the role the "Black Neo-Cons" played in the momentum of this conservative turn? This book asks its readers to take this question seriously. Symbolic representation is powerful in our media-driven society. Even if we stipulate that Black conservatives represent a small cohort of African Americans, do their actions in public have consequences for the larger political landscape? It seems that they do. In fact, their minority presence may have an even greater impact than the Black liberal majority does. In the modern era, they tend to hold positions with great influence and public presence.

We live in a nation that idolizes Horatio Alger. In early 2000 what were the consequences of simultaneously having an African American National Security Advisor, Condoleezza Rice, an African American Secretary of State, Colin Powell, Ron Christie as Bush's special assistant, Clarence Thomas on the Supreme Court, Alan Keyes running for both the Senate and President, Black Republicans running for high office in Maryland, Pennsylvania, Ohio, California, Chicago, Georgia, Mississippi, and Michigan, and intellectuals such as Thomas Sowell gaining media attention for his conservative economic policies? To my mind, the efforts of these and other Black conservatives are genuine; most often they genuinely desire to help this country and African Americans. However, politically savvy strategists, to curtail any progressive agenda, may be simultaneously utilizing them. After all, who better to criticize entitlement programs and affirmative action than Black political figures?

Entering the twenty-first century the GOP has intensified efforts to reach out to minority communities, particularly African American communities. In 2004 they started a campaign in which they recruited 10,000 young "team leaders" in order to disseminate Republican ideas and recruit African Americans from Black churches into the GOP. They started internship programs for minority voters and have devoted copious time to recruiting more African Americans as voters and potential candidates. We might stop to ask ourselves what this means for the future of African American leadership. Moving into the twenty-first century is it possible that more African Americans will be led toward the right? While Black conservatism is nothing new, the influx of Black Republicans in the public sphere, and the moderatism of Barack Obama, might be offering a glimpse into the future of Black leadership and African American political thought.

Part VI: The New Black Moderate: Obama and Beyond

Barack Obama's presidency has been met with skepticism and often hostility from progressive Black intellectuals and Black pundits, who question his ability to impact the Black community beyond mere symbolic representation. For some Obama is just a symbol—the embodiment of the success of the Civil Rights Movement, a post-racial society come to fruition—and buttresses the color-blindness of many Whites. He becomes a living breathing example that Horatio Alger lives and that with hard work and retention of the Protestant work ethic that anyone can succeed in the United States. This symbolism may have a positive impact on the Black community. However, again, many Black intellectuals are not so convinced. Leading Black public intellectual Cornell West said:

> Well, I think on a symbolic level I would give him an A in terms of uplifting the spirits and providing a sense of hope and possibility going into the inauguration and sustaining it up to a certain point. On a substantial level I would give him a C– when it comes to policy, when it comes to priority, when it comes to focusing on poor people and working people—which has to do with the vast majority of black people—that he has really not come through in any substantial and significant way.[18]

West's critiques are insightful. Obama's vision of bipartisan politics has been admirable but utopian nonetheless. Obama has accomplished what so many Black leaders have accomplished before him; he has created a moderate platform which sustains his political heartbeat but provides no relief to the body's failing organs. Obama has crafted a hybrid strategy for change that incorporates both liberal and conservative ideas. He recognizes problems facing many African Americans such as poverty, high dropout rates, incarceration, etc. He has offered policies that focus on government-sponsored programs and initiatives. At the same time he stresses personal responsibility. For example, he has been a huge proponent of the Fatherhood Initiative, stressing the importance of better parenting.

Overall, Black political leadership has been more conservative than we care to admit. What role has this played in the persistence of racism, policies that support the former, and the general lack of change to issues such as poverty? This book argues that African American political thought has always been underpinned by varying degrees of conservative ideology, namely self-help and cultural reform. How has the overall cultural conservatism of Black political leadership historically impacted Black people? Has its overall moderate trajectory helped Black people? On one hand Black leadership along within millions of activists brought about an end to slavery, Jim Crow, and assisted in the creation of meaningful reform such as the Civil Rights Act and Voting Rights Act. From another perspective poverty rates amongst African American remain close to 30 percent; Black men are being incarcerated at repugnant rates; dropout rates are high amongst Black youth. These are just some of the terrible problems that sill impact millions of Black folk. In light of this, what does this tell us about how well the strategies and philosophies of Black leaders have worked out for many African Americans? As we look to the future, it seems that although always buttressed by conservative social and cultural ideals, both African American political thought and Black leadership are moving further politically to the right. Readers will need to determine for themselves whether this shift will have positive or negative consequences for Black people.

*Editor's Note: the primary source documents throughout this text have been excerpted from longer texts. Any authors seeking copyright permission to duplicate materials in this book should be aware that these texts have been heavily edited.

Please note the paucity of primary source material in Chapter 8 on William Monroe Trotter reflects the poor documentation of his work. It is with great regret that I was not able to uncover further useful texts to include in this chapter.

Notes

1. On May 17, 2004 Bill Cosby gave a now infamous speech at the NAACP's fiftieth anniversary celebration of *Brown* v. *the Board of Education* at Constitution Hall in Washington, D.C. His diatribe colloquially has been dubbed the "pound-cake speech." In his speech in which he articulated classic conservative opinions, he told a fictitious story about a young Black child stealing a piece of pound cake. Subsequently in an altercation with police, he is shot. Outrage ensued amongst the Black community. To this Cosby remarked, "Well, what the hell was he doing with the pound cake in his hand?" Cosby argued (like many conservatives) that a major problem amongst Black people is incessant excuse making and lack of personal responsibility. He posited that Black families are in a shambles and do not properly parent. Children are not taught morals and ethics; they are not taught proper English and do not value education. In a more memorable but incredibly offensive line in another speech that followed at a Rainbow/Push coalition meeting, Cosby said, "your dirty laundry gets out of school at 2:30 every day. It's cursing on the way home, on the bus, train, in the candy store. They are cursing and grabbing each other and going nowhere." According to Cosby, Black people who experience poverty suffer from cultural pathology; they have copious children out of wedlock, cannot delay gratification, and do not value education and hard work. Until these internal problems are addressed there will be no change.
2. Jones, Angela. 2011. *African American Civil Rights: Early Activism and the Niagara Movement*. New York: Praeger.
3. Dawson, Michael C. 2001. *Black Visions: The Roots of Contemporary African American Political Ideologies*. Chicago: University of Chicago Press, p. 10.
4. Horatio Alger (1832–1899) was an American author. His name has become synonymous with the American Dream. Alger was famous for writing what we commonly call rags-to-riches tales. He published over 100 of these tales in which a young poor boy, through hard work, dedication, and thrift, pulls himself out of poverty and achieves the American Dream. Writers often utilize the term "the Horatio Alger Myth" to suggest that despite Alger's stories access to success is not without its roadblocks.
5. Wintz, Cary D. 1996. *Black Culture and the Harlem Renaissance*. Texas: Texas A& M University Press, p. 44.
6. The Weather Underground was a revolutionary organization that broke away from the more moderate organization Students for a Democratic Society in 1969. The group advocated the violent overthrow of the United States government, who they saw as imperialist capitalist oppressors who maintained their fascist state through the use of force. Before going underground its leaders were responsible for several bombings, including the bombing of the New York City police headquarters.

7. Black Marxists attempted to address Karl Marx's neglect of race in his critiques of capitalism and his vision of global revolution to abolish private property and institute Communism. Black Marxists attempted to utilize Marxism to address the problems of Black people. For an excellent account of Black Marxism see Robinson, Cedric. 1983. *Black Marxism: The Making of the Black Radical Tradition.* London: Zed Books.
8. Karl Marx referred to the wealthy or those who controlled the means of production as the bourgeoisie. During industrialization the bourgeoisie were factory owners.
9. According to Karl Marx the proletariat were the working class; they would eventually achieve consciousness of their exploitation by the bourgeoisie and once capitalism eventually and inevitably collapsed the proletariat would overthrow the bourgeoisie and assume control over the means of production. Private property would become public property and would be controlled by the workers.
10. Originally according to Karl Marx beneath the working class exists a group of people in society, an underclass, or a small group of criminals and degenerates called the lumpenproletariat. They would take no part in the revolution. This point became a point of contention for Black Power leaders. They argued that this was in fact a revolutionary group; they were a group that needed to be organized and mobilized. The lumpenproletariat would have nothing to lose by joining in revolution; they were your best candidates for revolution.
11. See   www.jointcenter.org/index.php/publications_recent_publications/national_opinion_polls/ 2008_national_opinion_poll.
12. See Graham, Lawrence Otis. 1999. *Our Kind of People: Inside America's Black Upper Class.* New York: Harper Perennial.
13. Parker, Star. "How GOP Can Win Black Vote." WorldNetDaily, November 9, 2004.
14. From the time when African Americans could all vote, after the passage of the Voting Rights Act 1965 and Twenty-fourth Amendment to the Constitution banning poll taxes, nationally the majority of African Americans voted in two presidential elections—1964 for Lyndon Baines Johnson and in 2008 for Barack Obama. Voter turnout rates remain incredibly low in local elections, mayoral, gubernatorial, and congressional races.
15. See Lincoln, C.E. and L.H. Mamiya. 1990. *The Black Church in the African American Experience.* Durham, NC: Duke University Press. Dyson, Michael Eric. 1996. *Race Rules: Navigating the Color Line.* Reading, MA: Addison-Wesley. McKinney, Richard. 1971. "The Black Church: Its Development and Present Impact." *The Harvard Theological Review*, Vol. 64, No. 4, pp. 452–481. Townsend Gilkes, Cheryl. 1998. "Plenty Good Room: Adaptation in a Changing Black Church." *Annals of the American Academy of Political and Social Science*, Vol. 588, pp. 101–121.
16. See Ward, Elijah G. 2005. "Homophobia, Hypermasculinity and the US Black Church." *Culture, Health & Sexuality*, Vol. 7, No. 5, pp. 493–504.
17. Lopez, Linda and Adrian D. Pantoja. 2004. "Beyond Black and White: General Support for Race-Conscious Policies among African Americans, Latinos, Asian Americans, and Whites." *Political Research Quarterly*, Vol. 57, No. 4, p. 635.
18. Wells, Kathleen. "A Conversation with Cornel West: Obama's First Year and the Marginalization of the Black Political Agenda." *The Huffington Post*, February 23, 2010.

PART I

THE ANTEBELLUM ERA
THE RISE OF ABOLITIONISM

1.
DAVID WALKER

David Walker (1785–1830) was born in Wilmington, North Carolina on September 25, 1785. The revolutionary abolitionist was born free. His mother was free and his father was a slave. Walker traveled and in 1826 settled in Boston, Massachusetts, the epicenter of the ensuing abolitionist movement. He became a frequent contributor and agent for the abolitionist African American newspaper, the *Freedom's Journal*. Walker managed a second-hand clothing store in order to financially support himself but made his name by publishing the *Appeal*.

David Walker's famous pamphlet, *Walker's Appeal*, was a vitriolic indictment of slavery. As you will see in this chapter, Walker condemned slavery and the capitalists who thrived off the exploitation and suffering of Africans. He called for insurgency and advocated retribution against the White oppressors. His message was revolutionary. Emancipation rested on the slaves; they would need to fight for their freedom.

Walker put copies of the *Appeal* in the pockets of the garments in his store. Because the store was near the waterfront on Brattle Street, he had access to seamen. These pamphlets were then circulated through the garments into Southern ports. Specifically, African American seamen helped circulate the pamphlet. After massive circulation, Walker's *Appeal* gave rise to penalties in states such as Georgia for circulating materials that would cause slaves to revolt. In fact, the Georgia legislature wanted Walker brought in dead or alive and offered a $10,000 reward for his capture. People pleaded with Walker to leave the United States and like many runaway slaves make his way to Canada. However, he refused to cower.

As you will see, the *Appeal* was powerful. It was Walker's call to arms that may have prompted the famous abolitionist Nat Turner into action. Walker spoke to audiences big and small advocating an overthrow of the total institution of slavery. However, it was the *Appeal* that channeled his voice to slaves themselves, not just free Blacks and White abolitionists.

Walker died on June 28, 1830, only a year after the first publication of the *Appeal*. There is no concrete evidence or consensus about how he died. There is convincing speculation that his untimely death was no accident. Some speculate that he was poisoned. Walker himself said in the preamble to the *Appeal* that he expected his work would cost him his life. However, others argued that he died of tuberculosis.

Overview of Ideas

David Walker was truly a revolutionary and the *Appeal* was his revolutionary manifesto. So revolutionary was this work that even Frederick Douglass, who believed political agitation would lead to emancipation, thought Walker's work was too revolutionary. Other White rabble-rousers and abolitionists such as Harriet Martineau and William Lloyd Garrison believed his advocation of revolt was appalling and that violence was never the answer.

Walker spoke in an unwavering tone denouncing the treatment and inequitable position of African slaves in the United States:

> we (colored people of the United States,) are the most degraded, wretched, and abject set of beings that ever lived since the world began; and I pray God that none like us ever may live again until time shall be no more.

Slavery was the cause of the wretched position of Africans in the United States. For Walker it was better to be dead, or no longer exist, than to be a slave.

Walker argued for an economic interpretation of both slavery and racism. The system is driven by avarice. African Americans "enriched their country with our blood and tears-have [*sic*] dug up gold and silver for them and their children, from generation to generation, and are in more miseries than any other people under heaven." He continued:

> I have been for years troubling the pages of historians, to find out what Our fathers have done to the *white Christians of America*, to merit such Condign punishments as they have inflicted on them, and do continue to inflict on us their children. But I must aver, that my researches have hitherto been to no effect. I have therefore, come to the immoveable conclusion, that they (Americans) have, and continue to punish us for nothing else, but for enriching them and their country.

Walker questions how people who call themselves Christians could behave like such evil savages. Religion plays an interesting role in his work and will play a pivotal role in many of the leaders' work covered in this text. Strategically, religion is utilized to appeal to Christians for the end of slavery on moral and religious grounds. Ending slavery becomes a religious imperative. Walker wrote, "God made man to serve Him *alone*, and that man should have no other Lord or Lords but Himself-that [*sic*] God Almighty is the *sole proprietors* or *master* of the WHOLE human family." Slaveholders become idolaters in Walker's eyes. The only master is God.

As you read Walker's words, remind yourself that that this was published in 1829; hopefully you will gain an appreciation of just how radical and revolutionary his words and his *Appeal* were. A man ahead of his time, we could argue that Walker was one of the first Black Nationalists. He wants an end to slavery but assures Whites:

> I would wish, candidly, however, before the Lord, to be understood, that I would not give a *pinch of snuff* to be married to any white person I ever saw in all the days of my life. And I do

say it, that the black man, or man of color, who will leave his own color … and marry a white woman, to be a double slave to her, just because she is *white*, ought to be treated by her as he surely will be, viz: as a NIGGER!!!!

Walker, advancing negritude, argued, "They think because they hold us in their infernal chains of slavery, that we wish to be white, or of their color—but they are dreadfully deceived." However, unlike many Black Nationalists, Walker was opposed to a solution based on a return to Africa.

Let no man of us budge one step, and let slave-holders come to beat us from our country. America is more our country, than it is the whites-we have enriched it with our *blood and tears*. … They must look sharp or this very thing will bring swift destruction upon them.

David Walker firmly criticized the means utilized by racist Whites to maintain hegemony. By keeping African Americans ignorant and uneducated this helped keep slaves passive. In fact, he indicted laws that prohibited Whites from teaching slaves to read or write. While Walker does not discuss a program for education, it seems his work suggests that education will be a vital part in emancipation. He also noted that Whites intentionally kept free Blacks from slaves because they knew that if slaves had first-hand knowledge that emancipation was possible, they would surely revolt. If a slave managed to gain his freedom and owned any property, if he died, despite the presence of kin, Whites would steal his property and possessions. They created laws to restrict all behaviors and ensure no political, economic, or social rights. Walker took on the government and publicly indicted Thomas Jefferson. "Mr. Jefferson [was] a much greater philosopher the world afforded, has in truth injured us more, and has been as great a barrier to our emancipation as any thing that has ever been advanced against us." He continued, "The whites have always been an unjust, jealous, unmerciful, avaricious and blood thirsty set of beings, always seeking after power and authority." Walker said, while Whites may refuse to acknowledge it, "this country is as much ours as it as the whites, whether they will admit it now or not, they will see and believe it by and by." He exposed the hypocrisy of paternalism and asked why Whites believed Blacks should be thankful to them—grateful for what; murdering their kin, raping their wives, and brutalizing their bodies?

Like all of the leaders in this text, Walker did not just identify the source of the problem (slavery) but identified a solution. Black folk needed to fight back.

I know well, that there are some talents and learning among the colored people of this country, which we have not a chance to develop [*sic*], in consequence of oppression; but our oppression ought not to hinder us from acquiring all we can. For we will have a chance to develop [*sic*] them by and by…. Our suffering will come to an *end*.

Walker calls for slaves to read the history of Hayti [*sic*] and how they were oppressed and murdered by Whites. He also reminded readers that Whites tried to enslave the Native Americans and questioned why Blacks were not fighting back the way the Native Americans did. He wanted Black folk to see what Whites were capable of all over the world and by inciting anger amongst Blacks it would call them to action.

Walker warned Whites also, "the whites want slaves, and want us for their slaves, but some of them will curse the day they ever saw us."

Walker argued if Whites refused to end their systematic brutalization of Africans it was time for Black folk to fight back. He wrote:

> believe this, that it is no more harm for you to kill a man, who is trying to kill you, than it is for you to take a drink of water when thirsty; in fact, the man who will stand still and let another murder him, is worse than an infidel, and if he has common sense, ought not to be pitied.

Walker appealed to Black folk to disseminate the message within these pages to as many other people as possible. Insurgency would require unity.

Despite critics who saw Walker's approach as too revolutionary, Walker said:

> treat us like men, and there is no danger but we will all live in peace and happiness together. ... For we are not like you, hard hearted, unmerciful, and unforgiving. ... But Americans, I declare to you, while you keep us and our children in bondage, and treat us like brutes, to make us support your families, we cannot be your friends.

Walker would like a peaceful accord. However, if Whites refused to change then Blacks would have to force that change and force Whites to live up to the beautiful words describing equality in the Declaration of Independence.

From the *Appeal*, 1830

Article I: Our wretchedness in consequence of slavery

My beloved brethren:—The Indians of North and of South America—the Greeks—the Irish, subjected under the king of Great Britain—the Jews, that ancient people of the Lord—the inhabitants of the islands of the sea—in fine, all the inhabitants of the earth, (except however, the sons of Africa) are called *men*, and of course are, and ought to be free. But we, (coloured people) and our children are *brutes!!* and of course are, and *ought to be* SLAVES to the American people and their children forever!! to dig their mines and work their farms; and thus go on enriching them, from one generation to another with our *blood* and our *tears!!!!*

I promised in a preceding page to demonstrate to the satisfaction of the most incredulous, that we, (coloured people of these United States of America) are the *most wretched, degraded* and *abject* set of beings that *ever lived* since the world began, and that the white Americans having reduced us to the wretched state of *slavery*, treat us in that condition *more cruel* (they being an enlightened and Christian people,) than any heathen nation did any people whom it had reduced to our condition. These affirmations are so well confirmed in the minds of all unprejudiced men, who have taken the trouble to read histories, that they need no elucidation from me.

Compare the above, with the American institutions. Do they not institute laws to prohibit us from marrying among the whites? I would wish, candidly, however, before the Lord, to be understood, that I would not give a *pinch of snuff* to be married to any white person I ever saw in all the days of my life. And I do say it, that the black man, or man of colour, who will leave his own colour (provided he can get one, who is good for any thing) and marry a white woman, to be a double slave to her, just because she is *white*, ought to be treated by her as he surely will be, viz: as a NIGGER!!!! It is not, indeed, what I care about inter-marriages with the whites, which induced me to pass this subject in review; for the Lord knows, that there is a day coming when they will be glad enough to get into the company of the blacks, notwithstanding, we are, in this generation, levelled by them, almost on a level with the brute creation: and some of us they treat even worse than they do the brutes that perish. I only made this extract to show how much lower we are held, and how much more cruel we are treated by the Americans, than were the children of Jacob, by the Egyptians.—

Need I mention the very notorious fact, that I have known a poor man of colour, who laboured night and day, to acquire a little money, and having acquired it, he vested it in a small piece of land, and got him a house erected thereon, and having paid for the whole, he moved his family into it, where he was suffered to remain but nine months, when he was cheated out of his property by a white man, and driven out of door! And is not this the case generally? Can a man of colour buy a piece of land and keep it peaceably? Will not some white man try to get it from him, even if it is in a *mud hole*? I need not comment any farther on a subject, which all, both black and white, will readily admit. But I must, really, observe that in this very city, when a man of colour dies, if he owned any real estate it most generally falls into the hands of some white person. The wife and children of the deceased may weep and lament if they please, but the estate will be kept snug enough by its white possessor.

But to prove farther that the condition of the Israelites was better under the Egyptians than ours is under the whites. I call upon the professing Christians, I call upon the philanthropist, I call upon the very tyrant himself, to show me a page of history, either sacred or profane, on which a verse can be found, which maintains, that the Egyptians heaped the *insupportable insult* upon the children of Israel, by telling them that they were not of the *human family.* Can the whites deny this charge? Have they not, after having reduced us to the deplorable condition of slaves under their feet, held us up as descending originally from the tribes of *Monkeys* or *Orang-Outangs?* O! my God! I appeal to every man of feeling—is not this insupportable? Is it not heaping the most gross insult upon our miseries, because they have got us under their feet and we cannot help ourselves? Oh! pity us we pray thee, Lord Jesus, Master.—Has Mr. Jefferson declared to the world, that we are inferior to the whites, both in the endowments of our bodies and our minds?[1] It is indeed surprising, that a man of such great learning, combined with such excellent natural parts, should speak so of a set of men in chains. I do not know what to compare it to, unless, like putting one wild deer in an iron cage, where it will be secured, and hold another by the side of the same, then let it go, and expect the one in the cage to run as fast as the one at liberty.

Millions of whom, are this day, so ignorant and avaricious, that they cannot conceive how God can have an attribute of justice, and show mercy to us because it pleased Him to make us black—which colour, Mr. Jefferson calls unfortunate!!!!!! As though we are not as thankful to our God, for having made us as it pleased himself, as they, (the whites,) are for having made them white. They think because they hold us in their infernal chains of slavery, that we wish to be white, or of their color—but they are dreadfully deceived—we wish to be just as it pleased our Creator to have made us, and no avaricious and unmerciful wretches, have any business to make slaves of, or hold us in slavery. How would they like for us to make slaves of, and hold them in cruel slavery, and murder them as they do us?—But is Mr. Jefferson's assertions true? viz. "that it is unfortunate for us that our Creator has been pleased to make us *black*." We will not take his say so, for the fact. The world will have an opportunity to see whether it is unfortunate for us, that our Creator *has made us* darker than the *whites*.

Fear not the number and education of our *enemies*, against whom we shall have to contend for our lawful right; guaranteed to us by our Maker; for why should we be afraid, when God is, and will continue, (if we continue humble) to be on our side?

The man who would not fight under our Lord and Master Jesus Christ, in the glorious and heavenly cause of freedom and of God—to be delivered from the most wretched, abject and servile slavery, that ever a people was afflicted with since the foundation of the world, to the present day—ought to be kept with all of his children or family, in slavery, or in chains, to be butchered by his *cruel enemies*.

I saw a paragraph, a few years since, in a South Carolina paper, which, speaking of the barbarity of the Turks, it said: "The Turks are the most barbarous people in the world—they treat the Greeks more like *brutes* than human beings." And in the same paper was an advertisement, which said: "Eight well built Virginia and Maryland *Negro fellows* and four *wenches* will positively be *sold* this day, *to the highest bidder!*" And what astonished me still more was, to see in this same *humane* paper!! the cuts of three men, with clubs and budgets on their backs, and an advertisement offering a considerable sum of money for their apprehension and delivery. I declare, it is really so amusing to hear the Southerners and Westerners of this country talk about *barbarity*, that it is positively, enough to make a man *smile*.[2]

I have been for years troubling the pages of historians, to find out what our fathers have done to the *white Christians of America*, to merit such condign punishment as they have inflicted on them, and do continue to inflict on us their children. But I must aver, that my researches have hitherto been to no effect. I have therefore, come to the immoveable conclusion, that they (Americans) have, and do continue to punish us for nothing else, but for enriching them and their country. For I cannot conceive of anything else. Nor will I ever believe otherwise, until the Lord shall convince me.

The world knows, that slavery as it existed among the Romans, (which was the primary cause of their destruction) was, comparatively speaking, no more than a *cypher*, when compared with ours under the Americans. Indeed I should not have noticed the Roman slaves, had not the very learned and penetrating Mr. Jefferson said, "when a master was murdered, all his slaves in the same house, or within hearing, were condemned to death."[3]—Here let me ask Mr. Jefferson, (but he is gone to answer at the bar of God, for the deeds done in his body while living,) I therefore ask the whole American people, had I not rather die, or be put to death, than to be a slave to any tyrant, who takes not only my own, but my wife and children's lives by the inches? Yea, would I meet death with avidity far! far!! in preference to such *servile submission* to the murderous hands of tyrants. Mr. Jefferson's very severe remarks on us have been so extensively argued upon by men whose attainments in literature, I shall never be able to reach, that I would not have meddled with it, were it not to solicit each of my brethren, who has the spirit of a man, to buy a copy of Mr. Jefferson's "Notes on Virginia," and put it in the hand of his son. For let no one of us suppose that the refutations which have been written by our white friends are enough—they are *whites*—we are *blacks*. We, and the world wish to see the charges of Mr. Jefferson refuted by the blacks *themselves*, according to their chance; for we must remember that what the whites have written respecting this subject, is other men's labours, and did not emanate from the blacks. I know well, that there are some talents and learning among the coloured people of this country, which we have not a chance to develop, in consequence of oppression; but our oppression ought not to hinder us from acquiring all we can. For we will have a chance to develope them by and by. God will not suffer us, always to be oppressed. Our sufferings will come to an *end*, in spite of all the Americans this side of *eternity*. Then we will want all the learning and talents among ourselves, and perhaps more, to govern ourselves.—"Every dog must have its day," the American's is coming to an end.

Article II: Our wretchedness in consequence of ignorance

The whites want slaves, and want us for their slaves, but some of them will curse the day they ever saw us. As true as the sun ever shone in its meridian splendor, my colour will root some of them out of the very face of the earth. They shall have enough of making slaves of, and butchering, and murdering us in the manner which they have. No doubt some may say that I write with a bad spirit, and that I being a black, wish these things to occur. Whether I write with a bad or a good spirit, I say if these things do not occur in their proper time, it is because the world in which we live does not exist, and we are deceived with regard to its existence.—It is immaterial however to me, who believe, or who refuse—though I should like to see the whites repent peradventure God may have mercy on them, some however, have gone so far that their cup must be filled.

Men of colour, who are also of sense, for you particularly is my APPEAL designed. Our more ignorant brethren are not able to penetrate its value. I call upon you therefore to cast your eyes upon the wretchedness of your brethren, and to do your utmost to enlighten them—*go to work and enlighten your brethren!*—Let the Lord see you doing what you can to rescue them and yourselves from degradation. Do any of you say that you and your family are free and happy, and what have you to do with the wretched slaves and other people? So can I say, for I enjoy as much freedom as any of you, if I am not quite as well off as the best of you. Look into our freedom and happiness, and see of what kind they are composed!! They are of the very lowest kind—they are the very *dregs!*—they are the most servile and abject kind, that ever a people was in possession of! If any of you wish to know how FREE you are, let one of you start and go through the southern and western States of this country, and unless you travel as a slave to a white man (a servant is a *slave* to the man whom he serves) or have your free papers, (which if you are not careful they will get from you) if they do not take you up and put you in jail, and if you cannot give good evidence of your freedom, sell you into eternal slavery, I am not a living man: or any man of colour, immaterial who he is, or where he came from, if he is not *the fourth from the negro race!!* (as we are called) the white Christians of America will serve him the same they will sink him into wretchedness and degradation for ever while he lives. And yet some of you have the hardihood to say that you are free and happy! May God have mercy on your freedom and happiness!! I met a coloured man in the street a short time since, with a string of boots on his shoulders; we fell into conversation, and in course of which, I said to him, what a miserable set of people we are! He asked, why?—Said I, we are so subjected under the whites, that we cannot obtain the comforts of life, but by cleaning their boots and shoes, old clothes, waiting on them, shaving them &c. Said he, (with the boots on his shoulders) "I am completely happy!!! I never want to live any better or happier than when I can get a plenty of boots and shoes to clean!!!" Oh! how can those who are actuated by avarice only, but think, that our Creator made us to be an inheritance to them for ever, when they see that our greatest glory is centered in such mean and low objects? Understand me, brethren, I do not mean to speak against the occupations by which we acquire enough and sometimes scarcely that, to render ourselves and families comfortable through life. I am subjected to the same inconvenience, as you all.—My objections are, to our *glorying* and being *happy* in such low employments; for if we are men, we ought to be thankful to the Lord for the past, and for the future. Be looking forward with thankful hearts to higher attainments than *wielding the razor* and *cleaning boots and shoes.* The man whose aspirations are not *above,* and even *below* these, is indeed, ignorant and wretched enough. I advanced it therefore to you, not as a *problematical,* but as an unshaken and for ever immovable *fact,* that your full glory and happiness, as well as all other coloured people under Heaven, shall never be fully consummated, but with the *entire emancipation of your enslaved brethren all over the world.* You may therefore, go to work and do what you can to rescue, or join in with tyrants to oppress them and yourselves, until the Lord shall come upon you all like a thief in the night. For I believe it is the will of the Lord that our greatest happiness shall consist in working for the salvation of our whole body. When this is accomplished a burst of glory will shine upon you, which will indeed astonish you and the world. Do any of you say this never will be done? I assure you that God will accomplish it—if nothing else will answer, he will hurl tyrants and devils into *atoms* and make way for his people. But O my brethren! I say unto you again, you must go to work and prepare the way of the Lord.

There is a great work for you to do, as trifling as some of you may think of it. You have to prove to the Americans and the world, that we are MEN, and not *brutes,* as we have been represented, and by millions treated. Remember, to let the aim of your labours among your brethren, and particularly the youths, be the dissemination of education and religion.[4] It is lamentable, that many of our children go to school, from four until they are eight or ten, and sometimes fifteen years of age, and leave school knowing but a little more about the grammar of their language than a horse does about handling a musket—and not a few of them are really so ignorant, that they are unable to answer a person correctly, general questions in geography, and to hear them read, would only be to disgust a man who has a taste for reading; which, to do well, as trifling as it may appear to some, (to the ignorant in particular) is a great part of learning. Some few of them, may make out to scribble tolerably well, over a half sheet of paper, which I believe has hitherto been a powerful obstacle in our way, to keep us from acquiring knowledge. An ignorant father, who knows no more than what nature has taught him, together with what little he acquires by the senses of hearing and seeing, finding his son able to write a neat hand, sets it down for granted that he has as good learning as any body; the young, ignorant gump, hearing his father or mother, who perhaps may be ten times more ignorant, in point of literature, than himself, extolling his learning, struts about, in the full assurance, that his attainments in literature are sufficient to take him through the world, when, in fact, he has scarcely any learning at all!!!!

It is a notorious fact, that the major part of the white Americans, have, ever since we have been among them, tried to keep us ignorant, and make us believe that God made us and our children to be slaves to them and theirs. *Oh! my God, have mercy on Christian Americans!!!*

Article IV: Our wretchedness in consequence of the colonizing plan

I say, from the beginning, I do not think that we were natural enemies to each other. But the whites having made us so wretched, by subjecting us to slavery, and having murdered so many millions of us, in order to make us work for them, and out of devilishness—and they taking our wives, whom we love as we do ourselves—our mothers, who bore the pains of death to give us birth—our fathers and dear little children, and ourselves, and strip and beat us one before the other—chain, hand-cuff, and drag us about like rattle-snakes—shoot us down like wild bears, before each other's faces, to make us submissive to, and work to support them and their families. They (the whites) know well, if we are *men*—and there is a secret monitor in their hearts which tells them we are—they know, I say, if we *are* men, and see them treating us in the manner they do, that there can be nothing in our hearts but death alone, for them, notwithstanding we may appear cheerful, when we see them murdering our dear mothers and wives, because we cannot help ourselves. Man, in all ages and all nations of the earth, is the same. Man is a peculiar creature—he is the image of his God, though he may be subjected to the most wretched condition upon earth, yet the spirit and feeling which constitute the creature, man, can never be entirely erased from his breast, because the God who made him after his own image, planted it in his heart; he cannot get rid of it. The whites knowing this, they do not know what to do; they know that they have done us so much injury, they are afraid that we, being men, and not brutes, will retaliate, and woe will be to them; therefore, that dreadful fear, together with an avaricious spirit, and the natural love in them, to be called masters, (which term will yet honour them with to their sorrow) bring them to the resolve that they will keep us in ignorance and wretchedness, as long as they possibly can,[5] and make the best of their time, while it lasts. Consequently they, themselves, (and not us) render themselves our natural enemies, by treating us so cruel. They keep us miserable now, and call us their property, but some of them will have enough of us by and by—their stomachs shall run over with us; they want us for their slaves, and shall have us to their fill. We are all in the world together!!—I said above, because we cannot help ourselves, (viz. we cannot help the whites murdering our mothers and our wives) but this statement is incorrect—for we can help ourselves; for, if we lay aside abject servility, and be determined to act like men, and not brutes—the murderers among the whites would be afraid to show their cruel heads. But O, my God!—in sorrow I must say it, that my colour, all over the world, have a mean, servile spirit. They yield in a moment to the whites, let them be right or wrong—the reason they are able to keep their feet on our throats. Oh! my coloured brethren, all over the world, when shall we arise from this death-like apathy?—And be men!! You will notice, if ever we become men, (I mean *respectable* men, such as other people are,) we must exert ourselves to the full. For remember, that it is the greatest desire and object of the greater part of the whites, to keep us ignorant, and make us work to support them and their families.—Here now, in the Southern and Western sections of this country, there are at least three coloured persons for one white, why is it, that those few weak, good-for-nothing whites, are able to keep so many able men, one of whom, can put to flight a dozen whites, in wretchedness and misery? It shows at once, what the blacks are, we are ignorant, abject, servile and mean—and the whites know it—they know that we are too servile to assert our rights as men—or they would not fool with us as they do. Would they fool with any other peoples as they do with us? No, they know too well, that they would get themselves ruined. Why do they not bring the inhabitants of Asia to be body servants to them? They know they would get their bodies rent and torn from head to foot. Why do they not get the Aborigines of this country to be slaves to them and their children, to work their farms and dig their mines? They know well that the Aborigines of this country, or (Indians) would tear them from the earth. The Indians would not rest day or night, they would be up all times of night, cutting their cruel throats. But my colour, (some, not all,) are willing to stand still and be murdered by the cruel whites. In some of the West-Indies Islands, and over a large part of South America, there are six or eight coloured persons for one white.[6] Why do they not take possession of those places? Who hinders them? It is not the avaricious whites—for they are too busily engaged in laying up money—derived from the blood and tears of the blacks. The fact is, they are too servile, they love to have Masters too well!! Some of our brethren, too, who seeking more after self aggrandisement, than the glory of God, and the welfare of their brethren, join in with our oppressors, to ridicule and say all manner of evils falsely against our Bishop. They think, that they are doing great things, when they can get in company with the whites, to ridicule and make sport of those who are labouring for their good. Poor ignorant creatures, they do not know that the sole aim and object of the whites, are only to make fools and slaves of them, and put the whip to them, and make them work to support them and their families. But I do say, that no man, can well be a despiser of Bishop Allen, for his public labours among us, unless he is a despiser of God and of Righteousness. Thus, we see, my brethren, the two very opposite positions of those great men, who have written respecting this "Colonizing Plan." (Mr. Clay and his slave-holding party,) men who are resolved to keep us in eternal wretchedness, are also bent upon sending us to Liberia. While the Reverend Bishop Allen, and his party, men who have the fear of God, and the wellfare of their brethren at heart. The Bishop, in particular, whose labours for the salvation of his brethren, are well known to a large part of those, who dwell in the United States, are completely opposed to the plan—and advise us to stay where we are. Now we have to determine whose advice we will take respecting this all important matter, whether we will adhere to Mr. Clay and his slave holding party, who have always been our oppressors and murderers, and who are for colonizing us, more through apprehension than humanity, or to this godly man who has done so much for our benefit, together with the advice of all the good and wise among us and the whites. Will any of us leave our homes and go to Africa? I hope not.[7] Let them commence their attack upon us as they did on our brethren in Ohio, driving and beating us from our country, and my soul for theirs, they will have enough of it. Let no man of us budge one step, and let slave-holders come to beat us from our country. America is more our country, than it is the whites—we have enriched it with our *blood and tears.* The greatest riches in all America have arisen from our blood and tears:—and will they drive us from our property and homes, which we have earned with our *blood?* They must look sharp or this very thing will bring swift destruction upon them. The Americans have got so fat on our blood and groans, that they have almost forgotten the God of armies. But let them go on.

Remember Americans, that we must and shall be free and enlightened as you are, will you wait until we shall, under God, obtain our liberty by the crushing arm of power? Will it not be dreadful for you? I speak Americans for your good. We must and shall be free I say, in spite of you. You may do your best to keep us in wretchedness and misery, to enrich you and your children; but God will deliver us from under you. And wo, wo, will be to you if we have to obtain our freedom by fighting. Throw away your fears and prejudices then, and enlighten us and treat us like men, and we will like you more than we do now hate you,[8] and tell us now no more about colonization, for America is as much our country, as it is yours.—Treat us like men, and there is no danger but we will all live in peace and happiness together. For we are not like you, hard hearted, unmerciful, and unforgiving. What a happy country this will be, if the whites will listen. What nation under heaven, will be able to do any thing with us, unless God gives us up into its hand? But Americans, I declare to you, while you keep us and our children in bondage, and treat us like brutes, to make us support you and your families, we cannot be your friends. You do not look for it, do you? Treat us then like men, and we will be your friends. And there is not a doubt in my mind, but that the whole of the past will be sunk into oblivion, and we yet, under God, will become a united and happy people. The whites may say it is impossible, but remember that nothing is impossible with God.

Remember, Americans, that as miserable, wretched, degraded, and abject as you have made us in preceding, and in this generation, to support you and your families, that some of you, (whites) on the continent of America, will yet curse the day that you were ever born. You want slaves, and want us for your slaves!!! My colour will yet, root some of you out of the very face of the earth!!!!

The Americans may say or do as they please, but they have to raise us from the condition of brutes to that of respectable men, and to make a national acknowledgement to us for the wrongs they have inflicted on us. As unexpected, strange, and wild as these propositions may to some appear, it is no less a fact, that unless they are complied with, the Americans of the United States, though they may for a little while escape, God will yet weigh them in a balance, and if they are not superior to other men, as they have represented themselves to be, he will give them wretchedness to their very heart's content.

Notes

1. [The reference is to Jefferson's *Notes on Virginia*, Query XIV. All of Walker's references to Jefferson are to this section of the *Notes*. Ed.]
2. See Dr. Goldsmith's History of Greece—page 9. See also, Plutarch's Lives. The Helots subdued by Agis, king of *Sparta*. [Walker's citation is to Oliver Goldsmith, *A History of Greece from the Earliest State to the Death of Alexander the Great*. Fifth American edition, 2 vols, in 1, Philadelphia, 1317. Ed.]
3. See his Notes on Virginia, page 210. [Cf. editor's note, page 10.]
4. Never mind what the ignorant ones among us may say, many of whom when you speak to them for their good, and try to enlighten their minds, laugh at you, and perhaps tell you plump to your face, that they want no instruction from you or any other Niger, and all such aggravating language. Now if you are a man of understanding and sound sense, I conjure you in the name of the Lord, and of all that is good, to impute their actions to ignorance, and wink at their follies, and do your very best to get around them some way or other, for remember they are your brethren; and I declare to you that it is for your interests to teach and enlighten them.
5. And still holds us up with indignity as being incapable of acquiring knowledge!!! See the inconsistency of the assertions of those wretches—they beat us inhumanely, sometimes almost to death, for attempting to inform ourselves, by reading the *Word* of our Maker, and at the same time tell us, that we are beings *void of intellect!!!!* How admirably their practices agree with their professions in this case. Let me cry shame upon you Americans, for such out-rages upon human nature!!! If it were possible for the whites always to keep us ignorant and miserable, and make us work to enrich them and their children, and insult our feelings by representing us as *talking Apes*, what would they do? But glory, honour and praise to Heaven's King, that the sons and daughters of Africa, will, in spite of all the opposition of their enemies, stand forth in all the dignity and glory that is granted by the Lord to his creature man.
6. For instance in the two States of Georgia, and South Carolina, there are, perhaps, not much short of six or seven hundred thousand persons of colour; and if I was a gambling character, I would not be afraid to stake down upon the board FIVE CENTS against TEN, that there are in the single State of Virginia, five or six hundred thousand Coloured persons. Four hundred and fifty thousand of whom (let them be well equipt for war) I would put against every white person on the whole continent of America. (Why? why because I know that the Blacks, once they get involved in a war, had rather die than to live, they either kill or be killed.) The whites know this too, which make them quake and tremble. To show the world further, how servile the coloured people are, I will only hold up to view, the one Island of Jamaica, as a specimen of our meanness. In that Island, there are three hundred and fifty thousand souls—of whom fifteen thousand are whites, the remainder, three hundred and thirty-five thousand are coloured people! and this Island is ruled by the white people!!!!!!!! (15,000) ruling and tyranizing over 335,000 persons!!!!!!!!—O! coloured men!! O! coloured men!!! O! coloured men!!!! Look!! look!!! at this!!!! and, tell me if we are not abject and servile enough, how long, O! how long my colour shall we be dupes and dogs to the cruel whites?—I only passed Jamaica, and its inhabitants, in review as a specimen to show the world, the condition of the Blacks at this time, now coloured people of the whole world, I beg you to look at the (15000 white,) and (Three Hundred and Thirty-five Thousand coloured people) in that Island, and tell me how can the white tyrants of the world but say that we are not men, but were made to be slaves and Dogs to them and their children forever!!!!!!!—why my friend only look at the thing!!!! (15000) whites keeping in wretchedness and degradation (335000) viz. 22 coloured persons for one white!!!!!!! when at the same time, an equal number (15000) Blacks, would almost take the whole of South America, because where they go as soldiers to fight death follows in their train.
7. Those who are ignorant enough to go to Africa, the coloured people ought to be glad to have them go, for if they are ignorant enough to let the whites *fool* them off to Africa, they would be no small injury to us if they reside in this country.
8. You are not astonished at my saying we hate you, for if we are men, we cannot but hate you, while you are treating us like dogs.

2.
MARIA STEWART

Maria Stewart (1803–1879) was a political activist, abolitionist, and feminist. Before she married James Stewart in 1826, Maria Miller grew up in Hartford, Connecticut. By the age of five, she lost both of her parents. As an orphan, she worked as a servant in a clergyman's home until she was fifteen. Even after Stewart left, like many African American women, she continued to work as a domestic. Like most of her Black counterparts, she acquired her education and became literate through religious instruction.

Stewart was only married to James Stewart, the veteran and entrepreneur, for three years before he died. She learned the hard way about living in a racist society. After her husband's death, the executors of his estate swindled his estate away from Maria Stewart. Interestingly, while the Stewart's were living in Boston they were acquainted with David Walker. In fact, when David Walker spoke of Whites taking the property and assets of Black men upon death and leaving their wives with nothing, he may very well having been referencing Stewart. Nonetheless, however little we know about their social relationship, we will emphatically see what a profound impact Walker had on Stewart.

Stewart became a public figure when in 1831 she began to contribute pieces for publication in William Lloyd Garrison's abolitionist newspaper, the *Liberator*. However, her pieces were put in the Ladies Department section. She soon became known as an abolitionist and a fighter for women's rights. She addressed audiences of men and women and became a strong public voice. After living in Boston for some time, Stewart went to New York. Stewart worked for Frederick Douglass's *North Star*. In 1835 a collection of her public addresses were published by William Lloyd Garrison. In 1837, she attended the Women's Anti-Slavery Convention and joined women's organizations. In 1878, the year before her death she published another collection of essays. Maria Stewart died in December 1879 in Washington, D.C.

Overview of Ideas

Like her counterparts, Maria Stewart's ideas were influenced by religion. In fact, Stewart, more so than her contemporaries, incorporated religious ideas into almost all her arguments for racial and gender equality. She even recognized this, "I suppose many of my friends will say, 'Religion is all your theme.'" However, she believed if you appealed to Whites as Christians they would realize that God would not want them to continue down the path of injustice.

Stewart was an abolitionist and a rabble-rouser. "African rights and liberty is a subject that ought to fire the breast of every free man of color in these United States, and excite in his bosom a lively, deep, decided and heart-felt interest." She argued African Americans needed to follow in David Walker's footsteps. "But where is the man that has distinguished himself in these modern days by acting wholly in the defence [*sic*] of African rights and liberty? There was one, although he sleeps, his memory lives." While Stewart's methods were different, she was undoubtedly influenced by David Walker, and continued to push Black folk to fight for an end to slavery. Like Walker, Stewart posited that Whites had benefited from Black labor for too long. "We have pursued the shadow, they have obtained the substance; we have performed the labor, they have received the profits; we have planted the vines, they have eaten the fruits of them." However, Black folk should not flee back to Africa but fight for citizenship in the country they helped build.

One of Stewart's basic strategies for emancipation hinged upon what Evelyn Brooks Higginbotham originally conceptualized as adhering to a *politics of respectability*. This meant that if Whites were going to abandon the system of slavery and realize that Blacks were not inferior then Black folks would have to demonstrate that they were equal through a refinement of behavior. Stewart argued that God knew African Americans were equal to Whites but Whites would have to learn this by seeing African American virtue and piety. "Were the American free people of color to turn their attention more assiduously to moral worth and intellectual improvement, this would be the result: prejudice would gradually diminish, and the whites would be compelled to say, unloose those fetters."

Although Stewart respected David Walker, she disagreed with him about method. She insisted to African Americans that revolutionary means were detrimental to progress. Despite the violence perpetrated by Whites, Blacks should not retaliate violently. God would judge them later. "Stand still and know that the Lord he is God. Vengeance is his, he will repay." Stewart called for a different tactic:

> Shall Afric's sons be silent any longer? Far be it from me to recommend to you either to kill, burn, or destroy. But I would strongly recommend to you to improve your talents; let not one [white] lie buried in the earth. Show forth your powers of mind. Prove to the world that "though black your skins as shades of night, your hearts are pure, your souls are white." … Prove to the world that you are neither ourang-outangs, or a species of mere animals, but that you possess the same powers of intellect as the proud-boasting American.

Interestingly, this strategic usage of the politics of respectability will be found in political thinkers including but not limited to: Stewart, Washington, Du Bois, King, and even Obama. Stewart might be cast as a conservative. What did she mean that Blacks should prove their souls were White? You decide.

In many ways, Stewart's reliance on the politics of respectability also foreshadowed the development of self-help ideology in Black political thought. Advancement required individual transformation and radical efforts to combat pathologies that developed amongst Black folk.

> I would implore our men, and especially our rising youth, to flee from the gambling board and the dance-hall; for we are poor, and have no money to throw away … it is astonishing to me that our fine young men are so blind to their own interest and the future welfare of their children as to spend their hard earnings for this frivolous amusement … suppress vice in all its abhorrent forms … we ought to follow the example of the whites in this respect. Nothing would raise our respectability, add to our peace and happiness, and reflect so much honor upon us, as to be ourselves the promoters of temperance.

Stewart is often noted as one of the first African American feminists. She called for women to unite and rally for their rights.

> Shall it any be longer said of the daughters of Africa, they have no ambition, they have no force? By no means. Let every female heart become united, and let us raise a fund ourselves; and at the end of one year and a half, we might be able to lay the corner stone for the building of a High School, that higher branches of knowledge might be enjoyed by us. … How long shall the fair daughters of Africa be compelled to bury their minds and talents beneath a load of iron pots and kettles.

Stewart foreshadows Du Bois by arguing that higher education for both Black men and women was essential. Black women no longer needed to be subservient to men—stuck in the world of domestic labor, both at work and at home. Why did women allow men to "enrich themselves with our hard earnings?" Women should make their own money, become their own bosses, and become educated. Stewart was a radical fighter for the rights of humanity—for both Black men and Black women.

———————

Religion And The Pure Principles Of Morality: The Sure Foundation On Which We Must Build, 1831

Feeling a deep solemnity of soul, in view of our wretched and degraded situation, and sensible of the gross ignorance that prevails among us, I have thought proper thus publicly to express my sentiments before you. I hope my friends will not scrutinize these pages with too severe an eye, as I have not calculated to display either elegance or taste in their composition, but have merely written the meditations of my heart as far as my imagination led; and have presented them before you in order to arouse you to exertion, and to enforce upon your minds the great necessity of turning your attention to knowledge and improvement.

I was born in Hartford, Connecticut, in 1803; was left an orphan at five years of age; was bound out in a clergyman's family; had the seeds of piety and virtue early sown in my mind, but was deprived of the advantages of education, though my soul thirsted for knowledge. Left them at fifteen years of age; attended Sabbath schools until I was twenty; in 1826 was married to James W. Stewart, was left a widow in 1829; was, as I humbly hope and trust, brought to the knowledge of the truth, as it is in Jesus, in 1830; in 1831 made a public profession of my faith in Christ.

From the moment I experienced the change, I felt a strong desire, with the help and assistance of God, to devote the remainder of my days to piety and virtue, and now possess that spirit of independence that, were I called upon, I would willingly sacrifice my life for the cause of God and my brethren.

All the nations of the earth are crying out for liberty and equality. Away, away with tyranny and oppression! And shall Africa's sons be silent any longer? Far be it from me to recommend to you either to kill, burn, or destroy. But I would strongly recommend to you to improve your talents; let not one lie buried in the earth. Show forth your powers of mind. Prove to the world that

Though black your skins as shades of night, your hearts are pure, your souls are white.

This is the land of freedom. The press is at liberty. Every man has a right to express his opinion. Many think, because your skins are tinged with a sable hue, that you are an inferior race of beings; but God does not consider you as such. He hath formed and fashioned you in his own glorious image, and hath bestowed upon you reason and strong powers of intellect. He hath made you to have dominion over the beasts of the field, the fowls of the air, and the fish of the sea [Genesis 1:26]. He hath crowned you with glory and honor; hath made you but a little lower than the angels [Psalms 8:5]; and according to the Constitution of these United States, he hath made all men free and equal. Then why should one worm say to another, "Keep you down there, while I sit up yonder; for I am better than thou?" It *is* not the color of the skin that makes the man, but it is the principles formed within the soul.

Many will suffer for pleading the cause of oppressed Africa, and I shall glory in being one of her martyrs; for I am firmly persuaded, that the God in whom I trust is able to protect me from the rage and malice of mine enemies, and from them that will rise up against me; and if there is no other way for me to escape, he is able to take me to himself, as he did the most noble, fearless, and undaunted David Walker.

Never will virtue, knowledge, and true politeness begin To Flow, till [*sic*] the pure principles of religion and morality are put into force. We have a great work to do. Never, no, never will the chains of slavery and ignorance burst, till we become united as one, and cultivate among ourselves the pure principles of piety, morality and virtue. O, ye daughters of Africa, awake! Awake! Arise! No longer sleep nor slumber, but distinguish yourselves. Show forth to the world that ye are endowed with noble and exalted faculties.

O, ye mothers, what a responsibility rests on you! You have souls committed to your charge, and God will require a strict account of you. It is you that must create in the minds of your little girls and boys a thirst for knowledge, the love of virtue, the abhorrence of vice, and the cultivation of a pure heart. The seeds thus sown will grow with their growing years; and the love of virtue thus early formed in the soul will protect their inexperienced feet from many dangers. O, do not say you cannot make any thing of your children; but say, with the help and assistance of God, we will try. Do not indulge them in their little stubborn ways; for a child left to himself bringeth his mother to shame. Spare not for their crying; thou shalt beat them with a rod, and they shall not die [Proverbs 23:13]; and thou shalt save their souls from hell. When you correct them, do it in the fear of God, and for their own good. They will not thank you for your false and foolish indulgence; they will rise up, as it were, and curse you in this world and, in the world to come, condemn you. It is no use to say you can't do this, or you can't do that; you will not tell your Maker so, when you meet him at the great day of account. And you must be careful that you set an example worthy of following, for you they will imitate. There are many instances, even among us now, where parents have discharged their duty faithfully, and their children now reflect honor upon their gray hairs.

Perhaps you will say that many parents have set pure examples at home, and they have not followed them. True, our expectations are often blasted; but let not this dishearten you. If they have faithfully discharged their duty, even after they are dead their works may live; their prodigal children may return to God and become heirs of salvation; if not, their children cannot rise and condemn them at the awful bar of God.

Perhaps you will say that you cannot send them to high schools and academies. You can have them taught in the first rudiments of useful knowledge, and then you can have private teachers who will instruct them in the higher branches; and their intelligence will become greater than ours, and their children will attain to higher advantages, and their children still higher; and then, though we are dead, our works shall live: though we are mouldering, our names shall not be forgotten.

Finally, my heart's desire and prayer to God is that there might come a thorough reformation among us. Our minds have too long grovelled in ignorance and sin. Come, let us incline our ears to wisdom, and apply our hearts to understanding; promote her, and she will exalt thee; she shall bring thee honor when thou dost embrace her. An ornament of grace shall she be to thy head, and a crown of glory shall she deliver to thee. Take fast hold of instruction; let her not go, keep her, for she is thy life [Proverbs 4:13]. Come, let us turn unto the Lord our God, with all our heart and soul, and put away every unclean and unholy thing from among us, and walk before the Lord our God, with a perfect heart, all the days of our lives: then we shall be a people with whom God shall delight to dwell; yea, we shall be that happy people whose God is the Lord.

I am of a strong opinion that the day on which we unite, heart and soul, and turn our attention to knowledge and improvement, that day the hissing and reproach among the nations of the earth against us will cease. And even those who now point at us with the finger of scorn, will aid and befriend us. It is of no use for us to sit with our hands folded, hanging our heads like bulrushes, lamenting our wretched condition; but let us make a mighty effort, and arise; and if no one will promote or respect us, let us promote and respect ourselves.

The American ladies have the honor conferred on them, that by prudence and economy in their domestic concerns, and their unwearied attention in forming the minds and manners of their children, they laid the foundation of their becoming what they now are. The good women of Wethersfield, Conn., toiled in the blazing sun, year after year, weeding onions, then sold the seed and procured enough money to erect them a house of worship, and shall we not imitate their examples, as far as they are worthy of imitation? Why cannot we do something to distinguish ourselves, and contribute some of our hard earnings that would reflect honor upon our memories, and cause our children to arise and call us blessed? Shall it any longer be said of the daughters of Africa, they have no ambition, they have no force? By no means. Let every female heart become united, and let us raise a fund ourselves; and at the end of one year and a half, we might be able to lay the corner stone for the building of a High School, that the higher branches of knowledge might be enjoyed by us; and God would raise us up, and enough to aid us in our laudable designs. Let each one strive to excel in good housewifery, knowing that prudence and economy are the road to wealth. Let us not say we know this, or we know that, and practise nothing, but let us practise what we do know.

How long shall the fair daughters of Africa be compelled to bury their minds and talents beneath a load of iron pots and kettles? Until union, knowledge and love begin to flow among us. How long shall a mean set of men flatter us with their smiles, and enrich themselves with our hard earnings, their wives' fingers sparkling with rings, and they themselves laughing at our folly? Until we begin to promote and patronize each other. Shall we be a by-word among the nations any longer? Shall they laugh us to scorn forever? Do you ask, what can we do? Unite and build a store of your own, if you cannot procure a license. Fill one side with dry goods, and the other with groceries. Do you ask where is the money? We have spent more than enough for nonsense, to do what building we should want. We have never had an opportunity of displaying our talents; therefore the world thinks we know nothing. And we have been possessed by far too mean and cowardly a disposition, though I highly disapprove of an insolent or impertinent one. Do you ask the disposition I would have you possess? Possess the spirit of independence. The Americans do, and why should not you? Possess the spirit of men, bold and enterprising, fearless and undaunted. Sue for your rights and privileges. Know the reason that you cannot attain them. Weary them with your importunities. You can but die if you make the attempt, and we shall certainly die if you do not. The Americans have practised nothing but head-work these 200 years, and we have done their drudgery. And is it not high time for us to imitate their examples, and practise head-work too, and keep what we have got, and get what we can? We need never to think that anybody is going to feel interested for us, if we do not feel interested for ourselves. That day we, as a people, hearken unto the voice of the Lord, our God, and walk in his ways and ordinances, and become distinguished for our ease, elegance and grace, combined with other virtues, that day the Lord will raise us up, and enough to aid and befriend us, and we shall begin to flourish.

Did every gentleman in America realize, as one, that they had got to become bondmen, and their wives, their sons, and their daughters, servants forever, to Great Britain, their very joints would become loosened, and tremblingly would smite one against another; their countenance would be filled with horror, every nerve and muscle would be forced into action, their souls would recoil at the very thought, their hearts would die within them, and death would be far more preferable. Then why have not Afric's sons the right to feel the same' Are not their wives, their sons, and their daughters, as dear to them as those of the white man's? Certainly God has not deprived them of the divine influences of his Holy Spirit, which is the greatest of all blessings, if they ask him. Then why should man any-longer deprive his fellow-man of equal rights and privileges? Oh, America, America, foul and indelible is thy stain! Dark and dismal is the cloud that hangs over thee, for thy cruel wrongs and injuries to the fallen sons of Africa. The blood of her murdered ones cries to heaven for vengeance against thee. Thou art almost become drunken with the blood of her slain; thou hast enriched thyself through her toils and labors; and now thou refuseth to make even a small return. And thou hast caused the daughters of Africa to commit whoredoms and fornications, but upon thee be their curse.

O, ye great and mighty men of America, ye rich and powerful ones, many of you will call for the rocks and mountains to fall upon you, and to hide you from the wrath of the lamb [Revelation 6:16], and from him that sitteth upon the throne; whilst many of the sable-skinned Africans you now despise will shine in the kingdom of heaven as the stars forever and ever. Charity begins at home, and those that provide not for their own are worse than infidels. We know-that you are raising contributions to aid the gallant Poles; we know that you have befriended Greece and Ireland; and you have rejoiced with France, for her heroic deeds of valor. You have acknowledged all the nations of the earth, except Hayti; and you may publish, as far as the East is from the West, that you have two millions of negroes, who aspire no higher than to bow at your feet, and to court your smiles. You may kill, tyrannize, and oppress as much as you choose, until our cry shall come up before the throne of God; for I am firmly persuaded, that he will not suffer you to quell the proud, fearless and undaunted spirits of the Africans forever; for in his own time, he is able to plead our cause against you, and to pour out upon you the ten plagues of Egypt. We will not come out against you with swords and staves, as against a thief [Matthew 26:55]; but we will tell you that our souls are fired with the same love of liberty and independence with which your souls are fired. We will tell you that too much of your blood flows in our veins, too much of your color in our skins, for us not to possess your spirits. We will tell you that it is our gold that clothes you in fine linen and purple, and causes you to fare sumptuously every day [Luke 16:19]; and it is the blood of our fathers, and the tears of our brethren that have enriched your soils. AND WE CLAIM OUR RIGHTS. We will tell you that we are not afraid of them that kill the body, and after that can do no more; but we will tell you whom we do fear. We fear Him who is able, after He hath killed, to destroy both soul and body in hell forever. Then, my brethren, sheath your swords, and calm your angry passions. Stand still and know that the Lord he is God. Vengeance is his, and he will repay. It is a long lane that has no turn. America has risen to her meridian. When you begin to thrive, she will begin to fall. God hath raised you up a Walker and a Garrison. Though Walker sleeps, yet he lives, and his name shall be had in everlasting remembrance. I, even I, who am but a child, inexperienced to many of you, am a living witness to testify unto you this day, that I have seen the wicked in great power, spreading himself like a green bay tree, and lo, he passed away; yea, I diligently sought him, but he could not be found [Psalms 37:35]; and it is God alone that has inspired my heart to feel for Africa's woes. Then fret not yourselves because of evil doers. Fret not yourselves because of the men who bring wicked devices to pass; for they shall be cut down as the grass, and wither as the green herb. Trust in the Lord, and do good; so shalt thou dwell in the land, and verily thou shalt be fed. Encourage the noble-hearted Garrison. Prove to the world that you are neither ourang-outangs, or a species of mere animals, but that you possess the same powers of intellect as the proud-boasting American.

I am sensible, my brethren and friends, that many of you have been deprived of advantages, kept in utter ignorance, and that your minds are now darkened; and if any one of you have attempted to aspire after high and noble enterprises, you have met with so much opposition that your souls have become discouraged. For this very cause, a few of us have ventured to expose our lives in your behalf, to plead your cause against the great; and it will be of no use, unless you feel for yourselves and then your little ones, and exhibit the spirits of men. Oh then, turn your attention to knowledge and improvement; for knowledge is power. And God is able to fill you with wisdom and understanding, and to dispel your fears. Arm yourselves with the weapons of prayer. Put your trust in the living God. Persevere strictly in the paths of virtue. Let nothing be lacking on your part, and in God's own time, and his time is certainly the best, he will surely deliver you with a mighty hand and with an outstretched arm.

I have never taken one step, my friends, with a design to raise myself in your esteem, or to gain applause. But what I have done, has been done with an eye single to the glory of God, and to promote the good of souls. I have neither kindred nor friends. I stand alone in your midst, exposed to the fiery darts of the devil, and to the assaults of wicked men. But though all the powers of earth and hell were to combine against me, though all nature should sink into decay, still I would trust in the Lord, and joy in the God of my salvation. For I am full persuaded that he will bring me off conqueror, yea, more than conqueror, through him who hath loved me and given himself for me.

Boston, October, 1831.

Lecture Delivered At Franklin Hall, 1832

Were the American free people of color to turn their attention more assiduously to moral worth and intellectual improvement, this would be the result: prejudice would gradually diminish, and the whites would be compelled to say, unloose those fetters!

> Though black their skins as shades of night
> Their hearts are pure, their souls are white.

Few white persons of either sex, who are calculated for anything else, are willing to spend their lives and bury their talents in performing mean, servile labor. And such is the horrible idea that I entertain respecting a life of servitude, that if I conceived of their [sic] being no possibility of my rising above the condition of servant, I would gladly hail death as a welcome messenger. O, horrible idea, indeed! to possess noble souls aspiring after high and honorable acquirements, yet confined by the chains of ignorance and poverty to lives of continual drudgery and toil. Neither do I know of any who have enriched themselves by spending their lives as house-domestics, washing windows, shaking carpets, brushing boots, or tending upon gentlemen's tables. I can but die for expressing my sentiments: and I am as willing to die by the sword as the pestilence; for I am a true born American; your blood flows in my veins, and your spirit fires my breast.

I observed a piece in the Liberator a few months since, stating that the colonizationists had published a work respecting us, asserting that we were lazy and idle. I confute them on that point. Take us generally as a people, we are neither lazy nor idle, and considering how little we have to excite or stimulate us, I am almost astonished that there are so many industrious and ambitious ones to be found; although I acknowledge, with extreme sorrow, that there are some who never were and never will be serviceable to society. And have you not a similar class among yourselves?

Again. It was asserted that we were "a ragged set, crying for liberty." I reply to it, the whites have so long and so loudly proclaimed the theme of equal rights and privileges, that our souls have caught the flame also, ragged as we are. As far as our merit deserves, we feel a common desire to rise above the condition of servants and drudges. I have learnt, by bitter experience, that continual hard labor deadens the energies of the soul, and benumbs the faculties of the mind; the ideas become confined, the mind barren, and, like the scorching sands of Arabia, produces nothing; or like the uncultivated soil, brings forth thorns and thistles.

Again, continual and hard labor irritates our tempers and sours our dispositions; the whole system becomes worn out with toil and fatigue; nature herself becomes almost exhausted, and we care but little whether we live or die. It is true, that the free people of color throughout these United States are neither bought nor sold, nor under the lash of the cruel driver; many obtain a comfortable support; but few, if any, have an opportunity of becoming rich and independent; and the enjoyments we most pursue are as unprofitable to us as the spider's web or the floating bubbles that vanish into air. As servants, we are respected; but let us presume to aspire any higher, our employer regards us no longer. And were it not that the King eternal has declared that Ethiopia shall stretch forth her hands unto God, I should indeed despair,

I do not consider it derogatory, my friends, for persons to live out to service. There are many whose inclination leads them to aspire no higher; and I would highly commend the performance of almost anything for an honest livelihood; but where constitutional strength is wanting, labor of this kind, in its mildest form, is painful. And doubtless many are the prayers that have ascended to Heaven from Afric's daughters for strength to perform their work. Oh, many are the tears that have been shed for the want of that strength! Most of our color have dragged out a miserable existence of servitude from the cradle to the grave. And what literary acquirement can be made, or useful knowledge derived, from either maps, books, or charts, by those who continually drudge from Monday morning until Sunday noon? O, ye fairer sisters, whose hands are never soiled, whose nerves and muscles are never strained, go learn by experience! Had we had the opportunity that you have had, to improve our moral and mental faculties, what would have hindered our intellects from being as bright, and our manners from being as dignified as yours? Had it been our lot to have been nursed in the lap of affluence and ease, and to have basked beneath the smiles and sunshine of fortune, should we not have naturally supposed that we were never made to toil? And why are not our forms as delicate, and our constitutions as slender, as yours? Is not the workmanship as curious and complete? Have pity upon us, have pity upon us, O ye who have hearts to feel for other's woes, for the hand of God has touched us. Owing to the disadvantages under which we labor, there are many flowers among us that are

> …born to bloom unseen
> And waste their fragrance on the desert air.

My beloved brethren, as Christ has died in vain for those who will not accept his offered mercy, so will it be vain for the advocates of freedom to spend their breath in our behalf, unless with united hearts and souls you make some mighty efforts to raise your sons and daughters from the horrible state of servitude and degradation in which they are placed. It is upon you that woman depends; she can do but little besides using her influence; and it is for her sake and yours that I have come forward and made myself a hissing and a reproach among the people [Jeremiah 29:18]; for I am also one of the wretched and miserable daughters of the descendants of fallen Africa. Do you ask, why are you wretched and miserable? I reply, look at many of the most worthy and most interesting of us doomed to spend our lives in gentlemen's kitchens. Look at our young men, smart, active and energetic, with souls filled with ambitious lire; if they look forward, alas! What are their prospects? They can be nothing but the humblest laborers, on account of their dark complexions; hence many of them lose their ambition, and become worthless. Look at our middle-aged men, clad in their rusty plaids and coats; in winter, every cent they earn goes to buy their wood and pay their rents; the poor wives also toil beyond their strength, to help support their families. Look at our aged sires, whose heads are whitened with the frosts of seventy winters, with their old wood-saws on their backs. Alas, what keeps us so? Prejudice, ignorance and poverty. But ah! methinks our oppression is soon to come to an end; yea, before the Majesty of heaven, our groans and cries have reached the ears of the Lord of Sabaoth [James 5:4]. As the prayers and tears of Christians will avail the finally impenitent nothing; neither will the prayers and tears of the friends of humanity avail us anything, unless we possess a spirit of virtuous emulation within our breasts. Did the pilgrims, when they first landed on these shores, quietly compose themselves and say, "The Britons have all the money and all the power, and we must continue their servants forever?" Did they sluggishly sigh and say, "Our lot is hard, the Indians own the soil, and we cannot cultivate it?" No; they first made powerful efforts to raise themselves, and then God raised up those illustrious patriots, WASHINGTON and LAFAYETTE, to assist and defend them. And, my brethren, have you made a powerful effort? Have you prayed the legislature for mercy's sake to grant you all the rights and privileges of free citizens, that your daughters may rise to that degree of respectability which true merit deserves, and your sons above the servile situations which most of them fill?

Address Delivered At The African Masonic Hall, 1833

African rights and liberty is a subject that ought to fire the breast of every free man of color in these United States, and excite in his bosom a lively, deep, decided and heart-felt interest. When I cast my eyes on the long list of illustrious names that are enrolled on the bright annals of fame among the whites, I turn my eyes within, and ask my thoughts, "Where are the names of our illustrious ones?" It must certainly have been for the want of energy on the pan of the free people of color, that they have been long willing to bear the yoke of oppression. It must have been the want of ambition and force that has given the whites occasion to say that our natural abilities are not as good, and our capacities by nature inferior to theirs. They boldly assert that did we possess a natural independence of soul, and feel a love for liberty within our breasts, some one of our sable race, long before this, would have testified it, notwithstanding the disadvantages under which we labor. We have made ourselves appear altogether unqualified to speak in our own defence, and are therefore looked upon as objects of pity and commiseration. We have been imposed upon, insulted and derided on every side; and now, if we complain, it is considered as the height of impertinence. We have suffered ourselves to be considered as dastards, cowards, mean, faint-hearted wretches; and on this account (not because of our complexion) many despise us, and would gladly spurn us from their presence.

These things have fired my soul with a holy indignation, and compelled me thus to come forward, and endeavor to turn their attention to knowledge and improvement; for knowledge is power. I would ask, is it blindness of mind, or stupidity of soul, or the want of education that has caused our men who are 60 or 70 years of age, never to let their voices be heard, nor their hands be raised in behalf of their color? Or has it been for the fear of offending the whites? If it has, O ye fearful ones, throw off your fearfulness, and come forth in the name of the Lord, and in the strength of the God of Justice, and make yourselves useful and active members in society; for they admire a noble and patriotic spirit in others; and should they not admire it in us? If you are men, convince them that you possess the spirit of men; and as your day, so shall your strength be. Have the sons of Africa no souls' Feel they no ambitious desires? Shall the chains of ignorance forever confine them? Shall the insipid appellation of "clever negroes," or "good creatures," any longer content them? Where can we find among ourselves the man of science, or a philosopher, or an able statesman, or a counsellor at law? Show me our fearless and brave, our noble and gallant ones. Where are our lecturers in natural history, and our critics in useful knowledge? There may be a few such men among us, but they are rare. It is true our fathers bled and died in the revolutionary war, and others fought bravely under the command of Jackson, in defence of liberty. But where is the mane that has distinguished himself in these modern days by acting wholly in the defence of African rights and liberty? There was one, although he sleeps, his memory lives.

I am sensible that there are many highly intelligent men of color in these United States, in the force of whose arguments, doubtless, I should discover my inferiority; but if they are blessed with wit and talent, friends and fortune, why have they not made themselves men of eminence, by striving to take all the reproach that is cast upon the people of color, and in endeavoring to alleviate the woes of their brethren in bondage? Talk, without effort, is nothing; you are abundantly capable, gentlemen, of making yourselves men of distinction; and this gross neglect, on your part, causes my blood to boil within me. Here is the grand cause which hinders the rise and progress of people of color. It is their want of laudable ambition and requisite courage.

Individuals have been distinguished according to their genius and talents, ever since the first formation of man, and will continue to be while the world stands. The different grades rise to honor and respectability as their merits may deserve. History informs us that we sprung from one of the most learned nations of the whole earth; from the seat, if not the parent, of science. Yes, poor despised Africa was once the resort of sages and legislators of other nations, was esteemed the school for learning, and the most illustrious men in Greece flocked thither for instruction. But it was our gross sins and abominations that provoked the Almighty to frown thus heavily upon us, and give our glory unto others. Sin and prodigality have caused the downfall of nations, kings and emperors; and were it not that God in wrath remembers mercy, we might indeed despair; but a promise is left us; "Ethiopia shall again stretch forth her hands unto God."

But it is of no use for us to boast that we sprung from this learned and enlightened nation, for this day a thick mist of moral gloom hangs over millions of our race. Our condition as a people has been low for hundreds of years, and it will continue to be so, unless by true piety and virtue, we strive to regain that which we have lost. White Americans, by their prudence, economy, and exertions, have sprung up and become one of the most flourishing nations in the world, distinguished for their knowledge of the arts and sciences, for their polite literature. While our minds are vacant and starve for want of knowledge, theirs are filled to overflowing. Most of our color have been taught to stand in fear of the white man from their earliest infancy, to work as soon as they could walk, and to call "master" before they could scarce lisp the name of mother. Continual fear and laborious servitude have in some degree lessened in us that natural force and energy which belong to man; or else, in defiance of opposition, our men, before this, would have nobly and boldly contended for their rights. But give the man of color an equal opportunity with the white from the cradle to manhood, and from manhood to the grave, and you would discover the dignified statesman, the man of science, and the philosopher. But there is no such opportunity for the sons of Africa, and I fear that our powerful ones are fully determined that there never shall be. Forbid, ye Powers on high, that it should any longer be said that our men possess no force. O ye sons of Africa, when will your voices be heard in our legislative halls, in defiance of your enemies, contending for equal rights and liberty? How can you, when you reflect from what you have fallen, refrain from crying mightily unto God, to turn away from us the fierceness of his anger, and remember our transgressions against us no more forever? But a god of infinite purity will not regard the prayers of those who hold religion in one hand, and prejudice, sin and pollution in the other; he will not regard the prayers of self-righteousness and hypocrisy. Is it possible, I exclaim, that for the want of knowledge we have labored for hundreds of years to support others, and been content to receive what they chose to give us in return? Cast your eyes about, look as far as you can see; all, all is owned by the lordly white, exept here and there a lowly dwelling which the man of color, midst deprivations, fraud, and opposition has been scarce able to procure. Like King Solomon, who put neither nail nor hammer to the temple, yet received the praise; so also have the white Americans gained themselves a name, like the names of the great men that are in the earth, while in reality we have been their principal foundation and support. We have pursued the shadow, they have obtained the substance; we have performed the labor, they have received the profits; we have planted the vines, they have eaten the fruits of them.

I would implore our men, and especially our rising youth, to flee from the gambling board and the dance-hall; for we are poor, and have no money to throw away. I do not consider dancing as criminal in itself, but it is astonishing to me that our fine young men are so blind to their own interest and the future welfare of their children as to spend their hard earnings for this frivolous amusement; for it has been carried on among us to such an unbecoming extent that it has become absolutely disgusting. "Faithful are the wounds of a friend, but the kisses of an enemy are deceitful [Proverbs 27:6]." Had those men among us who had an opportunity, turned their attention as assiduously to mental and moral improvement as they have to gambling and dancing, I might have remained quietly at home and they stood contending in my place. These polite accomplishments will never enroll your names on the bright annals of fame who admire the belle void of intellectual knowledge, or applaud the dandy that talks largely on politics, without striving to assist his fellow in the revolution, when the nerves and muscles of every other man forced him into the field of action. You have a right to rejoice, and to let your hearts cheer you in the days of your youth; yet remember that for all these things God will bring you into judgment. Then, O ye sons of Africa, turn your mind from these perishable objects, and contend for the cause of God and the rights of man. Form yourselves into societies. There are temperate men among you; then why will you any longer neglect to strive, by your example, to suppress vice in all its abhorrent forms? You have been told repeatedly of the glorious results arising from temperance, and can you bear to see the whites arising in honor and respectability without endeavoring to grasp after that honor and respectability also?

But I forbear. Let our money, instead of being thrown away as heretofore, be appropriated for schools and seminaries of learning for our children and youth. We ought to follow the example of the whites in this respect. Nothing would raise our respectability, add to our peace and happiness, and reflect so much honor upon us, as to *be* ourselves the promoters of temperance, and the supporters, as far as we are able, of useful and scientific knowledge. The rays of light and knowledge have been hid from our view; we have been taught to consider ourselves as scarce superior to the brute creation; and have performed the most laborious part of American drudgery. Had we as a people received one-half the early advantages the whites have received, I would defy the government of these United States to deprive us any longer of our rights.

I am informed that the agent of the Colonization Society has recently formed an association of young men for the purpose of influencing those of us to go to Liberia who may feel disposed. The colonizationists are blind to their own interest, for should the nations of the earth make war with America, they would find their forces much weakened by our absence; or should we remain here, can our "brave soldiers" and "fellow citizens," as they were termed in time of calamity, condescend to defend the rights of whites and be again deprived of their own, or sent to Liberia in return? Or, if the colonizationists are the real friends to Africa, let them expend the money which they collect in erecting a college to educate her injured sons in this land of gospel, light, and liberty; for it would be most thankfully received on our part, and convince us of the truth of their professions, and save time, expense, and anxiety. Let them place before us noble objects worthy of pursuit, and see if we prove ourselves to be those unambitious negroes they term us. But, ah, methinks their hearts are so frozen toward us they had rather their money should be sunk in the ocean than to administer it to our relief.

The unfriendly whites first drove the native American from his much loved home. Then they stole our fathers from their peaceful and quiet dwellings, and brought them hither, and made bond-men and bond-women of them and their little ones. They have obliged our brethren to labor, kept them in utter ignorance; nourished them in vice, and raised them in degradation; and now that we have enriched their soil, and filled their coffers, they say that we are not capable of becoming like white men, and that we can never rise to respectability in this country. They would drive us to a strange land. But before I go, the bayonet shall pierce me through. African rights and liberty is a subject that ought to fire the breast of every free man of color in these United States, and excite in his bosom a lively, deep, decided, and heartfelt interest.

3.
FREDERICK DOUGLASS

Frederick Douglass (1817–1895)[1] was born a slave in Maryland. In 1838 Douglass escaped from slavery and in the process he was jailed. While living in New England Douglass became actively involved in the abolitionist movement. He was a huge admirer of William Lloyd Garrison. In 1845 he published his autobiography, which he revised in 1882, and in December 1847 he founded his weekly abolitionist paper, the *North Star*. Douglass, like many of the African American political activists compiled in this volume, realized that the press was a powerful medium to mobilize the subaltern. In 1851 the *North Star* united with the *Liberty* newspaper and thereafter was known as the *Frederick Douglass Paper*. Douglass also published a magazine, *Douglass Monthly*. From 1870 to 1874, in order to reach more former slaves, he took over another weekly in Washington, D.C., *The New National Era*.

As Douglass matured as a political thinker he developed his own positions on abolition. In fact, he parted ways with his long time hero, William Lloyd Garrison. Douglass was far more moderate than Garrison and others in the abolitionist movement such as David Walker. As you will see in the readings in this chapter, rather than disparaging the church, Douglass believed the institution could be swayed to play a vital role in emancipation. Unlike Garrison and others, Douglass believed that democratic reform was possible. In fact, he held political positions; from 1877 to 1881 Douglass served as U.S. Marshall for the District of Columbia. He was also the minister of Haiti from 1889 to 1891. Finally while Garrison and many radical abolitionists posited that the Union should be dissolved, once again, Douglass saw the hope of resolve between the torn North and South. This is not to suggest that Douglass was a pacifist. Douglass was a radical. He was a former slave, vehemently demanding rights for African Americans and for women in general. Douglass died in Washington, D.C. on February 20, 1895; he was an American hero.

Overview of Ideas

Frederick Douglass, one of our nation's most famous abolitionists, called for an immediate end to slavery. Unlike David Walker, this end would be brought about through both democratic reform and moral reform. While Douglass's methods were less radical than Walker's, Douglass never wavered in the fight against slavery. All of the theorists in this section agreed with Douglass that "traffic in human flesh is a sin against God." By appealing to tenets of Christian faith, Douglass and others knew they could win allies in many Whites. However, Douglass indicts many churches and clergy members for not lending enough support, if any, to the movement. In fact, Douglass argues,

> the stronghold of Slavery is in the pulpit. Say what we may of politician and political parties, the power that holds the keys of the dungeon in which the bondman is confined, is the pulpit. It is that power which is dropping, dropping, constantly dropping on the ear of this people, creating and molding the moral sentiment of the land. This they have sufficiently under their control that they can change it from the spirit of hatred to that of love to mankind.

Preachers and clergymen have the power to help eradicate slavery but instead help reinforce it through dogmatic law and scripture. Too many Black folk are taught to not question slavery because after all they will be free upon salvation and in eternal life in Heaven. They are taught to be passive; they are told our parents dealt with the atrocities of slavery and we too can tolerate it and live through it until we get to Heaven. However, rather than abandoning the institution Douglass believed they could be made to see the sinful nature of slavery and speak out for its immediate end. Drawing from Christian principles Douglass posited that no violence was needed to meet the abolitionist movement's ends. "I have become a friend of that religion which teaches us to pray for our enemies ... I would not hurt a hair of a slaveholder's head." Douglass staunchly believed we could change the hearts and minds of racist Americans—making them understand slavery was immoral.

Douglass argued that slavery was a moral problem.

> Slavery must be abolished, and that can only be done by enforcing the great principles of justice. Vainly you talk about voting it down. When you cast your millions of ballots, you have not reached the evil. It has fastened its root deep into the heart of the nation, and nothing but God's truth and love can cleanse the land. We must change moral sentiment.

Frederick Douglass was not a trained social scientist. However, his work displayed an astute understanding of the social world. Douglass wrote that Whites were not prejudiced against Africans in the United States because of skin color. Rather their prejudice was a result of the discourses associated with blackness. "We are then a persecuted people; not because we are *colored* [emphasis his], but simply because that color has for a series of years been coupled in the public mind with the degradation of slavery and servitude." Whites subjugated Blacks because they adhered to sets of discourses, originally created to legitimize the system of slavery, that said that Africans were morally, culturally, and intellectually inferior. Therefore, it is these discourses that are the problem. Through behavior Black folk should demonstrate that these discourses are spurious.

An end to slavery would take a lot of action from Black folk themselves. Douglass relied heavily on conservative ideas related to self-help and individual transformation of pathologies. "Our white friends can and are rapidly removing the barriers to our improvement, which themselves have set up; but the main work must be commenced, carried on, and concluded by ourselves." It is interesting that self-help ideology developed under abolitionism. "We must rise or fall, succeed or fail, by our own merits."

Black people needed to prove that they were worthy of emancipation. We will see this idea woven in and out of African American political thought. Douglass told people to build character and show racist Whites how respectable African Americans are. Black people needed to show the United States "that we are men, worthy men, good citizens, good Christians, and ought to be treated as such." African Americans needed to refashion their behaviors and publicly demonstrate their Christian character in order to gain emancipation and become full-fledged citizens. However, behavioral change could not be the only strategy adopted by Black activists.

Throughout this text, almost all these leaders posited that the Black press was vital to emancipation. Supporting the Black press enables critical dialogue. African Americans needed to organize national conventions and utilize existing large fellowships to both discuss and debate their problems, calling for rights, and planning strategies for bringing about emancipation. Douglass said Black people needed to speak out and the Black press served as an extraordinary secular institution that could facilitate organization, protest, and debate.

Like his future counterparts, Douglass placed an emphasis on education. Even if education is kept from slaves via the Black Codes or if schools for freed slaves are limited, Black people must teach one another; teach their children. As a child Douglass learned this. After his slave master's wife illegally taught Douglass to read and write, Douglass continued to learn from young boys on the streets. There was a famous axiom that developed under slavery—"each one teach one." Even if African Americans were institutionally deprived of education it was the moral imperative of those African Americans who had been educated to teach other Black folk.

Again, while seemingly moderate, Douglass was also a supporter of women's rights, which made him incredibly radical. In response to the Seneca Falls Convention in 1848 and the growing first wave women's movement, he remarked that these women were able and dignified. He characterized the movement's leaders as brilliant. Douglass emphatically argued that women were entitled to the same rights as men. Women were just as intelligent as men. Women should be able to vote. Douglass posited that the same rights African American were entitled to should also be secured by women.

Martin Delany (see Part III) and others were already publicly advocating for a "back to Africa" movement. Douglass was opposed to a mass exodus from the United States. Slaves, while under deplorable circumstances, built this country. This country's land and wealth were built from the blood, sweat, and tears of Black folk. Why should they have to leave? Douglass noted that the Native Americans, the original "owners" and cultivators of this land, were robbed of their land, killed, maimed, raped, and forced into marginal spaces. African Americans must not meet the same fate. Therefore, despite pleas from both Whites and Blacks to not see the United States as a home, Douglass implored African Americans to see the United States as their home—a home worth fighting for. Whites and Blacks needed to find a way to live in harmony and erect equality between them.

It is evident that the white and black "must fall or flourish together." In the light of this great truth, laws ought to be enacted, and institutions established-all distinctions, founded on complexion, ought to be repealed, repudiated, and forever abolished-and every right, privilege, and immunity, now enjoyed by the white man, ought to be freely granted to the man of color.

Douglass vehemently opposed the burgeoning back-to-Africa movement; Africans needed to now be seen as Americans.

Douglass argued that Black people were Americans, who deserved full rights. He said all Black folk wanted was justice—not pity. Douglass demanded that African Americans not be treated like strangers, enemies, or barbarians. He asked for access to the same rights and resources as Whites. He required that Black children have equal access to schools, jobs, churches, and colleges. He demanded equal protection under the Constitution. For example, Douglass emphatically argued that Blacks should have the right to serve on juries, bear arms, not have to serve in an segregated army, and vote. Douglass argued that under a democracy, our urban republic is supposed to thrive from equality, not be riddled by inequalities. In order to realize full democracy slavery must be abolished. Douglass declared that Blacks would not stop until equality was realized. They would speak out in public and in the press. They will organize men and women from all backgrounds and appeal to the clergy to reach a wide audience. They will demand these rights from the government. Blacks must devote their own money and resources to this battle. Through all these means Black folk must fight to become recognized as American citizens.

Douglass confronted Americans' trepidation and fear that freeing slaves would promote chaos. Many Americans feared the worst; they feared that emancipation would leave slaves to become vagrants roaming the streets. Many feared that Blacks would become criminals and race relations would become strained to the extent that a race war would erupt in which Blacks who lacked resources would lose. Douglass tried to put these fears to rest. He posited that after emancipation the solution to what should happen with newly freed slaves was simple—leave them alone. Douglass argued that if society provided equal access to basic social institutions that all would be fine. However, the requirement to avoid the doomsday scenario offered by so many was for Whites to leave Black people alone. Black folk would persevere. They would work, attend school, and take care of their families and if Whites did not disturb these basic activities then no problems would arise. Peace would require that Whites accepted emancipation and justice—nothing more.

American Slavery, 1847

For sixteen years, Wm. Lloyd Garrison and a noble army of the friends of emancipation have been labouring in season and out of season, amid smiles and frowns, sunshine and clouds, striving to establish the conviction through this land, that to hold and traffic in human flesh is a sin against God. They have been somewhat successful; but they have been in no wise so successful as they might have been, had the men and women at the North rallied around them as they had a right to hope from their profession. They have had to contend not only with skilful politicians, with a deeply prejudiced and pro-slavery community, but with eminent Divines, Doctors of Divinity, and Bishops.

Instead of encouraging them as friends, they have acted as enemies. For many days did Garrison go the rounds of the city of Boston to ask of the ministers the poor privilege of entering their chapels and lifting up his voice for the dumb. But their doors were bolted, their gates barred, and their pulpits hermetically sealed. It was not till an infidel hall was thrown open, that the voice of dumb millions could be heard in Boston.

I take it that all who have heard at all on this subject, are well convinced that the stronghold of Slavery is in the pulpit. Say what we may of politicians and political parties, the power that holds the keys of the dungeon in which the bondman is confined, is the pulpit. It is that power which is dropping, dropping, constantly dropping on the ear of this people, creating and moulding [*sic*] the moral sentiment of the land.... There is nothing that will facilitate our cause more than getting the people to laugh at that religion which brings its influence to support traffic in human flesh. It has deceived us so long that it has overawed us.

For a long time when I was a slave, I was led to think from hearing such passages as "servants obey, &c." that if I dared to escape, the wrath of God would follow me.... If I could have the men at this meeting who hold such sentiments and could hold up the mirror to let them see themselves as others see them, we should soon make head against this pro-slavery religion.

I dwell mostly upon the religious aspect, because I believe it is the religious people who are to be relied on in this Anti-Slavery movement. Do not misunderstand my railing—do not class me with those who despise religion—do not identify me with the infidel. I love the religion of Christianity—which cometh from above—which is pure, peaceable, gentle, easy to be entreated, full of good fruits, and without hypocrisy. I love that religion which sends its votaries to bind up the wounds of those who have fallen among thieves.

I am not a man of war. The time was when I was. I was then a slave: I had dreams, horrid dreams of freedom through a sea of blood. But when I heard of the Anti-Slavery movement, light broke in upon my dark mind. Bloody visions fled away, and I saw the star of liberty peering above the horizon. Hope then took the place of desperation, and I was led to repose in the arms of Slavery. I said, I would suffer rather than do any act of violence—rather than that the glorious day of liberty might be postponed.

Since the light of God's truth beamed upon my mind, I have become a friend of that religion which teaches us to pray for our enemies—which, instead of shooting balls into their hearts, loves them. I would not hurt a hair of a slaveholder's head. I will tell you what else I would not do. I would not stand around the slave with my bayonet pointed at his breast, in order to keep him in the power of the slaveholder.

I am aware that there are many who think the slaves are very well off, and that they are very well treated, as if it were possible that such a thing could be. A man happy in chains! Even the eagle loves liberty.

As with the eagle, so with man. No amount of attention or finery, no dainty dishes can be a substitute for liberty. Slaveholders know this and knowing it, they exclaim,— "The South are surrounded by a dangerous population, degraded, stupid savages, and if they could but entertain the idea that immediate, unconditional death would not be their portion, they would rise at once and enact the St. Domingo tragedy. But they are held in subordination by the consciousness that the whole nation would rise and crush them." Thus they live in constant dread from day to day.

Friends, Slavery must be abolished, and that can only be done by enforcing the great principles of justice. Vainly you talk about voting it down. When you have cast your millions of ballots, you have not reached the evil. It has fastened its root deep into the heart of the nation, and nothing but God's truth and love can cleanse the land. We must change the moral sentiment. Hence we ask you to support the Anti-Slavery Society. It is not an organization to build up political parties, or churches, nor to pull them down, but to stamp the image of Anti-Slavery truth upon the community. Here we may all do something.

What Are the Colored People Doing for Themselves?, 1848

The present is a time when every colored man in the land should bring this important question home to his own heart. It is not enough to know that white men and women are nobly devoting themselves to our cause; we should know what is being done among ourselves. That our white friends have done, and are still doing, a great and good work for us, is a fact which ought to excite in us sentiments of the profoundest gratitude; but it must never be forgotten that when they have exerted all their energies, devised every scheme, and done all they can do in asserting our rights, proclaiming our wrongs, and rebuking our foes, their labor is lost—yea, worse than lost, unless we are found in the faithful discharge of our anti-slavery duties. If there be one evil spirit among us, for the casting out of which we pray more earnestly than another, it is that lazy, mean and cowardly spirit, that robs us of all manly self-reliance, and teaches us to depend upon others for the accomplishment of that which we should achieve with our own hands. Our white friends can and are; rapidly removing the barriers to our improvement, which themselves have set up; but the main work must be commenced, carried on, and concluded by ourselves. While in no circumstances should we undervalue or fail to appreciate the self-sacrificing efforts of our friends, it should never be lost sight of, that our destiny, for good or for evil, for time and for eternity, is, by an all-wise God, committed to us; and that all the help or hindrances with which we may meet on earth, can never release us from this high and heaven-imposed responsibility. It is evident that we be improved and elevated only just so fast and far as we shall improve and elevate ourselves. We must rise or fall, succeed or fail, by our own merits. If we are careless and unconcerned about our own rights and interests, it is not within the power of all the earth combined to raise us from our present degraded condition.

What we, the colored people, want, is *character*, and this nobody can give us. It is a thing we must get for ourselves. We must labor for it. It is gained by toil—hard toil. Neither the sympathy nor the generosity of our friends can give it to us. It is attainable—yes, thank God, it is attains able. "There is gold in the earth, but we must dig it"—so with character. It is attainable; but we must attain it, and attain it each for himself. I cannot for you, and you cannot for me.—What matters it to the mass of colored people of this country that they are able to point to their Peningtons, Garnets, Remonds, Wards, Purvises, Smiths, Whippers, Sandersons, and a respectable list of other men of character, which we might name, while our general ignorance makes these men exceptions to our race? Their talents can do little to give us character in the eyes of the world. We must get character for ourselves, as a people. A change in our political condition would do very little for us without this. Character is the important thing, and without it we must continue to be marked for degradation and stamped with the brand of inferiority. With character, we shall be powerful. Nothing can harm us long when we get character.—There are certain great elements of character in us which may be hated, but never despised. Industry, sobriety, honesty, combined with intelligence and a due self-respect, find them where you will, among black or white, must be *looked up to*—can never be *looked down upon.* In their presence, prejudice is abashed, confused and mortified. Encountering this solid mass of living character, our vile oppressors are ground to atoms. In its presence) the sneers of a caricaturing press, the taunts of natural inferiority, the mischievous assertions of Clay, and fine-spun sophisms of Calhoun, are innoxious, powerless and unavailing. In answer to these men and the sneers of the multitude, there is nothing in the wide world half so *effective*, as the presentation of a character precisely the opposite of all their representations. We have it in our power to convert the weapons intended for our injury into positive blessings. That we may sustain temporary injury from gross and general misrepresentation, is most true; but the Injury is but temporary, and must disappear at the approach of light, like mist from the vale. The offensive traits of character imputed to us, can only be injurious while they are true of us. For a man to say that sweet is bitter—that right is wrong—that light is darkness—is not to injure the 'truth, but to stamp himself a liar; and the like is true when they impute that of which we are not guilty. We have the power of making our enemies slanderers, and this we must do by showing ourselves worthy and respectable men.

We are not insensible to the various obstacles that throng the colored man's pathway to respectability. Embarrassments and perplexities, unknown to other men, are common to us. Though born on American soil, we have fewer privileges than aliens. The school-house, the work-shop, counting-house, attorney's office, and various professions, are opened to them, but closed to us. This, and much more, is true. A general and withering prejudice—a malignant and active hate, pursues us even in the best parts of this country. But a few days ago, one of our best and most talented men—and he a *lame man*, having lost an important limb—was furiously hurled from a car on the Niagara & Buffalo Railroad, by a band of white ruffians, who claim impunity for their atrocious outrage on the plea that New York law does not protect the rights of colored against a company of white men, and the sequel has proved them right; for the case, it appears, was brought before the grand jury, but that jury found no bill. We cannot at this time dwell on this aspect of the subject.

The fact that we are limited and circumscribed, ought rather to incite us to a more vigorous and persevering use of the elevating means within our reach, than to dishearten us. The means of education, though not so free and open to us as to white persons, are nevertheless at our command to such an extent as to make education possible; and these, thank God, are increasing. Let us educate our children, even though it should us subject to a coarser and scantier diet, and disrobe us of our few fine garments. "For the want of knowledge we are killed all the day." Get wisdom—get understanding, is a peculiarly valuable exhortation to us, and the compliance with it is our only hope in this land.—It is idle, a hollow mockery, for us to pray to God to break the oppressor's power, while we neglect the means of knowledge which will give us the ability to break this power.—God will help us when we help ourselves. Our oppressors have divested us of many valuable blessings and facilities for improvement and elevation; but, thank heaven, they have not yet been able to take from us the privilege of being honest, industrious, sober and intelligent. We may read and understand—we may speak and write—we may expose our wrongs—we may appeal to the sense of justice yet alive in the public mind, and by an honest, upright life, we may at last wring from a reluctant public the all-important confession, that we are men, worthy men, good citizens, good Christians, and ought to be treated as such.

The Rights of Women, 1848

One of the most interesting events of the past week, was the holding of what is technically styled a Woman's Rights Convention at Seneca Falls. The speaking, addresses, and resolutions of this extraordinary meeting was almost wholly conducted by women; and although they evidently felt themselves in a novel position, it is but simple justice to say that their whole proceedings were characterized by marked ability and dignity. No one present, we think, however much he might be disposed to differ from the views advanced by the leading speakers on that occasion, will fail to give them credit for brilliant talents and excellent dispositions. In this meeting, as in other deliberative assemblies, there were frequent differences of opinion and animated discussion; but in no case was there the slightest absence of good feeling and decorum. Several interesting documents setting forth the rights as well as the grievances of women were read. Among these was a Declaration of Sentiments, to be regarded as the basis of a grand movement for attaining the civil, social, political, and religious rights of women. We should not do justice to our own convictions, or to the excellent persons connected with this infant movement, if we did not in this connection offer a few remarks on the general subject which the Convention met to consider and the objects they seek to attain. In doing so, we are not insensible that the bare mention of this truly important subject in any other than terms of contemptuous ridicule and scornful disfavor, is likely to excite against us the fury of bigotry and the folly of prejudice. A discussion of the rights of animals would be regarded with far more complacency by many of what are called the *wise* and the *good* of our land, than would a discussion of the rights of women. It is, in their estimation, to be guilty of evil thoughts, to think that woman is entitled to equal rights with man. Many who have at last made the discovery that the Negroes have some rights as well as other members of the human family, have yet to be convinced that women are entitled to any. Eight years ago a number of persons of this description actually abandoned the anti-slavery cause, lest by giving their influence in that direction they might possibly be giving countenance to the dangerous heresy that woman, in respect to rights, stands on an equal footing with man. In the judgment of such persons the American slave system, with all its concomitant horrors, is less to be deplored than this *wicked* idea. It is perhaps needless to say, that we cherish little sympathy for such sentiments or respect for such prejudices. Standing as we do upon the watch-tower of human freedom, we cannot be deterred from an expression of our approbation of any movement, however humble, to improve and elevate the character of any members of the human family. While it is impossible for us to go into this subject at length, and dispose of the various objections which are often urged against such a doctrine as that of female equality, we are free to say that in respect to political say rights, we hold woman to be justly entitled to all we claim for man. We go farther, and express our conviction that all political rights which it is expedient for man to exercise, it is equally so for woman. All that distinguishes man as an intelligent and accountable being, is equally true of woman, and if that government only is just which governs by the free consent of the governed, there can be no reason in the world for denying to woman the exercise of the elective franchise, or a hand in making and administering the laws of the land. Our doctrine is that "right is of no sex." We therefore bid the women engaged in this movement our humble Godspeed.

The Destiny of Colored Americans, 1849

We deem it a settled point that the destiny of the colored man is bound up with that of the white people of this country; be the destiny of the latter what it may. It is idle—worse than idle, ever to think of our expatriation, or removal. The history of the colonization society must extinguish all such speculations. We are rapidly filling up the number of four millions; and all the gold of California combined, would be insufficient to defray the expenses attending our colonization. We are, as laborers, too essential to the interests of our white fellow-countrymen, to make a very grand effort to drive us from this country among probable events. While labor is needed, the laborer cannot fail to be valued; and although passion and prejudice may sometimes vociferate against us, and demand our expulsion, such efforts will only be spasmodic, and can never prevail against the sober second thought of self-interest. *We are here*, and here we are likely to be. To imagine that we shall ever be eradicated is absurd and ridiculous. We can be remodified, changed, and assimilated, but never extinguished. We repeat, therefore, that *we are here*; and that this is *our* country; and the question for the philosophers and statesmen of the land ought to be, What principles should dictate the policy of the action towards us? We shall neither die out, nor be driven out; but shall go with this people, either as a testimony against them, or as an evidence in their favor throughout their generations. We are clearly on their hands, and must remain there for ever. All this we say for the benefit of those who hate the Negro more than they love their country. In an article, under the caption of "Government and its Subjects," (published in our last week's paper,) we called attention to the unwise, as well as the unjust policy usually adopted, by our Government, towards its colored citizens. We would continue to direct attention to that policy, and in our humble way, we would remonstrate against it, as fraught with evil to the white man, as well as to his victim.

The white man's happiness cannot be purchased by the black man's misery. Virtue cannot prevail among the white people, by its destruction among the black people, who form a part of the whole community. It is evident that white and black "must fall or flourish together." In the light of this great truth, laws ought to be enacted, and institutions established—all distinctions, founded on complexion, ought to be repealed, repudiated, and for ever abolished—and every right, privilege, and immunity, now enjoyed by the white man, ought to be as freely granted to the man of color.

Where "knowledge is power," that nation is the most powerful which has the largest population of intelligent men; for a nation to cramp, and circumscribe the mental faculties of a class of its inhabitants, is as unwise as it is cruel, since it, in the same proportion, sacrifices its power and happiness. The American people, in the light of this reasoning, are, at this moment, in obedience to their pride and folly, (we say nothing of the wickedness of the act,) wasting one sixth part of the energies of the entire nation by transforming three millions of its men into beasts of burden.—What a loss to industry, skill, invention, (to say nothing of its foul and corrupting influence,) is *Slavery!* How it ties the hand, cramps the mind, darkens the understanding, and paralyses the whole man! Nothing is more evident to a man who reasons at all, than that America is acting an irrational part in continuing the slave system at the South, and in oppressing its free colored citizens at the North. Regarding the nation as an individual, the act of enslaving and oppressing thus, is as wild and senseless as it would be for Nicholas to order the amputation of the right arm of every Russian soldier before engaging in a war with France. We again repeat that Slavery is the peculiar weakness of America, as well as its peculiar crime; and the day may yet come when this visionary and oft repeated declaration will be found to contain a great truth.

The Claims of our Common Cause, 1853

Fellow citizens:

Met in convention as delegates, representing the Free Colored people of the United States; charged with the responsibility of inquiring into the general condition of our people, and of devising measures which may, with the blessing of God, tend to our mutual improvement and elevation; conscious of entertaining no motives, ideas, or aspirations, but such as are in accordance with truth and justice, and are compatible with the highest good of our country and the world, with a cause as vital and worthy as that for which (nearly eighty years ago) your fathers and our fathers bravely contended, and in which they gloriously triumphed—we deem it proper, on this occasion, as one method of promoting the honorable ends for which we have met, and of discharging our duty to those in whose name we speak, to present the claims of our common cause to your candid, earnest, and favorable consideration.

As an apology for addressing you, fellow-citizens! we cannot announce the discovery of any new principle adapted to ameliorate the condition of mankind. The great truths of moral and political science, upon which we rely, and which we press upon your consideration, have been evolved and enunciated by you. We point to your principles, your wisdom, and to your great example as the full justification of our course this day. That "all men are created equal": that "life, liberty, and the pursuit of happiness" are the right of all; that "taxation and representation" should go together; that governments are to protect, not to destroy, the rights of mankind; that the Constitution of the United States was formed to establish justice, promote the general welfare, and secure the blessing of liberty to all the people of this country; that resistance to tyrants is obedience to God—are American principles and maxims, and together they form and constitute the constructive elements of the American government. From this elevated platform, provided by the Republic for us, and for all the children of men, we address you. In doing so, we would have our spirit properly discerned. On this point we would gladly free ourselves and our cause from all misconception. We shall affect no especial timidity, nor can we pretend to any great boldness. We know our poverty and weakness, and your wealth and greatness. Yet we will not attempt to repress the spirit of liberty within us, or to conceal, in any wise, our sense of the justice and the dignity of our cause.

We are Americans, and as Americans, we would speak to Americans. We address you not as aliens nor as exiles, humbly asking to be permitted to dwell among you in peace; but we address you as American citizens asserting their rights on their own native soil. Neither do we address you as enemies, (although the recipients of innumerable wrongs); but in the spirit of patriotic good will. In assembling together as we have done, our object is not to excite pity for ourselves, but to command respect for our cause, and to obtain justice for our people. We are not malefactors imploring mercy; but we trust we are honest men, honestly appealing for righteous judgment, and ready to stand or fall by that judgment. We do not solicit unusual favor, but will be content with roughhanded "fair play." We are neither lame or blind, that we should seek to through off the responsibility of our own existence, or to cast ourselves upon public charity for support. We would not lay our burdens upon other men's shoulders; but we do ask, in the name of all that is just and magnanimous among men, to be freed from all the unnatural burdens and impediments with which American customs and American legislation have hindered our progress and improvement. We ask to be disencumbered of the load of popular reproach heaped upon us—for no better cause than that we wear the complexion given us by our God and our Creator.

We ask that in our native land, we shall not be treated as strangers, and worse than strangers.

We ask that, being friends of America, we should not be treated as enemies of America.

We ask that, speaking the same language and being of the same religion, worshipping the same God, owing our redemption to the same Savior, and learning our duties from the same Bible, we shall not be treated as barbarians.

We ask that, having the same physical, moral, mental, and spiritual wants, common to other members of the human family, we shall also have the same means which are granted and secured to others, to supply those wants.

We ask that the doors of the school-house, the workshop, the church, the college, shall be thrown open as freely to our children as to the children of other members of the community.

We ask that the American government shall be so administered as that beneath the broad shield of the Constitution, the colored American seaman, shall be secure in his life, liberty and property, in every State in the Union.

We ask that as justice knows no rich, no poor, no black, no white, but, like the government of God, renders alike to every man reward or punishment, according as his works shall be—the white and black man may; stand upon an equal footing before the laws of the land.

We ask that (since the right of trial by jury is a safeguard to liberty, against the encroachments of power, only as it is a trial by impartial men, drawn indiscriminately from the country) colored men shall not, in every instance, be tried by white persons; and that colored men shall not be either by custom or enactment excluded from the jury-box.

We ask that (inasmuch as we are, in common with other American citizens, supporters of the State, subject to its laws, interested in its welfare liable to be called upon to defend it in time of war, contributors to its wealth in time of peace) the complete and unrestricted right of suffrage, which is essential to the dignity even of the white man, be extended to the Free Colored man also.

Whereas the colored people of the United States have too long been retarded and impeded in the development and improvement of their natural faculties and powers, even to become dangerous rivals to white men, in the honorable pursuits of life, liberty and happiness; and whereas, the proud Anglo-Saxon can need no arbitrary protection from open and equal competition with any variety of the human family; and whereas, laws have been enacted limiting the aspirations of colored men, as against white men—we respectfully submit that such laws are flagrantly unjust to the man of color, and plainly discreditable to white men; and for these and other reasons, such laws ought to be repealed.

We especially urge that all laws and usages which preclude the enrollment of colored men in the militia, and prohibit their bearing arms in the navy, disallow their rising, agreeable to their merits and attainments are unconstitutional—the constitution knowing no color—are anti-Democratic, since Democracy respects men as equals—are unmagnanimous, since such laws are made by the many, against the few, and by the strong against the weak.

We ask that all those cruel and oppressive laws, whether enacted at the South or the North, which aim at the expatriation of the free people of color, shall be stamped with national reprobation, denounced as contrary to the humanity of the American people, and as an outrage upon the Christianity and civilization of the nineteenth century.

We ask that the right of pre-emption, enjoyed by all white settlers upon the public lands, shall also be enjoyed by colored settlers; and that the word *"white"* be struck from the pre-emption act. We ask that no appropriations whatever, state or national, shall be granted to the colonization scheme; and we would have our right to leave or to remain in the United States placed above legislative interference.

We ask that the Fugitive Slave Law of 1850, that legislative monster of modern times, by whose atrocious provisions the writ of *"habeas corpus,"* the "right of trial by jury," have been virtually abolished, shall be repealed.

We ask, that the law of 1793 be so construed as to apply only to apprentices, and others really owing service or labor; and not to slaves, who can *owe* nothing. Finally, we ask that slavery in the United States shall be immediately, unconditionally, and forever abolished.

To accomplish these just and reasonable ends, we solemnly pledge ourselves to God, to each other, to our country, and to the world, to use all and every means consistent with the just rights of our fellow men, and with the precepts of Christianity.

We shall speak, write and publish, organize and combine to accomplish them.

We shall invoke the aid of the pulpit and the press to gain them.

We shall appeal to the church and to the government to gain them.

We shall vote, and expend our money to gain them.

We shall send eloquent men of our own condition to plead our cause before the people.

We shall invite the co-operation of good men in this country and throughout the world—and above all, we shall look to God, the Father and Creator of all men, for wisdom to direct us and strength to support us in the holy cause to which we this day solemnly pledge ourselves.

Such, fellow-citizens are our aims, ends, aspirations and determinations. We place them before you, with the earnest hope, that upon further investigation, they will meet your cordial and active approval.

And yet, again, we would free ourselves from the charge of unreasonableness and self-sufficiency.

In numbers we are few and feeble; but in the goodness of our cause, in the rectitude of our motives, and in the abundance of argument on our side, we are many and strong.

We count our friends in the heavens above, in the earth beneath, among good men and holy angels. The subtle and mysterious cords of human sympathy have connected us with philanthropic hearts throughout the civilized world. The number in our own land who already recognize the justice of our cause, and are laboring to promote it, is great and increasing.

It is also a source of encouragement, that the genuine American, brave and independent himself, will respect bravery and independence in others. He spurns servility and meanness, whether they be manifested by nations or by individuals. We submit, therefore, that there is neither necessity for, nor disposition on our part to assume a tone of excessive humility. While we would be respectful, we must address you as men, as citizens, as brothers, as dwellers in a common country, equally interest with you for its welfare, its honor and for its prosperity.

To be still more explicit: We would, first of all, be understood to range ourselves no lower among our fellow-countrymen than is implied the high appellation of *"citizen."*

Notwithstanding the impositions and deprivations which have fettered us—notwithstanding the disabilities and liabilities, pending and impending—notwithstanding the cunning, cruel, and scandalous efforts to blot out that right, we declare that we are, and of right we ought to be *American citizens*. We claim this right, and we claim all the rights and privileges, and duties which, properly, attach to it.

It may, and it will, probably, be disputed that we are citizen. We may, and, probably, shall be denounced for this declaration, as making an inconsiderate, impertinent and absurd claim to citizenship; but a very little reflection will vindicate the position we have assumed, from so unfavorable, a judgment. Justice is never inconsiderate; truth is never impertinent; right is never absurd. If the claim we set up be just, true and right it will not be deemed improper or ridiculous in us so to declare it. Nor is it disrespectful to our fellow-citizens, who repudiate the aristocratic notions of the old world that we range ourselves with them in respect to all the rights and prerogatives belonging to American citizens. Indeed, believe, when you have duly considered this subject, you will commend us for the mildness and modesty with which we have taken our ground.

By birth, we are American citizens; by the principles of the Declaration of Independence, we are American citizens; within the meaning of the United States Constitution, we are American citizens; by the facts of history, and the admissions of American statesmen, we are American citizens; by the hardships and trials endured; by the courage and fidelity displayed by our ancestors in defending the liberties and in achieving the independence of our land, we are American citizens.

What Shall Be Done with the Slaves if Emancipated?, 1862

It is curious to observe, at this juncture, when the existence of slavery is threatened by an aroused nation, when national necessity is combining with an enlightened sense of justice to put away the huge abomination forever, that the enemies of human liberty are resorting to all the old and ten thousand times refuted objections to emancipation with which they confronted the abolition movement twenty-five years ago. Like the one stated above, these pro-slavery objections have their power mainly in the slavery-engendered prejudice, which every where pervades the country. Like all other great transgressions of the law of eternal rectitude, slavery thus produces an element in the popular and depraved moral sentiment favorable to its own existence. These objections are often urged with a show of sincere solicitude for the welfare of the slaves themselves. It is; said, what will you do with them? they can't take care of themselves; they would all come to the North; they would not work; they would become a burden upon the State, and a blot upon society; they'd cut their masters' throats; they would cheapen labor, and crowd out the poor white laborer from employment; their former masters would not employ them, and they would necessarily become vagrants, paupers and criminals, over-running all our alms houses, jails and prisons. The laboring classes among the whites would come in bitter conflict with them in all the avenues of labor, and regarding them as occupying places and filling positions which should be occupied and filled by white men; a fierce war of races would be the inevitable consequence, and the black race would, of course, (being the weaker,) be exterminated. In view of this frightful, though happily somewhat contradictory picture, the question is asked, and pressed with a great show of earnestness at this momentous crisis of our, nation's history, What shall be done with the four million slaves if they are emancipated?

This question has been answered, and can be answered in many ways. Primarily, it is a question less for man than for God—less for human intellect than for the laws of nature to solve. It assumes that nature has erred; that the law of liberty is a mistake; that freedom, though a nature want of the human soul, can only be enjoyed at the expense of human welfare, and that men are better off in slavery than they would or could be in freedom; that slavery is the natural order of human relations, that liberty is an experiment. What shall be done with them?

Our answer is, do nothing with them; mind your business, and let them mind theirs. Your *doing* with them is their greatest misfortune. They have been undone by your doings, and all they now ask, and really have need of at your hands, is just to let them alone. They suffer by every interference, and succeed best by being let alone. The Negro should have been let alone in Africa—let alone when the pirates and robbers offered him for sale in our Christian slave markets—(more cruel and inhuman than the Mohammedan slave markets)—let alone by courts, judges, politician, legislators and slave-drivers—let alone altogether, and assured that they were thus to be let alone forever, and that they must now make their own way in the world, just the same as any and every other variety of the human family. As colored men, we only ask to be allowed to *do* with ourselves, subject only to the same great laws for the welfare of human society which apply to other men, Jews, Gentiles, Barbarian, Sythian. Let us stand upon our own legs, work with our own hands, and eat bread in the sweat of our own brows. When you, our white fellow-countrymen, have attempted to do anything for us, it has generally been to deprive us of some right, power or privilege which you yourself would die before you would submit to have taken from you. When the planters of the West Indies used to attempt to puzzle the pure-minded Wilberforce with the question, How shall we get rid of slavery? his simple answer was, "quit stealing." In like manner, we answer those who are perpetually puzzling their brains with questions as to what shall be done with the Negro, "let him alone and mind your own business." If you see him plowing in the open field, leveling the forest, at work with a spade, a rake, a hoe, a pick-axe, or a bill— let him alone; he has a right to work. If you see him on his way to school, with spelling book, geography and arithmetic in his hands—let him alone. Don't shut the door in his face, nor bolt your gates against him; he has a right to learn—let him alone. Don't pass laws to degrade him. If he has a ballot in his hand, and is on his way to the ballot-box to deposit his vote for the man whom he thinks will most justly and wisely administer the Government which has the power of life and death over him, as well as others—let him *alone*; his right of choice as much deserves respect and protection as your own. If you see him on his way to the church, exercising religious liberty in accordance with this or that religious persuasion—let him alone.—Don't meddle with him, nor trouble yourselves with any questions as to what shall be done with him.

The great majority of human duties are of this negative character. If men were born in need of crutches, instead of having legs, the fact would be otherwise. We should then be in need of help, and would require outside aid; but according to the wiser and better arrangement of nature, our duty is done better by not hindering than by helping our fellow-men; or, in other words, the best way to help them is just to let them help themselves.

Note

1. Frederick Douglass acknowledges in his autobiography that it was hard for slaves to know their exact dates of birth. He was no different; Douglass wrote that he believed he was born in 1817. However, many historians date his birth to 1818. Douglass Frederick. 1885. *My Bondage and My Freedom*. New York: Miler, Orton, and Mulligan Publishers.

4.
ANNA JULIA COOPER

Anna Julia Cooper (1858–1964) worked throughout her life as an educator devoted to improving education for Black people. Cooper was highly educated; she received a B.A. and M.A. from Oberlin. She attended Columbia University and studied in Paris where she received a Ph.D.; at sixty-six years old Cooper was only the fourth Black woman in U.S. history to receive a Ph.D. Her educational background is important because it influenced her activism and strategies for social change. She believed in the power of higher education and the power of education in general in uplifting the race. From 1887–1930 she worked as an educator in Washington, D.C. Cooper was a teacher at St. Augustine's Normal School, Washington Colored High School, Wilberforce University, and devoted herself to public education. In 1901 she became principal of M Street School (formerly Washington Colored High School). For over a decade she was the president of Frelinghuysen University, founded in 1906, which was a group of schools aimed at educating working class Black adults. The school offered religious and academic training, as well as provided social services.

Cooper's activism was not just relegated to the classroom. Cooper was a great orator who extensively spoke publicly about quagmires impacting Black folk and women. For instance, in 1890, Cooper gave a tremendous speech, "The Higher Education of Women." The speech was given before the American Conference of Educators in order to make a case for the importance of educating women. In 1893 she delivered a speech in front of World's Congress of Representative Women in Chicago. She worked with various Black Women's Clubs. For example, she was a co-founder of the Colored Women's League (CWL). A year after co-founding the CWL in Washington, D.C., which later merged with the Federation of Afro-American Women to become the infamous National Association of Colored Women (NACW), in 1895 she assisted in the organization of the National Conference of Colorado Women. Cooper was not only an attendee at the first Pan-African Conference (1900), she gave one of the conference's most inspiring speeches. This chapter includes speeches given by Cooper so readers can experience her eloquence for themselves.

In 1892 Cooper published *A Voice from the South*. Her book was not only an excellent account of the interconnectedness of race, gender, and class in conditioning oppression but it undeniably made Cooper a pioneering Black feminist. She also published *L'Attitude de la France a l'Egard de l'Esclavage pendant la Revolution* (1925) and

Le Pelerinage de Charlemagne: Voyage a Jerusalem et a Constantinople (1925). Like her counterparts in this text, Cooper was committed to publishing writings about Black liberation. For example, in 1913, while working for a local settlement house in Washington, D.C., helping the Black poor, she published a pamphlet, "The Social Settlement: What it Is and What it Does." She was a contributor to the NAACP's *Crisis*. In *Crisis* she published "The Humor of Teaching" (1930) and "Angry Saxons and Negro Education" (1938). In response to World War II, Cooper published a pamphlet entitled "Hitler and the Negro," which was meant as a rallying cry for African Americans to join the war effort and to fight against global oppression. Her writings, work as an educator, and her activism clearly demonstrated her commitment to uplifting and changing the social position of Black people and women in America.

Overview of Ideas

Anna Julia Cooper believed that social progress required uplifting both women and African Americans. Cooper posited that women were oppressed all over the world despite the fact that it is women who "vitalize and inspire" civilization and society. Writing after emancipation Cooper realized that despite the freedom granted to slaves injustice still prevailed. Slavery cast Black folk into an inferior social position and into an economic underclass. Their impoverished status was not their fault. The United States needed to realize that women and African Americans were entitled to all the same rights as Whites; they have the same intelligence and same talents. Cooper, an early Black feminist, focused on how the education and uplift of Black women would be propitious for all African Americans and society.

> The black woman of to-day stands mute and wondering at the Herculean task devolving upon her. But the cycles wait for her. No other hand can move the lever. She must be loosed from her bands and set to work.

Women were vital to social progress. The Black church and educational institutions were the most powerful sources for generating political strength for Black women and African Americans. However, Cooper like many others saw moral transformation as a staple of African American advancement.

> A race cannot be purified from without. Preachers and teachers are helps ... [but] the time is ripe for action. Self-seeking and ambition must be laid on the alter. The battle is one of sacrifice and hardship.

It was time for African Americans, women and men, to stand together and fight for liberty and justice. However, these efforts must be grassroots and include self-help.

For Cooper, the United States was a developing capitalist superpower taken over by avarice. However, women managed to resist the temptations of luxury and worldly pleasures. Women, she argued, were more important to American society than ever. Women could help instill the morality missing in American consciousness. "Women's work and women's influence were needed as never before; needed to bring a heart power into this money getting, dollar-worshipping civilization; needed to bring a moral force into the utilitarian motives and interests of the time." Women were naturally moral and virtuous creatures who could teach the United States about the nation it should become. Speaking of women, Cooper argued, "in a reign of moral ideas she is easily queen." Women should emphatically be given access to the ballot box; their voices will only improve the country. Black women have a large goal to accomplish. Cooper notes that women have been relegated to the domestic "sphere … [of] the kitchen and the nursery" but today Black women have a larger task, not just to take care of their homes but to change their society.

What is interesting about Cooper is that while she was a pioneering feminist her logic was actually quite conservative. She argued that many of the discourses that second wave feminists worked so hard to debunk, such as being inherently sensitive, maternal, and nurturing, were accurate; this was her argument for why women needed to play large public roles. Women were better equipped to help African Americans and other Americans make the moral transformation necessary; only women could help build the character that this country so desperately needed.

Womanhood a Vital Element in the Regeneration and Progress of a Race, 1852

The vital agency of womanhood in the regeneration and progress of a race, as a general question, is conceded almost before it is fairly stated. I confess one of the difficulties for me in the subject assigned lay in its obviousness. The plea is taken away by the opposite attorney's granting the whole question.

"Woman's influence on social progress"—who in Christendom doubts or questions it? One may as well be called on to prove that the sun is the source of light and heat and energy to this many-sided little world.

Nor, on the other hand, could it have been intended that I should apply the position when taken and proven, to the needs and responsibilities of the women of our race in the South. For is it not written, "Cursed is he that cometh after the king?" and has not the King already preceded me in "The Black Woman of the South"?[1]

They have had both Moses and the Prophets in Dr. Crummell and if they hear not him, neither would they be persuaded though one came up from the South.

I would beg, however, with the Doctor's permission, to add my plea for the *Colored Girls* of the South:—that large, bright, promising fatally beautiful class that stand shivering like a delicate plantlet before the fury of tempestuous elements, so full of promise and possibilities, yet so sure of destruction; often without a father to whom they dare apply the loving term, often without a stronger brother to espouse their cause and defend their honor with his life's blood; in the midst of pitfalls and snares, waylaid by the lower classes of white men, with no shelter, no protection nearer than the great blue vault above, which half conceals and half reveals the one Care-Taker they know so little of. Oh, save them, help them, shield, train, develop, teach, inspire them! Snatch them, in God's name, as brands from the burning! There is material in them well worth your while, the hope in germ of a staunch, helpful, regenerating womanhood on which, primarily, rests the foundation stones of our future as a race.

It is absurd to quote statistics showing the Negro's bank account and rent rolls, to point to the hundreds of newspapers edited by colored men and lists of lawyers, doctors, professors, D. D's, LL D's, etc., etc., etc., while the source from which the life-blood of the race is to flow is subject to taint and corruption in the enemy's camp.

True progress is never made by spasms. Real progress is growth. It must begin in the seed. Then, "first the blade, then the ear, after that the full corn in the ear." There is something to encourage and inspire us in the advancement of individuals since their emancipation from slavery. It at least proves that there is nothing irretrievably wrong in the shape of the black man's skull, and that under given circumstances his development, downward or upward, will be similar to that of other average human beings.

But there is no time to be wasted in mere felicitation. That the Negro has his niche in the infinite purposes of the Eternal, no one who has studied the history of the last fifty years in America will deny. That much depends on his own right comprehension of his responsibility and rising to the demands of the hour, it will be good for him to see; and how best to use his present so that the structure of the future shall be stronger and higher and brighter and nobler and holier than that of the past, is a question to be decided each day by every one of us.

The race is just twenty-one years removed from the conception and experience of a chattel, just at the age of ruddy manhood. It is well enough to pause a moment for retrospection, introspection, and prospection [*sic*]. We look back, not to become inflated with conceit because of the depths from which we have arisen, but that we may learn wisdom from experience. We look within that we may gather together once more our forces, and, by improved and more practical methods, address ourselves to the tasks before us. We look forward with hope and trust that the same God whose guiding hand led our fathers through and out of the gall and bitterness of oppression, will still lead and direct their children, to the honor of His name, and for their ultimate salvation.

But this survey of the failures or achievements of the past, the difficulties and embarrassments of the present, and the mingled hopes and fears for the future, must not degenerate into mere dreaming nor consume the time which belongs to the practical and effective handling of the crucial questions of the hour; and there can be no issue more vital and momentous than this of the womanhood of the race.

Here is the vulnerable point, not in the heel, but at the heart of the young Achilles; and here must the defenses be strengthened and the watch redoubled.

We are the heirs of a past which was not our fathers' moulding. "Every man the arbiter of his own destiny" was not true for the American Negro of the past: and it is no fault of his that he finds himself to-day the inheritor of a manhood and womanhood impoverished and debased by two centuries and more of compression and degradation.

But weaknesses and malformations, which to-day are attributable to a vicious schoolmaster and a pernicious system, will a century hence be rightly regarded as proofs of innate corruptness and radical incurability.

Now the fundamental agency under God in the regeneration, the re-training of the race, as well as the ground work and starting point of its progress upward, must be the *black woman.*

With all the wrongs and neglects of her past, with all the weakness, the debasement, the moral thralldom of her present, the black woman of to-day stands mute and wondering at the Herculean task devolving upon her. But the cycles wait for her. No other hand can move the lever. She must be loosed from her bands and set to work.

Our meager and superficial results from past efforts prove their futility; and every attempt to elevate the Negro, whether undertaken by himself or through the philanthropy of others, cannot but prove abortive unless so directed as to utilize the indispensable agency of an elevated and trained womanhood.

The institution of the Church in the South to which she mainly looks for the training of her colored clergy and for the help of the "Black Woman" and "Colored Girl" of the South, has graduated since the year 1868, when the school was founded, *five young women*,[2] and while yearly numerous young men have been kept and trained for the ministry by the charities of the Church, the number of indigent females who have here been supported, sheltered and trained, is phenomenally small. Indeed, to my mind, the attitude of the Church toward this feature of her work is as if the solution of the problem of Negro missions depended solely on sending a quota of deacons and priests into the field, girls being a sort of *tertium quid* whose development may be promoted if they can pay their way and fall in with the plans mapped out for the training of the other sex. Now I would ask in all earnestness, does not this force potential deserve by education and stimulus to be made dynamic? Is it not a solemn duty incumbent on all colored church-men to make it so? Will not the aid of the Church be given to prepare our girls in head, heart, and hand for the duties and responsibilities that await the intelligent wife, the Christian mother, the earnest, virtuous, helpful woman, at once both the lever and the fulcrum for uplifting the race.

As Negroes and churchmen we cannot be indifferent to these questions. They touch us most vitally on both sides. We believe in the Holy Catholic Church. We believe that however gigantic and apparently remote the consummation, the Church will go on conquering and to conquer till the kingdoms of this world, not excepting the black man and the black woman of the South, shall have become the kingdoms of the Lord and of his Christ.

That past work in this direction has been unsatisfactory we must admit. That without a change of policy results in the future will be as meagre [*sic*], we greatly fear. Our life as a race is at stake. The dearest interests of our hearts are in the scales. We must either break away from dear old landmarks and plunge out in any line and every line that enables us to meet the pressing need of our people, or we must ask the Church to allow and help us, untrammelled [*sic*] by the prejudices and theories of individuals, to work agressively [*sic*] under her direction as we alone can, with God's help, for the salvation of our people.

The time is ripe for action. Self-seeking and ambition must be laid on the altar. The battle is one of sacrifice and hardship, but our duty is plain. We have been recipients of missionary bounty in some sort for twenty-one years. Not even the senseless vegetable is content to be a mere reservoir. Receiving without giving is an anomaly in nature. Nature's cells are all little workshops for manufacturing sunbeams, the product to be *given out* to earth's inhabitants in warmth, energy, thought, action. Inanimate creation always pays back an equivalent.

Now, *How much owest thou my Lord?* Will his account be overdrawn if he call for singleness of purpose and self-sacrificing labor for your brethren? Having passed through your drill school, will you refuse a general's commission even if it entail responsibility, risk and anxiety, with possibly some adverse criticism? Is it too much to ask you to step forward and direct the work for your race along those lines which you know to be of first and vital importance?

Will you allow these words of Ralph Waldo Emerson? "In ordinary," says he, "we have a snappish criticism which watches and contradicts the opposite party. We want the will which advances and dictates [acts]. Nature has made up her mind that what cannot defend itself, shall not be defended. Complaining never so loud and with never so much reason, is of no use. What cannot stand must fall; *and the measure, of our sincerity and therefore of the respect of men is the amount of health and wealth we will hazard in the defense of our right.*"

The Status of Woman in America, 1952

Time would fail to tell of the noble army of women who shine like beacon lights in the otherwise sordid wilderness of this accumulative period—prison reformers and tenement cleansers, quiet unnoted workers in hospitals and homes, among imbeciles, among outcasts—the sweetening, purifying antidotes for the poisons of man's acquisitiveness,—mollifying and soothing with the tenderness of compassion and love the wounds and bruises caused by his overreaching and avarice.

The desire for quick returns and large profits tempts capital ofttimes into unsanitary, well nigh inhuman investments,—tenement tinder boxes, stifling, stunting, sickening alleys and pestiferous slums; regular rents, no waiting, large percentages,—rich coffers coined out of the life-blood of human bodies and souls. Men and women herded together like cattle, breathing in malaria and typhus from an atmosphere seething with moral as well as physical impurity, revelling [*sic*] in vice as their native habitat and then, to drown the whisperings of their higher consciousness and effectually to hush the yearnings and accusations within, flying to narcotics and opiates—rum, tobacco, opium, binding hand and foot, body and soul, till the proper image of God is transformed into a fit associate for demons,—a besotted, enervated, idiotic wreck, or else a monster of wickedness terrible and destructive.

These are some of the legitimate products of the unmitigated tendencies of the wealth-producing period. But, thank Heaven, side by side with the cold, mathematical, selfishly calculating, so-called practical and unsentimental instinct of the business man, there comes the sympathetic warmth and sunshine of good women, like the sweet and sweetening breezes of spring, cleansing, purifying, soothing, inspiring, lifting the drunkard from the gutter, the outcast from the pit. Who can estimate the influence of these "daughters of the king," these lend-a-hand forces, in counteracting the selfishness of an acquisitive age?

To-day America counts her millionaires by the thousand; questions of tariff and questions of currency are the most vital ones agitating the public mind. In this period, when material prosperity and well earned ease and luxury are assured facts from a national standpoint, woman's work and woman's influence are needed as never before; needed to bring a heart power into this money getting, dollar-worshipping civilization; needed to bring a moral force into the utilitarian motives and interests of the time; needed to stand for God and Home and Native Land *versus gain and greed and grasping selfishness.*

There can be no doubt that this fourth centenary of America's discovery which we celebrate at Chicago, strikes the keynote of another important transition in the history of this nation; and the prominence of woman in the management of its celebration is a fitting tribute to the part she is destined to play among the forces of the future. This is the first congressional recognition of woman in this country, and this Board of Lady Managers constitute the first women legally appointed by any government to act in a national capacity. This of itself marks the dawn of a new day.

Now the periods of discovery, of settlement, of developing resources and accumulating wealth have passed in rapid succession. Wealth in the nation as in the individual brings leisure, repose, reflection. The struggle with nature is over, the struggle with ideas begins. We stand then, it seems to me, in this last decade of the nineteenth century, just in the portals of a new and untried movement on a higher plain and in a grander strain than any the past has called forth. It does not require a prophet's eye to divine its trend and image its possibilities from the forces we see already at work around us; nor is it hard to guess what must be the status of woman's work under the new regime.

In the pioneer days her role was that of a camp-follower, an additional something to fight for and be burdened with, only repaying the anxiety and labor she called forth by her own incomparable gifts of sympathy and appreciative love; unable herself ordinarily to contend with the bear and the Indian, or to take active part in clearing the wilderness and constructing the home.

In the second or wealth producing period her work is abreast of man's, complementing and supplementing, counteracting excessive tendencies, and mollifying over rigorous proclivities.

In the era now about to dawn, her sentiments must strike the keynote and give the dominant tone. And this because of the nature of her contribution to the world.

Her kingdom is not over physical forces. Not by might, nor by power can she prevail. Her position must ever be inferior where strength of muscle creates leadership. If she follows the instincts of her nature, however, she must always stand for the conservation of those deeper moral forces which make for the happiness of homes and the righteousness of the country. In a reign of moral ideas she is easily queen.

There is to my mind no grander and surer prophecy of the new era and of woman's place in it, than the work already begun in the waning years of the nineteenth century by the W. C. T. U. in America, an organization which has even now reached not only national but international importance, and seems destined to permeate and purify the whole civilized world. It is the living embodiment of woman's activities and woman's ideas, and its extent and strength rightly prefigure her increasing power as a moral factor.

The colored woman of to-day occupies, one may say, a unique position in this country. In a period of itself transitional and unsettled, her status seems one of the least ascertainable and definitive of all the forces which make for our civilization. She is confronted by both a woman question and a race problem, and is as yet an unknown or an unacknowledged factor in both. While the women of the white race can with calm assurance enter upon the work they feel by nature appointed to do, while their men give loyal support and appreciative countenance to their efforts, recognizing in most avenues of usefulness the propriety and the need of woman's distinctive co-operation, the colored woman too often finds herself hampered and shamed by a less liberal sentiment and a more conservative attitude on the part of those for whose opinion she cares most. That this is not universally true I am glad to admit. There are to be found both intensely conservative white men and exceedingly liberal colored men. But as far as my experience goes the average man of our race is less frequently ready to admit the actual need among the sturdier forces of the world for woman's help or influence. That great social and economic questions await her interference, that she could throw any light on problems of national import, that her intermeddling could improve the management of school systems, or elevate the tone of public institutions, or humanize and sanctify the far reaching influence of prisons and reformatories and improve the treatment of lunatics and imbeciles,—that she has a word worth hearing on mooted questions in political economy, that she could contribute a suggestion on the relations of labor and capital, or offer a thought on honest money and honorable trade, I fear the majority of "Americans of the colored variety" are not yet prepared to concede.

Fifty years ago woman's activity according to orthodox definitions was on a pretty clearly cut "sphere," including primarily the kitchen and the nursery, and rescued from the barrenness of prison bars by the womanly mania for adorning every discoverable bit of china or canvass with forlorn looking cranes balanced idiotically on one foot. The woman of to-day finds herself in the presence of responsibilities which ramify through the profoundest and most varied interests of her country and race. Not one of the issues of this plodding, toiling, sinning, repenting, falling, aspiring humanity can afford to shut her out, or can deny the reality of her influence. No plan for renovating society, no scheme for purifying politics, no reform in church or in state, no moral, social, or economic question, no movement upward or downward in the human plane is lost on her. A man once said when told his house was afire: "Go tell my wife; I never meddle with household affairs." But no woman can possibly put herself or her sex outside any of the interests that affect humanity. All departments in the new era are to be hers, in the sense that her interests are in all and through all; and it is incumbent on her to keep intelligently and sympathetically *en rapport* with all the great movements of her time, that she may know on which side to throw the weight of her influence. She stands now at the gateway of this new era of American civilization. In her hands must be moulded the strength, the wit, the statesmanship, the morality, all the psychic force, the social and economic intercourse of that era. To be alive at such an epoch is a privilege, to be a woman then is sublime.

Has America a Race Problem: If So, How Can It Best Be Solved?, 1852

Has America a Race Problem?
   Yes.
   What are you going to do about it?

Let it alone and mind my own business. It is God's problem and He will solve it in time. It is deeper than Gehenna. What can you or I do!

Are there then no duties and special lines of thought growing out of the present conditions of this problem?

Certainly there are. *Imprimis[sic]*; let every element of the conflict see that it represent a positive force so as to preserve a proper equipoise in the conflict. No shirking, no skulking, no masquerading in another's uniform. Stand by your guns. And be ready for the charge. The day is coming, and now is, when America must ask each citizen not "who was your grandfather and what the color of his cuticle," but "*What can you do?*" Be ready each individual element,—each race, each class, each family, each man to reply "I *engage to undertake an honest man's share.*"

God and time will work the problem. You and I are only to stand for the quantities *at their best*, which he means us to represent.

Above all, for the love of humanity stop the mouth of those learned theorizers, the expedient mongers, who come out annually with their new and improved method of getting the answer and clearing the slate: amalgamation, deportation, colonization and all the other ations [*sic*] that were ever devised or dreampt [*sic*] of. If Alexander wants to be a god, let him; but don't have Alexander hawking his patent plan for universal deification. If all could or would follow Alexander's plan, just the niche in the divine cosmos meant for man would be vacant. And we think that men have a part to play in this great drama no less than gods, and so if a few are determined to be white—amen, so be it; but don't let them argue as if there were no part to be played in life by black men and black women, and as if to become white were the sole specific and panacea for all the ills that flesh is heir to—the universal solvent for all America's irritations. And again, if an American family of whatever condition or hue takes a notion to reside in Africa or in Mexico, or in the isles of the sea, it is most un-American for any power on this continent to seek to gainsay or obstruct their departure; but on the other hand, no power or element of power on this continent, least of all a self-constituted tribunal of "recent arrivals," dossesses [*sic*] the right to begin figuring beforehand to calculate what it would require *to send* ten millions of citizens, whose ancestors have wrought here from the planting of the nation, to the same places at so much per head—at least till some one has consulted those heads.

We would not deprecate the fact, then, that America has a Race Problem. It is guaranty of the perpetuity and progress of her institutions, and insures the breadth of her culture and the symmetry of her development. More than all, let us not disparage the factor which the Negro is appointed to contribute to that problem. America needs the Negro for ballast if for nothing else. His tropical warmth and spontaneous emotionalism may form no unseemly counterpart to the cold and calculating Anglo-Saxon. And then his instinct for law and order, his inborn respect for authority, his inaptitude for rioting and anarchy, his gentleness and cheerfulness as a laborer, and his deep-rooted faith in God will prove indispensable and invaluable elements in a nation menaced as America is by anarchy, socialism, communism, and skepticism poured in with all the jail birds from the continents of Europe and Asia. I believe with our own Dr. Crummell that "the Almighty does not preserve, rescue, and build up a lowly people merely for ignoble ends." And the historian of American civilization will yet congratulate this country that she has had a Race Problem and that descendants of the black race furnished one of its largest factors.

Notes

1. Pamphlet published by Dr. Alex Crummell.
2. Five have been graduated since '86 two in '91, two in '92.

PART II

RECONSTRUCTION AND BEYOND
DEBATES OVER THE NEGRO PROBLEM AND THE CREATION OF CIVIL RIGHTS DISCOURSE

5.
ALEXANDER CRUMMELL

Alexander Crummell (1819–1898) was an Episcopalian priest, educator, and lecturer. Crummell grew up in a household of activists. The first Black newspaper, *Freedom's Journal*, was founded in his childhood home. Crummell was an exceptional public speaker. For example, in 1840 he was asked to be the keynote speaker in Albany at the Anti-Slavery New York State Convention of Negroes. As part of the abolitionist movement, he frequently spoke out against American slavery. Although a large part of his public speeches were aimed at raising funds for his ministries. In 1844 Crummell became an ordained priest. However, he was originally ostracized by the White Episcopalian diocese and Crummell left for England and in 1853 he graduated from Queens College in Cambridge. Readers will probably find that his educational background impacted his writing style. His most famous books included: *Future of Africa* (1862), *Greatness of Christ* (1882), and *Africa and America: Addresses and Discourses* (1891). Notable works published with the American Negro Academy were: "The Attitude of the American Mind Toward the Negro Intellect" (1898) and "Civilization: The Primal Need of the Race" (1898).

Crummell is most often reduced to being a man of letters. This extraordinary intellectual and educator founded the American Negro Academy (ANA) in 1897. First, it is important to recognize that although the organization was comprised of all highly educated males from around the globe, the goal of the organization was to promote higher education amongst African Americans and defend the rights of Black folk. The ANA promoted higher education as a primary solution to the "Negro Problem." Moreover, many of its members such as Crummell and W.E.B. Du Bois were active in the practical struggle for Black liberation. Moreover, Crummell was not just a man of letters. He spent twenty years of life working as a missionary in Liberia. Liberia was founded as a home for repatriated African slaves. There he worked to help achieve the vision of an independent Black Christian nation. For example, while in Liberia, at the Caldwell settlement, he assisted in the creation of a school and a church. Crummell remained devoted to the proliferation of education amongst African Americans. For example, at the College of Liberia, Crummell was a professor of philosophy and English. He ran educational outreach programs to foster empowerment. Just because a prodigious amount of his activism focused on helping Black people abroad does not render his efforts any less meaningful.

Overview of Ideas

Alexander Crummell was a staunch advocate of self-help ideology. He was an unapologetic writer whose often vitriolic tone conveyed a serious message about the necessity for racial solidarity. Crummell argued that often Blacks were urged to assimilate and reject their race or African heritage. He argued,

> the only place I know of in this land where you can "forget you are colored" is in the grave … if I forget that I am a black man, if you ignore the fact of race, and we both ostrich-like, stick our heads in the sand, or stalk along, high-headed, oblivious of the actual distinctions which *do* exist in American society, what are you or I to do for our social nature?

Crummell posited that social progress was dependent on racial unity and that Black people should utilize schools, churches, social and political organizations to foster social networks. By creating meaningful Black-only social, economic, and political ties African Americans would have power. But this was only one aspect of Crummell's self-help approach.

As many African Americans began to debate the need for full civil rights and advocated political agitation, Crummell argued for a different strategic approach.

> I know the natural resource of some minds, under these painful circumstances, to cry out, "Agitate! Agitate!" But *cui bono?* What advantage will agitation bring? … Character, my friends, is the grand, effective instrument which we are to use for the destruction of caste.

Here, Crummell promulgated that African Americans required moral and behavioral transformation. "What this race needs in this country is power … and that comes from character, and character is the product of religion, intelligence, virtue, family order, superiority, wealth, and the show of industrial forces." African Americans needed to band together, demonstrate their high moral character and adherence to the Protestant work ethic. Applied knowledge was paramount to Crummell. By living a pious and frugal life of hard work White Americans would come to see that African Americans were not an inferior class. Moreover, in industrious behavior Black folk could build themselves up economically and with economic power would eventually come political power.

A prodigious quagmire facing African Americans was that the abrupt end of slavery and the institutionalization of tenant farming systems; sharecropping re-ossified African American's fetters to the land and made them all but slaves again. Reminiscent of Karl Marx, Crummell critiques developing capitalism and warns African Americans about the

> danger of a labour system, semi-servile in its nature, and feudalistic in its working; binding the labourer to service, but allowing him the slenderest interest in the soil, and when possible, shutting him off from the ownership of the land.

Until African Americans could gain control over their own labor and the means of production, until they became owners, they would be doomed. Crummell like Marx posited that these economic conditions created under slavery create *alienation*; Black folk internalized their inferior position with the labor market and began to see them-selves as commodities whose rightful position was one of servitude to a master. In addition, capitalism perpetuates the idea that owners do not have to work or work hard and workers are degraded. In time, the idea that work is degrading leads indi-viduals, in this case African Americans, to despise work. Crummell argued it was important to teach Blacks that there is dignity in labor.

> Not until a people are able, by their own activities and skill, to raise themselves above want, and to meet the daily needs of home and family, can they take the next great step to the higher cultivation which comes be letters, refinement and religion; and which lifts them up to civility and power.

Most are familiar with the famous axiom—give a man a fish and he will eat for a day; teach a man how to fish and he will eat for life. This famous proverb is exactly what Crummell wanted to instill in Black people; self-sufficiency was the cornerstone of progress.

Crummell argued that African Americans needed to push and strive to acquire employment in various vocations. He argued that people should never be ashamed of any form of work; if you work hard then you are valuable. While all African Amer-icans should not be relegated to servitude if some still worked in this field it was not horrific. If employed in service work, Black folk could still learn basic cultural capital or household skills they could utilize in their own homes. In addition, working as a domestic forced African Americans to be neat and orderly; it taught them humility, often taught them basic English skills, and manners. Finally, in this work, or any work, Black people could acquire money and with the money they earned in honest labor they could purchase their own land later. In time, with hard work and perseverance Black people would be able to break into any sector in the labor market. All work is honorable. In the end, his simple prescription was this:

> the black race in this land cannot leap into might and majesty ... first, humble labour; then, gradual uprise; and then dogged and persistent effort, unfailing hope, living and undying aspi-ration, and pluck and audacious ambition, which brooks no limitations in the spheres of enter-prise!

Alexander Crummell was also a strong supporter of women's rights and to pub-licly advocate for the rights of women in the 1880s was certainly radical. Even before Ida B. Wells-Barnett, Crummell was an outspoken critic of rape against Black women. In fact, he argued that the plight of Black women in the South may have even been worse than for their male counterparts. While some Black men were able to escape the horrors of poverty and degrading living, Black women were doubly oppressed. Black women were treated like heifers bought and sold to primarily produce cattle. They were beaten, raped, and overworked. Even after emancipation their conditions had not improved. Crummell's solution was precise; he urged women from the North who had been educated, who had vocational training, and religious workers to teach women of the South what they had learned about thrift and work. They could teach them the skills they needed to run their own homes.

Like Anna Julia Cooper, Crummell said that all African Americans could not be uplifted without Black women. "Without them [Black women], no true nationality, patriotism, religion, cultivation, family life, or true social status is a possibility." Therefore, he argued that at least one industrial school should be opened in every Southern state just for Black women. He clarified that he was not talking about finishing schools but industrial schools, so poor Black women could enrich themselves and the lives of their children through trades and craftsmanship. Women should also become literate and learn a wide range of domestic tasks. Education slowly became a pivotal part of Crummell's political thought.

All African Americans required education in order to achieve progress. For some this meant industrial education. However, for those whose talents exceeded those of what Crummell called the average "noodles and numbskulls" higher education was a must. As Booker T. Washington (see Chapter 6) rose to prominence, Crummell wanted to distinguish himself; Crummell argued that Washington pushed only for industrial education at the expense of higher education for those who were able. He posited a need for further civilization which again required a refinement of culture and moral transformation. Crummell said Negroes needed "higher culture"; a bourgeois refinement of culture would open up doors, the doors to Yale and doors to economic opportunity.

The Social Principle among a People and Its Bearing on Their Progress, 1875

For, since, especially emancipation, *two* special heresies have influenced and governed the minds of colored men in this nation: (1) The one is the dogma which I have heard frequently from the lips of leaders, personal and dear, but mistaken, friends, *that the colored people of this country should forget, as soon as possible, that they A R E colored people:*—a fact, in the first place, which is an impossibility. Forget it, forsooth, when you enter a saloon and are repulsed on account of your color! Forget it when you enter a car, South or West, and are denied a decent seat! Forget it when you enter the Church of God, and are driven to a hole in the gallery! Forget it when every child of yours would be driven ignominiously from four-fifths of the common schools of the country! Forget it, when thousands of mechanics in the large cities would make a "strike" rather than work at the same bench, in the same yard, with a black carpenter or brick-maker! Forget it, when the boyhood of our race is almost universally deprived of the opportunity of learning trades, through prejudice! Forget it, when, in one single State, twenty thousand men dare not go to the polls on election-day, through the tyranny of caste! Forget it, when one great commonwealth offers a new constitution for adoption, by which a man like *Dumas* the younger, if he were a North Carolinian, could be indicted for marrying the foulest white woman in that State, and merely because she was white! Forget that you are colored, in these United States! Turn madman, and go into a lunatic asylum, and then, perchance, you may forget it! But, if you have any sense or sensibility, how is it possible for you, or me, or any other colored man, to live oblivious of a fact of so much significance in a land like this! The only place I know of in this land where you can "forget you are colored" is the grave!

But not only is this dogma folly, it is disintegrating and socially destructive. For shut out, for instance, as I am and you are from the cultivated social life of the superior classes of this country, if I forget that I am a black man, if you ignore the fact of race, and we both, ostrich-like, stick our heads in the sand, or stalk along, high-headed, oblivious of the actual distinctions which *do* exist in American society, what are you or I to do for our social nature? What will become of the measure of social life among ourselves which we now possess? Where are we to find our friends? Where find the circles for society and cheerful intercourse?

Why, my friends, the only way you, and I, and thousands of our people get domestic relations, marry wives and husbands, secure social relations, form good neighborhood and companionship, is by the very remembrance which we are told to scout and forswear.

2. The other dogma is the demand *that colored men should give up all distinctive effort, as colored men, in schools, churches, associations, and friendly societies*. But this, you will observe, is equivalent to a demand to the race to give up all civilization in this land and to submit to barbarism. The cry is: "Give up your special organization." "Mix in with your white fellow-citizens."

I wonder that the men who talk in the style I have referred to, forget that nine-tenths of the American people have become so poisoned and stimulated by the noxious influence of caste, that, in the present day, they would resist to the utmost before they would allow the affiliations, however remote, that implied the social or domestic principle.

Do not blink at the charge of inferiority. It is not a race peculiarity; and whatever its measure or extent in this country, it has been forced upon you. Do not deny it, but neutralize and destroy it, not by shrieks, or agonies, or foolish pretense; but by culture, by probity, and industry.

I know the natural resource of some minds, under these painful circumstances, to cry out, "Agitate! agitate!" But *cui bono*? What advantage will agitation bring? Everything has a value, according to its relation to its own natural and specific end. But what is the bearing of agitation to a purpose which is almost entirely subjective in its nature. For, as I take it, the object we must needs have in view, in the face of the disabilities which confront our race in this land, is the attainment of such general superiority that prejudice *must* decline. But agitation has no such force, possesses no such value. Agitation is the expenditure of force: our end and aim is the husbandry of all our vital resources.

Character, my friends, is the grand, effective instrument which we are to use for the destruction of caste: Character, in its broad, wide, deep, and high significance; character, as evidenced in high moral and intellectual attainments; as significant of general probity, honor, honesty, and self-restraint; as inclusive of inward might and power; as comprehending the attainments of culture, refinement, and enlightenment; as comprising the substantial results of thrift, economy, and enterprise; and as involving the forces of combined energies and enlightened cooperation. Make this, *not* the exceptional, but the common, general reality, amid the diverse, wide-spread populations of the colored people in this country; and then all the theories of inferiority, all the assumptions of your native and invincible degradation will pass, with wonderful rapidity, into endless forgetfulness; and the people of the very *next*, nay, multitudes, in the decline of *this* generation, when they look upon us, will wonder at the degrading facts of a past and wretched history. Only secure high, commanding, and masterly Character; and then all the problems of caste, all the enigmas of prejudice, all unreasonable and all unreasoning repulsion, will be settled forever, though you were ten times blacker than midnight! Then all false ideas concerning your nature and your qualities, all absurd notions relative to your capacity, shall vanish! Then every contemptuous fling shall be hushed, every insulting epithet be forgotten! Then, also, all the remembrances of a servile heritage, of ancestral degradation, shall be obliterated! Then all repulsive feelings, all evil dislikes shall fly away! Then, too, all timid disconcert shall depart from us, and all cramped and hesitant manhood shall die!

Dear brethren and friends, let there be but the clear demonstration of manly power and grand capacity in our race, in general, in this country; let there only be the wide out-flashings of art and genius, from their brains; and caste will slink, at once, oblivious to the shades. But no mere self-assertion, no strong, vociferous claims and clamor, can ever secure recognition and equality, so long as inferiority and degradation, if even cruelly entailed, abide as a heritage and a cancer. And I maintain we must *organize*, to the end that we may attain such character. The whole of our future on this soil depends upon that single fact of magnitude—character. Race, color, and all the incidents thereof have but little to do with the matter; and men talk idly when they say "we must forget that we are colored men." What is needed is not that *we* should forget this fact, but that we should rise to such elevation that the *people of the land* be forced to forget all the facts and theories of race, when they behold our thorough equality with them, in all the lines of activity and attainment, of culture and moral grandeur. The great necessity in this land is that its *white* population should forget, be made to forget, that we are *colored* men! Hence there is a work ahead of us, for the overthrow of caste, which will consume the best part of a century.

Everywhere throughout the Union wide and thorough organization of the people should be made, not for idle political logomachy [*sic*], but for industrial effort, for securing trades for youth, for joint-stock companies, for manufacturing, for the production of the great staples of the land, and likewise for the higher purposes of life, *i.e.*, for mental and moral improvement, and raising the plane of social and domestic life among us.

In every possible way these needs and duties should be pressed upon their attention, by sermons, by lectures, by organized societies, by state and national conventions; the *latter not* for political objects, but for social, industrial ends and attainments. I see nought in the future but that we shall be scattered like chaff before the wind before the organized labor of the land, the great power of capital, and the tremendous tide of emigration, unless, as a people, we fall back upon the might and mastery which come from the combination of forces and the principle of industrial co-operation. Most of your political agitation is but wind and vanity. *What this race needs in this country is* POWER—*the forces that may be felt.* And that comes from character, and character is the product of religion, intelligence, virtue, family order, superiority, wealth, and the show of industrial forces. THESE ARE FORCES WHICH WE DO NOT POSSESS. *We are the only class which, as a class,* IN THIS COUNTRY, IS WANTING IN THESE GRAND ELEMENTS.

The very first effort of the colored people should be to lay hold of them; and then they will take such root in this American soil that only the convulsive upheaving [*sic*] of the judgement-day [*sic*] can throw them out!

The Dignity of Labour, and Its Value to a New People, 1881

When I look at the present condition of the black race in this country, I see serious and formidable obstacles which array themselves in their way, preventing, so largely, the securing of land, and the acquisition of wealth; I am sorely troubled with misgivings, least the opposing forces may so far prevail as to keep their labour, for a long period to come, inferior, servile and unremunerative [*sic*].

Two special dangers threaten the race with respect to labour. *One* of these is the danger of a labour system, semi-servile in its nature, and feudalistic in its working; binding the labourer to service, but allowing him the slenderest interest in the soil, and when possible, shutting him off from the ownership of land.

The actual state of things, all through the south, justifies my fears. There is evidently a very wide conviction in the southern mind that the special function of the black man is to be a humble tiller of the soil; the mere functionary of the old landed proprietor. In making this statement I intend nothing offensive. I am speaking of the legitimate tendencies of human nature. Emancipation, you will remember was a terrible dislocation, it broke up everything suddenly and disastrously. It was like the upheaval of the great deep, by an earthquake. It tore up the foundations of systems which had had the rooting of two centuries and more. It left chaos on every side. The whites of the south felt it, and still feel it. All dislocations are injurious, and leave wounds and sorrows behind. They injure material interests, and they grievously confuse the brain. Herein lies the peril for the future. The old landed proprietor, bewildered as by an earthquake, mindful only of the past, unable to settle in the grooves of the future, holds on to the soil; holds on to his old notions as to the fit tillers of the soil; holds on to his old convictions of the natural place and destiny of the black race, as *the* tillers of the soil.

Hence arises the disposition, as by an instinct, to hold on to the soil, and to keep the black race from possessing it. "The Negro has no right to be a proprietor. He was born for service and for toil. If he does not know his place as a hewer of wood and a drawer of water, he must be taught it."

Now these convictions are the most natural conceivable. They are not the exclusive characteristic of southern gentlemen. Men of power and property act so everywhere. You will find the same sentiment among land owners in England; among planters in the West Indies; among manufacturers in New England; among proprietors in the East Indies; will you believe it? Yea, among black emigrants in Liberia surrounded by crude and ignorant pagans. Everywhere on earth men like to hold on to power; like to use their inferiors as tools and instruments; plume and pride themselves as superior beings; look with contempt upon the labouring classes, and strive by every possible means to use them to their own advantage.

Indeed, it is generally the selfish instinct of Capital to regard the labouring man as fit for use; regardless of his comfort, his rights, and his well being, as a man, a citizen and an immortal being. But not only have these opinions and this past system been injurious to the whites, but they have seriously affected *us*, as a people. They have injured us in two diverse and opposite ways. For, first they have served to settle in the minds of large numbers of our race the idea that servitude *is* the normal condition of the black man. Two centuries of service in this land has thoroughly driven this idea into the souls of thousands of our people; so that you can find numbers of black men and black women who really think that they themselves are inferior because they are black; that the race was born for inferiority; and that they reach the highest state of honour when they become servants of white men. These convictions have injured our race nearly as much in an *opposite* direction. They have bred the notion in another larger class, that labour is degrading; that superior people ought not to work; that as soon as one gets up a little in the world, soiled or horny hands, are vulgar and debasing; that those who can get a little learning, should give up hardy toil and aim after something higher!

Let me lay down here a few principles which may help us, as a people, to settle upon a solid basis this most important subject for the future. And, in this attempt, I wish to speak intelligently and with an eye to practicality.

First of all then, let me urge the primary importance of recognizing the duty and dignity of labour. Very many things have served to disturb such recognition. All the usages of society, all the habitudes of life, all the instructions of superiors, have tended to fasten upon us the idea of the degradation of labour. We have been brought up under a most artificial system, wherein on the one hand, all the glory and the beauty of life have been associated with ease, luxury and mastery; and where all the toil, the drudgery, the ignorance and the suffering, have been allied to the Negro and to servitude. What sort of a school was this, in which to learn the dignity of labour? Nay, rather was it not the very condition in which to convince the whole race that labour was the grandest curse of humanity? We cannot unlearn this conviction too speedily. For the very first step in a people's temporal prosperity is the material one of self-dependence, of personal support, through toil. Not until a people are able, by their own activities and skill, to raise themselves above want, and to meet the daily needs of home and family, can they take the next great step to the higher cultivation which comes by letters, refinement and religion; and which lifts them up to civility and power.

By concert, by general understanding, by wise forecast, by systematic action we must strive to introduce among the rising generation, every sort of trade and business which other men engage in. Can you tell me a single craft or calling in which white men are occupied, to which black men are utterly unfitted? Is there anything *they* do, which we can't do?

I have been referring this evening more especially to physical toil. I have said nothing concerning professional life, and the intellectual labours allied thereto; and simply for the reason that I fear there is too often extravagance among young men, in this regard. Work, I fear, is getting to be ungenteel [sic] in some classes among us; and so it comes to pass that many a good Barber, Caterer or Mechanic, is turned into a booby Doctor, or, a briefless [sic] Lawyer.

How much better if they had spent the time lost on law books in endeavoring to build up a business, or in farming; in successful catering, or the occupation of a trade.

Clever physicians we have. Keen and successful lawyers honour our race at the Bar. May their numbers be multiplied. We need a large school of such clever and efficient men. But you and I know instances not a few, where young men would have done a deal better by abiding in the callings of their parents; working with their hands; and throwing as much talent and respectability as possible in the old family craft, humble though it be.

If I could catch the ears of scores of such young men, whose vain ambition tires me, I would say—"Young men don't despise the humble positions of your parents. *All* the crafts of men are honourable. Dignify the toil of your family by your fine personal qualities. Raise their occupations, by genius and talent, to honour and competency. All work is honourable. Only throw brains, skill, energy and economy into your work; and it will lead you on to success, to comfort, and perchance to wealth.

May I join to this another suggestion: that is, that no man, no class of men, leap into superiority. Society never, anywhere, leaps into progress, greatness or power. The black race in this land cannot leap into might and majesty. It is to reach the higher planes in just the same way all other peoples have, in all the past of human history. The same conditions apply to us as to them. And these conditions are, first, humble labour; then, a gradual uprise; and then dogged and persistent effort, unfailing hope, living and undying aspiration, and pluck and audacious ambition, which brooks no limitations in the spheres of enterprise! In this process take the first step of the ladder! Never mind how lowly the duty may be. God has ordained that duty in the arrangements of society! Take it! Off with your coat. Bare your arms. Make a manly grasp of duty; do that duty, well and thoroughly, as a man; so that men of earth, and angels above you may see that it is work finished and complete!

The Black Woman of the South: Her Neglects and Her Needs, 1883

I do not stand here to-day to plead for the black man. He is a man; and if he is weak he must go to the wall. He is a man; he must fight his own way, and if he is strong in mind and body, he can take care of himself. But for the mothers, sisters, and daughters of my race I have a right to speak.

But I must remember that I am to speak not only of the neglects of the black woman, but also of her needs. And the consideration of her needs suggests the remedy which should be used for the uplifting of this woman from a state of brutality and degradation.

I have two or three plans to offer which, I feel assured, if faithfully used, will introduce widespread and ameliorating influences amid this large population.

(a) The *first* of these is specially adapted to the adult female population of the South, and is designed for immediate effect. I ask for the equipment and the mission of "sisterhoods" to the black women of the South. I wish to see large numbers of practical Christian women, women of intelligence and piety; women well trained in domestic economy; women who combine delicate sensibility and refinement with industrial acquaintance—scores of such women to go South; to enter every Southern State; to visit "Uncle Tom's Cabin;" to sit down with "Aunt Chloe" and her daughters; to show and teach them the ways and habits of thrift, economy, neatness, and order; to gather

them into "Mothers' Meetings" and sewing schools; and by both lectures and "talks" guide these women and their daughters into the modes and habits of clean and orderly housekeeping.

There is no other way, it seems to me, to bring about this domestic revolution.—We can not postpone this reformation to another generation. Postponement is the reproduction of the same evils in numberless daughters now coming up into life, imitators of the crude and untidy habits of their neglected mothers, and the perpetuation of plantation life to another generation. No, the effort must be made immediately, in *this* generation, with the rude, rough, neglected women of the times.

And it is to be done at their own homes, in their own huts. In this work all theories are useless. This is a practical need, and personal as practical. It is emphatically a personal work. It is to be done by example. The "Sister of Mercy," putting aside all fastidiousness, is to enter the humble and, per-chance, repulsive cabin of her black sister, and gaining her confidence, is to lead her out of the crude, disordered, and miserable ways of her plantation life into neatness, cleanliness, thrift, and self-respect. In every community women could be found who would gladly welcome such gracious visitations and instructors, and seize with eagerness their lessons and teachings. Soon their neighbors would seek the visitations which had lifted up friends and kinsfolk from inferiority and wretchedness. And then, erelong, whole communities would crave the benediction of these inspiring sisterhoods, and thousands and tens of thousands would hail the advent of these missionaries in their humble cabins. And then the seed of a new and orderly life planted in a few huts and localities, it would soon spread abroad, through the principle of imitation, and erelong, like the Banyan-tree, the beneficent work would spread far and wide through large populations. Doubtless they would be received, first of all, with surprise, for neither they nor their mothers, for two hundred years, have known the solicitudes of the great and cultivated for their domestic comfort. But surprise would soon give way to joy and exultation. Mrs. Fanny Kemble Butler, in her work, "journal of a Residence on a Georgian Plantation in 1838–39," tells us of the amazement of the wretched slave women on her husband's plantation when she went among them, and tried to improve their quarters and to raise them above squalor; and then of their immediate joy and gratitude.

There is nothing original in the suggestion I make for the "Sisters of Mercy." It is no idealistic and impractical scheme I am proposing, no new-fangled notion that I put before you. The Roman Catholic Church has, for centuries, been employing the agency of women in the propagation of her faith and as dispensers of charity. The Protestants of Germany are noted for the effective labors of holy women, not only in the Fatherland but in some of the most successful missions among the heathen in modern times. The Church of England, in that remarkable revival which has lilted her up as by a tidal wave, from the dead passivity of the last century, to an apostolic zeal and fervor never before known in her history, has shown, as one of her main characteristics, the wonderful power of "Sisterhoods," not only in the conversion of reprobates, but in the reformation of whole districts of abandoned men and women. This agency has been one of the most effective instrumentalities in the hands of that special school of devoted men called "Ritualists." Women of every class in that Church, many of humble birth, and as many more from the ranks of the noble, have left home and friends and the choicest circles of society, and given up their lives to the lowliest service of the poor and miserable. They have gone down into the very slums of her great cities, among thieves and murderers and harlots; amid filth and disease and pestilence; and for Christ's sake served and washed and nursed the most repulsive wretches; and then have willingly laid down and died, either exhausted by their labors or poisoned by infectious disease. Any one who will read the life of "Sister Dora" and of Charles Lowder, will see the glorious illustrations of my suggestion. Why can not this be done for the black women of the South?

(b) My *second* suggestion is as follows, and it reaches over to the future. I am anxious for a permanent and uplifting civilization to be engrafted on the Negro race in this land. And this can only be secured through the womanhood of a race. If you want the civilization of a people to reach the very best elements of their being, and then, having reached them, there to abide as an indigenous principle, you must imbue the *womanhood* of that people with all its elements and qualities. Any movement which passes by the female sex is an ephemeral thing. Without them, no true nationality, patriotism, religion, cultivation, family life, or true social status is a possibility. In *this* matter it takes *two* to make one—mankind is a duality. The *male* may bring, as an exotic, a foreign graft, say of a civilization, to a new people. But what then? Can a graft live or thrive of itself? By no manner of means. It must get vitality from the *stock* into which it is put; and it is the women who give the sap to every human organization which thrives and flourishes on earth.

I plead, therefore, for the establishment of at least one large "INDUSTRIAL SCHOOL" in every Southern State for the black girls of the South. I ask for the establishment of schools which may serve especially the *home* life of the rising womanhood of my race. I am not soliciting for these girls scholastic institutions, seminaries for the cultivation of elegance, conservatories of music, and schools of classical and artistic training. I want such schools and seminaries for the women of my race as much as any other race; and I am glad that there are such schools and colleges, and that scores of colored women are students within their walls.

But this higher style of culture is not what I am aiming after for *this* great need. I am seeking something humbler, more homelike and practical, in which the education of the hand and the use of the body shall be the specialties, and where the intellectual training will be the incident.

Let me state just here definitely what I want for the black girls of the South:

1. I want boarding-schools for the *industrial training* of one hundred and fifty or two hundred of the poorest girls, of the ages of twelve to eighteen years.
2. I wish the *intellectual* training to be limited to reading, writing, arithmetic, and geography.
3. I would have these girls taught to do accurately all domestic work, such as sweeping floors, dusting rooms, scrubbing, bed making, washing and ironing, sewing, mending, and knitting.
4. I would have the trades of dressmaking, millinery, straw-platting, tailoring for men, and such like, taught them.

5. The art of cooking should be made a specialty, and every girl should be instructed in it.
6. In connection with these schools, garden plats should be cultivated, and every girl should be required, daily, to spend at least an hour in learning the cultivation of small fruits, vegetables, and flowers.

I am satisfied that the expense of establishing such schools would be insignificant. As to their maintenance, there can be no doubt that, rightly managed, they would in a brief time be self-supporting. Each school would soon become a hive of industry, and a source of income. But the *good* they would do is the main consideration. Suppose that the time of a girl's schooling be limited to *three*, or perchance to *two* years. It is hardly possible to exaggerate either the personal family or society influence which would flow from these schools. Every class, yea, every girl in an outgoing class, would be a missionary of thrift, industry, common sense, and practicality. They would go forth, year by year, a leavening power into the houses, towns, and villages of the Southern black population; girls fit to be the thrifty wives of the honest peasantry of the South, the worthy matrons of their numerous households.

I am looking after the domestic training of the MASSES; for the raising up women meet to be helpers of *poor* men, the RANK AND FILE of black society, all through the rural districts of the South. The city people and the wealthy can seek more ambitious schools, and should pay for them.

Ladies and gentlemen, since the day of emancipation millions of dollars have been given by the generous Christian people of the North for the intellectual training of the black race in this land. Colleges and universities have been built in the South, and hundreds of youth have been gathered within their walls. The work of your own Church in this regard has been magnificent and unrivaled, and the results which have been attained have been grand and elevating to the entire Negro race in America. The complement to all this generous and ennobling effort is the elevation of the black woman. Up to this day and time your noble philanthropy has touched, for the most part, the male population of the South, giving them superiority, and stimulated them to higher aspirations. But a true civilization can only then be attained when the life of woman is reached, her whole being permeated by noble ideas, her fine taste enriched by culture, her tendencies to the beautiful gratified and developed, her singular and delicate nature lifted up to its full capacity; and then, when all these qualities are fully matured, cultivated, and sanctified, all their sacred influences shall circle around ten thousand firesides, and the cabins of the humblest freedmen shall become the homes of Christian refinement and of domestic elegance through the influence and the charm of the uplifted and cultivated black woman of the South!

The Prime Need of the Negro Race, 1897

UNFORTUNATELY, men often misconceive some of the larger *incidents* of life for its *problems*, and thus, unconsciously, they hinder the progress of the race.

Just such a mistake, if I err not, has arisen with regard to the solution of the "Negro Problem" in the South. It may be seen in the divergence of two classes of minds: the one maintains that industrialism is the solution of the Negro problem; and another class, while recognizing the need of industrial skill, maintains that culture is the true solution.

The thing of magnitude in the South, all must admit, is the civilization of a new race. The question is, then, how is this civilization to be produced? Is industrialism the prime consideration? Is the Negro to be built up from the material side of his nature?

But industrialism is no new thing in Negro life in this country. It is simply a change in the old phase of Southern Society. It is, in fact, but an incident; doubtless a large, and in some respects, a vital one. It would be the greatest folly to ignore its vast importance. Yet it is not to be forgotten that the Negro has been in this "school of labor" under slavery in America, fully two hundred and fifty years; and every one knows that it has never produced his civilization. That it was crude, previous to emancipation; that it is to be enlightened labor now, in a state of freedom, is manifestly but an alteration in the form of an old and settled order of life.

When the Negro passed from under the yoke he left a state of semi-barbarism behind him, put his feet for the first time within the domain of civilization, and immediately there sprang up before him a new problem of life. But that problem is not industrialism. That is simply the modification of an old condition; for it is but the introduction of intelligence into the crudeness of the old slave-labor system.

The other question, then, presents itself—is not the Negro's elevation to come from the quickening and enlightenment of his higher nature? Is it to come from below or from above?

It seems manifest that the major factor in this work for the Negro is his higher culture. There is not dispute as to the need of industrialism. This is a universal condition of life everywhere. But there is not need of an undue and overshadowing exaggeration of it in the case of the Negro.

And, first of all, industrialism itself is a *result* in man's civilization, not a cause. It may exist in a people and with much excellence for ages, and still that people may "lie in dull obstruction," semi-barbarous and degraded. We see in all history large populations moving in all the planes of industrial life, both low and high, and yet paralyzed in all the high springs of action, and for the simple reason that the hand of man gets its cunning from the brain. And without the enlightened brain what is the hand of man more than the claw of a bird or the foot of a squirrel? In fine, without the enlightened brain, where is civilization?

The Negro race, then, needs a new factor for its life and being, and this new factor must come from a more vitalizing source than any material condition. The end of industrialism is thrift, prosperity or gain. But civilization has a loftier object in view. It is to make men grander; it is to exalt them in the scale of being; and its main energy to this end is the "higher culture."

Observe, then, just here, that "every good gift and every perfect gift comes from above." I have no hesitation in using this text (albeit thus abbreviated) as an aphorism. And what I wish to say in its interpretation is this, viz., that all the greatness of men comes from altitudes. All the improvement, the progress, the culture, the civilization of men come from somewhere above. They never come from below!

Just as the rains and dews come down from the skies and fall upon the hills and plains and spread through the fields of earth with fertilizing power, so, too, with the culture of human society. Some exalted man, some great people, some marvelous migration, some extraordinary and quickening cultivation, or some divine revelation, "from above" must come to any people ere the processes of true and permanent elevation can begin among them. And this whole process I call civilization.

If a more precise and definite meaning to this word is demanded, I reply that I use it as indicative of letters, literature, science and philosophy. In other words, that this Negro race is to be lifted up to the acquisition of the higher culture of the age. This culture is to be made a part of its heritage; not at some distant day, but now and all along the development of the race. And no temporary fad of doubting or purblind philanthropy is to be allowed to make "industrial training" a substitute for it.

For, first of all, it is only a dead people who can be put into a single groove of life. And, next, every live people must have its own leaders as molders of its thought and determiners of its destiny: men, too, indigenous to the soil in race and blood.

For it is thought that makes the world—high, noble, prophetic, exalted and exalting thought. It is this that makes races and nations, industries and trades, farming and commerce; and not the reverse of this, i.e., that these make thought and civilization. And without thought, yea, scientific thought, peoples will remain everlastingly children and underlings, the mere tools and puppets of the strong.

And such thought, in these days, comes from the schools. The leaders of races must have wisdom, science, culture and philosophy. One such man has often determined the character and destiny of his race for centuries. This does not mean that noodles and numbskulls shall be sent to college; nor that every Negro shall be made a scholar; nor that there shall be a waste of time and money upon incapacity. No one can make a thimble hold the contents of a bucket! But what it does mean is this, that the whole world of scholarship shall be opened to the Negro mind; and that it is not to be fastened, temporarily or permanently to the truck-patch or to the hoe, to the anvil or to the plane; that the Negro shall be allowed to do his own thinking in any and every sphere, and not to have that thinking relegated to others. It means that when genius arises in this race and elects, with flaming torch, to push its way into the grand arcanum of philosophy or science or imagination, no bar shall be raised against its entrance. I submit:

1. That civilization is the foremost, deepest need of the Negro race.
2. That the "higher culture" is its grandest source.
3. That the gift to the Negro of the scientific mind, by Fisk and Clark and Lincoln, and Oberlin and Howard and Yale, and Harvard and other colleges, is of the most incalculable value to the black race.

6.
BOOKER T. WASHINGTON

Booker T. Washington (1856–1915) was one of the most prominent Black leaders in American history. His life exemplified the Horatio Alger tale; he was born a slave and by the end of his life he had had dinner at the White House. He gained the most notoriety from his founding of the Tuskegee Normal and Industrial Institute in Alabama (1881), his infamous book, *Up from Slavery* (1901), and his role as spokesman for Black people and advisor to both the Theodore Roosevelt and Taft administrations.

Washington attended the Hampton Agricultural Institute. The institute influenced his developing ideology and emphasis on industrial training as a means by which to assist newly freed slaves. After graduating in 1875, he worked as a teacher in West Virginia for two years before becoming faculty at Hampton. Washington went on to become the first teacher at the Tuskegee Institute and its principal from 1881 until his demise. Washington posited that education was paramount for the advancement of African Americans. He was responsible for the creation of copious new public schools for Black people in the rural South. At Tuskegee, Washington was engaged in praxis; he was actively involved in the vocational training of Black folk, so that they gained economic upward mobility and stability. In order to further his efforts he founded the National Negro Business League (NNBL) (1900). The same way Crummell's American Negro Academy worked to create a strong organization of academically accomplished men devoted to promoting higher education, the NNBL fostered social networks of Black entrepreneurs. Under Washington's direction the NNBL aimed to cultivate the development of an independent strong Black business class. The state and local chapters of the organization worked to help African Americans become a strong and viable economic class so that once they acquired economic upward mobility they could gain political power.

Overview of Ideas

In his famous "Atlanta Exposition Address" Booker T. Washington laid out his plan for African Americans, which is commonly referred to as accommodation. In his famous plea to African Americans, Washington told Black folk to "cast down your bucket where you are." Washington argued that leaving the United States, whether back to Africa or to another country, was not the answer.

> To those of my race who … underestimate the importance of cultivating friendly relations with the Southern white man, who is their next-door neighbor, I would say: "Cast down your bucket where you are"—cast it down in making friends in every manly way of the people of all races by whom we are surrounded.

Washington posited that Blacks and Whites should work together; socially this might take time but in the economy, and in basic social institutions, we should work together. He wrote, "in all things that are purely social we can be as separate as the fingers, yet one as the hand in all things essential to mutual progress." Black separatism was not the answer.

Washington's ideas about economic advancement have also been widely misunderstood. To be clear, Washington certainly did advocate (in the tradition of American liberalism) that African Americans would prosper by finding a trade and working hard. Classic American liberalism sees success as being achieved solely by individual effort. In the United States Horatio Alger stories are not fiction but a reality; with hard work, delayed gratification, and frugality anyone who tries can be successful. For Washington, African Americans needed to pull themselves up by their bootstraps. He tells African Americans to cast their buckets down in "agriculture, mechanics, in commerce, in domestic service, and in the professions." Washington argued that the overwhelming majority of African Americans worked with their hands and should continue to hone their skills and, like Crummell, he argued that they must take dignity in their labor. All energy should be put into their vocational skills:

> No race can prosper till it learns that there is as much dignity in tilling a field as in writing a poem … the opportunity to earn a dollar in a factory just now is worth infinitely more than then opportunity to spend a dollar in an opera house.

Higher education, as we will see advocated by other thinkers such as W.E.B. Du Bois, was not as important as learning basic cultural capital. With material prosperity African Americans would gain power.

Washington argued that through economic advancement we could displace racist discourses. If most Whites thought Blacks were lazy and prone to criminality, by working hard in a trade and building themselves up economically they would demonstrate to racist Whites that the racist discourses they relied so heavily on were spurious. Washington may have been accurate. Economic prosperity does produce model minorities in the eyes of Americans. For example, contemporary scholars have written about the rise of model minorities such as Asians and Jews.[1] Substantial and recognizable economic advancement allow members of oppressed groups to transcend much of the prejudice once inflicted upon them by bigots. For Washington, this was possible for Black people.

Washington is frequently misunderstood and misrepresented. Washington did put great emphasis on economic prosperity. However, he did believe that political rights were important. Washington was not opposed to integration; it was when integration should be struggled for and implemented that was the source of vitriolic debate. Washington advocated gradualism; integration would be best implemented after African

Americans gained substantial economic power. With new-found economic power political agitation would become easier. Moreover, his point was that "mere political agitation" was not enough. It would not be enough to lobby for civil rights. African Americans needed money to support these campaigns; they needed money to build their own communities; they needed to reform their own characters and behaviors. Without these other changes political agitation or political protest was futile. However, all claims that Washington was a sell-out, an accommodationist to segregation who thought political protest was not necessary, are misleading at best. In fact, Washington said segregation was unjust; it invites other unjust measures, and was unnecessary.

Washington argued that the disenfranchisement of African Americans was wrong. "Any law controlling the ballot, that is not absolutely just and fair to both races, will work more permanent injury to the whites than to the blacks." Interestingly, Washington often argued that African Americans were entitled to the same rights as Whites. However, strategically his arguments tended to focus on how Whites would benefit from allowing African Americans to gain equal access to basic institutions and rights. He emphasized the importance of providing equal education to Whites and Blacks. However, again, his logic was not based on pleas to Whites' Christian values or a moral imperative for Whites to act as humanitarians. He basically argued, if you believe Blacks are ignorant, than educate them and watch them enrich this country. Washington placated Whites; perhaps we could call him a "strategic sycophant." "First class training … will make us intelligent producers, and not only help us to contribute our proportion as taxpayers, but will result in retaining much money in the State." The United States and its White citizens had much to gain financially from the advancement of African Americans.

Washington was a gradualist. "The according of the full exercise of political rights is going to be matter of natural, slow growth, not an over-night, gourd-vine affair." He never told African Americans that voting was not important. In fact, he wrote, "I do not believe that the negro should cease voting, for a man can learn the exercise of self-government by ceasing to vote, any more than a boy can learn to swim by keeping out of the water." Change would be slow. Unlike leaders we will see in the coming chapters such as Trotter and Du Bois, Washington argued that African Americans could not jump directly from slavery to complete equality; he saw this process as coming over time and that strategically it would be best to achieve one realistic goal at a time.

With the Great Migration underway, in his last days Washington urged African Americans to stay in the South. Washington astutely realized that much of the opportunity ostensibly awaiting Blacks in the North was a mirage. Northern cities were plagued by overcrowding, disease, intense job competition, higher costs of living, inadequate housing, hypersegregation, and racism. Not only was the Northern utopia an illusion but there were advantages to remaining in the South. In the South, "Negroes are better able … to buy and own their own homes, to build their own communities, where they can have their own churches, schools, banks, and other places of business." Black folk had profuse opportunities for building wealth and strong communities in the South. If African Americans desired power by building wealth and strong networks in educational institutions and in churches, etc., they could realize this goal in the South.

Atlanta Exposition Address, 1895

Mr. President and Gentlemen of the Board of Directors and Citizens: One-third of the population of the South is of the Negro race. No enterprise seeking the material, civil, or moral welfare of this section can disregard this element of our population and reach the highest success. I but convey to you, Mr. President and Directors, the sentiment of the masses of my race when I say that in no way have the value and manhood of the American Negro been more fittingly and generously recognized than by the managers of this magnificent Exposition at every stage of its progress. It is a recognition that will do more to cement the friendship of the two races than any occurrence since the dawn of our freedom.

Not only this, but the opportunity here afforded will awaken among us a new era of industrial progress. Ignorant and inexperienced, it is not strange that in the first years of our new life we began at the top instead of at the bottom; that a seat in Congress or the state legislature was more sought than real estate or industrial skill; that the political convention or stump speaking had more attractions than starting a dairy farm or truck garden.

A ship lost at sea for many days suddenly sighted a friendly vessel. From the mast of the unfortunate vessel was seen a signal, "Water, water; we die of thirst!" The answer from the friendly vessel at once came back, "Cast down your bucket where you are." A second time the signal, "Water, water; send us water!" ran up from the distressed vessel, and was answered, "Cast down your bucket where you are." And a third and fourth signal for water was answered, "Cast down your bucket where you are." The captain of the distressed vessel, at last heeding the injunction, cast down his bucket, and it came up full of fresh, sparkling water from the mouth of the Amazon River. To those of my race who depend on bettering their condition in a foreign land or who underestimate the importance of cultivating friendly relations with the Southern white man, who is their next-door neighbour [sic], I would say: "Cast down your bucket where you are"—cast it down in making friends in every manly way of the people of all races by whom we are surrounded.

Cast it down in agriculture, mechanics, in commerce, in domestic service, and in the professions. And in this connection it is well to bear in mind that whatever other sins the South may be called to bear, when it comes to business, pure and simple, it is in the South that the Negro is given a man's chance in the commercial world, and in nothing is this Exposition more eloquent than in emphasizing this chance. Our greatest danger is that in the great leap from slavery to freedom we may overlook the fact that the masses of us are to live by the productions of our hands, and fail to keep in mind that we shall prosper in proportion as we learn to dignify and glorify common labour, and put brains and skill into the common occupations of life: shall prosper in proportion as we learn to draw the line between the superficial and the substantial, the ornamental gewgaws of life and the useful. No race can prosper till it learns that there is as much dignity in tilling a field as in writing a poem. It is at the bottom of life we must begin, and not at the top. Nor should we permit our grievances to overshadow our opportunities.

To those of the white race who look to the incoming of those of foreign birth and strange tongue and habits for the prosperity of the South, were I permitted I would repeat what I say to my own race, "Cast down your bucket where you are." Cast it down among the eight millions of Negroes whose habits you know, whose fidelity and love you have tested in days when to have proved treacherous meant the ruin of your firesides. Cast down your bucket among these people who have, without strikes and labour wars, tilled your fields, cleared your forests, builded [*sic*] your railroads and cities, and brought forth treasures from the bowels of the earth, and helped make possible this magnificent representation of the progress of the South. Casting down your bucket among my people, helping and encouraging them as you are doing on these grounds, and to education of head, hand, and heart, you will find that they will buy your surplus land, make blossom the waste places in your fields, and run your factories. While doing this, you can be sure in the future, as in the past, that you and your families will be surrounded by the most patient, faithful, law-abiding, and unresentful [*sic*] people that the world has seen. As we have proved our loyalty to you in the past, in nursing your children, watching by the sick-bed of your mothers and fathers, and often following them with tear-dimmed eyes to their graves, so in the future, in our humble way, we shall stand by you with a devotion that no foreigner can approach, ready to lay down our lives, if need be, in defense of yours, interlacing our industrial, commercial, civil, and religious life with yours in a way that shall make the interests of both races one. In all things that are purely social we can be as separate as the fingers, yet one as the hand in all things essential to mutual progress.

There is no defense or security for any of us except in the highest intelligence and development of all. If anywhere there are efforts tending to curtail the fullest growth of the Negro, let these efforts be turned into stimulating, encouraging, and making him the most useful and intelligent citizen. Effort or means so invested will pay a thousand per cent interest. These efforts will be twice blessed—"blessing him that gives and him that takes."

There is no escape through law of man or God from the inevitable:—

> The laws of changeless justice bind
>   Oppressor with oppressed;
> And close as sin and suffering joined
>   We march to fate abreast.

Nearly sixteen millions of hands will aid you in pulling the load upward, or they will pull against you the load downward. We shall constitute one-third and more of the ignorance and crime of the South, or one-third its intelligence and progress; we shall contribute one-third to the business and industrial prosperity of the South, or we shall prove a veritable body of death, stagnating, depressing, retarding every effort to advance the body politic.

Gentlemen of the Exposition, as we present to you our humble effort at an exhibition of our progress, you must not expect overmuch. Starting thirty years ago with ownership here and there in a few quilts and pumpkins and chickens (gathered from miscellaneous sources), remember the path that has led from these to the inventions and production of agricultural implements, buggies, steam-engines, newspapers, books, statuary, carving, paintings, the management of drug stores and banks, has not been trodden without contact with thorns and thistles. While we take pride in what we exhibit as a result of our independent efforts, we do not for a moment forget that our part in this exhibition would fall far short of your expectations but for the constant help that has come to our educational life, not only from the Southern states, but especially from Northern philanthropists, who have made their gifts a constant stream of blessing and encouragement.

The wisest among my race understand that the agitation of questions of social equality is the extremest [*sic*] folly, and that progress in the enjoyment of all the privileges that will come to us must be the result of severe and constant struggle rather than of artificial forcing. No race that has anything to contribute to the markets of the world is long in any degree ostracized. It is important and right that all privileges of the law be ours, but it is vastly more important that we be prepared for the exercise of these privileges. The opportunity to earn a dollar in a factory just now is worth infinitely more than the opportunity to spend a dollar in an opera-house.

In conclusion, may I repeat that nothing in thirty years has given us more hope and encouragement, and drawn us so near to you of the white race, as this opportunity offered by the Exposition; and here bending, as it were, over the altar that represents the results of the struggles of your race and mine, both starting practically empty-handed three decades ago, I pledge that in your effort to work out the great and intricate problem which God has laid at the doors of the South, you shall have at all times the patient, sympathetic help of my race; only let this be constantly in mind, that, while from representations in these buildings of the product of field, of forest, of mine, of factory, letters, and art, much good will come, yet far above and beyond material benefits will be that higher good, that, let us pray God, will come, in a blotting out of sectional differences and racial animosities and suspicions, in a determination to administer absolute justice, in a willing obedience among all classes to the mandates of law. This, coupled with our material prosperity, will bring into our beloved South a new heaven and a new earth.

Open Letter to the Louisiana Constitutional Convention, 1898

To the Louisiana State Constitutional Convention: In addressing you this letter.... More than one half of the people of your State are Negroes. No State can long prosper when a large percentage of its citizenship is in ignorance and poverty, and has no interest in government. I beg of you that you do not treat us as alien people. We are not aliens. You know us; you know that we have cleared your forests, tilled your fields, nursed your children and protected your families. There is an attachment between us that few understand. While I do not presume to be able to advise you, yet it is in my heart to say that if your Convention would do something that would prevent, for all time, strained relations between the two races, and would permanently settle the matter of political relations in our Southern States, at least, let the very best educational opportunities be provided for both races; and add to this the enactment of an election law that shall be incapable of unjust discrimination, at the same time providing that in proportion as the ignorant secure education, property and character, they will be given the right of citizenship. Any other course will take from one-half your citizens interest in the State, and hope and ambition to become intelligent producers and taxpayers—to become useful and virtuous citizens. Any other course will tie the white citizens of Louisiana to a body of death.

The Negroes are not unmindful of the fact that the white people of your State pay the greater proportion of the school taxes, and that the poverty of the State prevents it from doing all that it desires for public education; yet I believe you will agree with me, that ignorance is more costly to the State than education; that it will cost Louisiana more not to educate her Negroes than it will cost to educate them. In connection with a generous provision for public schools, I believe that nothing will so help my own people in your State as provision at some institution for the highest academic and normal training, in connection with thorough training in agriculture, mechanics and domestic economy. The fact is that 90 per cent of our people depend upon the common occupations for their living, and outside of the cities 85 per cent, depend upon agriculture for support. Notwithstanding this, our people have been educated since the war in everything else but the very thing that most of them live by. First-class training in agriculture, horticulture, dairying, stock-raising, the mechanical arts and domestic economy, will make us intelligent producers, and not only help us to contribute our proportion as taxpayers, but will result in retaining much money in the State that now goes outside for that which can be produced in the State. An institution that will give this training of the hand, along with the highest mental culture, will soon convince our people that their salvation is in the ownership of property, industrial and business development, rather than in mere political agitation.

The highest test of the civilization of any race is in its willingness to extend a helping hand to the less fortunate. A race, like an individual, lifts itself up by lifting others up. Surely no people ever had a greater chance to exhibit the highest Christian fortitude and magnanimity than is now presented to the people of Louisiana. It requires little wisdom or statesmanship to repress, to crush out.

The Negro and the Signs of Civilization, 1901

There are certain visible signs of civilization and strength which the world demands that each individual or race exhibit before it is taken seriously into consideration in the affairs of the world. Unless these visible evidences of ability and strength are forthcoming, mere abstract talking and mere claiming of "rights" amount to little. This is a principle that is as broad and old as the world and is not confined to the conditions that exist between the white man and the black man in the South. We may be inclined to exalt intellectual acquirements over the material, but all will acknowledge that the possession of the material has an influence that is lasting and unmistakable. As one goes through our Western States and sees the Norwegians in Minnesota, for example, owning and operating nearly one-third of the farms in the State; and then as he goes through one of the cities of Minnesota and sees block after block of brick stores owned by these Norwegians; as he sees factories and street railways owned and operated by these same people, and as he notes that as a rule these people live in neat, well-kept cottages where there are refinement and culture, on nice streets, that have been paid for, he can't help but have confidence in and respect for such people, no matter how he has been educated to feel regarding them. The material, visible and tangible elements in this case teach a lesson that almost nothing else can. It may be said in opposition to this view that this is exalting too high the material side of life. I do not take this view. Let us see what is back of this material possession. In the first place the possession of property is an evidence of mental discipline, mental grasp and control. It is an evidence of self-sacrifice. It is an evidence of economy. It is an evidence of thrift and industry. It is an evidence of fixedness of character and purpose. It is an evidence of interest in pure and intelligent government, for no man can possess property without having the deepest interest in all that pertains to local and national government. The black man who owns $50,000 worth of property in a town is going to think a good many times before he votes for the officer who will have the liberty of taxing his property. If he thinks that a colored law-maker will use his taxing power wrongfully, he is not likely to vote for him merely for the sentimental reason that he is a black man. The black man who owns $50,000 worth of property in a town is not likely to continue to vote for a Republican law-maker if he knows that a Democratic one will bring lower taxes and better protection to his property. Say or think what we will there is but one way for the Negro to get up and that is for him to pay the cost, and when he has paid the cost—paid the price of his freedom—it will appear in the beautiful, well-kept home, in the increasing bank account, in the farm, and crops that are free from debt, in the ownership of railroad and municipal stocks and bonds (and he who owns the majority of stock in a railroad will not have to ride in a "Jim Crow car"), in the well-kept store, in the well-fitted laundry, in the absence of mere superficial display. These are a few of the universal and indisputable signs of the highest civilization, and the Negro must possess them or be debarred. All mere abstract talk about the possibility of possessing them, or his intention to possess them, counts for little. He must actually possess them, and the only way to possess them is to possess them. From every standpoint of interest it is the duty of the Negro himself, and the duty of the Southern white man as well as the white man in the North, to see that the Negro be helped forward as fast as possible towards the possession of these evidences of civilization. How can it best be done? Where is the beginning to be made? It can be done by the Negro beginning right now and where he finds himself. What I am anxious for is for the Negro to be in actual possession of all the elements of the highest civilization, and when he is so possessed, the burden of his future treatment by the white man must rest upon the white man.

I repeat, let the Negro begin right where he is, by putting the greatest amount of intelligence, of skill and dignity into the occupations by which he is surrounded. Let him learn to do common things in an uncommon manner. Whenever in the South, for example, the Negro is the carpenter, [*sic*] let him realize that he cannot remain the carpenter unless people are sure that no one can excel him as a carpenter. This black carpenter should strive in every way possible to keep himself abreast of the best wood work done in the world. He should be constantly studying the best journals and books bearing on carpentry. He should watch for every improvement in his line. When this carpenter's son is educated in college or elsewhere, he should see that his son studies mechanical and architectural drawing. He should not only have his son taught practical carpentry, but should see that in addition to his literary education that he is a first class architect as well—that, if possible, he has an idea of landscape gardening and house furnishing. In a word, he should see that his son knows so much about wood work, house construction, and everything that pertains to making a house all that it should be, [sic] that his services are in constant demand. One such Negro in each community will give character to a hundred other Negroes. It is the kind of effort that will put the Negro on his feet. What I have said of carpentry, is equally true of dozens of occupations now within the Negro's hands. The second or third generation of this black man's family need not be carpenters, but can aspire successfully to something higher because the foundation has been laid.

It is not only the duty of the Negro to thus put himself in possession of the signs of civilization, but it is also the plainest duty of the white man, North and South, to help the Negro to do so in a more generous manner than ever before. One-third of the population of the South is black. Ignorance in any country or among any people is the sign of poverty, crime and incompetency [sic]. No State can have the highest civilization and prosperity with one-third of its population down. This one-third will prove a constant millstone about the neck of the other two-thirds. Every one-room Negro cabin in the South, where there is ignorance, poverty and stupidity, is an adverse advertisement of the State, the bad effects of which no white man in the next generation can escape.

Statement on Suffrage, 1903

Negro and the White

I believe it is the duty of the negro—as the greater part of the race is already doing—to deport himself modestly in regard to political claims, depending on the slow but sure influences that proceed from the possession of property, intelligence and high character for the full recognition of his political rights.

I think that the according of the full exercise of political rights is going to be a matter of natural, slow growth, not an over-night, gourd-vine affair. I do not believe that the negro should cease voting, for a man cannot learn the exercise of self-government by ceasing to vote, any more than a boy can learn to swim by keeping out of the water.

Suffrage Laws Unjust

I do not believe that any State should make a law that permits an ignorant and poverty-stricken white man to vote and prevents a black man in the same condition from voting.

Such a law is not only unjust, but it will react, as all unjust laws do, in time; for the effect of such a law is to encourage the negro [sic] to secure education and property, and at the same time it encourages the white man to remain in ignorance and poverty. I believe that in time, through the operation of intelligence and friendly race relations, all cheating at the ballot-box in the South will cease.

It will become apparent that the white man who begins by cheating a negro [*sic*] out of his ballot soon learns to cheat a white man out of his, and that man who does this ends his career of dishonesty by the theft of property or by some equally serious crime.

In my opinion, the time will come when the South will encourage all of its citizens to vote. It will see that it pays better, from every standpoint, to have healthy, vigorous life than to have that political stagnation which always results when one-half the population has no share and no interest in the government.

As a rule, I believe in universal, free suffrage, but I believe that in the South we are confronted with peculiar conditions that justify the protection of the ballot in many of the States, for a while at least, either by an educational test, a property test, or by both combined; but whatever tests are required they should be made to apply with equal and exact justice to both races.

The Negro in the North: Are His Advantages as Great as in the South?, 1907

My attention has been repeatedly called in recent years to the rapid increase of the Negro population in Northern cities, particularly in the larger cities of the North Atlantic States, that is, New England, New York, New Jersey, and Pennsylvania. These states have already considerably more than one-third of all the Northern Negroes and statistics show that from 1880 to 1900 this portion of the population increased one-third more rapidly than the white. The Negroes in Philadelphia increased in the ten years, between 1890 and 1900, from thirty to sixty-two thousand. The colored population in New York was 23,606 in 1890, but in 1900 it had risen to 60,666. Boston's colored population grew more slowly, but it has grown steadily. In 1880 the Negroes of Cambridge and Boston were 7,377, but in 1900 this number had increased to 15,497.

Under normal conditions I doubt whether the existence of 900,000 Negroes scattered over the whole Northern and Western country, and permanently settled on farms and in small towns, as they are to a very large degree in the South, would have attracted particular attention. But the fact is that the Negroes in the Northern States are, to a large extent, part of the floating population. While eighty-two per cent of the Southern Negroes are on farms and plantations in country districts, more than seventy per cent of the Northern Negroes are in cities.

This Negro element in the floating population of the Northern cities has grown so rapidly in recent years and has to such an extent complicated the problem of city life, already difficult enough, that some persons have come to regard it as a distinct menace.

City Life Unfavorable to Health and Morals

I have more than once said that the masses of the colored people are not yet fitted to survive and prosper in the great cities North and South to which so many of them are crowding. The temptations are too great and the competition with the foreign population with which they come in contact is too severe. Many of these young colored men and women, who leave the country for the city, go almost directly from the farms and plantations of the South, where they have been living on the same soil on which their fathers and mothers worked as slaves and under conditions not far removed from those that existed before emancipation. It is not difficult, under these circumstances, to understand that the colored immigrants from the South are not able at once to adjust themselves to the crowded, strenuous and complicated life of these great modern cities. The vital statistics, which are perhaps the best indicators we have in this matter, show that, of all the races now pouring into the larger American cities from various parts of the world, the Negro is the least prepared to meet the conditions of city life.

It should always be borne in mind that there is this difference between the Negro in the North and the average colored man living on plantations of the country districts in the South, that while he is ignorant he has not been degraded, as a rule, except in rare cases, by vicious habits. In the large cities of the North, it is true of a large element of the Negroes, as it is true of the same class of other races, that they have injured body and soul by degrading habits. There is a vast difference between pure ignorance and degradation.

My own conviction is that this problem, like others which the presence of the Negro race in this land has created, must find its solution ultimately on the farms and planta-tions of the Southern States. So far as I can understand the disposition of the masses of my own people they have determined to remain for all time upon the soil of the South-ern States, where their future, in my opinion, is inextricably bound up with the pros-perity of the soil. I do not believe that any large proportion of the Negro people intend to live permanently outside of the South, and I doubt very much if any laborer will be found to supplant permanently the Negro in the Southern cotton field. The problem of the Northern Negro will, to a very large extent, find its solution in the efforts now being made by the United States Department of Agriculture to improve the character and quality of the Negro farmers; in the efforts now being made to increase the number and efficiency of country schools; in the growing disposition among the better class of the white people to secure justice for the Negro and protect him against hectoring and abuse to which he is so often subjected, and finally in the encouragement the Negro is receiving in certain parts of the South to buy land, to build houses and permanently settle on the soil.

The security of the South against danger of race riots and the evils that causes them demands that every man, white and black, should, as far as possible, own a home; a hearth stone around which the interest of the family can find a center; and a perma-nent place of abode on which the wholesome influences of family life can find a prop.

I believe that those who are seeking a solution of the problem of the Northern Negro will find that they can co-operate in this direction with the more thoughtful class of the Southern people who find that the South is being slowly drained of the labor it needs in the fields and in the trades by emigration Northward.

I have spoken thus far of that part of the population which has but lately arrived in the North. It represents the element of unrest among the Negroes of the South. While a large number of these people have left the South upon a definite promise of higher wages or better treatment, a greater number are mere social drift, drawn into the cities with the tide that sets to the large centers of population from all over the United States.

While I do not deny that there are some advantages for the Negro in the North which he does not have in the South, there are also disadvantages. There are the advantages of better schools and better teachers. The Negro has, for example, the opportunity of using the public library, of entering the colleges and universities. The Northern cities are farther advanced, on the whole, in their methods of dealing with the problem of city life. The Northern people are not haunted by the fear of social equality, and are therefore able to take hold in a more practical way of the problem of uplifting backward races. The Northern cities are richer and more able to provide special education to meet the special needs of special classes of the population.

Difficulties in Finding Labor

But on the whole I am convinced that the condition of the great mass of Negroes in the Northern cities is not only worse than that of the Negroes on the farms in the South but worse than that of any other portion of the city population. The statistics show that the death rate is much larger among Negroes in the North than it is among the whites, and this greater death rate is, no doubt, the result, not of one, but a number of influences which, in the Northern cities, work to the detriment of the race. The Negro has greater difficulty there in finding satisfactory employment. Large numbers of Negro laborers are induced to leave the South to meet the emergencies of Northern industry. They were brought to Chicago to help dig the Chicago Drainage canal. They were imported to New York to work on the building of the subway. The labor unions, to whose interest it is to limit the supply of labor, have never been favorable to the employment of Negroes. The fact that Negroes are frequently brought North as "strike breakers" helps to intensify the prejudice against them. The tendency of all this is to force the Negro down to the lowest rung of the industrial ladder and to make him, in short, a sort of industrial pariah.

But in spite of these difficulties the facts show that a considerable number of exceptional colored men, spurred on by contact and competition with the swift and thrifty race about them, have made their way and been successful. The number of successful Negro business and professional men is probably larger in proportion to the Negro population in the North than it is in the South. Many of these have become men of influence in the communities in which they live and have worked quietly and steadily in their professions and in other directions for the benefit and building up of the Negro people.

Greater Opportunities in the South

But the Northern Negro who makes a success in business or in a profession must, in most instances, live beside and work for a people who have no special need of his talents. At best he can but perform for them a service that can be performed as well, if not better, by some one else. In the South, on the contrary, a Negro professional or business man has an opportunity to work for his own people who need his services and will respect and honor him for his work. Land is still cheap in the South. Negroes are better able there than in the North to buy and own their homes, to build their own communities, where they can have their own churches, schools, banks and other places of business, and where the masses of the people are not placed in such direct competition with a race centuries ahead of them in habits, instincts and education. In these communities the masses of the people are enabled to grow slowly and normally, and the educated Negro, the preacher, physician, teacher and business man has an opportunity in directing and controlling the development of his own people, to assist in building up his race and his country, and to gain for himself the honor and gratitude with which the world everywhere rewards real service.

But there is another disadvantage under which the Northern Negro labors which, while it is not so obvious, is none the less real. He is, in relation to the lives and interests of the masses of the Negro race, in a certain sense, an exile, condemned to witness from a distance their struggles to rise, but not able to give them any effectual aid. Very often it happens that the Northern Negro knows little or nothing, except what he can learn from the newspapers, of the actual condition under which the majority of the Negro population live. He hears much of the crime and violence and sees nothing of the deeper constructive forces which are working quietly in the minds and hearts of Southern people, black and white. His protests against what he regards as the wrongs committed against the members of his race in the South are often inspired by impatience and contempt for the Southern Negroes themselves who, as far as he can see, are willing patiently to suffer wrong.

The result has been that while Northern and Southern white people have been steadily coming closer together upon the race question, the Northern and Southern Negro seem to be steadily growing farther apart.

There is a radical group among the Northern Negroes, just as there is a radical section among Southern whites, who insist on making the racial question a political and sectional issue. They are seeking to solve the problem of the races by keeping the North and the South apart and preventing the co-operation of both sections and both races in the task of reconstruction.

My own opinion is that this policy is not only hopeless but mistaken. What the ultimate effect of any systematic effort to intensify the sectional and racial antagonisms that already exist might be I dare not say. Some persons have suggested that it would result in making the Negroes the permanent wards of the several states or of the United States. I do not believe that either the white people or the black people of the South are yet prepared to accept this solution. On the contrary I believe that the races that have lived and worked together for 250 years in slavery will be able, in spite of difficulties, to solve the problem of living together in freedom.

The Negro has too long been a battledore and shuttlecock of political parties. What the South at the present time needs most is racial and sectional peace. What the Negro wants is justice, protection and encouragement to put forth his best efforts in fruitful and productive labor for his own welfare and that of the country as a whole. This is not a sectional, but a national issue.

My View of Segregation Laws, 1915

In New Orleans, Atlanta, Birmingham, Memphis—indeed in nearly every large city in the South—I have been in the homes of negroes who live in white neighborhoods, and I have yet to find any race friction; the negro goes about his business, the white man about his. Neither the wives nor the children have the slightest trouble.

White people who argue for the segregation of the masses of black people forget the tremendous power of objective teaching. To hedge any set of people off in a corner and sally among them now and then with a lecture or a sermon is merely to add misery to degradation. But put the black man where day by day he sees how the white man keeps his lawns, his windows; how he treats his wife and children, and you will do more real helpful teaching than a whole library of lectures and sermons. Moreover, this will help the white man. If he knows that his life is to be taken as a model, that his hours, dress, manners, are all to be patterns for someone less fortunate, he will deport himself better than he would otherwise. Practically all the real moral uplift the black people have got from the whites—and this has been great indeed—has come from this observation of the white man's conduct. The South to-day is still full of the type of negro [*sic*] with gentle manners. Where did he get them? From some master or mistress of the same type [*sic*].

Summarizing the matter in the large, segregation is ill-advised because

1. It is unjust.
2. It invites other unjust measures.
3. It will not be productive of good, because practically every thoughtful negro resents its injustice and doubts its sincerity. Any race adjustment based on injustice finally defeats itself. The Civil War is the best illustration of what results where it is attempted to make wrong right or seem to be right.
4. It is unnecessary.
5. It is inconsistent. The negro is segregated from his white neighbor, but white business men are not prevented from doing business in negro neighborhoods.
6. There has been no case of segregation of negroes[*sic*] in the United States that has not widened the breach between the two races. Wherever a form of segregation exists it will be found that it has been administered in such a way as to embitter the negro [*sic*] and harm more or less the moral fibre [*sic*] of the white man. That the negro [*sic*] does not express this constant sense of wrong is no proof that he does not feel it.

It seems to me that the reasons given above, if carefully considered, should serve to prevent further passage of such segregation ordinances as have been adopted in Norfolk, Richmond, Louisville, Baltimore, and one or two cities in South Carolina.

Finally, as I have said in another place, as white and black learn daily to adjust, in a spirit of justice and fair play, those interests which are individual and racial, and to see and feel the importance of those fundamental interests which are common, so will both races grow and prosper. In the long run no individual and no race can succeed which sets itself at war against the common good; for "in the gain or loss of one race, all the rest have equal claim."

Note

1. See Feagin, Joe R. and Rosalind Chou. 2008. *The Myth of the Model Minority: Asian Americans Facing Racism*. Boulder: Paradigm Books. Also see Brodkin, Karen. 1998. *How the Jews Became White Folks: And What That Says About Race in America*. New Jersey: Rutgers University Press.

7.

IDA B. WELLS-BARNETT

Ida B. Wells-Barnett (1862–1931) struggled for racial justice throughout her life and was a famous crusader against lynching. In 1884 when Wells-Barnett was only twenty-two she was forcibly removed from her seat on a train by a conductor for the Chesapeake & Ohio Railroad Company. Wells-Barnett refused to give up her seat to a White passenger on the train. When the conductor tried to violently remove Wells-Barnett from her seat, she bit the conductor's arm. It took two other men to remove her. This story is emblematic of Wells-Barnett's entire career as an activist. She never ceased to fight against injustice. Wells-Barnett sued the Chesapeake & Ohio Railroad Company. While she won in the lower court and was awarded $500, in 1887 the Tennessee Supreme Court overturned the original verdict. Interestingly, it was her own personal struggle that launched her career as a journalist. Like her counterparts the press became a primary means to disseminate her ideas and in this case her personal battle with racism.

Wells-Barnett became active in the Black press. In 1889 she became a partner in Rev. R. Nightingale's newspaper, *Free Speech and Headlight*. Often under her pen name, Lola, she utilized *Free Speech* to educate Black people about lynching. For example, after the lynching of her friends, Thomas Moss, Calvin McDowell, and Henry Stewart, the owners of the People's Grocery whose success ostensibly threatened White businesses, she utilized the paper to both inform Black people in Memphis of the incident but also to implore Black residents to leave town to avoid the savage lynch mob. In fact, as a result the offices of the newspaper were attacked. Wells-Barnett published articles in various Black newspapers such as the weekly *The Living Way* and the African American powerhouse, the *New York Age*. In 1893 in response to the prohibiting of African American participation in the World's Fair in Chicago, Wells-Barnett, along with her soon-to-be husband Ferdinand Barnett, Frederick Douglass, and Irvine Garland Penn, published *The Reason Why the Colored American is Not in the World's Colombian Exposition*. In 1895 she published her famous pamphlet, *A Red Record*, which vehemently denounced and exposed the prevalence of lynching. In 1900 Wells-Barnett published *Mob Rule in New Orleans* which highlighted the pervasiveness of police violence against Black folk. However, Wells-Barnett did not just utilize the press and words to fight racial injustice; she battled everyday where the rubber met the road.

In 1896 Wells-Barnett assisted in the creation of the National Association of Colored Women. Wells-Barnett was a supporter of the Niagara Movement[1] and became involved in the Niagara Movement's successor the NAACP. However, Wells-Barnett, like William Monroe Trotter, also was cynical and unconvinced that the racially-mixed organization would adopt radical enough aims to initiate large-scale change in the lives of African Americans. For these reasons she eventually left the NAACP. Although Wells-Barnett is best known for her activism against lynching she was devoted to improving the lives of African Americans in many areas. As the Great Migration began and droves of African Americans migrated from the South to the North Wells-Barnett began to struggle for the rights of Black people in large cities whose lives were plagued by problems such as unemployment, poor working conditions, and horrific housing conditions. As a result, in 1910, she founded the Negro Fellowship League in order to assist in the acquisition of decent housing and jobs. Also a fighter for women's rights, particularly women's suffrage, in 1913 Wells-Barnett founded the Alpha Suffrage Club.

Ida B. Wells-Barnett participated in the mainstream suffrage movement. However, Black women were frequently marginalized by White middle class suffragettes and as a result Wells-Barnett created the Alpha Suffrage Club; it was the only suffrage club for Black women in Illinois. She struggled for the rights of the subaltern throughout her life; in fact, just one year before her death she ran for the Illinois state legislature. Although she did not win, it was just another example of her continued devotion to the full emancipation of Black people in the United States.

Overview of Ideas

Ida B. Wells-Barnett was a radical leader. Most well known for her campaigns against lynching she offered many prescriptions for the "Negro Problem." She, like many others, posited that a Black-owned press was vital to advancement. Newspapers could be utilized to teach African Americans about the importance of "self-help, thrift, and economy every week, they would be the teachers to those who had been deprived of school advantages ... and train [African Americans] to think for themselves." Black-owned newspapers would foster intellectual growth, monetary growth, and solidarity. Newspapers could also be utilized to thwart racial violence, namely lynching.

If African Americans had more knowledge about lynching they could protect themselves. If Americans knew how capriciously these violent acts were being carried out, maybe more sympathetic citizens would act. Lynching ran rampant in the South and was implemented by lawless mobs who would lynch any Black person regardless of gender or age. Lynch mobs often frivolously said they carried out these violent acts to avenge White female victims of rape. However, Wells-Barnett demonstrated that most often this claim was spurious. She was adamant about utilizing political agitation to force the government to address this horrific issue.

And yet this Christian nation, the flower of the nineteenth century civilization says it can do nothing to stop this inhuman slaughter. The general government is willingly powerless to send troops to protect the lives of its black citizens, but the state governments are free to use state troops to shoot them down like cattle, when the black men attempt to defend themselves.

In addition to being a crusader against lynching she actively fought for civil rights.

Ida B. Wells-Barnett championed equal rights for all. She posited that grassroots efforts were needed to achieve this aim. A unique contribution of Wells-Barnett was her emphasis on grassroots individual activism. Far too often we place the sole burden to address injustice on the government. Moreover, as we have already seen, when African American leaders focused on individual action it most often related to individual behavioral and moral reform. For Wells-Barnett, when she spoke to individuals she gave them prescriptions for how they could in small ways make a difference. Every individual must stand up and say everyone is entitled to life and liberty. For example, she argued that every individual has a right to vote. She took on the Republican Party for being passive and placating Southern racists. In fact, she encouraged Black folk to think and vote independently. She told African Americans to actively disseminate facts about lynching to any and all people they came in contact with. By spreading the facts we could change public opinion; again shifting public opinion did not require an act of Congress but individual action. Wells-Barnett encouraged individuals to place pressure on local civic organizations and churches to speak out against racial injustice.

Lynch Law in All its Phases, 1893

I am before the American people today through no inclination of my own, but because of a deep seated conviction that the country at large does not know the extent to which lynch law prevails in parts of the Republic nor the conditions which force into exile those who speak the truth. I cannot believe that the apathy and indifference which so largely obtains regarding mob rule is other than the result of ignorance of the true situation. And yet, the observing and thoughtful must know that in one section, at least, of our common country, a government of the people, by the people, and for the people, means a government by the mob; where the land of the free and home of the brave means a land of lawlessness, murder and outrage; and where liberty of speech means the license of might to destroy the business and drive from home those who exercise this privilege contrary to the will of the mob. Repeated attacks on the life, liberty and happiness of any citizen or class of citizens are attacks on distinctive American institutions; such attacks imperiling as they do the foundation of government, law and order, merit the thoughtful consideration of far sighted Americans; not from a standpoint of sentiment, not even so much from a standpoint of justice to a weak race, as from a desire to preserve our institutions.

The race problem or negro [sic] question, as it has been called, has been omnipresent and all pervading since long before the Afro American was raised from the degradation of the slave to the dignity of the citizen. It has never been settled because the right methods have not been employed in the solution. It is the Banquo's ghost of politics, religion, and sociology which will not down at the bidding of those who are tormented with its ubiquitous appearance on every occasion. Times without number, since invested with citizenship, the race has been indicted for ignorance, immorality and general worthlessness declared guilty and executed by its self constituted judges. The operations of law do not dispose of negroes [*sic*] fast enough, and lynching bees have become the favorite pastime of the South. As excuse for the same, a new cry, as false as it is foul, is raised in an effort to blast race character, a cry which has proclaimed to the world that virtue and innocence are violated by Afro-Americans who must be killed like wild beasts to protect womanhood and childhood.

Born and reared in the South, I had never expected to live elsewhere. Until this past year I was one among those who believed the condition of masses gave large excuse for the humiliations and proscriptions under which we labored; that when wealth, education and character became more feral among us, the cause being removed the effect would cease, and justice being accorded to all alike. I shared the general belief that good newspapers entering regularly the homes of our people in every state could do more to bring about this result than any agency. Preaching the doctrine of self help, thrift and economy every week, they would be the teachers to those who had been deprived of school advantages, yet were making history every day and train to think for themselves our mental children of a larger growth. And so, three years ago last June, I became editor and part owner of the *Memphis Free Speech*. As editor, I had occasion to criticize the city School Board's employment of inefficient teachers and poor school buildings for Afro-American children. I was in the employ of that board at the time, and at the close of that school term one year ago, was not re elected to a position I had held in the city schools for seven years. Accepting the decision of the Board of Education, I set out to make a race newspaper pay a thing which older and wiser heads said could not be done. But there were enough of our people in Memphis and surrounding territory to support a paper, and I believed they would do so. With nine months hard work the circulation increased from 1,500 to 3,500; in twelve months it was on a good paying basis. Throughout the Mississippi Valley in Arkansas, Tennessee and Mississippi on plantations and in towns, the demand for and interest in the paper increased among the masses. The newsboys who would not sell it on the trains, voluntarily testified that they had never known colored people to demand a paper so eagerly.

To make the paper a paying business I became advertising agent, solicitor, as well as editor, and was continually on the go. Wherever I went among the people, I gave them in church, school, public gatherings, and home, the benefit of my honest conviction that maintenance of character, money getting and education would finally solve our problem and that it depended us to say how soon this would be brought about. This sentiment bore good fruit in Memphis. We had nice homes, representatives in almost every branch of business and profession, and refined society. We had learned helping each other helped all, and every well conducted business by Afro-Americans prospered. With all our proscription in theatres, hotels and railroads, we had never had a lynching and did not believe we could have one. There had been lynchings and brutal outrages of all sorts in our state and those adjoining us, but we had confidence and pride in our city and the majesty of its laws. So far in advance of other Southern cities was ours, [*sic*] we were content to endure the evils we had, to labor and to wait.

The following table shows the number of men lynched from January 1, 1882, to January 1, 1892: In 1882, 52; 1883, 39; 1884, 53; 1885, 77; 1886, 73; 1887, 70; 1888, 72; 1889, 95; 1890, 100; 1891, 169. Of these 728 black men who were murdered, 269 were charged with rape, 253 with murder, 44 with robbery, 37 with incendiarism [*sic*], 32 with reasons unstated (it was not necessary to have a reason), 27 with race prejudice, 13 with quarreling with white men, 10 with making threats, 7 with rioting, 5 with miscegenation, 4 with burglary. One of the men lynched in 1891 was Will Lewis, who was lynched because "he was drunk and saucy to white folks." A woman [*sic*] who was one of the 73 victims in 1886, was hung in Jackson, Tenn., because the white woman for whom she cooked, died suddenly of poisoning. An examination showed arsenical poisoning. A search in the cook's room found rat poison. She was thrown into jail, and when the mob had worked itself up to the lynching pitch, she was dragged out, every stitch of clothing torn from her body, and was hung in the public court house square in sight of everybody. That white woman's husband has since died in the insane asylum, a raving maniac, and his ravings have led to the conclusion that he and not the cook, was the poisonier [*sic*] of his wife. A fifteen year old colored girl was lynched last spring, at Rayville, La., on the same charge of poisoning. A woman was also lynched at Hollendale, Miss. last [*sic*] spring, charged with being an accomplice in the murder of her paramour who had abused her. These were only two of the 159 persons lynched in the South from January 1, 1892, to January 1, 1893. Over a dozen black men have been lynched already since this new year set in, not yet two months old. It will thus be seen that neither age, sex nor decency [*sic*] are spared.

Although the impression has gone abroad that most of the lynchings take place because of assaults on white women only one third of the number lynched in the past ten years have been charged with that offense, to say nothing of those who were not guilty of the charge. And according to law none of them until proven [*sic*] so. But the unsupported word of any white person for any cause is sufficient to cause a lynching. So bold have the lynchers become masks are laid aside, the temples of justice and strongholds of law are invaded in broad daylight and prisoners taken out and lynched, while governors of states and officers of law stand by and see the work well done.

And yet this Christian nation, the flower of the nineteenth century civilization says it can do nothing to stop this inhuman slaughter. The general government is willingly powerless to send troops to protect the lives of its black citizens, but the state governments are free to use state troops to shoot them down like cattle, when in desperation the black men attempt to defend themselves, and then tell the world that it was necessary to put down a "race war."

Persons unfamiliar with the condition of affairs in the Southern States do not credit the truth when it is told them. They cannot conceive how such a condition of affairs prevails so near them with steam power, telegraph wires, and printing presses in daily and hourly touch with the localities where such disorder reigns. In a former generation the ancestors of these same people refused to believe that slavery was the "league with death and the covenant with hell." Wm. Lloyd Garrison declared it to be, until he was thrown into a dungeon in Baltimore, until the signal lights of Nat Turners lit the dull skies of Northampton County, and until sturdy old John Brown made his attack on

Harper's Ferry. When freedom of speech was martyred in the person of Elijah Lovejoy at Alton, when the liberty of free discussion in Senate in the Nation's Congress was struck down in the person of the fearless Charles Sumner, the Nation was at last convinced that slavery was not only a monster by a tyrant. That same tyrant is at work under a new name and guise. The lawlessness which has been here described is like unto that which prevailed under slavery. *The very same forces are at work now as then.* The attempt is being made to subject to a condition of civil and industrial independence, those whom the Constitution declares to be free men. The events which have led up to the present wide spread lawlessness in the South can be traced to the very first year Lee's conquered veterans marched from Appomattox to their homes in the Southland. They were conquered in war, but not in spirit. They believed as firmly as ever that it was their right to rule black men and dictate to the National Government. The Knights of White Liners, [sic] and the Ku Klux Klans were composed of veterans of the army who were determined to destroy the effect of all the slave had gained by the war. They finally accomplished their purpose in 1876. The right of the Afro American to vote and hold office remains in the Federal Constitution, but is destroyed in the constitution of the Southern states. Having destroyed the citizenship of the man, they are now trying to destroy the manhood of the citizen. All their laws are shaped to this end,—school laws railroad car regulations, those governing labor liens on crops, every device is adopted to make slaves of free men and rob them of their wages. Whenever a malicious law is violated in any of its parts, any farmer, any railroad conductor, or merchant can call together a posse of his neighbors and punish even with death the black man who resists and the legal authorities sanction what is done by failing to prosecute and punish the murders. The Repeal of the Civil Rights Law removed their last barrier and the black man's last bulwark and refuge. The rule of the mob is absolute.

Those who know this recital to be true, say there is nothing they can do they cannot interfere and vainly hope by further concession to placate the imperious and dominating part of our country in which this lawlessness prevails. Because this country has been almost rent in twain by internal dissension, the other sections seem virtually to have agreed that the best way to heal the breach is to permit the taking away of civil, political, and even human rights, to stand by in silence and utter indifference while the South continues to wreak fiendish vengeance on the irresponsible cause. They pretend to believe that with all the machinery of law and government in its hands; with the jails and penitentiaries and convict farms filled with pretty race criminals; with the well-known fact that no negro has ever been known to escape conviction and punishment for any crime in the South—still there are those who try to justify and condone the lynching of over a thousand black men in less than ten years an average of one hundred a year. The public sentiment of the country, by its silence in press, pulpit and in public meetings has encouraged this state of affairs, and public sentiment is stronger than law. With all this country's disposition to condone and temporize with the South and its methods; with its many instances of sacrificing principles to prejudice for the sake of making friends and healing the breach made by the late war; of going into the lawless country with capital to build up its waste places and remaining silent in the presence of outrage and wrong, the South is as vindictive and bitter as ever. She is willing to make friends as long as she is permitted to pursue unmolested and uncensored, her course of proscription, injustice, outrage and vituperation. The malignant misrepresentation of General Butler, the uniformly indecent and abusive assault of this dead man whose only crime was a defence [*sic*] of his country, is a recent proof that the South has lost none of its bitterness. The *Nashville American*, one of the leading papers of one of the leading southern cities, gleefully announced editorially that "'The Beast is dead.' Early yesterday morning, acting under the devil's orders, the angel of Death took Ben Butler and landed him in the lowest depths of hell, and we pity even the devil the possession has secured." The men who wrote these editorials are without exception young men who know nothing of slavery and scarcely anything of the war. The bitterness and hatred have been instilled in and taught them by their parents, and they are men who make and reflect the sentiment of their section. The South spares nobody else's feelings, and it seems a queer logic that when it comes to a question of right, involving lives of citizens and the honor of the government, the South's feelings must be respected and spared.

Do you ask the remedy? A public sentiment strong against lawlessness must be aroused. Every individual can contribute to this awakening. When a sentiment against lynch law as strong, deep and mighty as that roused by slavery prevails, I have no fear of the result. It should be already established as a fact and not as a theory, that every human being must have a fair trial for his life and liberty, no matter what the charge against him. When a demand goes up from fearless and persistent reformers from press and pulpit, from industrial and moral associations that this shall be so from Maine to Texas and from ocean to ocean, a way will be found to make it so.

In deference to the few words of condemnation uttered at the M.E. General conference last year, and by other organizations, Governors Hogg of Texas, Northern of Georgia, and Tillman of South Carolina, have issued proclamations offering rewards for the apprehension of lynchers. These rewards have never been claimed, and these governors knew they would not be when offered. In many cases they knew the ringleaders of the mobs. The prosecuting attorney of Shelby County, Tenn., wrote Governor Buchanan to offer a reward for the arrest of the lynchers of three young men murdered in Memphis. Everybody in that city and state knew well that the letter was written for the sake of effect and the governor did not even offer the reward. But the country at large deluded itself with the belief that the officials of the South and the leading citizens condemned lynching. The lynchings go on in spite of offered rewards, and in face of Governor Hogg's vigorous talk, the second man was burnt alive in his state with the utmost deliberation and publicity. Since he sent a message to the legislature the mob found and hung Henry Smith's stepson, because he refused to tell where Smith was when they were hunting for him. Public sentiment which shall denounce these crimes in season and out; public sentiment which turns capital and immigration from a section given over to lawlessness; public sentiment which insists on the punishment of criminals and lynchers by law must be aroused.

It is no wonder in my mind that the party which stood for their years as the champion of human liberty and human rights, the part of great moral ideas should suffer overwhelming defeat when it has proven recreant to its professions and abandoned a position it created; when although its followers were being outraged in every sense, it was afraid to stand for the right, and appeal to the American people to sustain them in it. It put aside the question of a free ballot and fair count of every citizen and give its voice and influence for the protection of the coat instead of the man who wore it, for the product of labor instead of the laborer; for the seal of citizenship rather than the citizen, and insisted upon the evils of free trade instead of the sacredness of speech. I am no politician but I believe if the Republican party had met issues squarely for human rights instead of the tariff it would have occupied a different position to day. The voice of the people is the voice of God, I long with all the intensity of my soul for the Garrison, Douglass, Sumner, Whittier, and Phillips who shall rouse this nation to a demand that from Greenland's icy mountains to the coral reefs of the Southern seas, mob rule shall be put down and equal and exact justice be accorded to every citizen of whatever race, who finds a home within the borders of the land of the free and the home of the brave.

Then no longer will our national hymn be sounding brass and a tinkling cymbal, but every member of this great composite nation will be a living, harmonious illustration of the words, and all can honestly and gladly join in singing:

> *My country! 'tis of thee,*
> *Sweet land of liberty*
> *Of thee I sing.*
> *Land where our fathers died,*
> *Land of the Pilgrim's pride,*
> *From every mountain side*
> *Freedom does ring.*

A Red Record, 1895

What can you do, reader, to prevent lynching, to thwart anarchy and promote law and order throughout our land?

1st. You can help disseminate the facts contained in this book by bringing them to the knowledge of every one with whom you come in contact, to the end that public sentiment may be revolutionized. Let the facts speak for themselves, with you as a medium.

2d. You can be instrumental in having churches, missionary societies, Y. M. C. A.'s, W. C. T. U.'s and all Christian and moral forces in connection with your religious and social life, pass resolutions of condemnation and protest every time a lynching takes place; and see that they are sent to the place where these outrages occur.

3d. Bring to the intelligent consideration of Southern people the refusal of capital to invest where lawlessness and mob violence hold sway. Many labor organizations have declared by resolution that they would avoid lynch infested localities as they would the pestilence when seeking new homes. If the South wishes to build up its waste places quickly, there is no better way than to uphold the majesty of the law by enforcing obedience to the same, [*sic*] and meting out the same punishment to all classes of criminals, white as well as black. "Equality before the law," must become a fact as well as a theory before America is truly the "land of the free and the home of the brave."

4th. Think and act on independent lines in this behalf, remembering that after all, it is the white man's civilization and the white man's government which are on trial.

5th. Congressman Blair offered a resolution in the House of Representatives, August, 1894. The organized life of the country can speedily make this a law by sending resolutions to Congress indorsing Mr. Blair's bill and asking Congress to create the commission. In no better way can the question be settled, and the Negro does not fear the issue.

Burning Human Beings Alive, 1900

Not only has life been taken by mobs in the past twenty years, but the ordinary procedure of hanging and shooting have been improved upon during the past ten years. Fifteen human beings have been burned to death in the different parts of the country by mobs. Men, women and children have gone to see the sight, and all have approved the barbarous deeds done in the high light of the civilization and *Christianity* of this country.

In 1891 Ed Coy was burned to death in Texarkana, Ark. He was charged with assaulting a white woman, and after the mob had securely tied him to a tree, the men and boys amused themselves for some time sticking knives into Coy's body and slicing off pieces, of flesh. When they had amused themselves sufficiently, they poured coal oil over him and the women in the case set fire to him. It is said that fifteen thousand people stood by and saw him burned. This was on a Sunday night, and press reports told how the people looked on while the Negro burned to death.

Feb. 1, 1893, Henry Smith was burned to death in Paris, Texas. The entire county joined in that exhibition. The district attorney himself went for the prisoner and turned him over to the mob. He was placed upon a float and drawn by four white horses through the principal streets of the city. Men, women and children stood at their doors and waved their handkerchiefs and cheered the echoes. They knew that the man was to be burned to death because the newspaper had declared for three days previous that this would be so. Excursions were run by all the railroads, and the mayor of the town gave the children a holiday so that they might see the sight.

Henry Smith was charged with having assaulted and murdered a little white girl. He was an imbecile, and while he had killed the child, there was no proof that he had criminally assaulted her. He was tied to a stake on a platform which had been built ten feet high, so that everybody might see the sight. The father and brother and uncle of the little white girl that had been murdered was upon that platform about fifty minutes entertaining the crowd of ten thousand persons by burning the victim's flesh with red-hot irons. Their own newspapers told how they burned his eyes out and, ran the red-hot iron down his throat, cooking his tongue, and how the crowd cheered wild delight. At last, having declared themselves satisfied, coal oil was poured over him and he was burned to death, and the mob fought over the ashes for bones and pieces of his clothes.

July 7, 1893, in Bardwell, Ky., C.J. Miller was burned to ashes. Since his death this man has been found to be absolutely innocent of the murder of the two white girls with which he was charged. But the mob would wait for no justification. They insisted that, as they were not sure he was the right man, they would compromise the matter by hanging him instead of burning. Not to be outdone, they took the body down and made a huge bonfire out of it.

July 22, 1893, at Memphis, Tenn., the body of Lee Walker was dragged through the street and burned before the court house. Walker had frightened some girls in a wagon along a country road by asking them to let him ride in their wagon. They cried out; some men working in a field near by said it was at attempt of assault, and of course began to look for their prey. There was never any charge of rape; the women only declared that he attempted an assault. After he was apprehended and put in jail and perfectly helpless, the mob dragged him out, shot him, cut him, beat him with sticks, built a fire and burned the legs off, then took the trunk of the body down and dragged further up the street, and at last burned it before the court house.

Sept. 20, 1893, at Roanoke, Va., the body of a Negro who had quarreled with a white woman was burned in the presence of several thousand persons. These people also wreaked their vengeance upon this helpless victim of the mob's wrath by sticking knives into him, kicking him and beating him with stones and otherwise mutilating him before life was extinct.

June 11, 1898, at Knoxville, Ark., James Perry was shut up in a cabin because he had smallpox and burned to death. He had been quarantined in this cabin when it was declared that he had this disease and the doctor sent for. When the physician arrived he found only a few smoldering embers. Upon inquiry some railroad hands who were working nearby revealed the fact that they had fastened the door of the cabin and set fire to the cabin and burned man and hut together.

Feb. 22, 1898, at Lake City, S.C., Postmaster Baker and his infant child were burned to death by a mob that had set fire to his house. Mr. Baker's crime was that he had refused to give up the post office, to which he had been appointed by the National Government. The mob had tried to drive him away by persecution and intimidation. Finding that all else had failed, they went to his home in the dead of night and set fire to his house, and as the family rushed forth they were greeted by a volley of bullets. The father and his baby were shot through the open door and wounded so badly that they fell back in the fire and were burned to death. The remainder of the family, consisting of the wife and five children, escaped with their lives from the burning house, but all of them were shot, one of the number made a cripple for life.

Jan. 7, 1898, two Indians were tied to a tree at Maud Post Office, Indian Territory, and burned to death by a white mob. They were charged with murdering a white woman. There was no proof of their guilt except the unsupported word of the mob. Yet they were tied to a tree and slowly roasted to death. Their names were Lewis McGeesy and Hond Martin. Since that time these boys have been found to be absolutely innocent of the charge. Of course that discovery is too late to be of any benefit to them, but because they were Indians the Indian Commissioner demanded and received from the United States Government an indemnity of $13,000.

April 23, 1899, at Palmetto, Ga., Sam Hose was burned alive in the presence of a throng, on Sunday afternoon. He was charged with killing a man named Cranford, his employer, which he admitted he did because his employer was about to shoot him. To the fact of killing the employer was added the absolutely false charge that Hose assaulted the wife. Hose was arrested and no trial was given him. According to the code of reasoning of the mob, none was needed. A white man had been killed and a white woman was said to have been assaulted. That was enough. When Hose was found he had to die.

The Atlanta Constitution, in speaking of the murder of Cranford, said that the Negro who was suspected would be burned alive. Not only this, but it offered $500 reward for his capture. After he had been apprehended, it was publicly announced that he would be burned alive. Excursion trains were run and bulletins were put up in the small towns. The Governor of Georgia was in Atlanta while excursion trains were being made up to take visitors to the burning. Many fair ladies drove out in their carriages on Sunday afternoon to witness the torture and burning of a human being. Hose's ears were cut off, then his toes and fingers, and passed round to the crowd. His eyes were put out, his tongue torn out and flesh cut in strips by knives. Finally they poured coal oil on him and burned him to death. They dragged his half-consumed trunk out of the flames, cut it open, extracted his heart and liver, and sold slices for ten cents each for souvenirs, all of which was published most promptly in the daily papers of Georgia and boasted over by the people of that section.

Oct. 19, 1889, at Canton, Miss., Joseph Leflore was burned to death. A house had been entered and its occupants murdered during the absence of the husband and father. When the discovery was made, it was immediately supposed that the crime was the work of a Negro, and the motive that of assaulting white women.

Bloodhounds were procured and they made a round of the village and discovered only one colored man absent from his home. This was taken to be proof sufficient that he was the perpetrator of the deed. When he returned home he was apprehended, taken into the yard of the house that had been burned down, tied to a stake, and was slowly roasted to death.

Dec. 6, 1899, at Maysville, Ky., Wm. Coleman also was burned to death. He was slowly roasted, first one foot and then the other, and dragged out of the fire so that the torture might be prolonged. All of this without a shadow of proof or scintilla of evidence that the man had committed the crime.

Thus have the mobs of this country taken the lives of their victims within the past ten years. In every single instance except one these burnings were witnessed by from two thousand to fifteen thousand people, and no one person in all these crowds throughout the country had the courage to raise his voice and speak out against the awful barbarism of burning human beings to death.

Men and women of America, are you proud of this record which the Anglo-Saxon race has made for itself? Your silence seems to say that you are. Your silence encourages a continuance of this sort of horror. Only by earnest, active, united endeavor to arouse public sentiment can we hope to put a stop to these demonstrations of American barbarism.

Lynching Record, 1900

The following table of lynchings has been kept year by year by the Chicago Tribune, beginning with 1882, and shows the list of Negroes that have been lynched during that time:

- 1882, Negroes murdered by mobs 52
- 1883, Negroes murdered by mobs 39
- 1884, Negroes murdered by mobs 53
- 1885, Negroes murdered by mobs 164
- 1886, Negroes murdered by mobs 136
- 1887, Negroes murdered by mobs 128
- 1888, Negroes murdered by mobs 143
- 1889, Negroes murdered by mobs 127
- 1890, Negroes murdered by mobs 171
- 1891, Negroes murdered by mobs 192
- 1892, Negroes murdered by mobs 241
- 1893, Negroes murdered by mobs 200
- 1894, Negroes murdered by mobs 190
- 1895, Negroes murdered by mobs 171
- 1896, Negroes murdered by mobs 131
- 1897, Negroes murdered by mobs 156
- 1898, Negroes murdered by mobs 127
- 1899, Negroes murdered by mobs 107

Of these thousands of men and women who have been put to death without judge or jury, less than one-third of them have been even accused of criminal assault. The world at large has accepted unquestionably the statement that Negroes are lynched only for assaults upon white women. Of those who were lynched from 1882 to 1891, the first ten years of the tabulated lynching record, the charges are as follows:

> Two hundred and sixty-nine were charged with rape; 253 with murder; 44 with robbery; 37 with incendiarism [*sic*]; 4 with burglary; 27 with race prejudice; 13 quarreled with white men; 10 with making threats; 7 with rioting; 5 with miscegenation; in 32 cases no reasons were given, the victims were lynched on general principles.

During the past five years the record is as follows:

> Of the 171 persons lynched in 1895 only 34 were charged with this crime. In 1896, out of 131 persons who were lynched, only 34 were said to have assaulted women. Of the 156 in 1897, only 32. In 1898, out of 127 persons lynched, 24 were charged with the alleged "usual crime." In 1899, of the 107 lynchings, 16 were said to be for crimes against women. These figures, of course, speak for themselves, and to the unprejudiced, fair-minded person it is only necessary to read and study them in order to show that the charge that the Negro is a moral outlaw is a false one, made for the purpose of injuring the Negro's good name and to create public sentiment against him.

If public sentiment were alive, as it should be upon the subject, it would refuse to be longer hoodwinked, and the voice of conscience would refuse to be stilled by these false statements. If the laws of the country were obeyed and respected by the white men of the country who charge that the Negro has no respect for law, these things could not be, for every individual, no matter what the charge, would have a fair trial and an opportunity to prove his guilt or innocence before a tribunal of law.

That is all the Negro asks—that is all the friends of law and order need to ask, for once the law of the land is supreme, [and] no individual who commits crime will escape punishment.

Individual Negroes commit crimes the same as do white men, but that the Negro race is peculiarly given to assault upon women, is a falsehood of the deepest dye. The tables given above show that the Negro who is saucy to white men is lynched as well as the Negro who is charged with assault upon women. Less than one-sixth of the lynchings last year, 1899, were charged with rape.

The Negro points to his record during the war in rebuttal of this false slander. When the white women and children of the South had no protector save only these Negroes, not one instance is known where the trust was betrayed. It is remarkably strange that the Negro had more respect for womanhood with the white men of the South hundreds of miles away, than they have today, when surrounded by those who take their lives with impunity and burn and torture, even worse than the "unspeakable Turk."

Again, the white women of the North came South years ago, threaded the forests, visited the cabins, taught the schools and associated only with the Negroes whom they came to teach, and had no protectors near at hand. They had no charge or complaint to make of the danger to themselves after association with this class of human beings. Not once has the country been shocked by such recitals from them as come from the women who are surrounded by their husbands, brothers, lovers and friends. If the Negro's nature is bestial, it certainly should have proved itself in one of these two instances. The Negro asks only justice and an impartial consideration of these facts.

Note

1. See Chapter 9 on Du Bois for further details. Also see Jones, Angela. 2011. *African American Civil Rights: Early Activism and the Niagara Movement*. Santa Barbara, CA: Praeger.

8.
WILLIAM MONROE TROTTER

William Monroe Trotter (1872–1934) was born into a family of activists; his father had been an active abolitionist. Like his father, Trotter was an important political figure in Boston, Massachusetts. For example, he helped register people to vote in Boston. Trotter helped organize anti-lynching campaigns. He also helped organize letter-writing campaigns and the lobbying of politicians. Although he was busy organizing in Boston, the Harvard graduate still kept ties to academia by writing and delivering papers. He wrote papers such as "Higher Education for the Negro." Trotter was an extraordinary intellectual and activist.

William Monroe Trotter assisted in the founding of the Boston Literary and Historical Association in 1901. In addition, Trotter served on the association's executive committee. He was also an active member of the Omar Khayyan Circle, an all-Black intellectual literary group. Trotter also saw the development of the Black press as paramount to the Black freedom struggle. Trotter, along with George W. Forbes, founded the radical newspaper, the *Guardian*. As editor, Trotter became known for his frequent diatribes about Booker T. Washington.

In 1903 Trotter was jailed for ostensibly causing the Boston Riot of 1903. Trotter, his sister Maude, and others were accused of causing a riot in a church during a public speech by Booker T. Washington. Trotter was known for his unwavering position against accommodation and his push for full civil rights through political agitation. For example, he led protests and campaigns against lynching, and plays and films that glorified the Ku Klux Klan.

Trotter was one of the twenty-nine founders of the Niagara Movement. In addition, he was the civil rights organization's press chairman. Although Trotter was extremely influential in establishing the Niagara Movement and in its early years, he left the organization in 1907 due to bitter fights with other key players in the organization. After his departure, he started the Negro American Political League and remained active in other groups such as the Massachusetts Racial Protective Association. Later, Trotter also started his own organization called the National Equal Rights League and refused to join the NAACP. Trotter refused to become part of the NAACP because of its White leadership and White financial backing and ostensibly pacifist agenda.

Trotter never ceased fighting for racial justice. Trotter led protests to the White House to protest segregation in Washington, D.C. In 1914 he led these protests to tell

Wilson that segregation in federal civil service was unacceptable. In 1915 Trotter led a campaign to boycott *The Birth of a Nation*, in Boston. He led this boycott in order to keep the movie from being shown in Boston. In 1919 Trotter wanted to attend the Paris Peace Conference in order to speak on behalf of racial justice to the organization. The State Department refused Trotter a passport in order to attend. However Trotter, with his dogged determination, disguised himself as a cook, got hired as a cook on a ship going to France, and managed to get to the Conference. Trotter's admirable dedication to the Black freedom struggle never wavered and never assuaged until his demise.

Overview of Ideas

William Monroe Trotter is one of the more radical figures to appear in this section. His important ideas and legacy are often flippantly neglected by the canon. Trotter is usually not included in these types of volumes on Black political thought. However, this is probably due to the paucity of political writing and documents found in the archives. Far more archival material has been compiled about his personal life than his political life.

Trotter was one of the leaders of the anti-Booker T. Washington and anti-accommodationist counterpublics[1] that began to develop in Boston, Massachusetts. He spearheaded the burgeoning movement to usurp Washington's growing political power. His political writings were evidence of this. In 1901 before W.E.B. Du Bois (most often given all the credit for mounting this debate) began to publicly challenge Washington, Trotter was there, at the turn of the twentieth century, publicly chastising Washington, denouncing accommodation, and articulating the foundations of integrationist ideology.

In the Boston *Guardian*, of which Trotter was the editor, he launched vitriolic attacks on Booker T. Washington, his associates, and expressed the need to cultivate an independent Black press as a primary strategy for the Negro Problem. He wrote, "the Guardian enters the journalistic field, no less to deliver our community ... a protest against allowing ourselves to be misrepresented at the bar of public opinion." He vowed to utilize his paper to unequivocally demand "the rights of citizenship ... which make all citizens joint heirs to equal rights and protections by the law of the land." Trotter told his readers that it was their duty to stand up, to be outraged, and publicly demand full and equal access to society's basic social institutions. Trotter always spoke in an unapologetic tone and was often deemed a crazy radical as a result. "The Guardian, therefore, will always speak out in no uncertain tones."

In public speeches Trotter was also a spokesman for full civil rights. He challenged the government and the legality of depriving African Americans of their constitutional rights. However, he wielded his most caustic diatribes for Booker T. Washington. Trotter never publicly advocated that African Americans required cultural transformation, a proposition too conservative for Trotter. He argued that Washington told Black folk "to cease from political activity and agitation until we learn to cultivate the soil, until we gain property, education, and character." Trotter argued this strategy would only lead African Americans back toward slavery and certainly not up from it. Recognizing that Washington's approach required gradualism, Trotter posited that waiting was not the answer; his slow approach was all but useless. Without political and civil rights now, African Americans could not and would not advance in any great number.

William Monroe Trotter was seen as such a radical that he was accused of starting a small riot in Boston in 1903 when Washington gave a speech in the Columbus Avenue African Methodist Episcopal Zion Church. Due to Trotter's stronghold in Boston, and over African American public opinion in Boston, people anticipated a very heated public forum and expected Trotter to lead the heckling of Washington. The plan, which never occurred before fighting ensued, the meeting broken up, and Trotter arrested, was for Trotter to challenge Washington from the floor and ask nine critical questions. Those questions are included in this chapter. The questions were emblematic of Trotter's radical ideas.

Trotter charged that Washington was in favor of disenfranchising African Americans. And again, without the ballot and power within the political sphere African Americans would have no legitimacy as a political constituency and therefore would have no means by which to acquire rights. He questioned, would African Americans just appeal to the better nature or moral character of White Americans? No, they would not. By securing political rights, they could apply pressure on politicians. Trotter also posited that Washington, a conservative in Trotter's eyes, said African Americans needed to be disciplined and Trotter said Washington was simply advocated pacifism. Washington's focus on self-sufficiency absolved American society and the government from its necessary role in solving the supposed Negro Problem and put the burden to correct the inequalities created under slavery on the backs of African Americans. For Trotter, Washington perpetrated racist discourses about African Americans, specifically enforcing the idea that Black people were in fact Sambos—lazy, dependant, and ignorant. He said, Washington, unlike himself did not stand up against violence against African Americans, specifically lynching. For these reasons, Trotter challenged his leadership abilities and the ability of his ideas to help Black folk progress.

The Boston *Guardian*, 1901

In making its bow to the public today, The Guardian congratulates in advance the constituency that it aspires to serve, upon the prospect of an organ which is to voice intelligently the needs and aspirations of the colored American. It has been long felt that the colored people of this section were allowing themselves to be caricatured rather than characterized by the vast number of poublications [*sic*] issuing forth weekly under the guise of newspapers. These papers know neither the needs of those they aspire to represent, nor how clearly to express what they do know. They are simply children crying in the night. Out of very shame, therefore, The Guardian enters the journalistic field, no less to deliver our community from this sad plight of affairs, than as a protest against allowing ourselves to be misrepresented at the bar of public opinion through incompetency [*sic*]. The mouth of the foolish is a present destruction. It is the province

of a well-conducted newspaper to reflect the lighter moods and pastimes of its constituency, no less than the most serious doings in their severer hours … but more important by far than all of these is the consideration of those ethical and moral questions
of the rights of citizenship, those grand fundamental postulates of government, which
make all citizens joint heirs to equal rights and protections by the laws of the land. And
in considering these we shall assume public opinion to be a natural product common
alike to all citizens, a public fountain free flowing for the use of all. Wherever, then, this
public product has been usurped or monopolized by any one class to the detriment of
the other, it is the duty of the outraged class to enter in an eternal protest against it.
Now it is to voice this eternal protest against having public opinion monopolized and
used forever to the detriment of the colored race in this country that The Guardian
has come into being. And if other classes of our citizens-the Germans, Italians and
Irish-feel it necessary to have papers to champion their rights, surely none will object
to the Colored race's making use of the same means in their own behalf. The Guardian,
therefore, will always speak out in no uncertain tones.

Speech at Old Faneuil Hall, 1902

While the national government takes no action to enforce the constitution when the
violations deprive Negroes of their citizenship: we shall henceforth no longer be silent.
Too long split and divided by the trimmers and compromisers [Washington and his
associates] in their own ranks, the Negroes of Massachusetts are and the Negroes of
the entire country are fast becoming united against the traitor within [Washington] and
the enemy without [racist whites]. In vain, henceforth, will they advise us to cease from
political activity and agitation until we learn to cultivate the soil, until we gain property,
education, and character. In vain will the aristocratic press … give praise and space to
the compromiser while shutting out the honest and manly Negro from its columns. Our
minds are made up. Our platform I, "No compromise on, no waiting a generation for
equal rights." WE believe a black American has as much right to vote as a white American; that the Negro should resist actively and with every means at his command the
taking away of his civil and political rights; that no apposition should be made between
earning a living, acquiring means or developing character on the one side and on the
other … equal participation with other men in the civil, political, and public life of the
community. Useless, henceforth, will it be for politicians or chief executives to select
Negro race trimmers as political leaders for the Negro. WE are solidly banded together
in the set determination to use and concentrate our thought, time, influence, means,
and political power upon the means of securing without delay our full rights under the
constitution. In government, in congressmen, in president, henceforth no sin shall be
so great, no policy so resented by us at the polls as that of residing to take action to
restore to the negro his constitutional rights, and to visit the deserved penalty upon those
who thus illegally disenfranchise us and enslave us. Let congress, quickly at least, end a
state of things under which disenfranchised men are counted to increase the power of
those who willfully rob them of their ballot. This much relief, at least, let them not be so
contemptuous of our power, as to refuse to apply. This injustice righted, the nullifiers of

the constitution thus shorn of their power, easier will be the task to do what remains, and much may not remain after this measure as ad its effect, to restore the negro his civil and political rights. WE solemnly affirm now that as our fight shall not cease as long as we or our posterity live, until the Negro has that equality of rights which some of us and our fathers and liberty-loving white men risked their lives in battle that it might be vouch-safed the Negro in the constitution of these United States.

Trotter's Challenge to Washington at the *Boston Riot* 1903

* Note: The introduction to Trotter's questions below is excerpted from Trotter's biography and was written by Stephen R. Fox and is reprinted here with permission of the publisher.

[Trotter] ... had some legitimate objections to Washington's leadership. The problem was to acquaint the public, white and black, with those objections. Louisville, despite being a radical debacle, was a beginning. In its aftermath the *New York Times* and the *Literary Digest*, two oracles of white opinion, took note of the anti-Washington movement.[2] Louisville was enemy territory, though, and Trotter hoped for better results by confronting Washington in Boston. Late in July the Boston branch of the National Negro Business League gave him the chance. The League announced plans for a public meeting to be held on July 30 in the Columbus Avenue African Methodist Episcopal Zion Church. William Lewis would preside, Harry Burleigh would sing, and Fortune and Washington would deliver the principal addresses. It would be Washington's first appearance before a Negro audience in Boston in some time.

In the *Guardian* office at 3 Tremont Row the editors drafted nine questions—challenges, actually—that Trotter would attempt to ask from the floor.

1. In your letter to the Montgomery Advertiser you said: "Every revised constitution throughout the southern states has put a premium upon intelligence, ownership of property, thrift and character." Did you not thereby indorse the disfranchising of our race?
2. In your speech before the Century club here in March you said: "Those are most truly free who have passed the most discipline." Are you not actually upholding oppressing our race as a good thing for us, advocating peonage?
3. Again, you say: "Black men must distinguish between the freedom that is forced and the freedom that is the result of struggle and self-sacrifice." Do you mean that the Negro should expect less from his freedom than the white man from his?
4. When you said: "It was not so important whether the Negro was in the inferior car as whether there was in that car a superior man not a beast," did you not minimize the outrage of the insulting Jim-crow car discrimination and justify it by the "bestiality" of the Negro?
5. In an interview with the Washington Post, June 25, as to whether the Negro should insist on his ballot, you are quoted as saying: "As is well known, I hold that no people in the same economic and educational condition as the masses of the black people of the south should make politics a matter of the first

importance in connection with their development." Do you not know that the ballot is the only self-protection for any class of people in this country?

6. In view of the fact that you are understood to be unwilling to insist upon the Negro having his every right (both civil and political), would it not be a calamity at this juncture to make you our leader?

7. Don't you know you would help the race more by exposing the new form of slavery just outside the gates of Tuskegee than by preaching submission?

8. Can a man make a successful educator and politician at the same time?

9. Are the rope and the torch all the race is to get under your leadership?

Notes

1. See Fraser, Nancy. 1992. "Rethinking the Public Sphere: A Contribution to the Critique of Actually Existing Democracy." In Craig Calhoun, ed., *Habermas and the Public Sphere*, Cambridge, MA: MIT Press, pp. 109–142. In response to Jurgen Habermas's normative and limited model of the public sphere, Fraser conceptualized what she calls *subaltern counterpublics* to refer to the spaces that individuals craft in the face of exclusion from the larger public sphere. In this case African American have crafted counterpublics in order to engage in public dialogue and political action even when marginalized by racist policies de jure and de facto. For a larger discussion of the creation of Black counterpublics and the role that figures such as Trotter played in their formation see Jones, Angela. 2011. *African American Civil Rights: Early Activism and the Niagara Movement*. New York: Praeger.

2. *New York Times*, July 3, 1903, p. 1; *Literary Digest*, XXVII (1903), 37–38.

9.
WILLIAM EDWARD BURGHARDT DU BOIS

William Edward Burghardt Du Bois (1868–1963) is best known as the first African American to receive a Ph.D. from Harvard. This is probably the least important element of Du Bois's legacy. More importantly, Du Bois was one of leading spokespersons for Black civil rights after the turn of the twentieth century. His famous book, *The Souls of Black Folk*, helped surmount a long lasting public debate over the role of higher education and political agitation in Black emancipation. Du Bois stood vehemently against Booker T. Washington and accomodationist ideology, or slower change vis-à-vis vocational training as the answer to the "Negro Problem."

Du Bois was one of the founders of the Niagara Movement and served as its general secretary from 1905 to 1910. With the Niagara Movement he assisted in the successful litigation of Jim Crow test cases, lobbied politicians, organized voting drives, and led protests against racial injustice in the military, education, economy, and government. He helped lead electoral campaigns to encourage Black folk to vote and to vote independently. Du Bois and the Niagara Movement asked African Americans to question their allegiance to the Republican Party. After the Niagara Movement completely disbanded in 1910 Du Bois worked actively to recruit African Americans to join the newly formed National Association for the Advancement of Colored People.

Du Bois had a tumultuous relationship with the NAACP. In 1909 Du Bois helped found the NAACP. There he served as a director of publicity and research and sat on the board of directors. He edited the journal of the NAACP, the *Crisis*, from 1910 to 1934. In 1934, after years of bickering with other key players over strategy, he left the organization. However, in 1944 after retiring from Atlanta University, Du Bois returned to the NAACP, as its director of special research and publicity. In 1945 Du Bois served as special consultant on behalf of the NAACP to the U.S. delegation for the founding conference of the United Nations. However, his return to the NAACP was short-lived. In 1948 he left the NAACP again and became the co-chairman of the Council of African Affairs.

Du Bois was active in the Black press. Du Bois founded a small paper called the *Moon*. In addition, he was one of the three founders and editors of Niagara's journal, the *Horizon*. Du Bois authored over three dozen books and countless articles. His contributions to both the academic and mainstream press are unparalleled by any other Black leader in this volume.

W.E.B. Du Bois was a Pan-Africanist. He was devoted to linking the quagmires faced by Black folk in the United States with the plight of oppressed Black people throughout the world. He was critical of imperialism and colonialism; he was an outspoken critic of White European control and tyranny of minorities all over the globe, particularly in Africa. In 1919 he called for the organization of the Pan-African Congress in Paris in order to further his Pan-Africanist goals. The conference was supposed to coincide with the Versailles Peace Conference. Du Bois saw the conference as a means by which to bring to the attention of the delegates the plight of the colonized and oppressed, in the hopes that the new League of Nations would address their problems. In 1921, 1923, 1927, and 1945 additional Pan-African Conferences were held.

Toward the end of Du Bois's life he simultaneously ran for political office and was targeted by the Justice Department. Du Bois always wanted to see the United States realize its full potential as a democracy. In 1950 Du Bois served as the chairman of the Peace Information Center. In this position he assisted in campaigns to ban the atomic bomb. In addition, in the same year Du Bois ran for U.S. Senate from New York, on the American Labor Party ticket. Du Bois was a casualty of McCarthyism. He was under suspicion for being a socialist. Du Bois publicly argued that our devotion to thwarting the spread of Communism was detracting from our nation's ability to annihilate the problems impacting oppressed people all over the world and at home. As he became more active in the anti-war and peace movement he became a target of the Justice Department. The Justice Department did eventually bring formal charges against Du Bois for his ostensibly subversive activities; however, he was acquitted. Du Bois increasingly grew tired of American racism and American apathy. After years of activism and hundreds of accolades he officially joined the Communist Party in 1961 and grew so tired of conditions in the United States that when he was ninety-three he moved to Ghana, Africa.

Overview of Ideas

While publicly challenging racism is a radical act, Du Bois's political thought was far more moderate than commonly noted. In the more radical strains of Du Bois's political thought he advocated Black Nationalism, specifically Cultural Nationalism. In one of Du Bois's most famous articles, "Strivings of the Negro People," later published in his book, *The Souls of Black Folk*, he coined his idea of *double consciousness*. Du Bois famously wrote:

> the Negro is a sort of seventh son, born with a veil, and gifted with second-sight in this American world, – a world which yields him no self-consciousness, but only lets him see himself through the revelation of the other world. It is a peculiar sensation, this double-consciousness, this sense of always looking at one's self through the eyes of others, of measuring one's soul by the tape of a world that looks on in amused contempt and pity.

According to Du Bois, slavery stripped Black folk of their cultural identities. As a result, it was vital for African American progress that Black folk cultivate and celebrate their African heritage. Rather than allowing racist Whites to define them, individuals of African descent needed to define themselves. Double consciousness was not the problem. In fact, Du Bois argued that part of the solution to the Negro Problem was to develop and celebrate an American identity and simultaneously develop and celebrate their African identity. In this process Black folk also needed to fight to ensure that their African identity did not impede their access to societal institutions and opportunity.

Du Bois also keenly observed and wrote extensively about the privileges that are assigned to racial groups such as Whites and the doors that are closed to others because of the social costs associated with being a member of other races such as Blacks. His own experiences in school amazed him when he realized that despite his accomplishments, his academic achievements, so many Whites would only see him as an inferior Black man. Du Bois first discussed what historians now call the *wages of whiteness.*[1] Du Bois realized that part of the solution to the Negro Problem would require making sure that the symbolic barrier of race, which he eloquently refers to as *the veil*, did not impede access to basic social institutions. Du Bois was a staunch public advocate for full integration.

Like William Monroe Trotter, Du Bois became an opponent of Booker T. Washington's gradualist strategy that pushed for vocational training and economic upward mobility as a means by which to attain political power in the future. Du Bois argued that without political power now there would be no advancement. In addition, Du Bois posited that by pushing African Americans into vocational education this would lead to the creation of a perpetual underclass of laborers. Instead, Black folk also required higher education. In Du Bois's famous, "Of Mr. Booker T. Washington and Others" he paid homage to Black leaders prior to Washington such as David Walker and Frederick Douglass. However, Du Bois argued that Washington failed to live up to their legacy. According to Du Bois, Washington, an educator, behaved far too much like a politician. His solutions and policies required far too much compromise. Moreover, through compromise Washington sold out the basic three requirements for real emancipation: political power, civil rights, and higher education. While figures such as Trotter wrote and spoke extensively about the need for civil and political rights, it was the professor Du Bois who spent copious amounts of time also pushing for higher education.

Du Bois pushed for the cultivation and nurturing of what he called the *talented tenth*. Du Bois posited that we train the best and brightest individuals of African descent to become a new generation of professionals, doctor, lawyers, politicians, etc. This group of highly educated Blacks would not just be a revolutionary vanguard of future leaders but serve as role models for younger generations of Black people. Higher education was key to the advancement of Black people.

> A university is a human invention for the transmission of knowledge and culture from generation to generation, through the training of quick minds and pure hearts, and for this work no other human invention will suffice, not even trade and industrial schools.

You cannot expect people to pull themselves up by their proverbial bootstraps without arming them with the skills and knowledge they need to compete and industrial education alone could never accomplish this tall order.

Education must not simply teach work—it must teach life. The Talented Tenth of the Negro race must be leaders of thought and missionaries of culture among their people. ... Negro colleges must train men for it. The Negro race, like all other races, is going to be saved by its exceptional men.

Du Bois's arguments here were evidence of his bourgeois sensibilities, for which he has been criticized for being elitist. His arguments suggested that poor Blacks would not be saved through grassroots activism amongst the subaltern but by the privileged of their own race.

As general secretary of the Niagara Movement, the all-Black civil rights organization, Du Bois labored arduously for civil rights.[2] However, his work with the organization further demonstrated that his strategies for progress were moderate; they incorporated intense political agitation for civil rights but also argued that advancement required reforming individual and cultural pathologies as well. As evidenced in the declaration of principles of the Niagara Movement, Du Bois, along with the members of the Niagara Movement, fought for: suffrage, full civil rights and access to public accommodations, equal access to economic institutions and labor unions, equal access to educational institutions, an end to discrimination in the legal system, access to equal and quality healthcare and housing, the rights of Black soldiers, an end to discrimination in the church, and an end to racism de jure and de facto. Publicly making these demands in 1905 was certainly radical. However, they also told Black people they had certain duties and that their pathological behavior had to be modified. They said African Americans had to refrain from their political apathy and vote, not be lazy and work hard, respect other people, obey the law and refrain from criminal activity, be clean and orderly in public, to send their children to school, and to respect themselves. According to Du Bois cultural transformation was an important strategy for social change. Many Black folk had been defeated by double consciousness and psychologically adopted and internalized the inferior positions forced upon them by racist Whites. This, coupled with the legacy of slavery, meant that many Black people had adopted poor cultural values and unproductive behaviors. Here, Du Bois adhered to conservative logic; African Americans needed to adopt bourgeois cultural values in order to be accepted and change themselves for the better.

Although ideological tension developed between Du Bois and rising Black Nationalists such as Marcus Garvey, who were not in favor of integration, they did agree that cultural nationalism was essential to progress. Du Bois incessantly called for race pride and pride in African heritage. He questioned White cultural hegemony. Equality would require economic, political, and social freedom. In order to acquire these freedoms African Americans needed to push the courts through Jim Crow test cases, lobby Congress and legislatures, and utilize democratic reform to realize equality and justice. As the editor of the *Moon*, the *Horizon*, and finally the *Crisis* under the NAACP, Du Bois advocated the need for an independent Black press to help shift public opinion. However, the struggle was not just in the economic and political realms of life. According to Du Bois, it was vital to revive African art and to bring Black arts into the public sphere. "We should resurrect forgotten ancient Negro art and history, and we should set the black man before the world as both a creative artists and a strong subject for artistic treatment." By fostering cultural nationalism, a celebration of Black art, the tide of public opinion could be swayed and Black folk would be taught how amazing and valuable their culture was for American society. Finally, people of African descent needed social equality.

Social equality would require social integration. However gradual this process, it was important for Black folk to have meaningful social interaction with other immigrant populations and oppressed peoples. In addition, unlike the overwhelming majority of Black Nationalists, Black activists should work with Whites in the struggle for true emancipation. As a founder of the NAACP, Du Bois was criticized by figures such as William Monroe Trotter and Marcus Garvey for his work with Whites. While for some working with Whites might lead to compromise, the development of pacifist strategies, and the relinquishing of self-sufficiency, Du Bois argued that sympathetic Whites were useful allies in their political struggles. "We cannot refuse to cooperate with white Americans and simultaneously demand the right to cooperate!" If full integration into American society was the goal then an integrated social movement would be required to achieve this goal.

As W.E.B. Du Bois matured his ideological and philosophical positions shifted. While Du Bois was never hostile to socialism, he did not really come to embrace it until later in his life, probably after witnessing so many failed attempts at legal and democratic reform from within the existing economic and political structure. While modern capitalism was problematic, traditional Marxism did not completely address the Negro Problem, as Marx's focus on class antagonisms came at the expense of racial antagonisms. Yes, the bourgeoisie exploits the proletariat. The working class, of which the average African American was a part of, was alienated, transformed into a mere commodity and forced to sell their labor power for low wages under terrible conditions. Capitalism is a system buttressed by pure avarice that simultaneously creates wealth for a few and creates masses of poor degraded people. This system is morally bankrupt because it thrives off of the backs of alienated laborers. And, like Marx, Du Bois agreed that, given the persistence of these horrific conditions, revolution would seem imminent. However, would the proletariat workers' revolution to bring about the overthrow of the bourgeoisie and capitalism, in favor of a classless society in which the means of production and private property are collective owned by the people actually benefit Black people?

Du Bois argued that Black people were a part of the oppressed proletariat. However, the proletariat in the United States was still very much segregated. In fact, race conditioned class exploitation. Therefore, while Black and White workers were certainly both exploited by capitalism, the wages of whiteness often gave White workers more access to privilege in the marketplace. Moreover, a large portion of the exploitation and brutality faced by Black folk was not just inflicted by the capitalists but was at the hands of White workers. Of course, capitalists had an incentive to fuel racial antagonisms between Black and White workers, to drive wages down and to thwart class consciousness that might lead to a united struggle. However, Marxism flippantly reduces these racial antagonisms to a manifestation of capitalist exploitation. Marxism fails to address the Negro Problem because White workers, including various "new White" immigrant groups such as the Irish, would fail to unite with Black workers in struggle. Resolving class struggle will not just bring racism to an end. The abolition of private property will not eliminate racist discourses. However, according to Du Bois this did not render socialism useless. If Marxism was modified to account for ways to practically address racial inequality then it might have use for Black people in the United States. However, while class unification might not be a reality, Du Bois did see racial unification as not only possible but necessary.

Du Bois posited that Pan-Africanism was essential to the struggles of the African Americans. Pan-Africanism meant that Black people in the United States needed to unite themselves and find common struggles with Black people all over the globe. Finding common ground with Black Nationalists, Du Bois argued that progress required complete cooperation with Africans and the Black Diaspora. This cooperation would lead to further cultural pride and political and economic strength.

Strivings of the Negro People, 1897

Between me and the other world there is ever an unasked question: unasked by some through feelings of delicacy; by others through the difficulty of rightly framing it. All, nevertheless, flutter round it. They approach me in a half-hesitant sort of way, eye me curiously or compassionately, and then, instead of saying directly, How does it feel to be a problem? they [*sic*] say, I know an excellent colored man in my town; or, I fought at Mechanicsville; or, Do not these Southern outrages make your blood boil? At these I smile, or am interested, or reduce the boiling to a simmer, as the occasion may require. To the real question, How [*sic*] does it feel to be a problem? I answer seldom a word.

And yet, being a problem is a strange experience,—peculiar even for one who has never been anything else, save perhaps in babyhood and in Europe. It is in the early days of rollicking boyhood that the revelation first bursts upon one, all in a day, as it were. I remember well when the shadow swept across me. I was a little thing, away up in the hills of New England, where the dark Housatonic winds between Hoosac and Taghanic to the sea. In a wee wooden schoolhouse, something put it into the boys' and girls' heads to buy gorgeous visiting-cards—ten cents a package—and exchange. The exchange was merry, till one girl, a tall newcomer, refused my card,—refused it peremptorily, with a glance. Then it dawned upon me with a certain suddenness that I was different from the others; or like, mayhap, in heart and life and longing, but shut out from their world by a vast veil. I had thereafter no desire to tear down that veil, to creep through; I held all beyond it in common contempt, and lived above it in a region of blue sky and great wandering shadows. That sky was bluest when I could beat my mates at examination-time, or beat them at a foot-race, or even beat their stringy heads. Alas, with the years all this fine contempt began to fade; for the world I longed for, and all its dazzling opportunities, were theirs, not mine. But they should not keep these prizes, I said; some, all, I would wrest from them. Just how I would do it I could never decide: by reading law, by healing the sick, by telling the wonderful tales that swam in my head,—some way. With other black boys the *strife* was not so fiercely sunny: their youth shrunk into tasteless sycophancy, [*sic*] or into silent hatred of the pale world about them and mocking distrust of everything white; or wasted *itself* in a bitter cry, Why did God make me an outcast and a stranger in mine own house? The "shades of the prison-house" closed round about us all: walls strait and stubborn to the whitest, but relentlessly narrow, tall, and unscalable to sons of night who must plod darkly on in resignation, or beat unavailing palms against the stone, or steadily, half hopelessly watch the streak of blue above.

After the Egyptian and Indian, the Greek and Roman, the Teuton and Mongolian, the Negro is a sort of seventh son, born with a veil, and gifted with second-sight in this American world,—a world which yields him no self-consciousness, but only lets him see himself through the revelation of the other world. It is a peculiar sensation, this double-consciousness, this sense of always looking at one's self through the eyes of others, of measuring one's soul by the tape of a world that looks on in amused contempt and pity. One ever feels his two-ness,—an American, a Negro; two souls, two thoughts, two unreconciled strivings; two warring ideals in one dark body, whose dogged strength alone keeps it *from* being torn asunder. The history of the American Negro is the history of this strife,—this longing to attain self-conscious manhood, to merge his double self into a better and truer self. In this merging he wishes neither of the older selves to be lost. He does not wish to Africanize America, for America has too much to teach the world and Africa; he does not wish to bleach his Negro blood in a flood of white Americanism, for he believes—foolishly, perhaps, but fervently—that Negro blood has yet a message for the world. He simply wishes to make it possible for a man to be both a Negro and an American without being cursed and spit upon by his fellows, without losing the opportunity of self-development.

Of Mr. Booker T. Washington and Others, 1903

Easily the most striking thing in the history of the American Negro since 1876 is the ascendancy of Mr. Booker T. Washington ... Mr. Washington represents in Negro thought the old attitude of adjustment and submission; but adjustment at such a peculiar time as to make his programme [sic] unique. This is an age of unusual economic development, and Mr. Washington's programme [sic] naturally takes an economic cast, becoming a gospel of Work and Money to such an extent as apparently almost completely to overshadow the higher aims of life. Moreover, this is an age when the more advanced races are coming in closer contact with the less developed races, and the race-feeling is therefore intensified; and Mr. Washington's programme practically accepts the alleged inferiority of the Negro races. Again, in our own land, the reaction from the sentiment of war time has given impetus to race-prejudice against Negroes, and Mr. Washington withdraws many of the high demands of Negroes as men and American citizens. In other periods of intensified prejudice all the Negro's tendency to self-assertion has been called forth; at this period a policy of submission is advocated. In the history of nearly all other races and peoples the doctrine preached at such crises has been that manly self-respect is worth more than lands and houses, and that a people who voluntarily surrender such respect, or cease striving for it, are not worth civilizing.

In answer to this, it has been claimed that the Negro can survive only through submission. Mr. Washington distinctly asks that black people give up, at least for the present, three things,—

First, political power,

Second, insistence on civil rights,

Third, higher education of Negro youth,—

and concentrate all their energies on industrial education, the accumulation of wealth, and the conciliation of the South. Thus policy has been courageously and insistently advocated for over fifteen years, and has been triumphant for perhaps ten years As a result of this tender of the palm-branch, what has been the return? In these years there have occurred:

1. The disfranchisement of the Negro.
2. The legal creation of a distinct status of civil inferiority for the Negro.
3. The steady withdrawal of aid from institutions for the higher training of the Negro.

These movements are not, to be sure, direct results of Mr. Washington's teachings; but his propaganda has, without a shadow of doubt, helped their speedier accomplishment. The question then comes: Is it possible, and probable, that nine millions of men can make effective progress in economic lines if they are deprived of political rights, made a servile caste, and allowed only the most meager [sic] chance for developing their exceptional men? If history and reason give any distinct answer to these questions, it is an emphatic *No*. And Mr. Washington thus faces the triple paradox of his career:

1. He is striving nobly to make Negro artisans business men and property-owners; but it is utterly impossible, under modern competitive methods, for workingmen and property-owners to defend their rights and exist without the right of suffrage.
2. He insists on thrift and self-respect, but at the same time counsels a silent submission to civic inferiority such as is bound to sap the man-hood of any race in the long run.
3. He advocates common-school and industrial training, and depreciates institutions of higher learning; but neither the Negro common-schools, nor Tuskegee itself, could remain open a day were it not for teachers trained in Negro colleges, or framed by their graduates.

The black men of America have a duty to perform, a duty stern and delicate,—a forward movement to oppose a part of the work of their greatest leader. So far as Mr. Washington preaches Thrift, Patience, and Industrial Training for the masses, we must hold up his hands and strive with him, rejoicing in his honors and glorying in the strength of this Joshua called of God and of man to lead the headless host. But so far as Mr. Washington apologizes for injustice, North or South, does not rightly value the privilege and duty of voting, belittles the emasculating effects of caste distinctions, and opposes the higher training and ambition of our brighter minds,—so far as he, the South, or the Nation, does this,—we must unceasingly and firmly oppose them. By every civilized and peaceful method we must strive for the rights which the world accords to men, clinging unwaveringly to those great words which the sons of the Fathers would fain forget: "We hold these truths to be self-evident: That all men are created equal; that they are endowed by their Creator with certain unalienable rights, that among these are life, liberty, and the pursuit of happiness."

The Talented Tenth, 1903

The Negro race, like all races, is going to be saved by its exceptional men. The problem of education, then, among Negroes must first of all deal with the Talented Tenth; it is the problem of developing the Best of this race that they may guide the Mass away from the contamination and death of the Worst, in their own and other races. Now the training of men is a difficult and intricate task. Its technique is a matter for educational experts, but its object is for the vision of seers. If we make money the object of man-training, we shall develop money-makers but not necessarily men; if we make technical skill the object of education, we may possess artisans but not, in nature, men. Men we shall have only as we make manhood the object of the work of the schools—intelligence, broad sympathy, knowledge of the world that was and is, and of the relation of men to it—this is the curriculum of that Higher Education which must underlie true life. On this foundation we may build bread winning, skill of hand and quickness of brain, with never a fear lest the child and man mistake the means of living for the object of life.

If this be true—and who can deny it—three tasks lay before me; first to show from the past that the Talented Tenth as they have risen among American Negroes have been worthy of leadership; secondly to show how these men may be educated and developed; and thirdly to show their relation to the Negro problem.

You misjudge us because you do not know us. From the very first it has been the educated and intelligent of the Negro people that have led and elevated the mass, and the sole obstacles that nullified and retarded their efforts were slavery and race prejudice; for what is slavery but the legalized survival of the unfit and the nullification of the work of natural internal leadership? ...

It is the fashion of today to sneer at them and to say that with freedom Negro leadership should have begun at the plow and not in the Senate—a foolish and mischievous lie; two hundred and fifty years that black serf toiled at the plow and yet that toiling was in vain till the Senate passed the war amendments; and two hundred and fifty years more the half-free serf of to-day may toil at his plow, but unless he have political rights and righteously guarded civic status, he will still remain the poverty-stricken and ignorant plaything of rascals, that he now is. This all sane men know even if they dare not say it.

And so we come to the present—a day of cowardice and vacillation, of strident wide-voiced wrong and faint hearted compromise; of double-faced dallying with Truth and Right. Who are today guiding the work of the Negro people? The "exceptions" of course. And yet so sure as this Talented Tenth is pointed out, the blind worshippers of the Average cry out in alarm: "These are exceptions, look here at death, disease and crime—these are the happy rule." Of course they are the rule, because a silly nation made them the rule: Because for three long centuries this people lynched Negroes who dared to be brave, raped black women who dared to be virtuous, crushed dark-hued youth who dared to be ambitious, and encouraged and made to flourish servility and lewdness and apathy. But nor even this was able to crush all manhood and chastity and aspiration from black folk. A saving remnant continually survives and persists, continually aspires, continually shows itself in thrift and ability and character. Exceptional it is to be sure, but this is its chiefest [*sic*] promise; it shows the capability of Negro blood, the promise of black men. Do Americans ever stop to reflect that there are in this land a million men of Negro blood, well-educated, owners of homes, against the honor of whose womanhood no breath was ever raised, whose men occupy positions of trust and usefulness, and who, judged by any standard, have reached the full measure of the best type of modern European culture? Is it fair, is it decent, is it Christian to ignore these facts of the Negro problem, to belittle such aspiration, to nullify such leadership and seek to crush these people back into the mass out of which by toil and travail, they and their fathers have raised themselves?

Can the masses of the Negro people be in any possible way more quickly raised than by the effort and example of this aristocracy of talent and character? Was there ever a nation on God's fair earth civilized from the bottom upward? Never; it is, ever was and ever will be from the top downward that culture filters. The Talented Tenth rises and pulls all that are worth the saving up to their vantage ground. This is the history of human progress; and the two historic mistakes which have hindered that progress were the thinking first that no more could ever rise save the few already risen; or second, that it would better the uprisen to pull the risen down.

How then shall the leaders of a struggling people be trained and the hands of the risen few strengthened? There can be but one answer: The best and most capable of their youth must be schooled in the colleges and universities of the land. We will not quarrel as to just what the university of the Negro should teach or how it should teach it—I willingly admit that each soul and each race-soul needs its own peculiar curriculum. But this is true: A university is a human invention for the transmission of knowledge and culture from generation to generation, through the training of quick minds and pure hearts, and for this work no other human invention will suffice, not even trade and industrial schools.

All men cannot go to college but some men must; every isolated group or nation must have its yeast, must have for the talented few centers of training where men are not so mystified and befuddled by the hard and necessary toil of earning a living, as to have no aims higher than their bellies, and no God greater than Gold. This is true training, and thus in the beginning were the favored sons of the freedmen trained.

Thus, again, in the manning of trade schools and manual training schools we are thrown back upon the higher training as its source and chief support. There was a time when any aged and wornout [*sic*] carpenter could teach in a trade school. But not so today. Indeed the demand for college-bred men by a school like Tuskegee, ought to make Mr. Booker T. Washington the firmest friend of higher training. Here he has as helpers the son of a Negro senator, trained in Greek and the humanities, and graduated at Harvard; the son of a Negro congressman and lawyer, trained in Latin and mathematics, and graduated at Oberlin; he has as his wife, a woman who read Virgil and Homer in the same class room with me; he has as college chaplain, a classical graduate of Atlanta University; as teacher of science, a graduate of Fisk; as teacher of history, a graduate of Smith,—indeed some thirty of his chief teachers are college graduates, and instead of studying French grammars in the midst of weeds, or buying pianos for dirty cabins, they are at Mr. Washington's right hand helping him in a noble work. And yet one of the effects of Mr. Washington's propaganda has been to throw doubt upon the expediency of such training for Negroes, as these persons have had.

Men of America, the problem is plain before you. Here is a race transplanted through the criminal foolishness of your fathers. Whether you like it or not the millions are here, and here they will remain. If you do not lift them up, they will pull you down. Education and work are the levers to uplift a people. Work alone will not do it unless inspired by the right ideals and guided by intelligence. Education must not simply teach work—it must teach Life. The Talented Tenth of the Negro race must be made leaders of thought and missionaries of culture among their people. No others can do this work and Negro colleges must train men for it. The Negro race, like all other races, is going to be saved by its exceptional men.

The Immediate Program of the American Negro, 1915

The immediate program of the American Negro means nothing unless it is mediate to his great ideal and the ultimate ends of his development. We need not waste time by seeking to deceive our enemies into thinking that we are going to be content with a half loaf, or by being willing to lull our friends into a false sense of our indifference and present satisfaction.

The American Negro demands equality—political equality, industrial equality and social equality; and he is never going to rest satisfied with anything less. He demands this in no spirit of braggadocio and with no obsequious envy of others, but as an absolute measure of self-defense and the only one that will assure to the darker races their ultimate survival on earth.

Only in a demand and a persistent demand for essential equality in the modern realm of human culture can any people show a real pride of race and a decent self-respect. For any group, nation or race to admit for a moment the present monstrous demand of the white race to be the inheritors of the earth, the arbiters of mankind and the sole owners of a heritage of culture which they did not create, nor even improve to any greater extent than the other great division of men—to admit such pretense for a moment is for the race to write itself down immediately as indisputably inferior in judgment, knowledge and common sense.

The equality in political, industrial and social life which modern men must have in order to live, is not to be confounded with sameness. On the contrary, in our case, it is rather insistence upon the right of diversity;—upon the right of a human being to be a man even if he does not wear the same cut of vest, the same curl of hair or the same color of skin. Human equality does not even entail, as is sometimes said, absolute equality of opportunity; for certainly the natural inequalities of inherent genius and varying gift make this a dubious phase. But there is a more and more clearly recognized minimum of opportunity and maximum of freedom to be, to move and to think, which the modern world denies to no being which it recognizes as a real man.

These involve both negative and positive sides. They call for freedom on the one hand and power on the other. The Negro must have political freedom; taxation without representation is tyranny. American Negroes of to-day are ruled by tyrants who take what they please in taxes and give what they please in law and administration, in justice and in injustice; and the great mass of black people must stand helpless and voiceless before a condition which has time and time again caused other peoples to fight and die.

The Negro must have industrial freedom. Between the peonage of the rural South, the oppression of shrewd capitalists and the jealousy of certain trade unions, the Negro laborer is the most exploited class in the country, giving more hard toil for less money than any other American, and have less voice in the conditions of his labor.

In social intercourse every effort is being made to-day from the President of the United States and the so-called Church of Christ down to saloons and boot-blacks to segregate [sic], strangle and spiritually starve Negroes so as to give them the least possible chance to know and share civilization.

These shackles must go. But that is but the beginning. The Negro must have power; the power of men, the right to do, to know, to feel and to express that knowledge, action and spiritual gift. He must not simply be free from the political tyranny of white folk, [sic] he must have the right to vote and to rule over the citizens, white and black, to the extent of his proven foresight and ability. He must have a voice in the new industrial democracy which is building and the power to see to it that his children are not in the next generation trained to be the mudsills of society. He must have the right to social intercourse with his fellows. There was a time in the atomic individualistic group when "social intercourse meant merely calls and tea-parties; to-day social intercourse means theatres, lectures, organizations, churches, clubs, excursions, travel, hotels,—it means in short Life; to bar a group from such methods of thinking, living and doing is to bar them from the world and bid them create a new world;—a task to which no single group is today equal; it is to crucify them and taunt them with not being able to live.

What now are the practical steps which must be taken to accomplish these ends?

First of all before taking steps the wise man knows the object and end of his journey. There are those who would advise the black man to pay little or no attention to where he is going so long as he keeps moving. They assume that God or his vice-gerent the White Man will attend to the steering. This is arrant nonsense. The feet of those that aimlessly wander land as often in hell as in heaven. Conscious self-realization and self-direction is the watchword of modern man, and the first article in the program of any group that will survive must be the great aim, equality and power among men.

The practical steps to this are clear. First we must fight obstructions; by continual and increasing effort we must first make American courts either build up a body of decisions which will protect the plain legal rights of American citizens or else make them tear down the civil and political rights of all citizens in order to oppress a few. Either result will bring justice in the end. It is lots of fun and most ingenious just now for courts to twist law so as to say I shall not live here or vote there, or marry the woman who wishes to marry me. But when to-morrow these decisions throttle all freedom and overthrow the foundation of democracy and decency, there is going to be some judicial house cleaning.

We must *secondly* seek in legislature and congress remedial legislation; national aid to public school education, the removal of all legal discriminations based simply on race and color, and those marriage laws passed to make the seduction of black girls easy and without legal penalty.

Third the human contact of human beings must be increased; the policy which brings into sympathetic touch and understanding, men and women, rich and poor, capitalist and laborer, Asiatic and European, must bring into closer contact and mutual knowledge the white and black people of this land. It is the most frightful indictment of a country which dares to call itself civilized that it has allowed itself to drift into a state of ignorance where ten million people are coming to believe that all white people are liars and thieves, and the whites in turn to believe that the chief industry of Negroes is raping white women.

Fourth only the publication of the truth repeatedly and incisively and uncompromisingly can secure that change in public opinion which will correct these awful lies. THE CRISIS, our record of the darker races, must have a circulation not of 35,000 chiefly among colored folk but of at least 250,000 among all men who believe in men. It must not be a namby-pamby box of salve, but a voice that thunders fact and is more anxious to be true than pleasing. There should be a campaign of tract distribution—short well written facts and arguments—rained over this land by millions of copies, particularly in the South, where the white people know less about the Negro than in any other part of the civilized world. The press should be utilized—the 400 Negro weeklies, the great dailies and eventually the magazines, when we get magazine editors who will lead public opinion instead of following afar with resonant brays. Lectures, lantern-slides and moving pictures, co-operating with a bureau of information and eventually becoming a Negro encyclopedia, all these are efforts along the line of making human beings realize that Negroes are human.

Such is the program of work against obstructions. Let us now turn to constructive effort. This may be summed up under (1) economic co-operation (2) a revival of art and literature (3) political action (4) education and (5) organization.

Under economic co-operation we must strive to spread the idea among colored people that the accumulation of wealth is for social rather than individual ends. We must avoid, in the advancement of the Negro race, the mistakes of ruthless exploitation which have marked modern economic history. To this end we must seek not simply home ownership, small landholding and saving accounts, but also all forms of co-operation, both in production and distribution, profit sharing, building and loan associations, systematic charity for definite, practical ends, systematic migration from mob rule and robbery, to freedom and enfranchisement, the emancipation of women and the abolition of child labor.

In art and literature we should try to loose the tremendous emotional wealth of the Negro and the dramatic strength of his problems through writing, the stage, pageantry and other forms of art. We should resurrect forgotten ancient Negro art and history, and we should set the black man before the world as both a creative artist and a strong subject for artistic treatment.

In political action we should organize the votes of Negroes in such congressional districts as have any number of Negro voters. We should systematically interrogate candidates on matters vital to Negro freedom and uplift. We should train colored voters to reject the bribe of office and to accept only decent legal enactments both for their own uplift and for the uplift of laboring classes of all races and both sexes.

In education we must seek to give colored children free public school training. We must watch with grave suspicion the attempt of those who, under the guise of vocational training, would fasten ignorance and menial service on the Negro for another generation. Our children must not in large numbers, be forced into the servant class; for menial service is still, in the main, little more than an antiquated survival of impossible conditions. It has always been as statistics show, a main cause of bastardy and prostitution and despite its many marvelous exceptions it will never come to the light of decency and honor until the house servant becomes the Servant in the House. It is our duty then, not drastically but persistently, to seek out colored children of ability and genius to open up to them broader, industrial opportunity and above all, to find that Talented Tenth and encourage it by the best and most exhaustive training in order to supply the Negro race and the world with leaders, thinkers and artists.

For the accomplishment of all these ends we must organize. Organization among us already has gone far but it must go much further and higher. Organization is sacrifice. It is sacrifice of opinions, of time, of work and of money, but it is, after all, the cheapest way of buying the most priceless of gifts—freedom and efficiency. I thank God that most of the money that supports the National Association for the Advancement of Colored People comes from black hands; a still larger proportion must so come, and we must not only support but control this and similar organizations and hold them unwaveringly to our objects, our aims and our ideals.

White Co-workers, 1920

There is one charge against the N.A.A.C.P. which is made, now openly and now by veiled innuendo, which it is necessary to answer plainly. It is said that this Association is not a Negro association, but is conducted by white people and that, therefore, it cannot effectively serve the cause of Negro freedom. The veiled assumption is that the efforts of the Negroes in the Association are controlled and largely nullified by whites.

The Association is not an exclusively Negro Association. We do not believe in the color line against either white or black. The N.A.A.C.P. is a union of American citizens of all colors and races who believe that Democracy in America is a failure if it proscribes Negroes, as such, politically, economically, or socially.

That all our officers and members are working wholeheartedly to this end is proven by the fact that this Association has done more for the emancipation of the Negro in the last ten years than any other organization of men, white, black or mixed, in the last half century. The record speaks for itself:

1. The overthrow of segregation
2. Defeat of intermarriage laws in twelve states
3. Cooperation in the "Grandfather" decision case
4. Model Civil Rights bills in New York and Michigan
5. The anti-lynching campaign
6. Movement for Negro Army officers
7. Preventing extradition where lynching was possible
8. Pan-African Congress
9. Spingam Medal
10. The CRISIS Magazine
11. Over a million pieces of literature, millions of letters, thousands of meetings, appeals, protests, etc.

We have not worked alone; what we have done has been in cooperation with numerous agencies and individuals outside our membership; but ours has been the impulse and initiative and most of the work.

Despite all this we admit frankly and freely that we have not yet settled the Negro problem. The Negro is still disfranchised, lynched, "Jim Crowed," robbed and insulted. But we did not expect to unravel the tangle of 300 years in 10; we *did* expect to start the unravelling and this the most churlish must credit us with doing.

If now anyone can suggest any improvement in our organization or method, we are eager to hear them; but we do not believe that the time has come, or ever will come, when we will not need the help of white Americans. To bar them from our organization would be a monstrous discrimination; it would advertise the fact that we can not or will not work with white people. If this is true, what are we doing in America or indeed in the modern world? What are we fighting for, if it is not the chance to stand with our white fellows, side by side and hand in hand, and fight for right?

We certainly *can* do this for we have. The N.A.A.C.P. consists of about 80,000 Negroes and 10,000 whites. Colored persons predominate on the Board of Directors, on the Committee of Executives and among the executive officers. Most of the white members of the board are there by the earnest invitation and insistence of the colored members, because of their influence and help. On the other hand, at no time has there been the slightest disposition to control the opinion of the colored members or officers. The policy of the N.A.A.C.P. has from the beginning been the policy proposed and advocated by the colored members of the Board and the white members have always been not only willing, but eager to promote the just demands of the Negroes as interpreted by their fellow members. In an experience of twenty-five years in organizations, boards and committees I have never been a member of a board which had more interesting or informing sessions and which, considering the volume and intricacy of its problems, had less friction and lack of good will.

What we have thus accomplished in the N.A.A.C.P. is a sample of what we aim to accomplish in the nation and the world. We propose, as black folk, to work with white folk and red and yellow in this land, as equal partners in promoting the common good; in the world we will to unite with all races and nations in a world Democracy of Humanity. But what shall be said if at the beginning of our world quest we refuse to work with any but Negroes for any object?

What is the meaning of such an attitude? Whither does it tend? Do we want to become American citizens or not? Do we want to share in a world state, or not? If we will neither of these things, then our whole aim and argument since 1863 has been wrong. What we really want is not to *fight* segregation, it *is* segregation. We want separate cities, colonies and states and eventually a separate nation. This is a possible aim. It is an aim which we may be driven by race prejudice sometime to adopt. But it is not our present aim and we cannot consistently or effectively at the same time pursue *both* these aims. We cannot refuse to cooperate with white Americans and simultaneously demand the right to cooperate!

Marxism and the Negro Problem, 1933

The task which Karl Marx set himself was to study and interpret the organization of industry in the modern world. One of Marx's earlier works, "The Communist Manifesto," issued in 1848, on the eve of the series of democratic revolutions in Europe, laid down this fundamental proposition.

"That in every historical epoch the prevailing mode of economic production and exchange, and the social organization necessarily following from it, form the basis upon which is built up, and from which alone can be explained, the political and intellectual history of that epoch; that consequently the whole history of mankind ... has been a history of class struggles, contest between exploiting and exploited, ruling and oppressed classes; that the history of these class struggles forms a series of evolution in which, now-a-days, a stage has been reached where the exploited and oppressed class (the proletariat) cannot attain its emancipation from the sway of the exploiting and ruling class (the bourgeoisie) without, at the same time, and once and for all, emancipating society at large from all exploitation, oppression, class-distinction and class-struggles."

All will notice in this manifesto phrases which have been used so much lately and so carelessly that they have almost lost their meaning. But behind them still is living and insistent truth. The *class struggle* of exploiter and exploited is a reality. The capitalist still today owns machines, materials, and wages with which to buy labor. The laborer even in America owns little more than his ability to work. A wage contract takes place between these two and the resultant manufactured commodity or service is the property of the capitalist.

What now has all this to do with the Negro problem? First of all, it is manifest that the mass of Negroes in the United States belong distinctly to the working proletariat. Of every thousand working Negroes less than a hundred and fifty belong to any class that could possibly be considered bourgeois. And even this more educated and prosperous class has but small connection with the exploiters of wage and labor. Nevertheless, this black proletariat is not a part of the white proletariat. Black and white work together in many cases, and influence each other's rates of wages. They have similar complaints against capitalists, save that the grievances of the Negro worker are more fundamental and indefensible, ranging as they do, since the day of Karl Marx, from chattel slavery, to the worst paid, sweated, mobbed and cheated labor in any civilized land.

And while Negro labor in America suffers because of the fundamental inequities of the whole capitalistic system, the lowest and most fatal degree of its suffering comes not from the capitalists but from fellow white laborers. It is white labor that deprives the Negro of his right to vote, denies him education, denies him affiliation with trade unions, expels him from decent houses and neighborhoods, and heaps upon him the public insults of open color discrimination.

It is no sufficient answer to say that capital encourages this oppression and uses it for its own ends. This may have excused the ignorant and superstitious Russian peasants in the past and some of the poor whites of the South today. But the bulk of American white labor is neither ignorant nor fanatical. It knows exactly what it is doing and it means to do it. William Green and Mathew Woll of the A.F. of L. have no excuse of illiteracy or religion to veil their deliberate intention to keep Negroes and Mexicans and other elements of common labor, in a lower proletariat as subservient to their interests as theirs are to the interests of capital.

This large development of a petty bourgeoisie within the American laboring class is a post-Marxian phenomenon and the result of the tremendous and world wide development of capitalism in the 20th Century. The market of capitalistic production has gained an effective world-wide organization. Industrial technique and mass production have brought possibilities in the production of goods and services which out-run even this wide market. A new class of technical engineers and managers has arisen forming a working class aristocracy between the older proletariat and the absentee owners of capital. The real owners of capital are small as well as large investors—workers who have deposits in savings banks and small holdings in stocks and bonds; families buying homes and purchasing commodities on installment; as well as the large and rich investors.

Of course, the individual laborer gets but an infinitesimal part of his income from such investments. On the other hand, such investments, in the aggregate, largely increase available capital for the exploiters, and they give investing laborers the capitalistic ideology. Between workers and owners of capital stand today the bankers and financiers who distribute capital and direct the engineers.

Thus the engineers and the saving better-paid workers, form a new petty bourgeois class, whose interests are bound up with those of the capitalists and antagonistic to those of common labor. On the other hand, common labor in America and white Europe far from being motivated by any vision of revolt against capitalism, has been blinded by the American vision of the possibility of layer after layer of the workers escaping into the wealthy class and becoming managers and employers of labor.

Thus in America we have seen a wild and ruthless scramble of labor groups over each other in order to climb to wealth on the backs of black labor and foreign immigrants.

The Irish climbed on the Negroes. The Germans scrambled over the Negroes and emulated the Irish. The Scandinavians fought forward next to the Germans and the Italians and "Bohunks" are crowding up, leaving Negroes still at the bottom chained to helplessness, first by slavery, then by disfranchisement and always by the Color Bar.

The second influence on white labor both in America and Europe has been the fact that the extension of the world market by imperial expanding industry has established a world-wide new proletariat of colored workers, toiling under the worst conditions of 19th century capitalism, herded as slaves and serfs and furnishing by the lowest paid wage in modern history a mass of raw material for industry. With this largess the capitalists have consolidated their economic power, nullified universal suffrage and bribed the white workers by high wages, visions of wealth and the opportunity to drive "niggers." Soldiers and sailors from the white workers are used to keep "darkies" in their "places" and white foremen and engineers have been established as irresponsible satraps in China and India, Africa and the West Indies, backed by the organized and centralized ownership of machines, raw materials, finished commodities and land monopoly over the whole world.

How now does the philosophy of Karl Marx apply today to colored labor? First of all colored labor has no common ground with white labor. No soviet of technocrats would do more than exploit colored labor in order to raise the status of whites. No revolt of a white proletariat could be started if its object was to make black workers their economic, political and social equals. It is for this reason that American socialism for fifty years has been dumb on the Negro problem, and the communists cannot even get a respectful hearing in America unless they begin by expelling Negroes.

On the other hand, within the Negro groups, in the United States, in West Africa, in South America and in the West Indies, petty bourgeois groups are being evolved. In South America and the West Indies such groups drain off skill and intelligence into the white group, and leave the black labor poor, ignorant and leaderless save for an occasional demagog.

In West Africa, a Negro bourgeoisie is developing with invested capital and employment of natives and is only kept from the conventional capitalistic development by the opposition and enmity of white capital, and the white managers and engineers who represent it locally and who display bitter prejudice and tyranny; and by white European labor which furnishes armies and navies and Empire "preference." African black labor and black capital are therefore driven to seek alliance and common ground.

In the United States also a petty bourgeoisie is being developed, consisting of clergymen, teachers, farm owners, professional men and retail businessmen. The position of this class, however, is peculiar: they are not the chief or even large investors in Negro labor and therefore exploit it only here and there; and they bear the brunt of color prejudice because they express in word and work the aspirations of all black folk for emancipation. The revolt of any black proletariat could not, therefore, be logically directed against this class, nor could this class join either white capital, white engineers or white workers to strengthen the color bar.

Under these circumstances, what shall we say of the Marxian philosophy and of its relation to the American Negro? We can only say, as it seems to me, that the Marxian philosophy is a true diagnosis of the situation in Europe in the middle of the 19th Century despite some of its logical difficulties. But it must be modified in the United States of America and especially so far as the Negro group is concerned. The Negro is exploited to a degree that means poverty, crime, delinquency and indigence. And that exploitation comes not from a black capitalistic class but from the white capitalists and equally from the white proletariat. His only defense is such internal organization as will protect him from both parties, and such practical economic insight as will prevent inside the race group any large development of capitalistic exploitation.

Meantime, comes the Great Depression. It levels all in mighty catastrophe. The fantastic industrial structure of America is threatened with ruin. The trade unions of skilled labor are double-tongued and helpless. Unskilled and common white labor is too frightened at Negro competition to attempt united action. It only begs a dole. The reformist program of Socialism meets no response from the white proletariat because it offers no escape to wealth and no effective bar to black labor, and a mud-sill of black labor is essential to white labor's standard of living. The shrill cry of a few communists is not even listened to, because and solely because it seeks to break down barriers between black and white. There is not at present the slightest indication that a Marxian revolution based on a united class-conscious proletariat is anywhere on the American far horizon. Rather race antagonism and labor group rivalry is still undisturbed by world catastrophe. In the hearts of black laborers alone, therefore, lie those ideals of democracy in politics and industry which may in time make the workers of the world effective dictators of civilization.

Pan-Africa and New Racial Philosophy, 1933

If … [B]lack American[s] [are] going to survive and live a life, [they] must calmly face the fact that however much he is an American there are interests which draw him nearer to the dark people outside of America than to his white fellow citizens.

And those interests are the same matters of color caste, of discrimination, of exploitation for the sake of profit, of public insult and oppression, against which the colored peoples of Mexico, South America, the West Indies and all Africa, and every country in Asia, complain and have long been complaining. It is, therefore, simply a matter of ordinary common sense that these people should draw together in spiritual sympathy and intellectual co-operation, to see what can be done for the freedom of the human spirit which happens to be incased in dark skin.

This was the idea that was back of the Pan-African Congresses, started in Paris directly after the war, and carried on for several years. These Congresses brought upon themselves the active enmity and disparagement of all the colony-owning powers. Englishmen, Frenchmen, Belgians and others looked upon the movement as a political movement designed to foment disaffection and strife and to correct abuse by force.

It is, therefore, imperative that the colored peoples of the world, and first of all those of Negro descent, should begin to concentrate upon this problem of their economic survival, the best of their brains and education. Pan-Africa means intellectual understanding and co-operation among all groups of Negro descent in order to bring about at the earliest possible time the industrial and spiritual emancipation of the Negro peoples.

Such a movement must begin with a certain spiritual housecleaning. American Negroes, West Indians, West Africans and South Africans must proceed immediately to wipe from their minds the preconcepts [*sic*] of each other which they have gained through white newspapers. They must cease to think of Liberia and Haiti as failures in government; of American Negroes as being engaged principally in frequenting Harlem cabarets and Southern lynching parties; of West Indians as ineffective talkers; and of West Africans as parading around in breech-clouts.

These are the pictures of each other which white people have painted for us and which with engaging naiveté we accept, and then proceed to laugh at each other and criticize each other before we make any attempt to learn the truth. There are, for instance, in the United States today several commendable groups of young people who are proposing to take hold of Liberia and emancipate her from her difficulties, quite forgetting the fact that Liberia belongs to Liberia. They made it. They suffered and died for it. And they are not handing over their country to any group of young strangers who happen to be interested. If we want to help Liberia, our business is to see in what respect the Liberians need help, and the persons best able to give this information are the Liberians themselves.

It is a large and intricate problem but the sooner we put ourselves in position to study it with a vast and increasing area of fact and with carefully guided and momentarily tested effort, the sooner we shall find ourselves citizens of the world and not its slaves and pensioners.

Notes

1. See Roediger, David R. 1991. *The Wages of Whiteness: Race and the Making of the American Working Class*. New York and London: Verso.
2. For full accounts of the Niagara Movement see Rudwick, Elliot. 1957. "The Niagara Movement." *The Journal of Negro History*, Vol. 42, No. 3, pp. 177–200. Jones, Angela. 2010. "The Niagara Movement 1905–1910: A Revisionist Approach to the Social History of the Civil Rights Movement." *The Journal of Historical Sociology*, Vol. 23, No. 3, pp. 453–500. Jones, Angela. 2011. *African American Civil Rights: Early Activism and the Niagara Movement*. Santa Barbara, CA: Praeger.

10.
ASA PHILIP RANDOLPH

Asa Philip Randolph (1889–1979) was a grassroots activist who was paramount in the Civil Rights Movement and became one of the most famous Black labor leaders primarily because of his work with the Brotherhood of Sleeping Car Porters. Randolph was a socialist and began his lifelong career as an activist in Harlem, New York. In 1910 Randolph officially joined the Socialist Party and stood on the infamous corner of Lenox Avenue and 135 Street, known as "soapbox corner," educating residents about class exploitation and encouraging Black residents to embrace socialism. In 1918 he left Harlem street corners and traveled across the United States giving speeches denouncing imperialism, war, and discussing the benefits of socialism. In 1920 he ran for New York State Comptroller on the Socialist ticket. In 1922 he also ran on the Socialist ticket for Secretary of the State of New York. Like many of his counterparts such as W.E.B. Du Bois Randolph found himself under investigation by the Department of Justice for his ostensibly radical proclivities and activities.

Randolph contributed to the Black press and labor activism. In 1917 Randolph became the editor of the *Hotel Messenger*, just called the *Messenger*, a monthly paper devoted to labor related issues. In the same year he began work organizing elevator operators. Randolph was becoming a powerful Black labor leader. From 1919 to 1921, as president of the National Brotherhood of Workers of America, Randolph organized Black shipyard workers into a union in Virginia. In 1925, Randolph became the president of the Brotherhood of Sleeping Car Porters. In 1955, Randolph became vice president of the AFL-CIO. He helped found the Negro American Labor Council (NALC). In addition, he was the NALC's president from 1960 to 1966. Randolph's organizing did not stop with organizing Black workers and unions.

Randolph was an extraordinary civil rights leader. In 1940 Randolph called for a March on Washington to protest the Roosevelt administration's apathy toward institutionalized racism; President Roosevelt declined to issue an executive order which would have made discrimination against African Americans in the defense industry illegal. Once the administration received word of the enormous momentum of the protest Roosevelt not only issued the order but created the Fair Employment Practices Commission to ensure the order was enforced. In addition, Randolph fought to end Jim Crow in the military. Here too, Randolph's organization pushed the president, this time Harry Truman, to begin to put an end to segregation in the armed forces. These were not the only marches Randolph helped to orchestrate. As chair of the marches' committee, Randolph was one of the main architects of the famous March on Washington in 1963. His lifetime efforts did not go unrecognized. Interestingly, despite advocating socialism publicly, President Lyndon Baines Johnson awarded him the Presidential Medal of Freedom in 1964.

Overview of Ideas

Asa Philip Randolph was one of the more radical leaders of this period. In an answer to the growing integrationist movement, Randolph introduced an economic perspective. Randolph, a socialist and labor leader, wanted African Americans and their leaders to recognize the important role labor reform would play in solving the Negro Problem.

Early in Randolph's political career he was vehemently opposed to democratic reform; he argued it was futile. His early philosophy was heavily driven from an economic perspective and as a socialist he saw no real use in advocating traditional political agitation such as voting drives, if Black people continued to support the binary system of electoral politics. According to Randolph both the Democratic and Republican parties had no interest in helping African Americans. Like Karl Marx, Randolph believed the government was an appendage of the bourgeoisie. Political parties and their candidates' votes and policies are bought by capitalists. Black people needed: better access to quality jobs, lower wages, access to quality and cheap clothing and shelter, etc. However, if politicians' interests are aligned with capitalists, whose interests are to maximize profits at all costs then why bother voting or engaging in political action if politicians have no interest in the problems facing both workers and Black people? Randolph told Black folk that their only hopes were with the Socialist Party.

The problems that Black people faced were largely the result of capitalism; a system based solely on the recognition of private property, whose sole purpose is the acquisition of wealth at all costs to the human community. For example, Randolph even argued that lynching was a result of capitalism. Class antagonisms fuel racial antagonisms. Capitalists have an incentive to maintain racial antagonisms. As long as Black and White workers are feuding there will be no common struggle against their oppressor, the capitalist. The struggles between White and Black workers are generally formed in the labor market. Competition over scarce jobs, resources, and wages exacerbates racial tensions. The government, the press, and even the church exacerbated these tensions by perpetuating racist discourses, calling Black people inferior, savage, prone to criminality, etc. Racist Whites then argued they had legitimate motives for violence against Black people such as lynching. However, the basis of these racial conflicts were economic and exploited by the capitalists to ensure greater profits.

> When the motive for promoting race prejudice is removed, viz., profits, by the social ownership, control and operation of the machinery and sources of production through the government, the government being controlled by the workers; the effects of prejudice, race riots, lynching, etc., will also be removed.

Under socialism lynching would cease to exist because its cause (tensions between workers ultimately derived from workplace competition) would have been eliminated.

Randolph promulgated that it was vital for the African American community to be united in struggle. Divisions amongst leadership and within the Black community thwarted progress. According to Randolph four distinct ideological camps developed within the African American community and again these divisions stifled unified struggle. First, there was what Randolph called a conservative or right-wing sect, led originally by Booker T. Washington and continued by individuals at the Tuskegee and Hampton Institutes and within the National Urban League. He said, "the Negro leaders of this group are largely satellites of their white benefactors, reflecting the views of conservative, imperial America." This group stressed economic uplift through thrift, delayed gratification, and hard work in a vocation. Second, Randolph argued there was a moderate group, most commonly associated with the NAACP and figures such as W.E.B. Du Bois. This group of political centrists did seek full civil rights along with the help of liberal Whites. To the far left were socialist leaders who saw the elimination of class conflict as the path for African Americans. Randolph saw himself as part of this camp. Finally, there was the group associated with Marcus Garvey's Back-to-Africa Movement. Randolph opposed the separatism advocated by this group.

> The Negro schools of thought are torn with dissension … all are engaged in a war of bitter recriminations, tearing each other limb from limb, while the wide, long-suffering Negro masses trudge aimlessly on, victims of the vanities, foibles, indiscretions and vaulting ambitions, ignorance and dishonesty of varying leaderships.

Without cooperative struggle the future looked bleak. Randolph suggested creating conferences at which these different contingencies might come together to see how to reconcile their respective demands and strategies. While Randolph proffered the need for unity amongst Black folk, like his counterpart Du Bois, they both agreed, unlike Black Nationalists such as Marcus Garvey, that working with Whites was important to a successful movement. Randolph argued that Blacks needed to work alongside Whites in common struggles such as: higher wages, improving working conditions, and shorter work days. In fact, Randolph was adamant that stereotyping Whites as all racist or all evil was deleterious. "All white peoples are no more alike than all Negroes." All Whites were not trying to retard the success of African American progress. In fact, many Whites would be powerful allies. Despite Randolph's insistence that Whites could and should be allies, he still understood the need for Black self-sufficiency, particularly within labor activism.

In "The Need of a Labor Background" Randolph demonstrates both his commitment to labor activism but also to Black Nationalism. He argued that historically, Blacks had attempted to organize and join unions. However, what they have lacked historically is the ability to garner leadership positions within these unions. For Randolph, working with White workers in unions and labor struggles was important. However, Black workers needed to also control unions. "While Negro workers have fought nobly in the ranks of white workers in long industrial struggles, they have not known what it means to have the responsibility for the moral and financial maintenance of struggle." While African Americans should be part of the American Labor Movement, they should be able to sustain themselves within that larger movement. Randolph said that Black workers needed to organize themselves; this would not be actively accomplished by White labor leaders. As part of a Black union, its members would learn self-sufficiency, pride, and what it means to "suffer and sacrifice for a group of black workers fighting for industrial justice." Because of Randolph's ideological affinity with socialism, most scholars do not acknowledge the elements of Black Nationalism, particularly economic nationalism in his work. Randolph wrote, "the economic self-organization of Negro workers, is most fundamental for the economic emancipation of the race."

Economic issues were one of the most pressing issues affecting African Americans. Writing during the Great Depression, Randolph urged to recognize the importance of labor struggle more than ever. High unemployment was a national issue. However, because of racism Blacks were adversely affected by unemployment. While unemployment could not be annihilated under capitalism, it could be reformed. Randolph noted that every sector of the labor market was being industrialized and mechanized; this meant that more and more workers would lose work. How could this problem be remedied? Sure, charity programs are helpful; however, without higher wages workers would continue to have no economic power—no ability to consume. In addition, workers needed to struggle for shorter work days and weeks, unfettered participation in labor unions (the primary solution to labor injustice), and social legislation (better pensions and labor laws). Finally, Randolph suggested the creation of workers' cooperatives. Major business were agglomerated and created large monopolies which paralyzed workers' ability to become entrepreneurs and stifled their agency as consumers because of price gauging. Workers are pushed further into the proletariat; therefore, by banding together and forming their own business networks and cooperatives they might be able to combat monopoly capital. Workers needed to fight back and organize. Like Du Bois, Randolph argued that education was necessary for workers to combat the dominance of the capitalist. In fact, he too argued that we needed "the best minds of the race to form a sort of Supreme Economic Council" to lead the fight and create the strategies to organize strong Black labor organizations.

The Negro in Politics, 1918

[H]ow is the Negro to know which party to support? Before answering this question may I observe that a party is a body of individuals who agree upon a political program and who strive to gain control of the government in order to secure its adoption. Its campaigns are made possible by a fund created by those persons who desire the adoption of its program. It is natural and plain then that those who supply the funds will control and direct the party.

Now, it is a fact of common knowledge that the Republican and Democratic parties receive their campaign funds from Rockefeller, Morgan, Schwab, Shonts, Ryan, Armour and other capitalists. It is also a fact of common knowledge, [*sic*] that the chief interests of these capitalists are: to make large profits by employing cheap labor and selling their goods at high prices to the public.

Thus, since the chief interests of the workers are more wages, less work, cheaper food, clothing and shelter, it is apparent that their chief interests are opposed to those of their employers—the capitalists which are represented by the Republican and Democratic parties.

Now, since almost all Negroes are workers, live on wages and suffer from the high cost of food, clothing and shelter, it is obvious that the Republican and Democratic parties are opposed to their interests.

But since neither the Republican nor Democratic parties represent the Negroes' interests, the question logically arises as to which party in American politics does?

I maintain that since the Socialist Party is supported financially by working men and working women and since its platform is a demand for the abolition of this class struggle between the employer and the worker, by taking over and democratically managing the sources and machinery of wealth production and exchange, to be operated for social service and not for private profits; and, further, since the Socialist Party has always, both in the United States and Europe, opposed all forms of race prejudice, that the Negro should no longer look upon voting the Republican ticket, as accepting the lesser of two evils; but that it is politically, economically, historically and socially logical and sound for him to reject both evils, the Republican and Democratic parties and select a positive good—Socialism.

The Negro, like any other class, should support that party which represents his chief interests. Who could imagine a brewer or saloonkeeper supporting the Prohibition party?

It's like an undertaker seeking the adoption of a law, if possible, to abolish death.

Such is not less ludicrous, however, than that of a Negro, living in virtual poverty, children without education, wife driven to the kitchen or the wash-tub: continually dispossessed on account of high rents, eating poor food on account of the high cost of food, working 10, 12 and 14 hours a day, and sometimes compelled to become sycophant and clownish for a favor, a "tip," supporting the party of Rockefeller, the party of his employer, whose chief interests are to overwork and underpay him. Let us abolish these contradictions and support our logical patty—the Socialist party.

The State of the Race, 1923

The state of the race, like the state of the world, is chaotic.... It is not unnatural that a group which is the last hired and the first fired, a group which works the hardest and receives the lowest pay, would show signs of moral deterioration under the stresses and strains of the present period of readjustment. Well might the race assemble in a parley to discuss its miserable plight, its apparent degeneration and the probable way out.

Our lines, defensive and offensive, have been pushed back on every sector, political, economic and social. Witness how the Dyer Anti-Lynching Bill, a supreme test of the race's virility and instinct to move forward, died because the overwhelming economic paralysis had sapped our *will* to battle for manhood rights.

Our political policies, the heritage of Civil War days, are barren of achievement. *The job-political-policy of the Old Crowd is insolvent, discredited, repudiated; still political statesmanship goes a-begging.*

In industry we have lost ground. Wages have dropped below other groups doing similar work because we lack bargaining power, which can only come with organization.

In business, our failures have been numerous and disastrous, including banks and enterprises of all kinds. Here we lack credit power, knowledge, and experience.

In the educational field the sinister monster of segregation rears its menacing head, in many cases securing our acquiescence, in others pressing us to yield through murder and threat.

Meanwhile, lynchings and riots and the indescribable depredations of the Ku Klux Klan are religiously employed to drive us back into the black night of moral slavery.

To the solution of these problems, the race has evolved many and diverse schools of thought, working assiduously at cross purposes. A word about them.

The conservative, or right wing, is led, in the field of education and general social policy, by the Tuskegee-Hampton-National Urban League-Howard University group. In this group, the idea of acquiring property, knowledge of trades and professions, and of being law-abiding, thrifty, home-buying, "cast-down-your-bucket-where-you-are" citizens, rather than of the protesting, insurgent variety, is stressed. The Negro leaders of this group are largely satellites of their white benefactors, reflecting the views of conservative, imperial America.

In the center stands the National Association for the Advancement of Colored People, articulating the opinion of liberal Negro America. Through this medium, liberal white America, in alliance with liberal Negro leaders, seek to achieve civil justice for the Negro.

The radical, or left wing, is represented through the MESSENGER and Crusader groups. With this section, political and economic radicalism is the dominant note, treating race as an incident of the larger world problem of class conflict. The radical black and white leaders combine to unite black and white workers.

Finally, there is the Garvey Movement, with its "back-to-Africa" program. The leader of this group has recently come into great disfavor on account of his interview with King Kleagle Clarke and his subsequent defense of the Ku Klux Klan. Such are, in brief, the broad streams of Negro thinking. Like their white correlatives, the Negro schools of thought are torn with dissension, giving birth to many insurgent factions in each. All are engaged in a war of bitter recriminations, tearing each other limb from limb, while the wide, long-suffering Negro masses trudge aimlessly on, victims of the vanities, foibles, indiscretions and vaulting ambitions, ignorance and dishonesty of varying leaderships.

To the foregoing picture of apparent, amazing race insanity the questions arise: whither are we trending? Is there any way out? What can be done to transform this internecine strife into constructive, co-operative effort?

First, may I observe that the Negro, like the capitalists and workers, like Nordics and Mongoloids, like various sects, cults and movements of all types, together with the great "power nations," is passing through a period of severe and relentless race dialectics, each wing, each leadership desperately striving with a sort of Machiavellian "might is right" creed, to establish a supreme mastery in leadership.

Out of this fierce competitive leadership—movement—struggle will be evolved a clearer vision, a firmer and a more rugged morale, an unconquerable will, and a finer and more comprehensive and scientific Race policy and technique of action. The progress of the mass is indifferent to leadership—egoisms. The race will move forward even though movements of well-merited honor and distinction for service fall into the discard. For social, like organic progress, in the main, responds to material imperatives.

I am not distressed, then, as to the ultimate issue of the race in these times of world readjustment, although I am conscious of a definite summons for a orientation in race policy and method, in harmony with the trend of the economic and social forces of the age. Thus a determination of the character and tendency of these socio-economic forces is the chief desideratum, since it is obvious that the march of the Race is advanced or retarded in proportion as it is guided by the most severely tested conclusions of modern science.

In conference after conference we must search for and work out the remedy. There should be specialized conferences whose agenda is economic, political, educational. But specialized parleys do not obviate the need of an All-Race Conference.

There are myriad questions of pressing immediacy which challenge the Race for an answer, an answer which should emanate from some representative body, embodying itself in a broad reasoned policy.

What, for instance, should be the attitude of the Negro in the United States on "the conflict between labor and capital," "immigration," "a future war," "the relation of Negroes to white leadership within and without the Race," "the problem of Negro business in periods of expansion and panics," "education in white and Negro schools and colleges," "radicalism among Negroes," "unemploy the white patrons when the Negro is in a dining room, a pullman car or a theatre as a guest than when he is there, as a servant. Because as a guest he occupies his own particular seat or berth as the other white guests do; whereas a servant, he moves freely among all of the white patrons constantly. Again, the Negro may live under the same roof with the rankest Bourbon Southern Negro hater as a servant; but no Negro must buy a house beside him and live as a neighbor, as an owner. Nor is it a question of economic status here. The Negro who purchases a house in a white neighborhood would be objected to were he a millionaire doctor or a plain ash-cart driver. A white common workman who was able to buy in an exclusive neighborhood would not be objected to, however. Why? Because there is always a desire to see an evidence of inferiority on the part of the Negro, and the capacity of a menial servant is reckoned as such an evidence [*sic*]. But again, why? The answer is simple. If the great laboring masses of people, black and white, are kept forever snarling over the question as to who is superior or inferior, they will never combine or they will take a long time to combine for the achievement of a common benefit: more wages, a shorter work-day and better working conditions. Combination between black and white working people in the South would mean the loss of millions in profits to railroads, cotton magnates, lumber barons and bankers. White railroad workers fear the Negro as a strikebreaker, but still refuse to take him into their unions because of the social pressure that decrees that Negroes are inferior to white men, and hence should be religiously denied contact. This is an instance of a direct blow at the very life of the race as a result of the mandate of segregation.

The Need of a Labor Background, 1927

Following the Civil War, the Negro workers showed considerable interest in organization. The fact that they had been suddenly transformed from a chattel to a wage slave, threw them into the labor market to compete with the white workers. The fires of race bitterness were burning fiercely, and the helpless freedmen were the victims of this bitterness. To offset this disadvantage, Negro workers banded themselves together into unions of their own as well as sought to join with their white brothers. Isaac Myers, according to Charles H. Wesley, in his Negro Labor in the United States, perhaps, the first Negro labor leader, was the leading spirit in the early Negro labor movements.

It is interesting to note, and it was natural, that the Negro labor unions were largely concerned with securing work, new industrial opportunities, rather than increased wages, although they wanted more pay.

Negroes, like the white workers of post-Civil War period, were distressingly unwitting of their way. But the rapidly developing industrial life of the country, the rise of higher forms of business organization, drove the American workers to build up their own organizations to fight for decent wages and working conditions. They also fought for certain civil and social legislation. Negroes, especially, were fighting hard to consolidate their civil status.

The National Labor Union, the first broad, national attempt of Negro workers to get together, was unfortunately turned from its economic program to politics. This doubtless was due to the failure of the efforts of labor, white and black, to get results.

Here and there, the Negro workers have cast their lot with organized labor, when permitted. They have developed but little organized labor psychology, due largely to the fact that they have not had the privilege of actually leading the workers in labor struggles. They are just beginning to experience what it means to face a formidable foe, to close their ranks and fight unflinchingly, under fire. While Negro workers have fought nobly in the ranks of white workers in long industrial struggles, they have not known what it means to have the responsibility for the moral and financial maintenance of a struggle. The Brotherhood of Sleeping Car Porters is supplying this first experience.

Upon this spirit and work must be built a broad Negro Labor movement, which, of course, will be a part, a conscious and articulate part of the American Labor Movement.

Not alone must Negro workers develop a labor union background, but the Negro public, too, must come to know what it means to suffer and sacrifice for a group of black workers fighting for industrial justice.

Such a labor background can best be developed through a definite systematic Negro labor movement, and experience shows that such a movement must be built up by

Negroes themselves. This must be done despite jurisdictional or any other question. Practically, all conditions hindering the economic advancement of Negro workers will vanish before the enlightened organization of Negro workers. Necessity will demonstrate the potency of this fact to white workers. Necessity will also demonstrate the fact that Negro workers must be self-organized. White workers cannot and will not organize them. The history of the Jewish, Italian and Irish workers shows that various groups of workers must organize themselves. In the process of self-organization and self-struggle, Negro workers will develop the necessary labor view-point sense of responsibility, a labor union morale and technique.

The economic self-organization of Negro workers, [*sic*] is most fundamental for the economic emancipation of the race. It also marks the beginning of the period when the Negro earnestly begins to help himself instead of merely looking for his friends to help him.

Hating All White People, 1927

"All coons look alike to me"—was once the title of a popular song which expressed the homely philosophy of a multitude of white people on the Negro. It typified their spiritual attitude toward the Negro as well as his physical effect upon their sense of right.

This opinion had economic consequences, too. Insurance companies made this a pretext or excuse for not insuring colored people, saying one Negro would die for another, and they could not, therefore, protect themselves against fraud. (Finger printing had probably not reached its present stage of accuracy in identification!)

Moreover, the theory had social consequences. When a crime was committed by one Negro, instead of taking pains to detect and to apprehend the real culprit, punishment meted out to "just any Negro" was regarded as sufficient. It was commonplace for a mob to lynch an innocent Negro, then later admit that a mistake had been made, while after the Chinese cynic's philosophy its members would soothe their slippery consciences with the consolation, "well, they are all bad fellows anyway!"

In physics there is a law which reads, Reaction is equal to action in the opposite direction. Which is also true of social physics—human psychology. Thus Negroes concluded that the way to fight fire is with fire. "All white people are alike," countered the Negro to the whites saying, "All coons look alike." Negroes grew to hate or distrust most white people. They acted trustfully in their presence, it is true, after that well known histrionic ability of weaker peoples, yet all the while they had reservations just as they believed and still believe that white people have reservations as to them. Abraham Lincoln gives a rather nice and succinct illustration of this principle in his Douglas debates. Said he, "When our fathers wrote in the Declaration of Independence 'all men are created equal,' they whispered behind their backs, 'all *white* men are created equal.'"

That both the white and the Negro opinion was and is erroneous is easy to expose by analysis, but more difficult to dispel by logic. In their sober moments most Negroes were always willing to admit that John Brown—who gave not only his own life, but the lives of his sons for Negro freedom—was not like all the Negro-hating whites. Today they accord to Clarence Darrow the high place of true friend, despite his being a Democrat and an agnostic—both of which are normally anathema to the Negro mind.

We are not, however, thrown for proof upon such isolated examples as John Brown, Lincoln, Sumner, Lovejoy, Greeley, Lowell, Beecher, Stowe, Garrison, and Darrow. For thinking colored people are well acquainted with Blaine's history of the Ku Klux Klan in the reconstruction period, wherein he points out how that notorious organization murdered over fifty thousand white union soldiers and Yankee teachers who went South to protect and instruct the freedom during those hectic and hazardous days. Likewise all Negroes, who have sojourned or been educated in the South, recall the splendid New England white teachers of Hampton, Howard, Fisk, Virginia Union, Atlanta, and other schools—remember with what industry they labored, with what devotion they toiled, with what unselfishness they chose to do a work for which there was little compensation except ostracism as "nigger-lovers," outside of the joy which one gleans from doing good deeds for others and performing what he considers his duty.

Chicago Negroes today would readily recall Darrow and Rosenwald, the late Victor F. Lawson, and Patrick O'Donnell, Mary McDowell and Jane Addams, and many others whose lives impress them as refuting the absurd principle that "all white people are alike."

A more powerful example as proof that homogeneity of opinion on the race question does not exist among all white people is to be found in a comparison of Negro treatment in different states. For instance, Mississippi has about 950,000 Negroes, and 800,000 whites. South Carolina, 900,000 Negroes, and 800,000 whites. New York has about 250,000 Negroes and 12,000,000 whites; Illinois 200,000 Negroes and 7,000,000 whites.

Mississippi and South Carolina, however, have Jim Crow cars, disfranchisement, discrimination in places of public accommodation and amusement, segregation in education and recreation, notwithstanding their racial populations are about equal numerically. Nevertheless, New York with a population of forty-eight whites to one Negro, and Illinois with thirty-five whites to one Negro, could, more easily than Mississippi and South Carolina adopt Jim Crow cars, disfranchise Negroes, discriminate again them in public accommodation and amusement, segregate in education and recreation. That they do not do so is based upon a difference of opinion among the white populations of those respective states.

In other words, all white peoples are no more alike than all Negroes. The person who asserts such rot writes himself down as either an ignorant or prejudiced bigot, whether he be white or black.

The Economic Crisis of the Negro, 1931

There is no absolute cure for unemployment under the present competitive economic system. But some fundamental remedies are applicable when the behavior of phenomena making for unemployment is adequately known.

Some Remedies

The machine is a challenge to the nation, not only to black and white workers, and this challenge cannot be met by charity, unemployment surveys and temporary jobs, however, important they may be for the *nonce*. No amount of charity is a remedy. Its [sic] a palliative. To feed the hungry and shelter the homeless is necessary but this should not obscure the fundamental problem.

The fact is the workers have worked themselves out of work and will repeat the process in the next five or six years. They have produced more goods and services than they can buy back with the wages they receive. The depression is not so much the result of over production as of under consumption. The people have a physical desire for goods they have no economic power to command.

High Wages

Obviously if the wage earners, the large majority of the population, cannot buy back what they produce which results in piling up large inventories, one remedy will consist in increasing the purchasing power by raising the wage scale. A word about this problem. In the decade from 1919 to 1929, the numbers of workers engaged in manufacturing decreased 449,775. Wages paid in 1929 showed an increase of $809,229,749 over 1919. Whereas the increase in the total value added by manufacture was $6,286,762,484. Put in another way, the employer was able to add $7.70 to the value of his goods for every dollar he gave to his employees in increased wages. The increase in the cost of raw materials in 1929 amounted to only $124,928,718 above the figures for 1919. Thus the value added by manufacture increased $5,352,604,017 more than the increase in raw materials and wages combined.

In 1914, the average wage in American manufacturing establishments was $589, the value added by manufacture per worker was $1,407. Five years later, in 1919, owing largely to the World War, wages had gone up to $1,162, but the value added by manufacture had increased to $2,756. In other words, the workers had received $573 more for creating $1,349 of additional value. Eight years later, in 1927, the average wage was $1,299 and value added by manufacture had gone up to $3,303. The worker was receiving $137 more wages than in 1919 but his production had increased $547 in value. Finally in 1929, the average wage was $1,318, and the value added by manufacture was $3,636. Here we find the workers' wages had increased $19 in two years and the value of his output had gone up $333. Herein lies [sic] the basic cause of recurring depressions. The problem can only be solved by the most scientific industrial statesmanship and social visions.

High wages (real wages) most significant as a remedy because wage earners are the most important and largest group of consumers in the country. Roughly, with their families, they represent 70 per cent of the population and receive an income of something more than 32 billion dollars a year or 36 per cent of the national income; with the earnings of the salaried workers, who represent about 13 per cent of the population, the two groups, while constituting 83 per cent or more of the population, receive only

57 per cent of the nation's income. And they purchase a great deal more than 57 per cent of the nation's consumer goods. On the other hand, the bond and share-holders and property owners, though representing 17 per cent or less of the population, receive about 43 per cent of the nation's income, and most of this income is reinvested in producers' capital, which is, in turn, a source of the production of more commodities the workers cannot buy, thereby, creating huge inventories and commodity congestion or industrial paralysis.

Shorter Work Day and Week

But high wages alone will not solve the problem of depressions. This fact is clearly recognized by the American Federation of Labor which is fighting for a 5-day week and by the Big Four Railroad Brotherhood Unions that have inaugurated a crusade for the 6-hour day. The 6-hour day may absorb nearly a quarter of a million idle rail workers. The progress of productive machinery, too, may eventually render the 4-hour day and the 4-day week practicable. How else will the surplus workers be employed?

Labor Unions

Obviously neither high wages nor the shorter work day or week will come without the struggle of those who will benefit from them. All history attests that every social, economic, political and religious reform has only been won through the utmost struggle, sacrifice and suffering. "Verily, there is no remission of sin except through blood."

Thus, labor organization is the primary and most effective factor in the solution of the problem of seasonal cyclical and technological unemployment, for it is only through the exercise of power, attainable through the organization of wage earners is it possible increasingly to exact higher wages and shorter hours of work. Labor alone will make the necessary struggle, sacrifice and undergo the suffering to stop its own exploitation. But the workers must be organized. Out of 41 million—only 5 million are organized and benefit from fairly high wages and shorter work hours.

Social Legislation

But labor may be helped. Old Age Pensions are essential to those who have paid their price to society in industry in blood, sweat, tears and toil and are no longer able to keep the pace. And while the aged should be pensioned, the deadline against the men of 45 in industry should be removed.

Employment could also be provided by raising the compulsory school age and the adoption of a Federal Child Labor Law which would affect over a million child laborers who are competitors of their fathers in the labor market.

Unemployment insurance, too, like sick, accident, death and fire insurance, should be formulated and enacted as a national measure by Congress. Private charities are far too inadequate. If unemployment, like sickness and death are unavoidable, insurance against it is indispensable.

Of course, free national employment exchanges and government works, planned over a long period, will help, but usually the political red tape incidental to developing public works, prevents the works from beginning until after the depression ends.

Twenty-five Year Plan

Beside the above-mentioned measures is the broad field of self-help by the people. In this field may be listed consumers and producers, cooperatives and workers' credit unions, to mobolize [*sic*] small units of capital into large volumes, for economic strength and protection.

Among Negroes as among farmers and economically weak groups, the Appian Way of private capitalism is difficult if not impossible to trod, especially, in view of the increasing concentration and centralization of financial and industrial power into fewer and fewer hands.

Through a process of interlocking directorships, about 1,000 corporations dominate American business, and at the top of these stand J.P. Morgan and Co., the Bankers Trust and Guarantee Companies, the First National, the National City and Chase National Banks, who have under their control over $74,000,000,000, of corporate assets, equal to more than one-quarter of all the corporate assets of the United States. They practically dominate the business life of the United States, Central and South Americas and exercise a tremendous control in all Europe, Asia and Africa. This amazing empire of capital is more powerful than any political empire or monarchy the world has even seen.

In this regime, the individual, black or white, is helpless. Negroes can only survive modern science and industrialism through consumers' and producers' cooperatives and labor organizations and through the support of labor and social legislation and political action in sympathy with the collective ownership, control and operation of the social productive and distributive instrumentalities in our industrial society. This, however, requires scientific intelligence and a new type of character which can only come through systematic and methodical planning to eventuate through a period of a quarter of a century, much of a piece in principle, with the Russian 5-Year Plan. Much time is needed for the tragedy of it all is that there are but few, either among the leadership or fellowship, who are aware of what is happening to our modern, industrial life.

Major factors in the plan should be workers' and adult education, and a leadership of courage, education and integrity and a will to sacrifice for the economic well-being of the masses.

To the development of such a plan the "best minds" of the race should be called to form a sort of Supreme Economic Council through which such a plan might be formulated and executed. No existing Negro organization can do it. It should embrace the "best brains" in all of the Negro movements, somewhat of the nature of Kelly Miller's Sanhedrin, but smaller. Probably more nearly like the League of Nations which assembles the worlds greatest experts to grapple with world problems such as the Young Plan. No single Negro organization is now strong enough to withstand the economic stress and strain of the coming years. United, scientific, courageous, honest and sacrificial endeavor alone can save the race. Have the leaders of church, school, press, politics, social service and race movements, the will and the spirit and world vision to meet this challenge? Either we accept the challenge, unite and rise or remain as we are and go down and perish. For, forsooth the old order passeth.

11.
BAYARD RUSTIN

Bayard Rustin (1912–1987) was a lifelong civil rights activist. The democratic socialist was one of the primary architects of the modern Civil Rights Movement. Rustin started his career as an activist in the American Friends Service Committee's activist training program. While attending City College in New York City in the late 1930s he joined the Young Communist League (YCL). Until 1941 Rustin worked with the YCL as a youth organizer fighting racial apartheid in the United States.

Bayard Rustin became a prolific public speaker. As the race relations secretary for the Fellowship of Reconciliation (FOR) he traveled the United States organizing meetings to foster positive race relations between antagonistic racial groups. He also served as field secretary for the Congress of Racial Equality (CORE). While working for CORE and FOR he organized Freedom Rides. The Freedom Rides consisted primarily of Northern activists who rode buses and trains throughout the South intentionally violating Jim Crow laws in protest. Like many of his counterparts, his direct action protests landed in him in jail on numerous occasions.

Rustin fought for the rights of various oppressed people, including racial minorities, women, and gays. For example, in 1942, when Japanese Americans were forced into what we conveniently call "internment camps," working with the FOR Rustin helped protect the property of the imprisoned Japanese Americans. In 1945 while still working for the FOR he organized the Free India Committee; as an advocate against imperialism and colonialism he stood aligned with India's movement for freedom from Great Britain. It was actually from this struggle that Rustin began to champion Gandhi's strategy of non-violence. In fact, while Martin Luther King Jr. is most often credited with introducing non-violence to the Civil Rights Movement, it was Rustin who originally vehemently pushed civil rights activists to utilize non-violence. In 1951 he played a pivotal role in the organization of the Committee to Support South African Resistance. He also joined the War Resisters League. Rustin fought for the rights of refugees; later in his career, he worked as the vice chairman of the International Rescue Committee fighting for basic resources such as food, shelter, and healthcare for refugees. He was also chairman of the human rights organization Executive Committee of Freedom House. Finally, Rustin was also a champion for gay rights long before the Gay Liberation Movement in the United States formally began. Rustin was often relegated to behind-the-scenes work and organizing because he was an openly gay man. In fact, he lost his job with the FOR because of his sexual orientation.

From behind the scenes Rustin became one of the leading architects of the mid-twentieth-century phase of the Civil Rights Movement. He helped organize the Prayer Pilgrimage for Freedom (1957), the National Youth marches for Integrated Schools (1958, 1959), and the March on Washington for Jobs and Freedom (1963). In 1964, Rustin assisted in founding the A. Philip Randolph Institute and never ceased labor organizing. He also served as co-chairman of the institute and president of the A. Philip Randolph Educational Fund. Until his demise Rustin never cased fighting for equality.

Overview of Ideas

Bayard Rustin was an advocate of non-violent protest and was famous for his public debates with Malcolm X over the issue. Rustin acknowledged why African Americans might be tempted to utilize aggressive or violent methods in protest. Imagine you were not only deprived of civil liberties but also harassed and physically harmed on a regular basis. How much can one be expected to tolerate? Rustin argued that while turning the cheek would be hard, like Gandhi recognized, "the Negro can attain progress only if he uses, in his struggle, nonviolent direct action." He posited that our ancestors had endured slavery; Black folk have a history of struggle and "enduring suffering." He said, "the Negro possesses qualities essential for nonviolent direct action." Of all people living in the United States, Black folk have successfully adapted the most and under the most horrific conditions.

Rustin did not just borrow the strategy of non-violence from Mahatma Gandhi; he also, like Gandhi, vehemently opposed war. In addition, like A. Philip Randolph, Rustin fought against segregation in the armed forces. He urged that protestors not just fight against Jim Crow and discrimination in travel accommodations but in every public institution. In fact, like Randolph and his abolitionist counterparts, he urged Black people to not fight in a segregated army or for a country that denied them basic rights.

As one of the architects of the March on Washington (1963) and of the mid-twentieth-century phase of the Civil Rights Movement, Rustin actively protested against racial injustice. Like Randolph, he posited that one of the greatest problems facing African Americans was unemployment. Unemployment was worse for Blacks than for Whites and competition over scarce jobs exacerbated race relations. Moreover, the tumultuous economy adversely affected all workers and the government seemed apathetic to their economic problems, namely, unemployment, poor conditions of labor, the automation of labor, and horrible wages. Rustin called upon the government and also advocated for grassroots activism to address these issues.

Rustin's basic solution for social change was full integration in all social institutions, including education, economy, housing, transportation, and military. He argued that it was futile to demand equal opportunities in a declining economy. Sure, Black folk could demand access to jobs but if those jobs were disappearing and/or all these jobs paid deplorable wages, maybe they would not be fighting the real problem. Rustin argued that more quality jobs were needed for all Americans. We needed to lobby and protest the government until they created large-scale programs to address mass unemployment and poverty. Because African Americans are hardest hit by America's economic quagmires they must play a large part in the struggle to rectify these atrocities. African Americans needed to force both the president and Congress to act. Rustin called for an enormous march to the Capitol building, where they would protest Congress. Leaders from civil rights organization, churches, etc. should all take meetings with congressmen and women. This would preferably be done on the same day; this way Congress will be overrun with African American activists making demands. In addition, a delegation should be sent to the White House to make demands. He also advocated having a mass protest rally reporting the outcome of these meetings and addressing the nation. In order to facilitate the March on Washington, and to ensure this plan, Rustin urged the following: that they have a clear statement of purpose, and an analysis of the economic problems impacting workers, particularly minorities, A. Philip Randolph should oversee these documents and they should be approved by the American Labor Council. These documents, plans, and logistics should be endorsed by Martin Luther King Jr., Roy Wilkins, and James Farmer and they should be called on for further monetary support. There must be a meeting combining the voices and interests of "labor, civil rights, church, women, and civic organizations" in which they, too, would make sure the official demands represented their constituencies. Finally, a press conference should be called to release these demands to the press and public. Unlike many of his counterparts, Rustin offered us a clear program for change, with prescriptions for direct action protest. However, his ability to do so was certainly enabled by those who came before him.

Rustin was luckier than his predecessors, in that he actually got to witness the objective results of the protests he led and helped shape. However, after the passage of the Civil Rights Act of 1964 and subsequent legislation eliminating racism de jure Rustin became increasing interested in racism de facto. He posited that it was essential to transform the protest movement that garnered those rights into a political movement. Rustin argued that what was needed now was not an isolated protest movement but a solid political movement to continue to meet the needs of African Americans and the American rabble. This was needed now more than ever. Racism de facto would be harder to fight. Now that barriers to success had ostensibly been removed it would be harder to justify race based programs. Activists would be needed to keep the government actively creating and maintaining programs to help end racism and ensure equal opportunity and access to basic social institutions. Speaking directly to leaders such as Malcolm X, Rustin posited that self-help ideology was the wrong direction. You cannot put the burden to solve racism de jure and poverty solely on the backs of the oppressed. Moreover, Black Nationalists lacked realistic strategy; calling for militancy was not a strategy. Like Randolph, Rustin proffered that what was needed now was an expansion of the public sector. He advocated for radical programs, which should include mass funding for education, housing, and anti-poverty programs. He said people need full employment; they need unfettered access to labor unions. Only a unification of progressive forces, containing people from various progressive movements, of different races and ethnic groups could achieve this.

As time passed, by the 1970s, as second wave feminism and gay liberation were burgeoning, Rustin was now able to be more publicly vocal about the civil rights of other oppressed minorities. While Rustin was always a staunch supporter of women's rights, as an openly gay man he was not able to be vocal about gay rights during the Civil Rights Movement. It was no accident that Martin Luther King was brought in as a figurehead for the movement and one of its primary architects—Rustin did not take a public role. In regards to the second wave of the women's movement, Rustin said that while he supported their efforts, they were not radical enough. They rightfully demanded reproductive freedom, day care centers for working class mothers, and equal opportunities in employment and education. However, these feminists failed to contextualize their demands or to see how they were all part of a larger problem in the United States. For example, demands for access to free abortions could be part of a larger movement for socialized medicine. Rather than lobbying for a few day care centers why not protest for greater funding for education and expansion of K-12 education to include day care? Rather than just demanding equal access to employment for women, why not demand full employment for all? Part of this problem stems from the bourgeois sensibilities and social position of its main leaders and participants. If middle class women dominated the movement it is no wonder why they did not make these larger demands. Finally, the marginalization of Black women from the dominant movement was inexcusable. Black women seem to better understand the larger problems in American society and therefore if placed in leadership roles within the movement would be more apt to incorporate the aims seen as most crucial to Rustin. Rustin understood that oppression for Black women was not just about their sex but conditioned by sex, race, and class.

Bayard Rustin also became extremely vocal about gay rights. Gay individuals are entitled to civil rights and the ability like all oppressed groups to "fight for their human rights." The gay and lesbian community needed to no longer be fearful, but should conquer their own self-loathing, overcome self-denial, and realize they had a political fight to wage. Just as Black civil rights activists were not fighting to get white-cloak-wearing racists to love them, gay activists were not either. However, what they could fight for and obtain is the right to end anti-gay violence and other forms of public gay bashing. They could fight for civil rights. Gay activists needed to lobby for legislation to protect their rights as equal citizens. Bayard Rustin fought for the rights of oppressed people throughout his life.

The Negro and Nonviolence, 1942

An increasingly militant group has it in mind to demand now, with violence if necessary, the rights it has long been denied. "If we must die abroad for democracy we can't have," I heard a friend of mine say, "then we might as well die right here, fighting for our rights."

This is a tragic statement. It is tragic also how isolated the average Negro feels in his struggle. The average Negro has largely lost faith in middle-class whites. In his hour of need he seeks not "talk" but dynamic action. He looks upon the middle-class idea of long-term educational and cultural changes with fear and mistrust. He is interested only in what can be achieved immediately by political pressure to get jobs, decent housing, and education for his children. He describes with disgust the efforts in his behalf by most middle-class Negro and white intellectuals as "pink tea methods—sometimes well-meanin' but gettin' us nowhere." It is for this reason, in part, that the March on Washington movement, aiming to become a mass movement, has tended toward "black nationalism." Its leadership, originally well motivated, now rejects the idea of including whites in its constituency or leadership. One local official said, "These are Negroes' problems and Negroes will have to work them out."

The March on Washington movement is growing but at best is only a partial answer to the present need. While the movement already exerts some real political pressure (President Roosevelt set up the FEPC at its request), it has no program, educational or otherwise, for meeting immediate conflict. To demand rights but not to see the potential danger in such a course, or the responsibility to develop a means of meeting that danger, seems tragic.

Many Negroes see mass violence coming. Having lived in a society in which church, school, and home problems have been handled in a violent way, the majority at this point are unable to conceive of a solution by reconciliation and nonviolence. I have seen schoolboys in Arkansas laying away rusty guns for the "time when." I have heard many young men in the armed forces hope for a machine-gun assignment "so I can turn it on the white folks." I have seen a white sailor beaten in Harlem because three Negroes had been "wantin' to get just one white" before they died. I have heard hundreds of Negroes hope for a Japanese military victory, since "it don't matter who you're a slave for."

These statements come not only from bitterness but from frustration and fear as well. In many parts of America the Negro, in his despair, is willing to follow any leadership seemingly sincerely identified with his struggle if he is convinced that such leadership offers a workable method. In this crisis those of us who believe in the nonviolent solution of conflict have a duty and an opportunity. In all those places where we have a voice, it is our high responsibility to indicate that the Negro can attain progress only if he uses, in his struggle, nonviolent direct action—a technique consistent with the ends he desires. Especially in this time of tension we must point out the practical necessity of such a course.

Nonviolence as a method has within it the demand for terrible sacrifice and long suffering, but, as Gandhi has said, "freedom does not drop from the sky." One has to struggle and be willing to die for it. J. Holmes Smith has indicated that he looks to the American Negro to assist in developing, along with the people of India, a new dynamic force for the solution of conflict that not merely will free these oppressed people but will set an example that may be the first step in freeing the world.

Certainly the Negro possesses qualities essential for nonviolent direct action. He has long since learned to endure suffering. He can admit his own share of guilt and has to be pushed hard to become bitter. He has produced, and still sings, such songs as "It's Me, Oh Lord, Standin' in the Need of Prayer" and "Nobody Knows the Trouble I've Seen." He follows this last tragic phrase by a salute to God—"Oh! Glory, Hallelujah." He is creative and has learned to adjust himself to conditions easily. But above all he possesses a rich religious heritage and today finds the church the center of his life.

Yet there are those who question the use of nonviolent direct action by Negroes in protesting discrimination, on the grounds that this method will kindle hitherto dormant racial feeling. But we must remember that too often conflict is already at hand and that there is hence a greater danger: the inevitable use of force by persons embittered by injustice and unprepared for nonviolence. It is a cause for shame that millions of people continue to live under conditions of injustice while we make no effective effort to remedy the situation.

Those who argue for an extended educational plan are not wrong, but there must also be a plan for facing *immediate* conflicts. Those of us who believe in nonviolent resistance can do the greatest possible good for the Negro, for those who exploit him, for America, and for the world by becoming a real part of the Negro community, thus being in a position to suggest methods and to offer leadership when troubles come.

Identification with the Negro community demands considerable sacrifice. The Negro is not to be won by words alone, but by an obvious consistency in words and deeds. The *identified* person is the one who fights side by side with him for justice. This demands being so integral a part of the Negro community in its day-to-day struggle, so close to it in similarity of work, so near its standard of living that when problems arise he who stands forth to judge, to plan, to suggest, or to lead is really at one with the Negro masses.

Our war resistance is justified only if we see that an adequate alternative to violence is developed. Today, as the Gandhian forces in India face their critical test, we can add to world justice by placing in the hands of thirteen million black Americans a workable and Christian technique for the righting of injustice and the solution of conflict.

Civil Disobedience, Jim Crow, and the Armed Forces, 1948

As a follower of the principles of Mahatma Gandhi, I am an opponent of war and of war preparations and an opponent of universal military training and conscription; but entirely apart from that issue I hold that segregation in any part of the body politic is an act of slavery and an act of war. Democrats will agree that such acts are to be resisted, and more and more leaders of the oppressed are responsibly proposing nonviolent civil disobedience and noncooperation [*sic*] as the means.

On March 22, 1948, A. Philip Randolph and Grant Reynolds, trusted Negro leaders, told President Truman that Negroes "do not propose to shoulder another gun for democracy abroad while they are denied democracy here at home." A few days later, when Mr. Randolph testified before the Senate Armed Services Committee, he declared that he openly would advise and urge Negro and white youth not to submit to Jim Crow military institutions. At this statement, Senator Wayne Morse interrupted and warned Mr. Randolph that "the Government would apply the legal doctrine of treason to such conduct."

This is a highly regrettable statement for a United States Senator to make. Certainly throughout Asia and Africa millions must have agreed with the lovers of freedom here who reasoned that if treason is involved, it is the treason practiced by reactionaries in the North and South who struggle to maintain segregation and discrimination and who thus murder the American creed. The organizers and perpetuators of segregation are as much the enemy of America as any foreign invader. The time has come when they are not merely to be protested. They must be resisted.

The world and the United States should know that there are many younger leaders, both black and white, in positions of responsibility who, not wishing to see democracy destroyed from within, will support Mr. Randolph and Mr. Reynolds.

We know that men should not and will not fight to perpetuate for themselves caste and second-class citizenship. We know that men cannot struggle for someone else's freedom in the same battle in which they fasten semi-slavery more securely upon themselves. While there is a very-real question whether any army can bring freedom, certainly a Jim Crow army cannot. On the contrary, to those it attempts to liberate, it will bring discrimination and segregation such as we are now exporting to Europe and to South America. To subject young men at their most impressionable age to a forced caste system, as now outlined in the Universal Military Training and Selective Service bills, not only is undemocratic but will prove to be suicidal.

Segregation in the military must be resisted if democracy and peace are to survive. Thus civil disobedience against caste is not merely a right but a profound duty. If carried out in the spirit of good will and non-violence, it will prick the conscience of America as Gandhi's campaigns stirred the hearts of men the world over.

Therefore, in the future I shall join with others to advise and urge Negroes and white people not to betray the American ideal by accepting Jim Crow in any of our institutions, including the armed services. Further, I serve notice on the government that, to the extent of my resources, I shall assist in the organization of disciplined cells across the nation to advise resistance and to provide spiritual, financial, and legal aid to resisters.

I sincerely hope that millions of Negroes and white people who cherish freedom will pledge themselves now to resist Jim Crow everywhere, including the military establishments. Thereby the United States may, in part, achieve the moral leadership in world affairs for which we so vigorously strive. I urge you to register this intention now with your Senators and Congressmen.

It is my supreme desire that those who resist will do so in that spirit which is without hatred, bitterness, or contention. I trust that all resisters will hold firm to the true faith that only good-will resistance, in the end, is capable of overcoming injustice.

Preamble to the March on Washington, 1963

1. The one hundred years since the signing of the Emancipation Proclamation have witnessed no fundamental government action to terminate the economic subordination of the American Negro. Today the ratio of unemployment among Negroes and whites remains two-to-one, while the income of Negroes is roughly half that of whites. Not only have these disparities remained constant over decades, but in the present period they have absolutely widened. Their effect on race relations generally can only frustrate the limited gains recently registered

in school integration and in equal accommodations in public facilities and transportation.

2. The condition of Negro labor is inseparable from that of white labor; the immediate crisis confronting black labor grows out of the unresolved crisis in the national economy. History shows that the peculiar disadvantages suffered by the Negro as the result of segregation and discrimination are alleviated in times of relatively full employment and aggravated when employment is high. So far the federal government has produced no serious answers to the problem of rising unemployment; each succeeding recession has produced an upward revision of minimal unemployment rates, and Congress and the White House appear complacent in the face of current unemployment figures of 6 percent.

3. The current crisis is overwhelmingly the result of structural unemployment. Thousands of workers have been displaced by automation, rendered economically functionless in modern industrial society. Negroes have been disproportionately victimized, for automation has attacked precisely those unskilled and semi-skilled jobs to which Negroes have traditionally been relegated. Moreover, the persistence of racial discrimination on a national scale has closed to Negroes who have lacked the training to compete for skilled jobs, even the limited opportunities for job retraining available to whites. Statistics speak clearly: 25 percent of the long-term unemployed are Negroes.

4. Automation coupled with a tremendous population increase is seriously limiting job opportunities for all youth particularly Negroes in the 16–21 age group. Fifty percent of Negro youth 16–21 are idle. A disproportionate number of the eight million school dropouts a year are Negroes.

5. These indisputable facts dictate certain strategies for the overall progress of the Negro in the present period:

   a. Integration in the fields of education, housing, transportation, and public accommodations will be of limited extent and duration so long as fundamental economic inequality along racial lines persists. Already the slowdown in the rate of progress in many of these fields is evident in the widespread characterization of recent gains as "tokenism." An economically disprivileged people is not able to utilize institutions and facilities geared to middle-class incomes and to an inflated economy. They cannot afford to patronize the better restaurants, integrated or not; their own financial circumstances segregate them from middle-class housing; they cannot afford to travel, whether buses are integrated or not, or send their children to college.

   b. The demand for "merit hiring" practices is obsolete. When a racial disparity in unemployment has been firmly established in the course of a century, the change-over to "equal opportunities" merely prevents a further divergence in the relative status of the races but does not wipe out the cumulative handicaps of the Negro worker. In addition, "equal opportunities" in a declining national economy means, at best, only an equal opportunity to share in the decline.

   c. Clearly there is no need for Negroes to demand jobs that do not exist. Nor do Negroes seek to displace white workers as both are being displaced by machines. Negroes seek instead, *as an integral part of their own struggle as a people*, the creation of more jobs for all Americans. Therefore, the project described below must be a massive effort involving coordinated participation by all progressive sectors of the liberal, labor, religious, and Negro communities. Only such an all-embracing effort can call for a broad national governmental action on a scale adequate to meet the problem of unemployment, especially as it relates to minority groups. At the same time, we believe that the Negro community has an especially important role to play. For the dynamic that has motivated Negroes to withstand with courage and dignity the intimidation and violence they have endured in their own struggle against racism, in all its forms, may now be the catalyst which mobilizes all workers behind demands for a broad and fundamental program of economic justice.

From Protest to Politics: The Future of the Civil Rights Movement, 1964

How can the (perhaps misnamed) civil rights movement deal with this problem? Before trying to answer, let me first insist that the task of the movement is vastly complicated by the failure of many whites of good will to understand the nature of our problem. There is widespread assumption that the removal of artificial racial barriers should result in the automatic integration of the Negro into all aspects of American life. This myth is fostered by facile analogies with the experience of various ethnic immigrant groups, particularly the Jews. But the analogies with the Jews do not hold for three simple but profound reasons. First, Jews have a long history as a literate people, a resource which has afforded them opportunities to advance in the academic and professional worlds, to achieve intellectual status even in the midst of economic hardship, and to evolve sustaining value systems in the context of ghetto life. Negroes, for the greater part of their presence in this country, were forbidden by law to read or write. Second, Jews have a long history of family stability, the importance of which in terms of aspiration and self-image is obvious. The Negro family structure was totally destroyed by slavery and with it the possibility of cultural transmission (the right of Negroes to marry and rear children is barely a century old). Third, Jews are white and have the *option* of relinquishing their cultural-religious identity, intermarrying, passing, etc. Negroes, or at least the overwhelming majority of them, do not have this option. There is also a fourth, vulgar reason. If the Jewish and Negro communities are not comparable in terms of education, family structure, and color, it is also true that their respective economic roles bear little resemblance.

I would advise those who think that self-help is the answer to familiarize themselves with the long history of such efforts in the Negro community, and to consider why so many foundered on the shoals of ghetto life. It goes without saying that any effort to combat demoralization and apathy is desirable but we must understand that demoralization in the Negro community is largely a common-sense response to an objective reality. Negro youths have no need of statistics to perceive, fairly accurately, what their odds are in American society. Indeed, from the point of view of motivation, some of the healthiest Negro youngsters I know are juvenile delinquents. Vigorously pursuing the American dream of material acquisition and status, yet finding the conventional means of attaining it blocked off, they do not yield to defeatism but resort to illegal (and often ingenious) methods. They are not alien to American culture. They are, in Gunnar Myrdal's phrase, "exaggerated Americans." To want a Cadillac is not un-American; to push a cart in the garment center is. If Negroes are to be persuaded that the conventional path (school, work, etc.) is superior, we had better provide evidence which is now sorely lacking. It is a double cruelty to harangue Negro youth about education and training when we do not know what jobs will be available for them. When a Negro youth can reasonably foresee a future free of slums, when the prospect of gainful employment is realistic, we will see motivation and self-help in abundant enough quantities.

Meanwhile, there is an ironic similarity between the self-help advocated by many liberals and the doctrines of the Black Muslims Professional sociologists, psychiatrists, and social workers have expressed amazement at the Muslims' success in transforming prostitutes and dope addicts into respectable citizens. But every prostitute the Muslims convert to a model of Calvinist virtue the ghetto replaces with two more. The Muslims, dedicated as they are to maintenance of the ghetto, are powerless to effect substantial moral reform. So too with every other group or program which is not aimed at the destruction of slums, their causes and effects. Self-help efforts must be geared, directly or indirectly, to mobilizing people into power units capable of effecting social change. That is, their goal must be genuine self-help, not merely self-improvement. Obviously, where self-improvement activities succeed in imparting to their participants a feeling of some control over their environment, those involved may find their appetites for change whetted; they may move into the political arena.

Let me sum up what I have thus far been trying to say. The civil rights movement is evolving from a protest movement into a full-fledged *social movement*—an evolution calling its very name into question. It is now concerned not merely with removing the barriers to full *opportunity* but with achieving the fact of *equality*. From sit-ins and Freedom Rides we have gone into rent strikes, boycotts, community organization, and political action. As a consequence of this natural evolution, the Negro today finds himself stymied by obstacles of far greater magnitude than the legal barriers he was attacking before: automation, urban decay, de facto school segregation. These are problems which, while conditioned by Jim Crow, do not vanish upon its demise. They are more deeply rooted in our socioeconomic order; they are the result of the total society's failure to meet not only the Negro's needs but human needs generally.

The Negro struggle has hardly run its course; and it will not stop moving until it has been utterly defeated or won substantial equality. But I fail to see how the movement can be victorious in the absence of radical programs for full employment, the abolition of slums, the reconstruction of our educational system, new definitions of work and leisure. Adding up the cost of such programs, we can only conclude that we are talking about a refashioning of our political economy. It has been estimated, for example, that the price of replacing New York City's slums with public housing would be $17 billion. Again, a multibillion-dollar federal public works program, dwarfing the currently proposed $2 billion program, is required to reabsorb unskilled and semi-skilled workers into the labor market and this must be done if Negro workers in these categories are to be employed. "Preferential treatment" cannot help them.

I am not trying here to delineate a total program, only to suggest the scope of economic reforms which are most immediately related to the plight of the Negro community. One could speculate on their political implications—whether, for example, they do not indicate the obsolescence of state government and the superiority of regional structures as viable units of planning. Such speculations aside, it is clear that Negro needs cannot be satisfied unless we go beyond what has so far been placed on the agenda. How are these radical objectives to be achieved? The answer is simple, deceptively so: *through political power.*

Neither that movement nor the country's twenty million black people can win political power alone. We need allies. The future of the Negro struggle depends on whether the contradictions of this society can be resolved by a coalition of progressive forces which becomes the *effective* political majority in the United States. I speak of the coalition which staged the March on Washington, passed the Civil Rights Act, and laid the basis for the Johnson landslide—Negroes, trade unionists, liberals, and religious groups.

The role of the civil rights movement in the reorganization of American political life is programmatic as well as strategic. We are challenged now to broaden our social vision, to develop functional programs with concrete objectives. We need to propose alternatives to technological unemployment, urban decay, and the rest. We need to be calling for public works and training, for national economic planning, for federal aid to education, for attractive public housing all—this on a sufficiently massive scale to make a difference. We need to protest the notion that our integration into American life, so long delayed, must now proceed in an atmosphere of competitive scarcity instead of in the security of abundance which technology makes possible. We cannot claim to have answers to all the complex problems of modern society. That is too much to ask of a movement still battling barbarism in Mississippi. But we can agitate the right questions by probing at the contradictions which still stand in the way of the Great Society. The questions having been asked, motion must begin in the larger society, for there is a limit to what Negroes can do alone.

Black Women and Women's Liberation, 1972

Contrary to popular impression, the woman most discriminated against is not the white suburban housewife but the mother of a ghetto household.... Black women, in reality, hear the drumroll of the movement for female equality much more loudly than do whites. And, contrary to popular myth, poor women respond to a majority of the issues of the feminist movement more fervently and in greater numbers than do the middle-class housewives and professionals who comprise the core of strength of women's activist groups.

But while endorsing the broad aims of feminists, black women differ sharply over which issues they consider most fundamental to equality. While white women find it difficult to define and quantify equality, black women see equality as a less elusive ideal. For black women believe that equality to a large degree can still be measured by more jobs, more and better-quality low and moderate-income housing, improved public education, quality health care, and programs to help the poor and elderly

I do not mean to imply that feminism's psychological implications do not concern black women. Black women are in fact more dissatisfied with their social roles. More deeply than whites they are distressed that their sexual role may have limited their chances for self-fulfillment, are convinced that doors to success which are open to men are shut for women, and often consider their years of schooling wasted.

These are not subjective evaluations: they are the innermost sentiments of black women as expressed in polls and studies. Yet to accept their validity is to raise significant questions about the course of the women's liberation movement today. For black women, no matter how profound their sympathy for the issues of feminist equality, have largely ignored the women's liberation movement.

When women's liberation rose to prominence several years ago there were those who warned that should it fail to alter the essentially middle-class nature of its appeal it would be unable to win the support of Negroes and white working-class women.

And while some feminist leaders have acknowledged this weakness we still find that black women, poor women, and working women, discriminated against and alienated as they are, remain unenthusiastic and occasionally antagonistic to women's liberation.

Too often they find that women's liberation is concerned with rhetoric and consciousness raising to the neglect of social change. Sometimes Gloria Steinem, Betty Friedan, and other leaders of women's rights arouse focus on issues so irrelevant to the personal lives of working people as to appear dilettantish.

But there is a more basic reason for black disenchantment. Black people, because they have lived with discrimination and struggled to overcome built-in prejudice, cannot relate to a cause which separates and isolates social problems on the basis of sex. They understand from personal experience that discrimination, poverty, and the miseries they bring are not sexually exclusive.

Thus while black women have remained conscious of the special problems they encounter as women, they are also cognizant that discrimination is essentially a matter of class and race.

This is reflected in their choice of social activism. In past years black women played important roles in the civil rights movement. They were the first to respond to Dr. King when he organized the Montgomery bus boycott and assumed leadership positions in this and many other campaigns.

More recently blacks have branched into other areas, organizing domestic workers, hospital workers, and school paraprofessionals, long the most impoverished and exploited of the female work force.

Thus in the most important areas of social activism—civil rights campaigns, labor organization, tenant rights groups, and the like—black women have carved remarkable records of accomplishment. Their leadership has been constructive and responsible, their militancy indisputable. And they bear with them the conviction that what they are doing is important not only in itself but also within the context of the larger movements for human dignity and sexual, racial, and social equality.

From Montgomery to Stonewall, 1986

In 1955 when Rosa Parks sat down and began the Montgomery Bus Protest, if anyone had said that it would be the beginning of a most extraordinary revolution, most people, including myself, would have doubted it.... Consider now gay rights. In 1969, in New York of all places, Greenwich Village, a group of gay people were in a bar. Recall that the 1960s was a period of extreme militancy—there were antiwar demonstrations, civil rights demonstrations, and women's rights demonstrations. The patrons of the bar added gay rights demonstration to the list. The events began when several cops moved into the bar to close it down, a very common practice in that period, forcing many gay bars to go underground. The cops were rough and violent, and, for the first time in the history of the United States, gays, as a collective group, fought back—and not just that night but the following night, and the next, and the night after that.

That was the beginning of an extraordinary revolution, similar to the Montgomery Bus Boycott in that it was not expected that anything extraordinary would occur. As in the case of the women who left the Russian factory, and as in the case of Rosa Parks who sat down in the white part of the bus, something began to happen. People began to protest. They began to fight for the right to live in dignity, the right to resist arbitrary behavior on the part of authorities, the right essentially to be one's self in every respect, and the right to be protected under law. In other words, people began to fight for their human rights.

Gay people must continue this protest. This will not be easy, in part because homosexuality remains an identity that is subject to a "we/they" distinction. People who would not say, "I am like this, but black people are like that," or "we are like this, but women are like that," or "we are like this, but Jews are like that," find it extremely simple to say, "homosexuals are like that, but we are like this." That's what makes our struggle the central struggle of our time, the central struggle for democracy and the central struggle for human rights. If gay people do not understand that, they do not understand the opportunity before them, nor do they understand the terrifying burdens they carry on their shoulders.

There are four burdens, which gays, along with every other despised group, whether it is blacks following slavery and reconstruction, or Jews fearful of Germany, must address. The first is to recognize that one must overcome fear. The second is overcoming self-hate. The third is overcoming self-denial. The fourth burden is more political. It is to recognize that the job of the gay community is not to deal with extremists who would castrate us or put us on an island and drop an H-bomb on us. The fact of the matter is that there is a small percentage of people in America who understand the true nature of the homosexual community. There is another small percentage who will never understand us. Our job is not to get those people who dislike us to love us. Nor was our aim in the civil rights movement to get prejudiced white people to love us. Our aim was to try to create the kind of America, legislatively, morally, and psychologically, such that even though some whites continued to hate us, they could not openly manifest that hate. That's our job today: to control the extent to which people can publicly manifest antigay sentiment.

12.
MARY McLEOD BETHUNE

Mary McLeod Bethune (1875–1955) was a famous educator and political activist. She was most well known for founding the Daytona Normal and Industrial Institute for Girls in 1904 and for her role as an advisor to Franklin D. Roosevelt. In 1923 Bethune's school merged with the Cookman Institute for Men and became Bethune–Cookman College. She served as Bethune–Cookman College's president until 1942. In addition to the notoriety she gained from her work as an educator she also gained political influence once appointed to work for Franklin D. Roosevelt's administration. From 1936 to 1943 Bethune worked as the Director of the Division of Negro Affairs of the National Youth Administration. This position allowed Bethune to continue her work in education, as she assisted young people gaining skills and jobs. In addition the appointment made her the first African American, male or female, to run a federal agency. She became a key advisor to Roosevelt as part of his "Black Cabinet," on issues related to race and African Americans in the United States.

Bethune was a spokeswoman for the rights of African Americans and women. She worked with the National Association of Colored Women (NACW). From 1917 to 1925 she served as the president of the NACW's Florida chapter. In 1924 Bethune even triumphed over Ida B. Wells-Barnett for the presidency of the organization. From 1920 to 1925 she was the president of the Southeastern Federation of Colored Women's Clubs. In 1935, she founded the National Council of Negro Women, an organization which like Bethune–Cookman College still thrives today.

Throughout her life Bethune worked vigorously with government agencies and non-governmental political action groups to enhance the lives of African Americans and to achieve her dream of improving American democracy. Bethune worked for: the National Child Welfare Commission, Commission on Home Building and Home Ownership, Special Advisor to President Franklin Roosevelt on Minority Affairs, Director of the Division of Negro Affairs National Youth Administration, Special Assistant to the Secretary of War for the selection of candidates for Officer Training School for WAACS, Committee of Twelve for National Defense, and was an Official Delegate to the second inauguration of William V.S. Tubman as President of Liberia. In the private sphere Bethune also worked with: the National Association for the Advancement of Colored People, National Urban League, Commission on Interracial Cooperation, Southern Conference for Human Welfare,

Southern Conference Educational Fund, League of Women Voters, and Americans for Democratic Action.

Overview of Ideas

Mary McLeod Bethune was a moderate political leader. Like many of her counterparts such as Randolph and Rustin she offered concrete solutions to the quagmires impacting Black folk. Writing in 1940 she argued that political participation and democratic reform was essential to future progress for African Americans. In fact she wrote to President Roosevelt suggesting the appointments of Black people to the Civil Service Commission, to the Council on Personal Administration, to National Defense, judges and district attorney positions, to the Department of Commerce, to the Department of Labor, Department of Agriculture, to the Federal Security Agency, to the Federal Works Agency, to Federal Loan Agencies, to the Public Health Department, and the Maritime Labor Board. African Americans are not represented in government and not just in Congress. Without political representation in various divisions and agencies within the federal government who would speak to the African American community's needs?

In 1951 Bethune also addressed President Truman. Strategically, reminiscent of Frederick Douglass and foreshadowing Barack Obama, she argued that winning the Cold War, defeating Communism, and strengthening our global relationships would not be enough to demonstrate that we were the pinnacle of democracy. "We believe that in order to overcome communism and to make the United States an impregnable citadel of freedom and democracy, our country must stand above reproach in the treatment it accords all of its peoples." By extending full rights and dignity to African Americans we would be demonstrating to the world that we live up to the principles we say we hold so dear; we would be the democracy we claim to be. Bethune said in order to accomplish this goal the Truman administration would need to end all racial segregation, particularly in the military, appoint qualified Black people to administrative and policy-making positions, appoint Black women and men to new government agencies as they are created, and have African Americans serve as diplomats and/or representatives of our country in global affairs.

According to Bethune, American democracy was incomplete. By struggling for racial equality and equal opportunity, "we will be cleansing the soul of nation that would lend the world to peace" and bring about true democracy. True democracy meant providing quality jobs, quality housing, and education. However, there are no free rides or handouts in this country.

Along with many conservatives and moderates, Bethune believed strongly that African Americans could not just rely on the government to correct the structural deficiencies and inequalities originally created by slavery. African Americans needed to build up their own communities. To be an American citizen required personal responsibility. "We have no right to be walking dead." Black people must participate in government, the economy, schools, etc. and become involved in making them better. Individuals must take responsibility for their own progress and the well-being of their community. Much like Booker T. Washington, Bethune posited that individuals must choose a vocation that allows them to contribute to society. The individual must be self-motivated. "His philosophy is the impetus which spurs him on to achievement." Opportunity and success are not just things afforded to individuals by the state; they are something the individual must strive for. She continually emphasized individual vigilance and perseverance. She emphasized personal responsibility. Citizenship is not just an entitlement; it is something you have to work for. Bringing about true democracy meant that African Americans needed to avail themselves of the political process and vote. In addition, women needed to step forward and assume leadership roles in democratic reform and social protest. "It must be the women of our race and our nation that must supply the driving force and the inspiration needed as we take the up-hill road to peace."

Bethune, a feminist and fighter for women's rights, spoke and wrote extensively about the contributions of Black women to American society. African American women have been the backbone of our society since their arrival in this country. They have contributed to the development and growth of every basic social institution, from the economy to the church. They have healed the sick and written books that have driven people to tears. For all these accomplishments Bethune declared, "I am glad that I am a Woman!" She, too, created schools for Black children, worked within government, and assisted in getting African Americans to vote. Women like Bethune were vital to the progress of African Americans and the United States as a whole.

Bethune, like most of her counterparts, emphasized the importance of education. Through education, African Americans could acquire the cultural capital, the knowledge they needed to be successful. In addition, integrated education would provide the necessary social contact between races to minimize racism and allow for races to begin living harmoniously with one another. In addition, as we will see with Martin Luther King Jr., faith and Christian principles such as love thy neighbor and brotherhood were needed to reconcile racial tensions. In addition, while not typically identified as a Pan-Africanist, Bethune did implore Black people to become unified. She wrote, "the problem of color is world-wide. It is found in Africa and Asia, Europe, and South America. I appeal to American Negroes—North, South, East and West—to recognize their common problems and unite to solve them." Only unity amongst Black people, amongst African American leadership, and by creating alliances and relationships with Whites could Black people reach their full potential.

Some of the Things Negroes Desire: A Memorandum to the President, 1940

MEMORANDUM   January 12, 1940

To: The President
From: Mary McLeod Bethune
Subject: Some of the Things Negroes Desire

1. Civil Service
    a) Elimination of the photograph and use of the finger print
    b) Appointment of a Negro to the Civil Service Commission

2. Appointment of Negro to be a member of the Council on Personnel Administration.
3. National Defense
    a) Appointment of Assistant to the Secretary of War. (During the last World War, Emmett J. Scott served as the Assistant to the Secretary.)
    b) Appointment of an appreciable percentage of Negroes, by Executive Order, to West Point and Annapolis, so that some of the candidates will be adjudged qualified.
5. Judiciary [*sic* no number 4 in original text]
    Appointment of Federal Judge in the United States
    Appointment of Negro United States District Attornies [*sic*]
6. Commerce
    Appointment of Negro in Administrative position in Department of Commerce
7. Labor
    Appointment of Negro in administrative position in Department of Labor
8. Agriculture
    Appointment of Negro in administrative position in Department of Agriculture
9. Federal Security Agency
    a) Negro Assistant to Administrator
    b) Appointment of additional personnel in Office of Education
    c) Appointment of administrative assistant to Social Security Board
10. Federal Works Agency
    Appointment of Negro administrative assistant to coordinate various divisions
11. Federal Loan Agency
    Appointment of Negro in Federal Housing and Home Owners Loan Corporation
12. United States Public Health
    Appointment of additional Negro personnel in Public Health Department
13. Maritime Labor Board
    Appointment of Negro in administrative position
14. Appointments of Negroes to positions that have been lost during the last seven years.
    1. Register of the Treasury
    2. Minister to Haiti
    3. Auditor of the Navy
    4. Collectors of Customs in the Port of New York Charleston, S.C. and others.

Americans All: Which Way America?, 1947

We are approaching a critical juncture in the history of the World, and the destiny of our Nation. One road can take us from suspicion of other nations, to disagreement, conflict and war of unimagined fervors that would blast civilization, as we know it, from the face of the Earth. That road is easy and all down hill. The other road is up-hill, tortuous and rocky and only for strong men to tread. It is the road of national and international understanding, resolving of differences, compromise, agreement and peace, which can lead to fields brighter in promise than the Sun of the Renaissance opened to man.

Which way, America? All of us are proud to see our nation assume its rightful place of world leadership. Proud to see our way of life help up before the men of all races and creeds and colors as a way of life that holds promise for the little men of the Earth everywhere. We are glad to fellow our leaders on the path of bringing Democracy to war-torn Europe and Asia—to Greece and Turkey—to China, Korea, Japan, Italy and Germany. We are proud to be part of a nation that stretches out the hand of Christian fellowship to raise up the brother who had fall on into the dust, and help him to help himself.

Is it to be the Democracy of the lynching mob and flaunted law? Of intimidation and threat and fear? Or, is it to be the Democracy of law and order, of the 14th Amendment really enforced, of the sanctity of the individual, of the protection of person and home against brute strength and fear? The shame of Monroe or Greenville is no more the business of Georgia or South Carolina only. Riot in the streets is no longer the concern of Detroit only. These blots on our escutcheon are now not only the concern of the entire nation, but they are now the business of Russia and China and of India— of the United Nations and the world. It is the concern of all of us, black and white alike, that America goes before the world with clean hands. He cannot find and bring to down-trodden nations the Holy Grail of peace and international accord while our hands are soiled with the lyncher's rope and the bull whip. We must all strive to hold high the integrity and sanctity of every individual like a flaming torch to a darkened world.

Will we take the up-hill road that leads to the Democracy of equal opportunity for all men—regardless of his station or the color of his eyes or of his skin or the nation of his origin? Or, is it to be the down-hill road, where there is a way of life only for him that hath, for the chosen few, for those of high birth, for the select, for those for the "right" religion or the "right" race? Our strength has arisen out of our way of keeping the door of opportunity wide open to all—so that the rail-splitter may rise to be President. That the unlettered may learn. That a man can go as far as his energy and skill and determination can take him. That the strength of each may be the strength of all. That the meek may inherit the kingdom. The chance for work, for jobs, for employment must be wide open so that each may enter and go forward in accordance with his abilities and without regard to race, creed, color or national origin. We must strive to hold wide open the door of equal opportunity so that all men may see the glory of America.

Is it to be the down road which leads to the Democracy of the slum and the blasted hearthstone, of the crowded ghetto, with its trail of congestion, ill health, delinquency and crime? Or, the up-hill road which leads to a way of life that gives every American a chance to have a decent home in which to raise his children and his family? Is it to be the life of open streets and playgrounds, of schools and hospitals, of smiling women and laughing children? Or, is it to be a Democracy that turns its [*sic*] back upon the filth and blight of our cities, [*sic*] that says people make the slums, that good homes are only for the few and the wealthy, that the rest are of no consequence? We must strive together to show the world that American strength lies in happy homes and clean streets and healthy families. We must strive manfully to take this kind of Democracy before the world—the way of security, of equality of opportunities, of equal chance for job and home; for health and education and recreation well within the reach of all. You and I must fight as never before to make our government realize the ideals upon which it was founded. We do this, not for Negroes or other minority races, [*sic*] we do this not only for the good of our city and our state and our nation. It is our obligation now to do it for the world. We must help save the soul of our own nation and its way of life so we can really save the world.

As Negroes, this is our great opportunity and our great obligation. We see all about us our boys home from the wars who fought to save Democracy, confused and frustrated because the Democracy they won is denied them. It is our job to rally them again to the ramparts to fight on to save that democracy at home. It means pressing on to get a chance for learning and training; it means hammering at the doors of opportunity until they open, as they must; it means preparing well and fighting for jobs.

It means saving and struggling to secure decent homes for our families, it means climbing farther up the way over which our fathers trod. Above all, it means hammering on the portals of government, it means qualifying, registering and voting so we can have the kind of government that we want and the kind of Democracy we want and the kind the world needs. We must do this for ourselves, but more important, for the strength and glory of the nation we want to see in the forefront of the world.

This is a call to battle, not of guns and blood, but of courage and of spirit and of peace. The world today needs audacity it needs audacious men and women in the high and noble sense. We must be audacious in fighting for Christian principles and dominating moral and spiritual enemies. The instrument used in the fight is faith. This will lift us to the far goal and carry us to goals that seem inexcessible [*sic*]. We call upon the people of the nation to assist in bringing leadership and strong public sentiment to lead us on to the high road where peace, security and justice will be found for all minority groups here in America. And, again as we have always done, it must be the women of our race and our nation that must supply the driving force and the inspiration needed as we take the up-hill road to peace. The united effort of women is paramount. For women have always been concerned with putting a floor on the necessities of life—namely, food, clothing, shelter. We can help provide the spiritual strength that buoyed up our fathers and grandfathers before us. We must help our boys and our men to know the way and find the light; bind up their wounds and wipe away their tears of defeat and frustration. We must rally them on no matter how dark the way. Today we will not only help a race to secure the fruits of full Democracy, but we will be cleansing the soul of a nation that would lead the world to peace. Let us then rededicate ourselves anew to the principles of true Democracy for all the people of the world.

Recent Achievements of Negro Women, 1947

The contributions which Negro women have made to the economic and cultural and spiritual development of this country, is a saga of American life that will go down, to be told and retold through grateful generations.

They have toiled in the fields, these women, to build an economy for others, and to maintain homes for their families. They have washed over tubs and ironed at night, [sic] that we, their children, might be educated. They have supported the churches and preached from the pulpits and sung in the choirs. They have started the schools and taught in them.

As doctors and as nurses they have ministered to the sick. Their voices have pleaded the cause of the oppressed in the courts of law. From the judge's bench they have listened with compassion and understanding to the pleadings of others.

They have been homemakers and businesswomen. They have been novelists and poets and musicians. They have been social workers and scientists, civic leaders and government officials. They have been artists of the stage and artists of the brush. What do we not owe to them? Our women!

I am glad that I am a woman! That I, too, have known what it means to work in the fields—in the hot sun. That I, too, have started schools and taught the children and sung in the choir, and directed programs of government, and showed my people how to use the ballot!

I close my eyes, and the grand old women pass in review—Phyllis Wheatley, the poet, Sojourner Truth, who helped spread the truth to make men free—Harriet Tubman, who led them to physical freedom.

I see educators—Lucy Laney in the South, Maria Baldwin in the North, Fanny Jackson Coppin in the African missions. I see the crusaders for women's advancement—Josephine Silome Yates, Josephine St. Pierre Ruffin, Mary Church Terrell, Margaret Murray Washington, Nannie Helen Burroughs—Ida B. Wells Barnett.

The line is long! Some have dropped out. Some are still here—struggling forward, with less stumbling; more surefooted; more efficient; better-trained; rising to new heights. Thank God for them all!

And what of our todays? When I open my eyes and look, at our todays, I realize that they are increasingly glorious, increasingly powerful. I realize, also, that they are rooted in the strength of the foundations sacrificially laid by those others, in our yesterdays!

Who are today's women who are building so surely our structure of modern life? What are they using for their bricks and mortar?

They are using education: Dr. Anna Cooper, whose Frelinghysen University in Washington, provides college opportunity at night, for those who must work by day; Maud Bousfield of Chicago, presiding over a great, public high school; Fannie Williams, who built an oasis of culture in the crowded slums of New Orleans; Margaret Bowen of New Orleans; Sadie Daniel of Washington, whose bio-biographies are as inspiring as her teaching; Arenia Mallory, who has brought light to the hinterlands of the great, dark, Mississippi Delta!

There are Artemesia Bowden of San Antonio and Madeline Foreman, whose biological knowledge has bridged the gap of race, and placed her at the head of her department in a large western college. Our Charlotte Hawkins Brown, still youthfully vigorous in mind, still sturdy in body, still planning, still building trained minds—cultured personalities.

All of these and many, many more, facing and mastering, day by day, the problems of health, of financial need, of personal development, of vocational guidance, that open the doors and point the way to well-rounded lives, to the flowering of talent and the fulfillment of dreams—to increased economic security.

They are using their legal knowledge in the courts of states all over the Union: Sadie Moselle Alexander, only Negro women member of the Philadelphia bar; L. Marion Poe, of Newport News, Virginia, Assistant Secretary of the National Bar Association and the first Negro woman to practice law in the State of Virginia; Jane Bolin, our first Negro woman judge, for eight years, now, on the bench of New York City's Court of Domestic Relations; Pauli Murray, who served as California's Assistant Attorney General; Elsie Austin of Ohio has served her State, also, as Assistant Attorney General; Georgia Jones Ellis, Assistant Corporation Counsel, and Edith Sampson Clayton, Assistant States Attorney, both of Chicago; Eunice Hunton Carter, formerly Assistant District Attorney of New York City; and Jeanne Cole, who practices before the Wayne County bar, in Detroit. We cannot do more, here, than to suggest the service that is being rendered—the structure that these fine women are helping to build.

In many instances, women in law have been women in politics. The women already mentioned, who have held high public office in legal capacities, have been in politics as well as in law. Sarah Pelham Speaks, criminal lawyer, has been in New York politics for twenty years or more, and has run for Congress from that State. Jeanetta Welch Brown of Detroit ran for the Michigan State Legislature at the last elections. Thomasina Johnson has touched Massachusetts politics, in Boston, her adopted home. Lola Ann Cullum has reached into politics in Texas. And we must remember that many of our women who are affecting American politics are <u>not</u> personally ambitious for public office. Many are ambitious only to see that those who do hold office <u>are fit</u>, and are truly representative of our communities and their needs, in all our affairs, from neighborhood to Nation!

Medicine is the brick and mortar for more than 200 Negro women physicians, using their skills to build strong, healthy people: Dorothy Ferebee, a practicing physician of Washington, and an instructor at the Howard University Medical School, where the enrollment of women has risen, in less than a decade, from a mere 3 to 4 percent, to 16 percent of all this school's medical students. There is Ruth Temple, health officer, of Los Angeles; Constance Yearwood, of Austin, Texas, first Negro woman to be appointed to the Texas State Health Department. Another Texas woman, Thelma Patten-Law, of Houston, is the president of her State medical association. In Virginia there is Zenobia Gilpin of Richmond; in New Jersey, Mae McCarroll of Newark, the first Negro appointed to the Newark Hospital, and Assistant <u>Epidemiologist</u> in the Newark City Health Department. In New York there are Dr. Petersen, Associate Director of the Union Health Center—working with organized labor; Myra Logan, women's specialist; and Catherine Lealtad. Dr. Lealtad has served with distinction in UNRRA, relieving suffering among the displaced persons of Central Europe. Again, these are only a few—only an indication of the contributions in this field.

In and out of classrooms, in the allied field of science, is a growing group of women-chemists, zoologists, physicists, biologists—women who have dared to be venturesome, who are making their contributions to society in line with their real aptitudes and abilities. Dr. Marie Clark, recently appointed Head of the Department of Botany at Howard University; Gladys Pinckney Fletcher, instructor in Organic Chemistry; Caroline Silence Woodruff, instructor in Biological Science; Blanche Ingraham and Ethel Battle in Analytical and General Chemistry; Dr. Marie Dailey—all teachers. There are Inez Hazel, of Boston, chemist, on the editorial staff of the Massachusetts Institute of Technology radar magazine; Angela Bornn, research chemist at the Princeton University laboratories; Marceil Daniel, research chemist at the University of Michigan laboratories; Miriam Mason Higgins, analytical and research chemist in the quartermaster Department at Chicago; Geraldine Pittman Woods, Doctor of Zoology from Harvard University. In the coming profession of medical technician we have Gwendolyn C. Lee, head of Chicago's Provident Hospital Bacteriology Section; Clover Oliver, laboratory chief at Freedom's Hospital in Washington, and others—all skilled—all moving ahead. And here again, we have only been able to suggest the full scope of current achievement.

In the time-honored field of nursing, Mabel Staupers and Estelle Riddle have done wonders in integrating the work of our women.

The field of business, pioneered by Maggie L. Walker of Richmond, Mme. C.J. Walker of Indianapolis, Annie Turnbo Malone of St. Louis and Chicago, and others, now includes such names as Mrs. Berry of Alexandria, Louisiana, proprietor of the finest market in that town; Mrs. Elliott of Muskogee, Oklahoma, owner and operator of a splendid, modern, women's apparel shop; Cecil Spaulding of Greensboro, North Carolina, Geneva K. Valentine of Washington and Lola Ann Cullum of Houston, Texas, all operating extensive real-estate businesses; Jessie Matthews Vann, publisher of one of our largest and most progressive papers, the Pittsburgh Courier; Jean Rhodes, owner of the Philadelphia Tribune; Mrs. Scott of the Atlanta World, our only Negro daily; Sarah Spencer Washington, whose beauty culture activities have become big business. These are only a few. In Washington, Jean Clore has a fine restaurant and cocktail lounge. Chicago has the beautiful Morris Eat Shoppe, Cocktail Lounge, and family party services; Susan Tokes operates Tokes Inn at Winchester, Virginia, in the heart of the apple country, for an exclusive clientele of both races.

We have done so many things! We have operated flying schools and gone down to the sea in ships—carrying freight and passengers down the Georgia Coast—Sea captains! We have gift shop businesses and drug stores, printing establishments, interior decorating and hand-made jewelry shops, modiste's [sic] shops—all owned and operated by women.

And we have contributed much to culture, directly, through such women as Meta Warwick Fuller and Selma Burke, sculptors, Laura Wheeler Waring and Lois Mailou Jones, painters. We have taught and we have created! Marian Anderson, Dorothy

Maynor, Carol Brice have reached new heights, carrying their message of the cultural contributions of Negroes wherever their glorious voices are heard. Lillian Evanti has internationalized her talent. Ethel Waters and Etta Moten have gone far in their special musical fields. Katherine Dunham with the dance, and Hilda Simms on the legitimate stage, have interpreted our problems and our moods. Hattie McManiel [*sic*] and Lena Horne have lowered barriers in the films.

Wherever men gather and make their homes, there is need for the sociologist and the social worker. Much outstanding work has been done in these fields by such women as Jane Hunter of Cleveland, Dorothy Height of the National Board of the YWCA, Eartha M.M. White, who has given her life to the underprivileged and unwanted of Florida; Pauline Redmond Coggs, now an instructor at the University of Wisconsin; Grace Towns Hamilton, Edmonia White Grant, Assistant Director of the Southern Conference for Human Welfare, Inabel Burns Lindsay, and, in the field of family life, Flemmie Kittrell and Mamie Phipps Clark, both with doctor's degrees in their chosen fields.

Journalism—a comparatively new field for our women, a decade ago, and generally looked upon then, as a short-cut to starvation, has, in recent years, attracted the talents of an interesting group of alert women. Carlotta Bass of California, Olive Diggs of Chicago, Hortense Young of Kentucky, Florence Murray, whose annual handbook is a "must" on every desk, Lucille Bluford, Gertrude Martin, Venice Spragg, Margery Lawson, and in the special field of women's interests, Rebecca Stiles Taylor, Toki Schalk, Consuelo Young and many others.

Women have made their contribution in the realm of government, also. Constance Daniel did her part, watching over loans and the welfare of tenant farmers and share-croppers and migrants, for the Department of Agriculture. Frances Williams did hers, guarding against price differentials at the Office of Price Administration; Vivian Carter Mason worked with Social Security, Corinne Robinson is still helping to keep our score straight at Housing, and Thomasina Walker Johnson, who developed with the Non-Partisan Council on Public Affairs, as its legislative representative, now occupies the key position at the Department of Labor. Patsy Graves is now at Agriculture in the field of Home Management.

The armed services had Negro women in every branch. We had to fight to get them there and we had to fight to keep them there; but they are still there.

We went overseas with the Red Cross—and we had our troubles there, too. But we got there. We made our way into every activity, and we observed and noted, wherever we went—and broadened our horizons.

In times of peace, many of us went abroad. Although few realize it, many Negro women of means were trained abroad, way back in the days of sailing ships—while America's doors of opportunity were still closed to them. These pioneers who studied and observed in foreign lands, before even the oldest of us here were born, have been followed by others, in increasing numbers, so that our eyes and minds have become attuned to the oneness of the world in which we live, and we seek, with a sure touch, spiritual and intellectual sisterhood with all women, of all races and of all nations.

The women of my race have stood shoulder to shoulder with our men—thinking together, counseling and <u>working</u>, in every field of endeavor, acknowledging no barriers of race of sex. Our achievements have only begun. They will continue as long as we press forward, with knowledge and understanding—<u>without</u> <u>fear</u>!

Statement to President Truman at the White House Conference on February 28, 1951

We are keenly aware of the increasing responsibility that rests upon the President of the United States as a result of the perilous world situation. So, we have not come to add to your cares, which are equally ours, but rather to make some suggestions which we believe will contribute something worthwhile to our moral health and to our national well being. We are solidly behind you and our government in the fight to stop the spread of communism and to maintain and improve our democratic way of life. We support the President of the United States in his declaring a state of national emergency and we accept in full the point of view expressed in his state of the union message.

Although we are not unmindful of the defects in our democracy, we believe that the United States of America is actually and potentially the greatest country on earth. Believing this, we want to play, in this crisis, our full role as American Citizens, unhampered and unfettered by those forces which weakens our democracy in the eyes of the world and which all too frequently give our enemies a justifiable reason to spread dangerous propaganda against us.

In this hour of global crisis, we should demonstrate to the world that we are a united people and that we are not only talking democracy and fighting for it across the earth, but that we are actually and sincerely demonstrating it in practice here at home. We are convinced that in order to defeat communism we must be militarily strong. But we are equally convinced that communism cannot be overcome by military might alone, however powerful that might may be—not even by the superior possession and use of atom and hydrogen bomb; nor by the use of the bacteriological implements of war.

In addition to military power, we believe that in order to overcome communism and to make the United States an impregnable citadel of freedom and democracy, our country must stand above reproach in the treatment it accords all of its peoples.

We believe that it would increase our national unity, weaken communist propaganda, strengthen our cause among the colored peoples of Asia, Africa, the Isles of the Sea, the West Indies, the United States and freedom-loving peoples everywhere, if you, Mr. President, would exercise the powers inherent in your office to extending the domain of democracy and to make possible the fullest use of the services of the Negro citizens in this hour of national emergency.

In the light of these convictions, we, a group of representative Negro Americans, have come today to request you to do six things:

1. To use your power and influence to abolish, immediately, racial segregation in the nation's capital. Washington is the capital of the greatest democratic country in the world and yet we are incessantly embarrassed by virtue of the fact that it is the most segregated national capital on the earth.

2. To appoint qualified Negroes on the administrative and policy making level of our government. We have had consultants and advisors, but we have had hardly any Negroes in government who actually shared in making and determining polices in the various branches of the government.
3. To integrate Negroes in all new agencies that are being established and will be established as a result of this emergency. New agencies and new positions are being created all the time—Negroes are usually the forgotten people. Especially do we urge that Washington tell regional and state offices which the Federal Government has and will set up with federal money that Negroes are to be utilized and integrated on the same basis as other peoples without regard to color, race or national origin.
4. To appoint Negroes more widely in the foreign and diplomatic service of our country. The contribution of Ralph Bunche to world peace is one of the many contributions that Negroes would make if given a chance.
5. To issue an Executive Order guaranteeing the maximum use of all manpower in all production efforts irrespective of color, race or national origin in the denfese emergency and provide an adequate machinery for its enforcement.
6. To abolish once and for all racial segregation of Negro soldiers in the United States Army.

We cannot make it too clear, Mr. President, that we come to you today not as Negroes defending Negroes. We come as American Citizens pleading for our country and concerned chiefly with advancing the cause of democracy and freedom in the United States and in the world. We believe, Sir, that the time is ripe for such actions as we have requested.

Respectfully submitted, we are:

Preparing Ourselves for Community Living, 1952

I bring to you, today, my soliciations and gratitude for the NATIONAL ASSOCIA-TION FOR THE ADVANCEMENT OF COLORED PEOPLE in commemoration of what it has done, and is continuing to do as pioneers in the field of human relations. I commend the movements in which you have built up the spirit of equality of opportunity for all.

We stand, today, at the doorway to a great world community through which we may enter to discover people, to create attitudes, to practice human relations, and to participate in the many and varied activities of a thriving humanity.

How important, then, is it, that every single one of us look circumspectly into ourselves, our tasks, and whatever area of the community we live. We must see to it, that as we enter this doorway, we are roundedly prepared to make a contribution to the enrichment of our neighborhood.

Our communities are the places we live in, where homes and firesides, churches and altars, factories and workbenches, playgrounds and activities, social work and human welfare, government and leadership, all are blended together in the promotion of the common good. Our communities are sometimes bounded by our narrow little selves, or by our door yards, or by our village streets, or by our city limits. Through the work of the National Association for the Advancement of Colored People our communities are extending their vision beyond these simple borders. In reality, our communities can stretch out to be as wide as our hearts are wide. Edna St. Vincent Millay has said it in these lines,

> "The heart can push the sea and land
> Farther away on either hand."

As our intellectual growth stretches out to broader horizons, our concept of the community is identified with a breadth of understanding, a sense of appreciation for human kind, and high regard for human personality. Human personality thrives and grows in the atmosphere of belonging. Each one must feel that he had a share in what is going on about him; each one must feel secure in his social relationships one with the other. This fostering of human rights is the kind of preparation which becomes the moral responsibility of leadership. One great imperative, today, is that we have citizens who can share in the thinking, the planning, and the organizational development of a community. These days demand strong leaders—fearless, courageous, far-visioned leaders,—who can follow through to their goals, not for selfish gain or personal power, but for the welfare of all mankind.

These basic considerations should be promoted by those who foster the promotion and enrichment of community life for the sake of brotherhood, justice, service, and equal opportunity. Whether our community in its physical aspects, is large or small, the fundamental undergirdings are the same. The people who are the members of the community must get to know, and to understand each other; they must be concerned about each other's welfare. The pursuit of happiness is for all. This common growth of acquaintance will make possible the quality of opportunity which we crave and work for, wherein no creed, class, or color will inhibit full participation from any member or group of members.

The community membership must be worthy of itself; one part cannot experience privileges and opportunities which are denied to the other part. The principles of sharing responsibility in our community are imperative to security and welfare.

Adequate preparation for living in our community depends upon education. We must become informed about what is going on around us. We must know when a source of information is a reliable one. We must learn to distinguish between information and propaganda. True citizenship means the assuming of our several responsibilities in the promotion of justice, economic efficiency, and social health.

We have no right to be the walking dead—just existing—without registering personal appreciation and reactions to and for the things that are going on around us. In order to be well informed, a citizen must seek satisfactory answers to the inquiries of his mind.

Who are the leaders? Where did they come from? How did they get to be leaders? For what do they stand? Is there spiritual, intellectual, and moral stature in them, sufficient to cope with the needs of a growing community? Do they have the world view?

Who are the workers? What is their work? How do the families live? What are the homes like? What are our chief resources? Who owns and operates the businesses? In whose hands rests the economic security of the community?

What are our schools like? Is our community a suitable laboratory for our schools? Are the leaders, parents, church leaders, and workers cooperating with the teachers and principals in building the kind of curriculum which we want for our children? Are our children and youth inspired to attend the schools and colleges, regularly, in order to realize the advancement they need? These are a few of the questions which the intelligent citizen must answer, if his community is to be an integral part of the unifying programs of the State, the nations, and the world.

Further, our preparation increases with experience and participation. Each of us has his individual task to accomplish. First there must be the choice of a vocation suitable to our interests and abilities. The youth must be inspired to choose vocations which make them happy and contributing members of the community. The preparation through vocational skills must be further endowed with vision and insight so that whatever our individual tasks are, the practice of them contributes of the success of the whole.

In the great struggle for existence, life in a community is continually threatened by disease, struggle, poverty, delinquency and war; there are economic upheavals of one sort or the other. The basic experiences which sustain men, and give them courage to hold on to their ideals, even when there is nothing in them "except the will that says to them hold on" must keep us fighting to overcome.

I am persuaded that each man can find for himself a philosophy of life which will give purpose and meaning to every activity in which he desires to engages. His philosophy is the impetus which spurs him on to achievement. Such an impetus has been the guide and inspiration for thousands and thousands of men and women who during the years have carried the torch, which had blazed the way for all of us even to this day.

We must prepare, not only to live in our little communities, but in America, with its tremendous responsibilities for leading the world. We must prepare to look critically at America, to envision how people outside of her look at this great moving community, composed of the 48 united communities, solving their problems together.

More and more, the responsibility of being a citizen challenges us. It is gratifying to me to be alive in a day like this when thousands and thousands, and thousands of my people can stand on their feet and look other men in the eyes, with courage and understanding, to express the needs and desires of their hearts. I see them now use the ballot, the weapon of freedom and equality, according to the dictates of their own hearts. This, my friends, is a status to which we have grown, and which we must safeguard if those who are to follow after us are to inherit that fullness of opportunity for which we pray.

May I challenge you to foster the atmosphere of first class citizenship by giving of your best to the tasks which are needful in this critical hour of history. This is a time that demands strange loyalties, courageous hearts, world vision, spiritual undergirding [*sic*], and steadfast devotion and loyalty to the constitution of our nation. This is the unifying force which makes our nation the larger community promoted for the people, by the people. This larger community calls for our allegiance in thought and in need. We need tall men, strong men, sun-crowned men whose feet are solidly on the ground, and whose hands are clasped in God's hands.

My Last Will and Testament, 1955

Sometimes as I sit communing in my study I feel that death is not far off. I am aware that it will overtake me before the greatest of my dreams—full equality for the Negro in our time—is realized. Yet, I face that reality without fear or regrets. I am resigned to death as all humans must be at the proper time. Death neither alarms nor frightens one who has had a long career of fruitful toil. The knowledge that my work has been helpful to many fills me with joy and great satisfaction.... So, as my life draws to a close, I will pass [this] on to Negroes everywhere in the hope that an old woman's philosophy may give them inspiration. Here, then is my legacy.

I LEAVE YOU LOVE. Love builds. It is positive and helpful. It is more beneficial than hate. Injuries quickly forgotten quickly pass away. Personally and racially, our enemies must be forgiven. Our aim must be to create a world of fellowship and justice where no man's skin, color or religion, is held against him. "Love thy neighbor" is a precept which could transform the world if it were universally practiced. It connotes brotherhood and, to me, brotherhood of man is the noblest concept in all human relations. Loving your neighbor means being interracial, interreligious and international.

I LEAVE YOU HOPE. The Negro's growth will be great in the years to come. Yesterday, our ancestors endured the degradation of slavery, yet they retained their dignity. Today, we direct our economic and political strength toward winning a more abundant and secure life. Tomorrow, a new Negro, unhindered by race taboos and shackles, will benefit from more than 330 years of ceaseless striving and struggle. Theirs will be a better world. This I believe with all my heart.

I LEAVE YOU THE CHALLENGE OF DEVELOPING CONFIDENCE IN ONE ANOTHER. As long as Negroes are hemmed into racial blocs by prejudice and pressure, it will be necessary for them to band together for economic betterment. Negro banks, insurance companies and other businesses are examples of successful, racial economic enterprises. These institutions were made possible by vision and mutual aid. Confidence was vital in getting them started and keeping them going. Negroes have got to demonstrate still more confidence in each other in business. This kind of confidence will aid the economic rise of the race by bringing together the pennies and dollars of our people and ploughing [sic] them into useful channels. Economic separatism cannot be tolerated in this enlightened age, and it is not practicable. We must spread out as far and as fast as we can, but we must also help each other as we go.

I LEAVE YOU A THIRST FOR EDUCATION. Knowledge is the prime need of the hour. More and more, Negroes are taking full advantage of hard-won opportunities for learning, and the educational level of the Negro population is at its highest point in history. We are making greater use of the privileges inherent in living in a democracy. If we continue in this trend, we will be able to rear increasing numbers of strong, purposeful men and women, equipped with vision, mental clarity, health and education.

I LEAVE YOU RESPECT FOR THE USES OF POWER. We live in a world which respects power above all things. Power, intelligently directed, can lead to more freedom. Unwisely directed, it can be a dreadful, destructive force. During my lifetime I have seen the power of the Negro grow enormously. It has always been my first concern that this power should be placed on the side of human justice.

Now that the barriers are crumbling everywhere, the Negro in America must be ever vigilant lest his forces be marshalled [*sic*] behind wrong causes and undemocratic movements. He must not lend his support to any group that seeks to subvert democracy. That is why we must select leaders who are wise, courageous, and of great moral stature and ability. We have great leaders among us today: Ralph Bunche, Channing Tobias, Mordecai Johnson, Walter White, and Mary Church Terrell. [The latter now deceased]. We have had other great men and women in the past: Frederick Douglass, Booker T. Washington, Harriet Tubman, and Sojourner Truth. We must produce more qualified people like them, who will work not for themselves, but for others.

I LEAVE YOU FAITH. Faith is the first factor in a life devoted to service. Without faith, nothing is possible. With it, nothing is impossible. Faith in God is the greatest power, but great, too, is faith in oneself. In 50 years the faith of the American Negro in himself has grown immensely and is still increasing. The measure of our progress as a race is in precise relation to the depth of the faith in our people held by our leaders. Frederick Douglass, genius though he was, was spurred by a deep conviction that his people would heed his counsel and follow him to freedom. Our greatest Negro figures have been imbued with faith. Our forefathers struggled for liberty in conditions far more onerous than those we now face, but they never lost the faith. Their perseverance paid rich dividends. We must never forget their sufferings and their sacrifices, for they were the foundations of the progress of our people.

I LEAVE YOU RACIAL DIGNITY. I want Negroes to maintain their human dignity at all costs. We, as Negroes, must recognize that we are the custodians as well as the heirs of a great civilization. We have given something to the world as a race and for this we are proud and fully conscious of our place in the total picture of mankind's development. We must learn also to share and mix with all men. We must make an effort to be less race conscious and more conscious of individual and human values. I have never been sensitive about my complexion. My color has never destroyed my self-respect nor has it ever caused me to conduct myself in such a manner as to merit the disrespect of any person. I have not let my color handicap me. Despite many crushing burdens and handicaps, I have risen from the cotton fields of South Carolina to found a college, administer it during its years of growth, become a public servant in the government of our country and a leader of women. I would not exchange my color for all the wealth in the world, for had I been born white I might not have been able to do all that I have done or yet hope to do.

I LEAVE YOU A DESIRE TO LIVE HARMONIOUSLY WITH YOUR FELLOW MEN. The problem of color is worldwide. It is found in Africa and Asia, Europe and South America. I appeal to American Negroes—North, South, East and West—to recognize their common problems and unite to solve them.

I pray that we will learn to live harmoniously with the white race. So often, our difficulties have made us hypersensitive and truculent. I want to see my people conduct themselves naturally in all relationships—fully conscious of their manly responsibilities and deeply aware of their heritage. I want them to learn to understand whites and influence them for good, for it is advisable and sensible for us to do so. We are a minority of 15 million living side by side with a white majority. We must learn to deal with these people positively and on an individual basis.

I LEAVE YOU FINALLY A RESPONSIBILITY TO OUR YOUNG PEOPLE. The world around us really belongs to youth for youth will take over its future management. Our children must never lose their zeal for building a better world. They must not be discouraged from aspiring toward greatness, for they are to be the leaders of tomorrow. Nor must they forget that the masses of our people are still underprivileged, ill-housed, impoverished and victimized by discrimination. We have a powerful potential in our youth, and we must have the courage to change old ideas and practices so that we may direct their power toward good ends.

Faith, courage, brotherhood, dignity, ambition, responsibility—these are needed today as never before. We must cultivate them and use them as tools for our task of completing the establishment of equality for the Negro. We must sharpen these tools in the struggle that faces us and find new ways of using them. The Freedom Gates are half-ajar. We must pry them fully open.

If I have a legacy to leave my people, it is my philosophy of living and serving. As I face tomorrow, I am content, for I think I have spent my life well. I pray now that my philosophy may be helpful to those who share my vision of a world of Peace, Progress, Brotherhood, and Love.

13.
MARTIN LUTHER KING Jr.

Martin Luther King Jr. (1929–1968) is probably the most famous civil rights leader in the United States. In 1955 King led and helped organize the Montgomery Bus Boycott, which was a successful direct action protest to desegregate buses. He served as president of the Montgomery Improvement Association. The famous boycott was ostensibly sparked when the now famous Rosa Parks refused to be "Jim-Crowed" on a public bus. King's house was bombed as a result of his efforts. However, his and thousands of other protestor's efforts were not in vain. On December 26, 1956 the buses in Montgomery were desegregated; the boycott was successful.

In 1957 King helped found the Southern Christian Leadership Conference. He also served as its first president. His most famous accomplishment came when in 1963 he helped organize the March on Washington for Jobs and Freedom along with Randolph, Rustin, and many others. This is where King delivered his famous "I Have a Dream" speech. In 1965 he organized another influential march. He organized the march from Selma to Montgomery for voting rights. This famous march has become known as Bloody Sunday; 600 protestors peacefully left Selma and upon arrival at the Edmund Pettus Bridge were met with tear gas and the billy clubs of angry law enforcement officials. The belligerent law enforcement officials beat the protesters and forcibly pushed them back into Selma. This was not the first or last time King or non-violent protestors were met with unprovoked violence. King himself was stoned, stabbed, and eventually shot. In 1968 he was assassinated at the Lorraine Hotel in Memphis, Tennessee. During his lifetime King was jailed frequently in his efforts to bring about justice and peace. However, his dogged determination won him the Nobel Peace Prize in 1964.

King was a prolific writer. In his lifetime he wrote countless speeches. One of his most famous pieces, "Letter From a Birmingham Jail," discussed the moral imperative of the clergy to stand up against racial injustice and insisted on non-violent protest as the most ideal means by which to fight injustice. In 1958 he published *Stride toward Freedom: The Montgomery Story*. In 1959 he published *The Measure of a Man*. In 1964 he released, *Why We Can't Wait*. In 1967 he published his fourth book, *Where do We Go From Here? Chaos or Community*.

Overview of Ideas

Martin Luther King Jr. needs no introduction. We only have to read his famous "I Have a Dream" speech to appreciate his charisma and optimism, which he seems to be most known for. However, King's ideas were far more complex than those we all probably learned in school. He is probably best known for his non-violent approach to direct action protest. King argued that physical violence was not necessary; in fact, it was counterproductive. Like Rustin, who also borrowed this strategy from Gandhi, King posited that non-violence was not the strategy of cowards; it was not passive. "The violent resister is just as opposed to the evil that he is standing against as the violent resister but he resists without violence." According to King, this method was spiritually aggressive and actually harder to implement than violent protest. To keep one's composure in the face of violence and hate was radical. To take the high road is always the more difficult path. However, this path was not an effort to humiliate your opponent. The goal of non-violent direct action is to gain your opponents' friendship and understanding. Violence was immoral. In addition, non-violent protest was an attack on an evil system, not on evil individuals. People are shaped by hegemonic discourses and the institutions that enforce them. Therefore, the goal must be to transform the institutions and discourses first and the people will follow. African Americans were waging a war for justice not against White people.

King argued that the chief weapon African Americans had in the struggle for freedom was love. "When we speak of love, we speak of understanding, good will toward *all* men." According to King, in waging a battle for civil rights religion would play a huge role. He suggested that African Americans should pray for guidance and support from God. For him, progress hinged upon the Civil Rights Movement being a spiritual movement. The struggle before African Americans was a moral struggle. Full integration was necessary to achieve justice, a morally superior society, and as Bethune also argued a true democracy.

In the 1960s, even after the 1954 *Brown v. the Board of Education*, which desegregated public schools, segregation and racism still persisted. According to King, part of the problem was that desegregation was not enough; desegregation did not mean these institutions would become integrated. "*Desegregation* is eliminative and negative, for it simply removes these legal and social prohibitions. Integration is creative … integration is the positive acceptance of desegregation and the welcomed participation of Negroes into the total range of human activities." Desegregation was the means to the end—integration. King argued that "integration demands that we recognize that a denial of freedom is a denial of life itself." Without integration there would be no true freedom.

Integration was necessary because it was ethical. All people are equal regardless of race. We are all human and all God's children. Every human is entitled to freedom—the freedom to act for themselves and not be restrained from improving their quality of life and their individual capacity. Integration was necessary because we are all part of one human family; integration helps us realize that human family. King posited that the protest could be utilized as a means by which to achieve the legal reform necessary to bring about integration.

King addressed a wide range of issues. However, they were not all related to civil rights and racial discrimination. As the Civil Rights Movement dwindled as a result of the gains it produced, the Civil Rights Act 1964, Voting Rights Act 1965, etc., King became more publicly vocal about issues such as poverty. He was concerned about the high rate of poverty and how it impacted both Whites and Blacks. Interestingly, King, as we will see, could be characterized as culturally and socially conservative but as the years progressed he became more radical about economic policy. In fact, his later writings suggest a likeness with Black socialists such as Randolph. Like Randolph, King argued that full employment was necessary. "I am now convinced that the simplest approach will prove to be the most effective—the solution to poverty is to abolish it directly by a now widely discussed measure: the guaranteed income." This income should be equivalent to the U.S. median income, not just a minimum wage that is barely enough to subsist. The rich have access to the resources they need; even the extremely poor have access to resources (even if diminutive) through welfare. However, the majority of Americans are left in the wind. Without eliminating poverty and class inequality how can we expect the individual to improve himself monetarily or to improve his character?

King was adamant that structural change was necessary. However, like many moderates he also drew from culturally and socially conservative logic and argued that change hinged upon African Americans transmogrifying their own "personal standards." Slavery and Jim Crow created many Black people who had no dignity and self-respect. In order to overcome the psychological warfare imposed by racism de jure and to gain the respect of Whites Black folk needed to improve their "shortcomings." Again, these shortcomings, this cultural pathology, immorality, inability to delay gratification, laziness, criminality, etc., were part of the legacy of slavery. Segregation caused these pathologies to flourish amongst many African Americans. However, desegregation will not be enough to eradicate these poor personal standards.

> Maybe we could be more sanitary; maybe we could be a little more clean ... you are not so poor that you cannot buy a five cents bar of soap.... We've got to lift our moral standards ... we must walk the street every day, and let people know that as we walk the street, we aren't thinking about sex every time we turn around ... we must improve our standards; improve our conduct; we must improve our sanitary conditions; we must even improve our cultural standards.

He argued that as structural barriers were being removed, Black individuals needed to seize these opportunities. Individual motivation was important to success. Individual and cultural transformation needed to accompany these structural changes. African Americans needed to work hard and delay gratification. King urged, if you became successful do not go out and buy extravagant luxury items, as many Black folk did. Instead Black people should save and invest it. "I look and I see how much money we spend on liquor and on beer and on all these alcoholic beverages. Right here in Alabama we spend enough money on liquor to endow three or four colleges." King, like many of his predecessors such as Du Bois, called for a hybrid strategy of change incorporating both structural change, individual, and cultural change.

Some Things We Must Do, 1957

*Editor's note—King delivered this speech at the Holt Street Baptist Church; the crowd responses are intentionally left within the text.

We all recognize the fact that we stand today on the threshold of the most amazing period of our nation's history. We look around and we see the walls of segregation gradually crumbling. (*That's right, That's right*) And let nobody fool you. All of the loud noises that you hear today in terms of nullification and interposition are merely the death groans of a dying system. (*Yes, Amen, All right*) As Dean Gomillion said so eloquently: "An old order is passing away (*Yeah*), and the new order is coming into being." (*Yeah*)

This evening, I'm not going to say anything about the role of the church; I'm not going to discuss the role of the federal government; I'm not going to discuss the role of white liberals, North and South. I just want to talk with you about some things that we must do (*Yes, Amen*), as Negroes. (*Yes*) We must realize that there is something that we can do to bring this new order into being. I think that was something of the greatness of Mahatma Gandhi, that he looked in the eyes of ordinary people, and he said to them that they had something. He looked at them and said: "You may be poor; you may be illiterate. You have something within your very being that can determine the very course of human events." And through that he was able to galvanize the forces of Indian people, and they were able to break aloose [*sic*] from the political domination and economic exploitation inflicted upon them by Britain. (*Yes*) And I come to you this evening and say you have something. What are the things that we can do? I just want to state them briefly, and go into them briefly, and I'm going to leave them with you.

Number one, we can maintain a continuing sense of dignity and self-respect. (*Yes*) This is important. And we will not achieve our freedom until we feel that we belong and that we have a sense of significance. Let no force, let no power, let no individuals, let no social system cause you to feel that you are inferior. (*Yeah*) You know, one of the great tragedies of this hour is that you have some Negroes who don't want to be free. (*Yes, Amen*) Did you know that? (*Yes*) There are Negroes in this Southland who have become so conditioned to the system of segregation that they prefer the fleshpots of Egypt (*Well*) to the challenges of the Promised Land. They lack a sense of dignity and self-respect.

Now that is why segregation is evil. I think, more than anything else; that is the basic reason. Segregation not only makes for physical inconveniences, but it does something spiritually to an individual. It distorts the personality and injures the soul. Segregation gives the segregator a false sense of superiority, and it gives the segregated a false sense of inferiority. But in the midst of this, we must maintain a sense of dignity and self-respect.

[M]y friends, if we are to be prepared for this new order and this new world which is emerging, we must believe that we belong. Every Negro must feel that he is somebody. (*All right, Yeah*) He must come to see that he is a child of God and that all men are made in God's image. (*Yes*) He must come to see that the basic thing about a man is not his specificity, but his fundamentum [*sic*] (*Yeah*), not the texture of his hair or the color of his skin, but the texture and quality of his soul. (*Yeah*) He must come to the point that he will believe with the eloquent poet:

> Fleecy locks and black complexion,
> Cannot forfeit nature's claim.
> Skin may differ, but affection,
> Dwells in black and white the same. (*All right, Yeah*)
> Were I so tall as to reach the poles,
> Or to grasp the ocean at a span,
> I must be measured by my soul. (*Yeah*)
> The mind is the standard of the man. (*All right*)

Tell your children that. (*Yes*) Say it to them at every hour, so they will be able to live in this age (*Yes*) with a sense of dignity (*Yeah*), and a sense of self-respect. (*Yeah*) This is something that we can do. (*Yeah*)

And the second thing: we must make ourselves worthy of the respect of others by improving our own personal standards. (*All right, Amen, That's right*) Now we must admit that we have some weaknesses (*Yes*) and some shortcomings (*Yeah*), and we must seek to gain the respect of others by improving on our shortcomings. (*Yes*) Now I realize, and I want to say this quickly, because I see a reporter here and I don't want to be misquoted. I want to say quickly that I realize that these standards in which we lag behind, whether they are cultural, whether they are moral, criminal, or what not, they are like they are because of segregation; I know that. (*That's right, Yeah*) They are here because of segregation (*Yes*); segregation is the causal factor. And it is a sort of torturous logic to argue for the tragic inequalities as a basis, as a result of inequality, as a basis for the continuation of inequality. (*Yeah*) See these things have been caused by segregation, and the thing to do is to remove the causal factor. (*All right*)

But in spite of this, we must admit that because segregation does exist and has existed for so many years, we must work on two fronts. And it presents a dual problem to the Negro. On the one hand, we must work to remove this system, which is the causal basis for our ills. We cannot let up; we cannot stop working to do away with segregation; we cannot retreat at that point. We must not rest until segregation and discrimination are banished from every area of our nation's life. (*Yes*) We've got to work, [*applause*] But we have another job. And that is to work to improve these standards that have been pushed back because of the system of segregation. We've got to work on two ends; we have both an internal problem and an external. One is to try to remove the system. The other is to work with these conditions that have come into being as a result of the system. We must work with them, and we've got to face this fact, my friends.

Let us be honest with ourselves, and say that we, our standards have lagged behind at many points. Negroes constitute ten percent of the population of New York City, and yet they commit thirty-five percent of the crime. St. Louis, Missouri: the Negroes constitute twenty-six percent of the population, and yet seventy-six percent of the persons on the list for aid to dependent children are Negroes. We have eight times more illegitimacy than white persons. We've got to face all of these things. We must work to improve these standards. We must sit down quietly by the wayside, and ask ourselves: "Where can we improve?" What are the things that white people are saying about us? They say that we want integration because we want to marry white people. Well, we know that is a falsehood. (*That's right*) We know that. We don't have to worry about that. (*All right*) Then on the other hand, they say some other things about us, and maybe there is some truth in them. Maybe we could be more sanitary; maybe we could be a little more clean. You may not have enough money to take a weekend trip to Paris, France, and buy all of the fascinating and enticing perfumes. You may not be able to do that, but you are not so poor that you cannot buy a five cents bar of soap (*Yeah*) so that you can wash before [*word inaudible*]. [*applause*]

And another thing my friends, we kill each other too much. (*All right, Yes*) We cut up each other too much. (*Yes, Yes sir*) There is something that we can do. We've got to go down in the quiet hour and think about this thing. We've got to lift our moral standards at every hand, at every point. You may not have a Ph.D. degree; you may not have an M.A. degree; you may not have an A.B. degree. But the great thing about life is that any man can be good, and honest, and ethical, and moral, and can have character. (*Well, Yes*) [*applause*]

We must walk the street every day, and let people know that as we walk the street, we aren't thinking about sex every time we turn around. (*No, That's right*) We are not animals (*No*) to be degraded at every moment. (*Yeah*) We know that we're made for the stars, created for eternity, born for the everlasting (*Yes*), and we stand by it. [*applause*] (*All right, All right*)

There are some things that we can do. (*Yes*) We must improve our standards (*Yeah*); improve our conduct; we must improve our sanitary conditions; we must even improve our cultural standards. There are many things that we can do. Opportunities are open now that were not open in the past, adult education and all of these things—we must take advantage of them. (*Yeah*) There are things that we can do to make ourselves respected by others. Let me rush on.

There's a third thing we must do, that we can do. We must achieve excellency in our various fields of activity and our various fields of endeavor. This is a new day, and that simply means that doors are opening now that were not open in the past. Opportunities stand before us now that did not stand before us in the past. And the great challenge before the Negro at this hour is to be ready to enter these doors as they open. (*Yes, All right*) Ralph Waldo Emerson said in an essay back in 1871 that if a man can write a better book or preach a better sermon or make a better mousetrap than his neighbor, even if he builds his house in the woods, the world will make a beaten path to his door. (*Yes*) We must get ready and do the job, the opportunities will stand there for us.

Now let me rush on to say that in this day we are going to compete with people, not Negro people. So don't set out to do a good Negro job. Do you see what I mean here? [*laughter*] That we are not out to be good Negro anything, especially at this hour. Set out to do a good job. I was in a fraternity meeting not long ago, and you know when you're pledging a fraternity, they ask you what you plan to do, or what are some of your ideals, and what is your life's work? What do you plan to do for life? And I remember very vividly, a fellow looked up and said, "Well, my aim is to be a good Negro high school principal." And I looked at him and said, "Brother, you aren't ready for this new order which is emerging, [*laughter*] You see, we are trying to get in an order where you won't have Negro high schools, and what do you mean, you're going to be a good Negro high school principal?" [*laughter*]

We've got to get ready to do a good job, a good job. Let us build up our standards of excellence in all of these areas. Businessmen, professional men—and when I say men, I'm speaking in a generic sense, I mean women also who are in these areas—set up your businesses and your professions on such a level that they will stand up anywhere. (*Yeah, All right*) Don't just set them up so that you go out begging people to come to trade with you because you're a Negro, but because you have a good business (*Yeah*), not because you're a Negro. Keep your business up and run it on a business basis, and keep it clean and well-developed so that people will come to your business (*Yeah*) because you have a good business, and not because you're a Negro (*That's right*) out here in need of a little help. You must do a good job. And I've said, you know, every-where along the way, I preach about this thing, that we must patronize Negro business. And that's not forming a new type of isolationism, but it simply means that we make jobs for other Negroes because we can't get jobs in these other places, in white busi-nesses, so often, so we must make jobs for ourselves.... Let's get ready to achieve excel-lence in all of these fields of activity.

We must use our growing economic security for worthy and meaningful ends. (*That's right*) We are making a little money now. We aren't making what we should make; standards are still low. Forty-three percent of the Negro families of America still make less than two thousand dollars a year, while just seventeen percent of the white families of America make less than two thousand dollars a year. Twenty-one percent of the Negro families of America still make less than one thousand dollars a year, while just seven percent of the white families of America make less than one thousand dollars a year. Eighty-eight percent of the Negro families of America still make less than five thousand dollars a year, while just sixty percent of the white families of America make less than five thousand dollars a year. So there is still a gap, and we have a long, long way to go to achieve economic justice. But in spite of that, we've come a long, long way. (*Yeah*) The average Negro wage earner today makes four times more than the average Negro wage earner of 1940. The annual income of the Negro is now at about seventeen billion dollars a year, more than the annual income of Canada, and more than all of the exports of the United States. We've come a long, long way.

Now, what are we going to do with this? That's the question. What are we going to spend this money for? Are we going to pool it in cooperative enterprises that will make for economic security for the race? Or are we going to waste it with meaning-less things? That's the question. Are we going to live above our standards? Now I can understand it. Are we going to live above our means? I can understand why we often do it. We often do it because we've been pushed around so much; we've been kicked about so much, until we get these big things that we often buy and can't afford in order to feed our repressed egos. So a Negro buys a Cadillac because it's as big as the white man's Cadillac and it can pass his on the highway, and when he sits up there, they're there together. I understand that. In many instances, he can't buy a home where he wants to buy it, and so he puts it in this other type of thing. I understand all of that.

In the midst of all of this, we must not let our psychological situation cause our values to be distorted. Let's live within our means. Save our money and invest it in meaningful ends. Did you ever stop to realize that according to the best economist, your automobile should not cost more than half of your annual income? Did you ever stop to realize that? That means if you make four thousand dollars a year, your car shouldn't cost much more than two thousand. Did you ever stop to realize that? Even your house, they tell us, shouldn't cost more than twice your annual income. So if you and your wife make six thousand dollars a year, your house shouldn't cost much more than twelve thousand. Did you ever stop to realize that? And yet we can find people making two thousand dollars a year riding around in a five thousand dollar car. There's something wrong with the sense of values there, isn't it? (*Yes*)

Now we must stop and see these things. And my friends, [*sic*] let us stop wasting money on frivolities. I look and see how much money we spend on liquor and on beer and on all of these alcoholic beverages. Right here in Alabama, we spend enough money on liquor to endow three or four colleges. (*That's right*) Right here in Alabama, in one state. (*That's right*) I said this, and I said it without any hesitation, to members of my fraternity. I remember three or four years ago, we met in Cleveland, Cleveland, Ohio for the convention, around the Christmas season. And that year, one of the sororities and another fraternity met with us there; we had a great meeting, a great session. At the end of the week, it was a bill that in one week, I want you to hear this, in one week a handful of Negroes spent five hundred thousand dollars for whiskey. (*Oh*) Now I thought about that. This was a tragedy that we spent more money in one week for whiskey than all of the sixteen million Negroes spent that whole year for the United Negro College Fund and the NAACP. (*Yeah*) Now that was a tragedy. (*Yeah*) That was a tragedy. (*Yeah*) Is this what we will do with our money? I know this is stinging, but this is something that we must do. This is something that we must do. (*Yeah*) Oh, it would be one of the tragedies of this century if it is revealed that the Negroes spent more money for frivolities than we spent for the cause of freedom and justice and for meaningful ends. (*All right*)

There is another point. In this period, we must develop intelligent, courageous and dedicated leadership. This is no day for the rabble rouser, whether he be Negro or white. We are grappling now with one of the most pressing and weighty social problems of the generation, and in the midst of such a weighty social problem, there is no place for misguided emotionalism. We must avoid the extremes of hotheadedness and Uncle Tomism (*That's right*), and somewhere develop the type of leadership to see the issues and that will move on calmly in the midst of strife-torn situations. Leaders are needed all over this South, in every community, all over this nation: intelligent, courageous, dedicated leadership. Not leaders in love with money, but in love with justice. Not leaders in love with publicity, but in love with humanity. I know if you're a leader, you're going to have to have money to live like everybody else. If you're a leader and you are in a situation that has the spotlight of the world, you will inevitably get some publicity. But these things must be incidental to the greater end. We must have in this hour leaders who are dedicated to the cause of freedom and justice, who have the love of humanity in their hearts.

> God give us leaders.
> A time like this demands great leaders.
> Leaders whom the lust of office does not kill;
> Leaders whom the spoils of life cannot buy;
> Leaders who possess opinions and a will;
> Leaders who will not lie;
> Leaders who can stand before a demagogue and damn his treacherous flatteries without winking.
> Tall leaders, sun-crowned, who live above the fog in public duty and in private thinking.

And finally, we must plunge deeper into the whole philosophy of nonviolence as we continue to move on in our quest for freedom. As I look at our situation and the situation of oppressed peoples all over the world, it seems to me that there are three ways that oppressed people can deal with their oppression. One is to rise up in armed revolt, one is to rise up with violence, and many people have used that method. It seems that violence has become something of the inseparable twin of western materialism. It's even become the hallmark of its grandeur. Violence nevertheless solves no social problems. It only creates new and more complicated ones. Yes, violence often brings about temporary victory, but never permanent peace. This evening as I stand before you, it seems that I can hear the voice crying through the vista of time, still saying to men in this generation: "He who lives by the sword, will perish by the sword." (*All right*) History is cluttered with the wreckage of nations and communities that failed to hear that command. Violence is not the way.

And this is the way (*Yes*) that will bring us once more into that society which we think of as the brotherhood of man. (*Yes*) This will be that day when white people, colored people, whether they are brown or whether they are yellow or whether they are black (*Yeah*), will all join together and stretch out with their arms (*Oh yeah*) and be able to cry out: "Free at last! (*Yeah*)

The Power of Nonviolence, 1957

From the very beginning there was a philosophy undergirding [*sic*] the Montgomery boycott, the philosophy of nonviolent resistance. There was always the problem of getting this method over because it didn't make sense to most of the people in the beginning. We had to use our mass meetings to explain nonviolence to a community of people who had never heard of the philosophy and in many instances were not sympathetic with it. We had meetings twice a week on Mondays and on Thursdays, and we had an institute on nonviolence and social change. We had to make it clear that nonviolent resistance is not a method of cowardice. It does resist. It is not a method of stagnant passivity and deadening complacency. The nonviolent resister is just as opposed to the evil that he is standing against as the violent resister but he resists without violence. This method is nonaggressive [*sic*] physically but strongly aggressive spiritually.

Not to Humiliate But to Win Over

Another thing that we had to get over was the fact that the nonviolent resister does not seek to humiliate or defeat the opponent but to win his friendship and understanding. This was always a cry that we had to set before people that our aim is not to defeat the white community, not to humiliate the white community, but to win the friendship of all of the persons who had perpetrated this system in the past. The end of violence or the aftermath of violence is bitterness. The aftermath of nonviolence is reconciliation and the creation of a beloved community. A boycott is never an end within itself. It is merely a means to awaken a sense of shame within the oppressor but the end is reconciliation, the end is redemption.

Then we had to make it clear also that the nonviolent resister seeks to attack the evil system rather than individuals who happen to be caught up in the system. And this is why I say from time to time that the struggle in the South is not so much the tension between white people and Negro people. The struggle is rather between justice and injustice, between the forces of darkness. And if there is a victory it will not be a victory merely for fifty thousand Negroes. But it will be a victory for justice, a victory for good will, a victory for democracy.

Another basic thing we had to get over is that nonviolent resistance is also an internal matter. It not only avoids external violence or external physical violence but also internal violence of spirit. And so at the center of our movement stood the philosophy of love. The attitude that the only way to ultimately change humanity and make for the society that we all long for is to keep love at the center of our lives. Now people used to ask me from the beginning what do you mean by love and how is it that you can tell us to love those persons who seek to defeat us and those persons who stand against us; how can you love such persons? And I had to make it clear all along that love in its highest sense is not a sentimental sort of thing, not even an affectionate sort of thing.

The Ethical Demands for Integration, 1962

The problem of race and color prejudice remains America's greatest moral dilemma. When one considers the impact it has upon our nation, internally and externally, its resolution might well determine our destiny. History has thrust upon our generation an indescribably important task—to complete a process of democratization which our nation has too long developed too slowly, but which is our most powerful weapon for world respect and emulation. How we deal with this crucial situation will determine our moral health as individuals, our cultural health as a region, our political health as a nation, and our prestige as a leader of the free world. The shape of the world today does not afford us the luxury of an anemic democracy. The price that America must pay for the continued oppression of the Negro is the price of its own destruction. The hour is late; the clock of destiny is ticking out; we must act now before it is too late.

Fanatical Death Throes

Happily, we have made some meaningful strides in breaking down the barriers of racial segregation. Ever since 1954, when the Supreme Court examined the legal body of segregation and pronounced it constitutionally dead, the system has been on the wane. Even the devout die-hards who used to cry "never," are now saying "later." Much of the tumult and the shouting interspersed with tirades against "race-mixing," "mongrelization of the races," and "outside agitators" represent the fanatical death throes of a dying system. As minimal as may be the "across-the-board" statistics, desegregation is in process. The bells of history are definitely tolling for segregation. I am convinced that in less than ten years desegregation will be a reality throughout the South.

Desegregation Not Enough

However, when the *desegregation* process is one hundred percent complete, the human relations dilemma of our nation will still be monumental unless we launch now the parallel thrust of the *integration* process. Although the terms desegregation and integration are often used interchangeably, there is a great deal of difference between the two. In the context of what our national community needs, *desegregation* alone is empty and shallow. We must always be aware of the fact that our ultimate goal is integration, and that desegregation is only a first step on the road to the good society. Perhaps this is the point at which we should define our terms.

Integration the Ultimate Goal

The word *segregation* represents a system that is prohibitive; it denies the Negro equal access to schools, parks, restaurants, libraries and the like. *Desegregation* is eliminative and negative, for it simply removes these legal and social prohibitions. Integration is creative, and is therefore more profound and far-reaching than desegregation. Integration is the positive acceptance of desegregation and the welcomed participation of Negroes into the total range of human activities. Integration is genuine intergroup [*sic*], interpersonal doing. Desegregation then, rightly, is only a short-range goal. Integration is the ultimate goal of our national community. Thus, as America pursues the important task of respecting the "letter of the law," i.e., compliance with desegregation decisions, she must be equally concerned with the "spirit of the law," i.e., commitment to the democratic dream of integration.

We do not have to look very far to see the pernicious effects of a desegregated society that is not integrated. It leads to "physical proximity without spiritual affinity." It gives us a society where men are physically desegregated and spiritually segregated, where elbows are together and hearts are apart. It gives us special togetherness and spiritual apartness. It leaves us with a stagnant equality of sameness rather than a constructive equality of oneness.

Therefore, our topic leads us to an analysis of the "oughtness" of integration. On the basis of what is right, why is integration an *end* and desegregation only a *means*? In the context of justice, freedom, morality and religion, what are the basic ethical demands of integration?

What Is Freedom?

What is freedom? It is, first, the capacity to deliberate or weigh alternatives. "Shall I be a teacher or a lawyer?" "Shall I vote for this candidate or the other candidate?" "Shall I be a Democrat, Republican or Socialist?" Second, freedom expresses itself in decision. The word decision like the word incision involves the image of cutting. Incision means to cut in, decision means to cut off. When I make a decision I cut off alternatives and make a choice. The existentialists say we must choose, that we are choosing animals; and if we do not choose we sink into thinghood and the mass mind. A third expression of freedom is responsibility. This is the obligation of the person to respond if he is questioned about his decisions. No one else can respond for him. He alone must respond, for his acts are determined by the centered totality of his being.

From this analysis we can clearly see the evilness of segregation. It cuts off one's capacity to deliberate, decide and respond.

The absence of freedom is the imposition of restraint on my deliberation as to what I shall do, where I shall live, how much I shall earn, the kind of tasks I shall pursue. I am robbed of the basic quality of man-ness. When I cannot choose what I shall do or where I shall live or how I shall survive, it means in fact that someone or some system has already made these a priori decisions for me, and I am reduced to an animal. I do not live; I merely exist. The only resemblances I have to real life are the motor responses and functions that are akin to humankind. I cannot adequately assume responsibility as a person because I have been made a party to a decision in which I played no part in making.

Now to be sure, this is hyperbole in some degree but only to underscore what actually happens when a man is robbed of his freedom. The very nature of his life is altered and his being cannot make the full circle of personhood because that which is basic to the character of life itself has been diminished.

Social Leprosy

This is why segregation has wreaked havoc with the Negro. It is sometimes difficult to determine which are the deepest—the physical wounds or the psychological wounds. Only a Negro can understand the social leprosy that segregation inflicts upon him. The suppressed fears and resentments, and the expressed anxieties and sensitivities make each day of life turmoil. Every confrontation with the restrictions imposed is another emotional battle in a never-ending war. He is shackled in his waking moments to tiptoe stance, never quite knowing what to expect next and in his subconscious he wrestles with this added demon.

Is there any argument to support the withdrawing of life-quality from groups because of the color of their skin, or the texture of their hair or any external characteristic which has nothing at all to do with life-quality? Certainly not on the grounds of morality, justice or religion. Nothing can be more diabolical than a deliberate attempt to destroy in any man his will to be a man and to withhold from him that something that constitutes his true reserve. Desegregation then is not enough for it only travels a part of the distance. It vouchsafes the lack of restriction against one's freedom but it does not prohibit the blocking of his total capacity. Only integration can do this, for it unchains the spirit and the mind and provides for the highest degree of life-quality freedom. I may do well in a *desegregated* society but I can never know what my total capacity is until I live in an *integrated* society. I cannot be free until I have had the opportunity to fulfill my total capacity untrammeled by any artificial hindrance or barrier.

Integration demands that we recognize that a denial of freedom is a denial of life itself.

Law Can Help

Let us never succumb to the temptation of believing that legislation and judicial decrees play only minor roles in solving this problem. Morality cannot be legislated, but behavior can be regulated. Judicial decrees may not change the heart, but they can restrain the heartless. The law cannot make an employer love an employee, but it can prevent him from refusing to hire me because of the color of my skin. The habits, if not the hearts of people, have been and are being altered everyday by legislative acts, judicial decisions and executive orders. Let us not be misled by those who argue that segregation cannot be ended by the force of law.

But acknowledging this, we must admit that the ultimate solution to the race problem lies in the willingness of men to obey the unenforceable. Court orders and federal enforcement agencies are of inestimable value in achieving desegregation, but desegregation is only a partial, though necessary step toward the final goal which we seek to realize, genuine intergroup [*sic*] and interpersonal living. Desegregation will break down the legal barriers and bring men together physically, but something must touch the hearts and souls of men so that they will come together spiritually because it is natural and right. A vigorous enforcement of civil rights laws will bring an end to segregated public facilities which are barriers to a truly desegregated society, but it cannot bring an end to fears, prejudice, pride, and irrationality, which are the barriers to a truly integrated society. Those dark and demonic responses will be removed only as men are possessed by the invisible, inner law which etches on their hearts the conviction that all men are brothers and that love is mankind's most potent weapon for personal and social transformation. True integration will be achieved by true neighbors who are willingly obedient to unenforceable obligations.

I Have a Dream, 1963

I am happy to join with you today in what will go down in history as the greatest demonstration for freedom in the history of our nation.

Fivescore years ago, a great American, in whose symbolic shadow we stand today, signed the Emancipation Proclamation. This momentous decree came as a great beacon light of hope to millions of Negro slaves who had been seared in the flames of withering injustice. It came as a joyous daybreak to end the long night of their captivity.

But one hundred years later, the Negro still is not free; one hundred years later, the life of the Negro is still sadly crippled by the manacles of segregation and the chains of discrimination; one hundred years later, the Negro lives on a lonely island of poverty in the midst of a vast ocean of material prosperity; one hundred years later, the Negro is still languished in the corners of American society and finds himself in exile in his own land.

So we've come here today to dramatize a shameful condition. In a sense we've come to our nation's capital to cash a check. When the architects of our republic wrote the magnificent words of the Constitution and the Declaration of Independence, they were signing a promissory note to which every American was to fall heir. This note was the promise that all men, yes, black men as well as white men, would be guaranteed the unalienable rights of life, liberty, and the pursuit of happiness.

It is obvious today that America has defaulted on this promissory note in so far as her citizens of color are concerned. Instead of honoring this sacred obligation, America has given the Negro people a bad check; a check which has come back marked "insufficient funds." We refuse to believe that there are insufficient funds in the great vaults of opportunity of this nation. And so we've come to cash this check, a check that will give us upon demand the riches of freedom and the security of justice.

We have also come to this hallowed spot to remind America of the fierce urgency of now. This is no time to engage in the luxury of cooling off or to take the tranquilizing drug of gradualism. Now is the time to make real the promises of democracy; now is the time to rise from the dark and desolate valley of segregation to the sunlit path of racial justice; now is the time to lift our nation from the quicksands [*sic*] of racial injustice to the solid rock of brotherhood; now is the time to make justice a reality for all God's children. It would be fatal for the nation to over look the urgency of the moment. This sweltering summer of the Negro's legitimate discontent will not pass until there is an invigorating autumn of freedom and equality.

Nineteen sixty-three is not an end, but a beginning. And those who hope that the Negro needed to blow off steam and will now be content, will have a rude awakening if the nation returns to business as usual.

There will be neither rest nor tranquility in America until the Negro is granted his citizenship rights. The whirlwinds of revolt will continue to shake the foundations of our nation until the bright day of justice emerges.

But there is something that I must say to my people who stand on the warm threshold which leads into the palace of justice. In the process of gaining our rightful place we must not be guilty of wrongful deeds.

Let us not seek to satisfy our thirst for freedom by drinking from the cup of bitterness and hatred. We must forever conduct our struggle on the high plane of dignity and discipline. We must not allow our creative protest to degenerate into physical violence. Again and again we must rise to the majestic heights of meeting physical force with soul force.

The marvelous new militancy which has engulfed the Negro community must not lead us to a distrust of all white people, for many of our white brothers, as evidenced by their presence here today, have come to realize that their destiny is tied up with our destiny and they have come to realize that their freedom is inextricably bound to our freedom. This offense we share mounted to storm the battlements of injustice must be carried forth by a biracial army. We cannot walk alone.

And as we walk, we must make the pledge that we shall always march ahead. We cannot turn back. There are those who are asking the devotees of civil rights, "When will you be satisfied?" We can never be satisfied as long as the Negro is the victim of the unspeakable horrors of police brutality.

We can never be satisfied as long as our bodies, heavy with fatigue of travel, cannot gain lodging in the motels of the highways and the hotels, of the cities. We cannot be satisfied as long as the Negro's basic mobility is from a smaller ghetto to a larger one.

We can never be satisfied as long as our children are stripped of their selfhood and robbed of their dignity by signs stating "for whites only." We cannot be satisfied as long as a Negro in Mississippi cannot vote and a Negro in New York believes he has nothing for which to vote. No, we are not satisfied, and we will not be satisfied until justice rolls down like waters and righteousness like a mighty stream.

I am not unmindful that some of you have come here out of excessive trials and tribulation. Some of you have come fresh from narrow jail cells. Some of you have come from areas where your quest for freedom left you battered by the storms of persecution and staggered by the winds of police brutality. You have been the veterans of creative suffering. Continue to work with the faith that unearned suffering is redemptive.

Go back to Mississippi; go back to Alabama; go back to South Carolina; go back to Georgia; go back to Louisiana; go back to the slums and ghettos of the northern cities, knowing that somehow this situation can, and will be changed. Let us not wallow in the valley of despair.

So I say to you, my friends, that even though we must face the difficulties of today and tomorrow, I still have a dream. It is a dream deeply rooted in the American dream that one day this nation will rise up and live out the true meaning of its creed—we hold these truths to be self-evident, that all men are created equal.

I have a dream that one day on the red hills of Georgia, sons of former slaves and sons of former slave-owners will be able to sit down together at the table of brotherhood.

I have a dream that one day, even the state of Mississippi, a state sweltering with the heat of injustice, sweltering with the heat of oppression, [*sic*] will be transformed into an oasis of freedom and justice.

I have a dream my four little children will one day live in a nation where they will not be judged by the color of their skin but by content of their character. I have a dream today!

I have a dream that one day, down in Alabama, with its vicious racists, with its governor having his lips dripping with the words of interposition and nullification, that one day, right there in Alabama, little black boys and black girls will be able to join hands with little white boys and white girls as sisters and brothers. I have a dream today!

I have a dream that one day every valley shall be exalted, every hill and mountain shall be made low, the rough places shall be made plain, and the crooked places shall be made straight and the glory of the Lord will be revealed and all flesh shall see it together.

This is our hope. This is the faith that I go back to the South with.

With this faith we will be able to hew out of the mountain of despair a stone of hope. With this faith we will be able to transform the jangling discords of our nation into a beautiful symphony of brotherhood.

With this faith we will be able to work together, to pray together, to struggle together, to go to jail together, to stand up for freedom together, knowing that we will be free one day. This will be the day when all of God's children will be able to sing with new meaning "my country 'tis of thee; sweet land of liberty; of thee I sing; land where my fathers died, land of the pilgrim's pride; from every mountain side, let freedom ring"— and if America is to be a great nation, this must become true.

So let freedom ring from the prodigious hilltops of New Hampshire.

Let freedom ring from the mighty mountains of New York.

Let freedom ring from the heightening Alleghenies of Pennsylvania.

Let freedom ring from the snow-capped Rockies of Colorado.

Let freedom ring from the curvaceous slopes of California.

But not only that.

Let freedom ring from Stone Mountain of Georgia.

Let freedom ring from Lookout Mountain of Tennessee.

Let freedom ring from every hill and molehill of Mississippi, from every mountain-side, let freedom ring.

And when we allow freedom to ring, when we let it ring from every village and hamlet, from every state and city, we will be able to speed up that day when all of God's children—black men and white men, Jews and Gentiles, Catholics and Protestants— will be able to join hands and to sing in the words of the old Negro spiritual, "Free at last, free at last; thank God Almighty, we are free at last."

Where We Are Going, 1967

In the treatment of poverty nationally, one fact stands out: There are twice as many white poor as Negro poor in the United States. Therefore I will not dwell on the experiences of poverty that derive from racial discrimination, but will discuss the poverty that affects white and Negro alike.

Up to recently we have proceeded from a premise that poverty is a consequence of multiple evils: lack of education restricting job opportunities; poor housing which stultified home life and suppressed initiative; fragile family relationships which distorted personality development. The logic of this approach suggested that each of these causes be attacked one by one. Hence a housing program to transform living conditions, improved educational facilities to furnish tools for better job opportunities, and family counseling to create better personal adjustments were designed. In combination these measures were intended to remove the causes of poverty.

While none of these remedies in itself is unsound, all have a fatal disadvantage. The programs have never proceeded on a coordinated basis or at a similar rate of development. Housing measures have fluctuated at the whims of legislative bodies. They have been piecemeal and pygmy. Educational reforms have been even more sluggish and entangled in bureaucratic stalling and economy-dominated decisions. Family assistance stagnated in neglect and then suddenly was discovered to be the central issue on the basis of hasty and superficial studies. At no time has a total, coordinated and fully adequate program been conceived. As a consequence, fragmentary and spasmodic reforms have failed to reach down to the profoundest needs of the poor.

In addition to the absence of coordination and sufficiency, the programs of the past all have another common failing—they are indirect. Each seeks to solve poverty by first solving something else.

I am now convinced that the simplest approach will prove to be the most effective—the solution to poverty is to abolish it directly by a now widely discussed measure: the guaranteed income.

Earlier in this century this proposal would have been greeted with ridicule and denunciation as destructive of initiative and responsibility. At that time economic status was considered the measure of the individual's abilities and talents. In the simplistic thinking of that day the absence of worldly goods indicated a want of industrious habits and moral fiber.

We have come a long way in our understanding of human motivation and of the blind operation of our economic system. Now we realize that dislocations in the market operation of our economy and the prevalence of discrimination thrust people into idleness and bind them in constant or frequent unemployment against their will. The poor are less often dismissed from our conscience today by being branded as inferior and incompetent. We also know that no matter how dynamically the economy develops and expands it does not eliminate all poverty.

We have come to the point where we must make the nonproducer a consumer or we will find ourselves drowning in a sea of consumer goods. We have so energetically mastered production that we now must give attention to distribution. Though there have been increases in purchasing power, they have lagged behind increases in production. Those at the lowest economic level, the poor white and Negro, the aged and chronically ill, are traditionally unorganized and therefore have little ability to force the necessary growth in their income. They stagnate or become even poorer in relation to the larger society.

The problem indicates that our emphasis must be two-fold. We must create full employment or we must create incomes. People must be made consumers by one method or the other. Once they are placed in this position, we need to be concerned that the potential of the individual is not wasted. New forms of work that enhance the social good will have to be devised for those for whom traditional jobs are not available.

In 1879 Henry George anticipated this state of affairs when he wrote, in Progress and Poverty:

"The fact is that the work which improves the condition of mankind, the work which extends knowledge and increases power and enriches literature, and elevates thought, is not done to secure a living. It is not the work of slaves, driven to their task either by the lash of a master or by animal necessities. It is the work of men who perform it for their own sake, and not that they may get more to eat or drink, or wear, or display. In a state of society where want is abolished, work of this sort could be enormously increased."

We are likely to find that the problems of housing and education, instead of preceding the elimination of poverty, will themselves be affected if poverty is first abolished. The poor transformed into purchasers will do a great deal on their own to alter housing decay. Negroes, who have a double disability, will have a greater effect on discrimination when they have the additional weapon of cash to use in their struggle.

Beyond these advantages, a host of positive psychological changes inevitably will result from widespread economic security. The dignity of the individual will flourish when the decisions concerning his life and in his own hands, when he has the assurance that his income is stable and certain, and when he know that he has the means to seek self-improvement. Personal conflicts between husband, wife and children will diminish when the unjust measurement of human worth on a scale of dollars is eliminated.

Two conditions are indispensable if we are to ensure that the guaranteed income operates as a consistently progressive measure. First, it must be pegged to the median income of society, not the lowest levels of income. To guarantee an income at the floor would simply perpetuate welfare standards and freeze into the society poverty conditions. Second, the guaranteed income must be dynamic; it must automatically increase as the total social income grows. Were it permitted to remain static under growth conditions, the recipients would suffer a relative decline. If periodic reviews disclose that the whole national income has risen, then the guaranteed income would have to be adjusted upward by the same percentage. Without these safeguards a creeping retrogression would occur, nullifying the gains of security and stability.

This proposal is not a "civil rights" program, in the sense that that term is currently used. The program would benefit all the poor, including the two-thirds of them who are white. I hope that both Negro and white will act in coalition to effect this change, because their combined strength will be necessary to overcome the fierce opposition we must realistically anticipate.

Our nation's adjustment to a new mode of thinking will be facilitated if we realize that for nearly forty years two groups in our society have already been enjoying a guaranteed income. Indeed, it is a symptom of our confused social values that these two groups turn out to be the richest and the poorest. The wealthy who own securities have always had an assured income; and their polar opposite, the relief client, has been guaranteed an income, however miniscule, through welfare benefits.

John Kenneth Galbraith has estimated that $20 billion a year would effect a guaranteed income, which he describes as "not much more than we will spend the next fiscal year to rescue freedom and democracy and religious liberty as these are defined by 'experts' in Vietnam."

The contemporary tendency in our society is to base our distribution on scarcity, which has vanished, and to compress our abundance into the overfed mouths of the middle and upper classes until they gag with superfluity. If democracy is to have breadth of meaning, it is necessary to adjust this inequity. It is not only moral, but it is also intelligent. We are wasting and degrading human life by clinging to archaic thinking.

The curse of poverty has no justification in our age. It is socially as cruel and blind as the practice of cannibalism at the dawn of civilization, when men ate each other because they had not yet learned to take food from the soil or to consume the abundant animal life around them. The time has come for us to civilize ourselves by the total, direct and immediate abolition of poverty.

PART III

BLACK NATIONALISM
ITS ROOTS AND DEVELOPMENT

14.
MARTIN R. DELANY

Martin R. Delany (1812–1885) was an abolitionist and one of the first documented Black Nationalists. Although Delany practiced medicine as a profession he became a well-known public orator and freedom fighter. Martin Delany like his counterparts saw the Black press as a primary means by which to raise awareness and address the problems of racial inequality. Initially, Delany published a weekly newspaper, *Mystery. Mystery* was an abolitionist paper. After four years, in 1847, Delany closed his paper and joined forces with Frederick Douglass at the *North Star.* Delany was probably best known not for his newspaper work but for publication of his 1852 book, *The Condition, Elevation, Emigration, and Destiny of the Colored People of the United States, Politically Considered.* The book, which is excerpted here, has become known as his manifesto for Black Nationalism, namely political nationalism. Interestingly, Delany also published fiction; however, even these works contained a political message. In response to Harriet Beecher Stowe's infamous *Uncle Tom's Cabin,* Delany wrote *Blake, or the Huts of America.* His book had a message of Black cultural nationalism. Delany was angered by *Uncle Tom's Cabin,* which he argued presented pathological images of Black folk; Delany posited that Stowe's book presented slaves as docile "Sambos." Instead, *Blake* focused on the insurgency of slaves. Delany's political work was not just discursive.

In 1854 Martin Delany assisted in the organization of the National Emigration Convention of Colored People; the convention was his attempt at praxis. Here, Delany advocated for the migration of newly freed slaves and all Blacks to Central and/or South America, the Caribbean, and regions in East Africa. In order to further his efforts he traveled to Africa in order to facilitate their emigration. At home and abroad he lectured about the need for political nationalism. However, in order to make life more tolerable for Blacks while still in the United States he also fought to improve existing conditions in the United States. For example, he took a job with the Freedman's Bureau in order to fight the disenfranchisement of Black people. While still in the United States, Delany posited the importance of political participation. In 1874 he ran for Lieutenant Governor in South Carolina; he only lost by a narrow margin.

Overview of Ideas

Martin Delany was one of the early founders of Black Nationalism, particularly political nationalism. His work was incredibly radical for the time in which he wrote, given that his contemporaries, abolitionists, were all focused on ending slavery and instituting integration. In *The Condition, Elevation, Emigration and Destiny of the Colored People of the United States*, Delany argued that while there are oppressed groups of people, who are denied basic rights and equality all over the globe, none have been treated as horrifically as Black people in the United States. Delany agreed with other abolitionists; in this ostensibly extraordinary republic, Africans were brought as slaves, not because they were inferior but to serve as free labor and racist discourses followed as a means by which to legitimize the oppression of Africans in the United States. However, what was the remedy? Unlike his abolitionist counterparts, the answer was not integration here in the United States. While abolitionists were beginning to call for integration, particularly access to political rights, Delany argued that political rights in the United States were almost all but useless. He said, "we may exercise the right of *voting* only, which to us, is but poor satisfaction; and we by no means cherish the privilege of voting somebody into office, to help make laws that degrade us." Instead political emancipation could be realized by establishing a nation for Black people, organized, and run by Black people. He was an originator of Black separatism.

The American Colonization Society along with many freed slaves sought refuge and emancipation in Liberia, outside of the Western Hemisphere. This was to become the home of freed slaves. However, Delany was skeptical about the success of emigration to Liberia. Instead he proffered that emigration to other parts of Africa and South and Central America were more ideal. Delany argued that the proposition to send slaves to Liberia was originated by racist Whites. In addition, Liberia was geographically not ideal. Most importantly, Liberia was not an independent country but an American satellite—the brainchild of racist American colonizationists. Instead, "Central and South America, are evidently the ultimate destination and future home of the colored race on this continent." These regions were rich in resources and had a better climate. In addition, the West Indies and Canada were also far better options than Liberia. "Will we go? Go we must, and go we will, as there is no alternative. To remain here in North America, and be crushed to the earth in vassalage and degradation, we never will."

In addition to emigration Delany was a strong proponent of self-sufficiency, a guiding principle in Black Nationalism. "Our Elevation is the work of our own hands. And Mexico, Central America, the West Indies, and South America, all present now, opportunities for the individual enterprise of our young men." Economic Nationalism, another quintessential component of Black Nationalism, suggests that Black people must be economically independent and strive to foster independent economic networks that will allow for stability, economic prosperity, and promote solidarity. Interestingly, like Booker T. Washington, Delany placed great emphasis on business and vocational education. In fact, unlike Du Bois amongst others, Delany understood people's desires to push their children into professional and higher education. However, Delany posited that practical business knowledge was paramount. Again, sounding a lot like Washington, "we should first be mechanics and common tradesmen, and professions as a matter of course would grow out of the wealth made thereby. Young men and women, must now prepare themselves for usefulness." Education should focus on political economy; Black folk must concern themselves with learning to acquire wealth. It is important to note that Delany saw this direction for both men and women. He said women should not be writing recipes when they can be writing invoices. This type of education, a focus on economic uplift, and the ability to control one's own political destiny will allow African Americans to transform their characters and heal their brutalized and crippled psyches. Slavery made Black people dependent and psychologically weak. However, according to Delany, relying on conservative logic, his platform would empower Black people and allow them to undergo much needed individual transformation, which, over time, would allow their children to escape cultural pathology.

The Condition, Elevation, Emigration, and Destiny of the Colored People of the United States, 1852

Chapter I. Condition of Many Classes in Europe Considered

That there have been in all ages and in all countries, in every quarter of the habitable globe, especially among those nations laying the greatest claim to civilization and enlightenment, classes of people who have been deprived of equal privileges, political, religious and social, cannot be denied, and that this deprivation on the part of the ruling classes is cruel and unjust, is also equally true. Such classes have ever been looked upon as inferior to their oppressors, and have ever been mainly the domestics and menials of society, doing the low offices and drudgery of those among whom they lived, moving about and existing by mere sufferance, having no rights nor privileges but those conceded by the common consent of their political superiors. These are historical facts that cannot be controverted, and therefore proclaim in tones more eloquently than thunder, the listful attention of every oppressed man, woman, and child under the government of the people of the United States of America.

In past ages there were many such classes, as the Israelites in Egypt, the Gladiators in Rome, and similar classes in Greece; and in the present age, the Gipsies in Italy and Greece, the Cossacs in Russia and Turkey, the Sclaves and Croats in the Germanic States, and the Welsh and Irish among the British, to say nothing of various other classes among other nations.

That there have in all ages, in almost every nation, existed a nation within a nation— a people who although forming a part and parcel of the population, yet were from force of circumstances, known by the peculiar position they occupied, forming in fact, by the deprivation of political equality with others, no part, and if any, but a restricted part of the body politic of such nations, is also true.

Such then are the Poles in Russia, the Hungarians in Austria, the Scotch, Irish, and Welsh in the United Kingdom, and such also are the Jews, scattered throughout not only the length and breadth of Europe, but almost the habitable globe, maintaining their national characteristics, and looking forward in high hopes of seeing the day when they may return to their former national position of self-government and independence, let that be in whatever part of the habitable world it may. This is the lot of these various classes of people in Europe, and it is not our intention here, to discuss the justice or injustice of the causes that have contributed to their degradation, but simply to set forth the undeniable facts, which are as glaring as the rays of a noon-day's sun, thereby to impress them indelibly on the mind of every reader of this pamphlet.

It is not enough, that these people are deprived of equal privileges by their rulers, but, the more effectually to succeed, the equality of these classes must be denied, and their inferiority by nature as distinct races, actually asserted. This policy is necessary to appease the opposition that might be interposed in their behalf. Wherever there is arbitrary rule, there must of necessity, on the part of the dominant classes, superiority be assumed. To assume superiority, is to deny the equality of others, and to deny their equality, is to premise their incapacity for self-government. Let this once be conceded, and there will be little or no sympathy for the oppressed, the oppressor being left to prescribe whatever terms at discretion for their government, suits his own purpose.

Such then is the condition of various classes in Europe; yes, nations, for centuries within nations, even without the hope of redemption among those who oppress them. And however unfavorable their condition, there is none more so than that of the colored people of the United States.

Chapter II. Comparative Condition of the Colored People of the United States

The United States, untrue to her trust and unfaithful to her professed principles of republican equality, has also pursued a policy of political degradation to a large portion of her native born countrymen, and that class is the Colored People. Denied an equality [*sic*] not only of political, but of natural rights, in common with the rest of our fellow citizens, there is no species of degradation to which we are not subject.

Reduced to abject slavery is not enough, the very thought of which should awaken every sensibility of our common nature; but those of their descendants who are freemen even in the non-slaveholding States, occupy the very same position politically, religiously, civilly and socially, (with but few exceptions,) as the bondman occupies in the slave States.

In those States, the bondman is disenfranchised, and for the most part, so are we. He is denied all civil, religious, and social privileges, except such as he gets by mere sufferance, and so are we. They have no part nor lot in the government of the country, neither have we. They are ruled and governed without representation, existing as mere nonentities among the citizens, and excrescences on the body politic—a mere dreg in community, and so are we. Where then is our political superiority to the enslaved? none, neither are we superior in any other relation to society, except that we are de facto masters of ourselves and joint rulers of our own domestic household, while the bondman's self is claimed by another, and his relation to his family denied him. What the unfortunate classes are in Europe, such are we in the United States, which is folly to deny, insanity not to understand, blindness not to see, and surely now full time that our eyes were opened to these startling truths, which for ages have stared us full in the face.

It is time that we had become politicians, we mean, to understand the political economy and domestic policy of nations; that we had become as well as moral theorists, also the practical demonstrators of equal rights and self-government. Except we do, it is idle to talk about rights, it is mere chattering for the sake of being seen and heard like the slave, saying something because his so called "master" said it, and saying just what he told him to say. Have we not now sufficient intelligence among us to understand our true position, to realise [sic] our actual condition, and determine for ourselves what is best to be done? If we have not now, we never shall have, and should at once cease prating about our equality, capacity, and all that.

[T]he African race had long been known to Europeans, in all ages of the world's history, as a long-lived, hardy race, subject to toil and labor of various kinds, subsisting mainly by traffic, trade, and industry, and consequently being as foreign to the sympathies of the invaders of the continent as the Indians, they were selected, captured, brought here as a laboring class, and as a matter of policy held as such. Nor was the absurd idea of natural inferiority of the African ever dreamed of, until recently adduced by the slave-holders and their abettors, in justification of their policy. This, with contemptuous indignation, we fling back into their face, as a scorpion to a vulture. And so did our patriots and leaders in the cause of regeneration know better, and never for a moment yielded to the base doctrine. But they had discovered the great fact, that a cruel policy was pursued towards our people, and that they possessed distinctive characteristics which made them the objects of proscription. These characteristics being strongly marked in the colored people, as in the Indians, by color, character of hair and so on, made them the more easily distinguished from other Americans, and the policies more effectually urged against us.

Chapter IX. Capacity of Colored Men and Women as Citizen Members of Community

The *will* of the man who sits in judgment on our liberty, is the law. To him is given *all power* to say, whether or not we have a right to enjoy freedom. This is the power over the slave in the South—this is now extended to the North. The will of the man who sits in judgment over us is the law; because it is explicitly provided that the *decision* of the commissioner shall be final, from which there can be no appeal.

The freed man of the South is even more secure than the freeborn of the North; because such persons usually have their records in the slave states, bringing their "papers" with them; and the slaveholders will be faithful to their own acts. The Northern freeman knows no records; he despises the "papers."

Depend upon no promised protection of citizens in any quarter. Their own property and liberty are jeopardised, and they will not sacrifice them for us. This we may not expect them to do.

Besides, there are no people who ever lived, love their country and obey their laws as the Americans.

Their country is their Heaven—their Laws their Scriptures—and the decrees of their Magistrates obeyed as the fiat of God. It is the most consummate delusion and mis-directed confidence to depend upon them for protection; and for a moment suppose even our children safe while walking in the streets among them.

A people capable of originating and sustaining such a law as this, are not the people to whom we are willing to entrust our liberty at discretion. What can we do? What shall we do? This is the great and important question:—Shall we submit to be dragged like brutes before heartless men, and sent into degradation and bondage?—Shall we fly, or shall we resist?

Ponder well and reflect.

A learned jurist in the United States, (Chief Justice John Gibson of Pennsylvania,) lays down this as a fundamental right in the United States: that "Every man's house is his castle, and he has the right to defend it unto the taking of life, against any attempt to enter it against his will, except for crime," by well authenticated process.

But we have no such right. It was not intended for us, any more than any other pro-vision of the law, intended for the protection of Americans. The policy is against us—it is useless to contend against it.

This is the law of the land and must be obeyed; and we candidly advise that it is useless for us to contend against it ... but we speak logically and politically, leaving morality and right out of the question—taking our position on the acknowledged popular, basis of American Policy; arguing from premise to conclusion. We must abandon all vague theory, and look at *facts* as they really are; viewing ourselves in our true political posi-tion in the body politic. To imagine ourselves to be included in the body politic, except by express legislation, is at war with common sense, and contrary to fact. Legislation, the administration of the laws of the country, and the exercise of rights by the people, all prove to the contrary. We are politically, not of them, but aliens to the laws and political privileges of the country. These are truths—fixed facts, that quaint theory and exhausted moralising, are impregnable to, and fall harmlessly before.

It is useless to talk about our rights in individual States: we can have no rights here as citizens, not recognised in our common country; as the citizens of one State, are entitled to all the rights and privileges of an American citizen in all the States—the nullity of the one necessarily implying the nullity of the other. These provisions then do not include the colored people of the United States; since there is no power left in them, whereby they may protect us as their own citizens. Our descent, by the laws of the country, stamps us with inferiority—upon us has this law worked *corruption of blood*. We are in the hands of the General Government, and no State can rescue us. The Army and Navy stand at the service of our enslavers, the whole force of which, may at any moment—even in the dead of night, as has been done—when sunk in the depth of slumber, called out for the purpose of forcing our mothers, sisters, wives, and children, or ourselves, into hopeless servitude, there to weary out a miserable life, a relief from which, death would be hailed with joy. Heaven and earth—God and Humanity!—are not these sufficient to arouse the most worthless among mankind, of whatever descent, to a sense of their true position? These laws apply to us—shall we not be aroused?

What then shall we do?—what is the remedy—is the important question to be answered? This important inquiry we shall answer, and find a remedy in when treating of the emigration of the colored people.

Chapter XVII. Emigration of the Colored People of the United States

That there have been people in all ages under certain circumstances, that may be benefited by emigration, will be admitted; and that there are circumstances "under which emigration is absolutely necessary to their political elevation, cannot be disputed.

This we see in the Exodus of the Jews from Egypt to the land of Judea; in the expedition of Dido and her followers from Tyre to Mauritania; and not to dwell upon hundreds of modern European examples—also in the ever memorable emigration of the Puritans, in 1620, from Great Britain, the land of their birth, to the wilderness of the New World, at which may be fixed the beginning of emigration to this continent as a permanent residence.

This may be acknowledged; but to advocate the emigration of the colored people of the United States from their native homes, is a new feature in our history, and at first view, may be considered objectionable, as pernicious to our interests. This objection is at once removed, when reflecting on our condition as incontrovertibly shown in a foregoing part of this work. And we shall proceed at once to give the advantages to be derived from emigration, to us as a people, in preference to any other policy that we may adopt. This granted, the question will then be, Where shall we go? This we conceive to be all-important—of paramount consideration, and shall endeavor to show the most advantageous locality; and premise the recommendation, with the strictest advice against any countenance whatever, to the emigration scheme of the so called Republic of Liberia.

Chapter XVIII. "Republic of Liberia"

We were disappointed—grievously disappointed, and proceed to show in short our objections to Liberia.

Its geographical position, in the first place, is objectionable, being located in the *sixth degree* of latitude North of the equator, in a district signally unhealthy, rendering it objectionable as a place of destination for the colored people of the United States. We shall say nothing about other parts of the African coast, and the reasons for its location where it is: it is enough for us to know the facts as they are, to justify an unqualified objection to Liberia.

In the second place, it originated in a deep laid scheme of the slaveholders of the country, to *exterminate* the free colored of the American continent; the origin being sufficient to justify us in impugning the motives.

Thirdly and lastly—Liberia is not an Independent Republic: in fact, it is not an independent nation at all; but a poor *miserable mockery*—a burlesque on a government— a pitiful dependency on the American Colonizationists, the Colonization Board at Washington city, in the District of Columbia, being the Executive and Government, and the principal man, called President, in Liberia, being the echo—a mere parrot of Rev. Robert [*sic*] R. Gurley, Elliott Cresson, Esq., Governor Pinney, and other leaders of the Colonization scheme—to do as they bid, and say what they tell him.[3] This we see in all of his doings.

Does he go to France and England, and enter into solemn treaties of an honorable recognition of the independence of his country; before his own nation has any knowledge of the result, this man called President, dispatches an official report to the Colonizationists of the United States, asking their gracious approval? Does king Grando, or a party of fishermen besiege a village and murder some of the inhabitants, this same "President," dispatches an official report to the American Colonization Board, asking for instructions—who call an Executive Session of the Board, and immediately decide that war must be waged against the enemy, placing ten thousand dollars at his disposal and war *actually declared in Liberia*, by virtue of the *instructions* of *the American Colonization Society*. A mockery of a government a disgrace to the office pretended to be held a parody on the position assumed. Liberia in Africa, is a mere dependency of Southern slaveholders, and American Colonizationists, and unworthy of any respectful consideration from us.

What would be thought of the people of Hayti, and their heads of government, if their instructions emanated from the American Anti-Slavery Society, or the British Foreign Missionary Board? Should they be respected at all as a nation? Would they be worthy of it? Certainly not. We do not expect Liberia to be all that Hayti is; but we ask and expect of her, to have a decent respect for herself to endeavor to be freemen instead of voluntary slaves. Liberia is no place for the colored freemen of the United States; and we dismiss the subject with a single remark of caution against any advice contained in a pamphlet, which we have not seen, written by Hon. James G. Birney, in favor of Liberian emigration. Mr. Birney is like the generality of white Americans, who suppose that we are too ignorant to understand what we want; whenever they wish to get rid of us, would drive us any where, so that we left them. Don't adhere to a word therein contained; we will think for ourselves. Let Mr. Birney go his way, and we will go ours. This is one of those confounded gratuities that is forced in our faces at every turn we make. We dismiss it without further comment and with it Colonization *in toto*—and Mr. Birney de facto.

Chapter XXI. Central and South America and the West Indies

Central and South America, are evidently the ultimate destination and future home of the colored race on this continent; the advantages of which in preference to all others, will be apparent when once pointed out.

Geographically, from the Northern extremity of Yucatan, down through Central and South America, to Cape Horn, there is a variation of climate from the twenty-second degree of North latitude, passing through the equatorial region; nowhere as warm as it is in the same latitude in Africa; to the *fifty-fifth degree of* South latitude, including a climate as cold as that of the Hudson Bay country in British America, colder than that of Maine, or any part known to the United States of North America; so that there is every variety of climate in South, as well as North America.

In the productions of grains, fruits, and vegetables, Central and South America are also prolific; and the best of herds are here raised. Indeed, the finest Merino sheep, as well as the principal trade in rice, sugar, cotton, and wheat, which is now preferred in California to any produced in the United States—the Chilian flour—might be carried on by the people of this most favored portion of God's legacy to man. The mineral productions excel all other parts of this continent; the rivers present the greatest internal advantage, and the commercial prospects, are without a parallel on the coast of the new world.

The advantages to the colored people of the United States, to be derived from emigration to Central, South America, and the West Indies, are incomparably greater than that of any other part of the world at present.

In the first place, there never have existed in the policy of any of the nations of Central or South America, an inequality on account of race or color, and any prohibition of rights, has generally been to the white, and not to the colored races. To the whites, not because they were white, not on account of their color but because of the policy pursued by them towards the people of other races than themselves. The population of Central and South America, consist of fifteen millions two hundred and forty thousand, adding the ten millions of Mexico; twenty-five millions two hundred and forty thousand, of which vast population, but *one-seventh* are whites, or the pure European race. Allowing a deduction of one-seventh of this population for the European race that may chance to be in those countries, and we have in South and Central America alone, the vast colored population of *thirteen millions one hundred and seventy-seven thousand;* and including Mexico, a *colored* population on this glorious continent of *twenty-one millions, six hundred and forty thousand.*

This vast number of people, our brethren—because they are precisely the same people as ourselves and share the same fate with us, as the case of numbers of them have proven, who have been adventitiously thrown among us—stand ready and willing to take us by the hand—nay, are anxiously waiting, and earnestly importuning us to come, that they may make common cause with us, and we all share the same fate. There is nothing under heaven in our way—the people stand with open arms ready to receive us. The climate, soil, and productions—the vast rivers and beautiful seacoast—the scenery of the landscape, and beauty of the starry heavens above—the song of the birds—the voice of the people say come—and God our Father bids us go.—Will we go? Go we must, and go we will, as there is no alternative. To remain here in North America, and be crushed to the earth in vassalage and degradation, we never will.

Chapter XXIII: Things as They are

> "And if thou boast TRUTH to utter,
> SPEAK, and leave the rest to God."

In presenting this work, we have but a single object in view, and that is, to inform the minds of the colored people at large, upon many things pertaining to their elevation, that but few among us are acquainted with. Unfortunately for us as a body, we have been taught to believe, that we must have some person to think for us, instead of thinking for ourselves. So accustomed are we to submission and this kind of training, that it is with difficulty, even among the most intelligent of the colored people, an audience may be elicited for any purpose whatever, if the expounder is to be a colored person; and the introduction of Subject is treated with indifference, if not contempt, when the originator is a colored person. Indeed, the most ordinary white person, is almost revered, while the most qualified colored person is totally neglected. Nothing from them is appreciated.

We have been standing comparatively still for years, following in the footsteps of our friends, believing that what they promise us can be accomplished, just because they say so, although our own knowledge should long since, have satisfied us to the contrary. Because even were it possible, with the present hate and jealousy that the whites have towards us in this country, for us to gain equality of rights with them; we never could have an equality of the exercise and enjoyment of those rights—because, the great odds of numbers are against us. We might indeed, as some at present, have the right of the elective franchise—nay, it is not the *elective franchise*, because the *elective franchise* makes the enfranchised, *eligible* to any position attainable; but we may exercise the right of *voting* only, which to us, is but poor satisfaction; and we by no means care to cherish the privilege of voting somebody into office, to help to make laws to degrade us.

In religion—because they are both *translators* and *commentators*, we must believe nothing, however absurd, but what our oppressors tell us. In Politics, nothing but such as they promulge; in Anti-Slavery, nothing but what our white brethren and friends say we must; in the mode and manner of our elevation, we must do nothing, but that which may be laid down to be done by our white brethren from some quarter or other; and now, even on the subject of emigration, there are some colored people to be found, so lost to their own interest and self-respect, as to be gulled by slave owners and colonizationists, who are led to believe there is no other place in which they can become elevated, but Liberia, a government of American slave-holders, as we have shown—simply, because white men have told them so ... we have therefore, laid this cursory treatise before our readers, with the hope that it may prove instrumental in directing the attention of our people in the right way, that leads to their Elevation. Go or stay—of course each is free to do as he pleases—one thing is certain; our Elevation is the work of our own hands. And Mexico, Central America, the West Indies, and South America, all present now, opportunities for the individual enterprise of our young men, who prefer to remain in the United States, in preference to going where they can enjoy real freedom, and equality of rights. Freedom of Religion, as well as of politics, being tolerated in all of these places.

Let our young men and women, prepare themselves for usefulness and business; that the men may enter into merchandise, trading, and other things of importance; the young women may become teachers of various kinds, and otherwise fill places of usefulness. Parents must turn their attention more to the education of their children. We mean, to educate them for useful practical business. Educate them for the Store and the Counting House—to do every-day practical business purposes. Consult the children's propensities, and direct their education according to their inclinations. It may be, that there is too great a desire on the part of parents, to give their children a professional education, before the body of the people, are ready for it. A people must be a business people, and have more to depend upon than mere help in people's houses and Hotels, before they are either able to support, or capable of properly appreciating the services, of professional men among them. This has been one of our great mistakes—we have gone in advance of ourselves. We have commenced at the superstructure of the building, instead of the foundation—at the top instead of the bottom. We should first be mechanics and common tradesmen, and professions as a matter of course would grow out of the wealth made thereby. Young men and women, must now prepare for usefulness the day of our Elevation is at hand—all the world now gazes at us and Central and South America, and the West Indies, bid us come and be men and women, protected, secure, beloved and Free.

The branches of education most desirable for the preparation of youth, for practical useful every-day life, are Arithmetic and good Penmanship, in order to be Accountants; and a good rudimental knowledge of Geography—which has ever been neglected, and under estimated—and of Political Economy; which without knowledge of the first, no people can ever become adventurous—nor of the second, never will be an enterprising people. Geography, teaches a knowledge of the world, and Political Economy, a knowledge of the wealth of nations; or how to make money. These are not abstruse sciences, or learning not easily acquired or understood; but simply, common School Primer learning, that every body may get. And, although it is the very Key to prosperity and success in common life, but few know any thing about it. Unfortunately for our people, so soon as their children learn to read a Chapter in the New Testament, and scribble a miserable hand, they are pronounced to have "Learning enough;" and taken away from School, no use to themselves, nor community. This is apparent in our Public Meetings, and Official Church Meetings; of the great number of men present, there are but few capable of filling a Secretaryship. Some of the large cities may be an exception to this. Of the multitudes of Merchants, and Business men throughout this country, Europe, and the world, few are qualified, beyond the branches here laid down by us as necessary for business. What did John Jacob Astor, Stephen Girard, or do the millionaires and the greater part of the merchant princes, and mariners, know about Latin and Greek, and the Classics? Precious few of them know any thing. In proof of this, in 1841, during the Administration of President Tyler, when the mutiny was detected on board of the American Man of War Brig Somers, the names of the Mutineers, were recorded by young S—a Midshipman in Greek. Captain Alexander Slidell McKenzie, Commanding, was unable to read them; and in his dispatches [*sic*] to the Government, in justification of his policy in executing the criminals, said that he "discovered some curious characters which he was unable to read," &c; showing thereby, that that high functionary, did not understand even the Greek Alphabet, which was only necessary, to have been able to read proper names written in Greek.

What we most need then, is a good business practical Education; because, the Classical and Professional education of so many of our young men, before their parents are able to support them, and community ready to patronize them, only serves to lull their energy, and cripple the otherwise, praiseworthy efforts they would make in life. A Classical education, is only suited to the wealthy, or those who have a prospect of gaining a livelihood by it. The writer does not wish to be understood, as underrating a Classical and Professional education; this is not his intention; he fully appreciates them, having had some such advantages himself; but he desires to give a proper guide, and put a check to the extravagant idea that is fast obtaining, among our people especially, that a Classical, or as it is termed, a "finished education," is necessary to prepare one for usefulness in life. Let us have an education, that shall practically develope [*sic*] our thinking faculties and manhood; and then, and not until then, shall we be able to vie with our oppressors, go where we may. We as heretofore, have been on the extreme; either no qualification at all, or a Collegiate education. We jumped too far; taking a leap from the deepest abyss to the highest summit; rising from the ridiculous to the sublime; without medium or intermission.

Let our young women have an education; let their minds be well informed; well stored with useful information and practical proficiency, rather than the light superficial acquirements, popularly and fashionably called accomplishments. We desire accomplishments, but they must be *useful.*

Our females must be qualified, because they are to be the mothers of our children. As mothers are the first nurses and instructors of children; from them children consequently, get their first impressions, which being always the most lasting, should be the most correct. Raise the mothers above the level of degradation, and the offspring is elevated with them. In a word, instead of our young women, transcribing in their blank books, recipes for *Cooking*; we desire to see them making the transfer of *Invoices of Merchandise.* Come to our aid then; the *morning of* our *Redemption* from degradation, adorns the horizon.

In our selection of individuals, it will be observed, that we have confined ourself entirely to those who occupy or have occupied positions among the whites, consequently having a more general bearing as useful contributors to society at large. While we do not pretend to give all such worthy cases, we gave such as we possessed information of, and desire it to be understood, that a large number of our most intelligent and worthy men and women, have not been named, because from their more private position in community, it was foreign to the object and design of this work. If we have said aught to offend, "take the will for the deed," and be assured, that it was given with the purest of motives, and best intention, from a true hearted man and brother; deeply lamenting the sad fate of his race in this country, and sincerely desiring the elevation of man, and submitted to the serious consideration of all, who favor the promotion of the cause of God and humanity.

Chapter XXIV: A Glance at Ourselves—Conclusion

In our own country, the United States, there are *three million five hundred thousand slaves*; and we, the nominally free colored people, are *six hundred thousand* in number; estimating one-sixth to be men, we have *one hundred thousand* able bodied freemen, which will make a powerful auxiliary in any country to which we may become adopted—an ally not to be despised by any power on earth. We love our country, dearly love her, but she don't love us—she despises us, and bids us begone, driving us from her embraces; but we shall not go where she desires us; but when we do go, whatever love we have for her, we shall love the country none the less that receives us as her adopted children.

For the want of business habits and training, our energies have become paralyzed; our young men never think of business, any more than if they were so many bondmen, without the right to pursue any calling they may think most advisable. With our people in this country, dress and good appearances have been made the only test of gentlemen and ladyship, and that vocation which offers the best opportunity to dress and appear well, has generally been preferred, however menial and degrading, by our young people, without even, in the majority of cases, an effort to do better; indeed, in many instances, refusing situations equally lucrative, and superior in position; but which would not allow as much display of dress and personal appearance. This, if we ever expect to rise, must be discarded from among us, and a high and respectable position assumed.

One of our great temporal curses is our consummate poverty. We are the poorest people, as a class, in the world of civilized mankind—abjectly, miserably poor, no one scarcely being able to assist the other. To this, of course, there are noble exceptions; but that which is common to, and the very process by which white men exist, and succeed in life, is unknown to colored men in general. In any and every considerable community may be found, some one of our white fellow-citizens, who is worth more than all the colored people in that community put together. We consequently have little or no efficiency. We must have means to be practically efficient in all the undertakings of life; and to obtain them, it is necessary that we should be engaged in lucrative pursuits, trades, and general business transactions. In order to be thus engaged, it is necessary that we should occupy positions that afford the facilities for such pursuits. To compete now with the mighty odds of wealth, social and religious preferences, and political influences of this country, at this advanced stage of its national existence, we never may expect. A new country, and new beginning, is the only true, rational, politic remedy for our disadvantageous position; and that country we have already pointed out, with triple golden advantages, all things considered, to that of any country to which it has been the province of man to embark.

Every other than we, have at various periods of necessity, been a migratory people, and all when oppressed, shown a greater abhorrence of oppression, if not a greater love of liberty, than we. We cling to our oppressors as the objects of our love. It is true that our enslaved brethren are here, and we have been led to believe that it is necessary for us to remain, on that account. Is it true, that all should remain in degradation, because a part are degraded? We believe no such thing. We believe it to be the duty of the Free, to elevate themselves in the most speedy and effective manner possible; as the redemption of the bondman depends entirely upon the elevation of the freeman; therefore, to elevate the free colored people of America, anywhere upon this continent; forebodes the speedy redemption of the slaves. We shall hope to hear no more of so fallacious a doctrine—the necessity of the free remaining in degradation, for the sake of the oppressed. Let us apply, first, the lever to ourselves; and the force that elevates us to the position of manhood's considerations and honors, will cleft the manacle of every slave in the land.

When such great worth and talents—for want of a better sphere—of men like Rev. Jonathan Robinson, Robert Douglass, Frederick A. Hindton, and a hundred others that might be named, were permitted to expire in a barbershop; and such living men as may be found in Boston, New York, Philadelphia, Baltimore, Richmond, Washington City, Charleston, (S.C.), New Orleans, Cincinnati, Louisville, St. Louis, Pittsburg, Buffalo, Rochester, Albany, Utica, Cleveland, Detroit, Milwaukie, Chicago, Columbus, Zanesville, Wheeling, and a hundred other places, confining themselves to Barber-shops and waiterships in Hotels; certainly the necessity of such a course as we have pointed out, must be cordially acknowledged; appreciated by every brother and sister of oppression; and not rejected as heretofore, as though they preferred inferiority to equality. These minds must become "unfettered," and have "space to rise." This cannot be in their present positions. A continuance in any position, becomes what is termed "Second Nature," it begets an *adaptation*, and *reconciliation* of mind to such condition. It changes the whole physiological condition of the system, and adapts man and woman to a higher or lower sphere in the pursuits of life. The offsprings of slaves and peasantry, have the general characteristics of their parents; and nothing but a different course of training and education, will change the character.

The slave may become a lover of his master; and learn to forgive him for continual deeds of maltreatment and abuse; just as the Spaniel would couch and fondle at the feet that kick him, because he has been taught to reverence them, and consequently, becomes adapted in body and mind to his condition. Even the shrubbery loving Canary, and lofty soaring Eagle, may be tamed to the cage, and learn to love it from habit of confinement. It has been so with us in our position among our oppressors; we have been so prone to such positions, that we have learned to love them. When reflecting upon this all important, and to us, all absorbing subject, we feel in the agony and anxiety of the moment, as though we could cry out in the language of a Prophet of old: "Oh that my head were waters, and mine eyes a fountain of tears, that I might weep day and night for the" degradation "of my people! Oh that I had in the wilderness a lodging place of way-faring men; that I might leave my people, and go from them!

The Irishman and German in the United States, are very different persons to what they were when in Ireland and Germany, the countries of their nativity. There their spirits were depressed and downcast; but the instant they set their foot upon unrestricted soil, free to act and untrammeled to move; their physical condition undergoes a change, which in time becomes physiological, which is transmitted to the offspring, who when born under such circumstances, is a *decidedly* different being to what it would have been, had it been born under different circumstances.

A child born under oppression, has all the elements of servility in its constitution; who when born under favorable circumstances, has to the contrary, all the elements of freedom and independence of feeling. Our children then, may not be expected, to maintain that position and manly bearing; born under the unfavorable circumstances with which we are surrounded in this country; that we so much desire. To use the language of the talented Mr. Whipper, "they cannot be raised in this country, without being stoop shouldered." Heaven's pathway stands unobstructed, which will lead us into a Paradise of bliss. Let us go on and possess the land, and the God of Israel will be our God.

The lessons of every school book, the pages of every history, and columns of every newspaper, are so replete with stimuli to nerve us on to manly aspirations, that those of our young people, who will now refuse to enter upon this great theatre of Polynesian adventure, and take their position on the stage of Central and South America, where a brilliant engagement, of certain and most triumphant success, in the drama of human equality awaits them; then, with the blood of *slaves*, write upon the lintel of every door in sterling Capitals, to be gazed and hissed at by every passer by—

> Doomed by the Creator
> To servility and degradation;
> The SERVANT of the *white* man,
> And despised of every nation!

15.
HENRY McNEAL TURNER

Henry McNeal Turner (1834–1915) began his public career as a missionary (and later a bishop) in the African Methodist Episcopal church. In 1863 President Abraham Lincoln appointed Turner as the Chaplain to Company B of the First Regiment of Colored Troops during the Civil War. He received another political appointment from Andrew Johnson; during reconstruction he was appointed to the Freedman's Bureau in Georgia. In 1868 Turner was elected to the Georgia state legislature. In 1887 he served as vice president for the American Colonization Society and later led major expeditions to Africa. As a contributor to the Black press, in 1889 he created the *Southern Christian Recorder*. In 1892 he also founded the *Voice of Missions*.

Overview of Ideas

Henry McNeal Turner was an early Black Nationalist who advocated emigration from the United States. Like Delany, Turner called for political nationalism, the creation of a Christian Black Nation, a Black nationality. Religion influenced his work and prescriptions for emigration. Turner indicted the United States for its apathy toward the plight of African Americans. No matter how hard Black people pushed themselves—no matter how much education they struggled to obtain, it did not matter; Black people would still be relegated to kitchens, the front of carriages, and the nurseries of White children. America offered no hope of real freedom; all it offered was degradation and continued persecution. Although the Thirteenth Amendment ostensibly freed Blacks from slavery, they were set free with no property, no education, no money, no forty acres and no mules. They continued to persist in a land where they were harassed, beaten, and left to the cruel hands of angry lynch mobs. The press exacerbated racist discourses by printing inaccurate stories of rape and presenting the Black man as a lascivious savage being whose sole desire in life was to commit crimes, rape White women, and take to indolence. This was no life. The only hope for Black folk was an exodus from this land of oppression.

Turner said his position was to

> found and establish a country or a government somewhere upon the continent of Africa, as I see no other place in the world to do it, where our young men and ladies can find a theatre

of activity and usefulness, and commence a career for the future that will meet the wants of prosperity, at the same time build up a center of Christian civilization that will help redeem the land of our ancestry.

Turner's writing is a quintessential example of the back-to-Africa approach articulated by Black Nationalists. Black people needed to reclaim Africa, their heritage, the agency to develop themselves autonomously and prosper as a result. While he did not argue that every Black person needed leave the United States, he said, for those who went, in Africa, Black people would become economically successful and politically empowered.

Turner's work highlighted the importance of Pan-Africanism to the struggle of Black people in America. Progress required unification with Black people in Africa. Moreover, Black separatism was necessary. It was naïve to not realize that "two alienated nations cannot occupy the same territory and be at peace, for one will dominate and ultimately tyrannize the other." Given Jim Crow in the United States, Whites would only continue to tyrannize Black folk. Logically, given these conditions, African Americans needed to craft their own nation. Turner recognized that particularly in the North some steps had been taken to educate Black people. As a representative of the Georgia state legislature, he had attempted to acquire funding for Black schools, garner funding for militias to protect Blacks from terrorists such as the Ku Klux Klan. Turner even campaigned for women's suffrage. Nonetheless, the level of diminutive funding being funneled into the so-called Negro Problem was not enough.

> If this country is to be our home, the Negro must be a self-controlling, automatic factor of the body politic or collective life of the nation. In other words, we must be full-fledged men; otherwise we will not be worth existence itself.

Unless Black people were made complete equals then staying in the United States was futile. Ergo, because this would not happen—in fact, from a legislative standpoint conditions seemed to be getting worse—and all attempts at protest and resistance failed, the only logical program was leaving.

Turner, too, argued that self-sufficiency was paramount. First, he argued like many other African American political thinkers that individual transformation was paramount. "We must adjust ourselves to our surroundings and put forth the utmost endeavor to improve our behavior, and merit the favor of God and man." Most importantly, he despised indifference. He encouraged African Americans to stand up for themselves. Cowardice would get you nowhere. He proposed national conventions; these conventions would be meeting grounds for Black people who were ready to fight back and ready to strategize. Turner advocated the creation of organizations and associations who would hold public meetings, craft circulars and pamphlets, particularly against lynching. As we saw later during the civil rights era, Turner said Black folk needed an independent Black owned and operated press to disseminate information and organize Black people. In addition, the Black church would play a vital role in organization. However, once organized Black people should demand at least 500 million dollars in reparations; although this country owed Black people over 40 billion dollars in wages. They could then utilize these funds for emigration. These funds could ensure the safe relocation of upwards of seven million willing Black people to Africa, specifically Liberia and middle class Blacks wishing to stay in the United States were welcome to stay. Moreover, Turner was pleased to see professional and upwardly mobile Blacks remain in the United States, as their petit bourgeoisie status would cripple their abilities and desires to assist in the establishment of a Black nation. There was no way for African Americans to achieve true self-consciousness in the United States. Turner was a pioneer of Black Nationalist thought.

Turner's Newspaper Writings

The *Christian Recorder*, January 25, 1883

We are bitten, we are poisoned, we are sick and we are dying. We need a remedy. Oh for some Moses to lift a brazen serpent, some goal for our ambition, some object to induce us to look up. Have we that object here? Is there any possibility of getting it here? I do not see it. Therefore I maintain that African colonization should be encouraged. Let the brave-hearted men, who are advanced enough to peril land and sea in search of better conditions, alone. Let them give us a respectable civil and Christian negro nation. Let them raise a banner standard that the world will respect and its glory and influence will tell upon the destinies of the race from pole to pole; our children's children can rest securely under the aegis, whether in Africa, Europe, Asia, America or upon the high seas.

The *Christian Recorder*, June 21, 1883

The truth is … something will have to be done … a revolution is inevitable … [O]ur present status, much less our condition, is intolerable; that it never has been endured in peace by any people since time began; that all the hush-and-be-quiet advocates offer no remedy for existing evils; that there must be an outlet, a theatre of manhood and activity established somewhere for our young men and women; that we cannot school and graduate our children eternally to be waiters, sleeping-car porters, field hands, boot blacks, washwomen, nurses of white children, chambermaids, room sweepers and for such like positions as will ruin our daughters and degrade our sons; that as long as we fill such a station of degradation there will never be accorded to us any recognition by the very class that we seek the recognition of; that people will not invite their cooks, nurses, chambermaids, carriage drivers and porters into their parlors to associate with their guests. All this and much more a large portion of our people see. I travel this country and talk with thousands and know whereof I speak. I have seen men sit down and cry because they were compelled to hire their daughters out as nurses and chambermaids, after spending all they had to give them an education. I have seen beautiful, angelic young graduates thus hired to return home after a few months of such service—well, I will not say, but you can think. The thinkers can think, anyway.

Now what is my position? Simply to found and establish a country or a government somewhere upon the continent of Africa, as I see no other place in the world to do it, where our young men and ladies can find a theatre of activity and usefulness, and commence a career for the future that will meet the wants of posterity, at the same time build up a center of Christian, civilization that will help redeem the land of our ancestry. All this jargon about "Bishop Turner trying to get all us colored people out of the United States," is not only nonsense, but absolutely false. But it seems that some people cannot understand how some of us can go without all going. The same parity of reasoning would imply, because some of us have been hung, all of us must be hung; because some of us go to the jail, penitentiary or hades, all must go. Such persons must think the negro race is a flock or herd of sheep; because one jumps off the London bridge, all must jump off and get drowned. No wonder Bishop Campbell says clanish-ness is the curse of the race. Every solitary writer who has been trying to excoriate me for my African sentiments, has done so under the huddle idea, "He wants us all to go to Africa." The idea of building up a government of a half million civilized Christian people upon the continent of Africa, where we can have our own high officials, digni-taries, artisans, mechanics, corporations, rail-roads, telegraphs, commerce, colleges, churches, &c., &c., has never entered the brain of these maligners and misrepresenters, nor have they ever thought of the glory that would accrue to the whole race from such a seat of power and influence.

The *Voice of Missions*, August 1893

To the friends of repatriation or Negro nationalization elsewhere: For four consecutive years I have been prompted by the impulse of an honest conviction, that the way we as a race are being decimated in this country by mobs, lynchers, and fire fiends, necessi-tates a national convention for the purpose of crystalizing our sentiments and unifying our endeavors for better or worse conditions.

For if we are the execrable demons, as is alleged through the public press daily, the facts should be impartially investigated and clearly established; and if we are an hon-orable people, inaugurate appliances for our reformation. At all events, while other people are saying and doing so much effecting our existence and destiny, we should make an effort both to say and do something ourselves, or consent to wear the brand of infamy and inferiority which is being charged upon us as a race. In plain words, if we are guilty we should know it, and admit it, and if not, deny it and try to stamp out the misrepresentation, or get out from under the calamitous conditions, which is the only escape I am able to see.

But being a bishop, and knowing that I was looked upon as the chief figurehead in the African emigrational movement, I hesitated to make any move in that direction, lest some non-progressive, apathetic and scullionized human fossil would raise the cry that I wanted a convention for the purpose of inducing all the colored people in this country, regardless of self-reliance or fitness, to get up and go to Africa, where they would inevitably contract the fever and die, apparently unconscious that we are daily being put to death here in the most fiendish manner known in the history of the world, and that we are being disgraced by quietly and cowardly submitting to it without raising a voice of protest. The people of England, France, and even Africa cannot understand our apathy and indifference, while death, destruction and extermination stalk abroad in our midst. An English nobleman said to me two months ago that we had better invoke the interference of other nations in our behalf than quietly submit to this reign of horror. For our silence in the midst of such terror is a declaration of its justice and of our endorsement.

I do not believe that there is any manhood future in this country for the Negro, and that his future existence, to say nothing of his future happiness, will depend upon his nationalization. The reasons, as I see them, are innumerable, certainly too numerous for discussion now. But knowing that thousands and tens of thousands see our present conditions and our future about as I do, and after waiting for four years or more for some of our colored statesmen or leaders to call a national convention or to propose some plan of speaking to the nation or to the world, or to project some measure that will remedy our condition, of will even suggest a remedy, and finding no one among the anti-emigrational party or anti-Negro nationalization party disposed to do so, and believing that further silence is not only a disgrace but a crime, I have about resolved to issue a call in the near future for a national convention to be held in the city of Cincinnati, where a spacious edifice is at our disposal, to meet some time in November, for the friends of African repatriation or Negro nationalization elsewhere, to assemble and adopt such measures for our future actions as may commend themselves to our better judgement. The call of the contemplated convention will have no application to party politics or to the stay-here portion of our race. They can project their own plans, resolve upon their own action, or do nothing as they are doing now. We will not interfere with them and they need not interfere with us unless they desire. But the Negro cannot remain here in his present condition and be a man, nor will it be possible to remain here a great while, for at the present rate his extermination is only a question of time.

Before issuing the call, however, I would be pleased to hear the opinions of prominent men who think as I do, from various parts of the country. You can write your approval upon post cards.

The *Voice of Missions*, December 1893

You are here assembled to consider and pass upon our condition as a distinct and specific race, yet a part of the aggregated people of the United States of America. I use the term specific race because of the special or specific legislation which has been enacted by the states, and the judicial decisions which apply and affect our rights and privileges in contradistinction to every other portion of the American people, whether claiming citizenship or occupying a place here as temporary inhabitants. The scum of creation can come to this country and receive kinder and more just treatment than we who were born and reared here. Thus the black, yet patient, loyal and ever faithful children of the United States are individualized and made the victims of class legislation, and the subjects of close discrimination, class proscription and race prejudice in a manner and to an extent that the world at present offers no parallel; and it is a question if history furnishes another instance.

Let us, by way of premises, itemize a few facts connected with our career in this country. We have been inhabitants of this continent for 273 years, and a very limited part of that time were we citizens—I mean from the ratification of the XIV amendment of the national constitution until the Supreme Court of the United States, Oct. 15th, 1883, declared that provision of the constitution null and void, and decitizenized us. Now, what does history set forth relative to our conduct and behavior during this our long residence?

While it is true that we were brought here as captive heathens, through the greed and avarice of the white man, to serve him as a slave, I believe that as over-ruling Providence suffered it to be because there was a great and grand purpose to be subserved, and that infinite wisdom intended to evolve ultimate good out of a temporary evil, and that in the ages to come, the glory of God will be made manifest and that millions will thank heaven for the limited toleration of American slavery. All of you may not accept my sentiments upon this point, but I believe there is a God, and that he takes cognizance of human events; for such a stupendous evil could not have existed so long, affecting the destiny of the unborn, without a glorious purpose in view.

However, since our forced introduction into this land, willingly or unwillingly, mankind will accord to us a fidelity to every interest that will command the respect of the world forever.... I know that thousands of our people hope and expect better times for the Negro in this country, but as one I see no signs of a reformation in our condition; to the contrary, we are being more and more degraded by legislative enactments and judicial decisions. Not a thing has been said or done that contemplates our elevation or the promotion of our manhood in twelve or fifteen years outside of promoting our education in erecting schools for our general enlightenment; but a hundred things have been done to crush out the last vestige of self-respect and to avalanche us with contempt. My remedy, without a change, is, as it would be folly to attempt resistance, and our appeals for better conditions are being unheeded, for that portion of us, at least, who feel we are self-reliant, to seek other quarters. There are many propositions before the colored people of this country. Some favor a partial African emigration, and I am one of that number; others favor Mexican emigration, Canadian emigration, Central and South American emigration, while Hon. John Temple Graves, one of our profoundest thinkers, most brilliant orators and broadest humanitarians in the country, advocates the setting apart of a portion of the public domain as a separate and distinct state, where we can have our own governors, United States senators, members of the lower house of Congress, and all the machinery of state, and thereby have a chance to speak for ourselves, where we can be heard, and give evidence of statesmanship to show to the world that we are capable of self-government, and where our educated sons and daughters can practicalize the benefits of their culture. The position of Mr. Graves may not commend itself to the favorable consideration of all present, any more than my African sentiments or the Mexican, Canadian or Central American theories, but we must do something. We must agree upon some project. We must offer some plan of action to our people or admit that we are too ignorant and worthless to do anything. This nation justly, righteously and divinely owes us for work and services rendered, billions of dollars, and if we cannot be treated as American people, we should ask for five hundred million dollars, at least, to begin an emigration somewhere, for it will cost, sooner or later, *far more than* that amount to keep the Negro down unless they reestablish slavery itself. Freedom and perpetual degradation are not in the economy of human events. It is against reason, against nature, against precedent and against God. A people who read, attend schools, receive the instruction of the pulpits, write for the public press, think and furnish famous orators, cannot be chained to degradation forever. They will be a menace to the land, and God himself, with all the laws of nature, will help them fight the injustice, and no pomp or boast of heraldry can prevent it, yet it may involve horror to both races. Money to leave and build up a nation of our own, where we can respect ourselves at least, or *justice* at the hands of the American nation, should be the watch word of every Negro in the land.

I have been more or less all over the world, and have mingled among people of many tongues, but I have never found such a condition of things as there is here in the United States.

I was told in England by old, gray-haired, and baldheaded white men, that they had never known of a man being lynched or put to death without due process of law. Yet every nation upon the face of the globe was represented there, as British ships go everywhere and return with representatives of all people, while in this country, so many of us are killed, that dead bodies hanging to some tree limb and pierced with bullets are so common that they are regarded as current events. What would have horrorized our fathers and mothers is passed by in these degenerate days as a natural occurrence. The Negro may be exterminated, but in the accomplishment of the heaven-defying job, a crop of imbruted children will grow up, who will annihilate each other. "For whatsoever a man soweth, that shall he also reap," is the declaration of the word of God, and all history confirms its truth.

The Negro, at best, in this country, occupies a very low plane. Look at the Greek, Latin and mathematical scholars employed as Pullman car porters and other college-bred young men, restricted to the sphere of a scullion, because color prejudice bars them from employment in harmony with their culture. Yet the Negro is the nearest competitor in aptitude, physical endurance, industrial application and punctuality to business, the white man has on the face of the globe; and because this fact is well known, the moment some ignorant white man gets into some legislature, he is offering a bill to increase the degradation of the Negro. For you never find such bills or resolutions emanating from first-class white gentlemen. All of these discriminating and proscribing laws that have been enacted against the colored people on these railroads have originated with what we used to call in the slave time "poor white trash." True, some of them since freedom have climbed up a little and have got to be congressmen and even governors of states, but it is the same old second-class roughs who can find nothing else to think or talk about but the ghost of the Negro. Yet the first-class white men and the entire nation, North and South, are responsible and the God of nations will so hold them. I refer to these facts merely to show you that degradation or extermination appears to hold a prominent place in the minds of the ruling powers of this country, and I cannot believe that our freedom, which cost so much blood and treasure, was intended for any such ultimatum.

But some of you may think I am over-gloomy, too despondent, that I have reached the plane of despair, and should anyone present so presume you will not be much at fault. For I confess that I have seen so much and know so much about American prejudice that I have no hope in the future success of my race in our present situation.

But you will discover that in this address I have largely spoken for myself. You will have time enough, and I know you have the ability to speak for yourselves. Should we differ, as we naturally will, let us defend our respective positions and sentiments with the best logical arguments we are able to advance. Slurs, philippics, witty utterances, light anecdotes, innuendoes, cutting remarks, sarcasm, tirades and bitter invectives should not be indulged in in this convention. Men of ability will not do it; they will have too many other things to say. Moreover, if we cannot now, surrounded as we are by mobs, lynchers, ropes, bullets, fire, proscription, color prejudice, decitizenship, blood, carnage, death and extermination, present a united front of action, although we may differ in opinions, then there is no unity of action in us and our destiny is a hopeless one.

You evidently see from the points I have endeavored to raise, and many more that I have not touched, that our condition in this country inferiorates us, and no amount of book-learning, divested of manhood, respect and manhood promptings will ever make us a great people; for, underlying all school culture, must exist the consciousness that I am somebody, that I am a man, that I am as much as anybody else, that I have rights, that I am a creature of law and order, that I am entitled to respect, that every avenue to distinction is mine. For where this consciousness does not form the substratum of any people, inferioration, retrogression and ultimate degradation will be the result. And seeing that this is our status in the United States today, it devolves upon us to project a remedy for our condition, if such a remedy is obtainable, or demand of this nation, which owes us billions of dollars for work done and services rendered, five hundred million dollars to commence leaving it; or endorse the petition of the colored lawyers' convention which was held in Chattanooga, Tenn., asking Congress for a billion dollars for the same purpose. For I can prove, by mathematical calculation, that this country owes us forty billion dollars for daily work performed. The one great desideratum of the American Negro is manhood impetus. We may educate and acquire general intelligence, but our sons and daughters will come out of college with all their years of training and drift to the plane of the scullion as long as they are restricted, limited and circumscribed by colorphobia. For abstract education elevates no man, nor will it elevate a race. What we call the heathen African will strut around his native land, three-fourths naked, and you can see by the way he stands, talks and acts, that he possesses more manhood than fifty of some of our people in this country, and any ten of our most distinguished colored men here; and until we are free from menace by lynchers ... we are destined to be a dwarfed people. Our sons and daughters will grow up with it in their very flesh and bones.

Much has been said, and many wild calculations have been made, by men of no education or of no brain, about the hundred million of dollars that we said, sometime ago, the colored people of this country should ask the general government for, to enable them to leave the United States, the lowest and meanest domain this side of hell, and there have been about as many white fools babbling over it as black, pretending to estimate the limited number that a hundred million would carry over to Africa. We are sure if the necessary ships could be gotten to running between the United States and Africa, the colored people could go as cheaply as the millions of whites have been brought from Europe to this country, averaging from ten to fifteen, eighteen and twenty dollars a head. Suppose we take the middle number and what would be the result, one hundred and five million of dollars would pay for the transportation of seven millions of emigrants to Africa, I mean Liberia being the objective point. If the general government will give us a hundred million dollars and let us charge, as we would, from five to ten dollars each, we will return to Africa the eight millions of colored people said to be in the United States, if they desire to go, and still have a few million left for incidental expenses.

Now, if these fault finders, ignorant critics, and blab-mouth objectors to every measure that has any sense in it wish to enter into the calculations, we are ready for them, and we will show this brainless crew that they had better be silent and let men and women who have some judgement and some intellect speak. Moreover, we do not want nor have we ever expressed a desire for all of these ignorant and scullionized Negroes to return to Africa. Two or three millions are about all that have sense enough and vim enough to return to Africa and accomplish anything for themselves, for the race and for God. The scullionized black man, be he illiterate or a graduate from some college, or a minister, or a doctor, or a lawyer, or a Bishop, or a congressman, or a diplomat, would do no good in building up a nation for the race, for the reason that this class believes that white is God and black is the devil, and if they were to go to Africa and find themselves in a country where they had no white men to look up to and fawn before, we would have to rid the country of them either by expatriating them or hanging them, for they have neither confidence in or respect for their own race. They desire to remain where white dominates, and in the land of jim-crow cars, lynchers, disfranchisement, newspaper abuse and villification, manufactured from bare-faced lies, and the meanest degradation known to the world's history.

16.
MARCUS GARVEY

Marcus Garvey (1887–1940) was born and raised in Jamaica and became one of the most influential Black leaders of the twentieth century. He was an outspoken critic of the United States and an advocate of Black Nationalism. An advocate of Pan-Africanism, in 1914 Garvey and Amy Ashwood started the Universal Negro Improvement Association (UNIA) in Jamaica and established the first UNIA in the United States in New York in 1917. While in New York, Garvey acquired a large auditorium in Harlem; the auditorium was called Liberty Hall. At Liberty Hall, he held meetings to spread his Black Nationalist message. In 1918 he founded the widely circulated newspaper, *Negro World*. The UNIA had no paucity of members; by 1919 they had over two million members and by 1924 they had over 600 branches with over six million members. In 1919 in order to practically implement his back-to-Africa plan, he started the Black Star Line to foster commerce and emigration in order to create a strong global Black economy. In addition, in 1919 he also founded the Negro Factories Corporation, which became incorporated in 1920. He organized local businesses and encouraged Black people to buy stock in the corporations. This, too, would foster Black economic independence. In fact, on August 25, 1919 Garvey staged a mass meeting to sell shares in the Black Star Line. It was not even by the close of this year that the FBI was laboring arduously to garner copious information on Garvey's efforts, with the intent to have him deported. So profound were his efforts that in addition to the government's efforts to deport Garvey, on October 21, 1919, George Tyler attempted to assassinate Garvey. The government finally got their wish and Garvey ended up serving three years in jail for mail fraud before finally being deported in 1927.

Overview of Ideas

Marcus Garvey was a staunch advocate of Black Nationalism and famous for his back-to-Africa approach to the Negro Problem. His tone was always fierce and uncompromising. However, while Garvey was militant he did not push for a violent revolution. He argued that White people have far too much power and resources to succumb to any violent coup. However, they could organize. Garvey called for Black unity:

> Since we are four hundr[e]d million strong, it is for us to organize that strong to protect our race
> … if there is a Negro who does not love the black race, to his race such a Negro is an outcast.

As a Pan-Africanist, Garvey argued for a global united effort of oppressed Black people.

Garvey posited that there were an extensive amount of quagmires facing Black people globally. However, these obstacles were not insurmountable. Black people had to fight: social marginalization, racism in the legal/penal system, imperialism and colonization, political disenfranchisement, segregation, the denial of labor rights and access to unions, and institutionalized racism in all other social institutions. While still in the United States, Black people needed to fight for and demand: civil rights, separate courts, all-Black juries, outlawing the word Nigger, and end to violence, a free and independent Black press, equal access to education, and recognition and celebration of Black history. As part of his Black Nationalist program he promulgated the need for cultural nationalism—a celebration of Black history and heritage. Finally, in advocating economic nationalism he wanted to foster Black global trade and economic independence. In advancing political nationalism, he called for an end to imperialism and colonialism and the reclaiming of Africa as a place for political emancipation.

Fighting racial injustice required self-help. Just like Booker T. Washington, both drew from American liberalism; Garvey promoted self-sufficiency or the individual's ability and necessity to make his or her own destiny. It was the destiny of Black people to reclaim their home in Africa.

> The Negro peoples of the world should be so determined to reclaim Africa and found a government there, so that if any black man in any part of the world is abused we can call the mighty power of Africa to come to our aid.... Tell me that I must live everlastingly under the domination of a white man, that I must bequeath to my children white overlordship, then I say, let me die now, Almighty God.

Garvey posited that God created all people equal. However, Whites refused to acknowledge this. To remain in a nation as an inferior, marginalized, disenfranchised, and brutalized people was irrational; autonomy would lead to true empowerment. In addition to political nationalism, the founding of a Black nation, Garvey also called for economic nationalism.

Relying again on self-sufficiency Garvey proffered that Africans in America needed to open up their own opportunities in the labor market. While Garvey was certainly radical, it is important to recognize that a dominant portion of his ideas relied upon an incredibly conservative ideal—that success and upward mobility is the sole responsibility of the individual; an individual who is highly motivated can overcome any structural limitations. Horatio Alger lives on, even in Garvey. By creating their own economic networks through independently owned and operated Black businesses Black people could prosper. Africa was so rich in natural resources and has been systematically raped and robbed through European conquest and colonialism. Garvey said he created the Black Star Line so Black people could return to Africa and save their homeland from the rapacious criminals bleeding her dry.

Garvey, like Malcolm X after him, seemed to speak primarily to working class Blacks and held contempt for Black people he called Big Negroes or what Malcolm X would later call House Negroes. These Black people thwarted the progress of the race. The modicum of privilege they ascertained most often through education and professional status garnered them upward mobility and rendered them in a state of false consciousness. Instead of sacrifice for their race, they engaged in conspicuous consumption in order to impress Whites. Although Garvey agreed in part with Washington's economic philosophy he said he had become one of these Big Negroes, an aristocrat. Black people did not need aristocrats; they needed humble servants to the cause. Garvey blamed most of his difficulties in implementing his solutions on these Big Negroes.

Garvey also held great contempt for W.E.B. Du Bois and interracial organizations of Big Negroes such as the National Association for the Advancement of Colored People. In fact, he said the NAACP was "a scheme to destroy the Negro Race." Garvey characterized leaders such as Du Bois as Uncle Toms who lacked true racial consciousness. Interestingly, the same charges hurled at Booker T. Washington by Du Bois and others that his affiliations with Whites were responsible for his ostensibly pacifist approach, would later come back to haunt them, as Garvey now made the same criticisms of them. More importantly, as a Black separatist, Garvey was vehemently opposed to White affiliation in a movement of Black people for freedom. In fact, unlike most of the integrationists previously covered, Garvey supported miscegenation laws. He saw interracial relations as racial suicide.

> We are fighting for the founding of a negro nation in Africa, so that there will be no clash between black and white and that each race will have a separate existence and civilization all its own without courting suspicion and hatred or eyeing each other with jealousy and rivalry within the borders of the same country.

According to Garvey, he was not promoting racism but rather diverting a race war. Garvey and other Black Nationalists did not skirt around the issue of race. Many contemporary and more moderate leaders have not always dealt with this issue as effectively or honestly. Throughout Garvey's readings, most profoundly demonstrated in "The Negro's Greatest Enemy," he displayed extreme disdain for America's light skinned Black leadership. At times it seemed as if he questioned their authenticity and ability to lead as a result. Readers might note for themselves if Garvey seemed obsessed with this issue. Nonetheless, he was interested in unifying the race and was troubled by the racial divisions within the Black community. Part of his strategy was to resolve these divisions. Garvey's ability to organize and bring together so many African Americans under one national organization was unparalleled.

Address to UNIA Supporters in Philadelphia, 1919

Mr. President, Lady President, Ladies and Gentlemen: Once more it is my pleasure to be with you. That you have turned out in such large numbers tonight proves beyond the shadow of a doubt that you good people of the race in Philadelphia are very much alive to the principles, to the aims, to the objects of the greatest movement among Negroes in the world today—the Universal Negro Improvement Association and African Communities League. It is the greatest movement in the world, because it is the only movement today that is causing the white man to tremble in his shoes. The white man has had the policies of our great men or the great leaders of the past. They have had the policies of Booker Washington, they have had the policies of the other great leaders of this country, of the West Indies and of Africa, but out of these policies nothing ever came to the Negro, and the white man was satisfied. They have buried our great leader in America, Booker Washington, and yet we have achieved nothing by way of our own initiative. They have buried the great leaders of the Negro race of other countries, and yet we have achieved nothing, except in the Republic of Haiti, where one Negro repelled them and established an independent republic. I speak of Haiti. They did not like Toussaint L'Overture [*sic*] because he had initiative. They lied to him, they deceived him, and when he had just a little faith still in them they destroyed that faith. They made a prisoner of him, took him to France, and there he died. Thank God, as Toussaint L'Ouverture in his time was able to inspire the other men of his country to carry on the work until Haiti was made a free country, so today we have inspired not one, not two, but hundreds of thousands to carry out the work even if they imprison one or kill one.

It is for me to say to you faithful members and followers of the Universal Negro Improvement Association in Philadelphia that the movement that you are in is a movement that is causing not merely the individual white man, but governments to be living in fear as touching the outcome of the Negro peoples of the world through their determination in the Universal Negro Improvement Association.

Last night, after I was through addressing my people in New York, about 5,000 of them jammed themselves into Liberty Hall, overtaxing the capacity of that building, and we had to turn away about 10,000, and there were fully 3,000 around the building, trying to get in last night. The biggest meeting we ever had in Harlem was last night, when we had fully between twenty and thirty thousand Negroes trying to get into Liberty Hall. After I was through addressing the good people there, one of the members brought me a letter he had received from his friend in Panama. They did not know that the Universal Negro Improvement Association has secret service men all over the world now, and the letter said that just two hours before he read a cable which was sent by the Canal Commission in Panama beseeching Washington not to give a passport to Marcus Garvey to visit Panama, because if he landed there, there would be trouble for the white man there. Now, you know who are the people who are controlling the Panama Canal under this administration. They are Southern white men. The chicken is going home to roost. We told those Southern crackers that one day the Negro would get even with them. You see how cowardly they are. Now, I am quite away in New York and they are begging the people here not to let me get out of New York to go there. But to show you how puzzled they are: My District Attorney friend in New York has been trying for many months to get me expelled from the country. Some want me to go and some don't want me to go. What must I do? To my mind, it is a question of being between hell and the powder house.

Now, that is what we can compliment ourselves for today. We have our foe, our ancient foe, puzzled. He does not know what to do with the New Negro; but the New Negro knows what to do with himself. And the thing that we are going to do is to blast a way to complete independence and to that democracy which they denied us even after we left the battlefields of France and Flanders. We, the New Negroes, say there is no turning back for us now. There is nothing else but a going forward, and if they squeal in America or anywhere else we are going forward. Why, we are not organized as four hundred millions yet, and they are so scared. Now, what will happen in the next five years when the entire four hundred millions will have been organized? All the lynching in the South will be a thing of the past. We are determined in this association to bring the white man to his senses. We are not going to fight and kill anybody because he has more than we have. But if there is anybody taking advantage of the Negro, whether he be white, red or blue, we are going to organize to stop him. We believe that white men have as much right to live as yellow men; we believe that yellow men have as much right to live as red men; we believe red men have as much right to live as black men, and we believe that black men have as much right to live as all men. Therefore, if any race of mankind says that the other race must die, it is time for that race that is dying to organize to prevent themselves from dying. And as for me, the sweetest life in the world to me is the life of my race. I cannot change my race overnight. You cannot change your race overnight. We have not been able to change our race for three hundred years. No one can change our race overnight. God created us what we are and we are going to remain what we are until Gabriel blows his horn.

Therefore we are of the Negro race and we are suffering simply because we are of the Negro race, and, since we are four hundred [*sic*] million strong, it is for us to organize that strong to protect our race. And I want you young men, you middle aged men and you old men of the race and women also to realize that this is the age of action—action on the part of each and every individual of every race. If there is a white man who does not love the white race, to his race he is an outcast; if there is a yellow man that does not love his race, to the yellow race he is an outcast: if there is a Negro who does not love the black race, to his race such a Negro is an outcast and should be trampled to death.

We have lived upon the farce of brotherhood for hundreds of years, and if there is anybody who has suffered from that farce it is the Negro. The white man goes forth with the Bible and tells us that we are all brothers, but it is against the world to believe, against all humanity to believe, that really there is but one brotherhood. And if there are six brothers in any family, at least those six brothers from natural tie ought to be honest in their dealings with each other to the extent of not seeing any of the six starve. If one has not a job, naturally the others would see to it that the one that is out of a job gets something to eat and a place to sleep so as to prevent him from starving and dying. This is brotherhood. Now there is one brother with all the wealth; he has more than he wants, and there is the other brother. What is he doing to the other brother? He is murdering the other brother. He is lynching the other brother, and still they are brothers. Now, if I have any brother in my family who has no better love for me than to starve me, to whip me and to burn me, I say, brother, I do not want your relationship at all. To hell with it.

No, sir, I strike against the idea of brotherhood as coming from that man. I believe in the brotherhood of man. I believe in the fatherhood of God, but as man sinned and lost his purpose ever since the fall of Adam and Eve, I also realize that man has lost his closest connection, his closest tie, with his God. And since man is human, since man has lost his instinct divine, I am not going to trust man. From the attitude of man, from the action of man today, I can see that every one is looking out for himself where the question of race comes in. The white race is looking out for the white race; the yellow race is looking out for the yellow race or Asiatic race. The time has come when the Negro should look out for himself and let the others look out for themselves. This is the new doctrine today. It is the doctrine of Europe. Europe is looking out for the white man. It is the doctrine of Asia. Asia is looking out for the yellow man. So should Africa look out for the black man, the Negro. And since they (the whites) have divided up Africa, having a part in America, a part in Canada, a part in the West Indies, a part in Central America, a part in South America and a part remaining in Africa, we are saying that the time has come that there should be a united Africa. And before a united Africa comes, Ethiopia, as scattered as she is, must stretch forth her hands unto God.

Tonight the Universal Negro Improvement Association is endeavoring to teach Negroes that the time has come for them to help themselves. We have helped the white man in this Western Hemisphere for over three hundred years until he has become so almighty that he respects not even God himself. The white man believes that there is only one God, and that is the white man. We have a different idea about God. We believe that there is but one God, and he is in a place called heaven. There is a heaven, we believe, and a God presides over that heaven, and as far as the Negro is concerned that God is the only being in the world whom we respect. We believe with Theodore Roosevelt, "FEAR GOD AND KNOW NO OTHER FEAR." And if every Negro in Philadelphia could just get that one thought into his or her mind, to fear God and him alone and let the world take care of itself, the better it would be for each and every one.

The white man comes before you in his imperial and majestic pomp and tries to impress upon you the idea that he is your superior. Who made him your superior? You stick his face with a pin and blood runs out. You stick the black man's face with a pin and blood runs out. Starve the white man and he dies. Starve the black man and he dies. What difference is there, therefore, in black and white. If you stick the white man, blood come[s] out. If you starve the white man he dies. The same applies to the black man. They said the white man was the superior being and the black man was the inferior being. That is the old time notion, but today the world knows that all men were created equal. We were created equal and were put into this world to possess equal rights and equal privileges, and the time has come for the black man to get his share. The white man has got his share and more than his share for thousands of years, and we are calling upon him now to give up that which is not his, so that we can have ours. Some of them will be wise enough and sensible enough to give up what is not theirs to save confusion. You know when a man takes what is not his, the one from whom he took that thing is going to take him to court so as to recover his loss. Now, the Negro is going to take somebody to a court of law one day. This court is not going to be presided over by the white man. It is the court to be presided over and decided by the sword. Yes; the sword will decide to whom belongs the right.

And I want you men of Africa, you men of the Negro race, to prepare for the day when Africa will call for a judgment. Africa is preparing to call for a judgment, and that judgment we must have, and it will be a judgment in favor of four hundred million oppressed people. And the marshal who will carry out the authority of the court will be the new Toussaint L'Ouverture with the sword and the banner of the new African Republic. You black men of Philadelphia sit here tonight as jurors in the case where judgment is to be given in favor of the Negro, and I am now asking you jurymen: Gentlemen of the jury, what is your verdict? Cries of: "Africa must be free!" Now, if Africa is to be free, it means, therefore, that Philadelphia has given her verdict as we have in New York. It is now for the judge to give his finding. The judge will give his finding after all the jurors of the Negro race, four hundred million, will have given their verdict. And then after the judge gives his finding he will have to find a marshal to serve the writ, who will require the New Negro to help him to serve this writ, because the man to whom this writ is to be served is of a desperate character, because he prefers to shed blood and take lives before he will give up what is not his. You have to spill blood in Africa before you get what is belonging to you.

Therefore, you will realize that the Universal Negro Improvement Association is no joke. It is a serious movement. It is as serious a movement as the movement of the Irish today to have a free Ireland; as the determination of the Jew to recover Palestine. The Negro peoples of the world should be so determined to reclaim Africa and found a government there, so that if any black man in any part of the world is abused we can call the mighty power of Africa to come to our aid. Men, a Negro government we had once, and a Negro government we must have again. Tell me that I must live ever-lastingly under the domination of a white man, that I must bequeath to my children white overlordship, then I say, let me die now, Almighty God. If there is no better future in the world for me than to be the slave of a white man, I say, take the life you gave me. I do not want it. You would not be my God if you created me to be a slave to other men; but you are my God and will continue to be my God if you created me an equal of all men.

Men, I want you to realize that the life you live was given you for a purpose; not for the purpose of being a slave, not for the purpose of being a serf, but for the purpose of being a man, and for that purpose you must live, or it is better you die.

Now I want to come to the practical, common sense side of this question. We have started an agitation all over the world. It is the agitation of self-reliance wherein the Negro must do for himself. I want you to understand that if you do not get behind this agitation and back it up morally and financially you are only flirting with your own downfall, because the world in which we live is today more serious than ever it was. White and yellow men have become more selfish today than they were before causing the terrible war, the terrible conflict, of 1914 to 1918. They destroyed all that they spent years and years to build and all the time and energy they gave us counted for nought because of the destruction. They have, therefore, lost their sympathies for other men. They have lost their sympathies for other races and have settled down to see nothing else but their own interest until they will have succeeded in rebuilding themselves. During this selfish, soulless age it falls to the province of the Negro to take the initiative and do for himself; otherwise he is going to die. He is going to d[ie] as I stand on this platform tonight economically in America; he is going to die economically under the yoke of Britain, of France and of Germany. He is going to die in the next one hundred years if he does not start out now to do for himself.

I want you to realize that this dear America, the greatest democracy in the world for white men, the greatest republic in the world for white men, that this America is becoming more prejudiced every day against the Negro. Month by month they are lynching more Negroes than they ever did before; month by month more riots are going on in the industrial sections of this country than ever before. This is an indication of the spirit of the people that are living today. It is the spirit that will be bequeathed to their children and to the unborn posterity of the white race. If you think that the white man is going to be more liberal to Negroes than they are at present, you are making a big mistake. Every succeeding generation of the white race is getting more prejudiced against the Negro. It is time, therefore, for the Negro to look out for the future for himself.

We have in America ninety million white fellow citizens, and they are lynching us by the dozen every day. In the next one hundred years you are going to have four hundred million people (white) in America. Now, if they are lynching twelve a day with their ninety millions, how many are they going to lynch when they are four hundred millions. I want you to figure this out for yourselves. And it is because our old time leaders failed to see this that we of the Universal Negro Improvement Association say that the old time leadership must go.

Again I want you to understand that economically we are flirting with our graves if we do not start out to make ourselves economically independent. This war brought about new conditions in America and all over the world. America sent hundreds of thousands of colored soldiers to fight the white man's battles, during which time she opened the doors of industry to millions of white American men and women and created a new problem in the industrial market. And now the war is over and those millions who took the places of the soldiers who have returned home say: "We are not going to give up our jobs. We are going to remain in the industrial life of the world.["] This makes it difficult for returned soldiers to get work now. There will be sufficient jobs now for returned soldiers and for white men, because abnormal conditions are still in existence, but in the next two years these abnormal conditions will pass away and the industries will not be opened up for so long. It means that millions are going to starve. Do you think the white industrial captains are going to allow the white men and the white women to starve and give you bread? To the white man blood is thicker than water.

Therefore, in the next two years there is going to be an industrial boomerang in this country, and if the Negroes do not organize now to open up economic and industrial opportunities for themselves there will be starvation among all Negroes. It is because we want to save the situation when this good time shall have passed by and the white man calls you, "My dear John, I haven't any job for you today," and you can leave the white man's job as a porter and go into the Negro factory as a clerk, you can leave the white man's kitchen and go into your home as the wife of a big Negro banker or a corporation manager.

That is why we want the Black Star Line so as to launch out to the Negro peoples of the world, and today the richest people of the world are the Negro people of Africa. Their minerals, their diamonds, their gold and their silver and their iron have built up the great English, French, German and Belgian Empires. Men, how long are we going to allow those parasites to suck the blood out of our children? How long? I answer for those who are active members of the Universal Negro Improvement Association and African Communities League, "Not one day longer." No parasite shall continue to feed off my body, because I want to have a healthy body. I have not sufficient blood to give to any parasite, because when I get sick I will need every drop of my blood to sustain me until I am well, so while I am well I will have to take off that parasite and throw it away. The time has come for the Negro to exert his energy to the utmost to do. Men and women of Philadelphia, the question is now for you to decide. Are you ready tonight or are you going to wait for two years more to be ready. The answer is, "You must be ready now[.]" Thank God, there are millions of us who are ready already, and when the Black Star Line sails out, by the demonstration of the Black Star Line spontaneously and simultaneously, millions will become [self sufficient] ... So tonight I want you men and women to understand that there is a chance for every one of you tonight to do service to your race, to humanity, before I leave this building for New York, and that is to help to launch on the 31st of this month the first ship of the Black Star Line. I want you all to buy as many shares as you can. If you can buy twenty, buy them; if you can buy fifteen, buy them; if you can buy ten, buy them. Buy as many as you possibly can, so as to render service to yourselves, service to your race, service to humanity.

Declaration of the Rights of the Negro Peoples of the World, 1920

Preamble

Be It Resolved, That the Negro people of the world, through their chosen representatives in convention assembled in Liberty Hall, in the City of New York and United States of America, from August 1 to August 31, in the year of Our Lord one thousand nine hundred and twenty, protest against the wrongs and injustices they are suffering at the hands of their white brethren, and state what they deem their fair and just rights, as well as the treatment they purpose to demand of all men in the future.

We complain:

1. That nowhere in the world, with few exceptions, are black men accorded equal treatment with white men, although in the same situation and circumstances, but, on the contrary, are discriminated against and denied the common rights due to human beings for no other reason than their race and color.

    We are not willingly accepted as guests in the public hotels and inns of the world for no other reason than our race and color.
2. In certain parts of the United States of America our race is denied the right of public trial accorded to other races when accused of crime, but are lynched and burned by mobs, and such brutal and inhuman treatment is even practiced upon our women.
3. That European nations have parcelled out among them and taken possession of nearly all of the continent of Africa, and the natives are compelled to surrender their lands to aliens and are treated in most instances like slaves.

4. In the southern portion of the United States of America, although citizens under the Federal Constitution, and in some States almost equal to the whites in population and are qualified land owners and taxpayers, we are, nevertheless, denied all voice in the making and administration of the laws and are taxed without representation by the State governments, and at the same time compelled to do military service in defense of the country.

5. On the public conveyances and common carriers in the southern portion of the United States we are jim-crowed and compelled to accept separate and inferior accommodations and made to pay the same fare charged for first-class accommodations, and our families are often humiliated and insulted by drunken white men who habitually pass through the jim-crow cars going to the smoking car.

6. The physicians of our race are denied the right to attend their patients while in the public hospitals of the cities and States where they reside in certain parts of the United States.
    Our children are forced to attend inferior separate schools for shorter terms than white children, and the public school funds are unequally divided between the white and colored schools.

7. We are discriminated against and denied an equal chance to earn wages for the support of our families, and in many instances are refused admission into labor unions and nearly everywhere are paid smaller wages than white men.

8. In the Civil Service and departmental offices we are everywhere discriminated against and made to feel that to be a black man in Europe, America and the West Indies is equivalent to being an outcast and a leper among the races of men, no matter what the character attainments of the black men may be.

9. In the British and other West Indian islands and colonies Negroes are secretly and cunningly discriminated against and denied those fuller rights of government to which white citizens are appointed, nominated and elected.

10. That our people in those parts are forced to work for lower wages than the average standard of white men and are kept in conditions repugnant to good civilized tastes and customs.

11. That the many acts of injustices against members of our race before the courts of law in the respective islands and colonies are of such nature as to create disgust and disrespect for the white man's sense of justice.

12. Against all such inhuman, unchristian and uncivilized treatment we here and now emphatically protest, and invoke the condemnation of all mankind.

In order to encourage our race all over the world and to stimulate it to overcome the handicaps and difficulties surrounding it, and to push forward to a higher and grander destiny, we demand and insist on the following Declaration of Rights:

1. Be it known to all men that whereas all men are created equal and entitled to the rights of life, liberty and the pursuit of happiness, and because of this we, the duly elected representatives of the Negro peoples of the world, invoking the aid of the just and Almighty God, do declare all men, women and children of our blood throughout the world free denizens, and do claim them as free citizens of Africa, the Motherland of all Negroes.

2. That we believe in the supreme authority of our race in all things racial; that all things are created and given to man as a common possession; that there should be an equitable distribution and apportionment of all such things, and in consideration of the fact that as a race we are now deprived of those things that are morally and legally ours, we believed it right that all such things should be acquired and held by whatsoever means possible.

3. That we believe the Negro, like any other race, should be governed by the ethics of civilization, and therefore should not be deprived of any of those rights or privileges common to other human beings.

4. We declare that Negroes, wheresoever they form a community among themselves should be given the right to elect their own representatives to represent them in Legislatures, courts of law, or such institutions as may exercise control over that particular community.

5. We assert that the Negro is entitled to even-handed justice before all courts of law and equity in whatever country he may be found, and when this is denied him on account of his race or color such denial is an insult to the race as a whole and should be resented by the entire body of Negroes.

6. We declare it unfair and prejudicial to the rights of Negroes in communities where they exist in considerable numbers to be tried by a judge and jury composed entirely of an alien race, but in all such cases members of our race are entitled to representation on the jury.

7. We believe that any law or practice that tends to deprive any African of his land or the privileges of free citizenship within his country is unjust and immoral, and no native should respect any such law or practice.

8. We declare taxation without representation unjust and tyran[n]ous, and there should be no obligation on the part of the Negro to obey the levy of a tax by any law-making body from which he is excluded and denied representation on account of his race and color.

9. We believe that any law especially directed against the Negro to his detriment and singling him out because of his race or color is unfair and immoral, and should not be respected.

10. We believe all men entitled to common human respect and that our race should in no way tolerate any insults that may be interpreted to mean disrespect to our race or color.

11. We deprecate the use of the term "nigger" as applied to Negroes, and demand that the word "Negro" be written with a capital "N."

12. We believe that the Negro should adopt every means to protect himself against barbarous practices inflicted upon him because of color.

13. We believe in the freedom of Africa for the Negro people of the world, and by the principle of Europe for the Europeans and Asia for the Asiatics, we also demand Africa for the Africans at home and abroad.

14. We believe in the inherent right of the Negro to possess himself of Africa and that his possession of same shall not be regarded as an infringement on any claim or purchase made by any race or nation.

15. We strongly condemn the cupidity of those nations of the world who, by open aggression or secret schemes, have seized the territories and inexhaustible natural wealth of Africa, and we place on record our most solemn determination to reclaim the treasures and possession of the vast continent of our forefathers.

16. We believe all men should live in peace one with the other, but when races and nations provoke the ire of other races and nations by attempting to infringe upon their rights war becomes inevitable, and the attempt in any way to free one's self or protect one's rights or heritage becomes justifiable.

17. Whereas the lynching, by burning, hanging or any other means, of human beings is a barbarous practice and a shame and disgrace to civilization, we therefore declare any country guilty of such atrocities outside the pale of civilization.

18. We protest against the atrocious crime of whipping, flogging and overworking of the native tribes of Africa and Negroes everywhere. These are methods that should be abolished and all means should be taken to prevent a continuance of such brutal practices.

19. We protest against the atrocious practice of shaving the heads of Africans, especially of African women or individuals of Negro blood, when placed in prison as a punishment for crime by an alien race.

20. We protest against segregated districts, separate public conveyances, industrial discrimination, lynchings and limitations of political privileges of any Negro citizen in any part of the world on account of race, color or creed, and will exert our full influence and power against all such.

21. We protest against any punishment inflicted upon a Negro with severity, as against lighter punishment inflicted upon another of an alien race for like offense, as an act of prejudice and injustice, and should be resented by the entire race.

22. We protest against the system of education in any country where Negroes are denied the same privileges and advantages as other races.

23. We declare it inhuman and unfair to boycott Negroes from industries and labor in any part of the world.

24. We believe in the doctrine of the freedom of the press, and we therefore emphatically protest against the suppression of Negro newspapers and periodicals in various parts of the world, and call upon Negroes everywhere to employ all available means to prevent such suppression.

25. We further demand free speech universally for all men.

26. We hereby protest against the publication of scandalous and inflammatory articles by an alien press tending to create racial strife and the exhibition of picture films showing the Negro as a cannibal.

27. We believe in the self-determination of all peoples.

28. We declare for the freedom of religious worship.

29. With the help of Almighty God we declare ourselves the sworn protectors of the honor and virtue of our women and children, and pledge our lives for their protection and defense everywhere and under all circumstances from wrongs and outrages.

30. We demand the right of an unlimited and unprejudiced education for ourselves and our posterity forever[.]

31. We declare that the teaching in any school by alien teachers to our boys and girls, that the alien race is superior to the Negro race, is an insult to the Negro people of the world.

32. Where Negroes form a part of the citizenry of any country, and pass the civil service examination of such country, we declare them entitled to the same consideration as other citizens as to appointments in such civil service.

33. We vigorously protest against the increasingly unfair and unjust treatment accorded Negro travelers on land and sea by the agents and employes [*sic*] of railroad and steamship companies, and insist that for equal fare we receive equal privileges with travelers of other races.

34. We declare it unjust for any country, State or nation to enact laws tending to hinder and obstruct the free immigration of Negroes on account of their race and color.

35. That the right of the Negro to travel unmolested throughout the world be not abridged by any person or persons, and all Negroes are called upon to give aid to a fellow Negro when thus molested.

36. We declare that all Negroes are entitled to the same right to travel over the world as other men.

37. We hereby demand that the governments of the world recognize our leader and his representatives chosen by the race to look after the welfare of our people under such governments.

38. We demand complete control of our social institutions without interference by any alien race or races.

39. That the colors, Red, Black and Green, be the colors of the Negro race.

40. Resolved, That the anthem "Ethiopia, Thou Land of Our Fathers etc.," shall be the anthem of the Negro race.

41. We believe that any limited liberty which deprives one of the complete rights and prerogatives of full citizenship is but a modified form of slavery.

42. We declare it an injustice to our people and a serious impediment to the health of the race to deny to competent licensed Negro physicians the right to practice in the public hospitals of the communities in which they reside, for no other reason than their race and color.

43. We call upon the various government[s] of the world to accept and acknowledge Negro representatives who shall be sent to the said governments to represent the general welfare of the Negro peoples of the world.

44. We deplore and protest against the practice of confining juvenile prisoners in prisons with adults, and we recommend that such youthful prisoners be taught gainful trades under human supervision.

45. Be it further resolved, That we as a race of people declare the League of Nations null and void as far as the Negro is concerned, in that it seeks to deprive Negroes of their liberty.

46. We demand of all men to do unto us as we would do unto them, in the name of justice; and we cheerfully accord to all men all the rights we claim herein for ourselves.

47. We declare that no Negro shall engage himself in battle for an alien race without first obtaining the consent of the leader of the Negro people of the world, except in a matter of national self-defense.

48. We protest against the practice of drafting Negroes and sending them to war with alien forces without proper training, and demand in all cases that Negro soldiers be given the same training as the aliens.

49. We demand that instructions given Negro children in schools include the subject of "Negro History," to their benefit.
50. We demand a free and unfettered commercial intercourse with all the Negro people of the world.
51. We declare for the absolute freedom of the seas for all peoples.
52. We demand that our duly accredited representatives be given proper recognition in all leagues, conferences, conventions or courts of international arbitration wherever human rights are discussed.
53. We proclaim the 31st day of August of each year to be an international holiday to be observed by all Negroes.
54. We want all men to know that we shall maintain and contend for the freedom and equality of every man, woman and child of our race, with our lives, our fortunes and our sacred honor.

Motive of the NAACP Exposed, 1923

The policy of the Universal Negro Improvement Association is so clean-cut, and my personal views are so well known, that no one, for even one moment, could reasonably accuse us of having any other desire than that of working for a united Negro race.

Some of us make the mistake to state in America, the West Indies and Africa that the nearer we approach the white man in color the greater our social standing and privilege, and that we should build up an "aristocracy" based upon caste of color and not achievement in race. It is well known, although no one is honest enough to admit it, that we have been, for the past thirty years at least, but more so now than ever, grading ourselves for social honor and distinction on the basis of color. That the average success in the race has been regulated by color and not by ability and merit; that we have been trying to get away from the pride of race into the atmosphere of color worship, to the damaging extent that the whole world has made us its laughing stock.

There is no doubt that a race that doesn't respect itself forfeits the respect of others, and we are in the moral-social position now of losing the respect of the whole world.

There is a subtle and underhand propaganda fostered by a few men of color in America, the West Indies and Africa to destroy the self-respect and pride of the Negro race by building up what is commonly known to us as a "blue vein" aristocracy and to foster same as the social and moral standard of the race. The success of this effort is very much marked in the West Indies, and coming into immediate recognition in South Africa, and is now gaining much headway in America under the skillful leadership of the National Association for the Advancement of "Colored" People and their silent but scattered agents.

The observant members of our race must have noticed within recent years a great hostility between the National Association for the Advancement of "Colored" People and the Universal "Negro" Improvement Association, and must have wondered why Du Bois writes so bitterly against Garvey and vice versa. Well, the reason is plainly to be seen after the following explanation:

Du Bois represents a group that hates the Negro blood in their veins, and has been working subtly to build up a caste aristocracy that would socially divide the race into two groups: One the superior because of color caste, and the other the inferior, hence the pretentious work of the National Association for the Advancement of "Colored" People. The program of deception was well arranged and under way for success when Marcus Garvey arrived in America, and he, after understudying the artful doctor and the group he represented, fired a "bomb" into the camp by organizing the Universal "Negro" Improvement Association to cut off the wicked attempt of race deception and distinction, and to in truth build up a race united in spirit and ideal with the honest desire-of adjusting itself to its own moral-social pride and national self-respect. When Garvey arrived in America and visited the office of the National Association for the Advancement of "Colored" People to interview Du Bois, who was regarded as a leader of the Negro people and who had recently visited the West Indies, he was dum[b]founded when, on approach to the office but for Mr. Dill and Dr. Du Bois himself and the office boy, he could not tell whether he was in a white office or that of the National Association for the Advancement of "Colored" People. The whole staff was either white or very near white, and thus Garvey got his first shock of the advancement hypocrisy. There was no representation of the race there that anyone could recognize. The advancement meant that you had to be as near white as possible, otherwise there was no place for you as stenographer, clerk or attendant in the office of the National Association for the Advancement of "Colored" People. After a short talk with Du Bois, Garvey became so disgusted with the man and his principles that the thought he never contemplated entered his m[i]nd—that of remaining in America to teach Du Bois and his group what real race pride meant … Now, what does all this mean? It is to relate the hidden program and motive of the National Association for the Advancement of "Colored" People and to warn Negro America of not being deceived by a group of men who have as much love for the Negro blood in their veins as the devil has for holy water.

The National Association for the Advancement of "Colored" People is a scheme to destroy the Negro Race, and the leaders of it hate Marcus Garvey because he has discovered them at their game and because the Universal Negro Improvement Association, without any prejudice to color or caste, is making headway in bringing all the people together for their common good. They hate Garvey because the Universal Negro Improvement Association and the Black Star Line employed every shade of color in the race, according to ability and merit, and put the N.A.A.C.P. to shame for employing only the "lightest" of the race. They hate Garvey because he forced them to fill Shilady's place with a Negro. They hate Garvey because they had to employ "black" Pickens to cover up their scheme after Garvey had discovered it; they hate Garvey because they have had to employ brown-skin "Bob" Bagnall to make a showing to the people that they were doing the "right" thing by them; they hate Garvey because he has broken up the "Pink Tea Set"; they hate Garvey because they have been forced to recognize mulatto, brown and black talent in the association equally with the lighter element; they hate Garvey because he is teaching the unity of race, without color superiority or prejudice. The gang thought that they would have been able to build up in America a buffer class between the white and the Negro, and thus in another fifty years join with the powerful race and crush the blood of their mothers, as is being done in South Africa and the West Indies … But now we have reached the point where the entire race must get together and stop these schemers at their game. Whether we are light, yellow, black or what not, there is but one thing for us to do, and that is to get together and build up a race. God made us in His own image and He had some purpose when He thus created us. Then why should we seek to destroy ourselves? If a few Du Boises and De Lissers do not want their progeny to remain of our race, why not be satisfied to abide their time and take their peaceful exit? But why try in this subtle manner to humiliate and destroy our race?

We as a people, have a great future before us. Ethiopia shall once more see the day of her glory, then why destroy the chance and opportunity simply to be someone else?

Let us work and wait patiently, for our day of racial triumph will come. Let us not divide ourselves into castes, but let us all work together for the common good. Let us remember the sorrow of our mothers. Let us forget not that it is our duty to remedy any wrong that has already been done, and not of ourselves perpetuate the evil of race destruction. To change our race is no credit. The Anglo-Saxon doesn't want to be a Japanese; the Japanese doesn't want to be a Negro. Then, in the name of God and all that is holy, why should we want to be somebody else?

Let the National Association for the Advancement of Colored People stop its hypocrisy and settle down to real race uplift.

If Du Bois, Johnson, Pickens and Bagnall do not know, let me tell them that they are only being used to weaken the race, so that in another fifty or a hundred years the race can easily be wiped out as a social, economic and political force or "menace." The people who are directing the affairs of the National Association for the Advancement of "Colored" People are keen observers and wise leaders. It takes more than ordinary intelligence to penetrate their motive, hence you are now warned.

All the "gas" about anti-lynching and "social equality" will not amount to a row of pins; in fact, it is only a ruse to raise money to capitalize the scheme and hide the real motive. Negroes, watch your step and save yourselves from deception and subsequent extermination.

What We Believe, 1924

The Universal Negro Improvement Association advocates the uniting and blending of all Negroes into one strong healthy race. It is against miscegenation and race suicide.

It believes that the Negro race is as good as any other, and therefore should be as proud of itself as others are.

It believes in the purity of the Negro race and the purity of the white race.

It is against rich blacks marrying poor whites.

It is against rich or poor whites taking advantage of Negro women.

It believes in the spiritual Fatherhood of God and the Brotherhood of Man.

It believes in the social and political physical separation of all people to the extent that they promote their own ideals and civilization, with the privilege of trading and doing business with each other. It believes in the promotion of a strong and powerful Negro nation.

It believes in the rights of all men.

Universal Negro Improvement Assn.
Marcus Garvey
President-General

17.
MALCOLM X

Malcolm X (1925–1965) was not always a political figure. While historians suggest he exaggerated his criminal past, after dropping out of high school, Malcolm became involved in drug dealing, gambling, and prostitution rings. In 1946 he was sentenced to between eight and ten years for armed robbery. While serving what ultimately amounted to six years in prison, he converted to Islam. Like many Black Nationalists, Malcolm X changed his name, Malcolm Little, to reject his "slave name." Many Black Nationalists, particularly members of the radical Nation of Islam (NOI), changed their last names to an X; the X represented their unidentified name or the one stolen from them along with other aspects of their identity and culture during slavery. In 1953, the same year of his name change, he was appointed the Assistant Minister of the Nation of Islam's Detroit Temple. Brother Malcolm made his ascendancy through the ranks of the Nation of Islam expeditiously. By 1954 he was appointed the Minster of the Nation of Islam New York Temple. In 1957 he founded the Nation of Islam newspaper, *Muhammad Speaks*. As membership in the NOI grew tremendously, many people attributed its growth to the young charismatic leader. Malcolm had become the public face of the NOI. However, antagonisms developed between Malcolm X and the NOI's leader, Elijah Muhammad.

Malcolm was distressed when he learned that his mentor, Elijah Muhammad, had supposedly engaged in numerous extramarital affairs and even fathered children with his mistresses. Malcolm refused to play any role in covering up his nefarious behavior. In addition, in 1963 Malcolm made ostensibly insensitive remarks about the assassination of President Kennedy (see "God's Judgment of White America" in this chapter and discussion below). In what became known as "the chickens come home to roost speech" Malcolm X said that American racism had run so rampant that not only were Black people being brutalized and murdered as a result but even Kennedy lost his life as a result of American racial hate. However, many said that Malcolm was justifying his assassination or suggesting it was karma for hundreds of years of White brutalization of Black people. Despite the tumultuous relationships between Malcolm and members of the NOI, he still remained active. In 1963 he led the Unity Rally in Harlem. However, his problems within the NOI created a schism, which resulted in Malcolm's departure from the NOI. In March 1964 Malcolm X left the NOI and started the Muslim Mosque, Inc. In this group many former disgruntled members of the NOI found a new home.

The next month he made his famous hajj to Mecca where he made a large transformation in his ideas about race relations; he became more open to interracial relations in the political sphere. Now a Sunni Muslim he condemned all racial intolerance and prejudice. In May 1964 he started the Organization of Afro-American Unity, which was a Harlem-based political organization. His work, ideas, and unapologetic tone scared many Americans. On February 14, 1965, his home was firebombed and one week later he was assassinated in the Audubon Ballroom in Harlem, New York.

Overview of Ideas

Malcolm X was a radical spokesman for Black Nationalists and originally the Nation of Islam. He argued that cultural nationalism was vital to the progress of African Americans. Black people have been stripped of their heritage and history. He said a major factor that differentiated White people and Black people were that White people knew their history. It was taught and celebrated in their schools, in their homes, and in their society. African Americans did not have this option. Whether Black people were educated in segregated Black schools or in the Ivy halls of Harvard they all learned White man's history. This educational process furthered the alienation of Black people from themselves and their true identities. In the Nation of Islam under Elijah Muhammad, Malcolm said Black people were beginning to learn their history. Once Black people were reunited with their history, they would know themselves and then be equipped to fight against the White man. This lack of education made Black people childlike.

American society through its racist policies has aimed to keep Black people in an inferior position, economically, politically, and socially. By dominating decision-making you render the Black population a group of dependents, like children. Black people have been reduced to children "because a child is someone who sits around and waits for his father to do for him what he should be doing for himself." With the exception of churches, Black people have built nothing for themselves. According to Malcolm X, it was time for Black people to build institutions of their own. It was time they reunited with their real father. Black people and their integrationist leaders are overly concerned with making positive relationships with White people instead of the Black people and Africans in their original homeland. And why? White people had brutalized and slaughtered millions of people. They oppressed and exploited human beings for profit. For this, White people were a race of devils.

In his famous speech, "God's Judgment of White America" he continued his indictment of the race of White devils.

> So we of this present generation are also witnessing how the enslavement of millions of black people in this country is now beginning White America to her hour of judgment, to her downfall as a respected nation ... it is only a matter of time before White America too will be utterly destroyed by her own sins.

God was going to finally punish the United States her lack of humanity and cruelty. "The hour of judgment and doom is upon White America for the evil seeds of slavery and hypocrisy she has shown." The United States committed its greatest sin against

Black people and it was time to pay. This apocalyptic vision was not just supported by Islamic text but also by Christian text. Americans should refrain from their usual hubris; as the axiom tells us, pride comes before the fall.

Given that Malcolm made this speech immediately following John F. Kennedy's death many perceived these comments as almost blasphemous. Many claimed Malcolm X was saying Kennedy' death was retribution and implied that he deserved to die. This reactionary response missed Malcolm's point. John F. Kennedy made attempts, however diminutive or futile, to assuage racial injustice and doing so cost him his life. Kennedy was another casualty in a long line of people, overwhelmingly Black people, whose lives had been taken by American racists.

Interestingly, Malcolm X noted that he was astonished that White people were so resistant to the conversion of so many African Americans from Christianity to Islam. The NOI preached conservative cultural values, ones that surprisingly even staunch modern conservatives also advocate with fervor. Malcolm X said Elijah Muhammad taught his followers to delay gratification. They were not allowed to consume alcohol or drugs, smoke cigarettes, have sex outside of marriage, gamble, lie, and commit crimes. Why would Americans oppose this? The quagmire did not lie with their Muslim conversion; Black people were learning the importance of individual transformation. According to Malcolm X, Whites were angry because Black people's cultural roots were being restored. With racial empowerment the status quo would be shaken at its core.

Malcolm X, a Pan-Africanist, cautioned Americans that Black people all over the globe were uniting and increasing both their wealth and power. However, the United States had two choices to escape its ill fate. First, they could repent and join Islam, which Malcolm said would not happen. Second, and ultimately the only real solution, was "the complete separation of these twenty-two million ex-slaves from our white slave master, and the return of these ex-slaves to our own land, where we can then live in peace and security among our own people." The answer was separatism, not integration. Moreover, like early advocates of Black Nationalism, such as Martin Delany, the government should finance the transportation and all resources needed to make the pilgrimage back to Africa. Moreover, like Marcus Garvey, Malcolm agreed that no good would come of continued existence on the same soil. Separation would foster peace.

Malcolm X argued that White-influenced civil rights organizations and their leaders were espousing the idea that integration would solve the problems facing African Americans. However, this was only a strategy to keep paternalism in its place, to keep the Black child dependent on his White father figure. The government will continue to make promises of civil rights and various freedoms and African Americans would soon learn they had been written bad checks. Much like Marcus Garvey, Malcolm X was enraged by civil rights leadership; he saw them as bourgeois Uncle Toms who were leading Black people in the wrong direction.

Like Marcus Garvey, Malcolm saw integrated civil rights organizations as pacifists and sell-outs. In fact, Brother Malcolm saw the Civil Rights Movement as a huge charade. After the march on Washington, where A. Philip Randolph, Bayard Rustin, and Martin Luther King Jr. all stood proud, Malcolm X said the march was "run by whites in front of a statue of a president who has been dead for a hundred years and who didn't like us when he was alive." In a famous parable, Malcolm X compared the Civil Rights Movement to a cup of coffee; he said a cup of freshly brewed coffee is Black and it is hot. Add milk and it becomes tepid. This is what happened to the Black freedom struggle. White liberals now controlled the movement. Fighting for the needs of working class Blacks could only solve the struggle against racial injustice. Instead, the Civil Rights Movement was being led by middle class "white-minded" Blacks and their White liberal comrades. Malcolm X was an organizer of the Black working classes and poor.

Famously, Malcolm X told a story about the House Negro and Field Negro during slavery. During slavery, light-skinned slaves tended to work in the master's house as servants, mammies, etc. The dark-skinned slaves primarily labored in the fields. Imagine for a moment a master's plantation house raging in flames. From the field, one could hear slaves rejoicing. As the master stood watching his house engulfed in voracious flames, the House Negro turned to master and exclaimed, "Master our house is on fire." The light-skinned House Negro, with their modicum of privilege, was falsely conscious of their social position. The House Negro, like the leaders of the mainstream Civil Rights Movement, stood beside their masters instead of aligning themselves with their oppressed brethren in the fields. Malcolm X's focus was on organizing Field Negroes; the mainstream Civil Rights Movement organized House Negroes. Malcolm realized what Black Nationalists who came after him during Black Power did. They both realized the importance of organizing the lumpenproletariat; they had nothing to lose.

Malcolm X has been widely misunderstood in popular American discourse. He has been depicted as a violent revolutionary calling for death to all White people. First, Malcolm redefined what it meant to be a revolutionary. Colloquially, hearing the word revolutionary conjures up images of guns and bloodshed. According to Malcolm, a revolutionary was someone who did not just seek to reform an oppressive system or regime; a revolutionary is someone who seeks to institute an entirely new system, a system of his or her own design. Calling for and creating an independent Black nation was revolutionary. This is precisely what civil rights activists did not understand. Voting would lead nowhere; the two-party system allowed for no representation for Black people; both parties' apathy toward African American interests were blatant. Moreover, the political system was rigged through mechanisms such as gerrymandering, which refers to the practice of restructuring voting districts once a minority population gains too much control and influence over the voting district. A revolutionary was cognizant that democratic reform would not meet the needs of Black people in the United States.

Second, Malcolm never suggested that Black people capriciously cause harm to or murder White people. However, a group of people regularly abused and brutalized has a human right to defend themselves. In addition, if Black Nationalists' efforts to organize and constitute their own nation were met with hostility and violence, which Malcolm legitimately anticipated, then in defense of their freedom Black people would retaliate. This was the reality of revolution. With his usual wit and candor Malcolm gave an example; if you were peacefully protesting and a police officer turned a ravaging dog on you and that dog came at you, teeth gnashing, would you be right to shoot that dog? Of course you would. Malcolm argued civil rights protesters led by the "Big Negroes" or House Negroes would allow the dog to bite you. Historically, the revolutionary efforts of marginalized and oppressed groups are always met with enmity by the hegemonic forces.

Finally, to be a revolutionary meant to control one's own destiny. Revolution has always been over land; revolutions struggle to gain control over the land and to take back control from colonial and/or imperialist powers. Again, according to Malcolm X, Black Nationalism was comprised of three basic tenets. First, Black people needed to create and control their own nation. The economic philosophy of Black Nationalism meant that "we should control the economy of our community." By owning their own businesses, stores, banks, etc., Black people would be responsible for employing other Black people. With thriving businesses Black communities would thrive. This approach fosters self-sufficiency and independence. Malcolm insisted African Americans did not need to beg the White man for jobs or programs to create jobs for them; they could create their own jobs. Finally, as discussed earlier, Malcolm was adamant that change had to come from within and much of that change was cultural and moral.

> The social philosophy of black nationalism only means that we have to get together and remove the evils, the vices, alcoholism, drug addiction, and other evils that are destroying the moral fiber of our community. WE ourselves have to lift the level of our community, the standard of our community to a higher level, make our own society beautiful so that we will be satisfied in our own social circles and won't be running around here trying to knock our way into a social circle where we're not wanted.

A strict conservative moral ethos would invoke positive change in the Black community. Moreover, it was high time Black people became more concerned with building meaningful social networks with other Black people and not laboring so hard to fit in with Whites.

After leaving the NOI and his life-altering hajj to Mecca, Malcolm began to focus more on alliances with other non-White oppressed groups. As a Pan-Africanist Malcolm always saw the struggles of Black people in the United States as connected with those of the entire Black Diaspora. However, in 1964 Malcolm began to publicly claim that this worldwide revolution would also include all non-White oppressed people. This meant the global revolution would consist of people from Africa, Asia, and Latin America. Groups who were colonized on different continents by Europeans all shared a common struggle. They were all fighting for human rights. Oppressed groups have been divided for too long; this was the greatest strategy colonial imperialist powers have had—to divide and conquer. Malcolm astutely noted that too many Black people saw themselves as minorities. However, if you put the struggles of African Americans in a global context you will begin to see that, in fact, White people are the minority. Finally, by forging a united global revolution for human rights, it would make it possible to bring the case to the United Nations. The United States could then be charged with human rights violations. Malcolm said the United States should be charged with genocide. Although his philosophy changed slightly in regards to race, Malcolm always remained an uncompromising revolutionary.

Black Man's History, 1962

There's a basic difference in why we are treated as we are: one knows his history and one doesn't know his history! The American so-called Negro is a soldier who doesn't know his history; he's a servant who doesn't know his history; he's a graduate of Columbia, or Yale, or Harvard, or Tuskeegee, who doesn't know his history. He's confined, he's limited, he's held under the control and the jurisdiction of the white man who knows more about the history of the Negro than the Negro knows about himself. But when you and I wake up, as we're taught by The Honorable Elijah Muhammad, and learn our history, learn the history of our kind, and the history of the white kind, then the white man will be at a disadvantage and we'll be at an advantage.

The only thing that puts you and me at a disadvantage is our lack of knowledge concerning history. So one of the reasons, one of the missions, one of the objectives of The Honorable Elijah Muhammad here in America is not only to teach you and me the right religions but to teach you and me history. In fact, do you know that if you and I know history we know the right religion? The only way that you can become confused, that you can become mixed up and not know which religion belongs to God, is if you don't know history. In fact, you have to know history to know something about God. You have to know history to know something about God's religion. You have to know history to know something about God's people. You have to know history to know something about God's plans and God's purposes, and, as I say, the only people who don't know history are the American so-called Negroes.

The so-called Negro are childlike people—you're like children. No matter how old you get, or how bold you get, or how wise you get, or how rich you get, or how educated you get, the white man still calls you what? Boy! Why, you *are* a child in his eyesight! And you are a child. Anytime you have to let another man set up a factory for you and you can't set up a factory for yourself, you're a child; anytime another man has to open up businesses for you and you don't know how to open up businesses for yourself and your people, you're a child; anytime another man sets up schools and you don't know how to set up your own schools, you're a child. Because a child is someone who sits around and waits for his father to do for him what he should be doing for himself, or what he's too young to do for himself, or what he is too dumb to do for himself. So the white man, knowing that here in America all the Negro has done—I hate to say it, but it's the truth—all you and I have done is build churches and let the white man build factories.

You and I build churches and let the white man build schools. You and I build churches and let the white man build up everything for himself. Then after you build the church you have to go and beg the white man for a job, and beg the white man for some education. Am I right or wrong? Do you see what I mean? It's too bad but it's true. And it's history. So it shows that these childlike people—people who would be children, following after the white man—it says in the last day that God will raise up

Elijah, and Elijah's job will be to turn the hearts of these children back toward their fathers. Elijah will come and change our minds; he'll teach us something that will turn us completely around. When Elijah finds us we'll be easy to lead in the wrong direction but hard to lead in the right direction. But when Elijah gets through teaching the Lost Sheep, or the Lost People of God, he'll turn them around, he'll change their minds, he'll put a board in their back, he'll make them throw their shoulders back and stand upright like men for the first time. It says he'll turn the hearts of these children toward their fathers and the hearts of the fathers toward the children. This is something that The Honorable Elijah Muhammad is doing here in America today. You and I haven't thought in terms of our forefathers. We haven't thought of our fathers. Our fathers, brother, are back home. Our fathers are in the East. We're running around here begging the Great White Father. You never hear of black people in this country talking or speaking or thinking in terms of connecting themselves with their own kind back home. They are trying to make contact with the white man, trying to make a connection with the white man, trying to connect, trying to make a connection with a kidnapper who brought them here, trying to make a connection with, actually, the man who enslaved them. You know that's a shame—it's pitiful—but it's true.

So, brothers and sisters, my time has expired. I just wanted to point out that the white man, a race of devils, was made six thousand years ago. This doesn't mean to tell you that this implies any kind of hate. They're just a race of devils. They were made six thousand years ago, they were made to rule for six thousand years, and their time expired in the year 1914. The only reason God didn't remove them then was because you and I were here in their clutches and God gave them an extension of time—not *them* an extension of time, but they received an extension of time to give the wise men of the East the opportunity to get into this House of Bondage and "awaken" the Lost Sheep. Once the American so-called Negroes have been awakened to a knowledge of themselves and of their own God and of the white man, then they're on their own. Then it'll be left up to you and me whether we want to integrate into this wicked race or leave them and separate and go to our own. And if we integrate we'll be destroyed along with them. If we separate then we have a chance for salvation. So on that note, in the name of Allah, and His Messenger The Honorable Elijah Muhammad, I bring my talk to a close, "As-Salaam-Alaikum."

Gods Judgment of White America, 1963

(The Chickens Are Coming Home to Roost)

The Honorable Elijah Muhammad teaches us that as it was the evil sin of slavery that caused the downfall and destruction of ancient Egypt and Babylon, and of ancient Greece, as well as ancient Rome, so it was the evil sin of colonialism (slavery, nineteenth-century European style) that caused the collapse of the white nations in present-day Europe *as world powers*. Unbiased scholars and unbiased observers agree that the wealth and power of white Europe has rapidly declined during the nineteen-year period between World War II and today.

So we of this present generation are also witnessing how the enslavement of millions of black people in this country is now bringing White America to her hour of judgment, to her downfall as a respected nation. And even those Americans who are blinded by childlike patriotism can see that it is only a matter of time before White America too will be utterly destroyed by her own sins, and all traces of her former glory will be removed from this planet forever.

The Honorable Elijah Muhammad teaches us that as it was divine will in the case of the destruction of the slave empires of the ancient and modern past, America's *judgment* and *destruction* will also be brought about by divine will and divine power. Just as ancient nations paid for their sins against humanity, White America must now pay for her sins against twenty-two million "Negroes." White America's worst crime is her hypocrisy and her deceit. White America pretends to ask herself: "What do these Negroes want?" White America knows that four hundred years of cruel bondage has made these twenty-two million ex-slaves too (mentally) blind to see what they really want.

White America should be asking herself: "What does God want for these twenty-two million ex-slaves?" Who will make White America know what God wants? Who will present God's plan to White America?

What is God's solution to the problem caused by the presence of twenty-two million unwanted ex-slaves here in America? And who will present God's solution?

We, the Muslims who follow The Honorable Elijah Muhammad, believe wholeheartedly in the God of justice. We believe in the Creator, whose divine power and laws of justice created and sustain the universe.

We believe in the all-wise Supreme Being: the great God who is called "Jehovah" by the monotheistic Hebrews. We do not believe in the Trinity (or "plurality of gods") as advocated by the polytheistic Christians. We who are Muslims call God by his true name: Allah, the great God of the universe, the Lord of all the worlds, the Master of the Day of Judgment.

The Honorable Elijah Muhammad teaches us that Allah is the true name of the divine Supreme Being, and that Islam is an Arabic word which means complete submission to God's will, or obedience to God's guidance.

We who are Muslims believe in this religion that is described in the Arabic language by the word "Islam." This religion, Islam, teaches us submission to God's will and obedience to God's guidance. It gives us the moral discipline that makes it easy for us to walk the path of truth and righteousness.

"Muslim" is an Arabic word, and it describes a person whose religion is Islam. A Muslim is one who practices complete submission and obedience to God's will.

Here in America the word "Muslim" is westernized or anglicized and pronounced "Moslem." Muslim and Moslem are actually the same word. The true believers in Allah call themselves Muslims, but the nonbelieving infidels refer to Muslims as Moslems or Muhammadans. Many of the weak, backsliding Muslims who come to this country have also adopted some of these same pronunciations coined for them by the infidels.

But we don't condemn these "orthodox" Muslims, because the reward of the believer, as well as the chastisement of the nonbeliever and the backslider, come only from

Allah. Allah is the only judge. He alone is master of this Day of Judgment in which we now live.

Why is the American white man so set against the twenty-two million "Negroes" learning about the religion of Islam? Islam is the religion that elevates the morals of the people who want to do right. Just by teaching us the religion of Islam, and by showing us how to live the life of a Muslim, The Honorable Elijah Muhammad is turning hundreds of thousands of American "Negroes" away from drunkenness, drug addiction, nicotine, stealing, lying, cheating, gambling, profanity, filth, fornication, adultery, and the many other acts of immorality that are almost in-separable from this indecent Western society.

The hour of judgment and doom is upon White America for the evil seeds of slavery and hypocrisy she has sown; and God himself has declared that no one shall escape the doom of this Western world, except those who accept Allah as God, Islam as his only religion, and The Honorable Elijah Muhammad as his Messenger to the twenty-two million ex-slaves here in America, twenty-two million "Negroes" who are referred to in the symbolism of the Scriptures as the Lost Sheep, the Lost Tribes, or the Lost People of God.

White America is doomed! God has declared that The Honorable Elijah Muhammad is your only means of escape. When you reject The Honorable Elijah Muhammad, when you refuse to hear his message or heed his warning, you are closing your only door of escape. When you cut yourself off from him, you cut yourself off from your only way out of the divine disaster that is fast approaching White America.

Before your pride causes you to harden your heart and further close your ears, and before your ignorance provokes laughter, search the Christian Scriptures. Search even the histories of other nations that sat in the same positions of wealth, power, and authority that these white Americans now hold ... and see what *God* did to them. If God's unchanging laws of justice caught up with every one of the slave empires of the past, how dare you think White America can escape the harvest of unjust seeds planted by her white forefathers against our black fore-fathers here in this land of slavery! ... The time is past when the white world can exercise unilateral authority and control over the dark world. The independence and power of the dark world is on the increase; the dark world is rising in wealth, power, prestige, and influence. It is the rise of the dark world that is causing the fall of the white world.

As the white man loses his power to oppress and exploit the dark world, the white man's own wealth (power or "world") decreases. His world is on its way down; it is on its way out ... and it is the will and power of God himself that is bringing an end to the white world.

You and I were born at this turning point in history; we are witnessing the fulfill-ment of prophecy. Our present generation is witnessing the end of colonialism, Euro-peanism, Westernism, or "White-ism" ... the end of white supremacy, the end of the evil white man's unjust rule.

I must repeat: The end of the world only means the end of a certain "power." The end of colonialism ends the world (or power) of the colonizer. The end of European-ism ends the world (or power) of the European ... and the end of "White-ism" ends the world (or power) of THE WHITE MAN.

Judgment day is the final hour when God himself sits in the seat of justice and judges these white nations (or the white world) according to the deeds they committed and the seeds they sowed when they themselves sat in the seat of power.

According to the Christian Bible, Judgment Day is that final hour when God will cause "those who led others into captivity to go into captivity themselves" ... and "those who killed others with the sword to be killed by the sword of justice themselves."

Justice only means that the wicked slave master must reap the fruit (or harvest) of the evil seeds of slavery he has planted. This is justice! Other slave empires received justice, and now White America must receive justice. According to White America's own evil past, which is clearly recorded on the pages of history, so shall God judge her today ... In like manner God has prepared a Doomsday (a day of slaughter, a lake of fire) for this sinful white world of colonizers, enslavers, oppressors, exploiters, lynchers ... and all others who refuse to repent and atone at the end of this white world.

God has also prepared a refuge, a haven of salvation, for those who will accept his last Messenger and heed his last warning.

White America is doomed! Death and devasting destruction hang at this very moment in the skies over America. But why must her divine execution take place? Is it too late for her to avoid this catastrophe? ... Is it possible for America to escape this divine disaster? If America can't atone for the crimes she has committed against the twenty-two million "Negroes," if she can't undo the evils she has brutally and mercilessly heaped upon our people these past four hundred years, then America has signed her own doom ... and our own people would be foolish to accept her deceitful offers of integration into her doomed society at this late date!

How can America atone for her crimes? The Honorable Elijah Muhammad teaches us that a desegregated theater or lunch counter won't solve our problems. Better jobs won't even solve our problems. An integrated cup of coffee isn't sufficient pay for four hundred years of slave labor, and a better job in the white man's factory or position in his business is, at best, only a temporary solution. The only lasting or permanent solution is complete separation on some land that we can call our own.

The Honorable Elijah Muhammad teaches us that the race problem can easily be solved, just by sending these twenty-two million ex-slaves *back to our own homeland* where we can live in peace and harmony with our own kind. But this government should provide the transportation, plus everything else we need to get started again in our own country. This government should provide everything we need in machinery, materials, and finance; enough to last us for from twenty to twenty-five years, until we can become an independent people *in our own country*.

If this white government is afraid to let her twenty-two million ex-slaves go back to our country and to our own people, then America must set aside some separate territory here in the Western Hemisphere, where the two races can live apart from each other, since we certainly don't get along peacefully while we are here together.

The size of the territory can be judged according to our own population. If our people number one-seventh of America's total population, then give us one-seventh of this land. We don't want any land in the desert, but where there is rain and much mineral wealth.

We want fertile, productive land on which we can farm and provide our own people with sufficient food, clothing, and shelter. This government must supply us with the machinery and other tools needed to dig into the earth. Give us everything we need for them for from twenty to twenty-five years, until we can produce and supply our own needs.

If we are a part of America, then part of what she is worth belongs to us. We will take our share and depart, then this white country can have peace. *What is her net worth?* Give us our share in gold and silver and let us depart and go back to our homeland in peace.

We want no integration with this wicked race that enslaved us. We want complete separation from this race of devils. But we should not be expected to leave America and go back to our homeland empty-handed. After four hundred years of slave labor, we have some back pay coming, a bill owed to us that must be collected.

If the government of White America truly repents of its sins against our people, *and atones by giving us our true share, only then can America save herself!*

But if America waits for Almighty God himself to step in and force her into a just settlement, God will take this entire continent away from her; and she will cease to exist as a nation. Her own Christian Scriptures warn her that when God comes He can give the "entire Kingdom to whomsoever He will" ... which only means that the God of Justice on Judgment Day can give this entire continent to whomsoever He wills!

White America, wake up and take heed, before it is too late!

Message to the Grass Roots, 1963

Revolution is bloody, revolution is hostile, revolution knows no compromise, revolution overturns and destroys everything that gets in its way. And you, sitting around here like a knot on the wall, saying, "I'm going to love these folks no matter how much they hate me." No, you need a revolution. Whoever heard of a revolution where they lock arms, as Rev. Cleage was pointing out beautifully, singing "We Shall Overcome"? You don't do that in a revolution. You don't do any singing, you're too busy swinging. It's based on land. A revolutionary wants land so he can set up his own nation, an independent nation. These Negroes aren't asking for any nation—they're trying to crawl back on the plantation.

When you want a nation, that's called nationalism. When the white man became involved in a revolution in this country against England, what was it for? He wanted this land so he could set up another white nation. That's white nationalism. The American Revolution was white nationalism. The French Revolution was white nationalism. The Russian Revolution too—yes, it was—white nationalism. You don't think so? Why do you think Khrushchev and Mao can't get their heads together? White nationalism. All the revolutions that are going on in Asia and Africa today are based on what?—black nationalism. A revolutionary is a black nationalist. He wants a nation. I was reading some beautiful words by Rev. Cleage, pointing out why he couldn't get together with someone else in the city because all of them were afraid of being identified with black nationalism. If you're afraid of black nationalism, you're afraid of revolution. And if you love revolution, you love black nationalism.

To understand this, you have to go back to what the young brother here referred to as the house Negro and the field Negro back during slavery. There were two kinds of slaves, the house Negro and the field Negro. The house Negroes—they lived in the house with master, they dressed pretty good, they ate good because they ate his food— what he left. They lived in the attic or the basement, but still they lived near the master; and they loved the master more than the master loved himself. They would give their life to save the master's house—quicker than the master would. If the master said, "We got a good house here," the house Negro would say, "Yeah, we got a good house here." Whenever the master said "we," he said "we." That's how you can tell a house Negro.

If the master's house caught on fire, the house Negro would fight harder to put the blaze out than the master would. If the master got sick, the house Negro would say, "What's the matter, boss, *we* sick?" *We* sick! He identified himself with his master, more than his master identified with himself. And if you came to the house Negro and said, "Let's run away, let's escape, let's separate," the house Negro would look at you and say, "Man, you crazy. What you mean, separate? Where is there a better house than this? Where can I wear better clothes than this? Where can I eat better food than this?" That was that house Negro. In those days he was called a "house nigger." And that's what we call them today, because we've still got some house niggers running around here.

This modern house Negro loves his master. He wants to live near him. He'll pay three times as much as the house is worth just to live near his master, and then brag about "I'm the only Negro out here." "I'm the only one on my job." "I'm the only one in this school." You're nothing but a house Negro. And if someone comes to you right now and says, "Let's separate," you say the same thing that the house Negro said on the plantation. "What you mean, separate? From America, this good white man? Where you going to get a better job than you get here?" I mean, this is what you say. "I ain't left nothing in Africa," that's what you say. Why, you left your mind in Africa.

On that same plantation, there was the field Negro. The field Negroes—those were the masses. There were always more Negroes in the field than there were Negroes in the house. The Negro in the field caught hell. He ate leftovers. In the house they ate high up on the hog. The Negro in the field didn't get anything but what was left of the insides of the hog. They call it "chitt'lings" nowadays. In those days they called them what they were—guts. That's what you were—gut-eaters. And some of you are still gut-eaters.

The field Negro was beaten from morning to night; he lived in a shack, in a hut; he wore old, castoff clothes. He hated his master. I say he hated his master. He was intelligent. That house Negro loved his master, but that field Negro—remember, they were in the majority, and they hated the master. When the house caught on fire, he didn't try to put it out; that field Negro prayed for a wind, for a breeze. When the master got sick, the field Negro prayed that he'd die. If someone came to the field Negro and said, "Let's separate, let's run," he didn't say "Where we going?" He'd say, "Any place is better than here." You've got field Negroes in America today. I'm a field Negro. The masses are the field Negroes. When they see this man's house on fire, you don't hear the little Negroes talking about "*our* government is in trouble." They say, "*The* government is in trouble." Imagine a Negro: "*Our* government"! I even heard one say "*our* astronauts." They won't even let him near the plant—and "*our* astronauts"! "*Our* Navy"—that's a Negro that is out of his mind, a Negro that is out of his mind.

Just as the slavemaster of that day used Tom, the house Negro, to keep the field Negroes in check, the same old slavemaster today has Negroes who are nothing but modern Uncle Toms, twentieth-century Uncle Toms, to keep you and me in check, to keep us under control, keep us passive and peaceful and nonviolent. That's Tom making you nonviolent. It's like when you go to the dentist, and the man's going to take your tooth. You're going to fight him when he starts pulling. So he squirts some stuff in your jaw called novocaine [*sic*], to make you think they're not doing anything to you. So you sit there and because you've got all of that novocaine [*sic*] in your jaw, you suffer—peacefully. Blood running all down your jaw, and you don't know what's happening. Because someone has taught you to suffer—peacefully.

The white man does the same thing to you in the street, when he wants to put knots on your head and take advantage of you and not have to be afraid of your fighting back. To keep you from fighting back, he gets these old religious Uncle Toms to teach you and me, just like novocaine [*sic*], to suffer peacefully. Don't stop suffering—just suffer peacefully. As Rev. Cleage pointed out, they say you should let your blood flow in the streets. This is a shame. You know he's a Christian preacher. If it's a shame to him, you know what it is to me.

There is nothing in our book, the Koran, that teaches us to suffer peacefully. Our religion teaches us to be intelligent. Be peaceful, be courteous, obey the law, respect everyone; but if someone puts his hand on you, send him to the cemetery. That's a good religion. In fact, that's that old-time religion. That's the one that Ma and Pa used to talk about: an eye for an eye, and a tooth for a tooth, and a head for a head, and a life for a life. That's a good religion.

The Ballot or the Bullet, 1964

Although I'm still a Muslim, I'm not here tonight to discuss my religion. I'm not here to try and change your religion. I'm not here to argue or discuss anything that we differ about, because it's time for us to submerge our differences and realize that it is best for us to first see that we have the same problem, a common problem—a problem that will make you catch hell whether you're a Baptist, or a Methodist, or a Muslim, or a nationalist. Whether you're educated or illiterate, whether you live on the boulevard or in the alley, you're going to catch hell just like I am. We're all in the same boat and we all are going to catch the same hell from the same man. He just happens to be a white man. All of us have suffered here, in this country, political oppression at the hands of the white man, economic exploitation at the hands of the white man, and social degradation at the hands of the white man.

Now in speaking like this, it doesn't mean that we're anti-white, but it does mean we're anti-exploitation, we're anti-degradation, we're anti-oppression. And if the white man doesn't want us to be anti-him, let him stop oppressing and exploiting and degrading us ... I am one who doesn't believe in deluding myself. I'm not going to sit at your table and watch you eat, with nothing on my plate, and call myself a diner. Sitting at the table doesn't make you a diner, unless you eat some of what's on that plate. Being here in America doesn't make you an American. Being born here in America doesn't make you an American. Why, if birth made you American, you wouldn't need any legislation, you wouldn't need any amendments to the Constitution, you wouldn't be faced with civil-rights filibustering in Washington, D.C., right now. They don't have to pass civil-rights legislation to make a Polack an American.

No, I'm not an American. I'm one of the 22 million black people who are the victims of Americanism. One of the 22 million black people who are the victims of democracy, nothing but disguised hypocrisy. So, I'm not standing here speaking to you as an American, or a patriot, or a flag-saluter, or a flag-waver—no, not I. I'm speaking as a victim of this American system. And I see America through the eyes of the victim. I don't see any American dream; I see an American nightmare.

So, what I'm trying to impress upon you, in essence, is this: You and I in America are faced not with a segregationist conspiracy, we're faced with a government conspiracy. Everyone who's filibustering is a senator—that's the government. Everyone who's finagling in Washington, D.C., is a congressman—that's the government. You don't have anybody putting blocks in your path but people who are a part of the government. The same government that you go abroad to fight for and die for is the government that is in a conspiracy to deprive you of your voting rights, deprive you of your economic opportunities, deprive you of decent housing, deprive you of decent education. You don't need to go to the employer alone, it is the government itself, the government of America, that is responsible for the oppression and exploitation and degradation of black people in this country. And you should drop it in their lap. This government has failed the Negro. This so-called democracy has failed the Negro. And all these white liberals have definitely failed the Negro.

So, where do we go from here? First, we need some friends. We need some new allies. The entire civil-rights struggle needs a new interpretation, a broader interpretation. We need to look at this civil-rights thing from another angle—from the inside as well as from the outside. To those of us whose philosophy is black nationalism, the only way you can get involved in the civil-rights struggle is give it a new interpretation. That old interpretation excluded us. It kept us out. So, we're giving a new interpretation to the civil-rights struggle, an interpretation that will enable us to come into it, take part in it. And these handkerchief-heads who have been dillydallying and pussy-footing and compromising—we don't intend to let them pussyfoot and dillydally and compromise any longer. How can you thank a man for giving you what's already yours? How then can you thank him for giving you only part of what's already yours?… When we begin to get in this area, we need new friends, we need new allies. We need to expand the civil-rights struggle to a higher level—to the level of human rights. Whenever you are in a civil-rights struggle, whether you know it or not, you are confining yourself to the jurisdiction of Uncle Sam. No one from the outside world can speak out in your behalf as long as your struggle is a civil-rights struggle. Civil rights comes within the domestic affairs of this country. All of our African brothers and our Asian brothers and our Latin-American brothers cannot open their mouths and interfere in the domestic affairs of the United States. And as long as it's civil rights, this comes under the jurisdiction of Uncle Sam.

But the United Nations has what's known as the charter of human rights, it has a committee that deals in human rights. You may wonder why all of the atrocities that have been committed in Africa and in Hungary and in Asia and in Latin America are brought before the UN, and the Negro problem is never brought before the UN. This is part of the conspiracy. This old, tricky, blue-eyed liberal who is supposed to be your and my friend, supposed to be in our corner, supposed to be subsidizing our struggle, and supposed to be acting in the capacity of an adviser, never tells you anything about human rights. They keep you wrapped up in civil rights. And you spend so much time barking up the civil-rights tree, you don't even know there's a human-rights tree on the same floor. When you expand the civil-rights struggle to the level of human rights, you can then take the case of the black man in this country before the nations in the UN.

The political philosophy of black nationalism means that the black man should control the politics and the politicians in his own community; no more. The black man in the black community has to be re-educated into the science of politics so he will know what politics is supposed to bring him in return. Don't be throwing out any ballots. A ballot is like a bullet. You don't throw your ballots until you see a target, and if that target is not within your reach, keep your ballot in your pocket. The political philosophy of black nationalism is being taught in the Christian church. It's being taught in the NAACP. It's being taught in CORE meetings. It's being taught in SNCC [Student Nonviolent Coordinating Committee] meetings. It's being taught in Muslim meetings. It's being taught where nothing but atheists and agnostics come together. It's being taught everywhere. Black people are fed up with the dillydallying, pussyfooting, compromising approach that we've been using toward getting our freedom. We want freedom *now*, but we're not going to get it saying "We Shall Overcome." We've got to fight until we overcome.

The economic philosophy of black nationalism is pure and simple. It only means that we should control the economy of our community. Why should white people be running all the stores in our community? Why should white people be running the banks of our community? Why should the economy of our community be in the hands of the white man? Why? If a black man can't move his store into a white community, you tell me why a white man should move his store into a black community. The philosophy of black nationalism involves a re-education program in the black community in regards to economics. Our people have to be made to see that any time you take your dollar out of your community and spend it in a community where you don't live, the community where you live will get poorer and poorer, and the community where you spend your money will get richer and richer. Then you wonder why where you live is always a ghetto or a slum area. And where you and I are concerned, not only do we lose it when we spend it out of the community, but the white man has got all our stores in the community tied up; so that though we spend it in the community, at sundown the man who runs the store takes it over across town somewhere. He's got us in a vise.

So the economic philosophy of black nationalism means in every church, in every civic organization, in every fraternal order, it's time now for our people to become conscious of the importance of controlling the economy of our community. If we own the stores, if we operate the businesses, if we try and establish some industry in our own community, then we're developing to the position where we are creating employment for our own kind. Once you gain control of the economy of your own community, then you don't have to picket and boycott and beg some cracker downtown for a job in his business.

The social philosophy of black nationalism only means that we have to get together and remove the evils, the vices, alcoholism, drug addiction, and other evils that are destroying the moral fiber of our community. We ourselves have to lift the level of our community, the standard of our community to a higher level, make our own society beautiful so that we will be satisfied in our own social circles and won't be running around here trying to knock our way into a social circle where we're not wanted.

Last but not least, I must say this concerning the great controversy over rifles and shotguns. The only thing that I've ever said is that in areas where the government has proven itself either unwilling or unable to defend the lives and the property of Negroes, it's time for Negroes to defend themselves. Article number two of the constitutional amendments provides you and me the right to own a rifle or a shotgun, it is constitutionally legal to own a shotgun or a rifle. This doesn't mean you're going to get a rifle and form battalions and go out looking for white folks, although you'd be within your rights—I mean, you'd be justified; but that would be illegal and we don't do anything illegal. If the white man doesn't want the black man buying rifles and shotguns, then let the government do its job. That's all ... if I die in the morning, I'll die saying one thing: the ballot or the bullet, the ballot or the bullet.

18.
STOKLEY CARMICHAEL/KWAME TOURE

Stokley Carmichael/Kwame Toure (1941–1998) began his political career as an activist. At Howard University he was active in the Non-Violent Action Group. He was active in the Freedom Rides orchestrated by the Congress on Racial Equality to protest segregation in public transportation. Carmichael went on to work full time for the Student Nonviolent Coordinating Committee, which was the most militant or radical organization of the major civil rights organizations. First, he served as a regional coordinator during voter registration drives in Mississippi. He also worked arduously in Lowndes County, Alabama, in their extensive voter registration campaigns. In 1966 he went on to become SNCC's chairman. He held this appointment for one year. In 1967 he became honorary prime minister of the Black Panther Party. In 1969 Carmichael, now calling himself Kwame Toure, moved to West Africa, Guinea. In 1971 he assisted in the organization of the All African People's Revolutionary Party in which he fought for the creation of an all-African run socialist republic. He became President Ahmed Sekou Toure's aid. This is also part of where he took his name from. He also borrowed his new first name from Kwame Nkrumah, former leader of Ghana. As a Pan-Africanist he was invested in the unification of people of African descent. However, his goal became to also unite them under socialism so that they could better improve the economic, political, social, and cultural conditions in Africa. Throughout his life, like many of his counterparts, he was so devoted to better the global position of Black people that he was arrested over two dozen times. Carmichael/Toure was a radical.

Overview of Ideas

Stokley Carmichael was a leading voice in the Black Power movement. As chairman of the Student Nonviolent Coordinating Committee, Carmichael saw the Civil Rights Movement moving in a new direction. He emphasized the growing need to shift strategy from non-violent direct action campaigns such as the voting drives that characterized Freedom Summer and the movement's most successful campaigns. Carmichael attempted to integrate a Black Nationalist approach into the Civil Rights Movement. He later became more vocal about socialist reform.

Carmichael, like Malcolm X, was interested in organizing young Black people from urban ghettoes. Poor marginalized Black people were growing increasing livid and frustrated with the lack of change in the United States. Institutionalized racism still continued. Brutality still continued. All the marches and protests had not annihilated this.

> After years of this, we are almost at the same point—because we demonstrated from a point of weakness. We cannot be expected any longer to march and have our heads broken in order to say to whites: come on, you're nice guys. For you are not nice guys. We have found you out.

Unlike Frederick Douglass, or Booker T. Washington or Martin Luther King Jr. who strategically appealed to Whites on moral, Christian, and humanitarian grounds, Carmichael emphasized that these efforts to take the "high ground" to appeal to the better nature of Whites was unsuccessful. It was time for a new approach or a new strategy and that was Black Power.

According to Carmichael the slogan Black Power was widely misunderstood. Black Power was not utilized to advance a new racist movement against Whites; it was not the same as when a Southern White man cloaked in a white sheet screamed White power. Black Power merely referred to an organized movement to address class inequality and racial inequality that would lead to the self-empowerment of Black people. Black Power meant achieving a political voice. It meant financing your own political movements. Black Power meant being able to vote for Black candidates and having representation throughout the government. It meant being able to elect officials who would actually act in the interests of Black people. Black Power meant finally defending oneself against unprovoked violence. Like Malcolm X, Carmichael argued that violence in self-defense was not just legitimate but necessary. White power already existed; in fact, it controlled every basic societal institution. It was time for Black Power to exist as well. Black Power merely meant that Black people could exert influence over society and control their own destinies.

Black Power recognized that the quagmire impacting African Americans was not just caused by racism but by class inequality. In addition, the focus on integration was problematic. Integration suggested that equality would be achieved when Black children could attend White schools or Black families could move into White neighborhoods. Carmichael astutely noted that this reinforced the idea that White was right. In praxis, integration meant that maybe the Little Rock Nine[1] would be educated with White students but the overwhelming number of Black children would still be left to attend inferior schools. Integration did not mean White people would be running to live with and attend schools with Blacks. The Civil Rights Movement and its integrationist platform made gains. However, those gains primarily benefited middle class Blacks and rural Southerners. Life for the urban poor was worse than ever. Again, class inequality was a larger part of the problem.

Carmichael was a staunch advocate of economic nationalism. However, he modified economic nationalism as articulated as articulated by Garvey or Malcolm X. Interestingly, we may hear more of A. Philip Randolph in Carmichael's words.

> Black people do not want to "take over" this country. They don't want to "get whitey" ... but our vision is not merely of a society in which all black men have enough to buy the good things of

life. When we urge that black money go into black pockets ... we want to see money go back into the community and used to benefit it ... the society we seek to build among black people, then, is not a capitalist one.

Carmichael did not just advocate for economic self-improvement within the capitalist order. Because Carmichael posited that communal enterprise and living was important he also was a critic of capitalism. As Carmichael matured politically he became more vocal and more frequently denounced capitalism. Drawing from Karl Marx, unlike his earlier Black Nationalist counterparts, Carmichael argued that the capitalist mode of production was responsible for the fact that millions of Black people lived in squalor. After his migration to Africa, Carmichael, then Toure, was adamant that Mao and Guevara were inspirations. He came to embrace Communism and was active in anti-imperialist struggle.

Like his other Black Nationalist counterparts, Carmichael emphasized the importance of cultural or social nationalism. Black Power also indicated that Black people needed to reclaim their history and identities as people of African descent. Other ethnic groups who immigrated to the United States formed ethnic enclaves and Africans in the United States should be doing this as well. In addition, just as Malcolm warned, the middle class liberal Civil Rights Movement was promoting participation in a binary system of politics, in which neither political party served the interests of Blacks. With this, Black Power also meant political nationalism. While in the United States this entailed political independence, control over offices, and full representation in American democracy.

The task of making America truly the global emblem of democracy and justice was the job of White people, not Black people. Carmichael said all human beings were born free. It was White people who denied freedom and rights to Black people. Therefore, civil rights legislation was not for Black people; it was for White people. It was to tell White people what Black people already knew; that they were human beings entitled to human rights. White people needed the civil rights movement. The radical Carmichael, rebuking the cultural conservativism found in so much of African American political thought, argued that "we are oppressed as a group because we are black, not because we are lazy or apathetic, not because we're stupid or we stink ... we are oppressed because we are black." The Negro Problem was a structural problem related to class warfare and racism. White people caused the Negro Problem; it was not the result of the behavior of Black people. Carmichael asked the public if White people would ever surmount their own racism. However, he said, Black people were now tired of asking them nicely to change; Black people were now going to take what was rightfully theirs.

What We Want, 1966

One of the tragedies of the struggle against racism is that up to now there has been no national organization that could speak to the growing militancy of young black people in the urban ghetto. There has been only a civil rights movement, whose tone of voice was adapted to an audience of liberal whites. It served as a sort of buffer zone between them and angry young blacks. None of its so-called leaders could go into a rioting community and be listened to. In a sense, I blame ourselves—together with the mass media—for what has happened in Watts, Harlem, Chicago, Cleveland, and Omaha. Each time the people in those cities saw Martin Luther King get slapped, they became angry; when they saw four little black girls bombed to death, they were angrier; and when nothing happened, they were steaming. We had nothing to offer that they could see, except to go out and be beaten again. We helped to build their frustration.

For too many years, black Americans marched and had their heads broken and got shot. They were saying to the country, "Look, you guys are supposed to be nice guys and we are only going to do what we are supposed to do—why do you beat us up, why don't you give us what we ask, why don't you straighten yourself out?" After years of this, we are at almost the same point—because we demonstrated from a position of weakness. We cannot be expected any longer to march and have our heads broken in order to say to whites: Come on, you're nice guys. For you are not nice guys. We have found you out.

An organization which claims to speak for the needs of a community—as does the Student Nonviolent Coordinating Committee—must speak in the tone of that community, not as somebody else's buffer zone. This is the significance of Black Power as a slogan. For once, black people are going to use the words they want to use—not just the words whites want to hear. And they will do this no matter how often the press tries to stop the use of the slogan by equating it with racism or separatism.

An organization which claims to be working for the needs of a community—as SNCC does—must work to provide that community with a position of strength from which to make its voice heard. This is the significance of Black Power beyond the slogan.

Black Power can be clearly defined for those who do not attach the fears of white America to their questions about it. We should begin with the basic fact that black Americans have two problems: they are poor and they are black. All other problems arise from this two-sided reality: lack of education, the so-called apathy of black men. Any program to end racism must address itself to that double reality.

Almost from its beginning, SNCC sought to address itself to both conditions with a program aimed at winning political power for impoverished Southern blacks. We had to begin with politics because black Americans are a propertyless people in a country where property is valued above all. We had to work for power, because this country does not function by morality, love, and nonviolence, but by power. Thus we determined to win political power, with the idea of moving on from there into activity that would have economic effects. With power, the masses could *make or participate in making* the decisions which govern their destinies, and thus create basic change in their day-to-day lives.

But if political power seemed to be the key to self-determination, it was also obvious that the key had been thrown down a deep well many years earlier. Disenfranchisement, maintained by racist terror, made it impossible to talk about organizing for political power in 1960. The right to vote had to be won, and SNCC workers devoted their energies to this from 1961 to 1965. They set up voter registration drives in the

Deep South. They created pressure for the vote by holding mock elections in Missis-sippi in 1963 and by helping to establish the Mississippi Freedom Democratic Party (MFDP) in 1964. That struggle was eased, though not won, with the passage of the 1965 Voting Rights Act. SNCC workers could then address themselves to the question: Who can we vote for, to have our needs met—how do we make our vote meaningful?

SNCC had already gone to Atlantic City for recognition of the Mississippi Freedom Democratic Party by the Democratic convention and been rejected; it had gone with the MFDP to Washington for recognition by Congress and been rejected. In Arkan-sas, SNCC helped thirty Negroes to run for school board elections; all but one were defeated, and there was evidence of fraud and intimidation sufficient to cause their defeat. In Atlanta, Julian Bond ran for the state legislature and was elected—twice— and unseated—twice. In several states, black farmers ran in elections for agricultural committees which make crucial decisions concerning land use, loans, etc. Although they won places on a number of committees, they never gained the majorities needed to control them.

All of the efforts were attempts to win Black Power. Then, in Alabama, the oppor-tunity came to see how blacks could be organized on an independent party basis. An unusual Alabama law provides that any group of citizens can nominate candidates for county office, and if they win 20 per cent of the vote, may be recognized as a county political party. The same then applies on a state level. SNCC went to organize in several counties, such as Lowndes, where black people—who form 80 per cent of the popula-tion and have an average annual income of $943—felt they could accomplish nothing within the framework of the Alabama Democratic Party because of its racism and because the qualifying fee for the 1966 elections was raised from $50 to $500 in order to prevent most Negroes from becoming candidates. On May 3, 1966, five new county "freedom organizations" convened and nominated candidates for the offices of sheriff, tax assessor, members of the school boards.[2] Their ballot symbol was the black panther: a bold, beautiful animal, representing the strength and dignity of black demands today. A man needs a black panther on his side when he and his family must endure—as hundreds of Alabamans have endured—loss of job, eviction, starvation, and some-times death for political activity. He may also need a gun, and SNCC reaffirms the right of black men everywhere to defend themselves when threatened or attacked. As for initiating the use of violence, we hope that such programs as ours will make that unnecessary; but it is not for us to tell black communities whether they can or cannot use any particular form of action to resolve their problems. Responsibility for the use of violence by black men, whether in self-defense or initiated by them, lies with the white community.

This is the specific historical experience from which SNCC's call for Black Power emerged on the Mississippi march in July 1966. But the concept of Black Power is not a recent or isolated phenomenon: it has grown out of the ferment of agitation and activity by different people and organizations in many black communities over the years. Our last year of work in Alabama added a new concrete possibility. In Lowndes County, for example, Black Power will mean that if a Negro is elected sheriff, he can end police brutality. If a black man is elected tax assessor, he can collect and channel funds for the building of better roads and schools serving black people—thus advancing the move from political power into the economic arena. In such areas as Lowndes, where black men have a majority, they will attempt to use it to exercise control. This is what they seek: control. Where Negroes lack a majority, Black Power means proper representation and sharing of control. It means the creation of power bases from which black people can work to change statewide or nationwide patterns of oppression through pressure from strength—instead of weakness. Politically, Black Power means what it has always meant to SNCC: the coming-together of black people to elect representatives and *to force those representatives to speak to their needs*. It does not mean merely putting black faces into office. A man or woman who is black and from the slums cannot be automatically expected to speak to the needs of black people. Most of the black politicians we see around the country today are not what SNCC means by Black Power. The power must be that of a community, and emanate from there.

SNCC today is working in both North and South on programs of voter registration and independent political organizing. In some places, such as Alabama, Los Angeles, New York, Philadelphia, and New Jersey, independent organizing under the black panther symbol is in progress. The creation of a national "black panther party" must come about; it will take time to build, and it is much too early to predict its success. We have no infallible master plan and we make no claim to exclusive knowledge of how to end racism; different groups will work in their own different ways. SNCC cannot spell out the full logistics of self-determination, but it can address itself to the problem by helping black communities define their needs, realize their strength, and go into action along a variety of lines which they must choose for themselves. Without knowing all the answers, it can address itself to the basic problem of poverty, to the fact that in Lowndes County 86 white families own 90 per cent of the land. What are black people in that county going to do for jobs; where are they going to get money? There must be reallocation of land, of money.

Ultimately, the economic foundations of this country must be shaken if black people are to control their lives. The colonies of the United States—and this includes the black ghettos within its borders, North and South—must be liberated. For a century, this nation has been like an octopus of exploitation, its tentacles stretching from Mississippi and Harlem to South America, the Middle East, southern Africa, and Vietnam; the form of exploitation varies from area to area but the essential result has been the same—a powerful few have been maintained and enriched at the expense of the poor and voiceless colored masses. This pattern must be broken. As its grip loosens here and there around the world, the hopes of black Americans become more realistic. For racism to die, a totally different America must be born.

This is what the white society does not wish to face; this is why that society prefers to talk about integration. But integration speaks not at all to the problem of poverty—only to the problem of blackness. Integration today means the man who "makes it," leaving his black brothers behind in the ghetto. It has no relevance to the Harlem wino or to the cottonpicker making three dollars a day.

Integration, moreover, speaks to the problem of blackness in a despicable way. As a goal, it has been based on complete acceptance of the fact that in order to have a decent house or education, blacks must move into a white neighborhood or send their children to a white school. This reinforces, among both black and white, the idea that "white" is automatically better and "black" is by definition inferior. This is why integration is a subterfuge for the maintenance of white supremacy. It allows the nation to focus on a handful of Southern children who get into white schools, at great price, and to ignore the 94 per cent who are left behind in unimproved all-black schools. Such situations will not change until black people have power—to control their own school boards, in this case. Then Negroes become equal in a way that means something, and integration ceases to be a one-way street. Then integration doesn't mean draining skills and energies from the ghetto into white neighborhoods; then it can mean white people moving from Beverly Hills into Watts, white people joining the Lowndes County Freedom Organization. Then integration becomes relevant.

Black people do not want to "take over" this country. They don't want to "get Whitey"; they just want to get him off their backs, as the saying goes. It was, for example, the exploitation by Jewish landlords and merchants which first created black resentment toward Jews—not Judaism. The white man is irrelevant to blacks, except as an oppressive force. Blacks want to be in his place, yes, but not in order to terrorize and lynch and starve him. They want to be in his place because that is where a decent life can be had.

But our vision is not merely of a society in which all black men have enough to buy the good things of life. When we urge that black money go into black pockets, we mean the communal pocket. We want to see money go back into the community and used to benefit it. We want to see the cooperative concept applied in business and banking. We want to see black ghetto residents demand that an exploiting landlord or storekeeper sell them, at minimal cost, a building or a shop that they will own and improve cooperatively; they can back their demand with a rent strike, or a boycott, and a community so unified behind them that no one else will move into the building or buy at the store. The society we seek to build among black people, then, is not a capitalist one. It is a society in which the spirit of community and humanistic love prevail. The word "love" is suspect; black expectations of what it might produce have been betrayed too often. But those were expectations of a response from the white community, which failed us. The love we seek to encourage is within the black community, the only American community where men call each other "brother" when they meet. We can build a community of love only where we have the ability and power to do so: among blacks.

As for white America, perhaps it can stop crying out against "black supremacy," "black nationalism," "racism in reverse," and begin facing reality. The reality is that this nation is racist; that racism is not primarily a problem of "human relations" but of an exploitation maintained—either actively or through silence—by the society as a whole. Can whites, particularly liberal whites, condemn themselves? Can they stop blaming us, and blame their own system? Are they capable of the shame which might become a revolutionary emotion?

We have found that they usually cannot condemn themselves, and so we have done it. But the rebuilding of this society, if at all possible, is basically the responsibility of whites—not blacks. We won't fight to save the present society, in Vietnam or anywhere else. We are just going to work, in the way *we* see fit, and on goals *we* define, not for civil rights but for all our human rights.

Toward Black Liberation, 1966

One of the most pointed illustrations of the need for Black Power, as a positive and redemptive force in a society degenerating into a form of totalitarianism, is to be made by examining the history of distortion that the concept has been given by the national media of publicity. In this "debate," as in everything else that affects our lives, Negroes are dependent on, and at the discretion of, forces and institutions within the white society that have little interest in representing us honestly. Our experience with the national press has been that when they have managed to escape a meretricious special interest in "Git Whitey" sensationalism and race-war mongering, individual reporters and commentators have been conditioned by the enveloping racism of the society to the point where they are incapable of objective observation and reporting of racial *incidents*, much less the analysis of *ideas*. But this limitation of vision and perceptions is an inevitable consequence of the dictatorship of definition, interpretation, and consciousness, along with the censorship of history that the society has inflicted upon the Negro—and itself.

Our concern for Black Power addresses itself directly to this problem: the necessity to reclaim our history and our identity from the cultural terrorism and depredation of self-justifying white guilt.

To do this we shall have to struggle for the right to create our own terms to define ourselves and our relationship to the society, and to have these terms recognized. This is the first necessity of a free people, and the first right that any oppressor must suspend. The white fathers of American racism knew this—instinctively it seems—as is indicated by the continuous record of the distortion and omission in their dealings with the red and black men. In the same way that Southern apologists for the "Jim Crow" society have so obscured, muddied and misrepresented the record of the Reconstruction period, until it is almost impossible to tell what really happened, their contemporary counterparts are busy with the recent history of the civil rights movement.

Traditionally, for each new ethnic group, the route to social and political integration in America's pluralistic society has been through the organization of their own institutions with which to represent their communal needs within the larger society. This is simply stating what the advocates of Black Power are saying. The strident outcry, *particularly* from the liberal community, that has been evoked by this proposal can be understood only by examining the historic relationship between Negro and white power in this country.

Negroes are defined by two forces: their blackness and their powerlessness. There have been, traditionally, two communities in America: the white community, which controlled and defined the forms that all institutions within the society would take, and the Negro community, which has been excluded from participation in the power decisions that shaped the society, and has traditionally been dependent upon and subservient to the white community.

This has not been accidental. The history of every institution of this society indicates that a major concern in the ordering and structuring of the society has been the maintaining of the Negro community in its condition of dependence and oppression. This has not been on the level of individual acts of discrimination—individual whites against individual Negroes—but total acts by the white community against the Negro community. This fact cannot be too strongly emphasized—that racist assumptions of white superiority have been so deeply ingrained in the structure of the society that it infuses its entire functioning, and is so much a part of the national subconscious that it is taken for granted and is frequently not even recognized. It is more than a figure of speech to say that the Negro community in America is the victim of white imperialism and colonial exploitation.

It is white power that makes the laws, and it is violent white power in the form of armed white cops that enforces those laws with guns and nightsticks. The vast majority of Negroes in this country live in captive communities and must endure these conditions of oppression because, and only because, *they are black and powerless.* Without bothering to go into the historic factors that contribute to this pattern—economic exploitation, political impotence, discrimination in employment and education—one can see that to correct this pattern will require far-reaching changes in the basic power-relationships and the ingrained social patterns within the society. The question, of course, is: What kinds of changes are necessary, and how is it possible to bring them about?

In recent years the answer to these questions that has been given by most articulate groups of Negroes and their white allies, the "liberals" of all stripes, has been in terms of something called "integration." According to the advocates of integration, social justice will be accomplished by "integrating the Negro into the mainstream institutions of the society from which he has been traditionally excluded." It is very significant that each time I have heard this formulation it has been in terms of "the Negro," the individual Negro, rather than in terms of the community.

This concept of integration had to be based on the assumption that there was nothing of value in the Negro community, so the thing to do was to siphon off the "acceptable" Negroes into the surrounding middle-class white community. It is true that the student demonstrations in the South during the early sixties, out of which SNCC came, had a similar orientation. But while it is hardly a concern of a black sharecropper, dishwasher, or welfare recipient whether a certain fifteen-dollar-a-day motel offers accommodations to Negroes, the overt symbols of white superiority and the imposed limitations on the Negro community had to be destroyed. Now black people must look beyond these goals, to the issue of collective power.

Such a limited class orientation was reflected not only in the program and goals of the civil rights movement, but in its tactics and organization. It is very significant that the two oldest and most "respectable" civil rights organizations have constitutions which *specifically* prohibit partisan political activity. CORE once did, but changed that clause when it changed its orientation toward Black Power. But this is perfectly understandable in terms of the strategy and goals of the older organizations. The civil rights movement saw its role as a kind of liaison between the powerful white community and the dependent Negro one. The dependent status of the black community apparently was unimportant since—if the movement was successful—it was going to blend into the white community anyway. We made no pretense of organizing and developing institutions of community power in the Negro community, but appealed to the conscience of white institutions of power. The posture of the civil rights movement was that of the dependent, the suppliant. The theory was that without attempting to create any organized base of political strength itself, the civil rights movement could influence national legislation and national social patterns by forming coalitions with various "liberal" pressure organizations in the white community—liberal reform clubs, labor unions, church groups, progressive civic groups, and at times one or other of the major political parties.

I think we all have seen the limitations of this approach. We have repeatedly seen that political alliances based on appeals to conscience and decency are chancy things, simply because institutions and political organizations have no consciences outside their own special interests. The political and social rights of Negroes have been and always will be negotiable and expendable the moment they conflict with the interests of our "allies." If we do not learn from history, we are doomed to repeat it, and that is precisely the lesson of the Reconstruction. Black people were allowed to register, vote, and participate in politics because it was to the advantage of powerful white allies to promote this. But this was the result of white decision, and it was ended by other white men's decision before any political base powerful enough to challenge that decision could be established in the Southern Negro community. (Thus at this point in the struggle Negroes have no assurance—save a kind of idiot optimism and faith in a society whose history is one of racism—that if it were to become necessary, even the painfully limited gains thrown to the civil rights movement by the Congress will not be revoked as soon as a shift in political sentiments should occur.)

The major limitation of this approach was that it tended to maintain the traditional dependence of Negroes, and of the movement. We depended upon the good will and support of various groups within the white community whose interests were not always compatible with ours. To the extent that we depended on the financial support of other groups, we were vulnerable to their influence and domination.

Also, the program that evolved out of this coalition was really limited and inadequate in the long term, and one which affected only a small select group of Negroes. Its goal was to make the white community accessible to "qualified" Negroes and presumably each year a few more Negroes armed with their passport—a couple of university degrees—would escape into middle-class America and adopt the attitudes and life styles of that group; and one day the Harlems and the Watts would stand empty, a tribute to the success of integration. This is simply neither realistic nor particularly desirable. You can integrate communities, but you assimilate individuals. Even if such a program were possible its result would be, not to develop the black community as a functional and honorable segment of the total society, with its own cultural identity, life patterns, and institutions, but to abolish it—the final solution to the Negro problem. Marx said that the working class is the first class in history that ever wanted to abolish itself. If one listens to some of our "moderate" Negro leaders it appears that the American Negro is the first *race* that ever wished to abolish itself. The fact is that what must be abolished is not the black community, but the dependent colonial status that has been inflicted upon it. The racial and cultural personality of the black community must be preserved and the community must win its freedom while preserving its cultural integrity. This is the essential difference between integration as it is currently practiced and the concept of Black Power.

What has the movement for integration accomplished to date? The Negro graduating from M.I.T. with a doctorate will have better job opportunities available to him than to Lynda Bird Johnson. But the rate of unemployment in the Negro community is steadily increasing, while that in the white community decreases. More educated Negroes hold executive jobs in major corporations and federal agencies than ever before, but the gap between white income and Negro income has almost doubled in the last twenty years. More suburban housing is available to Negroes, but housing conditions in the ghetto are steadily declining. While the infant mortality rate of New York City is at its lowest rate ever in the city's history, the infant mortality rate of Harlem is steadily climbing. There has been an organized national resistance to the Supreme Court's order to integrate the schools, and the federal government has not acted to enforce that order. Less than 15 per cent of black children in the South attend integrated schools; and Negro schools, which the vast majority of black children still attend, are increasingly decrepit, overcrowded, understaffed, inadequately equipped and funded.

The rate of school dropouts is increasing among Negro teenagers, who then express their bitterness, hopelessness, and alienation by the only means they have—rebellion. As long as people in the ghettos of our large cities feel that they are victims of the misuse of white power without any way to have their needs represented—and these are frequently simple needs (to get the welfare inspectors to stop kicking down your doors in the middle of the night, the cops to stop beating your children, to get the landlord to exterminate the vermin in your home, the city to collect your garbage)—we will continue to have riots. These are not the products of Black Power, but of the absence of any organization capable of giving the community the power, the Black Power, to deal with its problems.

SNCC proposes that it is now time for the black freedom movement to stop pandering to the fears and anxieties of the white middle class in the attempt to earn its "good will," and to return to the ghetto to organize these communities to control themselves. This organization must be attempted in Northern and Southern urban areas as well as in the rural black-belt counties of the South. The chief antagonist to this organization is, in the South, the overtly racist Democratic Party, and in the North the equally corrupt big city machines.

The standard argument presented against independent political organization is, "But you are only 10 per cent." I cannot see the relevance of this observation, since no one is talking about taking over the country, but taking control over our own communities.

The fact is that the Negro population, 10 per cent or not, is very strategically placed because of—ironically—segregation. What is also true is that Negroes have never been able to utilize the full voting potential of our numbers. Where we can vote, the case has always been that the white political machine stacks and gerrymanders the political subdivisions in Negro neighborhoods, so the true voting strength is never reflected in political strength. Would anyone looking at the distribution of political power in Manhattan ever think that Negroes represented 60 per cent of the population there?

Just as often the effective political organization in Negro communities is absorbed by tokenism and patronage—the time-honored practice of "giving" certain offices to selected Negroes. The machine thus creates a "little machine," which is subordinate and responsive to it, in the Negro community. These Negro political "leaders" are really vote deliverers, more responsible to the white machine and the white power structure than to the community they allegedly represent. Thus the white community is able to substitute patronage control for audacious Black Power in the Negro community.

This is precisely what Johnson tried to do even before the Voting Rights Act of 1966 was passed. The national Democrats made it very clear that the measure was intended to register Democrats, not Negroes. The President and top officials of the Democratic Party called in almost one hundred selected Negro "leaders" from the Deep South. Nothing was said about changing the policies of the racist state parties, nothing was said about repudiating such leadership figures as Eastland and Ross Barnett in Mississippi or George Wallace in Alabama. What was said was simply, "Go home and organize your people into the local Democratic Party—*then* we'll see about poverty money and appointments." (Incidentally, for the most part the war on poverty in the South is controlled by local Democratic ward heelers—outspoken racists who have used the program to change the form of the Negroes' dependence. People who were afraid to register for fear of being thrown off the farm are now afraid to register for fear of losing their children's Head Start places.)

We must organize black community power to end these abuses, and to give the Negro community a chance to have its needs expressed. A leadership that is truly "responsible"—not to the white press and power structure, but to the community— must be developed. Such leadership will recognize that its power lies in the unified and collective strength of that community. This will make it difficult for the white leadership group to conduct its dialogue with individuals in terms of patronage and prestige, and will force them to talk to the community's representatives in terms of real power.

The single aspect of the Black Power program that has encountered most criticism is this concept of independent organization. This is presented as third-partyism which has never worked, or a withdrawal into black nationalism and isolationism. If such a program is developed it will not have the effect of isolating the Negro community but the reverse. When the Negro community is able to control local offices, and negotiate with other groups from a position of organized strength, the possibility of meaningful political alliances on specific issues will be increased. That is a rule of politics and there is no reason why it should not operate here. The only difference is that we will have the power to define the terms of these alliances.

The next question usually is, "So—can it work, can the ghettos in fact be organized?" The answer is that this organization must be successful, because there are no viable alternatives—not the war on poverty, which was at its inception limited to dealing with effects rather than causes, and has become simply another source of machine patronage. And "integration" is meaningful only to a small chosen class within the community.

The revolution in agricultural technology in the South is displacing the rural Negro community into Northern urban areas. Both Washington, D.C., and Newark have Negro majorities. One-third of Philadelphia's population of two million people is black. "Inner city" in most major urban areas is already predominantly Negro, and with the white rush to suburbia, Negroes will in the next three decades control the heart of our great cities. These areas can become either concentration camps with a bitter and volatile population, whose only power is the power to destroy, or organized and powerful communities able to make constructive contributions to the total society. Without the power to control their lives and their communities, without effective political institutions through which to relate to the total society, these communities will exist in a constant state of insurrection. This is a choice that the country will have to make.

Berkeley Speech, 1966

In a much larger view, SNCC says that white America cannot condemn herself for her criminal acts against black America. So black people have done it—you stand condemned. The institutions that function in this country are clearly racist; they're built upon racism. The questions to be dealt with then are: How can black people inside this country move? How can white people who say they're not part of those institutions begin to move? And how then do we begin to clear away the obstacles that we have in this society, to make us live like human beings?

Several people have been upset because we've said that integration was irrelevant when initiated by blacks, and that in fact it was an insidious subterfuge for the maintenance of white supremacy. In the past six years or so, this country has been feeding us a "thalidomide drug of integration," and some Negroes have been walking down a dream street talking about sitting next to white people. That does not begin to solve the problem. We didn't go to Mississippi to sit next to Ross Barnett [former Governor of Mississippi], we did not go to sit next to Jim Clark [sheriff of Selma, Alabama], we went to get them out of our way. People ought to understand that; we were never fighting for the right to integrate, *we were fighting against white supremacy*. In order to understand white supremacy we must dismiss the fallacious notion that white people can give anybody his freedom. A man is born free. You may enslave a man after he is born free, and that is in fact what this country does. It enslaves blacks after they're born. The only thing white people can do is *stop denying black people their freedom*.

I maintain that every civil rights bill in this country was passed for white people, not for black people. For example, I am black. I know that. I also know that while I am black I am a human being. Therefore I have the right to go into any public place. White people didn't know that. Every time I tried to go into a public place they stopped me. So some boys had to write a bill to tell that white man, "He's a human being; don't stop him." That bill was for the white man, not for me. I knew I could vote all the time and that it wasn't a privilege but my right. Every time I tried I was shot, killed or jailed, beaten or economically deprived. So somebody had to write a bill to tell white people,

"When a black man comes to vote, don't bother him." That bill was for white people. I know I can live anyplace I want to live. It is white people across this country who are incapable of allowing me to live where I want. You need a civil rights bill, not me. The failure of the civil rights bill isn't because of Black Power or because of the Student Nonviolent Coordinating Committee or because of the rebellions that are occurring in the major cities. That failure is due to the whites' incapacity to deal with their own problems inside their own communities.

And so in a sense we must ask, How is it that black people move? And what do we do? But the question in a much greater sense is, How can white people who are the majority, and who are responsible for making democracy work, make it work? They have failed miserably on this point. They have never made democracy work, be it inside the United States, Vietnam, South Africa, the Philippines, South America, Puerto Rico, or wherever America has been. We not only condemn the country for what it has done internally, but we must condemn it for what it does externally. We see this country trying to rule the world, and someone must stand up and start articulating that this country is not God, and that it cannot rule the world.

The white supremacist attitude, which you have either consciously or subconsciously, is running rampant through society today. For example, missionaries were sent to Africa with the attitude that blacks were automatically inferior. As a matter of fact, the first act the missionaries did when they got to Africa was to make us cover up our bodies, because they said it got them excited. We couldn't go bare-breasted any more because they got excited! When the missionaries came to civilize us because we were uncivilized, to educate us because we were uneducated, and to give us some literate studies because we were illiterate, they charged a price. The missionaries came with the Bible, and we had the land; when they left, they had the land, and we still have the Bible. That's been the rationalization for Western civilization as it moves across the world—stealing, plundering and raping everybody in its path. Their one rationalization is that the rest of the world is uncivilized and they are in fact civilized. But the West is un-civ-i-lized. And that still runs on today, you see, because now we have "modern-day missionaries," and they come into our ghettos—they Head Start, Upward Lift, Bootstrap, and Upward Bound us into white society. They don't want to face the real problem. A man is poor for one reason and one reason only—he does not have money. If you want to get rid of poverty, you give people money. And you ought not to tell me about people who don't work, and that you can't give people money if they don't work, because if that were true, you'd have to start stopping Rockefeller, Kennedy, Lyndon Baines Johnson, Lady Bird Johnson, the whole of Standard Oil, the Gulf Corporation, all of them, including probably a large number of the board of trustees of this university. The question, then, is not whether or not one can work; it's *Who has power to make his or her acts legitimate?* That is all. In this country that power is invested in the hands of white people, and it makes their acts legitimate.

We are now engaged in a psychological struggle in this country about whether or not black people have the right to use the words they want to use without white people giving their sanction. We maintain the use of the words Black Power—let them address themselves to that. We are not going to wait for white people to sanction Black Power.

We're tired of waiting; every time black people try to move in this country, they're forced to defend their position beforehand. It's time that white people do that. They ought to start defending themselves as to why they have oppressed and exploited us. A man was picked as a slave for one reason—the color of his skin. Black was automatically inferior, inhuman, and therefore fit for slavery, so the question of whether or not we are individually suppressed is nonsensical, and it's a downright lie. We are oppressed as a group because we are black, not because we are lazy or apathetic, not because we're stupid or we stink, not because we eat watermelon or have good rhythm. We are oppressed because we are black.

We must wage a psychological battle on the right for black people to define themselves as they see fit, and organize themselves as they see fit. We don't know whether the white community will allow for that organizing, because once they do they must also allow for the organizing inside their own community. It doesn't make a difference, though—we're going to organize our way. The question is how we're going to facilitate those matters, whether it's going to be done with a thousand policemen with submachine guns, or whether it's going to be done in a context where it's allowed by white people warding off those policemen. Are white people who call themselves activists ready to move into the white communities on two counts, on building new political institutions to destroy the old ones that we have, and to move around the concept of white youth refusing to go into the army? If so, than we can start to build a new world. We must urge you to fight now to be the leaders of today, not tomorrow. This country is a nation of thieves. It stands on the brink of becoming a nation of murderers. We must stop it. We must stop it. We must stop it.

We are on the move for our liberation. We're tired of trying to prove things to white people. We are tired of trying to explain to white people that we're not going to hurt them. We are concerned with getting the things we want, the things we have to have to be able to function. The question is, Will white people overcome their racism and allow for that to happen in this country? If not, we have no choice but to say very clearly, "Move on over, or we're going to move on over you."

Notes

1. The Little Rock Nine refers to a group of African American students who were the first to attend the Little Rock Central High School. Despite the 1954 *Brown* v. *the Board of Education* landmark decision that declared segregation in public schools unconstitutional, many schools still thwarted the entrance of Black students. In the famous case of the Little Rock Nine, President Eisenhower had to intervene because the Arkansas National Guard on the orders of Arkansas governor, Orval Faubus, blocked their entrance into the school in 1957.
2. The Lowndes County Freedom Organization slate lost that election by a narrow margin amid much violence on election day. They received enough votes, however, to qualify as an official party in Alabama, and are now called the Lowndes County Freedom Party.

19.

THE BLACK PANTHERS

Founders Huey P. Newton and Bobby Seale

Huey P. Newton (1942–1989) with Bobby Seale (born 1936) founded the Black Panther Party for Self Defense (BPP) in 1966 in response to the perceived pacifism of the dominant civil rights organizations and their sole focus on non-violent direct action protest to obtain full integration. Seale became chairman and Newton took the position of minister of defense. In October 1966 Newton and Seale wrote the Ten-Point program in which they delineated the goals and objectives of the BPP. In January 1967 they opened up their first office in Oakland, California. When the BPP was founded they had six members; the BPP eventually had over 5,000 members with forty-five chapters throughout the United States.

The Black Panthers opened up Black Panther recruitment centers, patrolled neighborhoods protecting Black citizens from police brutality, created food programs for the poor, held rent strikes, sponsored anti-drug programs, assisted in school programs, opened free clinics, and held clothing drives. Despite all of their amazing grassroots efforts to help poor Black people and build-up Black communities, Seale and the BPP became widely known in American society when, in 1967, a cohort of Black Panthers ascended the California State Capitol, armed, in order to protest racist gun control laws and to protest the curtailment of their Second Amendment right to bear arms, particularly in self-defense. In fact, the FBI under J. Edgar Hoover named the BPP the number one danger to national security. Agencies such as COINTELPRO did not hide their intent to raze the organization.

In April 1967 they created the Black Panther newspaper, *Black Community News Service*, whose circulation reached over a quarter of a million every week. Like many of their counterparts the founders were jailed. However, the circumstances of Newton's arrest were quite different and were the source of controversy and protest. In Oakland on October 28, 1967, police officer John Frey stopped Huey P. Newton. The police engaged in frequent stops of Panther members, in an effort to disarm the revolutionary group and thwart their patrols; the BPP patrolled Black neighborhoods, protecting its citizens, particularly from police brutality. Details of the case are nebulous. Another police officer, Herbert Heanes, had arrived on scene as back-up. Once other police arrived both officers had been shot and they later found Newton shot in his abdomen in a nearby hospital.

Newton was charged with the killing of Frey, assault on Heanes, and kidnapping because he had taken a bystander's car to take himself to the hospital. He was convicted of voluntary manslaughter and sentenced to between two and fifteen years. In 1970 he won his appeal and received a new trial. However, after two mistrials California declined to continue to prosecute. During the ordeal the "Free Huey" movement emerged. Newton became a revolutionary icon due to the trial, the media frenzy surrounding it, and the protests that also emerged. Unfortunately, after his revolutionary career with the BPP ended due in large part to the government's sophisticated efforts as implemented by COINTELPRO he became a recluse, at least from politics. In addition, after he obtained a Ph.D. in 1980 he became involved in drugs. His addiction to crack-cocaine may have contributed to his death as a known drug dealer, Tyronne Robinson, killed him.

In 1968 in Chicago, Seale participated in the protests at the Democratic National Convention. In 1969 along with seven other protestors, he was prosecuted for ostensibly attempting to start a riot at the convention. During the course of the tumultuous trial late that year, Seale was sentenced to four years in prison. However, his sentence was a result of outbursts in the courtroom during the trial, which ultimately found him bound and gagged during the trial. He was imprisoned on sixteen counts of contempt of court. In 1971 the original conspiracy charges related to the 1968 protests were dropped because the jury could not render a verdict. Despite the hung jury, he was not released from jail until the next year when the contempt charges were suspended. His incarceration did not intimidate him. In 1973 Seale unsuccessfully ran for mayor in Oakland, California. He left the failing Black Panthers the following year.

Overview of Ideas

The Black Panther Party and its founders were revolutionaries. Like all other Black Nationalists, they argued that Black people needed to control the social institutions within their own community. However, unlike other Black Nationalists they did not push for cultural nationalism and avoided the conservative strain in Black Nationalism that suggested that cultural and moral change was vital. In fact, Huey P. Newton called cultural nationalism "Pork Chop" nationalism. At the time cultural Black Nationalists, most notably Amiri Baraka (Leroi Jones), founder of the Black Arts Repertory Theater and School, posited that Black people needed to learn about their heritage, take pride in their heritage, and celebrate Black culture. The development of a distinct Black aesthetic was important to progress. Through the arts, Black folk who had become victims of racial warfare, many of whom had internalized the racist discourses that pervaded society, would come to feel empowered. Moreover, the arts were a healthy realm in which to express Black fury. For most Panthers, namely Newton, this cultural program would not improve the real quagmires that Black people faced everyday. The arts, eating soul food, or wearing a dashiki would not need lead to political emancipation.

Instead, the BPP argued that the government needed to create full employment. Either the government should create jobs or the means of production should be removed from the hands of private industry in order to foster full employment. They also posited that Black people were entitled to reparations. General Sherman's plan for former slaves to be given forty acres and a mule never came to fruition; it was time for the United States government, as it had done with other oppressed groups (Native Americans and Japanese Americans), to provide reparations to African Americans.

The BPP was adamant that the American fascist regime needed to be stopped. For example, the Panthers vehemently opposed the war in Vietnam. The United States was imperialist; they utilized extreme force to impose their will, desires, and policies on other nations in order to feed their hunger for global domination and empire. In fact, the totalitarian government acting as an appendage of the capitalist class sought the same domination at home; this is what Bobby Seale called *domestic imperialism*. They instituted a brute police force here at home in order to maintain complete domination of the American people. The government utilized the courts, law enforcement, numerous national security and intelligence agencies, and the supposed justice system to buttress their domination. This is why groups such as the Black Panthers were monitored, falsely incarcerated, and even in the case of leaders such as Fred Hampton, were assassinated. By 1970 thirty members of the BPP were accused of crimes with capital punishment sentences, forty more faced sentences of life in prison, another fifty-five faced long jail terms, and an additional 155 were either in jail or were being pursued by law enforcement.[1] Many were falsely incarcerated. According to Michael Parenti:

> from 1968 to 1971 over three hundred members of the Black Panther Party … were arrested, many held without bail, or trial for a long duration. At least ten former Panthers were convicted on fabricated evidence and coerced testimony that was subsequently recanted, served thirty years each in prison.[2]

The Black Panthers were designated public enemies because they were one of only a few groups to have ever challenged this fascist government through revolutionary means.

The Black Panthers were highly organized. The media constantly perpetuated misnomers about Panthers being recklessly violent hypermasculine racist revolutionaries. Again, violence was utilized for self-defense. In an interview, Seale said:

> Panther party training in the area of self-defense includes a study of gun laws, safe use of weapons, and there is a strict rule that no party member can use a weapon except in the case of an attack on his life.[3]

In addition, the BPP argued that riots were counterproductive and lacked organization. All efforts to bring about their demands should be timed and organized.

The BPP were often chastised for their uncompromising and vitriolic tone and their use of words like pig to describe police and capitalists. However, Seale once said,

> people, especially white people, have to come to understand that the language of the ghetto is a language of its own and as the party—whose members for the most part come from the ghetto—seeks to talk to the people, it must speak the people's language.[4]

Strategically, this was a point that most leaders of the mid-twentieth-century phase of the Civil Rights Movement neglected. Images of Black Panthers in black leather, fists clenched and adopting a militant stance often caused people to see the group as hypermasculine chauvinists. However, the group and its leaders were far from this. They defended the rights of women. They specifically defended the rights of Black women and retained a large female membership. Women, like Black people, were oppressed by the American fascist state. Finally, the Black Panthers, like many Black Nationalists, were typecast as racists. They emphatically said that while there were no White members in the Black Panthers they worked with radical White groups. In addition, they worked to organize all oppressed and exploited workers, including Whites and other ethnic groups. They defended the rights of all oppressed groups such as Native Americans and Chicano people to control their own destinies. They had a global vision.

The BPP did not just reserve their critiques and protests for racist Whites in the United States. Their critique was far more sophisticated. The BPP chastised imperialism and colonization. Black people all over the world were being colonized. In the United States, Africans were utilized to build the country and maintain the country's prosperity. However, the ability of the American government to brutalize and exploit Black people depended upon hegemony. In order to have total control over a group of people you must find ingenious ways to get them to consent to their own oppression. In the United States many Black people had been convinced that they were inferior, taught to be subservient, and even in protest are taught to utilize passive methods in protest. Directing his comments to leaders of the Civil Rights Movement Newton said,

> the Black leaders serve the oppressor by purposefully keeping the people submissive, passive, and non-violent, turning a deaf ear to the cries of the suffering and downtrodden, the unemployed and welfare recipients who hunger for liberation by any means necessary.

Why would you utilize your oppressor's rules to relinquish their fetters on you? Why wouldn't you utilize the means that best serve your interests? Why beg your oppressor for freedom?

The United States government has always had its own militia to serve their interests and ensure acquiescence to authority. Police departments regularly harass and brutalize Black people. They ensure compliance and suppress all insurgency. They said the government was afraid of them. They were the first organized effort to thwart this brutality and defend themselves against government-sponsored violence. Newton said that Black people were now being armed with the "basic tool of liberation: the gun."[5] Historically all major advances made by exploited and oppressed groups have been through revolutionary means. Black liberation would be no different.

The goals and objectives of Black Power advocates were quite different from their integrationist counterparts. They argued that civil rights leaders fought for the right to sit near White people in restaurants; they fought for the right to move into bourgeois neighborhoods. Meanwhile, most Black people could not afford the rent in a deplorable tenement building. It was time to speak for the Black poor and fight against the structural forces keeping them in poverty.

The BPP argued that Black people required political power. However, previous Black leaders have misunderstood what political power is. Political power is acquired through having access to: economic power, land, and/or military power. Black people have been systematically denied access to all three basic forms of power. Therefore, a Black revolution would seek these ends. Black people do not need to vote for leaders who do not represent their interests or who will not help them gain access to political power. In our capitalist nation, which is driven by pure avarice, Black people needed to utilize force to acquire access to economic power. Capitalism must be annihilated and the means of production taken from private hands and given to the people. According to the Panthers, Communism was the answer and like their Black Nationalist counterparts were organizing the lumpenproletariat. This actually separated the Panthers from Karl Marx. Marx focused on mobilizing the proletariat or the working class and saw the lumpenproletariat, the underclass, as a useless unproductive body of criminals and derelicts. The BPP argued that this was an important group to organize; not only were they oppressed and desperate but they had nothing to lose.

The BPP was invested in organizing the underclass. Leaders such as Huey P. Newton stood out amongst his contemporaries in his support and public call for camaraderie with both women's and gay liberation groups. He advocated respect for and unity with all oppressed groups. In fact, Newton warned activists to not allow their own homophobia and heterosexism to interfere with political action. Newton said homosexuals were probably the most oppressed group in society. "The women's liberation front and gay liberation front are our friends, they are potential allies, *and we need as many allies as possible.*"6 Newton posited it was advantageous to align the Black Power movement with as many oppressed groups as possible.

The Black Panther Party were "revolutionary intercommunalists." First, the Panthers identified themselves as Black Nationalists and believed that they needed to create their own nation. Then they called themselves revolutionary nationalists, in that they believed both Black Nationalism and socialism combined were the solution to the supposed Negro Problem. A third transition occurred; they started referring to themselves as Internationalists, in that they saw the plight of Black people in the United States as linked with people all over the world oppressed by imperialism, colonization, and capitalism. However, because these oppressed groups did not have nations of their own, it seemed futile to employ terms that suggest that they were nations seeking solidarity. Revolutionary Intercommunalism suggested that oppressed groups throughout the world would unite, take control of the means of production, overthrow the bourgeois imperialist powers, and redistribute wealth amongst the communities of the world. The BPP and their founders were global revolutionaries.

The Ten Point Platform and Program of the Black Panther Party, 1966

1. **WE WANT FREEDOM. WE WANT POWER TO DETERMINE THE DESTINY OF OUR BLACK AND OPPRESSED COMMUNITIES.**
    We believe that Black and oppressed people will not be free until we are able to determine our destinies in our own communities ourselves, by fully controlling all the institutions which exist in our communities.

2.   **WE WANT FULL EMPLOYMENT FOR OUR PEOPLE.**
We believe that the federal government is responsible and obligated to give every person employment or a guaranteed income. We believe that if the American businessmen will not give full employment, then the technology and means of production should be taken from the businessmen and placed in the community so that the people of the community can organize and employ all of its people and give a high standard of living.

3.   **WE WANT AN END TO THE ROBBERY BY THE CAPITALISTS OF OUR BLACK AND OPPRESSED COMMUNITIES.**
We believe that this racist government has robbed us and now we are demanding the overdue debt of forty acres and two mules. Forty acres and two mules were promised 100 years ago as restitution for slave labor and mass murder of Black people. We will accept the payment in currency which will be distributed to our many communities. The American racist has taken part in the slaughter of our fifty million Black people. Therefore, we feel this is a modest demand that we make.

4.   **WE WANT DECENT HOUSING, FIT FOR THE SHELTER OF HUMAN BEINGS.**
We believe that if the landlords will not give decent housing to our Black and oppressed communities, then housing and the land should be made into cooperatives so that the people in our communities, with government aid, can build and make decent housing for the people.

5.   **WE WANT DECENT EDUCATION FOR OUR PEOPLE THAT EXPOSES THE TRUE NATURE OF THIS DECADENT AMERICAN SOCIETY. WE WANT EDUCATION THAT TEACHES US OUR TRUE HISTORY AND OUR ROLE IN THE PRESENT-DAY SOCIETY.**
We believe in an educational system that will give to our people a knowledge of the self. If you do not have knowledge of yourself and your position in the society and in the world, then you will have little chance to know anything else.

6.   **WE WANT COMPLETELY FREE HEALTH CARE FOR All BLACK AND OPPRESSED PEOPLE.**
We believe that the government must provide, free of charge, for the people, health facilities which will not only treat our illnesses, most of which have come about as a result of our oppression, but which will also develop preventive medical programs to guarantee our future survival. We believe that mass health education and research programs must be developed to give all Black and oppressed people access to advanced scientific and medical information, so we may provide our selves [*sic*] with proper medical attention and care.

7.   **WE WANT AN IMMEDIATE END TO POLICE BRUTALITY AND MURDER OF BLACK PEOPLE, OTHER PEOPLE OF COLOR, All OPPRESSED PEOPLE INSIDE THE UNITED STATES.**
We believe that the racist and fascist government of the United States uses its domestic enforcement agencies to carry out its program of oppression against black people, other people of color and poor people inside the united States [*sic*]. We believe it is our right, therefore, to defend ourselves against such

armed forces and that all Black and oppressed people should be armed for self defense [*sic*] of our homes and communities against these fascist police forces.

8. **WE WANT AN IMMEDIATE END TO ALL WARS OF AGGRESSION.**
    We believe that the various conflicts which exist around the world stem directly from the aggressive desire of the United States ruling circle and government to force its domination upon the oppressed people of the world. We believe that if the United States government or its lackeys do not cease these aggressive wars it is the right of the people to defend themselves by any means necessary against their aggressors.

9. **WE WANT FREEDOM FOR ALL BLACK AND OPPRESSED PEOPLE NOW HELD IN U. S. FEDERAL, STATE, COUNTY, CITY AND MILITARY PRISONS AND JAILS. WE WANT TRIALS BY A JURY OF PEERS FOR All PERSONS CHARGED WITH SO-CALLED CRIMES UNDER THE LAWS OF THIS COUNTRY.**
    We believe that the many Black and poor oppressed people now held in United States prisons and jails have not received fair and impartial trials under a racist and fascist judicial system and should be free from incarceration. We believe in the ultimate elimination of all wretched, inhuman penal institutions, because the masses of men and women imprisoned inside the United States or by the United States military are the victims of oppressive conditions which are the real cause of their imprisonment. We believe that when persons are brought to trial they must be guaranteed, by the United States, juries of their peers, attorneys of their choice and freedom from imprisonment while awaiting trial.

10. **WE WANT LAND, BREAD, HOUSING, EDUCATION, CLOTHING, JUSTICE, PEACE AND PEOPLE'S COMMUNITY CONTROL OF MODERN TECHNOLOGY.**
    When, in the course of human events, it becomes necessary for one people to dissolve the political bonds which have connected them with another, and to assume, among the powers of the earth, the separate and equal station to which the laws of nature and nature's God entitle them, a decent respect to the opinions of mankind requires that they should declare the causes which impel them to the separation.
    We hold these truths to be self-evident, that all men are created equal; that they are endowed by their Creator with certain unalienable rights; that among these are life, liberty, and the pursuit of happiness. That to secure these rights, governments are instituted among men, deriving their just powers from the consent of the governed; that, whenever any form of government becomes destructive of these ends, it is the right of the people to alter or to abolish it, and to institute a new government, laying its foundation on such principles, and organizing its powers in such form as to them shall seem most likely to effect their safety and happiness. Prudence, indeed, will dictate that governments long established should not be changed for light and transient causes; and, accordingly, all experience hath shown that mankind are most disposed to suffer, while evils are sufferable, than to right themselves by abolishing the forms to which they are accustomed. But,

when a long train of abuses and usurpation, pursuing invariably the same object, evinces a design to reduce them under absolute despotism, it is their right, it is their duty, to throw off such government, and to provide new guards for their future security.

In Defense of Self-Defense, 1967
Huey P. Newton

Historically the power structure has demanded that Black leaders cater to their desires and to the ends of the imperialistic racism of the oppressor. The power structure has endorsed those Black leaders who have reduced themselves to nothing more than apologizing parrots. They have divided the so-called Black leaders within the political arena. The oppressors sponsor radio programs, give space in their racist newspapers, and show them the luxury enjoyed only by the oppressor. The Black leaders serve the oppressor by purposely keeping the people submissive, passive, and non-violent, turning a deaf ear to the cries of the suffering and downtrodden, the unemployed and welfare recipients who hunger for liberation by any means necessary.

Historically there have been a few Black men who have rejected the handouts of the oppressor and who have refused to spread the oppressor's treacherous principles of deceit, gradual indoctrination, and brainwashing, and who have refused to indulge in the criminal activity of teaching submission, fear, and love for an enemy who hates the very color Black and is determined to commit genocide on an international scale.

There has always existed in the Black colony of Afro-America a fundamental difference over which tactics, from the broad spectrum of alternatives, Black people should employ in their struggle for national liberation.

One side contends that Black people are in the peculiar position where, in order to gain acceptance into the "mainstream" of American life, they must employ no tactic that will anger the oppressor Whites. This view holds that Black people constitute a hopeless minority and that salvation for Black people lies in developing brotherly relations. There are certain tactics that are taboo. Violence against the oppressor must be avoided at all costs because the oppressor will retaliate with superior violence. So Black people may protest, but not protect. They can complain, but not cut and shoot. In short, Black people must at all costs remain non-violent.

On the other side we find that the point of departure is the principle that the oppressor has no rights that the oppressed is bound to respect. Kill the slavemaster, destroy him utterly, move against him with implacable fortitude. Break his oppressive power by any means necessary. Men who have stood before the Black masses and recommended this response to the oppression have been held in fear by the oppressor. The Blacks in the colony who were wed to the non-violent alternative could not relate to the advocates of implacable opposition to the oppressor. Because the oppressor always prefers to deal with the less radical, i.e., less dangerous, spokesmen for his subjects. He would prefer that his subjects had no spokesmen at all, or better yet, he wishes to speak for them himself. Unable to do this practically, he does the next best thing and endorses spokesmen who will allow him to speak through them to the masses.

Paramount among his imperatives is to see to it that implacable spokesmen are never allowed to communicate their message to the masses. Their oppressor will resort to any means necessary to silence them.

The oppressor, the "endorsed spokesmen," and the implacables form the three points of a triangle of death. The oppressor looks upon the endorsed spokesmen as a tool to use against the implacables to keep the masses passive within the acceptable limits of the tactics he is capable of containing. The endorsed spokesmen look upon the oppressor as a guardian angel who can always be depended upon to protect him from the wrath of the implacables, while he looks upon the implacables as dangerous and irresponsible madmen who, by angering the oppressor, will certainly provoke a blood bath in which they themselves might get washed away. The implacables view both the oppressors and the endorsed leaders as his deadly enemies. If anything, he has a more profound hatred for the endorsed leaders than he has for the oppressor himself, because the implacables know that they can deal with the oppressor only after they have driven the endorsed spokesmen off the scene.

Historically the endorsed spokesmen have always held the upper hand over the implacables. In Afro-American history there are shining brief moments when the implacables have outmaneuvered the oppressor and the endorsed spokesmen and gained the attention of the Black masses. The Black masses, recognizing the implacables in the depths of their despair, respond magnetically to the implacables and bestow a devotion and *loyalty* to them that frightens the oppressor and endorsed spokesmen into a panic-stricken *frenzy*, often causing them to leap into a rash act of murder, imprisonment, or exile to silence the implacables and to get their show back on the road.

The masses of Black people have always been deeply entrenched and involved in the basic necessities of life. They have not had time to abstract their situation. Abstractions come only with leisure, the people have not had the luxury of leisure. Therefore, the people have been very aware of the true definition of politics. Politics is merely the desire of individuals and groups to satisfy their basic needs first: food, shelter, and clothing, and security for themselves and their loved ones. The Black leaders endorsed by the power structure have attempted to sell the people the simpleminded theory that politics is holding a political office; being able to move into a $40,000 home; being able to sit near White people in a restaurant (while in fact the Black masses have not been able to pay the rent of a $40.00 rat-infested hovel).

The Black leaders have led the community to believe that brutality and force could be ended by subjecting the people to this very force of self-sacrificing demonstrations. The Black people realize brutality and force can only be inflicted if there is submission. The community has not responded in the past or in the present to the absurd, erroneous and deceitful tactics of so-called legitimate Black leaders. The community realizes that force and brutality can only be eliminated by counterforce through self-defense. Leaders who have recommended these tactics have never had the support and following of the *down*-trodden Black masses who comprise the bulk of the community. The grass roots, the downtrodden of the Black community, though rejecting the hand-picked "handkerchief heads" endorsed by the power structure have not had the academic or administrative knowledge to form long resistance to the brutality.

Marcus Garvey and Malcolm X were the two Black men of the twentieth century who posed an implacable challenge to both the oppressor and the endorsed spokesmen.

In our time, Malcolm stood on the threshold with the oppressor and the endorsed spokesmen in a bag that they could not get out of. Malcolm, implacable to the ultimate degree, held out to the Black masses the historical, stupendous victory of Black collective salvation and liberation from the chains of the oppressor and the treacherous embrace of the endorsed spokesmen. Only with the gun were the Black masses denied this victory. But they learned from Malcolm that with the gun they can recapture their dreams and make them a reality.

The heirs of Malcolm now stand millions strong on their corner of the triangle, facing the racist dog oppressor and the soulless endorsed spokesmen. The heirs of Malcolm have picked up the gun and taking first things first are moving to expose the endorsed spokesmen so the Black masses can see them for what they are and have always been. The choice offered by the heirs of Malcolm to the endorsed spokesmen is to repudiate the oppressor and to crawl back to their own people and earn a speedy reprieve or face a merciless, speedy, and most timely execution for treason and being "too wrong for too long."

Black Soldiers as Revolutionaries to Overthrow the Ruling Class, 1969
Bobby Seale

This is the county jail, city prison, San Francisco, California. And this is Bobby Seale, the Chairman of the Black Panther Party of which Huey P. Newton is the Minister of Defense, and Eldridge Cleaver is the Minister of Information. I am presently incarcerated here as a political prisoner in the same manner that our Minister of Defense, Huey P. Newton, is incarcerated in another prison here in California known as C.M.C. (south of San Francisco 200 miles). And I wanted to send a message from jail here as a political prisoner.

We are here in America, brothers, (Black G.I.'s, who this message is to), trying to rid ourselves of the oppressive conditions that we've been subjected to for 400 years. And now they have Black brothers with their lives on the line, dying and fighting a people who are only wanting for themselves, self-determination in their own homeland and to unify their country and unify their people. And the only reason that Black G.I.'s are over there, or Brown G.I.'s, or Red (Indian-American) G.I.'s, Chicanos, and even white G.I.'s, the only reason you're there is because the fascist, ruling class circles of America (the avaricious, big-time, businessmen, the big rich men; the demagogic, lying politicians, the misleading politicians who mislead and try to lie to the people) are the ones who put you there and the ones who mean to keep you there. They're the ones making fascists out of you brothers. And it's correct that the Vietnamese should defend themselves and defend their land and fight for the right to self-determination, because they have NEVER oppressed us. They have NEVER called us "nigger". They have NEVER done anything wrong to us. The leadership of the Vietnamese is that of heroic people. This is also true of the Vietnamese people who are heroic people, fighting for their right self-determination.

And so, the same goes for Black people here in American living in wretched ghettos and oppression. We have been struggling for 400 years, as many of you Black brothers are well aware. I know you dream about home. But when you come home, come home and realize that you have a fight here, that we have the right to control our destinies in our Black community; as the Chicano people have a right to control their destinies in their Chicano community or areas and places where they live; as the American Indians have a right to control their destiny; as the poor, oppressed white people have a right to control their destiny (many poor, oppressed white people must realize that it's the ruling class). The Indian-Americans, the Chicano-Americans, the Latino-Americans and Brown people, and Black people in America are beginning to move more and more in opposition to the oppressive conditions that the SAME avaricious businessmen and demagogic, lying politicians create and maintain—that exploitation. The workers of this country are beginning to move more and more, day by day, step by step from a lower to a higher level in opposing the ruling class circles, because they (the ruling class circles) are the ones who keep the racism going. They are the ones who keep people hating each other because of skin color, etc.

The Black Panther Party, brothers, does not fight racism with racism. There are no white people in the Black Panther Party but we do have alliances with white radical student groups who have stood up in protest against that war for your sake and for all the G.I.'s sake. We wanted them back home. We wanted to bring them back home as a means to end that war, demanding and protesting that the G.I.'s come back home and the war end.

The Black brothers, Vietnam Black G.I.'s, must understand and feel desire to oppose oppression right here at home domestically. Oppose fascism. The cops occupy our community just like a foreign troop occupies territory. Just like, you are a foreign troop there in Vietnam, occupying territory at the directions of the fascist ruling class and their military leaders who are also a part of the fascist ruling class. Not at the will of the people of America are you there. You're there because the imperialist U.S. aggressors (and that's exactly what they are) have sent you there. And we'll be glad when you come back, because here you must fight the pigs who occupy our community. In every major city and metropolis throughout America police forces have been doubled, tripled, and quadrupled wherever Black people live; where the large populations of Chicano people live; where the large populations of people who are protesting and opposing war, are protesting and opposing the poverty and the murder and brutality that's committed against Black people in the Black community. Wherever the case, these police forces have been tripled and quadrupled with machine guns, AR-15s (the same kinds of guns you brothers got and are carrying over there) magnums (you can stand up and shoot 10 demonstrators with one bullet with a .357 or a .44 magnum) that these cops carry here.

They're not solving the problems of the people, the U.S. government, the local government, the federal government, and the city governments. All they're doing is putting money out for more arms. And now a state of DOMESTIC imperialism exists here to the extent that genocide can begin to be committed tomorrow, if they decide.

We'll be glad when you come home. We oppose the war here, we say, "Power to the People." We want all the people to move to have proletarian democracy—workers democracy (a real people's democracy), and not capitalistic, exploiting democracy for the minority ruling class. There are only 800 big, rich businessmen who control this imperialistic regime in America. There are numerous demagogic politicians, from the local government to the federal government. There are approximately half a million or more local police, some more millions of national guardsmen. But they are used against, not to protect the people. They're used to murder and to brutalize the people, such as at the National Democratic Convention back in August of 1968.

The numerous amounts of brutality that are going on, and you brothers haven't even heard about them. The political prisoners that Black Panther Party members have been made (We have over 50 political prisoners here.) all because the Ten Point Platform and Program of the Black Panther Party began to be implemented. And what was the Ten Point Platform and Program of the Black Panther Party?

From the very beginning of the Party the Ten Point Platform has always read: We want freedom. We want the right to determine our destiny in our own Black community. Number two: We want full employment for our people. Number three: We want the end to oppression and the exploitation of the Black community by the capitalists in our communities. Number four: We want decent housing fit for shelter of human beings. Five says: We want a decent education. It says we want decent education that teaches us about the true nature of this decadent American society, an education that teaches us our true history and our role in the present day society. And number six says: We want all Black men to be exempt from military service. That's what we demand here of this government. (We really want you home, brothers). Number seven says: We want an immediate end to police brutality and murder of Black people. The last two points of the Program covers our right to fair trial by peers as it says in the Constitution of the United States.

It's important Black brothers that we understand the need to come home. It's important that we understand that the Vietnamese people are only fighting for the right to self-determination in their land. It's important, brothers, that we understand it's the fascist ruling class circle who have you there, who got you fighting there. It's important, brothers, that you understand that your fight is really right here at home in America. So when you come back, you'll be fighting against the oppression that we've been subjected to for 400 years. So I will wind this statement up and probably, hopefully, send some more. Better yet, I think I should say a few more things concerning Black G.I.'s and the history of this country.

In the Civil War when there was a fight between the North and the South, in that Civil War, 186,000 Black people enlisted in the military service. We were promised freedom, justice, and equality; and we never received it. During World War I there were over 350,000 Black Americans in World War I. And we were promised freedom, justice, and equality; and we never received it. In World War II some 850,000 almost a million Black Americans fought in that war as Black G.I.'s. And we were promised freedom, justice, and equality; and we never received it. Then there was the Korean War the fascist ruling class aggressors put together. And we fought there. Now, here it is again—another war against a people who are trying to fight for the right of their self-determination. They don't even promise you "freedom, justice, and equality" anymore. Kinda bad now, brothers.

If we would only begin to realize the necessity of not being a tool for the fascist aggressor! And that doesn't only go for Black G.I.'s. That goes for Mexican-American G.I.'s, Chicano brothers, rather; that goes for the Indian American G.I.'s and Chinese-American G.I.'s; and that goes for even the poor white American G.I.'s who have to understand. That goes for even the G.I.'s who have some humanistic understanding about a people's right to survive and a right to determine their own destiny in their own land, like the average human being who can understand that Black people have been oppressed for 400 years here in America—all G.I.'s. And the Chicano people are oppressed, and the Indian-Americans are oppressed.

You guys know that. Every last one of you know that. You cats come from off the block, you Black brothers. And I know you. You know me just as well as I know you. The many times we use to break off into parties and be fighting and carrying on. Some of you would be blowing joints, and drinking and carrying on and being sharp, trying to get you some clean clothes, and chasing them sisters out there. You ain't no different from other brothers; only we just turned political. We just turned political. We're being made political prisoners because we're standing up out there against this fascist ruling class, against those fascist, racist pigs who occupy our community like a foreign troop occupies territory. We're the same, but we're just in two different places. We should be here fighting here at home. They protest over here for the freedom of political prisoners. You should all be closer at protesting over there for the freedom of political prisoners in America.

Power to the people. Power to the people; that's what we say. Power to all the people. And get rid of the power, take the power away from the minority ruling class circles, the imperialists and fascists here in America. The same thing they're doing over there to the Vietnamese people, they're getting ready to upstep and do to Black American people. The same thing; the same kind of weapons, vicious weapons. They have tanks; they have nerve gas and everything else prepared. And it's time that we understand and realize this. All the masses of the people and the G.I.'s and the people at home are the ones who have to protest the war, are the ones who have to protest the injustices right here at home.

So you brothers who are dreaming about coming back home, when you get back home, you're going to see that same oppression. They're going to promise you a job; but you're going to be out of a job. In some cases they're going to try to give some of you dishonorable discharges for one reason or another and tell you that you can't get a job when you get back. But all you have to do is tell him it wasn't no jobs here when you left. And that's why you got off into that thing anyway. You went into the service for the same reason I went into it at one time over 10 years ago, some fourteen years, now; 'cause it wasn't no jobs, it wasn't nothing to do, and you didn't have any money in your pocket and you was frustrated with your surroundings and basically your environment. That's the reason most of you brothers went in there. It was a way to get a chance to do something. And you feel you'd go in the Army and some guy'd sell you some insidious notion about being a man, and all that kind of crap. And you were already a man. You're a human being. That's the first basis for being a man; it's being a human being, and not going out trying to prove how many colored peoples you can kill in a foreign land. That's not being a man; that's being a fascist. And that's what the fascist power structure does.

So to ALL Black American G.I.'s, it's very important that you understand the need to come home; the need to relate to the struggle here; the need for the people and us to get mobilized and to amass together to free the political prisoners; the need to fight for community control of police where the people will have control, not of the same police, but fire those in now and set up community control operations. The Breakfast for Children Programs. Understand that the demagogic politicians are lying. They're lying on the Party. They've attacked the Party; they've attacked our offices. And in some cases we've had to defend ourselves with weapons because we vowed that we would stand and defend ourselves, to defend our people and teach our people the correct methods to resist the pig power structure here in America, the fascist ruling class, the exploiters. That's what they are—oppressors.

So, power to the people, brothers. And please come on home, brothers. And when you get home, we'll be waiting for you.

Speech Delivered at Boston College, 1970
Huey P. Newton

Power to the people, brothers and sisters. I would like to thank you for my presence here tonight because you are responsible for it. I would be in a maximum-security penitentiary if it were not for the power of the people.

I would like to petition you to do the same for Bobby Seale, our Chairman, for Ericka Huggins, for Angela Davis, for the New York 21 and the Soledad Brothers. For all political prisoners and prisoners of war. On the 28th and 29th of November we will have a People's Revolutionary Constitutional convention in Washington, D.C. We cannot have that convention if the people do not come. After all, the people are the makers of world history and responsible for everything. How can we have a convention if we have no people? Some believe a people's convention is possible without the people being there. As I recall, that was the case in 1777.

Tonight, I would like to outline for you the Black Panther Party's program and explain how we arrived at our ideological position and why we feel it necessary to institute a Ten-Point Program. A Ten-Point Program is not revolutionary in itself, nor is it reformist. *It is a survival program*. We, the people, are threatened with genocide because racism and fascism are rampant in this country and throughout the world. And the ruling circle in North America is responsible. We intend to change all of that, and in order to change it, there must be a total transformation. But until we can achieve that total transformation, we must exist. In order to exist, we must survive; therefore, we need a survival kit: the Ten-Point Program. It is necessary for our children to grow up healthy with functional and creative minds. They cannot do this if they do not get the correct nutrition. That is why we the United States, or North America, became an empire it changed the whole composition of the world. There were other nations in the world. But "empire" means that the ruling circle who lives in the empire (the imperialists) control other nations. Now some time ago there existed a phenomenon we called—well, I call—primitive empire. An example of that would be the Roman Empire because the Romans controlled all of what was thought to be the known world. In fact they did not know all of the world, therefore some nations still existed independent of it. Now, probably all of the world is known. The United States as an empire necessarily controls the whole world either directly or indirectly.

If we understand dialectics we know that every determination brings about a limitation and every limitation brings about a determination. In other words, while one force may give rise to one thing it might crush other things, including itself. We might call this concept "the negation of the negation." So, while in 1917 the ruling circle created an industrial base and used the system of capitalism they were also creating the necessary conditions for socialism. They were doing this because in a socialist society it is necessary to have some centralization of the wealth, some equal distribution of the wealth, and some harmony among the people.

Now, I will give you roughly some characteristics that any people who call themselves a nation should have. These are economic independence, cultural determination, control of the political institutions, territorial integrity, and safety.

In 1966 we called our Party a Black Nationalist Party. We called ourselves Black Nationalists because we thought that nationhood was the answer. Shortly after that we decided that what was really needed was revolutionary nationalism, that is, nationalism plus socialism. After analyzing conditions a little more, we found that it was impractical and even contradictory. Therefore, we went to a higher level of consciousness. We saw that in order to be free we had to crush the ruling circle and therefore we had to unite with the peoples of the world. So we called ourselves Internationalists. We sought solidarity with the peoples of the world. We sought solidarity with what we thought were the nations of the world. But then what happened? We found that because everything is in a constant state of transformation, because of the development of technology, because of the development of the mass media, because of the fire power of the imperialist, and because of the fact that the United States is no longer a nation but an empire, nations could not exist, for they did not have the criteria for nationhood. Their self-determination, economic determination, and cultural determination has been transformed by the imperialists and the ruling circle. They were no longer nations. We found that in order to be Internationalists we had to be also Nationalists, or at least acknowledge nationhood. Internationalism, if I understand the word, means the interrelationship among a group of nations. But since no nation exists, and since the United States is in fact an empire, it is impossible for us to be Internationalists. These transformations and phenomena require us to call ourselves "inter communalists" *because nations have been transformed into communities of the world.* The Black Panther Party now disclaims internationalism and supports intercommunalism.

Marx and Lenin felt, with the information they had, that when the non-state finally came to be a reality, it would be caused or ushered in by the people and by communism. A strange thing happened. The ruling reactionary circle, through the consequence of being imperialists, transformed the world into what we call "Reactionary Intercommunalism." They laid siege upon all the communities of the world, dominating the institutions to such an extent that the people were not served by the institutions in their own land. The Black Panther Party would like to reverse that trend and lead the people of the world into the age of "Revolutionary Intercommunalism." This would be the time when the people seize the means of production and distribute the wealth and the technology in an egalitarian way to the many communities of the world.

We see very little difference in what happens to a community here in North America and what happens to a community in Vietnam. We see very little difference in what happens, even culturally, to a Chinese community in San Francisco and a Chinese community in Hong Kong. We see very little difference in what happens to a Black community in Harlem and a Black community in South Africa, a Black community in Angola and one in Mozambique. We see very little difference.

So, what has actually happened, is that the non-state has already been accomplished, but it is reactionary. A community by way of definition is a comprehensive collection of institutions that serve the people who live there. It differs from a nation because a community evolves around a greater structure that we usually call the state, and the state has certain control over the community if the administration represents the people or if the administration happens to be the people's commissar. It is not so at this time, so there's still something to be done. I mentioned earlier the "negation of the negation," I mentioned earlier the necessity for the redistribution of wealth. We think that it is very important to know that as things are in the world today socialism in the United States will never exist. Why? It will not exist because it cannot exist. It cannot at this time exist anyplace in the world. Socialism would require a socialist state, and if a state does not exist how could socialism exist? So how do we define certain progressive countries such as the People's Republic of China? How do we describe certain progressive countries, or communities as we call them, as the Democratic People's Republic of Korea? How do we define certain communities such as North Vietnam and the provisional government in the South? How do we explain these communities if in fact they too cannot claim nation-hood? We say this: we say they represent the people's liberated territory. They represent a community liberated. But that community is not sufficient, it is not satisfied, just as the National Liberation Front is not satisfied with the liberated territory in the South. It is only the ground-work and preparation for the liberation of the world—seizing the wealth from the ruling circle, equal distribution and proportional representation in an intercommunal framework. This is what the Black Panther Party would like to achieve with the help of the power of the people, because without the people nothing can be achieved.

I stated that in the United States socialism would never exist. In order for a revolution to occur in the United States you would have to have a redistribution of wealth not on a national or an international level, but on an intercommunal level.

Notes

1. See Akinyele Omowale Umoja. 2001. "Repression Breeds Resistance." In Kathleen Cleaver and George Katsiaficas. Eds. *Liberation, Imagination, and the Black Panther Party*. New York: Routledge. Also see Reed, T.V. 2005. *The Art of Protest: Culture and Activism from the Civil Rights Movement to the Streets of Seattle*. Minneapolis: University of Minnesota Press.
2. Parenti, Michael. 2010. 9th Edition. *Democracy for the Few*. New York: Wadsworth.
3. Seale, Bobby. 1970. "Bobby Seale Explains Panther Politics: An Interview." In Philip S. Foner. Ed. *The Black Panthers Speak*. Cambridge: DeCapo Press, p. 86.
4. Ibid., p. 82.
5. Newton, Huey P. 1967. *In Defense of Self Defense*. In David Hilliard and Donald Weise. Eds. 2002. *The Huey P. Newton Reader*. New York: Seven Stories Press, p. 137.
6. Newton, Huey P. 1970. "The Womren's Liberation and Gay Liberation Movements." In David Hilliard and Donald Weise. Eds. 2002. *The Huey P. Newton Reader*. New York: Seven Stories Press, p. 159.

PART IV

BLACK RADICAL FEMINISM

20.
CLAUDIA JONES

Claudia Jones (1915–1964) was a revolutionary Communist and feminist. By the time Jones was twenty years old she was actively involved in grassroots activism. She was actively involved in protesting the unjust convictions of the Scottsboro Nine.[1] Jones became active in Harlem, New York. There, she attended rallies and, in 1936, Jones officially joined the Communist Party. She became involved in the Young Communist League and its youth movement.

Over the years Jones held many positions within the Communist Party. In 1937 she was the Secretary of the Executive Committee of Young Communist League. By 1938 she was the New York State Chair of the Young Communist League. By the time she became the organization's Educational Director of the Young Communist League in 1941 she was becoming a well-known revolutionary. Jones became a target of the FBI's Communist witch-hunts and over the years was arrested countless times for her revolutionary efforts and fought off deportation until the end of 1955. In 1947 she became the secretary of the women's commission within the Communist Party. Jones, a passionate feminist, was involved in other women's organizations. She worked within the Congress of American Women and National Council of Negro Women. She worked with these groups organizing protests and rallies. Jones recruited around the United States and labored to bring workers, women, and Black folk together in struggle.

Jones, like so many of the leaders in this book, was a proponent of utilizing the press to battle injustice. Even in her early organizing days, she edited the paper of the Federated Youth Clubs of Harlem. In 1943 she became the editor of *Spotlight* and editor-in-chief of *Weekly Review*. In 1945 she also became editor of Negro Affairs for the *Daily Worker*. In 1954 despite imprisonment and heart disease she still continued her work; she became the editor of the *Negro Affairs Quarterly*. After her deportation and migration to London, the native Trinidadian not only worked with Communists, West Indian, and Caribbean groups but also worked on a paper there, the *Caribbean News*. In 1958 she created the *West Indian Gazette* and went on to edit both the *West Indian Gazette* and *Afro-Asian Caribbean News*. All of this work furthered her Pan-Africanist goals and her commitment to organizing Afro-Asian and Caribbean communities against imperialism and global exploitation. In addition to her political activism, she also demonstrated cultural nationalism and organized cultural festivals, specifically London's first Caribbean carnivals.

Overview of Ideas

Claudia Jones was a Marxist-Leninist. As an active member of the Communist Party, she posited that the "Negro Question" was "the question of a nation oppressed by American imperialism." The supposed "Negro Problem" was not just a problem for Black people; the same forces oppressing Black people, oppressed workers of all races and ethnic groups. The solution to the "Negro Problem" was socialism; this meant the overthrow of capitalism and the emergence of "self-determination to the oppressed peoples." In fact, Jones advocated global socialism and the eventual merger of formerly oppressed nations around the world.

Democracy in the United States would only be realized if Black people and the working class were united in struggle against capitalist exploitation. Moreover, progressives, namely working class revolutionaries, must fight harder for the rights of Black people. Jones adroitly explained why it was in the interests of progressives, specifically the White working classes, to fight on behalf of African Americans. U.S. imperialist capitalists, to divide and conquer the working classes, crafted racist discourses in the United States. Therefore, to fight against racism was to challenge the imperialist capitalist forces oppressing all workers. Integrated struggle was mandatory for liberation. In addition, Jones argued that many progressives welcomed integrated political struggle but not social integration. They were happy to see Black and White activists holding hands in political struggle but not holding hands intimately. Unlike other Black radicals, namely Black Nationalists, Jones advocated interracial social bonds.

Claudia Jones was an innovative thinker. While influenced by Marx and Lenin, like Angela Davis, she ingeniously incorporated the issues of race and gender into her understanding of class exploitation. According to Jones, Black people experienced "double oppression"; they were both wage slaves to the bourgeoisie and oppressed under White supremacy. However, Jones was hopeful about the condition of Black folk. As more Black people joined unions and as industrialization, particularly in the Black Belt, created an even larger working class, Black people would become more unified and more likely to achieve self-determination.

Black women, too, experienced super-exploitation; they experienced oppression along class, racial, and gender lines. Departing from traditional Marxism and drawing heavily from Lenin, Jones posited the importance of being attentive to the special problems faced by women, particularly Black women and not reducing their experiences of oppression to simply class exploitation. By meaningfully inculcating Black women into the anti-fascist, anti-imperialist, and anti-capitalist struggle of the Communist Party, particularly amongst its leadership, the movement would become stronger. Black women are a force to be reckoned with.

> The bourgeoisie is fearful of the militancy of the Negro woman and for good reason. The capitalist know, far better than many progressives seem to know, that once Negro women undertake action, the militancy of the whole Negro people and thus of the anti-imperialist coalition, is greatly enhanced.

Historically Black women have been powerful matriarchs; they have defended their family and community since the enslavement of Black people in the United States. As a result the bourgeoisie have intensified their exploitation of Black women. Historically, while Black women were required to maintain jobs to support their families, White women have most often been freed from toil. When White women were working they were more likely to enjoy better conditions of labor and better wages than Black women. As Davis highlighted, because Black women have been relegated to domestic work and menial labor their experiences as part of the laboring class have been particularly repugnant. It was essential to fight for jobs, better wages, and better conditions of labor for Black women. Moreover, popular discourse, too, as found in the media, perpetuated stereotypes such as the mammy that legitimized and reified Black women's inferior positions in labor. In order to counteract massive efforts to subordinate Black women in the labor market, it was essential to organize Black women. However, this organization cannot just extend to the organization of Black women in factories; it must extend to Black women in the service industry. Labor organizing and unionization was paramount. Existing labor movements could no longer ignore issues that were conditioned by race.

Like her Black radical feminist counterparts, Jones argued that what she called *bourgeois feminism* spoke primarily to the needs of middle class White women and ignored the super-exploitation of black women. In addition, "according to bourgeois feminism, women's oppression stems, not from the capitalist system, but from men." Jones's goal was to expose this as a lie. Part of Claudia Jones's platform was to organize American women into the anti-war and larger peace movement:

> A fundamental condition for rallying the masses of American women into the peace camp is to free them from the influence of the agents of imperialism and to arouse their sense of internationalism with million upon millions of their sisters the world over.

Jones's objective was to get women, particularly bourgeois feminists, to see their alliances with oppressed women of other lower classes and other races.

Just as they had done with race, capitalists manipulated sexist discourse to advance and maintain their own avarice. They told disgruntled male workers that the reasons they were unemployed or underemployed was because women were taking their jobs and needed to return to the kitchen. Jones implored all workers to see past these insidious tactics and to see them for what they were—again, a ploy to divide and conquer the working classes. In fact, Jones argued that sexism had even become a problem amongst progressives. Even Communist men were not seeking to annihilate male supremacy. Jones reminded them that while focusing on class exploitation was a basic imperative of the movement, so was tackling White and male supremacy. Until all three interconnected facets of oppression were faced head-on there would be no real emancipation for anyone. This was the type of knowledge that needed to be disseminated in order to combat false consciousness, which functioned like a spell that too many potential revolutionaries were under.

As we have seen throughout this text, Jones, too, argued that education was a necessary part of the solution to the "Negro Question." However, for Jones, educational institutions required complete transformation. They currently were indoctrinating young people with deleterious ideas. Students were being taught racism and pro-fascist ideology. The current system stifled the ability of progressive teachers to create new generations of critical thinkers. Students were given access to watered-down, sanitized versions of American history. They were not taught to question authority or demand better education. These mechanisms helped maintain the fascist state.

On the Right to Self-Determination for Negro People in the Black Belt, 1946

Even the worst enemies of the Communist Party cannot fail to admit that we have been in the forefront of the struggle for equality of the Negro people. It was the Communist Party which fourteen years ago made the name of Scottsboro ring around the world. It was the Communist Party, which was the first, since the overthrow of the Reconstruction governments, to raise in the heart of the South the issue of full Negro freedom.

What galvanized our Party to become the initiator and vanguard of these struggles? It was our understanding of the Negro question in the United States as a *special* question, as an issue whose solution requires *special* demands, in addition to the general demands of the American working class.

It was essentially this understanding that found Communists in the forefront of the struggle to combat the imperialist ideology of "white supremacy" which is today endangering the unity of the labour-democratic coalition and of the working class itself. It was essentially this knowledge that taught white American workers to fight for Negro rights in their own self-interest, to understand that to fight against white chauvinism is to fight against imperialist ideologies and practices of America's ruling class which serves to separate Negro and white workers. It was this understanding that taught Negro workers to fight against petty-bourgeois nationalism—a result of white chauvinist ideology—and to have both Negro and white workers form strong bonds of unity with each other.

It was our understanding of the Negro question as a *national* question, that is, as the question of a nation oppressed by American imperialism, in the ultimate sense as India is oppressed by British imperialism and Indonesia by Dutch imperialism. It was our knowledge, grounded in Lenin's teachings, that every aspect of Negro oppression in our country stems from the existence of an *oppressed nation*, in the heart of the South, the Black Belt.

We knew that the semi-slavery of the Southern sharecroppers; the inferior status of the Negro people in industry, North and South, the existence of Jim Crow in the armed forces; the Jim Crow practices of New York and Chicago, as well as of Birmingham and Tampa; the shooting two months ago of a Harlem child by a trigger-happy cop—all can be traced back step by step to the continued existence of an oppressed Negro nation within our borders.

Wherein do the Negro people in the Black Belt constitute an oppressed nation? To answer this question, we must first determine the characteristics of a nation. Marxist-Leninists hold that "a nation is a historically evolved, stable community of language, territory, economic life and psychological make-up manifested in a community of culture."

The Black Belt, an area in which the Negro people form a majority, came into existence with the growth of cotton culture and plantation economy. As the area of cotton cultivation moved over Westward in the days before the Civil War, so did the area of the plantation that consisted of a white-master family with its slaves.

The Civil War, which abolished chattel slavery, failed either to break up this area of Negro majority or to fully liberate the Negro people within it. Retaining their plantation lands, the ex-slaveholders soon forced to return to these lands of their former slaves as sharecroppers. A series of laws passed by Southern states—the crop lien laws, the jumping contract laws and so on—prevented and still prevent the free migration of the Negro people. Scarcely less than before the Civil War, is the Black Belt a prison-house of the Negroes; the chains which hold them now are the invisible chains of poverty, the legal chains of debt-slavery and when the landlords deem it necessary, the iron shackles of the chain gang.

The Civil War might have broken the bars of the Black Belt; it did not, for the Northern capitalists, who had gained a united market and field of exploitation throughout the nation as a result of the Civil War, were terrified by the simultaneous rise of Southern democracy, the Northern labour movement and radical agrarian organizations. They betrayed the Negro people and the Southern white masses and turned the South back to semi-slavery.

The migrations of the 1870s, of the First World War and of the Second World War, did not appreciably diminish the proportion by which the Negroes find themselves a majority today in the Black Belt—these are virtually the same. It cannot be said that this majority is accidental, or that the Negro people continue as an oppressed people within the Black Belt by inertia or by choice. They continue so because the sheriff's posse of the twentieth century is carrying on, under new forms, the work of the slave-catchers of the nineteenth. The majority remains a majority by force.

This community in which the Negro people are a majority is neither racial nor tribal, it is composed of a significant minority of whites as well. The territory stretches contiguously westward from the Eastern shore of Maryland and lies within Maryland, Virginia, North Carolina, South Carolina, Georgia, Florida, Alabama, Mississippi, Louisiana, Tennessee, Arkansas and Texas.

Following the Civil War, boundary lines were definitely shaped by the defeated slaveholders to prohibit the full participation of the Negroes and poor whites in political life. If it is true in the North, where certain election districts are "gerrymandered" to prohibit the full expression of the Negro vote (and of the white vote as well), it was no less true of the Black Belt, where the majority of the inhabitants were Negroes and represented its basic core.

As to the other characteristics of nationhood: Have the Negro people, for example, a common language? They have a common language—English. If it be argued that this is the language of the entire country, we say that this is true. A common language is necessary to nationhood,—a different language is not. When the American colonies separated from Britain, they had a common language, which was the same as that of their oppressors. Surely no one will argue that our community of language with our British oppressors should have kept us indefinitely in the status of a colonial people.

Is there an American Negro culture? The peculiar oppression of the Negro people and their striving for freedom have been expressed in a native way, in spirituals, work-songs, literature, art and dance. This does not mean that American Negro culture is not part of American culture generally. Negro culture is part of the general stream of American culture, but it is a distinct current in that stream, it arose out of the special historical development and unique status of the Negro people,—no other people in America could have developed this particular culture.

Have the Negro people a stable community of economic life? First, let us discuss what is meant by a common economic life. It is sometimes said that people have a common economic life when they make their living in the same way—they are all sharecroppers, or they are all workers. Actually, a common economic life with reference to a nation or community under capitalism means that the nation or community has within it the class and social relations that characterize society, it has capitalists, workers, farmers and intellectuals, ranged according to their position in the production relations. In this case it means that a Negro must be able to hire a Negro, buy from a Negro, sell to a Negro and service a Negro

Such class stratification exists among the Negro people in the Black Belt. There is a Negro bourgeoisie, it is not a big bourgeoisie, the bourgeoisie of an oppressed nation never is, it is one of the results of national oppression that the bourgeoisie of oppressed nations is retarded by the oppressors. The market of the Negro bourgeoisie is founded upon Jim Crowism, it functions chiefly in life insurance, banking and real estate. Its leadership among the Negro people is reflected in an ideology—petty-bourgeois nationalism, whose main purpose is to mobilize the Negro masses under its own influence.

By these distinguishing features, therefore, the Negro people in the Black Belt constitute a nation. They are an historically developed community of people, with a common language, a common territory and a common economic life, all of which are manifest in a common culture.

As far back as 1913, Lenin emphasized that the Negro people constitute an oppressed nation. In an unfinished essay on the national and colonial question he made a *direct* reference to the Negro people as an *oppressed nation*, stating:

> In the United States 11.1 per cent of the population consists of Negroes (and also mulattoes and Indians) who must be considered an oppressed nation, inasmuch as the equality, won in the Civil War of 1861–65 and guaranteed by the constitution of the Republic, has in reality been more and more restricted in many respects in the main centres of the Negro population (in the South) with the transition from the progressive, pre-monopolistic capitalism of 1860–1870 to the reactionary monopolistic capitalism (imperialism) of the latest epoch.
>
> (V. I. Lenin, *Miscellany*, Collected Works, Vol. XXX, Russian Edition.)

Browder's Revision of Leninist Teachings

In discussing the right of self-determination for Negroes in the Black Belt, we surely cannot ignore the revisionist position taken by Earl Browder, as set forth in his article in *The Communist* for January, 1944, which was presented as a declaration of policy for American Communists. There Browder wrote:

> … It was in view of the gathering world crisis that we Communists at that time—in the early 30s raised the issue of self-determination At that time, we necessarily faced the possibility that the Negro people, disappointed in their aspirations for full integration into the American nation, might find their only alternative in separation and in the establishment of their own state in the Black Belt, in the territory in which they are a majority. We raised this as one of the rights of the Negro people, in case the Negro people found this was the only way to satisfy their aspirations.

Browder further wrote:

> The crisis of history has taken a turn of such character that the Negro people in the United States have found it possible to make their decision once and for all. Their decision is for their complete integration into the American nation as a whole and not for separation.

Browder thus denied that the right of self-determination for Negroes in the Black Belt was any longer an issue, since, according to him, the Negro people had already made their historic choice!

What was the fallacy on which Browder's premise was based?

Browder's fallacy was inherently connected with a false estimate of the relationship of forces in our nation and the world Clearly, if a rosy future was to be envisioned in which a "peaceful" capitalism would voluntarily relinquish its exploitations, solve its contradictions, etc, the Leninist programme which showed that the very essence of imperialism was the distinction and conflict between oppressed and oppressing nations no longer applied to our country!

Moreover, Browder based his premise, not on evaluating the right of self-determination as it applies to the Negro people in the Black Belt, but on one of its aspects, separation. That he saw fit to discuss the whole question from the standpoint of a practical political matter, confirms this. His treatment of these two demands as being identical needs examination.

Is separation identical with self-determination? The right to separation is inherent in the right to self-determination, whether that right is eventually exercised or not. It becomes a practical political matter only when the concrete objective conditions for that choice are at hand. Therefore, to identify self-determination with separation, or to substitute one for the other, is tantamount to forcing on the Negro people a choice, which they are clearly not in an objective position to make—which, in other words, though a right, is not necessarily a function of their exercise of self-determination!

It is obvious from this that the right of self-determination is not something one can dangle, withdraw, or put forward again as a sheerly objective factor. Either the objective historic conditions of nationhood exist, in which such a right remains inviolate, or they do not. Either the objective conditions exist for the choice to be made by the oppressed nation (either for separation, autonomy, amalgamation, etc.), or they do not. Thus, and only thus, can we approach the issue as a practical political matter.

How then, does the question of integration apply? Are the Negro people demanding integration in American political life? Most certainly they are! But this is no new phenomenon insofar as the Negro people are concerned. Negro Americans have been fighting for integration for over two hundred years. Every *partial* fight—whether expressed in the demand of the Reconstruction leaders, together with the white workers and farmers in the South for land, or in the present day demands of Negroes in Atlanta to enforce the Supreme Court ruling against the "white primary" laws, whether it be the fight against lynching and poll-tax disfranchisement, or the recent successful campaign, conducted in Negro-white unity to re-elect Benjamin J. Davis, Jr., to the New York City Council—is a step towards integration

But integration cannot be considered a substitute for the right of self-determination. National liberation is not synonymous with integration, neither are the two concepts mutually exclusive.

What does integration really mean? Integration, that is, *democratic* integration, means breaking down the fetters that prohibit the full economic, political and social participation of Negroes in all phases of American life. This does not mean that a merger, or an assimilative process necessarily takes place. In a general sense, the struggle for integration waged today by the Negro people is directed toward achieving *equal rights*—economic, political and social.

But the basic difference, in fact the touchstone of programmatic difference, between the liberals (as well as the Social-Democrats) and the Communists hinges on the application of the programme of equal rights to the Black Belt, and therefore, to the *source of Negro oppression* throughout the country—a difference based on diametrically opposed concepts of the nature of the question.

In the North, the struggle for equal rights for the Negro people is chiefly that of heightening the fight to secure equal participation in every sphere of American life. The problems of the Negro people in the North are akin to those of an oppressed national minority. Particularly here, the fight for equal rights as a—whole in enhanced by the presence of a large and growing Negro proletariat, in the area of the most highly developed capitalism, as well as by the participation of the advanced workers throughout the country for equal rights for Negroes. In fact, it is the existence of a strong Negro proletariat-represented today by close to one million organized trade unionists – that provides the intimate link between the American working class as a whole and the struggle for emancipation and land for the oppressed Negro people and white workers in the Black Belt.

In the Black Belt the problem is chiefly that of wiping out the economic, political and social survivals of slavery, of the *enforcement* of equal rights. Without the necessary *enforcement* of equal rights for the Negro people in the Black Belt, including social equality, it is folly to speak of integration as being equal to the achievement of national liberation. Hence, equal rights for the Negro people in the Black Belt can be achieved only through enforcement, through their exercise of the right of self-determination.

The right of self-determination does not exclude the struggle for partial demands, it pre-supposes an energetic struggle for concrete partial demands, linked up with the daily needs and problems of the wide masses of the Negro people and the white workers in the Black Belt. The fight for such partial demands, moreover, is a struggle for democracy. It does not divert or overshadow the working class struggle against exploitation, it is an aid to it.

It is only by helping to interconnect the partial demands with the right of self-determination that we Communists, in concert with other progressive forces, can contribute guidance to the struggle for complete equality for the Negro people.

An End to the Neglect of the Problems of Negro Women, 1949

An outstanding feature of the present stage of the Negro liberation movement is the growth in the militant participation of Negro women in all aspects of the struggle for peace, civil rights and economic security. Symptomatic of this new militancy is the fact that Negro women have become symbols of many present-day struggles of the Negro people This growth of militancy among Negro women has profound meaning, both for the Negro liberation movement and for the emerging anti-fascist, anti-imperialist coalition.

To understand this militancy correctly, to deepen and extend the role of Negro women in the struggle for peace and for all interests of the working class and the Negro people, means primarily to overcome the gross neglect of the special problems of Negro women. This neglect has too long permeated the ranks of the labour movement generally, of Left-progressives and also of the Communist Party. The most serious assessment of these shortcomings by progressives, especially by Marxist-Leninists, is vitally necessary if we are to help accelerate this development and integrate Negro women in the progressive and labour movement and in our own Party.

The bourgeoisie is fearful of the militancy of the Negro woman and for good reason. The capitalists know, far better than many progressives seem to know, that once Negro women undertake action, the militancy of the whole Negro people and thus of the anti-imperialist coalition, is greatly enhanced.

Historically, the Negro woman has been the guardian, the protector, of the Negro family. From the days of the slave traders down to the present, the Negro woman has had the responsibility of caring for the needs of the family, of militantly shielding it from the blows of Jim Crow insults, of rearing children in an atmosphere of lynch terror, segregation and police brutality and of fighting for an education for their children. The intensified oppression of the Negro people, which has been the hallmark of the postwar reactionary offensive, cannot therefore but lead to an acceleration of the militancy of the Negro woman. As mother, as Negro, and as worker, the Negro woman fights against the wiping out of the Negro family, against the Jim Crow ghetto existence which destroys the health, morale and the very life of millions of her sisters, brothers and children.

Viewed in this light, it is not accidental that the American bourgeoisie has intensified its oppression, not only of the Negro people in general, but of Negro women in particular. Nothing so exposes the drive to *fascization* in the nation as the callous attitude which the bourgeoisie displays and cultivates toward Negro women. The vaunted boast of the ideologists of Big Business—that American women possess "the greatest equality" in the world is exposed in all its hypocrisy when one sees that in many parts of the world, particularly in the Soviet Union, the New Democracies and the formerly oppressed land of China, women are attaining new heights of equality. But above all else, Wall Street's boast stops at the water's edge where Negro and working class women are concerned. Not equality, but degradation and super-exploitation: this is the actual lot of Negro women!

Consider the hypocrisy of the Truman Administration, which boasts about "exporting democracy throughout the world" while the state of Georgia keeps a widowed Negro mother of twelve children under lock and key. Her crime? She defended her life and dignity aided by her two sons—from the attacks of a "white supremacist." Or ponder the mute silence with which the Department of Justice has greeted Mrs. Amy Mallard, widowed Negro school-teacher, since her husband was lynched in Georgia because he had bought a new Cadillac and become, in the opinion of the "white supremacists," "too uppity." Contrast this with the crocodile tears shed by the US delegation to the United Nations for Cardinal Mindszenty, who collaborated with the enemies of the Hungarian People's Republic and sought to hinder the forward march to fuller democracy by the formerly oppressed workers and peasants of Hungary. Only recently, President Truman spoke solicitously in a Mother's Day Proclamation about the manifestation of "our love and reverence" for all mothers of the land. The so-called "love and reverence" for the mothers of the land by no means includes Negro mothers who, like Rosa Lee Ingram, Amy Mallard, the wives and mothers of the of the Trenton Six, or the other countless victims, dare to fight back, against lynch law and "white supremacy" violence.

Economic Hardships

Very much to the contrary, Negro women—as workers, as Negroes, and as women—are the most oppressed stratum of the whole population.

In 1940, two out of every five Negro women, in contrast to two out of every eight white women, worked for a living. By virtue of their majority status among the Negro people, Negro women not only constitute the largest percentage of women heads of families, but, are the main breadwinners of the Negro family. The large proportion of Negro women in the labour market is primarily a result of the low-scale earnings of Negro men. This disproportion also has its roots in the treatment and position of Negro women over the centuries.

Following emancipation and persisting to the present day, a large percentage of Negro women—married as well as single—were forced to work for a living. But despite the shift in employment of Negro women from rural to urban areas, Negro women are still generally confined to the lowest-paying jobs. The Women's Bureau, US Department of Labour, *Handbook of Facts for Women Workers* (1948, Bulletin 225), shows white women workers as having median earnings more than twice as high as those of non-white women and non-white women workers (mainly Negro women) as earning less than $500 a year! In the rural South, the earnings of women are even less. In three large Northern industrial communities, the median income of white families ($1,720) is also 60 per cent higher than that of Negro families ($1,095). The super exploitation of the Negro woman worker is thus revealed not only in that she receives, as woman, less than equal pay for equal work with men, but also in that the majority of Negro women get less than half the pay of white women. Little wonder, then, that in Negro communities the conditions of ghetto-living—low salaries, high rents, high prices, etc.—virtually become an iron curtain hemming in the lives of Negro children and undermining their health and spirit! Little wonder that the maternity death rate for Negro women is triple that of white women! Little wonder that one out of every ten Negro children born in the United States does not grow to manhood or womanhood!

The low scale of earnings of the Negro woman is directly related to her almost complete exclusion from virtually all fields of work except the most menial and underpaid, namely, domestic service. Revealing are the following data given in the report of 1945, *Negro Women War Workers* (Women's Bureau, US Department of Labour, Bulletin 205): Of a total 7½ million Negro women, over a million are in domestic and personal service. The overwhelming bulk—about 918,000—of these women workers are employed in private families and some 98,000 are employed as cooks, waitresses and in like services in other than private homes. The remaining 60,000 workers in service trades are in miscellaneous personal service occupations (beauticians, boarding house and lodging-house keepers, charwomen, janitors, practical nurses, housekeepers, hostesses and elevator operators).

The next largest number of Negro women workers are engaged in agricultural work. In 1940, about 245,000 were agricultural workers. Of them, some 128,000 were unpaid family workers.

Industrial and other workers numbered more than 96,000 of the Negro Women reported. Thirty-six thousand of these women were in manufacturing, the chief groups being 11,300 in apparel and other fabricated textile products, 1,000 in tobacco manufactures and 5,600 in food and related products

Clerical and kindred workers in general numbered only 13,000. There were only 8,300 Negro women workers in civil service.

The rest of the Negro women who work for a living were distributed along the following lines: 50,000 teachers, 6,700 nurses and student nurses, 1,700 social and welfare workers, 120 dentists, pharmacists and veterinarians, 129 physicians and surgeons, 200 actresses, 100 authors, editors and reporters, 39 lawyers and judges, 400 librarians and other categories likewise illustrating the large-scale exclusion of Negro women from the professions.

During the anti-Axis war, Negro women for the first time in history had an opportunity to utilize their skills and talents in occupations other than domestic and personal service. They became trailblazers in many fields. Since the end of the war, however, this has given way to growing unemployment, to the wholesale firing of Negro women, particularly in basic industry.

This process has been intensified with the development of the economic crisis. Today, Negro women are being forced back into domestic work in great numbers. In New York State, for example, this trend was officially confirmed recently when Edward Corsi, Commissioner of the State Labour Department, revealed that for the first time since the war, domestic help is readily obtainable. Corsi in effect admitted that Negro women are not voluntarily giving up jobs, but rather are being systematically pushed out of industry. Unemployment, which has always hit the Negro woman first and hardest, plus the high cost of living, is what compels Negro women to re-enter domestic service today Accompanying this trend is an ideological campaign to make domestic work palatable. Daily newspaper advertisements which base their arguments on the claim that most domestic workers who apply for jobs through USES "prefer this type of work to work in industry," are propagandizing the "virtues" of domestic work, especially of "sleep-in positions."

Inherently connected with the question of job opportunities where the Negro woman is concerned, is the special oppression she faces as Negro, as woman and as worker. She is the victim of the white chauvinist stereotype as to where her place should be. In film, radio and the press, the Negro woman is not pictured in her real role as breadwinner, mother and protector of the family, but as a traditional "mammy" who puts the care of children and families of others above her own. This traditional stereotype of the Negro slave mother, which to this day appears in commercial advertisements, must be combated and rejected as a device of the imperialists to perpetuate the white chauvinist ideology that Negro women are "backward," "inferior" and the "natural slaves" of others.

Historical Aspects

Actually, the history of the Negro woman shows that the Negro mother under slavery held a key position and played a dominant role in her own family grouping. This was due primarily to two factors: the conditions of slavery, under which marriage, as such, was non-existent and the Negro's social status was derived from the mother and not the father, and the fact that most of the Negro people brought to these shores by the slave traders came from West Africa where the position of women, based on their actual participation in property control, was relatively higher in the family than that of European women.

Early historians of the slave trade recall the testimony of travelers indicating that the love of the African mother for her child was unsurpassed in any part of the world. There are numerous stories attesting to the self-sacrificial way in which East African mothers offered themselves to the slave traders in order to save their sons and Hottentot women refused food during famines until after their children were fed.

It is impossible within the confines of this article to relate the terrible sufferings and degradation undergone by Negro mothers and Negro women generally under slavery. Subject to legalized rape by the slave owners, confined to slave pens, forced to march for eight to fourteen hours with loads on their backs and to perform back-breaking work even during pregnancy, Negro women bore a burning hatred for slavery and undertook a large share of the responsibility for defending and nurturing the Negro family.

The Negro mother was mistress in the slave cabin and despite the interference of master or overseer, her wishes in regard to mating and in family matters was paramount. During and after slavery, Negro women had to support themselves and the children, necessarily playing an important role in the economic and social life of her people.

The Negro Woman Worker

The negligible participation of Negro women in progressive and trade-union circles is thus all the more startling. In union after union, even in those unions where a large concentration of workers are Negro women, few Negro women are to be found as leaders or active workers. The outstanding exceptions to this are the Food and Tobacco Workers' Union and the United Office and Professional Workers' Union.

But why should these be exceptions? Negro women are among the most militant trade unionists. The sharecroppers' strikes of the 30s were spark-plugged by Negro women. Subject to the terror of the landlord and white supremacist, they waged magnificent battles together with Negro men and white progressives in that struggle of great tradition led by the Communist Party Negro women played a magnificent part in the pre-CIO days in strikes and other struggles, both as workers and as wives of workers, to win recognition of the principle of industrial unionism, in such industries as auto, packing, steel, etc. More recently, the militancy of Negro women unionists is shown in the strike of the packing-house workers and even more so, in the tobacco workers' strike—in which such leaders as Moranda Smith and Velma Hopkins emerged as outstanding trade unionists. The struggle of the tobacco workers led by Negro women later merged with the political action of Negroes and whites which led to the election of the first Negro in the South (in Winston-Salem, NC) since Reconstruction days.

It is incumbent on progressive unionists to realize that in the fight for equal rights for Negro workers, it is necessary to have a special approach to Negro women workers, who, far out of proportion to other women workers, are the main bread-winners in their families. The fight to retain the Negro woman in industry and to upgrade her on the job is a major way of struggling for the basic and special interests of the Negro woman worker. Not to recognize this feature is to miss the special aspects of the effects of the growing economic crisis, which is penalizing Negro workers, particularly Negro women workers with special severity.

The Domestic Worker

One of the crassest manifestations of trade-union neglect of the problems of the Negro women worker has been the failure, not only to fight against relegation of the Negro woman to domestic and similar menial work, but also to *organize* the domestic worker. It is merely lip-service for progressive unionists to speak of organizing the unorganized without turning their eyes to the serious plight of the domestic worker, who; unprotected by union standards, is also the victim of exclusion from all social and labour legislation. Only about one in ten of all Negro women workers are to be found in states having minimum-wage laws. All of the arguments heretofore projected with regard to the real difficulties of organizing the domestic workers—such as the "casual" nature of their employment, the difficulties of organizing day workers, the problem of organizing people who work in individual households, etc., must be overcome forthwith. There is a danger that Social-Democratic forces may enter this field to do their work of spreading disunity and demagogy, unless progressives act quickly.

The lot of the domestic worker is one of unbearable misery. Usually, she has no definition of tasks in the household where she works. Domestic workers may have "thrown in," in addition to cleaning and scrubbing, such tasks as washing windows, caring for the children, laundering, cooking, etc. and all at the lowest pay. The Negro domestic worker must suffer the additional indignity, in some areas, of having to seek work in virtual "slave markets" on the streets where bids are made, as from a slave block, for the hardiest workers. Many a domestic worker, on returning to her own household, must begin housework anew to keep her own family together.

Who was not enraged when it was revealed in California, in the heinous case of Dora Jones, that a Negro woman domestic was enslaved for more than 40 years in "civilized" America? Her "employer" was given a minimum sentence of a few years and complained that the sentence was for "such a long period of time." But could Dora Jones, Negro domestic worker, be repaid for more than 40 years of her life under such conditions of exploitation and degradation? And how many cases, partaking in varying degrees of the condition of Dora Jones, arc still tolerated by progressives themselves!

Only recently, in the New York State Legislature, legislative proposals were made to "fingerprint" domestic workers. The Martinez Bill did not see the light of day, because the reactionaries were concentrating on other repressive legislative measures, but here we see clearly the imprint of the African "pass" system of British imperialism (and of the German Reich in relation to the Jewish people!) being attempted in relation to women domestic workers.

It is incumbent on the trade unions to assist the Domestic Workers Union in every possible way to accomplish the task of organizing the exploited domestic workers, the majority of whom are Negro women. Simultaneously, a legislative fight for the inclusion of domestic workers under the benefits of the Social Security Law is vitally urgent and necessary. Here, too, recurrent questions regarding "administrative problems" of applying the law to domestic workers should be challenged and solutions found.

The continued relegation of Negro women to domestic work has helped to perpetuate and intensify the chauvinism directed against all Negro women. Despite the fact that Negro women may be grand mothers or mothers, the use of the chauvinist term "girl" for adult Negro women is a common expression. The very economic relationship of Negro women to white women, which perpetuates "madam-maid" relationships, feeds chauvinist attitudes and makes it incumbent on white women progressives and particularly Communists, to fight consciously against all manifestations of white chauvinism, open and subtle.

Chauvinism on the part of progressive white women is often expressed in their failure to have close ties of friendship with Negro women and to realize that this fight for equality of Negro women is in their own self-interest, inasmuch as the super-exploitation and oppression of Negro women tends to depress the standards of all women. Too many progressives and even some Communists, are still guilty of exploiting Negro domestic workers, of refusing to hire them through the Domestic Workers' Union (or of refusing to help in its expansion into those areas where it does not exist) and generally of participating in the vilification of "maids" when speaking to their bourgeois neighbours and their own families. Then, there is the expressed "concern" that the exploited Negro domestic worker does not "talk" to, or is not "friendly" with, her employer, or the habit of assuming that the duty of the white progressive employer is to "inform" the Negro woman of her exploitation and her oppression which she undoubtedly knows quite intimately. Persistent challenge to every chauvinist remark as concerns the Negro woman is vitally necessary, if we are to break down the understandable distress on the part of Negro women who are repelled by the white chauvinism they often find expressed in progressive circles.

International Women's Day and the Struggle for Peace, 1950

Women in the Struggle For Peace and Security

On International Women's Day this year, millions of women in the world-wide camp of peace headed by the mighty land of Socialism will muster their united forces to make March 8, 1950, a day of demonstrative struggle for peace, freedom and women's rights.

In our own land, there will be over fifty celebrations. On New York's Lower East Side, original site of this historic American-born day of struggle for equal rights for women, and in major industrial states, such as Illinois, Ohio, Michigan, Pennsylvania, California, Massachusetts and Connecticut, broad united-front meetings of women for peace will be held "Save the Peace!" "Halt Production of the A-Bomb!" "Negotiate with the Soviet Union to Outlaw Atomic Weapons!"—these are the slogans of women in the USA on International Women's Day.

A Rich Heritage of Struggle

Before 1908 and since, American women have made lasting contributions in the struggle for social progress: against slavery and Negro oppression, for equal rights for women and women's suffrage, against capitalist exploitation, for peace and for Socialism. Special tribute must be paid those heroic women who gave their lives in the struggle for Socialism and freedom: Elsie Smith, Anna Damon, Rose Pastor Strokes, Fanny Sellins, Williana Burroughs and Grace Campbell. In this period of the US monopoly drive to war and world domination, reaction pays unwilling tribute to the role of Communist women leaders by its deportation delirium. The present-day struggles of progressive and Communist women merge with the traditions and contributions of such great anti-slavery fighters as Harriet Tubman and Sojourner Truth, of such militant women proletarians as the textile workers of 1848, of such women pioneers as Susan B. Anthony and Elizabeth Cady Stanton, of such builders of America's progressive and working class heritages as Kate Richards O'Hare, Mother Jones, Ella Reeve Bloor, Anita Whitney and Elizabeth Gurley Flynn.

March 8 was designated International Women's Day by the International Socialist Conference in 1910, upon the initiative of Clara Zetkin, the heroic German Communist leader, who later electrified the world with her brave denunciation of the Nazis in Hitler's Reichstag in 1933. Already in 1907, Lenin demanded that the woman question be specifically mentioned in Socialist programme because of the special problems, needs and demands of toiling women. Present at the 1910 conference as a representative of the Russian Social-Democratic Labour Party, Lenin strongly supported and urged adoption of the resolution inaugurating International Women's Day. Thus did the American-initiated March 8 become International Women's Day.

The opportunist degeneration of the leadership of the Second International inevitably reduced the struggle for the emancipation of women to a paper resolution. Interested only in catching votes, the Socialist parties paid attention to the woman question only during elections.

Lenin and Stalin restored and further developed the revolutionary Marxist position on the woman question. Thus, Stalin declared:

> There has not been a single great movement of the oppressed in history in which working women have not played a part. Working women, who are the most oppressed of all the oppressed, have never stood aloof, and could not stand aloof, from the great match of emancipation.
>
> (*Joseph Stalin: A Political Biography*, p. 65)

Lenin and Stalin taught that the position of working women in capitalist society as "the most oppressed of all the oppressed" makes them more than a reserve, makes them a full-fledged part, of the "regular army" of the proletariat Stalin wrote:

> ... The female industrial workers and peasants constitute one of the biggest reserves of the working class ... Whether this female reserve goes with the working class or against it will determine the fate of the proletarian movement ... The first task of the proletariat and of its vanguard, the Communist Party, therefore, is to wage a resolute struggle to wrest women, the women workers and peasants, from the influence of the bourgeoisie, politically to educate and to organize the women workers and peasants under the banner of the proletariat ... But working women ... are something more than a reserve. They may and should become ... a regular army of the working class ... fighting shoulder to shoulder with the great army of the proletariat...
>
> (Stalin, *ibid.*)

Women Under Socialism

Complete emancipation of women is possible only under Socialism. It was only with the October Socialist Revolution that, for the first time in history, women were fully emancipated and guaranteed their full social equality in every phase of life.

Women in the USSR are accorded equal rights with men in all spheres of economic, state, cultural, social and political life (New Soviet Constitution, Article 122).

But equal rights in the USSR are not just formal legal rights, which, under bourgeois democracy, are curtailed, where not denied in reality by the very nature of capitalist exploitation. In the Soviet Union, full enjoyment of equal rights by women is *guaranteed* by the very nature of the Socialist society, in which class divisions and human exploitation are abolished. In bourgeois democracies, equal rights for women constitute at best a programmatic demand to be fought for, and constant struggle is necessary to defend even those rights that are enacted into law.

In the USSR equal-rights articles in the law of the land are but codifications of already existing and guaranteed reality. No wonder Soviet women express such supreme confidence in Socialism and such love for the people. Their respect for other nations, their profound sympathy with the oppressed peoples fighting for national liberation, is based on the firm conviction that their Socialist country is the decisive factor and leader in the struggle for peace

Marxism-Leninism rejects as fallacious all petty-bourgeois equalitarian notions. Equal rights under Socialism do not mean that women do not have special protection and social care necessitated by their special function (child bearing, etc.) and special needs which do not apply to men.

Party Tasks

Following Comrade Foster's article in *Political Affairs*, nine Party Conferences on Work Among Women were held with the active participation of district Party leaders. Two major regional schools to train women cadres were held. An all-day conference on Marxism-Leninism and the Woman Question held at the Jefferson School of Social Science last summer was attended by 600 women and men. These developments evidence a thirst for knowledge on Marxist-Leninist teachings on the woman question.

But it must be frankly stated that it is necessary to combat all and sundry male supremacist ideas still pervading the labour and progressive movements and our Party. The uprooting of this ideology, which emanates from the ruling class and is sustained by centuries of myths pertaining to the "biological inferiority" of women, requires a sustained struggle. Failure to recognize the special social disabilities of women under capitalism is one of the chief manifestations of male supremacy. These special forms of oppression particularly affect the working women, the farm women and the triply oppressed Negro women, – but, in varying degrees, they help to determine the inferior status of women in all classes of society.

Progressive and Communist men must become vanguard fighters against male supremacist ideas and for equal rights for women. Too often we observe in the expression and practice of labour-progressive, and even some Communist men glib talk about women "as allies" but no commensurate effort to combat male supremacy notions which hamper woman's ability to struggle for peace and security. Too many labour-progressive men, not excluding some Communists, resist the full participation of women, avow bourgeois "equalitarian" notions as regards women, tend to avoid full discussion of the woman question and shunt the problem aside with peremptory decisions. What the promotion of a sound theoretical understanding of this question would achieve for our Party is shown by the initial results of the cadre training schools and seminars on the woman question, many of whose students have begun seriously to tackle male supremacist notions in relation to the major tasks of the movement and in relation to their own attitudes.

The manifestation of bourgeois feminism in the progressive women's movement and also in our Party is a direct result of the prevalence of male superiority ideas and shows the need for our women comrades to study the Marxist-Leninist teachings on the woman question. According to bourgeois feminism, woman's oppression stems, not from the capitalist system, but from men. Marxism-Leninism, just as it rejects and combats the petty-bourgeois "equalitarianism" fostered by Social-Democracy, so it has nothing in common with the bourgeois idiocy of "the battle of the sexes" or the irrational Freudian "approach" to the woman question. These false ideologies must be combated by women labour-progressives and in the first place by women Communists. Key participants in the fight against these ideologies, and in the fight to enlist the masses of women for the pro-peace struggle, must be the advanced trade-union women and women Communists on all levels of Party leadership. All Communist women must, as Lenin said, "themselves become part of the mass movement," taking responsibility for the liberation of women.

We must guarantee that women cadres end isolation from the masses women, by assigning these cadres to tasks of work among women, on a mass and Party basis. The Women's Commissions of the Party must be strengthened. A Party departments and Commissions must deal more consistently with these questions, putting an end to the false concept that work among women represents "second-class citizenship" in our Party. A key responsibility of a Women's Commissions is increased attention and support to the growing movements of youth.

We must gauge our Party's work among women by our effectiveness in giving leadership and guidance to out cadres in mass work, with a view to concentrating among working class women and building the Party. To this end, further, working class and Negro women forces need to be promoted in all spheres of Party work and mass activity.

An examination of our work among women is necessary in all Party districts. There is need of Party conferences on the problems of working women and housewives. The good beginnings of examining the long neglected problems of Negro women must become an integral part of all our future work among women. This arises as an imperative task in the light of the militancy and tenacity of Negro women participating in struggles on all fronts.

Experience shows that a major area of our work should and must be in the field of education, where monopoly reaction and the Roman Catholic hierarchy concentrate in a policy of inculcating militarist, racist, pro-fascist ideology in the minds of our children, of victimizing progressive teachers, of conducting witch-hunts, etc. Where good work has been carried on in this sphere, victories have been won, as in the defeat of reactionary legislative measures directed at progressive teachers. In developing struggles to alleviate the frightful conditions of schooling, particularly in Negro, Puerto Rican, Mexican and other working class communities, Communist and progressive women have an important task to perform and an opportunity for developing an exceedingly broad united front for successful endeavor.

By connecting the struggle against the seemingly little issues of crowded schoolrooms, unsanitary conditions, lack of child care facilities, etc., with the issues of reactionary content of teaching—racism, jingoism, etc.—the political consciousness of the parent masses can be raised to the understanding of the interconnection between the demand for lunch for a hungry child and the demand of the people for economic security, between the campaign for the dismissal of a Negro-hating, anti-Semitic Mae Quinn from the school system and the fight of the people for democratic rights, between the protest against a jingoistic school text and the broad fight of the people for peace.

In keeping with the spirit of International Women's Day, tremendous tasks fall upon our Party. The mobilization of the masses of Americans, together with the enlisting and activation of women cadres, for heightened struggles for peace and for the special needs of oppressed womanhood, in indispensable to the building and strengthening of the anti-fascist, anti-imperialist, anti-war coalition. In working for a stronger peace movement among the women as such, we much draw the masses of women into the impending 1950 election campaign and thereby, on the basis of their experiences in the struggle, help raise their political consciousness to the understanding of the bipartisan demagogy and the hollowness of Truman's tall promises. Large masses of women can thus be brought to a full break with the two-party system of monopoly capital and to adherence to the third-party movement. In the course of this development, with our Party performing its vanguard task, advanced sections among the working class women will attain the level of Socialist consciousness and will, as recruited Communists, carry on their struggle among the broad masses of women upon the scientific conviction that the final guarantee of peace, bread and freedom, and the full emancipation of subjected womankind, will be achieved only in a Socialist America.

Note

1. The Scottsboro Nine refers to a group of nine young Black boys who, on March 25, 1935, were arrested originally for assault after getting into an altercation with White men aboard a train. They were subsequently charged with the rape of two White women, Victoria Price and Ruby Bates, who had also been on the train. The incident became a media frenzy; a lynch mob formed outside the Scottsboro jail in Alabama. On March 30 a grand jury indicted all nine boys on the word of the two women. By April 7 two of the boys, Clarence Norris and Charlie Weems, were tried, found guilty, and ultimately sentenced to death. The next day Haywood Patterson also met the same fate. By April 9 Olen Montgomery, Ozie Powell, Willie Roberson, Eugene Williams, and Andy Wright were all also convicted and sentenced to death. Only one of the boys, Roy Wright, who was thirteen years old, escaped the death sentence; his trial ended in a hung jury. The case drew attention from activists who protested the outcome of the case. Many were outraged at how quickly the cases were tried and that such young boys were being sentenced to death constituted cruel and unusual punishment, a clear violation of the Eighth Amendment. These protests led to a stay in the executions of the eight young men. Despite the recantation of Ruby Bates, the Alabama Supreme Court upheld their convictions. However, the court did give Eugene Williams a new trial because he was so young at the time of prosecution. The U.S. Supreme Court granted the remaining boys a new trial because they were denied counsel during their speedy trials. The new trials and subsequent battles went on for years. The Scottsboro Defense Committee was formed in December 1935. However, again, despite testimony from Bates that neither her or Price had been raped, in the end, in 1936 Patterson was found guilty and sentenced to seventy-five years in prison. Clarence Norris was sentenced to death. Andy Wright received ninety-nine years. Charley Weems was convicted again and sentenced to seventy-five years. Ozie Powell received twenty years on the original assault charges but the rape charges against him were dropped. Finally, the rape charges against Montgomery, Roberson, Williams, and Roy Wright were dropped. This case was one of the greatest miscarriages of justice in American history and vividly demonstrated the degree to which racism was embedded in our justice system.

21.
FLORYNCE "FLO" KENNEDY

Florynce "Flo" Kennedy (1916–2000) was an outspoken activist for the rights of African Americans, women, sex workers, and members of the LGBT community. Robert Abrams, Borough President of the Bronx in 1976, in an interview with Kennedy, said:

> Flo Kennedy has been described as one of the loudest, rudest, and most audacious people you can find anywhere. Yet while that may be true, I see to find her one of the softest, kindest people I know. So I guess she is an absolutely irrepressible and incongruous person. People who may be meeting her for the first time will get to know what I am talking about.[1]

In the mid-1950s Kennedy became involved with the Young Democrats but she found them to be organized and run bureaucratically and strategically passive. She also worked with the organization Young Activists Now. Kennedy graduated from Columbia Law School and represented artists such as Billie Holiday. Along with TAN she helped successfully protest Atlantic and Columbia Records. They organized pickets where they smashed records. Their efforts were to get these major record labels to hire more Black and Puerto Rican young people. In 1966 she founded the Media Workshop and was a lead organizer behind many protests of radio and media corporations.

Kennedy was a dedicated activist throughout her life. She worked with the Coalition against Racism and Sexism. In 1966 she organized a trip from New York to Maryland in which they were protesting the arrest of H. Rap Brown, who like Seale had been charged with attempting to start a riot. She attended anti-war conferences, Black political caucuses meetings, and all four Black Power conferences. She was frequently invited to give speeches about Black Power and racism, feminism, gay rights, and sex workers' rights.

Although some inaccurately credit Kennedy with assisting in the foundation of the National Organization of Women (NOW), she did work extensively with the organization until she, along with another radical activist, Ti-Grace Atkinson, left. In November of 1971 she founded the Feminist Party. She found NOW and its members timid and passive. She felt they refused to speak out aggressively against war, for the rights of lesbians, and prostitutes. In fact, in her autobiography she called them "retarded." Kennedy on the other hand was known for being outspoken and charismatic. She often dressed in outlandish clothing and frequently utilized obscenities.

In 1972 Kennedy was arrested for her involvement in the Women against Richard Nixon demonstration. She was forcefully knocked down by police officers during her arrest. Despite charges being dropped she still brought suit against the police department, specifically Sergeant Rooney, who as a result was censured for his actions. She never stopped her crusades against the media. In 1973 in her usual outlandish style, Kennedy and protestors gave out "toilet paper awards" made of toilet paper to what she called "pigocrats in the media," media moguls who produced racist, sexist, and mind-numbing programming aimed at maintaining the status quo. In 1975 she organized the March against Media Arrogance. Kennedy never wavered on her commitment to social justice.

Overview of Ideas

Florynce "Flo" Kennedy was one of the most radical women of her generation. She took the tone of the Black Panthers and amplified it. Kennedy successfully integrated feminism into the Black Power movement. She argued that both Black people and women were oppressed and were exploited in similar ways. Kennedy posited that both groups were exploited in the marketplace; they were both subject to inferior wages, inferior conditions of labor, and were both treated as expendable commodities. Women and Black men were estranged and alienated from one another; instead of recognizing their common oppressor, their capitalist employers, they competed, seeing the other as their problem. She posited that both groups were similarly marginalized from other social institutions. Blacks and women were marginalized from politics. Both groups needed better access to education, healthcare, and housing. Both groups had their sexuality policed. Stereotypes of Black people and women were rampant in the media. Both were trapped by these stereotypes that said women needed to know their place, in the kitchen and nursery, and at the same time also said that Black people, too, needed to know their place. While activists from both camps tended to ignore one another or worse yet focused on their differences, Kennedy promulgated that it was imperative to focus on their similarities and join forces in struggle. Kennedy was intent on exposing the "divide and conquer" strategy utilized by the government and capitalists. For instance, Kennedy wrote about Jews and Blacks; she felt it was unfortunate that these two widely oppressed groups were pitted against one another, instead of unifying in struggle.

As noted by previous Black Nationalists, the domination of the oppressed requires their compliance. Kennedy forced people to question hegemony or to question why the oppressed would participate in their own oppression. She called this the pathology of the oppressed. "It should be noted, from the jump, that there can be no really pervasive system of oppression, such as that in the United States, without the consent of the oppressed." Women, for example, often submitted quietly to their roles as dishwashers and wet nurses. They did not have to be forced and even if they had no maternal calling they assumed an unwanted role as mother. Kennedy calls this role the BPBP—barefoot, pregnant and behind the plow. Women often consented to exploitation in the labor market. They accepted the jobs offered to them as nuns and nurses, even if they were not the jobs they'd enjoy. Women submitted to oppression by their own husbands. For example, sexism de facto still required their husbands to get housing. Women needed to fight against their continued treatment as chattel rather than falling into acquiescence.

Kennedy did not just reserve her criticisms for the government and societal institutions. She critiqued other movements and activists. She saw mainstream civil rights activists as pacifists just like Black Nationalists. She said civil rights activists such as Bayard Rustin still defended "pig establishments." Martin Luther King Jr., who was also part of what she called the "nigger nobility," preached non-violence. She, like Black Nationalists and Black Power advocates, argued that this turn-the-other-cheek approach was too passive and not useful. In fact, she said it is like, "eating shit and calling it chocolate." You cannot allow the government and its militia who enforces their "pigocratic values" to brutalize you. You must fight back.

Kennedy, who staunchly defended women's reproductive freedoms, took on Black Nationalists, specifically the Black Panthers. Because many Black Nationalists saw abortion as a means by which to covertly commit Black genocide they did not support abortion and birth control campaigns. According to Kennedy, giving young Black women access to abortion would allow them to go on and finish school instead of dropping out. An abortion would allow more women to become revolutionaries because they would be free to join progressive movements. Kennedy argued that many Black Nationalists' opposition to abortion was evidence of male chauvinism. They still also held steadfastly to the hegemonic idea that women were best suited for motherhood. Finally, she convincingly argued that Black Nationalists wanted self-sufficiency and independence; they wanted far less government interference in the lives of black people. By allowing the government to tell women what they could or could not do with their bodies, she asked, wasn't that a violation of the basic tenets of their struggle? However, Kennedy did recognize that the issue of race played a role in shaping the debate over abortion.

Kennedy criticized the dominant women's movement. She questioned the notion of sisterhood. Merely being a woman did not make you a comrade. Kennedy saw the middle class dominated women's movement as passive; they adhered to a culturally conservative logic. In fact, as a proponent of the rights of sex workers, she saw the mainstream movement as sexually repressed. Mainstream feminists rebuked sex workers from the movement and why? These were women who often made more money than most women engaged in a behavior that allowed them autonomy and agency over their own bodies. Housewives sold their bodies. Local governments worried about prostitution instead of grappling with much larger problems. This type of tactic is a distraction from truly detrimental problems facing our society.

Accentuating the Similarities of the Societal Position of Women and Negroes, 1946

Editing below is from her autobiography; this editing was not done by the author.

. . . The similarities of the societal positions of women and Negroes are fundamental rather than superficial. The obvious differences are accentuated by the fact that women are supposed to occupy a privileged position. No such pretense is usually made where the Negro is concerned, but a dispassionate consideration of the economic, sociological, historical, psychological, political, and even physiological aspects reveals some rather startling parallels.

The majority of both groups are generally dependent economically upon the dominant group. Great lengths are attained to insure these dependencies. The necessity for an F.E.P.C. (Fair Employment Practices Committee) in a "Democracy," and support clauses in divorce codes, which according to Hobhouse existed in pre-Christian societies, and which Monica Hunter, Naomi M. Griffen, Ruth Benedict, and Cora Du Bois refer to in their accounts of various primitive societies, may be accepted as proof of the excessive abuses prevalent.

More than any other aspect of culture, the economic factor determines cultural development and direction. The political and social implications of this fact are infinite. It is therefore of primary importance to examine carefully the means by which women as a group and Negroes as a group are rendered *hors de combat* by being deprived of economic equality and independence. The far-reaching effects of their economic incompetencies leave not the minutest detail of their lives unaffected.

Women and Negroes are less apt to be hired and more apt to be fired than a similarly equipped member of the currently dominant group. Exceptions are made for extraordinary competence or during emergencies such as wartime or political revolutions. Both women and Negroes command lower wages, and are usually confined to lower-bracket positions.

In times of economic stress working women and Negroes arouse the resentment of those of the dominant group who are unemployed. Thus a returned serviceman may be especially upset to find his job occupied by a woman or Negro. Without entering into a which-came-first-the-chicken-or-the-egg argument, it seems sufficient to point out that rivalry for jobs provides a source of serious friction

Industry frequently adds insult to injury by exploiting the subordinate group to lower wage scales or break strikes. A dual purpose is served, since this divide-and-rule technique further alienates society from those women or Negroes thus exploited. It goes without saying that the disdain is directed not at the employer but at the tool.

Both groups are barred from many specialized fields. Prestige of a position tends to decline upon their entrance. The withholding of training and education precludes development of potentialities. Exclusion from intimate situations where powerful combines are made places a definite barrier in their path. Even those women or Negroes who have attained some prominence in a preferential field are only tolerated in exclusive clubs, at banquets, or on golf courses with equally distinguished members of the dominant group. In the isolated instances where such chummy relationships prevail, the adoption of patronage and subtle condescension saves the day for the dominants.

The preeminence of those exceptionals among the weaker group is paradoxically viewed. Many conflicting theories and rationalizations are encountered: "Determination will win" ... "The majority (e.g. of women or Negroes) are inferior; these are the exceptions that prove the rule" ... (bosh) ... "This woman has a masculine mind" ... or ... "This Negro has 'white' blood" ... what "Negro" hasn't? "Women are getting all the best jobs" ... "Negroes are 'taking over' the theatre" ...

This magnifying of hard-won advancement makes it seem that a weak gnarled tree that pushes through the concrete in Brooklyn is a threat to miles of centuries-old forests which have flourished in fertile lands where the best of expert care has been lavished.

How are subordinate groups kept in subordination? Is their suppression a reflection of the will of all of the dominants? Do those who are submerged struggle to reach the level of their "betters"? If not, why not? How, if at all, are the submerged groups rewarded? How punished? Why do not the "superiors" crush them entirely? Women are much loved; Negroes are generally ignored, distrusted, pitied, or even disliked; do not these differences make any attempt to draw parallels seem a bit ridiculous?...

The psychological implications are vastly important in any consideration of personal-social relationships. The geographical, temperamental, financial, political, social, psychological, physiological, and historical are but a few of the most abstract factors which enter into every formula. For example: a customer is asking for a pound of butter... Alabama or New York?... Humbly or peremptorily?... Mink coat or Union Square special?... New Deal and O.P.A. or Republicans and "free enterprise"?... Does the butcher read *P.M.* or the *Daily News*? Is he young or old?... a Coughlin-Bilbo fan or Henry Wallace devotee?... All generalizations ignore these variables...

Social sanctions take many forms. There are written laws governing franchise, property, political participation, and legal articulation. Social legislation reflects the comparative insignificance of women and Negroes. Educational budgets and medical care for Negroes or women have long been unequal. In housing, Negro districts are invariably slumlike. The kitchen where the average housewife spends the majority of her time is often the least spacious, attractive, comfortable, or even practical room of the house. Overwork is the lot of most of the members of the subordinate groups. When their health suffers due to this insanitary environment, their poor health immediately becomes the "reason" for their exclusion from desirable endeavor or choice programs...

The unwritten laws are often more convenient and certainly more difficult to combat. Some are rational, most are nonrational or irrational. Many paradoxes and inconsistencies exist. There are great discrepancies between theory and practices.

Nonsupport cases belie the exaltation of motherhood so often heard. Societal penalties and punishments are more severe for sex "transgressions" by women or Negroes. Both are regarded as evil and dangerous. The Christian and other religious influences, and the white southerner, are but two sources from which such ideas have come. Overemphasis of the potency of women and Negroes in personal-societal relations serves to place an almost insurmountable barrier between these groups whenever it is advantageous. Sex taboos do not prevent miscegenation, but usually guarantee secrecy and therefore minimize the possibilities for legalized union and familial solidarity. There's no denying that sex drives are frequently far more democratic than contemporary societal pretense.

Paradoxically, criminal action by women or Negroes may be approached with extraordinary leniency; depending upon the offense, a paternal we-don't-expect-much-of-you attitude is frequently encountered. A Negro who cohabits with a white southern woman is almost certainly doomed to die; a Negro who kills another Negro in a brawl may be rescued by his white employer. In rare conformance with the theory that they are the weaker sex, women may receive preferential treatment in criminal courts.

Indeed, so numerous are the devices employed to delineate and emphasize the desired role that it is difficult to account for the many digressions that exist. Fiction and nonfiction, movies (with silly Billy Burke and groveling Ingrid Bergman, shuffling Stepin Fetchit, and Mammy Louise Beavers as "typical" women and Negroes), radio, drama, myths and legends, gossip and rumor, implication and innuendo leave little to the average imagination as to what is acceptable to "society."

A passive woman or Negro is presented with a ready-made role. Choice may be made from a wide range of conceptualizations which are considered ideal and/or average. Individual distinctions are minimized. Accomplishment outside circumscribed areas is discouraged.

Clothing is designed to accentuate the societal roles which have been chosen for the weaker group. Any concerted attempt to emulate or imitate the dominant group in dress is frowned upon—or laughed at. Women in slacks or a well-dressed Negro in a small southern town may be subjected to numerous embarrassments.

Religious participation is encouraged. Futile, blind alley endeavor is sponsored. Docility, forbearance, reticence, faithfulness, blind loyalty, silent suffering, acceptance of the *status quo*, and recognition of the divine right of the dominants are drama-tized and applauded by society. Eager for status, the subordinate group accepts the role assigned by the powers-that-be. *Hence comes the irony.*

The subordinates become the enthusiastic sponsors of the campaign for their own suppression!

Endless complexity results from the fact that the majority of a subordinate-group, though rejecting the ignominious position, will accept and popularize the devices through which the suppression is maintained...

Thus, the longer the history of an inferior position, the greater the necessity for a break with tradition. Little effort is required by either group to further the submergence of those chosen, once religion and the prescribed pattern are accepted. The program becomes self-perpetuating. The desire to be identified with the dominant group results in the least significant of the societal underlings' becoming the unpaid guardians and champions of their exploiters' theories.

Rewards for conformance are spurious or superficial. Security and independence for the entire group are never expected or offered without a death struggle. The inevi-tability of the societal position is accepted by many of the most militant opposers to inequality.

Reforms are usually much too little and centuries too late. Reforms are at best not the result of intellectual conviction but of emotional effort. The recognitions of rights are considered concessions; sentimental reasons are offered to explain long-overdue justices. Progress results from struggle. Little fundamental change can be cited. Superficial progress has been merely a shifting of emphasis rather than an alteration of balance. Progress has seemed to some extent related to societal advancement.

Women and Negroes are but two of hundreds of groups within groups which occupy subordinate positions.

Foremost authorities to the contrary notwithstanding, I am convinced that the glorification—without qualification—of family life militates against the achievement of full equality for women. It would be interesting to see how many marriages would result without the church, *True Stories*, Myrna Loy, sex myths, and the *Ladies' Home Journal*. It would be more interesting to see how many monogamous marriages would endure if polygamy were legalized and popularized, and children's support were guaranteed by the states.

If women weren't coaxed and lured from industry and professions by societal cupids, those who are unsuited to marriage and breeding could direct their energies into other channels. Without pleading a case for a doctrine of individualism, it would seem that a recognition of the infinite variations among women and Negroes will lessen the occurrence of the every-girl-should-marry, women's-place-is-in-the-home philosophy as well as the more diabolical but no less effective keep-the-Negro-in-his-place attitude. Few societies at any cultural level provide for an acceptance of an independent life for large numbers of unmarried women. Emancipation for women and Negroes would seem to be contingent upon the emancipation of societal thought. This is, of course, question-begging at its worst, since there remains to be solved the problem of how to revolutionize the theories and thinking of "civilized" society.

If a study of this type has any value, it lies in the possible counteraction to the divide-and-rule technique which minority dominants invariably employ. Recognition of the similarity of their position can hasten the formation of alliances to combat the forces which advocate the suppression of many for the aggrandizement of the few.

The continuation of conscious or unconscious subordination of one group by another will hasten the coarsening of the moral fibre [sic] of society. Psychological maladjustments result from the difficulty of reconciling pretense with practice. Personal-social behavior is cramped when societal sanctions and taboos are at too great variance with logic and humanitarian proclivities.

Societal impoverishment inevitably results from policies of discrimination, segregation, and limitation. That such policies are absolutely necessary disproves the much-publicized contention that women and/or Negroes are "naturally" inferior. Bitterness and societal unrest arise out of attempts to exclude women and Negroes from full participation in societal endeavor.

No amount of segregation separates one unit of society from society as a whole. Thus, general societal health is ever contingent upon the health of its least significant member.

Exclusivistic tendencies deprive society of innumerable skills and contributions. The dissatisfied minorities within the subordinate groups provide an ever-present threat to societal peace. Need it again be necessary to call the attention of those who defend the *status quo* to the fact that it has never been a question of whether or not a subordinate group is capable of self-rule and equal right, but rather whether or not any group is worthy of the right to dominance and autocracy?

Institutionalized Oppression vs. the Female, 1970[2]

People who have trouble accepting the thesis that women are an oppressed group might be somewhat placated by my theory of the *circularity of oppression*. It should be noted, from the jump, that there can be no really pervasive system of oppression, such as that in the United States, without the consent of the oppressed. People who have not withdrawn consent usually deny that they are oppressed. It follows. However, although the concept of circularity fails to suggest that some groups are far more restricted, segregated, boycotted, ostracized, and insulted than others, it does succeed in suggesting one reason for the uncomfortably solid basis for the male backlash.

Men are outraged, turned off, and wigged out, by threats that women might withdraw consent to oppression, because they—men—subconsciously (and often consciously) know that they—men—are oppressed. Women, as they loudly proclaim their rejection of further oppression, will arouse men to turn upon the established order. First, women will ignore or take care of the male backlash by any means necessary. In acknowledging their oppression, women will do well to reject their own roles in the hierarchy of institutionalized oppression.

At least one answer to the failure of any number of people, especially women, to accept as a fact the contention that women are oppressed, might lie in their experience of having been the victim of an oppressive woman, i.e., women being utilized as agents for oppressors.

Women are frequently oppressive in one-to-one situations. In those cases the oppressees tend to be their children, other family members, especially husbands, superintendents, or other domestic or nonpolitical public servants, e.g., waiters.

I see our society, however defined, as an excellent example of institutionalized oppression. *Where a system of oppression has become institutionalized it is unnecessary for individuals to be oppressive.* So it is that where Blacks are concerned (there we go again analogizing women and Black people; it's too perfect to ignore) whites can say, "But I never feel the slightest prejudice!" So, also, a man may say, "I'd hire a woman art director in a minute!"

Even if thousands of white male personnel directors made such declarations, such is the System that the overwhelming majority of art directors in major advertising agencies would be white and male. Just by nobody doing nothing the old bullshit mountain just grows and grows. Chocolate-covered, of course. We must take our little teaspoons and get to work. We can't wait for shovels.

It may be the church, the husband, the TV series, or a sister-in-law who persuades the pregnant woman that she should run for cover the second she dons a maternity dress. Surely the personnel director does not decree that she hover over the crib, the creeper, the crawler, and the cuddly until puberty. Women in their brainwashed consensual condition frequently act out their role of hovering mother without any noticeable pressure from anyone. Note "noticeable."

Dictates, from so many sources that you couldn't even count them, wind like soft cotton-candy fiberglass to bind the woman to the BPBP status—Barefoot-Pregnant-and-Behind-the-Plow. Although the BPBP status of peasant days now translates into various updated versions, there is little doubt that sex and the female ability to bear children is a frequent rationalization for ever so many of the (at least) fifty-seven varieties of rationale for oppressing women. What difference does it make whether the rationalizations arise from suspicion, tradition, or competition? It's women's job to put their power to work to slow it down or break it up.

Very usually consent to oppression is obtained by the issuance of a license to oppress. Since not all women seek a license to oppress, and since children are frequently the objects for women's oppression and not all women have access to children, consent is sometimes obtained through the ennoblement of suffering and sacrifice. Quite often, women consent to the system of oppression in exchange for a Vaseline-dispensing franchise. The franchise for dispensation of Vaseline is not wholly distinguishable from the honor of sacrifice and suffering, but has the added dimension of giving the female a superior status. She ministers to the suffering natives in her role as missionary, nun, or nurse, in exchange for which she suffers a second-class treatment from male missionaries, priests, or doctors. But she is so superior to the natives, novitiates, sinners, and bedridden that she glides serenely through the bullshit as if it were a field of daisies.

Magazine articles ponder the question of whether a wife can be a mother *and* a career woman. Never any problem being a *wife, hostess, chauffeur, gardener, cook, home typist, nurse, seamstress, social secretary, purchasing agent,* and/or *baby-manufacturing machine.* A woman may be discouraged from studying law. "The books are *so* heavy." But do they weigh more than a six-month-old baby? TV commercials reduce the female worth by depicting the young wife crying over sink spots and water marks on goblets. What will his mother say? Make a good pudding so's you'll be loved. Get a strong deodorant! Women get so excited, they smell! Poor dears.

Men are scarcely less peripheral and irrelevant in their day-to-day or weekend activities than women. They should be prepared to join with women to force society to liberate everybody from irrelevant, peripheral, societal bullshit. But for the foreseeable future some women will act as if getting in on the corruption is more desirable than ending it.

Freud was at his most fraudulent (forgive, I couldn't help it) when he talked about women's frustrations and hostility in terms of "penis envy." One would have thought that even the most pompous and fatuous of asses would have gathered that women were less interested in standing at urinals than in standing on an equal basis before the bar of justice! As with most, if not all, systems of injustice and institutionalized oppression, the law had a leading role in oppressing women. It still has.

Some considerable time ago, anachronistic laws depriving women of most, if not all, civil and property laws were rewritten or repealed. But try to rent an apartment without a husband's (or some man's) signature. I can't begin to tell how many times a woman, separated from her husband, had to get him to sign a lease or help her get a charge account. Brothers or fathers often have to co-sign or countersign auto loans or chattel mortgages. This comes as a superirony, when, as is occasionally the case, the woman in question earns more, or has a longer and/or more impressive work record.

As a rule, of course, the men, especially if they're white, do have the better jobs and the more impressive work record. That's because of sex bigotry, the buddy system, and various other below-the-belt Establishmentarian characteristics.

Women with really good jobs and connections are often kowtowed to, like the "Negro" who has "made it." Women who know what's good for them lapse into old role styles when they really need or desperately want something, like an apartment, or a part in a play, or a really cool job.

The kind of female who doesn't pull punches even to get an important Precious becomes known as strident, strong, a ball-breaker, or crazy. If they survive the ridicule, scarcasm, hostility, demotions, and demerits, such women frequently fare better than the pliables. But the casualty rate is high.

Survivors of the gamut often are among those most impatient with feminism or female liberation. They scrambled their way up and why can't anybody else? Such women are gleefully quoted by the Establishment, even as the "Uncles" Roy Wilkins and Bayard Rustin are widely quoted when they take Black activists to task or defend pig Establishmentarians.

I predict that the Harriet Van Hornes who sniff at such beautiful zaps as the 1968 women's liberation demonstration against the Miss America Pageant, or the hollow, bewigged, superchic Pamela Masons who seem so bright and brittle until they have to deal with the matter of women's liberation, will meet with less tolerance than the Uncle Toms and the white maggots who feed off the few edibles in the garbage dump that the civil rights "fight" turned out to be.

Just as the students bypassed some of the turn-the-other-cheek, beat-me-daddy-eight-to-the-bar bullshit that Black people grooved on, so, I predict, women will begin almost where the students left off, and *they* are starting more fires than get into the papers.

Some of the same reasons might account for the speed with which the women's movement will take off, once it taxies the field for a season or two. Students and women, unlike Black people, didn't see themselves as oppressed; therefore when they were niggerized they didn't respond with a shuffle and a "S'cuse me, boss." Of course, Black students are in the vanguard of the student movement. This, if my theory is right, is because they knew they were scheduled for oppression and withdrew their consent: "Hell, no, we won't go," "No Vietnamese ever called me Nigger," etc. So Black students were indeed not representative of the Black community, or the shit would have hit the fan a long time ago.

But women are doers, and dreamers, and activists by the nature of their permissible roles. They do most of the buying, most of the lying ("Honey, call them and say I have to see an out-of-town client on the weekend"; "Dear, say I have a virus"—Hangover Hal; "Say we'll send the rent in on Friday"; "Change the appointment 'til next week") and a major portion of the hassling: with the landlord, merchants, family, etc. Women are more ready than most for the liberation struggle. We have only to direct our hostility from the vertical *down* (the kids, the merchants, the family, co-workers, and other women), and from the horizontal—to the vertical *up*. According to my *modus operandi* this means systems and institutions less than people.

Kicking ass should be only where an ass is protecting the System. Ass-kicking should be undertaken regardless of the sex, the ethnicity, or the charm of the oppressor's agent. As the struggles intensify, the oppressor tends to select more attractive agents, frequently from among the oppressed.

It is for this reason that I have considerable difficulty with the sisterhood mystique: "We are all sisters," "Don't criticize a 'sister' publicly," etc. When a female judge asks my client where the bruises are when she complains about being assaulted by her husband (as did Family Court Judge Sylvia Jaffin Liese), and makes smart remarks about her being overweight, and when another female judge is so hostile that she disqualifies herself but refuses to order a combative husband out of the house (even though he owns property elsewhere with suitable living quarters)—these judges are not my sisters. And if the same pair of female Family Court judges concur in decisions to return a three-year-old child to her mother and stepfather only a few months before the child's body is recovered from the river and her stepfather accused of her death? (Foster parents had pleaded to keep the child and had pointed to the evidences of physical abuse, to no avail.) No, these judges are not my sisters. Such females, in my opinion, are agents of an oppressive System, which the Family represents without a doubt.

Every form of bigotry can be found in ample supply in the legal system of our country. It would seem that Justice (usually depicted as a woman) is indeed blind to racism, sexism, war, and poverty.

Dean Willis Reese, a lanky man who talks with a lisp in a shrill voice and walks with a switch, hastened to assure me that I was being refused admission to Columbia Law School in 1948 not because I was Black, but I because I was a woman. I leaned on the ethnic angle, saying that some of my more cynical friends thought I was being discriminated against because I was a Negro (we weren't saying "Black" in those days), and in any case it felt the same. Law school admissions opened the door just wide enough for *me*, but not for my friend Pat Jones, who was a Barnard graduate, with a slightly higher law aptitude level and slightly lower undergraduate average, but white.

Many senior partners, or hiring partners in Establishment law firms still have the nerve to say they don't normally hire women. Some, perhaps most, firms will accept a woman if she is in the upper percentile of her law school class. (So, also, they'll accept supersmart Jews.)

Of course, the law schools assist by screening out the women and the Blacks "from the gitgo." Nowadays the tokens have become a trickle. Much of the clash of Black students on campus and the predictable upcoming clashes involving women is due to the "expectancy gap" which prevails when a bigot decides to go straight. The crabgrass liberal-bigot anticipates a good sport, a dazzled recipient with damp hands and misty eyes near to overflowing with gratitude—but is confronted by a cool, if not coldly suspicious, potential foe—a creditor sullenly receiving a minuscule payment of an unconscionably late I.O.U. Black students now—and female students in seasons to come—will break up the bank.

Black Genocide, 1971

The overwhelmingly white Women's Liberation contingent was rather nonplussed by the failure of the Black community and the Third World people to join in on the struggle to repeal the New York State abortion laws. Outside the white community there was scarcely an audible rustle for or against reform, or repeal of laws or practices relating to abortion. In short, the Black community seemed preoccupied with other problems or totally uninvolved. To the extent that the views of the Black community were publicly expressed, they were almost always diametrically opposed to the ideas encountered in the eye of the storm for abortion repeal. On several radio programs Black men and women (and, in at least one case, people from the Muslim community) denounced abortion as racist genocide, directed at Black people.

Moreover, there was an immediate and emphatic response by the Black Panther party a few days after the new abortion law became effective. This response was reminiscent of the position taken at the Black Power Conference in 1967, in Newark, New Jersey, where there was a consensus that birth control and abortion were both forms of Black genocide. At that time there was a workshop on "Black women and the Home" from which a rather generally worded statement was issued:

> …Black women commit themselves to: a self-preservation and continuity through educating and exposing to our people the genocidal practices by racist societies."[3]

This resolution was predicated on considerable discussion in which it was very clear that the consensus was against contraception.

Some revolutionaries in the Black community take the position that Black revolutionary forces will be decimated by birth control and abortion. Dire predictions about "population explosions" or sudden offers of long-denied birth control information only serve to confirm well-founded suspicions of racist motives.

Many of the arguments emanating from the Black community have been set forth by Brenda Hyson in the July 4, 1970, issue of *The Black Panther*. This article is a well-articulated exposition of views held by many varied Black groups. Her article was directed at the abortion law passed by the New York State Legislature, effective July 1, 1970.

The *Panther* article took a dim view of the idea that the new law was a victory:

> "…Perhaps it is a victory for the white middle-class mother who wants to have a smaller family, thereby enabling her to have more material goods or more time to participate in whatever fancies her at the moment. But most of all it is a victory for the oppressive ruling class who will use this law to kill off Black and other oppressed people before they are born."

This *Panther* view was similar to that stated in the Manifesto from the 1967 National Conference on Black Power:

> "Black people who live under imperialist governments in America, Asia, Africa and Latin America stand at the cross-roads of either an expanding revolution or ruthless extermination. It is incumbent for us to get our own house in order to fully utilize the potentialities of the revolution or to resist our own execution."[4]

The *Panther* article also expressed an emotional and sentimental view of the Black family. Brenda Hyson labeled the true problem as capitalist greed:

"Black women love large families, and the only reason that they would want to eliminate them is to rid them of the pain and the agony of trying to survive. Why in a country where farmers like Eastland are given large sums of public funds to not grow food, where food is actually burned, must Black mothers kill their unborn children? So they won't go hungry? Absurd! Eliminating ourselves is not the solution to the hunger problem in America nor any other problem that could exist from a so-called unwanted pregnancy in the context of this capitalistic society. The solution lies in overthrowing this system and returning the means of production back to the people—REVOLUTION."

The specter of enforced abortions is almost upon us. Pregnant women in New York, prior to the new law, had sometimes been told that they could get an abortion only if they agreed to be sterilized. Women on welfare are sometimes threatened with being removed from the rolls if they have had a relationship with a man, let alone have another child. Cynicism about the new abortion law is related to cynicism about the law generally. As the Panther writer so well put it:

"The abortion law hides behind the guise of helping women, when in reality it will attempt to destroy our people. How long do you think it will take for voluntary abortion to turn into involuntary abortion, into compulsory sterilization? Black people are aware that laws made supposedly to ensure our well-being are often put into practice in such a way that they ensure our deaths. The current welfare laws are one of the classic examples."

Finally, the article strongly decried the poor health services available at hospitals and other treatment facilities, about which there can be no dispute.

Notable exceptions to those who equate abortion with Black genocide include Black women such as Florence Rice of the Harlem Consumer Education Council, Shirley Chisholm, first Black congresswoman, and the many Black women who contacted us for abortion information during the course of the case. Among them were several youngsters under sixteen. The *amicus* brief filed by Emily Goodman had as one of its signators Percy E. Sutton, Borough President of Manhattan and a former New York State assemblyman, who was one of the first sponsors of abortion law reform in the New York State Assembly.

In our opinion the Black genocide argument is subject to certain objections. Of girls who drop out of high school, a large proportion are from the Black or nonwhite communities and a major reason for leaving school is pregnancy, which competes with economics and boredom to motivate the dropout.

Black majorities in places like South Africa and Mississippi are not noticeably revolutionary. No evidence has come to our attention that mothers of large broods led the rebellions in Watts, Detroit, or Newark, although Mothers for Adequate Welfare in Roxbury precipitated the Boston rebellion with their sit-in.

Women hampered by children tend not to be in the vanguard, and male revolutionaries frequently abandon their children when the going gets rough. Perhaps the thought is that the parents will continue to consent to oppression, but will reproduce large numbers of children who will snatch them from the claws of the oppressors in their old age. This concept of breeding revolutionaries, rather then revolutions, is appropriate in a society where the old people do the voting and the youngsters do the fighting and dying. Breeding revolutions can be fatal, whereas breeding revolution-aries is not too far removed from a cultural past where Black women were encouraged to be breeding machines for their slave masters.

It might shock Black radicals to entertain the possibility that religious programming combined with certain of the slaver's social values, plus a soupçon of male chauvin-ism, account for the volume of the contention that a legalization of a women's right to terminate an unwanted pregnancy is Black genocide. In any case, Friends of the Fetus in the Black Community have permitted a number of potential revolutionaries to lan-guish in orphanages and foster homes, despite widely broadcast pleas for rescue (for revolutionary or whatever purpose).

If abortion or other forms of birth control are used by oppressors against a certain class of people, there might easily come a time when all women will have to fight against the imposition of abortions. Like any other problem, abortion must be approached openly and dialectically and not in a mechanistic manner. Enforced sterilization is not merely a nightmare of the future, since it has often been ordered in the case of welfare mothers, and has been used as well as a precondition for an abortion.

We favor the right of women. Black and white, to have the choice of deciding whether they wish to have babies. To the degree that Black people equate the repeal of abortion laws with compulsory sterilization, they obviously must oppose it. However, among the silent majority there would appear to be bleeding women in the emergency rooms of hospitals who could use the help of those who have been espousing the Black genocide theory.

A further irony in the Black genocide position is that here it is the opponents of governmental control of Black communities who urge the continuation of state inter-ference in the personal lives of Black people. It would seem more understandable for these anti-Establishmentarians to seek community control of such matters. This control might better result if abortion laws were repealed and free choice prevailed.

Nevertheless, the white women's movement must be careful not to use the Black women's plight to make their case for them. White women must let the Black move-ment formulate its own ideas and strategies in its own time and way.

That Black women are beginning to publicly oppose the Black genocide position is further evidenced by a recent article in *Black America*:

> "Don't call me sister if you can't call me wife. Dig it! This is not a catch phrase, or one of the ten top Black sayings of the week. This is a sentiment taking a strong hold on many sisters who are no longer willing to be the punch line of some brother's joke. The sisters say it and they mean business. No more fatherless Black babies, no more weeping Black unwed mothers. Sisters are firm in this stand, and they warn, 'Don't cry Black Genocide!'"[3]

Nobody Ever Died From a Blow Job, 1976

Talking about sexual recreation reminds me that a very average prostitute in almost any part of this country can get $100 a night minimum, or if she is fairly well-known she might make as much as $500. A run-of-the-mill file clerk nets about $100 a week, and a run-of-the-mill housewife will get zero a week for filing, fucking, ironing, having the baby, nursing the baby, baby-sitting, and the whole megillah. In my opinion, a government that cannot provide full employment for women who don't have degrees, and even those who do, has a pretty big nerve making the most lucrative occupation a crime. Recently, when I was lecturing in the Midwest, I talked to a young woman who was in law school and also worked in a massage parlor. She told me she was somewhat conflicted as to whether to bother finishing law school, because she was earning more in a massage parlor than she would after five years of law school. And she was serious. I have the feeling that if she continued at law school, it would be because society disapproves of people who work in massage parlors, and that if she continued to work there she might very soon need a lawyer herself to prevent her going to jail. I think that neither the feminists nor the church nor the government nor anybody else has the right to say to women that they cannot choose whichever endeavor, for whatever reason, is best suited to their lives.

Prostitutes are accused even by feminists of selling their bodies; but prostitutes don't sell their bodies, they rent their bodies. Housewives sell their bodies when they get married—they cannot take them back—and most courts do not regard the taking of a woman's body by her husband against her will as rape. And I am inclined to think that the right to get up and go home afterwards might almost be worth sleeping with strangers for money, instead of going out to work in a laundry, or carrying around some stranger's shit floating in a shallow pan of piss, as nurses do. Yet you rarely hear the church come down on nurses—in fact, it sponsors nurses. I'm sure there is no nurse who has been working in a hospital for more than a year who hasn't washed some strange man's ass, and I think that a whore might find fucking a stranger not too much less pleasant than that, or, even worse, getting crotch-grabbed by a patient.

Now, even when I was young I wasn't good-looking, so I was never confronted with the possibility of becoming a prostitute, and I am not suggesting that I want my child or my sister or even my feminist friends all to become prostitutes. But I just don't see that women have such fascinating jobs, for the most part, that a job that pays ten times as much as most others should be outlawed.

Society's concern to eliminate prostitution from the scene is very political, in my opinion. In Boston during the World Series there was a kind of sweep of the "Combat Zone," the area where the prostitutes are. And in New York before a major convention like the 1976 Democratic Convention, you always have our brilliant municipal officials running around talking about "cleaning up" this or that erogenous zone—in this case, Times Square. And the mayor, the corrupt police, and the "good people" form an almost solid phalanx between the whores and those of us who think the city has better things to do than chase whores. Instead of worrying about the massage parlors, why doesn't the government think about cleaning up Times Square by getting rid of tobacco and alcohol? There's a billboard, which dominates the whole area, of a man blowing smoke out over Times Square to encourage people to smoke, but tobacco kills 52,000 people a year from lung cancer, and there's no telling how many lives have been ruined through drinking. But to my knowledge, no one has ever died of a blow job, except, Margo St. James tells me, a whore who choked to death recently on the West Coast, and a few men who have died of heart attacks—but what better way to go, if that's how you get your jollies?

Notes

1. Kennedy, Flo. 1976. *Color Me Flo: My Hard Life and Good Times*. New Jersey: Prentice-Hall, p. 109.
2. Resolution from the National Conference on Black Power. These resolutions represented the distillation of the first major national dialogue by 1,300 Black Americans on the creative possibilities inherent in the concept of Black Power. There were a great number of resolutions from the seventeen workshops—at which there were delegates from 39 states, Bermuda, and 190 organizations.
3. Carolyn Jones, "Abortion and Black Women," *Black America*, Vol. 1, No. 5, September 1970.

22.
SHIRLEY CHISHOLM

Shirley Chisholm (1924–2005) devoted her life to fighting for the subaltern, including the poor, Black people, minorities of various other ethnic groups, farm workers, and women. In the early 1960s Chisholm was an advocate for quality education and focused on early intervention as an educational consultant for the New York City Bureau of Child Welfare. She was a first-class activist; she worked within the Brooklyn, New York Democratic Party, the Bedford-Stuyvesant Political League, the League of Women Voters, and the National Organization of Women. However, her grassroots activism eventually led her into electoral politics. In 1964 she was voted into the New York State Assembly and in her most extraordinary accomplishment, Chisholm became the first African American women seated in Congress in 1968.

Never the meek woman, like her counterparts in this section, despite being a freshman congressperson, Chisholm was outspoken from the minute she arrived. Her campaign slogan had been "unbought and unbossed" and she was determined to let her actions buttress her campaign slogan. From the outset she proclaimed to her fellow congresspersons that she was going to vote no on all bills that appropriated funding for the Department of Defense instead of funding education and anti-poverty programs. She vehemently opposed the war in Vietnam. While in Congress she served on the Agriculture Committee, Veterans' Affairs Committee, and the Education and Labor Committees. With her feet firmly planted in Washington politics she went on to become a founder of the National Women's Political Caucus and the Congressional Black Caucus. As a powerful player in these committees Chisholm, along with John Conyers after years of struggle, were able to get Congress to pass the measure making Martin Luther King Jr.'s birthday a national holiday. In another great milestone, in 1972 Chisholm campaigned for President of the United States on the Democratic ticket. Although, she did not even come close to winning the primary, she was a seven-term congressperson who demonstrated through both word and deed that Black women were powerful. Even after she retired in 1982, she did not stop fighting for the rights of marginalized Americans. From 1984 to 1992 she served as the chairwoman for the National Political Congress of Black Women.

Overview of Ideas

Chisholm was a staunch advocate for the rights of the poor and oppressed minorities, including Haitian immigrants, Native Americans, Hispanics, African Americans, and women just to name a few. Because of her political position and aspirations she was not always able to engage the vitriolic vernacular of her counterparts but the battles she waged for justice were just as fierce and uncompromising. However, because of her political position, she was able to be a pioneer. She was not just a pioneer because she was the first African American woman to be elected to Congress; she was a pioneer because she was one of the first women to bring feminism onto the Capitol building's congressional floor.

Chisholm recognized that there is a matrix of oppression at work in the United States and that race, class, and gender conditioned an individual's experiences in our society. In politics and in the economy women were incessantly treated as inferior and were fettered to discourses that had them bound to feminine labor and perpetually cast as intellectually inferior emotional housemaids. Due in large part to the Civil Rights Movement, the United States was beginning to confront its racial schisms and racial inequalities. She said racism was starting to be seen by many as unacceptable. However, sexism was not just tolerated but it was acceptable. In order to address society's rampant sexism, particularly as it manifested itself in basic social institutions: economy, government, education, etc., there was a remedy; it was the Equal Rights Amendment.

Women did not require protection; they required laws to guarantee equal rights. "What we need are laws to protect working people, to guarantee them fair pay, safe working conditions, protection against sickness and layoffs, and provision for dignified, comfortable retirement. Men and women need these things equally." Chisholm recognized that enacting new laws would not change the hearts and minds of all Americans and sexism de facto would surely still persist. However, these laws would certainly ensure equality in the labor market and other vital institutions. Chisholm's emphasis on electoral politics and legal reform distinguish her from her counterparts. Readers should decide if her methods make her more moderate than Flo Kennedy who advocated constant direct action protest and Angela Davis who advocated revolutionary protest.

Along with her emphasis on sexism came an astute attention to the insidious ways in which racism conditioned sexism. Like her counterparts she was quite critical of the second wave women's movement and its platform. "The black woman cannot be discussed in the same context as her Caucasian counterpart because of the twin jeopardy of race and sex which operates against her, and the psychological and political consequences which attend them." She argued that the movement's leaders often neglected the bread-and-butter issues of Black women in favor of bourgeois issues such as utilizing Ms. instead of Mrs. Many White feminists may have neglected that while they were finding jobs as secretaries and teachers (while confined to feminine labor), they were not being relegated to dirty service work the way Black women still were. And while women made less than their male counterparts for the same work, Black women made substantially less than them. Moreover, just as the women's movement neglected the issues of Black women, so did the Black liberation movement. She also astutely noted that the disunity between Black men and women were deleterious and only served the status quo.

Like her Black radical feminist counterparts she was critical of capitalism. Although not as outspoken against the system itself as her counterparts, she was quite vocal about the degree to which hired lobbyists and representatives of capital had been able to buy votes in Washington and rig the political game. When she ran for president she declared that she would never act in the interests of the bourgeoisie but only in the interests of her constituents. The political savvy, Black radical feminist made sure to tell Americans that while she did not want to just be seen as the "Black candidate" she was proud to be both Black and a women. While certainly not as radical as Black Nationalism, she still shared with Black Power activists a commitment to unifying oppressed groups in the struggle for employment, quality housing, access to health-care, access to quality education and free day care, and other social services. Moreover, like Black Nationalists she appealed to the youth and urbanites and not just to middle and upper class constituencies with money for campaign donations. Not your average politician, Shirley Chisholm brought Black radical feminism to Washington.

Equal Rights For Women, 1969

Address To The United States House Of Representatives, Washington, DC: May 21, 1969

Mr. Speaker, when a young woman graduates from college and starts looking for a job, she is likely to have a frustrating and even demeaning experience ahead of her. If she walks into an office for an interview, the first question she will be asked is, "Do you type?"

There is a calculated system of prejudice that lies unspoken behind that question. Why is it acceptable for women to be secretaries, librarians, and teachers, but totally unacceptable for them to be managers, administrators, doctors, lawyers, and Members of Congress.

The unspoken assumption is that women are different. They do not have executive ability orderly minds, stability, leadership skills, and they are too emotional.

It has been observed before, that society for a long time, discriminated against another minority, the blacks, on the same basis—that they were different and inferior. The happy little homemaker and the contented "old darkey" on the plantation were both produced by prejudice.

As a black person, I am no stranger to race prejudice. But the truth is that in the political world I have been far oftener discriminated against because I am a woman than because I am black.

Prejudice against blacks is becoming unacceptable although it will take years to elim-inate it. But it is doomed because, slowly, white America is beginning to admit that it exists. Prejudice against women is still acceptable. There is very little understanding yet of the immorality involved in double pay scales and the classification of most of the better jobs as "for men only."

More than half of the population of the United States is female. But women occupy only 2 percent of the managerial positions. They have not even reached the level of tokenism yet No women sit on the AFL-CIO council or Supreme Court There have been only two women who have held Cabinet rank, and at present there are none. Only two women now hold ambassadorial rank in the diplomatic corps. In Congress, we are down to one Senator and 10 Representatives.

Considering that there are about 3 1/2 million more women in the United States than men, this situation is outrageous.

It is true that part of the problem has been that women have not been aggressive in demanding their rights. This was also true of the black population for many years. They submitted to oppression and even cooperated with it. Women have done the same thing. But now there is an awareness of this situation particularly among the younger segment of the population.

As in the field of equal rights for blacks, Spanish-Americans, the Indians, and other groups, laws will not change such deep-seated problems overnight. But they can be used to provide protection for those who are most abused, and to begin the process of evolutionary change by compelling the insensitive majority to reexamine it's unconscious attitudes.

It is for this reason that I wish to introduce today a proposal that has been before every Congress for the last 40 years and that sooner or later must become part of the basic law of the land—the equal rights amendment.

Let me note and try to refute two of the commonest arguments that are offered against this amendment. One is that women are already protected under the law and do not need legislation. Existing laws are not adequate to secure equal rights for women. Sufficient proof of this is the concentration of women in lower paying, menial, unrewarding jobs and their incredible scarcity in the upper level jobs. If women are already equal, why is it such an event whenever one happens to be elected to Congress?

It is obvious that discrimination exists. Women do not have the opportunities that men do. And women that do not conform to the system, who try to break with the accepted patterns, are stigmatized as "odd" and "unfeminine." The fact is that a woman who aspires to be chairman of the board, or a Member of the House, does so for exactly the same reasons as any man. Basically, these are that she thinks she can do the job and she wants to try.

A second argument often heard against the equal rights amendment is that it would eliminate legislation that many States and the Federal Government have enacted giving special protection to women and that it would throw the marriage and divorce laws into chaos.

As for the marriage laws, they are due for a sweeping reform, and an excellent beginning would be to wipe the existing ones off the books. Regarding special protection for working women, I cannot understand why it should be needed. Women need no protection that men do not need. What we need are laws to protect working people, to guarantee them fair pay, safe working conditions, protection against sickness and layoffs, and provision for dignified, comfortable retirement. Men and women need these things equally. That one sex needs protection more than the other is a male supremacist myth as ridiculous and unworthy of respect as the white supremacist myths that society is trying to cure itself of at this time.

Speech in Favor of the Equal Rights Amendment, 1970

Mr. Speaker, House Joint Resolution 264, before us today, which provides for equality under the law for both men and women, represents one of the most clear-cut opportunities we are likely to have to declare our faith in the principles that shaped our Constitution. It provides a legal basis for attack on the most subtle, most pervasive, and most institutionalized form of prejudice that exists. Discrimination against women, solely on the basis of their sex, is so widespread that is seems to many persons normal, natural and right.

Legal expression of prejudice on the grounds of religious or political belief has become a minor problem in our society. Prejudice on the basis of race is, at least, under systematic attack. There is reason for optimism that it will start to die with the present, older generation. It is time we act to assure full equality of opportunity to those citizens who, although in a majority, suffer the restrictions that are commonly imposed on minorities, to women.

The argument that this amendment will not solve the problem of sex discrimination is not relevant. If the argument were used against a civil rights bill, as it has been used in the past, the prejudice that lies behind it would be embarrassing. Of course laws will not eliminate prejudice from the hearts of human beings. But that is no reason to allow prejudice to continue to be enshrined in our laws—to perpetuate injustice through inaction.

The amendment is necessary to clarify countless ambiguities and inconsistencies in our legal system. For instance, the Constitution guarantees due process of law, in the 5th and 14th amendments. But the applicability of due process of sex distinctions is not clear. Women are excluded from some State colleges and universities. In some States, restrictions are placed on a married woman who engages in an independent business. Women may not be chosen for some juries. Women even receive heavier criminal penalties than men who commit the same crime. What would the legal effects of the equal rights amendment really be? The equal rights amendment would govern only the relationship between the State and its citizens—not relationships between private citizens. The amendment would be largely self-executing, that is, and Federal or State laws in conflict would be ineffective one year after date of ratification without further action by the Congress or State legislatures.

Opponents of the amendment claim its ratification would throw the law into a state of confusion and would result in much litigation to establish its meaning. This objection overlooks the influence of legislative history in determining intent and the recent activities of many groups preparing for legislative changes in this direction.

State labor laws applying only to women, such as those limiting hours of work and weights to be lifted would become inoperative unless the legislature amended them to apply to men. As of early 1970 most States would have some laws that would be affected. However, changes are being made so rapidly as a result of title VII of the Civil Rights Act of 1964, it is likely that by the time the equal rights amendment would become effective; no confliction State laws would remain.

In any event, there has for years been great controversy as to the usefulness to women of these State labor laws. There has never been any doubt that they worked a hardship on women who need or want to work overtime and on women who need or want better paying jobs, and there has been no persuasive evidence as to how many women benefit from the archaic policy of the laws. After the Delaware hours law was repealed in 1966, there were no complaints from women to any of the State agencies that might have been approached.

Jury service laws not making women equally liable for jury service would have been revised. The selective service law would have to include women, but women would not be required to serve in the Armed Forces where they are not fitted any more than men are required to serve. Military service, while a great responsibility, is not without benefits, particularly for young men with limited education or training.

Since October 1966, 246,000 young men who did not meet the normal mental or physical requirements have been given opportunities for training and correcting physical problems. This opportunity is not open to their sisters. Only girls who have completed high school and meet high standards on the educational test can volunteer. Ratification of the amendment would not permit application of higher standards to women.

Survivorship benefits would be available to husbands of female workers on the same basis as to wives of male workers. The Social Security Act and the civil service and military service retirement acts are in conflict. Public schools and universities could not be limited to one sex and could not apply different admission standards to men and women. Laws requiring longer prison sentences for women than men would be invalid, and equal opportunities for rehabilitation and vocational training would have to be provided in public correctional institutions. Different ages of majority based on sex would have to be harmonized. Federal, State, and other governmental bodies would be obligated to follow nondiscriminatory practices in all aspects of employment, including public school teachers and State university and college faculties.

What would be the economic effects of the equal rights amendment? Direct economic effects would be minor. If any labor laws applying only to women still remained, their amendment or repeal would provide opportunity for women in better-paying jobs in manufacturing. More opportunities in public vocational and graduate schools for women would also tend to open up opportunities in better jobs for women.

Indirect effects could be much greater. The focusing of public attention on the gross legal, economic, and social discrimination against women by hearings and debates in the Federal and State legislatures would result in changes in attitude of parents, educators, and employers that would bring about substantial economic changes in the long run.

Sex prejudice cuts both ways. Men are oppressed by the requirements of the Selective Service Act, by enforced legal guardianship of minors, and by alimony laws. Each sex, I believe, should be liable when necessary to serve and defend this country. Each has a responsibility for the support of children.

There are objections raised to wiping out laws protecting women workers. No one would condone exploitation. But what does sex have to do with it. Working conditions and hours that are harmful to women are harmful to men; wages that are unfair for women are unfair for men. Laws setting employment limitations on the basis of sex are irrational, and the proof of this is their inconsistency from State to State. The physical characteristics of men and women are not fixed, but cover two wide spans that have a great deal of overlap. It is obvious, I think, that a robust woman could be more fit for physical labor than a weak man. The choice of occupation would be determined by individual capabilities, and the rewards for equal works should be equal.

This is what it comes down to: artificial distinctions between persons must be wiped out of the law. Legal discrimination between the sexes is, in almost every instance, founded on outmoded views of society and the pre-scientific beliefs about psychology and physiology. It is time to sweep away these relics of the past and set further generations free of them.

Federal agencies and institutions responsible for the enforcement of equal opportunity laws need the authority of a Constitutional amendment. The 1964 Civil Rights Act and the 1963 Equal Pay Act are not enough; they are limited in their coverage—for instance, one excludes teachers, and the other leaves out administrative and professional women. The Equal Employment Opportunity Commission has not proven to be an adequate device, with its power limited to investigation, conciliation, and recommendation to the Justice Department. In its cases involving sexual discrimination, it has failed in more than one-half. The Justice Department has been even less effective. It has intervened in only one case involving discrimination on the basis of sex, and this was on a procedural point. In a second case, in which both sexual and racial discrimination were alleged, the racial bias charge was given far greater weight.

Evidence of discrimination on the basis of sex should hardly have to be cited here. It is in the Labor Department's employment and salary figures for anyone who is still in doubt. Its elimination will involve so many changes in our State and Federal laws that, without the authority and impetus of this proposed amendment, it will perhaps take another 194 years. We cannot be parties to continuing a delay. The time is clearly now to put this House on record for the fullest expression of that equality of opportunity which our founding fathers professed. They professed it, but they did not assure it to their daughters, as they tried to do for their sons.

The Constitution they wrote was designed to protect the rights of white, male citizens. As there were no black Founding Fathers, there were no founding mothers—a great pity, on both counts. It is not too late to complete the work they left undone. Today, here, we should start to do so.

In closing I would like to make one point. Social and psychological effects will be initially more important than legal or economic results. As Leo Kanowitz has pointed out:

> *Rules of law that treat of the sexes per se inevitably produce far-reaching effects upon social, psychological and economic aspects of male-female relations beyond the limited confines of*

legislative chambers and courtrooms. As long as organized legal systems, at once the most respected and most feared of social institutions, continue to differentiate sharply, in treatment or in words, between men and women on the basis of irrelevant and artificially created distinctions, the likelihood of men and women coming to regard one another primarily as fellow human beings and only secondarily as representatives of another sex will continue to be remote. When men and women are prevented from recognizing one another's essential humanity by sexual prejudices, nourished by legal as well as social institutions, society as a whole remains less than it could otherwise become.

Announcement Seeking Democratic Nomination for President, 1972

January 25, 1972 in Brooklyn at the Concord Baptist Church

I stand before you today as a candidate for the Democratic nomination for the Presidency of the United States of America.

I am not the candidate of black America, although I am black and proud. I am not the candidate of the women's movement of this country, although I am a woman, and I am equally proud of that.

I am not the candidate of any political bosses or fat cats or special interests.

I stand here now without endorsements from many big name politicians or celebrities or any other kind of prop. I do not intend to offer to you the tired and glib clichés, which for too long have been an accepted part of our political life. I am the candidate of the people of America. And my presence before you now symbolizes a new era in American political history.

I have always earnestly believed in the great potential of America. Our constitutional democracy will soon celebrate its 200th anniversary, effective testimony, to the longevity to our cherished constitution and its unique bill of rights, which continues to give to the world an inspirational message of freedom and liberty.

Fellow Americans, we have looked in vain to the Nixon administration for the courage, the spirit, the character and the words to lift us. To bring out the best in us, to rekindle in each of us our faith in the American dream. Yet all we have received in return is just another smooth exercise in political manipulation, deceit and deception, callousness and indifference to our individual problems and a disgusting playing of devices politics. Pinning the young against the old, labor against management, north against south, black against white. The abiding concern of this administration has been one of political expediency, rather than the needs of man's nature.

The president has broken his promises to us, and has therefore lost his claim to our trust and confidence in him. I cannot believe that this administration would ever have been elected four years ago, if we had known then what we know today. But we are entering a new era, in which we must, as Americans, must demand stature and size in our leadership—leadership, which is fresh, leadership, which is open, and leadership, which is receptive to the problems of all Americans.

I have faith in the American people. I believe that we are smart enough to correct our mistakes. I believe that we are intelligent enough to recognize the talent, energy, and dedication, which all American including women and minorities have to offer. I know from my travels to the cities and small towns of America that we have a vast potential, which can and must be put to constructive use in getting this great nation together. I know that millions of Americans, from all walks of life agree with me that leadership does not mean putting the ear to the ground, to follow public opinion, but to have the vision of what is necessary and the courage to make it possible, building a strong and just society, which in its diversity and is noble in its quality of life.

I stand before you today, to repudiate the ridiculous notion that the American people will not vote for qualified candidates, simply because he is not right or because she is not a male. I do not believe that in 1972, the great majority of Americans will continue to harbor such narrow and petty prejudice.

I am convinced that the American people are in a mood to disc [*sic*] the politics and political personalities of the past.

I believe that they will show in 1972, and thereafter, that they intend to make individual judgments on the merits of a particular candidate, based on that candidates intelligence, character, physical ability, competence, integrity, and honesty. It is, I feel the duty of responsible leaders in this country to encourage and maximize, not to dismiss and minimize such judgment.

Americans all over are demanding a new sensibility, a new philosophy of government from Washington. Instead of sending spies to snoop on participants on Earth Day, I would welcome the efforts of concerned citizens of all ages to stop the abuse of our environment. Instead of watching a football game on television, while young people beg for the attention of their President, concerning our actions abroad, I would encourage them to speak out, organize for peaceful change, and vote in November. Instead of blocking efforts to control huge amounts of money given political candidates by the rich and the powerful, I would provide certain limits on such amounts and encourage all people of this nation to contribute small sums to the candidates of their choice. Instead of calculating political cost of this or that policy, and of weighing in favors of this or that group, depending on whether that group voted for me in 1968, I would remind all Americans at this hour of the words of Abraham Lincoln, "A house divided, cannot stand."

We Americans are all fellow countrymen. One day confronting the judgment of history in our country. We are all God's children and a bit of each of us is as precious as the will of the most powerful general or corporate millionaire. Our will can create a new America in 1972, one where there is freedom from violence and war, at home and abroad, where there is freedom from poverty and discrimination, where there exists at least a feeling, that we are making progress and assuring for everyone medical care, employment, and decent housing. Where we more decisively clean up our streets, our water, and our air. Where we work together, black and white, to rebuild our neighborhoods and to make our cities quiet, attractive, and efficient and fundamentally where we live in the confidence that every man and every woman in America has at long last the opportunity to become all that he was created of being, such as his ability.

In conclusion, all of you who share this vision, from NY to CA, from WI to FL, are brothers and sisters on the road to national unity and a new America. Those of you who were locked outside of the convention hall in 1968, those of you who can now vote for the first time, those of you who agree with me that the institutions of this country belong to all of the people who inhabit it. Those of you who have been neglected, left out, ignored, forgotten, or shunned aside for whatever reason, give me your help at this hour. Join me in an effort to reshape our society and regain control of our destiny as we go down the Chisholm Trail for 1972.

The Black Woman in Contemporary America, 1974

Speech at the University of Missouri in Kansas City

Ladies and gentlemen, and brothers and sisters all—I'm very glad to be here this evening. I'm very glad that I've had the opportunity to be the first lecturer with respect to the topic of the black woman in contemporary America. This has become a most talked-about topic and has caused a great deal of provocation and misunderstandings and misinterpretations. And I come to you this evening to speak on this topic not as any scholar, not as any academician, but as a person that has been out here for the past twenty years, trying to make my way as a black and a woman, and meeting all kinds of obstacles.

The black woman's role has not been placed in its proper perspective, particularly in terms of the current economic and political upheaval in America today. Since time immemorial the black man's emasculation resulted in the need of the black woman to assert herself in order to maintain some semblance of a family unit. And as a result of this historical circumstance, the black woman has developed perseverance; the black woman has developed strength; the black woman has developed tenacity of purpose and other attributes which today quite often are being looked upon negatively. She continues to be labeled a matriarch. And this is indeed a played-upon white sociological interpretation of the black woman's role that has been developed and perpetrated by Daniel Moynihan and other sociologists.

Black women by virtue of the role they have played in our society have much to offer toward the liberation of their people. We know that our men are coming forward, but the black race needs the collective talents and the collective abilities of black men and black women who have vital skills to supplement each other.

It is quite perturbing to divert ourselves on the dividing issue of the alleged fighting that absorbs the energies of black men and black women. Such statements as "the black woman has to step back while her black man steps forward" and "the black woman has kept back the black man" are grossly, historically incorrect and serves as a scapegoating technique to prevent us from coming together as human beings—some of whom are black men and some are black women.

The consuming interests of this type of dialogue abets the enemy in terms of taking our eyes off the ball, so that our collective talents can never redound in a beneficial manner to our ethnic group. The black woman who is educated and has ability cannot be expected to put said talent on the shelf when she can utilize these gifts side-by-side with her man. One does not learn, nor does one assist in the struggle, by standing on the sidelines, constantly complaining and criticizing. One learns by participating in the situation—listening, observing and then acting.

It is quite understandable why black women in the majority are not interested in walking and picketing a cocktail lounge which historically has refused to open its doors a certain two hours a day when men who have just returned from Wall Street gather in said lounge to exchange bits of business transactions that occurred on the market. This is a middle-class white woman's issue. This is not a priority of minority women. Another issue that black women are not overly concerned about is the "M-S" versus the "M-R-S" label. For many of us this is just the use of another label which does not basically change the fundamental inherent racial attitudes found in both men and women in this society. This is just another label, and black women are not preoccupied with any more label syndromes. Black women are desperately concerned with the issue of survival in a society in which the Caucasian group has never really practiced the espousal of equalitarian principles in America.

An aspect of the women's liberation movement that will and does interest many black women is the potential liberation, is the potential nationalization of daycare centers in this country. Black women can accept and understand this agenda item in the women's movement. It is important that black women utilize their brainpower and focus on issues in any movement that will redound to the benefit of their people because we can serve as a vocal and a catalytic pressure group within the so-called humanistic movements, many of whom do not really comprehend the black man and the black woman.

An increasing number of black women are beginning to feel that it is important first to become free as women, in order to contribute more fully to the task of black liberation. Some feel that black men—like all men, or most men—have placed women in the stereotypes of domestics whose duty it is to stay in the background—cook, clean, have babies, and leave all of the glory to men. Black women point to the civil rights movement as an example of a subtle type of male oppression, where with few exceptions black women have not had active roles in the forefront of the fight. Some like Coretta King, Katherine Cleaver, and Betty Shabazz have come only to their positions in the shadows of their husbands. Yet, because of the oppression of black women, they are strongest in the fight for liberation. They have led the struggle to fight against white male supremacy, dating from slavery times. And in view of these many facts it is not surprising that black women played a crucial role in the total fight for freedom in this nation. Ida Wells kept her newspaper free by walking the streets of Memphis, Tennessee, in the 1890s with two pistols on her hips. And within recent years, this militant condition of black women, who have been stifled because of racism and sexism, has been carried on by Mary McLeod Bethune, Mary Church Terrell, Daisy Bates, and Diane Nash.

The black woman lives in a society that discriminates against her on two counts. The black woman cannot be discussed in the same context as her Caucasian counterpart because of the twin jeopardy of race and sex which operates against her, and the psychological and political consequences which attend them. Black women are crushed by cultural restraints and abused by the legitimate power structure. To date, neither the black movement nor women's liberation succinctly addresses itself to the dilemma confronting the black who is female. And as a consequence of ignoring or being unable to handle the problems facing black women, black women themselves are now becoming socially and politically active.

Undoubtedly black women are cultivating new attitudes, most of which will have political repercussions in the future. They are attempting to change their conditions. The maturation of the civil rights movement by the mid '60s enabled many black women to develop interest in the American political process. From their experiences they learned that the real sources of power lay at the root of the political system. For example, black sororities and pressure groups like the National Council of Negro Women are adept at the methods of participatory politics—particularly in regard to voting and organizing. With the arrival of the '70s, young black women are demanding recognition like the other segments of society who also desire their humanity and their individual talents to be noticed. The tradition of the black woman and the Afro-American subculture and her current interest in the political process indicate the emergence of a new political entity.

Historically she has been discouraged from participating in politics. Thus she is trapped between the walls of the dominant white culture and her own subculture, both of which encourage deference to men. Both races of women have traditionally been limited to performing such tasks as opening envelopes, hanging up posters and giving teas. And the minimal involvement of black women exists because they have been systematically excluded from the political process and they are members of the politically dysfunctional black lower class. Thus, unlike white women, who escape the psychological and sociological handicaps of racism, the black woman's political involvement has been at most a marginal role.

But within the last six years, the Afro-American subculture has undergone tremendous social and political transformation and these changes have altered the nature of the black community. They are beginning to realize their capacities not only as blacks, but also as women. They are beginning to understand that their cultural well-being and their social well-being would only be affirmed in connection with the total black struggle. The dominant role black women played in the civil rights movement began to allow them to grasp the significance of political power in America. So obviously black women who helped to spearhead the civil rights movement would also now, at this juncture, join and direct the vanguard which would shape and mold a new kind of political participation.

This has been acutely felt in urban areas, which have been rocked by sporadic rebellions. Nothing better illustrates the need for black women to organize politically than their unusual proximity to the most crucial issues affecting black people today. They have struggled in a wide range of protest movements to eliminate the poverty and injustice that permeates the lives of black people. In New York City, for example, welfare mothers and mothers of schoolchildren have ably demonstrated the commitment of black women to the elimination of the problems that threaten the well-being of the black family. Black women must view the problems of cities such as New York not as urban problems, but as the components of a crisis without whose elimination our family lives will neither survive nor prosper. Deprived of a stable family environment because of poverty and racial injustice, disproportionate numbers of our people must live on minimal welfare allowances that help to perpetuate the breakdown of family life. In the face of the increasing poverty besetting black communities, black women have a responsibility. Black women have a duty to bequeath a legacy to their children. Black women have a duty to move from the periphery of organized political activity into its main arena.

I say this on the basis of many experiences. I travel throughout this country and I've come in contact with thousands of my black sisters in all kinds of conditions in this nation. And I've said to them over and over again: it is not a question of competition against black men or brown men or red men or white men in America. It is a questions of the recognition that, since we have a tremendous responsibility in terms of our own families, that to the best of our ability we have to give everything that is within ourselves to give—in terms of helping to make that future a better future for our little boys and our little girls, and not leave it to anybody.

Francis Beal describes the black woman as a slave of a slave. Let me quote: "By reducing the black man in America to such abject oppression, the black woman had no protector and she was used—and is still being used—in some cases as the scapegoat for the evils that this horrendous system has perpetrated on black men. Her physical image has been maliciously maligned. She has been sexually molested and abused by the white colonizer. She has suffered the worst kind of economic exploitation, having been forced to serve as the white woman's maid and wet-nurse for white offspring, while her own children were more often starving and neglected. It is the depth of degradation to be socially manipulated, physically raped and used to undermine your own household—and then to be powerless to reverse this syndrome."

However, Susan Johnson notes a bit of optimism. Because Susan, a brilliant young black woman, has said that the recent strides made by the black woman in the political process is a result of the intricacies of her personality. And that is to say that as a political animal, she functions independently of her double jeopardy. Because confronted with a matrifocal past and present, she is often accused of stealing the black male's position in any situation beyond that of housewife and mother. And if that were not enough to burden the black woman, she realizes that her political mobility then threatens the doctrine of white supremacy and male superiority so deeply embedded in the American culture.

So choosing not to be a victim of self-paralysis, the black woman has been able to function in the political spectrum. And more often than not, it is the subconsciousness of the racist mind that perceives her as less harmful than the black man and thus permits her to acquire the necessary leverage for political mobility. This subtle component of racism could prove to be essential to the key question of how the black woman has managed some major advances in the American political process.

It is very interesting to note that everyone—with the exception of the black woman herself—has been interpreting the black woman. It is very interesting to note that the time has come that black women can and must no longer be passive, complacent recipients of whatever the definitions of the sociologists, the psychologists and the psychiatrists will give to us. Black women have been maligned, misunderstood, misinterpreted—who knows better than Shirley Chisholm?

And I stand here tonight to tell to you, my sisters, that if you have the courage of your convictions, you must stand up and be counted. I hope that the day will come in America when this business of male versus female does not become such an over-riding issue, so that the talents and abilities that the almighty God have given to people can be utilized for the benefit of humanity.

One has to recognize that there are stupid white women and stupid white men, stupid black women and stupid black men, brilliant white women and brilliant white men, and brilliant black women and brilliant black men. Why do we get so hung-up in America on this question of sex? Of course, in terms of the black race, we understand the historical circumstances. We understand, also, some of the subtle maneuverings and machinations behind the scenes in order to prevent black women and black men from coming together as a race of unconquerable men and women.

And I just want to say to you tonight, if I say nothing else: I would never have been able to make it in America if I had paid attention to all of the doomsday-criers about me. And I want to say in conclusion that as you have this conference here for the next two weeks, put the cards out on the table and do not be afraid to discuss issues that perhaps you have been sweeping under the rug because of what people might say about you. You must remember that once we are able to face the truth, the truth shall set all of us free.

In conclusion, I just want to say to you, black and white, north and east, south and west, men and women: the time has come in America when we should no longer be the passive, complacent recipients of whatever the morals or the politics of a nation may decree for us in this nation. Forget traditions! Forget conventionalisms! Forget what the world will say whether you're in your place or out of your place. Stand up and be counted. Do your thing, looking only to God—whoever your God is—and to your consciences for approval. I thank you.

23.
ANGELA Y. DAVIS

Angela Y. Davis (1944–) is a radical feminist, Communist, and revolutionary voice within progressive organizations such as the Black Panthers. Angela Davis, currently distinguished professor emeritus at the University of California, Santa Cruz, is a remarkable intellectual, although she has never just reserved her ideas for academics and students. She is an activist first and foremost. What good are revolutionary ideas if we do not actively try to implement them?

Davis began her career as an activist with the Student Nonviolent Coordinating Committee. However, she left the group to join the Black Panther Party. She was involved in both organizations' west coast chapters. However, Davis was disconcerted with these organizations' conservative approaches to gender and sexual politics. Since her days as a student, Karl Marx and Friedrich Engels always influenced Davis and in 1968 she formally joined the Communist Party. Davis sat on the Communist Party's Central Committee for twenty-three years. In fact, her active membership caused Ronald Reagan, amongst others, to attempt to have her removed from her position at the University of California. However, this did not stop Davis. In fact, she ran for vice president twice, in 1980 and 1984 on the Communist ticket.

Davis is famous for being on the FBI's ten most wanted list. (This is certainly far from the most important fact about her accomplishments or legacy.) She found herself on the list after she became heavily involved in the Soledad Brothers case. The Soledad Brothers refers to the case of George Jackson, Fleeta Drumgo, and John Clutchette, who were activists like Davis, in the prisoners' rights movement. In 1970 they were spuriously charged with the murder of a prison guard (after years of agitation they were ultimately acquitted). Davis, who was now actively engaged in the prisoners' rights movement and specifically in the Soledad Brothers case, was being harassed. She received frequent death threats and as a result sought out a personal security team comprised of other activists. Davis legally purchased much of the weaponry utilized by her security team. At the same time, Jonathan Jackson, brother of George Jackson and now friend and security personnel to Angela Davis, committed a now infamous crime.

Jackson desired to make a grandiose statement about the atrocities in the prison system; so, he stormed into a California court armed and took a judge, district attorney, and a few members of a jury hostage. Also removed from the court were three prisoners on trial. Jackson and his accomplices attempted to bring them to their getaway van in the court parking lot and were fired upon by San Quentin prison guards. The gunfire left the judge, Jackson, and two of the prisoners dead. The kidnapped district attorney, jurors, and the other prisoner were seriously wounded. Although Davis played no actual role in the events, because she had purchased the guns utilized in the massacre she was named as an accomplice. For two months, Davis went underground and this is when she found herself on the FBI's infamous list. By October 1970 she had been captured and then spent sixteen months in jail before she was even released on bail.

Davis was ultimately charged with kidnapping and conspiracy. Progressives who took up her cause, such as the National United Committee to Free Angela Davis, along with her defense lawyers argued that Davis was not being charged for these actual crimes but she was being charged for being an effective radical leader. Davis, who actively aided her lawyers in her own defense, utilized her own deplorable experiences to expose the atrocities within the prison system. With the support of the Congressional Black Caucus and countless activists in February of 1972, she was finally granted bail and on June 4, 1972 she was acquitted of all charges. Throughout her life she has continued to work for justice. Davis was one of the founders of the Critical Resistance, a group devoted to abrogating the prison industrial complex; she has worked as an executive board member of the Women of Color Resource Center. She has worked for Justice Now, an organization devoted to providing legal assistance to incarcerated women and another organization similar to Justice Now called Sisters Inside. Whatever disagreements individuals may have over her ideological trajectory or strategies, one cannot deny that Davis has devoted her life to the struggle for human rights.

Overview of Ideas

Angela Davis was a revolutionary who fought arduously for Black liberation, an end to exploitation of all workers and other marginalized groups, particularly women. As a Black Power activist, she firmly articulated the need for revolutionary means to end oppression. Democratic reform was impossible. Democracy and capitalism are two mutually exclusive entities. Democracy does not and cannot exist under capitalism. Moreover, capitalism was the primary source of oppression in the United States. Therefore, as Marxists argue, you cannot resolve society's most deleterious quagmires such as crime, poverty, racism, and sexism without annihilating them at their roots—capitalism.

Historically, revolutionary and often illegal means have been required to overturn injustice. The history of slavery tells us that in order to escape the ghastly fetters of slavery individuals had to utilize illegal measures to escape. Brave men and women had to craft ingenious strategies, often illegal, to circumvent racist laws such as the Black Codes. Unfortunately, again, democratic reform does not always work and alternative means must be sought. According to Davis, the valiant individuals who fight against repressive policy and institutions, when caught, are not criminals; they are political prisoners. The individuals who ran the Underground Railroad, although engaged in ostensibly criminal activity were political prisoners. Martin Luther King Jr., Bobby Seale, Huey P. Newton, Angela Davis, and all other leaders in this volume incarcerated for fighting for justice were all political prisoners.

> Nixon's and J. Edgar Hoover's pronouncements lead one to believe that they would readily accept … fascist legal theory. Anyone who seeks to overthrow oppressive institutions, whether or not he has engaged in an overt illegal act, is *a prior* a criminal who must be buried away in one of America's dungeons.

When arrested while engaged in protest, you were solely being arrested for "political boldness" not the actual crime for which you were charged. "The political act is defined as criminal in order to discredit radical or revolutionary movements." As the Black Power movement grew the more the fascist state would utilize imprisonment as a tool to thwart the gains of the movement. This is what facilitated the increase in government "frame-ups" of key leaders.

Davis has become one the most outspoken critics of the prison system in the United States. The prison industrial complex has become a tool for the suppression of dissent and a mechanism to produce wealth for the capitalist class. The state chooses to incarcerate its poor, the large majority of whom are people of color, who commit crimes most often as a last resort in the face of poverty. This class, the lumpenproletariat, for classical Marxists is a futile class of criminals and vagrants. However, Angela Davis, like her comrades in the BPP, saw them as a viable revolutionary class. Part of her solution to resolving the problems impacting Black people was to mobilize this group of people.

Davis foreshadowed that the mass incarceration of people of color would continue to worsen. Racism plagued the entire justice system. However, there is no incentive for the state to remedy this calamity. More and more Blacks, Chicanos, and Puerto Ricans were finding themselves incarcerated. They, too, were becoming political prisoners. As victims of the exploitative capitalist marketplace, they found themselves impoverished, often incarcerated as a result, and then utilized as slave labor in penitentiaries. For example, prisoners will make as low as forty cents per hour. The state too, sees the revolutionary potential of this class and therefore utilizes the penal system and the prison industrial complex as a means by which to suppress their revolutionary potential. Part of the impending revolution required an end to "the prison system in its present form." The current prison system does not even attempt to rehabilitate the citizens who enter its gates. It is merely a punishment industry. We have witnessed the corporatization of the punishment industry. Prison labor is being outsourced; private companies are able to utilize prison labor. Davis continues to fight for the human rights of prisoners. She actively fights for the end of the prison industrial complex and issues that stem from it such as felony disenfranchisement, where convicted felons in many states permanently lose their right to vote. In addition, women are one of the fastest growing prison populations in the United States. As a result, she has also spoken out against the sexual abuse of women in prison. In addition to her commitment to the Black Liberation movement and prisoners' rights movement, Davis also struggled for the rights of women.

Angela Davis was an outspoken critic of the women's movement. However, unlike Flo Kennedy, her criticisms were not just of issues related to platform and strategy. Davis indicted the women's movement and its leaders for their neglect of both race and class. Black women were marginalized from second wave feminism. The White leadership of the women's movement thought that the "triple oppression" faced by women of color was not relevant to their lives. Women of color, particularly Black women, endured a matrix of oppression condition by their membership in a marginalized racial, gender, and class group. The dominant women's movement was bourgeois and allowed their social position and the privilege that came from it to blind them to the harsh realities facing many other women. Even when the movement fought for issues ostensibly impacting all women, it ignored race and class. For example, in the case of abortion rights, the movement ignored issues of forced sterilization that impacted poor women and women of color. Davis's goal was to demonstrate that the women's movement needed to be more attentive to issues related to both class and race. Moreover, addressing these issues would also benefit White middle class women.

The women's movement needed to reconcile itself with the labor movement. Women have been by far impacted the most by conservative welfare reform, union-busting, layoffs, and other labor issues. What has been coined the "feminization of poverty," the increasing likelihood that women will live in poverty, is not just a labor issue; it is a woman's issue. In addition, while dismissed by the women's movement as a racial issue, affirmative action also benefits women. In fact, Davis's pleas eventually caught on. White middle class women have benefited from affirmative action by far the most since its inception under the Lyndon Baines Johnson administration's Great Society.

Davis argued that the demands of the women's movement needed to stretch far beyond the much-needed battle for abortion rights and reproductive freedoms. She proposed the introduction of accessible day care. She was an advocate of reform within American educational institutions. Public schools should fight against racism within their structure and curriculum. For example, bilingual public education was mandatory. If these types of programs were implemented then women on the bottom of the social strata would benefit. When women on the bottom benefit it simultaneously makes advances for the women above them in the social hierarchy.

Davis's prescriptions for the women's movement were a reflection of her larger concerns about the extreme exploitation and dire poverty caused by capitalism. Davis argued that even the first wave women's movement for suffrage missed this point as well. The middle class White women fighting for the right to vote were often baffled by the working class women of all races who thought the suffrage movement was futile, if they did not have money to buy bread. This is the same point Davis made about the modern women's movement. The empowerment of women hinged upon a struggle that sought to tackle labor issues, homophobia, conservative immigration reform, ageism, and discrimination against differently-abled people. Davis accurately argued in the 1980s that a third wave of the women's movement was brewing. It was this third wave that would need to take up this multifaceted platform in order for future progress and empowerment to be realized. In the spirit of Pan-Africanism, this new movement must align itself with the struggles of oppressed women globally. Finally, this new movement must adhere to socialist principles. These principles must include recognizing the need for free accessible healthcare for all, free education from kindergarten to postgraduate level, and housing reform such as what we currently see in Cuba. In Cuba, housing will never cost a family or individual more than 10 percent of their income. According to Davis, without addressing these fundamental bread-and-butter issues we will not achieve progress.

Future progress depends upon a set of very specific political strategies. First, Davis argues that future movements must be intergenerational and young and old activists must learn to work proactively side by side. Crucially, older activists must learn to allow younger people to take the helm and lead them. In addition, as noted previously, progressive activists must build bridges across racial and ethnic lines. Identity politics has thwarted the progress of the modern left in the United States. For example, Davis points out that modern issues such as immigrants' rights and campaigns against prisons have the ability to effectively achieve this goal. Finally, Davis argues for the importance of a cultural dimension in political activism. Modern political movements and organizations should utilize modern media and cultural forms to achieve their goals, organize and recruit members. After all, picket signs and newsletters are not the only way to disseminate a message. Music, art, poetry, etc. are all-important strategies in protest and need to be utilized more frequently and effectively. Angela Davis continues to be a strong voice in progressive politics in the United States.

Political Prisoners, Prisons, and Black Liberation, 1971

Despite a long history of exalted appeals to man's inherent right of resistance, there has seldom been agreement on how to relate *in practice* to unjust, immoral laws and the oppressive social order from which they emanate. The conservative, who does not dispute the validity of revolutions deeply buried in history, invokes visions of impending anarchy in order to legitimize his demand for absolute obedience. Law and order, with the major emphasis on order, is his watchword. The liberal articulates his sensitiveness to certain of society's intolerable details, but will almost never prescribe methods of resistance which exceed the limits of legality—redress through electoral channels is the liberal's panacea.

In the heat of our pursuit for fundamental human rights, Black people have been continually cautioned to be patient. We are advised that as long as we remain faithful to the *existing* democratic order, the glorious moment will eventually arrive when we will come into our own as full-fledged human beings.

But having been taught by bitter experience, we know that there is a glaring incongruity between democracy and the capitalist economy which is the source of our ills. Regardless of all rhetoric to the contrary, the people are not the ultimate matrix of the laws and the system which govern them—certainly not Black people and other nationally oppressed people, but not even the mass of whites. The people do not exercise decisive control over the determining factors of their lives.

Official assertions that meaningful dissent is always welcome, provided it falls within the boundaries of legality, are frequently a smokescreen obscuring the invitation to acquiesce in oppression. Slavery may have been unrighteous, the constitutional provision for the enslavement of Blacks may have been unjust, but conditions were not to be considered so unbearable (especially since they were profitable to a small circle) as to justify escape and other acts proscribed by law. This was the import of the fugitive slave laws.

Needless to say, the history of the United States has been marred from its inception by an enormous quantity of unjust laws, far too many expressly bolstering the oppression of Black people. Particularized reflections of existing social inequities, these laws have repeatedly borne witness to the exploitative and racist core of the society itself. For Blacks, Chicanos, for all nationally oppressed people, the problem of opposing unjust laws and the social conditions which nourish their growth, has always had immediate practical implications. Our very survival has frequently been a direct function of our skill in forging effective channels of resistance. In resisting, we have sometimes been compelled to openly violate those laws which directly or indirectly buttress our oppression. But even when containing our resistance within the orbit of legality, we have been labelled criminals and have been methodically persecuted by a racist legal apparatus.

Under the ruthless conditions of slavery, the Underground Railroad provided the framework for extra-legal anti-slavery activity pursued by vast numbers of people, both Black and white. Its functioning was in flagrant violation of the fugitive slave laws; those who were apprehended were subjected to severe penalties. Of the innumerable recorded attempts to rescue fugitive slaves from the clutches of slave-catchers, one of the most striking is the case of Anthony Burns, a slave from Virginia, captured in Boston in 1853. A team of his supporters in attempting to rescue him by force during the course of his trial, engaged the police in a fierce courtroom battle. During the gun fight a prominent abolitionist, Thomas Wentworth Higginson, was wounded. Although the rescuers were unsuccessful in their efforts, the impact of this incident "...did more to crystallize Northern sentiment against slavery than any other except the exploit of John Brown, 'and this was the last time a fugitive slave was taken from Boston. It took 22 companies of state militia, four platoons of marines, a battalion of United States artillerymen, and the city's police force ... to ensure the performance of this shameful act, the cost of which, to the Federal government alone, came to forty thousand dollars.'"[1]

Throughout the era of slavery, Blacks as well as progressive whites recurrently discovered that their commitment to the anti-slavery cause frequently entailed the overt violation of the laws of the land. Even as slavery faded away into a more subtle yet equally pernicious apparatus to dominate Black people, 'illegal' resistance was still on the agenda. After the Civil War, the Black Codes, successors to the old slave codes, legalized convict labor, prohibited social intercourse between Blacks and whites, gave white employers an excessive degree of control over the private lives of Black workers, and generally codified racism and terror. Naturally, numerous individual as well as collective acts of resistance prevailed. On many occasions, Blacks formed armed teams to protect themselves from white terrorists who were, in turn, protected by law enforcement agencies, if not actually identical with them.

By the second decade of the twentieth century, the mass movement headed by Marcus Garvey, proclaimed in its Declaration of Rights that Black people should not hesitate to disobey all discriminatory laws. Moreover, the Declaration announced, they should utilize all means available to them, legal or illegal, to defend themselves from legalized terror as well as Ku Klux Klan violence. During the era of intense activity around civil rights issues, systematic disobedience of oppressive laws was a primary tactic, The sit-ins were organized trangressions of racist legislation.

All these historical instances involving the overt violation of the laws of the land converge around an unmistakable common denominator. At stake has been the collective welfare and survival of a people. There is a distinct and qualitative difference between one breaking a law for one's own individual self-interest and violating it in the interests of a class or a people whose oppression is expressed either directly or indirectly through that particular law. The former might be called a criminal (though in many instances he is a victim), but the latter, as a reformist or revolutionary, is interested in universal social change. Captured, he or she is a political prisoner.

The political prisoner's words or deeds have in one form or another embodied political protests against the established order and have consequently brought him into acute conflict with the state. In light of the political content of his act, the 'crime' (which may or may not have been committed) assumes a minor importance. In this country, however, where the special category of political prisoners is not officially acknowledged, the political prisoner inevitably stands trial for a specific criminal offense, not for a political act. Often the so-called crime does not even have a nominal existence. As in the 1914 murder frame-up of the IWW organizer, Joe Hill, it is a blatant fabrication, a mere excuse for silencing a militant crusader against oppression. In all instances however, the political prisoner has violated the unwritten law which prohibits disturbances and upheavals in the status quo of exploitation and racism. This unwritten law has been contested by actually and explicitly breaking a law or by utilizing constitutionally protected channels to educate, agitate and organize the masses to resist.

A deep-seated ambivalence has always characterized the official response to the political prisoner. Charged and tried for a criminal act, his guilt is always political in nature. This ambivalence is perhaps best captured by Judge Webster Thayer's comment upon sentencing Bartolomeo Vanzetti to 15 years for an attempted payroll robbery: "This man, although he may not have actually committed the crime attributed to him, is nevertheless morally culpable, because he is the enemy of our existing institutions."[2]— (The very same judge incidentally, sentenced Sacco and Vanzetti to death for a robbery and murder of which they were manifestly innocent.) It is not surprising that Nazi Germany's foremost constitutional lawyer, Carl Schmitt, advanced a theory which generalized this *a priori* culpability. A thief, for example, was not necessarily one who has committed an overt act of theft, but rather one whose character renders him a thief (*wer nach seinem wesen ein Dieb ist*). Nixon's and J. Edgar Hoover's pronouncements lead one to believe that they would readily accept Schmitt's fascist legal theory. Anyone who seeks to overthrow oppressive institutions, whether or not he has engaged in an overt illegal act, is *a priori* a criminal who must be buried away in one of America's dungeons.

Even in all Martin Luther King's numerous arrests, he was not so much charged with the nominal crimes of trespassing, disturbance of the peace, etc., but rather with being an enemy of Southern society, an inveterate foe of racism. When Robert Williams was accused of a kidnapping, this charge never managed to conceal his real offense—the advocacy of Black people's incontestable right to bear arms in their own defense.

The offense of the political prisoner is his political boldness, his persistent challenging—legally or extra-legally—of fundamental social wrongs fostered and reinforced by the state. He has opposed unjust laws and exploitative, racist social conditions in general, with the ultimate aim of transforming these laws and this society into an order harmonious with the material and spiritual needs and interests of the vast majority of its members.

Nat Turner and John Brown were political prisoners in their time. The acts for which they were charged and subsequently hanged, were the practical extensions of their profound commitment to the abolition of slavery. They fearlessly bore the responsibility for their actions. The significance of their executions and the accompanying widespread repression did not lie so much in the fact that they were being punished for specific crimes, nor even in the effort to use their punishment as an implicit threat to deter others from similar *armed* acts of resistance. These executions and the surrounding repression of slaves, were intended to terrorize the anti-slavery movement in general; to discourage and diminish both legal and illegal forms of abolitionist activity. As usual, the effect of repression was miscalculated and in both instances, anti-slavery activity was accelerated and intensified as a result.

Nat Turner and John Brown can be viewed as examples of the political prisoner who has actually committed an act which is defined by the state as "criminal." They killed and were consequently tried for murder. But did they commit murder? This raises the question of whether American revolutionaries had *murdered* the British in their struggle for liberation. Nat Turner and his followers killed some 65 white people, yet shortly before the Revolt had begun, Nat is reputed to have said to the other rebelling slaves: "Remember that ours is not war for robbery nor to satisfy our passions, it is a *struggle for freedom*. Ours must be deeds not words.[3]

The very institutions which condemned Nat Turner and reduced his struggle for freedom to a simple criminal case of murder, owed their existence to the decision, made a half century earlier, to take up arms against the British oppressor.

The battle for the liquidation of slavery had no legitimate existence in the eyes of the government and therefore the special quality of deeds carried out in the interests of freedom was deliberately ignored. There were no political prisoners, there were only criminals; just as the movement out of which these deeds flowed was largely considered criminal.

Likewise, the significance of activities which are pursued in the interests of liberation today is minimized not so much because officials are unable to *see* the collective surge against oppression, but because they have consciously set out to subvert such movements. In the Spring of 1970, Los Angeles Panthers took up arms to defend themselves from an assault initiated by the local police force on their office and on their persons. They were charged with criminal assault. If one believed the official propaganda, they were bandits and rogues who pathologically found pleasure in attacking policemen. It was not mentioned that their community activities—educational work, services such as free breakfast and free medical programs—which had legitimized them in the Black community, were the immediate reason for which the wrath of the police had fallen upon them. In defending themselves from the attack waged by some 600 policemen (there were only 11 Panthers in the office) they were not only defending their lives, but even more important their accomplishments in the Black community surrounding them and in the broader thrust for Black Liberation. Whenever Blacks in struggle have recourse to self-defense, particularly armed self-defense, it is twisted and distorted on official levels and ultimately rendered synonymous with criminal aggression. On the other hand, when policemen are clearly indulging in acts of criminal aggression, officially they are defending themselves through 'justifiable assault' or 'justifiable homicide'.

The ideological acrobatics characteristic of official attempts to explain away the existence of the political prisoner of do not end with the equation of the individual political act with the individual criminal act. The political act is defined as criminal in order to discredit radical and. revolutionary movements. A political event is reduced to a criminal event in order to affirm the absolute invulnerability of the existing order. In a revealing contradiction, the court resisted the description of the New York Panther 21 trial as 'political,' yet the prosecutor entered as evidence of criminal intent, literature which represented, so he purported, the political ideology of the Black Panther Party.

The legal apparatus designates the Black liberation fighter a criminal, prompting Nixon, Agnew, Reagan *et al.* to proceed to mystify with their demagogy millions of Americans whose senses have been dulled and whose critical powers have been eroded by the continual onslaught of racist ideology.

As the Black Liberation Movement and other progressive struggles increase in magnitude and intensity, the judicial system and its extension, the penal system, consequently become key weapons in the state's fight to preserve the existing conditions of class domination, therefore racism, poverty and war.... The prison is a key component of the state's coercive apparatus, the overriding function of which is to ensure social control. The etymology of the term 'penitentiary' furnishes a clue to the controlling idea behind the 'prison system' at its inception. The penitentiary was projected as the locale for doing penitence for an offense against society, the physical and spiritual purging of proclivities to challenge rules and regulations which command total obedience. While cloaking itself with the bourgeois aura of universality—imprisonment was supposed to cut across all class lines, as crimes were to be defined by the act, not the perpetrator—the prison has actually operated as an instrument of class domination, a means of prohibiting the have-nots from encroaching upon the haves.

The occurrence of crime is inevitable in a society in which wealth is unequally distributed, as one of the constant reminders that society's productive forces are being channeled in the wrong direction. The majority of criminal offenses bear a direct relationship to property. Contained in the very concept of property, crimes are profound but suppressed social needs which express themselves in anti-social modes of action. Spontaneously produced by a capitalist organization of society, this type of crime is at once a protest against society and a desire to partake of its exploitative content. It challenges the symptoms of capitalism, but not its essence.

Some Marxists in recent years have tended to banish 'criminals' and the lumpenproletariat as a whole from the arena of revolutionary struggle. Apart from the absence of any link binding the criminal to the means of production, underlying this exclusion has been the assumption that individuals who have recourse to anti-social acts are incapable of developing the discipline and collective orientation required by revolutionary struggle.

With the declassed character of lumpenproletarians in mind, Marx had stated that they are as capable of "the most heroic deeds and the most exalted sacrifices, as of the basest banditry and the dirtiest corruption."[4] He emphasized the fact that the Provisional Government's Mobile Guards under the Paris Commune—some 24,000 troops—were largely formed out of young lumpenproletarians from 15 to 20 years of age. Too many Marxists have been inclined to overvalue the second part of Marx's observation—that the lumpenproletariat is capable of the basest banditry and the dirtiest corruption—while minimizing or indeed totally disregarding his first remark, applauding the lumpen for their heroic deeds and exalted sacrifices.

Especially today when so many Black, Chicano and Puerto Rican men and women are jobless as a consequence of the internal dynamic of the capitalist system, the role of the unemployed which includes the lumpenproletariat in revolutionary struggle must be given serious thought. Increased unemployment, particularly for the nationally oppressed, will continue to be an inevitable by-product of technological development. At least 30 per cent of Black youth are presently without jobs. In the context of class exploitation and national oppression it should be clear that numerous individuals are compelled to resort to criminal acts, not as a result of conscious choice—implying other alternatives—but because society has objectively reduced their possibilities of subsistence and survival to this level. This recognition should signal the urgent need to organize the unemployed and lumpenproletariat, as indeed the Black Panther Party as well as activists in prison have already begun to do.

In evaluating the susceptibility of the Black and Brown unemployed to organizing efforts, the peculiar historical features of the U.S., specifically racism and national oppression, must be taken into account. There already exists in the Black and Brown communities, the lumpenproletariat included, a long tradition of collective resistance to national oppression.

Moreover, in assessing the revolutionary potential of prisoners in America as a group, it should be borne in mind that not all prisoners have actually committed crimes. The built-in racism of the judicial system expresses itself, as Du Bois has suggested, the railroading of countless innocent Blacks and other national minorities into the country's coercive institutions.

One must also appreciate the effects of disproportionate long prison terms on Black and Brown inmates. The typical criminal mentality sees imprisonment as a calculated risk for a particular criminal act. One's prison term is more or less rationally predictable. The function of racism in the judicial-penal complex is to shatter that predictability. The Black burglar, anticipating a 2 to 4 year term may end up doing 10 to 15 years, while the white burglar leaves after two years.

Within the contained, coercive universe of the prison, the captive is confronted with the realities of racism, not simply as individual acts dictated by attitudinal bias; rather he is compelled to come to grips with racism as an institutional phenomenon collectively experienced by the victims. The disproportionate representation of the Black, and Brown communities, the manifest racism of parole boards, the intense brutality inherent in the relationship between prison guards and Black and Brown inmates—all this and more cause the prisoner to be confronted daily, hourly, with the concentrated, systematic existence of racism.

For the innocent prisoner, the process of radicalization should come easy; for the 'guilty' victim, the insight into the nature of racism as it manifests itself in the judicial-penal complex can lead to a questioning of his own past criminal activity and a re-evaluation of the methods he has used to survive in a racist and exploitative society. Needless to say, this process is not automatic, it does not occur spontaneously. The persistent educational work carried out by the prison's political activists plays a key role in developing the political potential of captive men and women.

Prisoners—especially Blacks, Chicanos, and Puerto Ricans—are increasingly advancing the proposition that they are *political* prisoners. They contend that they are political prisoners in the sense that they are largely the victims of an oppressive politico-economic order, swiftly becoming conscious of the causes underlying their victimization. The Folsom Prisoners' Manifesto of Demands and Anti-Oppression Platform attests to a lucid understanding of the structures of oppression within the prison—structures which contradict even the avowed function of the penal institution: "The program we are submitted to, under the ridiculous title of rehabilitation, is relative to the ancient stupidity of pouring water on the drowning man, in as much as we are treated for our hostilities by our program administrators with their hostility as medication." The Manifesto also reflects an awareness that the severe social crisis taking place in this country, predicated in part on the ever-increasing mass consciousness of deepening social contradictions, is forcing the political function of the prisons to surface in all its brutality. Their contention that prisons are being transformed into the "fascist concentration camps of modern America," should not be taken lightly, although it would be erroneous as well as defeatist in a practical sense, to maintain that fascism has irremediably established itself.

The point is this, and this is the truth which is apparent in the Manifesto: The ruling circles of America are expanding and intensifying repressive measures designed to nip revolutionary movements in the bud as well as to curtail radical-democratic tendencies, such as the movement to end the war in Indochina. The government is not hesitating to utilize an entire network of fascist tactics, including the monitoring of congressmen's telephone calls, a system of 'preventive fascism,' as Marcuse has termed it, in which the role of the judicial-penal systems looms large. The sharp edge of political repression, cutting through the heightened militancy of the masses, and bringing growing numbers of activists behind prison walls, must necessarily pour over into the contained world of the prison where it understandably acquires far more ruthless forms.

It is a relatively easy matter to persecute the captive whose life is already dominated by a network of authoritarian mechanisms. This is especially facilitated by the indeterminate sentence policies of many states, for politically conscious prisoners will incur inordinately long sentences on their original conviction. According to Louis S. Nelson, warden of San Quentin Prison, "...if the prisons of California become known as 'schools for violent revolution,' the Adult Authority would be remiss in their duty not to keep the inmates longer." (S.F. *Chronicle*, May 2, 1971). Where this is deemed inadequate, authorities have recourse to the whole spectrum of brutal corporal punishment, including out and out murder. At San Quentin, Fred Billingslea was teargassed to death in February, 1970. W. L. Nolan, Alvin Miller, and Cleveland Edwards were assassinated by a prison guard in January, 1970 at Soledad Prison. Unusual and inexplicable suicides have occurred with incredible regularity in jails and prisons throughout the country.

It should be self-evident that the frame-up becomes a powerful weapon within the spectrum of prison repression, particularly because of the availability of informers, the broken prisoners who will do anything for a price. The Soledad Brothers and the Soledad 3 are leading examples of frame-up victims. Both cases involve militant activists who have been charged with killing Soledad prison guards. In both cases, widespread support has been kindled within the California prison system. They have served as occasions to link the immediate needs of the Black community with a forceful fight to break the fascist stronghold in the prisons and therefore to abolish the prison system in its present form.

The pivotal struggle which must be waged in the ranks of the working class is consequently the open, unreserved battle against entrenched racism. The white worker must become conscious of the threads which bind him to a James Johnson, Black auto worker, member of UAW, and a political prisoner presently facing charges for the killings of two foremen and a job setter.[5] The merciless proliferation of the power of monopoly capital may ultimately push him inexorably down the very same path of desperation. No potential victim of the fascist terror should be without the knowledge that the greatest menace to racism and fascism is unity!

Facing our Common Foe: Women and the Struggle against Racism, 1984[6]

It is too frequently assumed that white people are obligated to recognize Black people's leadership only when Afro-American equality is at issue—or that Chicanos, Puerto Ricans, Native Americans, and Asian-Pacific people are only qualified to speak on behalf of their own people and not on the conditions of society and humanity at large. It is imperative that those sectors of the women's movement that largely reflect the particular aspirations of their white middle-class constituencies challenge these erroneous assumptions. All too often—historically as well as at present—white leaders of the women's movement presume that when Black women raise our voices about the triple oppression we suffer, our message is at best of marginal relevance to their experiences. They have falsely presumed that women's issues can be articulated in isolation from issues associated with the Black movement and the labor movement. Their theories and practice have frequently implied that the purest and most direct challenge to sexism is one exorcised of elements related to racial and economic oppression—as if there were such a phenomenon as abstract womanhood abstractly suffering sexism and fighting back in an abstract historical context. In the final analysis, that state of abstraction turns out to be a very specific set of conditions: white middle-class women suffering and responding to the sexist attitudes and conduct of white middle-class men and calling for equality with those particular men. This approach leaves the existing socioeconomic system with its fundamental reliance on racism and class bias unchallenged.

It is possible for white women—especially those associated with the capitalist or middle classes—to achieve their own particular goals without securing any ostensible progress for their racially oppressed and working-class sisters.

In order for the women's movement to meet the challenges of our times, the special problems of racially oppressed women must be given strategic priority. During the early phases of the contemporary women's movement, women's liberationist issues were so narrowly construed that most white women did not grasp the importance of defending Black women from the material and ideological assaults emanating from the government. White women who were then primarily involved in the consciousness-raising process failed to comprehend the relationship between the welfare rights movement and the larger battle for women's emancipation. Neither did they understand the importance of challenging the propagandistic definition of Black women as "emasculating matriarchs" as a struggle in which all women who identified with women's liberation ought to have participated. Today, we can no longer afford to dismiss the racist influences that pervade the women's movement, nor can we continue to succumb to the belief that white women will be unable eternally to grasp the nature of the bonds that link them to their sisters of color.

It is no longer permissible for white women to justify their failure to struggle jointly with women of color by offering such frail excuses as, "We invited them to our meeting, but they just don't seem to be interested in women's issues." During the late 1960's and early 1970's, it was frequently suggested in women's liberation circles that Black, Chicana, and Puerto Rican women were not interested in feminist issues because our awareness of male supremacy was not so advanced as that of the white women who hastened to participate in the antisexist consciousness-raising process. However, their articulation of the problem in these terms reflected their own particular class and racial backgrounds. Women of color—and white working-class women as well—suffered the effects of sexism in different ways than their sisters associated with the women's liberation movement and consequently felt that middle-class white women's issues were largely irrelevant to their own lives.

Economic issues certainly may not seem as central to white middle-class women as to women whose children may become irreparably malnourished if they are unable to find a job—or if they do not receive the welfare subsidies or food stamps so drastically reduced by the Reagan administration. The demand for jobs, the fight against plant shutdowns and against union-busting—these are women's struggles. While these struggles are waged by the labor movement as a whole, women have a special interest in them because we have been most severely hurt—particularly if we happen to be Black or Brown—by the Reagan administration's economic policies.

Students and professional women must learn to accept leadership from women who are actively involved in the labor movement. Women's groups not directly associated with the labor movement should, for example, seek to aid and support those women who are involved in strike activities. Consider the Chicana and Native American women who went out on strike, along with their brother miners, against Phelps Dodge in Morenci, Arizona. Alberta Chavez, who heads the women miners' and wives of miners' organization, had criminal charges imposed on her as she womaned a picket-line in defiance of the police. Ms. Chavez appealed to women throughout the country for support.

In order to cultivate a strong women's presence in our movements against racism, women must resolutely defend affirmative action from such callous attacks as those mounted by the Reagan administration. Women and men of all racial and economic backgrounds should remember that the Black liberation movement formulated the strategy of affirmative action for the purpose of furthering the struggle against racism—and that this strategy was subsequently taken up by the women's movement as a means of facilitating the campaign against sexist discrimination. Affirmative action on the job as well as on the campus must not only be defended, but ultimately must be expanded so that it will assist all who currently suffer the discrimination wrought by our racist, sexist, capitalist society and government.

Women of color are particularly in need of an extensive, accessible child-care system. Such a system should be federally funded, nonracist, and nonsexist, and should be made available to all who need it. As we raise our demands for child care, we must simultaneously conduct an ongoing campaign against racism in the public-school system, insisting upon the implementation of bilingual public education on all levels.

We must not presume that authentic solidarity will automatically flow from the recognition of the simple fact that women of color are the most oppressed human beings in our society. Certainly, white women *should* feel compelled to lend their support to our struggles, but if they do not understand how their causes are substantially advanced by the victories won by women of color, they may inadvertently fall into ideological traps of racism even as they honestly attempt to challenge racist institutions. White women who labor under the illusion that only with their assistance will their "poor Black sisters" rise out of their deprivation—as if we need a Great White Sister Savior—have fallen prey to prevailing racist attitudes, and their activism could well prove more detrimental to our cause than beneficial. White women activists in the battered women's movement must especially beware of racist overtones in their conduct, of which they may be entirely unaware but to which women of color are highly sensitized. Lesbian organizations that are predominantly white should strive to understand the special impact of homophobia on women of color.

For the purpose of clarifying how middle-class white women benefit from the gains of their working-class sisters and sisters of color, try to visualize a simple pyramid, laterally divided according to the race and social class of different groups of women. White women are situated at the top—the bourgeoisie first, under which we place the middle classes and then white working-class women. Located at the very bottom are Black and other racially oppressed women, the vast majority of whom come from working-class backgrounds. Now, when those at the very apex of the pyramid achieve victories for themselves, in all likelihood the status of the other women remains unchanged. This dynamic has proven true in the cases of Sandra Day O'Connor and Jeane Kirkpatrick, who both achieved "firsts" as women in their respective fields. On the other hand, if those at the nadir of the pyramid win victories for themselves, it is virtually inevitable that their progress will push the entire structure upward. The forward movement of women of color almost always initiates progressive change for all women.

Working-class women, and women of color in particular, confront sexist oppression in a way that reflects the real and complex objective interconnections between economic, racial, and sexual oppression. Whereas a white middle-class woman's experience of sexism incorporates a relatively isolated form of this oppression, working-class women's experiences necessarily place sexism in its context of class exploitation—and Black women's experiences further contextualize gender oppression within the realities of racism.

Let us consider one of the most visible issues associated with the women's movement today within the framework of its relationship to the campaign against racism—the attempt to force women to surrender the right to control their bodies. Not only does the "pro-life" movement oppose the constitutional amendment that would guarantee women equal rights, they are pushing for a constitutional ban on abortions that, in effect, would extinguish women's most fundamental—and, ironically, most sacred—right: to determine what comes of and from their own bodies.

Terrorist tactics have been overtly encouraged and shamelessly implemented in the anti-abortion campaign of the so-called "right-to-lifers." During a peak year of the 1980s, there were some 147 incidents of violence and/or harassment—ranging from verbal abuse to the use of explosives to physically destroy the clinics—directed against abortion clinics and women seeking their services. In 1982, a group called the Army of God kidnapped the owner of a clinic in Illinois along with his wife. The two were held hostage for eight days, while their captors threatened to kill them if President Reagan did not announce an end to legal abortions. Incidents such as these facilitated Reagan's manipulation of the abortion issue to encourage more widespread support of ultraright positions.

In considering the issue of abortion from a progressive vantage point, it is not enough to challenge the conservative factions that would deny women the right to control the biological processes of their bodies. It is also incumbent upon us to carefully examine the strategical and tactical approaches of the movement that strive to defend this basic right of all women. We must first ask why there have been so few women of color in the ranks of the abortion rights movement. And we must go on to consider a related issue: Why, with all the raging controversy surrounding women's right to abortion, has an equally burning question—that of women's right to be free of sterilization abuse—been virtually ignored? As a result of the 1977 Hyde Amendment, which withdrew federal funding for abortions, the likelihood that poor women will be forced to submit to sterilization surgery—knowingly or unknowingly—has increased, in spite of the fact that they may wish to remain capable of bearing children in the future. And how can we explain the fact that while there is presently no federal funding for abortions, over 90 percent of the cost of sterilization surgery is covered by the federal government? Sterilization abuse is sometimes blatant, but usually it occurs in more subtle ways, and its victims are most often Puerto Rican, Chicana, Native American, Black, and poor white women. One advocate of involuntary sterilization, the Nobel Prize-winning physicist William Shockley, has deemed 85 percent of Black Americans "genetically disadvantaged" and thus candidates for sterilization. Such policies must be challenged because we must protect not only women's right to limit the size of their families, but also their right to *expand* their families if and when they so desire.

This is only one example of the many ways in which we must formulate issues so as to ensure that they reflect the experiences of women of color. Certainly, there are many more issues related to the women's movement that, if explored, would demonstrate the extent to which racism often influences the way those issues are framed and publicly articulated. Such racist influences, as long as they pervade the women's movement, will continue to obstruct the building of multiracial organizations and coalitions. Thus, the *eradication* of those influences is a fundamental prerequisite to all endeavors undertaken by the women's movement. This process of exorcising racism from our ranks will determine whether the women's movement will ultimately have a part in bringing about radical changes in the socioeconomic structures of this country.

Let Us All Rise Together: Radical Perspectives on Empowerment for Afro-American Women, 1988[7]

The concept of empowerment is hardly new to Afro-American women. For almost a century, we have been organized in bodies that have sought collectively to develop strategies illuminating the way to economic and political power for ourselves and our communities. During the last decade of the nineteenth century, after having been repeatedly shunned by the racially homogeneous women's rights movement, Black women organized their own Club Movement. In 1895—five years after the founding of the General Federation of Women's Clubs, which consolidated a club movement reflecting concerns of middle-class White women—one hundred Black women from ten states met in the city of Boston, under the leadership of Josephine St. Pierre Ruffin, to discuss the creation of a national organization of Black women's clubs. As compared to their White counterparts, the Afro-American women issuing the call for this national club movement articulated principles that were more openly political in nature. They defined the primary function of their clubs as an ideological as well as an activist defense of Black women—and men—from the ravages of racism. When the meeting was convened, its participants emphatically declared that, unlike their White sisters, whose organizational policies were seriously tainted by racism, they envisioned their movement as one open to all women:

> Our woman's movement is woman's movement in that it is led and directed by women for the good of women and men, for the benefit of *all* humanity, which is more than any one branch or section of it. We want, we ask the active interest of our men, and, too, we are not drawing the color line; we are women, American women, as intensely interested in all that pertains to us as such as all other American women; we are not alienating or withdrawing, we are only coming

to the front, willing to join any others in the same work and cordially inviting and welcoming any others to join us.[8]

The following year, the formation of the National Association of Colored Women's Clubs was announced. The motto chosen by the Association was "Lifting As We Climb."[9]

The nineteenth-century women's movement was also plagued by classism. Susan B. Anthony wondered why her outreach to working-class women on the issue of the ballot was so frequently met with indifference. She wondered why these women seemed to be much more concerned with improving their economic situation than with achieving the right to vote.[10] As essential as political equality may have been to the larger campaign for women's rights, in the eyes of Afro-American and White working-class women it was not synonymous with emancipation. That the conceptualization of strategies for struggle was based on the peculiar condition of White women of the privileged classes rendered those strategies discordant with working-class women's perceptions of empowerment. It is not surprising that many of them told Ms. Anthony, "Women want bread, not the ballot."[11] Eventually, of course, working-class White women, and Afro-American women as well, reconceptualized this struggle, defining the vote not as an end in itself—not as the panacea that would cure all the ills related to gender-based discrimination—but rather as an important weapon in the continuing fight for higher wages, better working conditions, and an end to the omnipresent menace of the lynch mob.

Today, as we reflect on the process of empowering Afro-American women, our most efficacious strategies remain those that are guided by the principle used by Black women in the club movement. We must strive to "lift as we climb." In other words, we must climb in such a way as to guarantee that all of our sisters, regardless of social class, and indeed all of our brothers, climb with us. This must be the essential dynamic of our quest for power—a principle that must not only determine our struggles as Afro-American women, but also govern all authentic struggles of dispossessed people. Indeed, the overall battle for equality can be profoundly enhanced by embracing this principle.

Afro-American women bring to the women's movement a strong tradition of struggle around issues that politically link women to the most crucial progressive causes. This is the meaning of the motto, "Lifting As We Climb." This approach reflects the often unarticulated interests and aspirations of masses of women of all racial backgrounds. Millions of women today are concerned about jobs, working conditions, higher wages, and racist violence. They are concerned about plant closures, homelessness, and repressive immigration legislation. Women are concerned about homophobia, ageism, and discrimination against the physically challenged. We are concerned about Nicaragua and South Africa. And we share our children's dream that tomorrow's world will be delivered from the threat of nuclear omnicide. These are some of the issues that should be integrated into the overall struggle for women's rights if there is to be a serious commitment to the empowerment of women who have been rendered historically invisible. These are some of the issues we should consider if we wish to lift as we climb.... We must begin to create a revolutionary, multiracial women's movement that seriously addresses the main issues affecting poor and working-class women. In order to tap the potential for such a movement, we must further develop those sectors of the movement that are addressing seriously issues affecting poor and working-class women, such as jobs, pay equity, paid maternity leave, federally subsidized child care, protection from sterilization abuse, and subsidized abortions. Women of all racial and class backgrounds will greatly benefit from such an approach.

I want to suggest, as I conclude, that we link our grass-roots organizing, our essential involvement in electoral politics, and our involvement as activists in mass struggles to the long-range goal of fundamentally transforming the socioeconomic conditions that generate and persistently nourish the various forms of oppression we suffer. Let us learn from the strategies of our sisters in South Africa and Nicaragua. As Afro-American women, as women of color in general, as progressive women of all racial backgrounds, let us join our sisters—and brothers—across the globe who are attempting to forge a new socialist order—an order which will reestablish socioeconomic priorities so that the quest for monetary profit will never be permitted to take precedence over the real interests of human beings. This is not to say that our problems will magically dissipate with the advent of socialism. Rather, such a social order should provide us with the real opportunity to further extend our struggles, with the assurance that one day we will be able to redefine the basic elements of our oppression as useless refuse of the past.

Notes

1. William Z. Foster, *The Negro People in American History*, International Publishers, New York, 1954, pp. 169–170 (quoting Herbert Aptheker).
2. 'Louis Adamic, *Dynamite: The History of Class Violence in America*, Peter Smith, Gloucester, Mass., 1963, p. 312.
3. Herbert Aptheker, *Nat Turner's Slave Rebellion*, Grove Press, N.Y. 1968, p. 45. According to Aptheker these are not Nat Turner's exact words.
4. Karl Marx: *The Class Struggle in France in Handbook of Marxism*, International Publishers, New York: 1935, p. 109.
5. See Chapter Five on political prisoners for the details of James Johnson's case.
6. Address to a conference on "Women and the Stuggle Against Racism" sponsored by the Minnesota Coalition for Battered Women, November 15, 1984.
7. Address given to the National Women's Studies Association annual conference, Spellman College, June 25, 1987. Originally published under the title "Radical Perspectives on Empowerment for Afro-American Women," *Harvard Educational Review* 25, no. 3, August 1988. Copyright 1988 by the President and Fellows of Harvard College. All rights reserved.
8. Gerda Lerner, *Black Women in White America* (New York: Pantheon Books, 1972), p. 443.
9. These clubs proliferated the progressive political scene during this era. By 1916—twenty years later—50,000 women in 28 federations and over 1,000 clubs were members of the National Association of Colored Women's Clubs. See Paula Giddings's discussion of the origins and evolution of the Black Women's Club Movement in *When and Where I Enter* (New York: William Morrow, 1984), Chapters IV–VI.
10. Miriam Schneir, ed., *Feminism: The Essential Historical Writings* (New York: Vintage, 1972), pp. 138–142.
11. Ibid.

PART V

MODERN BLACK CONSERVATIVES
WHY BLACK "NEO-CONS" MATTER

24.
CLARENCE THOMAS

Clarence Thomas (born 1948) replaced Thurgood Marshall on the Supreme Court in 1991. He became the second African American to serve on the high court. For many liberals and progressives, the nomination of Thomas, a staunch conservative, to replace Marshall, a pioneer in the struggle for civil rights, was a travesty. Before he was appointed to the Supreme Court he began his life in Georgia. Thomas's life was the quintessential Horatio Alger tale.

Thomas's mother was a maid; his father abandoned the family when he was only two years old. He attended an African American Catholic school, followed by a seminary school, and then went on to the Immaculate Conception Abbey and Holy Cross. He graduated from Yale Law School in 1974. He began an impressive career in law. From 1974 to 1977 he was assistant attorney general in Missouri. From 1977 to 1979 he practiced law with the Monsanto Company. He was incredibly influenced by and adopted many of his conservative views from Republican senator John C. Danforth. He worked as a legislative assistant for the senator from 1979 to 1981. From 1981 to 1982 Thomas worked as assistant secretary in the U.S. Department of Education. Beginning in 1982 he served for eight years as the chairman of the Equal Employment Opportunity Commission. While on the Commission he shifted the Commission's focus. Thomas advocated self-reliance and personal responsibility and as a result had the commission focus more on individual discrimination lawsuits and less on pursuing class action discrimination lawsuits. In 1990, President George H. Bush appointed Thomas to the U.S. Court of Appeals for the federal district in Washington, D.C. Thomas seemed like a shoo-in for the Supreme Court.

Thomas was confirmed by a narrow vote in the Senate, 52–48, after the Senate judiciary committee was deadlocked at a 7–7 vote. Once nominated for the Supreme Court, Anita Hill, who worked for Thomas at the Equal Employment Opportunity Commission and the Department of Education, accused him of sexual harassment. Hill was an accomplished lawyer and law professor. To this day, Thomas continues to deny these charges. Thomas famously said that his public persecution was tantamount to a "high-tech lynching." The media depicted Hill as a disgruntled angry Black woman and Thomas the victim of a liberal lynch mob. In the end, after countless hours of testimony and detailed accounts of inappropriate sexual comments and propositions, Hill, who had her own aspirations and desires to one day sit on the federal bench, was publicly humiliated and called a liar and Thomas was eventually confirmed to the court.

Overview of Ideas

Clarence Thomas along with Atonin Scalia is one of the most conservative members of the Supreme Court, if not the most conservative. In two monumental cases, *Planned Parenthood of Southeastern Pennsylvania* v. *Casey* (1992) and *Missouri* v. *Jenkins* (1995), Thomas asserted himself as a staunch conservative. In Casey, Thomas made his opinion on abortion clear; he as part of the dissenting opinion argued that *Roe* v. *Wade* should be reversed. In Jenkins, Thomas said, "the federal courts ... should avoid using racial equality as a pretext for solving social problems that do not violate the Constitution." Thomas continues to criticize "judicial activism," the federal government's intervention in state affairs, and the paternalistic intervention into the lives of individuals. In Jenkins, Thomas also said:

> desegregation has not produced the predicted leaps forward in black educational achievement. There is no reason to think that black students cannot learn as well when surrounded by members of their own race as when they are in an integrated environment.

Thomas posited that having all-black schools that were successful would serve as role models for African Americans and demonstrate that self-sufficiency is paramount.

Thomas is an advocate of personal responsibility. In 1980 Thomas attended a conservative conference organized by Thomas Sowell, a famous conservative African American economist. At this conference, in front of a packed room of Black conservatives, Thomas made several comments that became the subject of controversy and initiated media frenzy. Thomas said, "I marched. I protested. I asked the government to help black people ... I did all those things. But it hasn't worked. It isn't working. And someone needs to say that."[1] According to Thomas, expanding the welfare state does not help Black people; in fact, it stifles individual motivation. Clarence Thomas continues to be a critical opponent of affirmative action, rent control, minimum wage laws, school busing programs, and welfare. In fact, referencing his sister, he said:

> she gets mad when the mailman is late with her welfare check ... that is how dependent she is. What's worse is that now her kids feel entitled to the check too. They have no motivation for doing better or getting out of that situation.[2]

What made these comments particularly horrific was that he neglected to tell the audience that while he was at Yale Law, his sister was working hard to support her and her children after her ex-husband abandoned her. She worked two minimum wage jobs trying to support her family. When their aunt had a stroke, she quit these jobs to care for her and this is when she went on welfare.

Thomas frequently utilizes his personal background and experiences as anecdotal evidence to buttress his arguments. For example, in an effort to support his arguments about self-sufficiency and personal responsibility he said:

I remember being called in the first report period—we got report cards every six weeks—and all but told that I was inherently inferior. Therefore, I had to work harder. I knew that it was a way of downgrading me, but in fact it spurred me on. I did not think anybody should get away with calling me "inherently inferior." So I performed very well.

According to Thomas, African Americans face discrimination in public institutions. However, African Americans, then, must work harder and demonstrate through action that they are not inferior. He argues that institutions should never create quotas, change their rules, or lower their standards to address the legacy of racism de jure in the United States. The solution to poverty and overcoming prejudices is the responsibility of the individual and not the state. Clarence Thomas harkens back to his earliest memories as a child; he tells stories of watching matriarchs in his family and neighborhood working long hard hours under repugnant conditions of labor to support their families. Again, he strategically utilizes these anecdotes to suggest that the Protestant work ethic—hard work in a vocational calling and thrift—is what makes individuals successful in society. African Americans must adopt this work ethic. African Americans require resourcefulness, like his mother, who never wasted any part of the pig when cooking for their family. Moreover, the solution to the Negro Problem lies in tenacity; African Americans should never let their circumstances, however deplorable, be an excuse for failure. Self-pity is the enemy of success.

Thomas, like many Black conservatives, is flippantly reduced to being a "House Negro" or a sell-out to the White political establishment. Thomas recognizes that racial discrimination exists. He recognizes the inequalities present under capitalism:

That mean, callous world out there is still very much filled with discrimination. It still holds out a different life for those who do not happen to be the right race or the right sex. It is a world in which the "haves" continue to reap more dividends than the "have-nots", and the powerful wield more influence than the powerless.

His solutions to these problems are just different than his liberal critics. Rather than favoring a top-down government-implemented solution, like many of his predecessors, he emphasizes self-help. He argues that many young people become enthralled in a culture of commodity fetishism that is also hedonistic. They are not taught the importance of "obligations and responsibilities." It is the job of the family to teach hard work, thrift, and morals. Secularization and the decline of the nuclear structure of the African American family contribute too many of the social problems that poor Black people face. This is an internal problem; this is not the government's problem.

Thomas says he is constantly outraged by what African Americans have had to and still continue to endure in this country. He says, "I am here to say that discrimination, racism, and bigotry have gone no place and probably never will." However, he says that means Black folk must fight harder. Is this fair? Probably not. But does sitting around crying and complaining that the unjust nation has forced you too work harder actually help change your situation? This will get Black people nowhere, Thomas says. Excuses will get you nowhere.

Clarence Thomas has challenged racism within the Republican Party and amongst conservatives. Thomas argues that more Black folk would vote conservative and align themselves with conservatives if they were not marginalized from these circles. Conservatives need to work harder to demonstrate why Black people have far more in common with conservatives than many acknowledge. Liberals are the only people who actively recruit Black people; this has been the great mistake of conservatism.

According to Thomas, many African Americans actually adhere to conservative ideologies. However, many Blacks "hate or fear" conservatives. According to Thomas, the media has played a large role in convincing African Americans that the Republican Party and conservatism is antithetical to their interests. The media continues to paint Black conservatives as sell-outs and Uncle Toms. Thomas continues to fight the idea that conservative Blacks "might as well be White." He continues to posit that there is diversity amongst African American political thought. He continues to fight the misnomer that all Blacks must be Democrats or liberals.

Being Educated Black, 1980

I attended one of the black schools which Dr. Sowell profiled, St. Pius X High School in Savannah, Georgia. The interesting thing about the school is this: as a result of racial integration, as a result of the requirement that all high schools be integrated in the city of Savannah, they closed down St. Pius X High School because there was no cross-integration from the white community, and approximately 300 students who could afford to go to St. Pius X High School were put out. They were told to go to Benedictine Military Academy, which cost maybe ten times as much for some students. I think we had some very intelligent people who were displaced to what I would consider inferior schools. We did have the bad physical plant; we did have the constant problems with paying bills, and so forth, and we did have the poor books. We also had an excellent education.

The Black Spot on the White Horse

I later attended Holy Cross College. It was very interesting because, prior to that, I had attended an all-white seminary in Savannah. I was the only black there during the mid-1960s and I was referred to, not too politely, as the black spot on the white horse. At that time there was no mercy shown to blacks and there were no changes made in the curriculum. We were simply required to go on and perform as the other students. I remember being called in the first report period—we got report cards every six weeks—and all but told that I was inherently inferior. Therefore, I had to work harder. I knew that it was a way of downgrading me, but in fact it spurred me on. I did not think anybody should get away with calling me "inherently inferior." So I performed very well.

We Attempted to Change Everything

We did some interesting things at Holy Cross College. I think we did some interesting things across this country when I was in college. We attempted to change everything, including the practices at schools. When we saw that black students were not surviving, we attributed that to discrimination and immediately tried to change the grade requirements. We tried to eliminate courses like metaphysics, sciences, and similar ones. We wound up with some poorly educated black kids and we still did not improve the grades and we still did not lower the flunk-out rate. It was a tremendously depressing and disappointing experience. I'm glad to hear Professor Sowell document and explain these facts, because for so long I knew something was wrong. A lot of us knew something was wrong, but we simply did not know precisely what it was.

We Have Some Hope

I believe that the problem will definitely not be solved with an external answer. I do not believe that an institution can change its numbers, change its quotas, change its courses, or reduce its standards and make us better. I do believe that we have some hope, some possibility of accomplishing something if we begin to internalize the solution to the problem, to think in terms of solving it ourselves. It may not be successful, but I can assure you that if we do not take responsibility ourselves we will not have any hope at all.

Black People Need to Look to Themselves for Solutions

We have an interesting problem at the institution on whose board I serve. Most of the black students are lumped at the end of the class. My question, after ten years of experience with black students, is why are they all at the end of the class? We have changed course requirements, we have given remedial assistance, and hopefully we have created better students. But they are still lumped at the bottom of the class. Personally, I believe that, as black people beginning the 1980s, we need to look more to ourselves for solutions, not forgetting the preclusive practices that have occurred, but definitely putting the primary role, the primary responsibility for the solution to these problems, on ourselves.

Savannah State College Commencement Address, 1985

President Rayburn, members of the faculty, distinguished guests, relatives, friends, and most importantly, graduates. It is with great pleasure and a sense of gratitude that I stand before you all today. I regret only that my grandparents, Myers and Christine Anderson, are not here. Not too many years ago, attending Savannah State was a distant dream for me. This institution, the bricks, the mortar, the books, the professors stood as a testament to a race in the defiance of a *system* designed to keep a race ignorant—a *system* bent on establishing racial dominance. Savannah State College, its legacy, its tradition, its history made it possible for those of us who grew up in its benevolent shadows to believe that we could take another giant step away from slavery, that we could leap across the great chasm of bigotry and hatred, that we could one day have what the *other* America had, endless opportunities in a bountiful country. *Yes*, I grew up here in Savannah. *Yes*, I was born not far from here (in Pinpoint) [*sic*]. I am a child of those marshes, a son of this soil. I am a descendant of the slaves whose labors made the dark soil of the South productive. I am the great, great grandson of a freed slave, whose enslavement continued after my birth. I am, my friends, the product of hatred and love—the hatred of the social and political structure which dominated the segregated, hate-filled city of my youth *and* the love of some people—my mother, my grandparents, my neighbors and relatives—who said *by* their actions "You can make it, but first, you must endure." You *can survive*, but first, you must endure. You *can live*, but first, you must endure. You must endure the unfairness—you must endure the hatred—you must endure the bigotry—you must endure the segregation. You must endure the indignities.

I watched the strongest man in the world endure *so* that he could raise his two grandsons, *so* that he could make something of his life; and *so* that his two grandsons (my brother and me) could do the same with ours. I watched a quiet strong grandmother slave away in the kitchen, clean house, cook *and endure*, so we could make it. I watched through a child's eyes as my young mother, Miss Mariah, Miss Bec, Miss Gladys, Miss Gertrude, Cousin Hattie, Cousin Bea, Cousin Julie all worked countless hours in other people's kitchens, with aching feet and pain-filled heads for little pay and no benefits—but they *endured* so that we who watched them could make it.

They loved us not only with kisses and hugs but with example. I have watched these women line up in the early morning—in the cold—in the dark—in the rain to catch the bus to work. I have watched them in the evenings standing on solitary corners with their shopping bags in the heat and humidity waiting for the bus where they would crowd in the back, with no air-conditioning—or if they were lucky, they would ride in the back seat of their employer's car. They endured *this* to get home dead tired so they could raise *their* families, clean their houses, cook their dinners. And we, we had the nerve to wonder why they needed a goodie, a standback or a BC with a coke. But *endure* they did—and through the eyes of children, we watched.

I haven't mentioned those women who shucked oysters, picked crabs, headed shrimp, hoed corn, raised chickens. I haven't mentioned those men who held two or even three jobs. I haven't mentioned Mr. Miller (both father and son) who worked *all* the time. I haven't mentioned Mr. Sam Williams and Mr. Ben Wise who ran businesses and carried fuel oil like my grandfather. I haven't mentioned all those people who could fix anything or build anything. They endured Savannah and all it had to offer.

I watched through the eyes of a child as my race took that part of life that was left and survived. I often think about the renewed interest in soul food. Take, for example, what we ate from the pig; the foot, the tail, the head, the ears, the neck, and intestines. I have yet to mention any part that anyone else wanted. If someone was having pork shoulder or ham for dinner, we would say "Yeah, they're eating high on the hog." To this day I marvel at what my mother could do with some neckbones and pigtails—and what my grandmother could do with chicken feet.

These are my greatest teachers. My role models. Their lives have been my greatest and most important classes. They made every effort to rise above the life they were left to wallow in. Even though they had to live in poverty or near poverty, they rejected squalor and self-pity. They refused to give in to the seemingly hopeless circumstances, *and* they never gave up. They rose up like a phoenix from the ashes of bigotry and hatred. They endured—they survived. And, we were the beneficiaries of their survival, for we had no choice but to learn the values which made their survival possible *and* the hostility and bigotry which we could expect as we grew older and took our turn at being adults. I learned from people whose condition and status were self-evident but who *refused* to accept as inevitable the rational consequences of their lot.

Today I stand before you as one who had the same beginnings as yourselves—as one who has walked a little farther down the road, climbed a little higher up the mountain. I come back to you, who must now travel this road and climb this jagged, steep mountain that lies ahead. I return as a messenger—a front-runner, a scout. My friends, what lies ahead of you is even tougher than what is now behind you.

That mean, callous world out there is still very much filled with discrimination. It still holds out a different life for those who do not happen to be the right race or the right sex. It is a world in which the "haves" continue to reap more dividends than the "have-nots", and the powerful wield more influence than the powerless.

You will enter a world in which more than one-half of all Black children are born primarily to youthful mothers and out of wedlock. You will enter a world in which the Black teenage unemployment rate as always is more than double that of white teenagers. Yours will be a world in which computers and computer technology are a way of life. Any discrimination, like sharp turns in a road, become [*sic*] critical because of the tremendous speed at which we are travelling toward and into the high-tech world of a service economy.

Because I was once as youthful as you all are, I am familiar with the omniscience of youthful arrogance. Mr. "Know-t-All" [*sic*] is what my grandfather called me when he [*sic*] grew weary of me. Accepting this tendency as a given. I urge you to listen anyway.

There is a tendency among young upwardly mobile, intelligent minorities today to forget. We *forget* the sweat of our forefathers. We *forget* the blood of the marchers, the prayers and hope of our race. We *forget* who brought us into this world. We *overlook* who put food in our mouths and clothes on our backs. We forget commitment to excellence. We *procreate* with pleasure and retreat from the responsibilities of the babies we produce. We subdue, we seduce, but we don't respect ourselves, our women, our babies. How do we expect a race that has been thrown into the gutter of socio-economic indicators to rise above these humiliating circumstances if we hide from responsibility for our own destiny. The truth of the matter is we have become more interested in designer jeans and break-dancing than we are in obligations and responsibilities.

Over the past 15 years, I have watched as others have jumped quickly at the opportunity to make excuses for Black Americans. It is said that Blacks cannot start businesses because of discrimination. But, I remember businesses on East Broad and West Broad that were run in spite of bigotry. It is said that we can't learn because of bigotry. But I know for a fact that tens of thousands of Blacks were educated at historically Black colleges, in spite of discrimination. And there are some who would have closed this College in the name of desegregation when they opened up the competitive school as a junior college to keep from going to Savannah State. We learned to read in spite of segregated libraries. You didn't dare go to the Savannah Public Library—Carnegie is where you went. We built homes in spite of segregated neighborhoods. We learned how to play basketball (and did we ever learn!!), even though we couldn't go to the NBA. And you had better not go into Daffin Park.

You ask what am I saying. Simply put, I am saying that we have lost something. We look for role models in all the wrong places. We refuse to reach back in our not too distant past for the lessons and values we need to carry us into the uncertain future. We prefer the speculations of seers and clairvoyants to the certainty of past experience. We ignore what has permitted Blacks in this country to survive the brutality of slavery and the bitter rejection of segregation. We overlook the reality of positive values and run to the mirage of promises, visions and dreams.

I do not stand before you poised for debate. I do not dare come to this city, which only two decades ago clung so tenaciously to segregation, bigotry, and Jim Crowism, to convince you all of the fairness of this society. My memory is too precise—my recollection too keen to venture down that path of self-delusion. I am not blind to our history—nor do I turn a deaf ear to the pleas and cries of Black Americans. Often I must struggle to contain my outrage at what has happened to Black Americans—what continues to happen—what we let happen and what we do to ourselves. If I let myself go, I would rage in the words of Frederick Douglass:

> "At a time like this, scorching irony, not convincing argument, is needed. Oh! Had I the ability, and could reach the nation's ear, I would today pour out a fiery stream of biting ridicule, blasting reproach, withering sarcasm and stern rebuke. For it is not light that is needed, but fire; it is not the gentle shower, but thunder. We need the storm, the whirlwind, and the earthquake. The feeling of the nation must be quickened; the conscience of the nation must be roused; the propriety of the nation must be started; the hypocrisy of the nation must be exposed; and its crimes against God and man must be denounced."

I often hear rosy platitudes about this country—much of which is true. It is the greatest country on earth. It does have more freedoms than any other nation. It is the richest and the most powerful country. All of this is true, and makes me proud, but how are we Black Americans to feel when we have so little in a land with so much. How is Black America to respond to the celebration of the wonders of this great nation. Again, in the words of Frederick Douglass:

> "To him, your celebration is a sham; your boasted liberty, an unholy license; your national greatness, swelling vanity; your sounds of rejoicing are empty and heartless; your denunciation of tyrants, *brass-fronted* impudence; your shouts of liberty and equality, hollow mockery; your prayers and hymns, your sermons and thanksgivings, with all your religious parade and solemnity, are to Him mere bombast, fraud, deception, impiety, and hypocrisy…"

No, I have no delusions about discrimination, racism, or bigotry. I am not among those who believed that this unholy triumvirate went some place—disappeared. I watched, however, as those three demons were summoned up or sent away to suit the whims and motives of politicians and so-called leaders. When the parties they supported were in power, they would push the demons back. When their opponents came to power, they would again summon up this unholy alliance as the reason why Blacks could make no progress. Well, I am here to say that discrimination, racism, and bigotry have gone no place and probably never will. What does that mean for us—for you graduates? Does it mean that you roll over and give up? Does it mean you do nothing until these hideous creatures of hate are destroyed? Does it mean you accept no responsibility for your future? For your lives?

You know, in 1964, when I entered the Seminary on the Isle of Hope, I was the only Black in my class and one of two in the school. A year later, I was the only one in the school. Not a day passed that I was not pricked by that ever-present trident of prejudice.

But I had an advantage over Black students and kids today, I had never heard any excuses made. Nor had I seen my role models take comfort in excuses. The women who worked in those kitchens and waited on the bus knew it was prejudice which caused their plight, but that didn't stop them from working. My grandfather knew why his business wasn't more successful, but that didn't stop him from getting up at two in the morning to carry ice, wood, and fuel oil. Sure, they knew it was bad. They knew all too well that they were held back by prejudice. But they weren't pinned down by it. They fought against discrimination under the leadership of W. W. Law and the NAACP. Equally important, they fought against the awful effects of prejudice by doing all they could do in spite of this obstacle. They could still send their children to school, they could still respect and help each other, they could still moderate their use of alcohol; they could still be decent, law-abiding citizens. I had the benefit of people who knew they had to walk a straighter line, climb a taller mountain, and carry a heavier load. They took all that segregation and prejudice would allow them *and* at the same time fought to remove these awful barriers.

You all have a much tougher road to travel. Not only do you have to contend with the ever-present bigotry, you must do so with a recent tradition that almost requires you to wallow in excuses. You now have a popular national rhetoric which says that you can't learn because of racism, you can't raise the babies you make because of racism, you can't get up in the mornings because of racism. You commit crimes because of racism. Unlike me you must not only overcome the repressiveness of racism, you must also overcome the lure of excuses. You have twice the job I had.

In Greek mythology, sirens with their bewitching sweetness, lured ships to their destruction on dangerous rocky coastlines. There will be many, many such sirens in your lives. They will attempt to lure you to the rocks of certain destruction and definite failure. They will try to convince you that others have total control over your lives— that politicians here, in Atlanta, and in Washington have more to do with your success than you do.

They don't. Do not be lured by their sirens and purveyors of misery who profit from constantly regurgitating all that is wrong with Black Americans and blaming these problems on others. Do not succumb to this temptation of always blaming others. Do not become obsessed with all that is wrong with our race. Rather, become obsessed with looking for solutions to our problems. Be tolerant of all positive ideas, their number is much smaller than the countless number of problems to be solved. We need *all* the hope we can get.

Most importantly, draw on that great lesson and those positive role models who have gone down this road before us. We are badgered and pushed by our friends and peers to do unlike our parents and grandparents—we are told not to be old fashioned. But they have weathered the storm. It is up to us now to learn how. Countless hours of research are spent to determine why Blacks fail or why we commit crimes. Why can't we spend a few hours learning how those closest to us have survived and helped us get this far? As your frontrunner, I have gone ahead and taken a long, hard look. I have seen two roads from my perch a few humble feet above the maddening crowd. On the first, a race of people is rushing mindlessly down a highway of sweet, intoxicating destruction, with all its bright lights and grand promises, constructed by social scientists and politicians. To the side, there is a seldom used, overgrown road leading through the valley of life with all its pitfalls and obstacles, with all its hatred and discrimination. It is a difficult "winding, meandering" road, full of ups and downs, with no promise of certain success. But it is a road of hope and opportunity. It is the road—the old fashioned road—travelled by those who endured slavery—who endured Jim Crowism—who endured hatred. It is the road that *might* reward hard work and discipline; that *might* reward intelligence; that *might* be fair and provide equal opportunity. But there are no guarantees.

You must choose. The lure of the highway is seductive and enticing, but the destruction is certain. To travel the road of hope and opportunity is hard and difficult, but there is a chance that you might somehow, someway, with the help of God—make it!

Two decades from now you must face your children and other graduates who must choose. Will you say I was destroyed by the life of the fast highway, or will you be able to say in the words of Robert Frost:

> "Two roads diverged in the woods, and I—I took the one less travelled by, and that has made all the difference."

The roads are there. The challenge is clear. The choice is yours. I wish you good luck and Godspeed!

Why Black Americans Should Look to Conservative Policies, 1987

Much has been said about blacks and conservatism. Those on the Left smugly assume blacks are monolithic and will by force of circumstances always huddle to the left of the political spectrum. The political Right watches this herd mentality in action, concedes that blacks are monolithic, picks up a few dissidents, and wistfully shrugs at the seemingly unbreakable hold of the liberal Left on black Americans. But even in the face of this, a few dissidents like Tom Sowell and J.A. Parker stand steadfast, refusing to give in to the cult mentality and childish obedience that hypnotize black Americans into a mindless, political trance. I admire them, and only wish I could have a fraction of their courage and strength.

Many pundits have come along in recent years, who claim an understanding of why so many blacks think right and vote left. They offer "the answer" to the problem of blacks failing to respond favorably to conservatism. I, for one, am not certain there is such a thing as "the answer." And, even if there is, I assure you I do not have it.

I have only my experiences and modest observations to offer. First, I may be somewhat of an oddity. I grew up under state-enforced segregation, which is as close to totalitarianism as I would like to get. My household, notwithstanding the myth fabricated by experts, was strong, stable, and conservative. In fact, it was far more conservative than many who fashion themselves conservatives today. God was central. School, discipline, hard work, and knowing right from wrong were of the highest priority. Crime, welfare, slothfulness, and alcohol were enemies. But these were not issues to be debated by keen intellectuals, bellowed about by rousing orators, or dissected by pollsters and researchers. They were a way of life; they marked the path of survival and the escape route from squalor.

Family Policy, Not Social Policy. Unlike today, we debated no one about our way of life—we lived it. I must add that my grandparents enforced the no-debate rule. There were a number of concerns I wanted to express. In fact, I did on a number of occasions at a great price. But then, I have always found a way to get in my two cents.

Of course, I thought my grandparents were too rigid and their expectations were too high. I also thought they were mean at times. But one of their often stated goals was to raise us so that we could "do for ourselves," so that we could stand on our "own two feet." This was not their social policy, it was their family policy—for their family, not those nameless families that politicians love to whine about. The most compassionate thing they did for us was to teach us to fend for ourselves and to do that in an openly hostile environment. In fact, the hostility made learning the lesson that much more urgent. It made the difference between freedom and incarceration; life and death; alcoholism and sobriety. The evidence of those who failed abounded, and casualties lay everywhere. But there were also many examples of success—all of whom, according to my grandfather, followed the straight and narrow path. I was raised to survive under the totalitarianism of segregation, not only without the active assistance of government but with its active opposition. We were raised to survive in spite of the dark oppressive cloud of governmentally sanctioned bigotry. Self-sufficiency and spiritual and emotional security were our tools to carve out and secure freedom. Those who attempt to capture the daily counseling, oversight, common sense, and vision of my grandparents in a governmental program are engaging in sheer folly. Government cannot develop individual responsibility, but it certainly can refrain from preventing or hindering the development of this responsibility.

No Prescription for Success. I am of the view that black Americans will move inexorably and naturally toward conservatism when we stop discouraging them; when they are treated as a diverse group with differing interests; and when conservatives stand up for what they believe in rather than stand against blacks. This is not a prescription for success, but rather an assertion that black Americans know what they want, and it is not timidity and condescension. Nor do I believe gadget ideas such as enterprise zones are of any consequence when blacks who live in blighted areas know that crime, not lack of tax credits, is the problem. Blacks are not stupid. And no matter how good an idea or proposal is, no one is going to give up the comfort of the leftist status quo as long as they view conservatives as antagonistic to their interest, and conservatives do little or nothing to dispel the perception. If blacks hate or fear conservatives, nothing we say will be heard. Let me relate my experience as a designated black/conservative/Republican/Reagan appointee in the civil rights area—our soft underbelly as far as our opponents are concerned.

I begin by noting that there was much that many of us who have been in this Administration since the beginning could and should have done. This is at least as true for me as for anyone else. For example, I believe firmly that I should have taken a more aggressive stand against opponents of free enterprise and opponents of the values that are central to success in this society. For me, even more important, I should have been more aggressive in arguing my points with fellow members of the Administration and with those who shared my political and ideological bent. With that said, let us take a look at my perception of the past six years.

High Hopes. In 1980 when Ronald Reagan was elected, I was a staffer for Senator John Danforth of Missouri. After the election, Thomas Sowell called to invite me to a conference in San Francisco, later named the Fairmont Conference. It was his hope, and certainly mine, that this conference would be the beginning of an alternative group—an alternative to the consistently leftist thinking of the civil rights and the black leadership. To my knowledge, it was not intended that this group be an antagonist to anyone, but rather that it bring pluralism to the thinking and to the leadership of black Americans. At the conference at the Fairmont Hotel in San Francisco, there was much fanfare, considerable media coverage, and high hopes. In retrospect, however, the composition of the conference, the attendees, and their various motives for being there should have been an indication of the problems we would encounter in providing alternative thinking in our society. Some of us went because we felt strongly that black Americans were being fed a steady diet of wrong ideas, wrong thinking, and certainly nothing approaching pluralism. There were some others, however, who appeared there solely to gain strategic political position(s) in the new Administration. This would be the undoing of a great idea. But even so, hopes were high, expectations and spirits were high, and morale was high. For those of us who had wandered in the desert of political and ideological alienation, we had found a home, we had found each other. For me, this was also the beginning of public exposure that would change my life and raise my blood pressure—and anxiety level. After returning from San Francisco, the Washington Post printed a major op-ed article about me and my views at the Fairmont Conference. Essentially, the article listed my opposition to busing and affirmative action as well as my concerns about welfare. The resulting outcry was consistently negative.

Castigated and Ridiculed. Many black Republicans with whom I had enjoyed a working and amicable relationship on Capitol Hill were now distant, and some were even hostile. Letters to the Editor castigated and ridiculed me. I was invited to a panel presentation by one organization, "Black Women's Agenda," and scolded by none other than then Congressman Harold Washington of Chicago. Although initially shocked by the treatment I received, my spirits were not dampened. I was quite enthusiastic about the prospects of black Americans with different ideas receiving exposure. It was in this spirit in 1981 that I joined the Administration as an Assistant Secretary in the Department of Education. I had, initially, declined taking the position of Assistant Secretary for Civil Rights simply because my career was not in civil rights and I had no intention of moving into this area. In fact, I was insulted by the initial contact about the position as well as my current position. But policies affecting black Americans had been an all-consuming interest of mine since the age of 16.

I always found it curious that, even though that my background was in energy, taxation, and general corporate regulatory matters, I was not seriously sought after to move into one of those areas. But be that as it may, I was excited about the prospects of influencing change. The early enthusiasm was incredible. We had strategy meetings among blacks who were interested in approaching the problems of minorities in our society in a different way—among blacks who saw the mistakes of the past and who were willing to admit error and redirect their energies in a positive way. There was also considerable interest (among some white organizations) in black Americans who thought differently. But, by and large, it was an opportunity to be excited about the prospects of the future—to be excited about the possibilities of changing the course of history and altering the direction of social and civil rights policies in this country. Of course, for much of the media and for many organizations, we were mere curiosities. One person asked rhetorically, "Why do we need blacks thinking like whites?" I saw the prospects of proselytizing many young blacks who, like myself, had been disenchanted with the Left; disenchanted with the so-called black leaders; and discouraged by the inability to effect change or in any way influence the thinking of black leaders in the Democratic Party.

Honeymoon Over. But all good things must come to an end. During my first year in the Administration, it was clear that the honeymoon was over. The emphasis in the area of civil rights and social policies was decidedly negative. In the civil rights arena, we began to argue consistently against affirmative action. We attacked welfare and the welfare mentality. These are positions with which I agree. But, the emphasis was unnecessarily negative. It had been my hope and continues to be my hope that we would espouse principles and policies which by their sheer force would preempt welfare and race-conscious policies.

The winds were not taken out of our sails, however, until early 1982 when we changed positions in the Supreme Court to support a tax exemption for Bob Jones University which had been previously challenged because of certain racial policies. Although the point being made in the argument that the administrative and regulatory arm of government should not make policies through regulations was a valid point, it was lost in the overall perception that the racial policies of Bob Jones University were being defended. In addition, the perception that the Administration did not support an extension of the Voting Rights Act aggravated our problems.

I was intrigued by several events that surrounded both the Bob Jones decision and the handling of the Voting Rights Act. As you probably remember, the decision to change positions in the Bob Jones University was made public on Friday afternoon simultaneously with the AT&T breakup. On the following Monday, I expressed grave concerns in a previously scheduled meeting that this would be the undoing of those of us in the Administration who had hoped for an opportunity to expand the thinking of and about black Americans. A fellow member of the Administration said rather glibly that, in two days, the furor over Bob Jones would end. I responded that we had sounded our death knell with that decision. Unfortunately, I was more right than he was.

With respect to the Voting Rights Act, I always found it intriguing that we consistently claimed credit for extending it. Indeed, the President did sign it. Indeed, the President did support the extension of the Voting Rights Act. But by failing to get out early and positively in front of the effort to extend the Act, we allowed ourselves to be put in the position of opposing a version of the Voting Rights Act that was unacceptable, and hence we allowed the perception to be created that this Administration opposed the Voting Rights Act, not simply a version of it.

My Friend Attacked. Needless to say, the harangues to which we were subjected privately, publicly, and in all sorts of forums were considerable after these two policy decisions. There was no place that any of us who were identified as black conservatives, black Republicans, or black members of the Administration could go without being virtually attacked and certainly challenged with respect to those two issues specifically and the Administration generally. I remember a very good friend of mine complaining to me that he had been attacked simply for being my friend. Apparently the attack was so intense he simply left the event he was attending. They also made his date leave.

If that were not enough, there was the appearance within the conservative ranks that blacks were to be tolerated but not necessarily welcomed. There appeared to be a presumption, albeit rebuttable, that blacks could not be conservative. Interestingly, this was the flip side of the liberal assumption that we consistently challenged: that blacks were characteristically leftist in their thinking. As such, there was the constant pressure and apparent expectation that even blacks who were in the Administration and considered conservative publicly had to prove themselves daily. Hence, in challenging either positions or the emphases on policy matters, one had to be careful not to go so far as to lose his conservative credentials—or so it seemed. Certainly, pluralism or different points of view on the merits of these issues was not encouraged or invited-especially from blacks. And, if advice was given, it was often ignored. Dissent bore a price—one I gladly paid. Unfortunately, I would have to characterize the general attitude of conservatives toward black conservatives as indifference—with minor exceptions. It was made clear more than once that, since blacks did not vote right, they were owed nothing. This was exacerbated by the mood that the electoral mandate required a certain exclusivity of membership in the conservative ranks. That is, if you were not with us in 1976, do not bother to apply.

For blacks the litmus test was fairly clear. You must be against affirmative action and against welfare. And your opposition had to be adamant and constant or you would be suspected of being a closet liberal. Again, this must be viewed in the context that the presumption was that no black could be a conservative.

Caricatures and Sideshows. Needless to say, in this environment little or no effort was made to proselytize those blacks who were on the fence or who had not made up their minds about the conservative movement In fact it was already hard enough for those of us who were convinced and converted to survive. And, our treatment certainly offered no encouragement to prospective converts. It often seemed that to be accepted within the conservative ranks and to be treated with some degree of acceptance, a black was required to become a caricature of sorts, providing sideshows of anti-black quips and attacks. But there was more—much more—to our concerns than merely attacking previous policies and so-called black leaders. The future, not the past was to be influenced.

It is not surprising, with these attitudes, that there was a general refusal to listen to the opinions of black conservatives. In fact, it appeared often that our white counterparts actually hid from our advice. There was a general sense that we were being avoided and circumvented. Those of us who had been identified as black conservatives were in a rather odd position. This caused me to reflect on my college years. The liberals, or more accurately, those on the Left spent a great of time, energy, and effort recruiting and proselytizing blacks by playing on the ill treatment of black Americans in this country. They would devise all sorts of programs and protests in which we should participate. But having observed and having concluded that these programs and protests were not ours and that they were not in the best interest of black Americans, there was no place to go. There was no effort by conservatives to recruit the same black students. It seemed that those with whom we agreed ideologically were not interested and those with whom we did not agree ideologically persistently wooed us. I, for one, had the nagging suspicion that our black counterparts on the Left knew this all along and just sat by and waited to see what we would do and how we would respond. They also knew that they could seal off the credibility with black Americans by misstating our views on civil rights and by fanning the flames of fear among blacks. That is precisely what they did.

Assuring Alienation. I failed to realize just how deep-seated the animosity of blacks toward black conservatives was. The dual labels of black Republicans and black conservatives drew rave reviews. Unfortunately the raving was at us, not for us. The reaction was negative, to be euphemistic, and generally hostile. Interestingly enough, however, our ideas themselves received very positive reactions, especially among the average working-class and middle-class black American who had no vested or proprietary interest in the social policies that had dominated the political scene for the past 20 years. In fact, I was often amazed with the degree of acceptance. But as soon as Republican or conservative was injected into the conversation, there was a complete about face. The ideas were okay. The Republicans and conservatives, especially the black ones, were not.

Our black counterparts on the Left and in the Democratic Party assured our alienation. Those of us who were identified as conservative were ignored at best. We were treated with disdain, regularly castigated, and mocked; and of course we could be accused of anything without recourse and with impunity. I find it intriguing that there has been a recent chorus of pleas by many of the same people who castigated us, for open-mindedness toward those black Democrats who have been accused of illegalities or improprieties. This open-mindedness was certainly not available when it came to accusing and attacking black conservatives, who merely had different ideas about what was good for black Americans and themselves.

Ideological Litany. The flames were further fanned by the media. I often felt that the media assumed that, to be black, one had to espouse leftist ideas and Democratic politics. Any black who deviated from the ideological litany of requisites was an oddity and was to be cut from the herd and attacked. Hence, any disagreement we had with black Democrats or those on the Left was exaggerated. Our character and motives were impugned and challenged by the same reporters who supposedly were writing objective stories. In fact, on numerous occasions, I have found myself debating and arguing with a reporter, who had long since closed his notebook, put away his pen, and turned off his tape recorder. I remember one instance when I first arrived at the Department of Education, a reporter, who happened to be white, came to my office and asked: "What are you all doing to cut back on civil rights enforcement?" I said, "Nothing! In fact, here is a list of all the things we are doing to enforce the law properly" and not just play numbers games." He then asked, "You had a very rough life, didn't you?" To this, I responded that I did not; that I did indeed come from very modest circumstances but that I had lived the American dream; and that I was attempting to secure this dream for all Americans, especially those Americans of my race who had been left out of the American dream. Needless to say, he wrote nothing. I have not always been so fortunate.

Burying Positive News. There was, indeed, in my view, a complicity and penchant on the part of the media to disseminate indiscriminately whatever negative news there was about black conservatives and ignore or bury the positive news. It is ironic that six years ago, when we preached self-help, we were attacked ad infinitem. Now it is common among the black Democrats to act as though they have suddenly discovered our historical roots and that self-help is an integral part of our roots. We now have permission to talk about self-help. The media were also recklessly irresponsible in printing unsubstantiated allegations that portrayed us as anti-black and anti-civil rights.

Unfortunately, it must have been apparent to the black liberals and those on the Left that conservatives would not mount a positive (and I underscore positive) civil rights campaign. They were confident that our central civil rights concern would give them an easy victory since it was confined to affirmative action—that is being against affirmative action. They were certain that we would not be champions of civil rights or would not project ourselves as champions of civil rights. Therefore, they had license to roam unfettered in this area claiming that we were against all that was good and just and holy, and that we were hell bent on returning blacks to slavery. They could smirk at us black conservatives because they felt we had no real political or economic support. And, they would simply wait for us to self-destruct or disappear, bringing to an end the flirtation of blacks with conservatism.

Interestingly enough, I had been told within the first month of going to the Department of Education in 1981 that we would be attacked on civil rights and that we would not be allowed to succeed. It was as though there was a conspiracy between opposing ideologies to deny political and ideological choices to black Americans. For their part, the Left exacted the payment of a very high price for any black who decided to venture from the fold. And among conservatives, the message was that there is no room at the inn. And if there is, only under very strict conditions.

Conservatives Must Open the Door. It appears that we are welcomed by those who dangled the lure of the wrong approach and we are discouraged by those who, in my view, have the right approach. But conservatives must open the door and lay out the welcome mat if there is ever going to be a chance of attracting black Americans. There need be no ideological concessions, just a major attitudinal change. Conservatives must show that they care. By caring I do not suggest or mean the phony caring and tear-jerking compassion being bandied about today. I, for one, do not see how the government can be compassionate, only people can be compassionate, and then only with their own money, their own property, or their own effort, not that of others. Conservatives must understand that it is not enough just to be right.

Notes

1. Williams, Juan. "Black Conservatives, Center Stage." December 16, 1980, p. A21.
2. Ibid.

25.
ALAN KEYES

Alan Keyes (born 1950) is an African American conservative who has devoted nearly four decades of his life to public service. He received a Ph.D. from Harvard. In 1979 Keyes worked for the U.S. Foreign Service in India. In 1980 he continued his service in Zimbabwe. From 1981 to 1985 he was an ambassador to the UN. Ronald Reagan appointed him Ambassador to the Economic and Social Council of the UN. He, like Steele, was incredibly influenced by Reagan. Keyes and Reagan had a special relationship. From 1985 to 1987 Keyes served as Reagan's Assistant Secretary for International Organization Affairs. Reagan once said, "I've never known a more stout-hearted defender of a strong America than Alan Keyes." This type of endorsement enhanced his political career and, after serving in these roles, Keyes decided to run for political office.

In 1988, 1992, and 2004 Keyes ran for the U.S. Senate. In the 2004 election in Illinois, he lost to the charismatic newcomer, Barack Obama. He ran for president in 1996, 2000, and 2008. He failed to secure the Republican nomination on all three occasions. Keyes remains a vibrant voice in conservative politics and has been highly criticized by liberals. For example, in 2005, his private life was highly scrutinized by political kibitzers. Keyes has been an outspoken critic of gay marriage and gay rights. His daughter, Maya, publicly identified herself as a lesbian and Keyes was not supportive.

Overview of Ideas

Alan Keyes, like most conservatives, identifies individual responsibility as key to remedying many of the social problems that face our nation, particularly that face Black people. The war on poverty, the war on drugs, teen pregnancy, mass incarceration as a result of the influx of crime, high dropout rates, the rise of matriarchal families and family dysfunction are all because our society and the communities hardest hit by these epidemics suffer from a "crisis of character." Far too many individuals do not display enough restraint and nurture every whim that their Ids conjure up. Our society is in moral decay. If people truly want to eradicate these problems and improve their lives they must improve themselves, their characters, and have their moral compasses rewired.

Keyes argues we are a society completed removed from the illustrious vision created by the Founding Fathers. They envisioned and prescribed a self-governing society. However, we have become a secularized hedonistic society. We have let our desires and passions overcome us. They have become so out of control that we require the state to impose laws to constrain us; we have lost the power to self-govern ourselves and to delay gratification. The Protestant ethic has been all but lost. Until people learn to constrain themselves we will continue to see the aforementioned quagmires worsen. For example, Keyes argues that sexual desire must be restrained in order to maintain social order. Our Judeo-Christian society did not need its government and its legal branches to dictate moral code. However, the moral fabric of our society is deteriorating.

Keyes's basic arguments have important implications for the Black community. According to Keyes, liberal Black leadership has been misleading African Americans. They have been led to believe that marching in protests and becoming involved in radical coalitions and organizations that lobby the government for support is the remedy to all their problems. Keyes suggests that the key to improving the problems impacting many black people lies in harnessing "the black community's traditional emphasis on family, religious faith, and self-reliance." Black people have been taught to depend on the welfare state and not on their own communities and institutions. If the church and the family were strong and the basis of the African American community, the way it once was, these problems would necessarily assuage. "Though the black family structure survived all the assaults of racism and economic repression, it has virtually collapsed under the crushing weight of the welfare mentality spawned by liberal paternalism." The welfare state and its numerous programs have thwarted motivation and, as Thomas also argued, create an ideology of victimhood amongst Black people, which assaults their ability to self-govern themselves.

Large-scale welfare programs have rendered a once empowered community helpless; it has revitalized the paternalism of the plantation. Moreover, these welfare programs have created a class schism amongst African Americans, whereby middle-class and affluent Blacks no longer aid their lower class brethren because they know the government has replaced the community in helping ailing families. Keyes compares the Black community to the Jewish community; he casts the Jewish community as a model minority. According to Keyes, Jews had utilized self-help community-based networks to achieve upward mobility and integration. If Black people embraced the same approach, instead of relying on welfare state socialism they would be able to advance as many Jews have. Instead, the Black community suffers from a cultural crisis. It has spawned a culture that celebrates criminality, is anti-education, and cannot delay gratification. The Black community must return to the Christian values that were formerly the bedrock of the community.

Keyes posits the need for Republican strategists within the party to make better efforts to reach out to the Black community. Again, historically the Black community is deeply rooted in conservative Christian principles. Black people overwhelmingly agree with the GOP's positions on issues such as abortion, gay marriage, etc. Republican politicians must work harder to reach out to African American ministers and congregations. Conservatives should work more with Black institutions; they will find strong allies in these communities.

Excerpts from *Our Character, Our Future: Reclaiming America's Moral Destiny,* 1996

The Crisis of Character

> Freedom without restraint will inevitably become disorder

The moral requirements of freedom are clear. According to the *Declaration of Independence,* our freedom comes from a transcendent authority—from the Creator. That means that the kind of freedom our Founding Fathers envisioned cannot be exercised without discipline. If it comes from a certain authority, it has to be exercised with some respect for that authority.

So there is a discipline inherent in the American conception of freedom. We do not have the right to do anything we please, because if we act in that way, we will be rejecting and undercutting the authority from which our freedom ultimately comes. American freedom necessarily contains within it the seeds of discipline and responsibility. These are the indispensable counterparts of our exercise of choice, and our exercise of liberty—which means that we have to have within ourselves the moral capacity to exercise that discipline.

Thus, the moral requirements of freedom are at bottom what the Founders called self-government. Self-government begins with self-control—that is to say, it begins with the ability of each of us to restrain our own passions and our own inclinations. Self-government demands at one and the same time the willingness to postpone our material gratification to the extent necessary for economic success and the discretion to limit our passions to the extent necessary to live in peace with our fellow citizens. Both of these things are prerequisites of recognizing in the individual the right to make choices for himself or herself.

The real crisis of our times is therefore, a crisis of character. It is a crisis that has been caused by our inability to admit the moral requirement of freedom. It is a crisis that has been caused by our insistence on marginalizing Truth.

This crisis of character has wrought a tremendous number of consequences—in almost every area of life. It has of course wrought dire consequences in our deteriorating family structures. But it has also wrought seriously debilitating social, political, and legal consequences.

Notice for instance, our growing obsession with rights of various kinds—covering everything from a fixation on psychosocial victimization to wholesale charges of sexual harassment in the workplace, from litigious gender equity issues to the radical gay rights agenda. All of these are directly related to this crisis of character—to the eroding moral condition of the country and of the people.

Why is that the case? To a large degree it is because we can no longer trust one another to exercise self-government.

Take, for example, the furor over sexual harassment and the myriad tangential issues that it has suddenly raised in American social life—like the codes of dating conduct and other standards for political correctness now emerging in many businesses. At one university, administration officials were actually proposing specific rules for how to move from one level of intimacy to another. Apparently, you are now supposed to stop and ask permission for each new advance across certain boundaries of intimacy. Have we really arrived at the situation where anybody who wants to go out on a date without strict legal adherence to this juridical code—or perhaps, the presence of their lawyer—is in real legal jeopardy?

This could make for some interesting dates: at each stage in the game we would all have to negotiate the terms for moving from one stage to the next; or perhaps the two parties would just sit it out while the two lawyers worked out the terms and signed the agreement.

Such a scenario is obviously absurd—and yet it is practically what we have come to these days. We still recognize it as absurd though because somewhere, deep down, we continue to believe that there ought to be certain human relationships that can be managed by individuals without the intervention of government, courts, law, the state, outside powers.

That is a natural assumption for us to make. In fact, we make that kind of assumption all the time—in all kinds of areas from the arena of family life to our interpersonal relationships. And yet, it is getting more and more dangerous to do so.

The way things are moving in the so-called children's rights movement for instance, we will not even be able to get up and hug our daughter good morning without the presence of a lawyer—or at least without taking videotapes to make sure that no unwarranted charges can be brought against us.

There is in this kind of trend, evidence not only of a kind of absurdity, evidence not only of an external push in the name of sundry group rights, but also evidence of something far deeper than that. There is evidence of a radical society-wide distrust—the sense that, at a certain level, we can't be alone with each other. I have to wonder for instance, why anyone would allow a one-on-one meeting between individuals of opposite sexes, without videotape or a witness there. These days that is a risky proposition—taking your life in your hands, or at the very least, your career.

The fact is, we can no longer maintain the expectation that people will govern themselves, that they will exercise self-control. It almost seems as if we just can't trust anyone any more.

Where has this level of radical distrust come from? To a large degree it results from a certain alteration in our concept of the human person. And that alteration can be understood if we look at another of these areas where group rights are being asserted—and that is the gay rights agenda.

Normally the terms of this discussion revolve around whether we do or do not approve of the sexual activities that a small group of individuals engage in. But let's look at it from another perspective altogether. People are now coming forward and are basically telling us that for purposes of discrimination, sexual orientation—or, more accurately, sexual behavior—must be treated like race.

Is that at all legitimate? When I got up this morning I was a black guy. When I go to bed tonight, in all probability I will still be a black guy. And no matter how much I try to talk myself out of it in the meantime, this is still going to be the case. That is because by definition this business of race is something that is really beyond my control. I know in the past people used to refer to people as being of the "colored persuasion." But that was simply a manner of speaking—and a very inaccurate manner at that. Persuasion really has nothing to do with it whatsoever.

So, if we are going to say that sexual orientation is to be treated like race for purposes of discrimination, then we're obviously saying that sexual orientation—read, behavior—is like race, a condition beyond the individual's control.

The problem of course is that such a notion would necessarily undermine all principles of sexual responsibility and accountability—principles that are essential for certain kinds of intimate relationships, such as marriage.

When we get married we take a vow—there is an explicit understanding that we will be faithful. But if our orientation—read, behavior—is beyond our control, then when we walk out and see an attractive member of the opposite sex and we give in to temptation, who can blame us? If we should come home after the affair and our spouse detects the telltale signs and starts to call us to account we could just turn to them and you say, "Well, you, you can't raise that issue. I have an adulterous orientation. It's just something you'll have to accept."

Now, if you think that this line of reasoning is simply-absurd, all you have to do is recall the recent *Time* magazine cover story that proclaimed, "Infidelity: It's In the Genes." There are indeed those who believe that we are held in the grip of indomitable animal instinct and we cannot help but do what comes naturally.

If we accept this kind of reasoning though, why we should be expected to draw the line at sexual passion? Isn't that rather unfair—discriminatory even? If we're going to have special legal protections for homosexuals, shouldn't everybody else's uncontrollable sexual orientations be protected? Shouldn't adulterers, pedophiles, rapists, and other sorts of sexual aberrants be eligible for the same benefits? Shouldn't we all be able to demand that our uncontrollable sexual behaviors be accorded the same respect and freedom from discrimination that is being demanded for gays?

And further, shouldn't that same principle of equality apply to other human passions? Alter all, what is it that distinguishes sexual orientation from other emotional or behavioral orientations? What if I am someone who is disposed to fly into a rage whenever anything fails to go my way? You could say I had an anger orientation, and that passion should be treated with respect. Or what if I am someone who is disposed to become uncontrollably jealous, when somebody gets something that I want? So I have a jealousy orientation. Why wouldn't that be subject to the same kind of respect? I don't understand why it is that we would want to accord one passion this kind of special legal and cultural categorization and not give it to all the passions—since it seems to me that to a certain degree they all have an equal standing in this regard: if we can't control one why is it that we can control the rest?

Of course, if we were to accept this convoluted logic we would be left with the concept of the human person which accents strict external regimentation: we are basically people out of control. Though that may sound a bit far-fetched, in fact, I think in just about every respect our society is moving in that direction.

The modern rights movement has actually bought a concept of the human person that basically denies free will and responsibility. We are not people capable of controlling our passions and our reactions to the situations and circumstances around us.

That being the case, the only way in which we can be rendered safe for one another, is for our behavior to be externally controlled and surveyed.

And we then have the problem of constructing the mechanisms for this kind of external control—ergo, restrictive regulations and controls in virtually every area of life.

What we have actually done in adopting this premise is to discard the essential assumption of self-government. This means we are now operating under a regime where genuine freedom is no longer possible. So, we have begun to substitute a regime of governmental intrusion that in the end will become little more than arbitrary rule—especially since we tend to identify the standards of law with the decisions of lawyers and the precedents of the courts.

We are trusting that kind of arbitrariness because we can no longer trust one another, and we no longer trust one another because we can no longer make assumptions about the common character of decency that we share as a people.

Thus we are facing a deep-seated moral crisis—a crisis that manifests itself partly in principle and partly in practice.

In principle it manifests itself as a rejection of the idea that there is a foundation in our lives for human justice and the observance of human justice. Most Americans once believed that there was such a foundation—but our leaders, politicians, and statesmen don't want to talk about it anymore because they claim that it involves bringing religion into politics. Indeed, there was a time when most Americans held to the notion that the only sure and secure foundation for freedom was God—the Source of unalienable rights and the Policeman stationed in every human heart. On that basis, the great American experiment in liberty originally involved the development of a moral regime that was relatively universal.

But apparently, we don't believe in that sort of thing anymore. As a result, we are attempting to reinvent America. We are trying to substitute for that basic premise all kinds of structures of legal and external control.

The problem, of course, is that it won't work. It never has. It never will. Throughout all of human history, the only thing that does work, the only thing that makes provision for freedom in human societies, is moral character. No matter how ingenious we are, no matter how creative we are, we will never find a substitute for character that is compatible with freedom.

And all we will be doing it we try, is to construct the elaborate legal rationalizations for the imposition of an ever-increasing degree of totalitarian tyranny and control. Sadly, we have already proven that—and only too well.

Indeed, the moral requirements of freedom are clear.

The Race Card and Liberalism

> Domination by the state has undermined black America's traditional reliance on family and church

The cover of a recent issue of *Emerge* magazine—which styles itself *Black America's Newsmagazine*—offers a doctored photo of Supreme Court Justice Clarence Thomas wearing a sly look, with a handkerchief tied around his head.

The cover story bears the headline "Betrayed: Clarence Thomas' Former Support-ers." Both the cover photo and the article smack of the diseased mentality of the liberal black establishment in America today. Name calling and ridicule take the place of common sense and reason in the establishment's attacks on black Americans who don't subscribe to the party line. The gist of the article is simple. Some liberal blacks supported Justice Thomas' elevation to the Supreme Court because they thought he would alter his conservative views once confirmed. He hasn't. His votes on the court have been entirely consistent with his known and expressed views prior to his confir-mation. Therefore, he duped them, and they feel betrayed.

In America, during the Clinton reign of lies, the sight of a public figure who is exactly what he appears to be may seem like cause for chagrin, particularly to the establish-ment blacks who supported Mr. Clinton so enthusiastically during the election.

Black liberals still suffer from the bigoted belief that anyone who disagrees with them must be pretending. This despite the fact that their approach to the problems of black America has not only failed, but has produced enormous tragedy in the black community. They march in gay pride parades, preach condom distribution, destroy black pride with their continual litany of black hopelessness and failure.

Abandoning the black community's traditional emphasis on family religious faith, and self-reliance, they assiduously pursue a strategy of dependence on gov-ernment spending and government power. Their materialistic liberalism shoulders aside the black American value system that gives primacy to morality and spiritual-ity. Large-scale reliance on the welfare system obscures the community's traditional belief in hard work, self-reliance and self-improvement as the keys to survival and progress.

Most importantly, domination by the impersonal structures of the bureaucratic state has undermined or pushed aside black America's traditional reliance on family and church as the roots of personality and security.

When they surrendered to big government paternalism, the black liberal leadership abandoned the foundations of black America's moral identity, which were in fact the foundations of our survival as individuals and as a people.

The results have been devastating. Though the black family structure survived all the assaults of racism and economic repression, it has virtually collapsed under the crush-ing weight of the welfare mentality spawned by liberal paternalism. The black work ethic survived the degenerative influence of decades of wickedly creative discourage-ments to economic initiative and enterprise. Yet it has been dangerously weakened by the liberal ideology of victimization, which makes racism an all too easy excuse for spiritual sloth and physical self-destruction.

The liberal black establishment hates Justice Thomas because he openly departs from their failed ideology. He and other black conservatives—including, I suppose, myself—are like the little boy in the old fairy tale. Through our unwillingness to silently accept their irrational dogma, we pose the risk of revealing that this emperor has no clothes, and, what is more, leaving the black community naked to its enemies.

The black liberal leaders attend summits with gang chieftains. They dance with glee when riotous thugs escape the consequences of their acts. They fight to have the justice system deal more leniently with the criminals who prey upon the streets and neighbor-hoods where decent black folks struggle to survive. Instead of self-control, they preach condom distribution, pushing black youth in particular into a deadly game of sexual Russian Roulette.

All the while the people who have always been the true heart and soul of the black community are ignored—the kids who hit the books instead of the streets, the people who fill the churches instead of the jails, the men who go to the altar instead of the nightclubs, facing up to the difficulties of marriage and real fatherhood even though it means burdensome work and responsibility. No summits are called that speak to their interests. Indeed, on issues from abortion to school choice, from gay rights to excessive taxation, their feelings are trampled upon and their values betrayed. But that's a cover story you won't read in *Emerge*.

Welfarism and Ethnic Enmity

> A sense of helplessness breeds enormous frustration

The tragic and violent clashes between blacks and Jews in places such as the Crown Heights neighborhood in Brooklyn are unhappily not the product of a unique and isolated set of circumstances.

As I have traveled the country during the past two years, I have heard more and more about the rising tensions, misunderstandings, and angry passions afflicting black and Jewish relations in urban neighborhoods, on college campuses, and in the work-place.

It's hard for me to understand why these two groups should be at odds. Both are minorities, have experienced harsh discrimination, and because of that experience, share a deep commitment to equal justice, civil rights and social progress.

Through the prolonged holocaust of the slave trade, blacks plumbed the depths of greedy inhumanity. In the Nazi extermination camps, Jews felt the awful weight of unbridled human evil. This terrible parallel should contain the seeds of an unbreakable bond between the two peoples, for we have both looked the devil in the eye, yet never given him our souls.

But it doesn't seem to work that way any more, Jews have been oppressed, but today the Jewish community is, on the whole, one of America's most impressive stories of material success. Meanwhile, nearly half the black community continues to be mired in poverty and crime, its social fabric disintegrating. Mobs of young blacks roam the streets in Crown Heights and appear to resent and hate Jews, who have become for them a symbol of the success and influence they have not achieved.

Yet Jewish community leaders, intellectuals and political activists have always been in the forefront of the liberal movements that sought greater government action to deal with the economic and social problems of poor blacks. Jewish voters have sup-ported the liberal advocates of these programs, and seconded their arguments that more of our society's resources should be devoted to state-sponsored action to help the poor. Given that record, many people in the Jewish community are bewildered, and themselves increasingly resentful and angry about the unwarranted expressions of anti-Semitism coming from black communities and seconded or tolerated by many black leaders.

I believe that, unwittingly, Jewish supporters of the government–dominated welfare state approach to the economic and social problems of the black community helped to create the mentality that now produces anger and anti-Semitism in black neighborhoods. Welfare state socialism encourages a sense of powerlessness and helplessness in its clients and their communities. This sense of helplessness breeds enormous frustration and makes people susceptible to demagogic appeals that offer scapegoats instead of workable solutions.

"Since I can't get up, I'll bring you down." It's not an answer, but at least it's something to do.

Welfare state socialism also inhibits the social integration of the black community across class lines, in ways that would impel successful blacks to build the structures that reach back into the community in order to draw others along with them.

Middle-class blacks have acted as if political support for government action and programs is an effective substitute for their own organizational efforts. That's why the agendas of groups such as the NAACP and the Black Caucus have become increasingly irrelevant to the real challenges faced in black communities. There is a vacuum where the black community needs an active, effective middle-class network dedicated to community action.

Jewish people can do something to help remedy this void. Well-intentioned Jewish people, as well as middle-class blacks who really care about the community's future, could reconsider their allegiance to welfare state socialism. If it works so well, why didn't the Jewish community rely upon it? Instead, Jews developed one of the most effective self-help networks in the world. The key to its success is the ability to mobilize the successful people in the Jewish community in support of efforts to aid the rest. Blacks need to do the same.

The critical mass of successful and well-to-do blacks exists today. Jewish leaders and activists understand the technology for mobilizing such community elites better than anyone. Both communities need to concentrate on developing cooperative programs to allow blacks to share in and master that technology.

Then the successful black middle class can begin to deal with underclass resentment in the right way, by developing the internal structures of self-help that will address its causes.

Blacks and the GOP

Republicans and conservatives should make a major effort to break with the past

We may never know the whole truth behind the flap caused by reported efforts of certain Republican Party operatives to bribe black clergymen in New Jersey—efforts designed to discourage blacks from voting. At first the chief strategist for the party, Ed Rollins, quipped that they had indeed made the payments. Later he denied it.

So, did the Republicans actually cross the line in their efforts to suppress black voter turnout on Election Day? Did any of New Jersey's black clergy agree to aid and abet the self-disenfranchisement of the state's black voters?

Whatever answers emerge over time, the whole flap should impress on everyone the ugly consequences of the present almost institutionalized enmity between the black community and the Republican Party. It hurts Republicans, it hurts black Americans, and it damages the political system as a whole.

The Republican campaign may not have gone to the illegitimate extremes Ed Rollins claimed in their efforts to "lighten the turnout" in the black community. Anyone familiar with Republican politics knows, though, that reducing black voter turnout is a standard goal, and hoped-for outcome, of Republican strategists. This complicates life enormously for black Republicans, since it means folks in the GOP leadership will work at cross-purposes with any efforts to carry the Republican message into heavily black precincts. They will even undercut a potentially successful black Republican candidacy out of fear that increased black interest in the election will work to the detriment of other Republicans on Election Day. This may explain why the only-black Republicans in Congress today come from districts where black voters aren't a critical factor.

This self-defeating approach results from the myopic unwillingness of some GOP leaders and political consultants to abandon defensive tactics against the black community, and go on the offensive in search of black support. This myopia persists despite every indication that black voters share many of the GOP's conservative values and issue positions. A third to half of blacks in polling samples routinely identify themselves as conservative. On issues such as crime and welfare reform, majorities of voting blacks have supported views in line with GOP positions. Even on an issue such as abortion, roughly half of the black electorate voices opposition to unlimited abortion rights, though black Americans are a special target of the pro-abortion propagandists.

These facts don't translate into electoral support at least in part because the GOP doesn't actively pursue black support. To be sure, at meetings and conferences black conservatives are put on display in support of Republican issue positions. But interest in black conservatives isn't a two-way street. In the real world, what counts most is the mobilization of organizational and financial networks in support of the efforts black Americans are making to address problems that particularly burden the black community—such as the disintegration of family life—in ways that reflect conservative values and principles. Many black churches, for instance, are making heroic efforts to re-establish the traditional strength of the black family, to rebuild the strong ethic of work and sacrifice that was characteristic in the black American community before the pernicious effects of the bureaucratic welfare state. Republicans should be seeking out and supporting the black ministers and congregations who are mounting these efforts, instead of fantasizing about bribing the clergy to suppress black voter participation.

Republicans and conservatives should make a major effort to break with past defensive attitudes and behavior. One step might be the establishment of an activist, grassroots-oriented institute to identify and give financial support to ongoing efforts by black Americans that represent workable alternatives to the debilitating, family-killing, spirit destroying dependency fostered by the liberal welfare state. The key here is to work with the black churches—not as political pawns to be manipulated as the Democrats do—at election time with bribes and government patronage, but as the independent institutions through which black Americans have traditionally worked for the betterment of their community.

The other day I happened to say something about the black community to a friendly acquaintance at one of the conservative-leaning think tanks in Washington. He began his response by noting in an offhand way that "well, there's really no such thing as the black community is there?" He meant, I think, that not all black Americans think alike—a very good point—but he also meant that, apart from negative things like discrimination and poverty, black Americans have nothing in common—an untrue and, therefore, a very bad point.

Conservatives and Republicans need to overcome their unwillingness to see the black community—as distinct from a few black individuals—in a positive light, in order to start working with the black community's institutions toward positive goals. The Rollins flap could produce something more beneficial than fodder for the media talk shows if it helps to open more eyes to this necessity.

26.
MICHAEL STEELE

Michael Steele (born 1958) is an African American politician and lawyer. Steele is a conservative who has been incredibly influential in the American Republican Party. He was the first African American to serve as the chairperson of the Republican National Committee. He served as chairman from 2009 to 2011. Prior to this, in 1993 he co-founded the Republican Leadership Council. He also was chairman of the Grand Old Party Political Action Committee. From 2003 to 2007 he served as the Lieutenant Governor in Maryland. He was also the first African American to hold this position. In 2006 Steele ran for U.S. Senate in Maryland. Finally, Steele has not reserved all his work for Washington. In 2010 Steele created the Fire Pelosi Bus Tour. For a period of six weeks, Steele visited over 100 cities throughout the United States encouraging people to vote, vote Republican, and thwart the rising power of the Democrats in Washington. There was an emphasis on Republicans gaining control of Congress and specifically replacing the Speaker of the House, Nancy Pelosi.

Overview of Ideas

Michael Steele's primary argument, like most conservatives, is that upward mobility and success is determined by individual effort and the government should never impinge upon individual rights. According to Steele, the American Dream is alive and well and achievable for all. However, the American Dream cannot just be equated with wealth or large homes and fancy cars. Our fascination with acquiring material things is deleterious. We cannot just teach that good individual choices create monetary success because it has far greater consequences for our lives and society. When individuals are taught to take responsibility for their own choices it means a better life for their families and communities. This is the message that must be disseminated within many African American communities.

Like Thomas and other Black conservatives, Steele's personal narrative of watching his sharecropper mother endure hardship only to preserve and achieve the American Dream is utilized to suggest that access to opportunity is unfettered in the United States. He often tells audiences about his mother, Maebell, who taught him the principles and values required to be successful. Again, one does not become successful because of a government-sponsored jobs program but because of the principles that motivate them into action. Steele posits that prosperity requires thrift and strong moral character. Blaming those who have more wealth than you or who employ you for your own misfortune will only keep you from growing both spiritually and economically. Two simple principles will aid any ailing American: individual rights and action. Every individual has the human right to better themselves with no intervention from the state (unless needed to maintain order) and every individual who seeks to better their life has the ability to change their lives through individual action. Their own moral compass, not the mandates of the government, must dictate a person's individual choices.

Steele argues that liberals, Democrats, and civil rights leaders failed the poor, various minorities, and specifically African Americans. He posits that these groups

> assumed they could simply legislate compassion, mandate acceptance, and everything for black Americans would turn around. They were wrong. Human experience teaches that real change must first take root in our hearts, and hearts change by choice, not by force.

These groups tell African Americans it is the job of the government to pay them back or worse yet to save them. Steele astutely points out an interesting point. He argues it is curious that liberals would adhere to the "White Man's burden." Originally, the White Man's Burden suggested that it was the task of White men to "civilize" "inferior" populations of people. According to Steele, it is the obligation of African Americans to fight, to get degrees, jobs, to start their own businesses, and create their own opportunity. He argues that Black people have been taught since entering school, perhaps even before, that they are victims of an oppressive society that hates them and offers them no real hope for the future. Steele says this lie must cease to be disseminated. We indoctrinate young Black people into a cult of victimhood. Like Thomas argued, this psychology of victimhood is the problem. "Success comes only when we stop feeling sorry for ourselves, stop bellyaching about our circumstances, accept reality for what it is, and use our talents to the best of our ability."

To be clear, Steele does not argue that all welfare or state-sponsored assistance should end. There are people who are truly desperate and so impoverished that they require assistance. However, taken too far, an extensive welfare state removes the incentive to work. Welfare programs must be cut back so as to allow the individual to help themselves. Although seemingly simplistic, Steele argues that life is not fair. However, you must fight harder in the face of adversity. That is the American way. Advancement, particularly for African Americans, will come from hard work, devoting oneself to one's family, and laboring to enhance their own communities. Aid must be bottom-up not top-down. "We can truly help those in need by keeping a safety net for the most disadvantaged, while reducing ineffective government handouts and encouraging more targeted, efficient assistance by local organizations, communities, churches, and private charities." According to Steele, communities must help themselves; again, self-sufficiency is paramount. What devastated communities need is not structural transformation but cultural transformation. Steele, drawing from Christianity as we saw in the abolitionist era, argues for a return to traditional values. He places emphasis on the nuclear family.

Inspired by Ronald Reagan, Steele argues that helping the poor, specifically the Black poor, requires bolstering the capitalist class. Many of the leaders in the previous chapters have critiqued capitalism; Steele focuses on the ways in which capitalism is not the adversary of Black folk. In fact, if left alone, never stifled by government interventions, prosperity is inevitable. Steele like Keyes was incredibly influenced by Reagan's "supply-side" or "trickle-down" economics. If businesses are unhampered they will be able to create more jobs. If businesses make more profit and generate more wealth, they can create more jobs. This would mean that the wealth created by corporations would then trickle down to the working and middle classes. (The effectiveness and validity of this perspective remains a huge source of contention between conservatives and liberals.)

As chairman of the Republican National Committee, Steele is critical of liberal policies, particularly of the Democratic Party. Once Barack Obama became president, Steele became even more critical of the party and the high level of spending being implemented by the government. He argues that people were captivated by charm and misguided by Obama's promises of hope and change. In fact, he argues that it is time for the Republican Party to stand up and take the country back as Obama is leading us toward socialism. Steele argues that spending borrowed money and creating an enormous deficit will not help the poor, people whose homes have been foreclosed, etc. Instead, Steele is a proponent of the famous axiom, "a rising tide lifts all boats." If the private sector is allowed to prosper then so will everyone else.

Excerpts from *Right Now: A 12-Step Program For Defeating the Obama Agenda*, 2009

Inventory Our Principles

We arrive at our moral and political principles through self-examination, through our experiences with our families and communities, and through the study of history. We conserve what is best—hence the word "conservative"—and seek patterns so we might learn what truly makes something good or valuable. But where do we first learn how to live a dignified life and what really matters in the world?

I learned this from a sharecropper's daughter. Her folks had to pull her out of school in the fifth grade to work in the cotton fields of South Carolina. She worked her whole life to provide for her family, never making more than minimum wage.

That woman is my mother, Maebell.

Through the remarkable example of her life, her will, and her experiences, my mother taught me the value of self-discipline and self-reliance matched with compassion for those in need. She said that one of the best ways to meet your obligation to others is to live life as if everybody were watching what you do or say.

She taught me to know God, to respect others and myself, and to keep that "pecking order" in mind in all things. Cultivating this mindset of respect for self, generosity of spirit, love for God, and caring for others is, to me, the real American dream.

But as I look around today, I see many people setting aside that dream for a false promise.

While hard work and careful planning often lead to material wealth, there is a growing perception that we are naturally entitled to prosperity regardless of our effort, and that fabulous wealth is far more common than it really is. What's worse, many people—especially our young—now believe the heartbreaking lie that money, power, fame, and material things are the keys to a happy life.

But money is not a cure-all, power does not bring satisfaction, fame is not noble, and material things cannot fill the God-shaped hole in the human heart.

For many folks—and believe me, I know the temptation—life's priorities are out of whack. But the answer isn't simply to show that poor choices have poor consequences. We must help people understand that they have the right to choose how to live their own lives, and that good choices can have great consequences not only for themselves, but also for their family, community, and nation.

As Republicans, our first job ought to be setting that example in our own lives. I learned it by watching my mother live that way every day. Come to think of it, she always had two jobs: doing whatever it was she had to do—picking cotton, washing laundry, or being a wife and mother—and providing an example for my sister, me, and anyone else who happened to notice.

Maebell has not lived a life of ease and comfort, but for her it still has been the American dream: to live by her own choices—her own hope and heart—and to hold herself to a high and noble standard. Ask her if she has lived a good life. She will tell you her answer before you get the question out of your mouth: *Yes, baby.*

People who want to live life with hope and heart must remember that the American dream is not possessions, rewards, or recognitions, but a life of seeking both opportunity and service. The American dream is a life well-lived.

And the best news of all about the American dream is this: it is available to anyone willing to claim it. It is a legacy to which everyone has a right. Your name doesn't have to be Rockefeller or Vanderbilt or even Oprah to stake your claim.

That dream has taken me on a long and wonderful journey from seeing my mother leave home every morning for hand work at the laundry, to watching her smile as I took the oath of office to become lieutenant governor of the state of Maryland and then the first African-American chairman of the Republican National Committee. As the son of an abusive, alcoholic father, that dream led me from the childhood terror of seeing my father hurting my mother, to being a proud father of my own children and sharing every day of life with a loving, caring, and beautiful wife. And as an African-American, I proudly see that dream has led black people from historic, institutional oppression, to opportunity across the spectrum of culture and economics, and to a life of success and true happiness for a man like me.

People ask me, "How did all this happen for you?"

I always tell 'em the same thing: it was Maebell.

Maebell raised me to understand and appreciate some enduring principles:

- You cannot bring about prosperity by discouraging thrift.
- You cannot strengthen the weak by weakening the strong.

- You cannot help the wage earner by pulling down the wage payer.
- You cannot further the brotherhood of man by encouraging class hatred.
- You cannot help the poor by destroying the rich.
- You cannot build character and courage by taking away man's initiative and incentive.
- You cannot help men in the long run by doing for them what they should do for themselves.

Maebell didn't make these up herself—these principles have been attributed to various people, including President Lincoln. And to me, they are a whole lot more than Mother's smart advice. They help make me who I am—and, when I stumble, they remind me of the man I want to be.

But what is the ultimate source of those principles? From what fundamental idea do they flow? Read through them again, and I think their foundation will become clear. They recognize the obligation we have to others. They reject the casting of blame. They call for elevation of self, not the denigration of others. Overall, they call for us to reach for something better within ourselves, not to drag down the best in others in the name of parity. What's more, if you think about each of these things, everyday experience tells you they work. Therefore, I believe our principles must have two simple but profound qualities, one that prescribes their purpose and another that prescribes their execution: our principles must promote freedom, and they must inspire action.

Freedom, by definition, is the right to conduct our lives as we see fit. It is the most basic human right, and it is a *natural right*—that is, it belongs to us by virtue of our birth as human beings, not as citizens of some country or adherents of some ideology, and not because it has been granted to us by a person, group, or government. In other words, every human being in every nation is born with the right to be free. That does not mean we all get to exercise that right, because not all of us are citizens of a nation that protects the right to freedom. But freedom will always be non-negotiable and the greatest "good" thing that exists.

Long before "Live free or die" became the motto of New Hampshire, General John Stark declared it in 1809 in a letter to fellow veterans of the American Revolution. It resonates with Americans in general and with Republicans in particular because it is such a clear distillation of America's founding idea. Note that General Stark didn't say, "Live sort of free," or "I'd gladly trade living free for some 'free' healthcare and a retirement package and a government-managed economy."

Yet two hundred years later a whole lot of Americans are happy to trade little pieces of freedom for what they think is greater security—conceding parts of their economic liberty, their physical safety, and more. And as Benjamin Franklin wrote a generation before the founding, "Those who sacrifice liberty for security deserve neither."

At a time when many Americans are compromising their freedom, Republican principles must promote it. No political party can claim a stronger commitment to freedom and liberty than the Republican Party—we are the Party of Lincoln.

When women and men were bound in chains, it was the Republican Party that took action to end slavery. Our forebears carried out this profoundly moral act because it was the right thing to do. It was a devastating political choice, but political expediencies should never—and in this case did not—keep us from doing what's right.

And when we do what's right, we gain sincere, long-term supporters. But let's be clear, I'm talking about principled acts, not pandering and empty promises. The Republican Party didn't come about because a handful of individuals in the 1850s put forward a laundry list of pet programs. If they had, they could have taken their ideas to the Democrats, the Whigs, the Liberty Party, the Free Soil Party, or the Know-Nothings. They were willing to disagree among themselves on tactics, but as committed opponents of slavery, they were without a home, so they organized a party based on that principle. That way, like-minded citizens could stand together and have a voice in shaping the future of the young nation.

This principle-driven identity is what the Republican Party has lost and what we now must regain.

As Republicans, we can disagree among ourselves on how best to put principles into action. Such disagreement is good and necessary, because debate, discussion, and advocacy are how we improve policy. But any principle we embrace must form the foundation for debate, not become the topic of debate. We must hold the principle in common, it must be grounded in freedom, and it must lead to effective policy.

But what should that principle be? Does one stand out more than others? Yes it does: individual rights. The fight for individual rights is what brought our nation into existence and gave root to our party one hundred years later. It is the foundation of Western civilization, and a pure expression of absolute respect for human dignity. It is, above all else, the principle to which the Republican Party must return.

The other quality that our principles must have is "action," and by this I mean that we must act on what we propose, our proposals must be effective, and they must work the way we say they will. This may sound obvious, but for many politicians and special interests, whether something actually works is often an afterthought. Many of them only want to win—for themselves, their cause, their group, or their personal opinions.

As Republicans, we must do better. It is not enough to advocate some plan because it reflects an ideology we like. Democrats do that, and look what it's doing to our freedoms. If we advocate an idea, it must not be enough for us to think it sounds "conservative." We need to know, and not simply hope, that it's going to do what we promise when it's put into practice.

To borrow a famous phrase, the "audacity of hope" can inspire, but without the work to back it up, "hope" never created anything—never put a roof over someone's head, never helped someone find a job, never fed a hungry family, never made a man or woman free. A fellow may hope that he will fly when he jumps off a mountain, but gravity doesn't care about hope. Pretty words won't make you fly, and audacity won't save you from a crushing fall.

The "hope" so many talk about now isn't much more than hero worship. These days, "hope" means an empty promise that all your wishes will come true. Remember the news stories in the 2008 election campaign about people who believed that Obama would pay their gas bills and make our enemies into friends just by shaking hands? Since those heady days, the bloom has come off that rose, thankfully.

Real hope is an informed confidence rooted in history, experience, and knowledge. Man has known this for centuries. St. Paul identified it in the Bible when he described faith not as blind optimism, but as the evidence of things not seen. Another generation is about to learn that hard lesson for itself.

Conservatives don't need to reinvent that wheel. One of the reasons conservatism succeeds is its respect for history and the real world. We look for guidance from what has been proven over time. Thousands of years of recorded human experience provide an awesome record of what works and what doesn't. It's a practical guide to achieving real change by saving us the wasted effort of reinventing success or repeating failure.

We need to defend individual rights in order to limit government power. Government's natural tendency is always to grow, justifying new programs through an ever-expanding definition of what is necessary for society. Call it "government by whim"—and look where it's leading.

The government already tells us how much water our toilets can flush and what kind of light bulbs we can buy—for our own good, it says. A friend of mine in Fairfax County, Virginia, can't install a new staircase rail in his own home because it isn't "wheelchair-friendly"—never mind that no one in his house uses a wheelchair, and never mind that he owns the house. The same government that "gives" you bicycle paths and museums is always finding more expansive ways to define what is "for the good of the community."

And these proposals for never-ending nanny state regulations are getting more intrusive and more invasive every day. Alabama officials have proposed a fat tax on overweight city employees; California regulators sought to ban the sale of dark colored cars; also in the Sunshine State, the California Energy Commission lobbied to require private homes to use special thermostats that allow the utility company to control your home temperature. Every time one of these outrageous proposals is rejected (usually after receiving some unexpected and unwelcome publicity), two new ones pop up to replace it.

When it seemed we were getting something for nothing, we didn't speak out. Who doesn't want some new civic bauble paid for by someone else? But all this paved the way for what's happening today. Washington has gone from protecting our individual rights to granting us ever more limited permission to exercise them.

President Gerald Ford put it best when he said, "A government big enough to give you everything you want is strong enough to take everything you have." I fear that Americans don't take that to heart. In a recent Rasmussen survey, a mere 53 percent of Americans agreed that capitalism is better than socialism, so we may be a lot closer than we realize to surrendering our rights for good, one little bit at a time—and that's a scary thought.

It's time for Republicans to articulate our principles. Let us once again stand for individual rights as the foundation of freedom and real liberty. We should remind people what we stand to lose at the hands of an ever-encroaching government. And let's also declare what we can gain from freedom and individual liberty: we can keep more of what we earn; we can better afford to educate our children and have more choices about what kind of education they will receive; we can cultivate a healthier economy with more jobs; and we can choose our healthcare program instead of lining up for a government-run "one-size-fits-all" system.

When the government's reach is limited by the will of the people, we can have the environment cared for by local conservationists instead of ideological extremists who don't care about preserving local jobs and communities. We can reduce the harm and divisiveness of political correctness by removing its legal sanction. We can limit the power of "empathetic" judges who disrespect the rule of law. We can expand school choice, exposing the hypocrites who extol the wonders of public education while sending their own kids to private school. (Are you listening, President Obama?) And we can truly help those in need by keeping a safety net for the most disadvantaged, while reducing ineffective government handouts and encouraging more targeted, efficient assistance by local organizations, communities, churches, and private charities.

It is time for America to part ways with liberal groupthink, hypocrisy, and hero worship. It is time for Republicans to return to our founding principle: the protection of individual rights, leading to liberty and justice for all.

Take Back the Culture

America should be a place where men and women can fully and freely exercise the right to live as they choose, even when others disagree with those choices. That's just what Republicans believe.

Democrats might *say* they want that too, but far more often their policies aim to constrain your personal freedom. Sometimes they do it by outlawing what they don't like, from simple light bulbs to "hate speech." Other times they foreclose on economic opportunity by heaping new regulations on people and businesses, often cynically presenting their restrictions as "more opportunity and choice." And still other times they try to "encourage" you to engage in what they believe to be virtuous behavior, using the government's taxation and subsidizing powers to get you to eat the "right" foods, buy the "right" cars, and the like. Insidiously, through all these mechanisms, they encourage a culture that diminishes and denigrates all but their own moral choices.

Personal morality should be a personal matter, not a government matter, as long as a persons choices do not damage or destroy the lives of others (as abortion does, for instance), or carry crippling social and economic consequences (such as drug use), or interfere with the ability to govern (as the various sex scandals in both parties do).

Liberals have developed their own moral code, however, and they are using all the weapons at their disposal—the news media, the education system, popular entertainment, you name it—to instill it in the rest of us. They seem determined to tear down any remaining vestiges of traditional morality. Their relentless mocking of Christianity, of course, is the prime example. If Hollywood or the *New York Times* treated Islam or other religions with the unconcealed contempt they reserve for Christianity, their own liberal activist allies would be calling for hate crimes prosecutions.

We discussed liberal intolerance before, but it's worth revisiting in the context of the so-called culture war. The ground under this war has changed, and leading Democrats have buried the old notion of "tolerance"—at least when it comes to tolerating traditional values, the practice of Christianity, and the primacy of the nuclear family. They present the cultural foundations of American society less often as ideals to strive for than as rotten pillars of a morally corrupt nation or the butt of vulgar jokes.

Open hostility to traditional morality deeply infects liberalism today, revealing liberals to be far more intolerant than those they criticize. For all their talk about diversity, liberals actively oppose the most important kind of diversity a free society can have: diversity of opinion. They really just regard "tolerance" as a useful rhetorical weapon to flay conservatives for not agreeing with their agenda.

It is time to take back the culture, but in a different way than we have considered before. We should not sit idly by while the Left continues to denigrate traditional moral and religious values. To borrow from the president's playbook, we need to call them out on it. We should point out how their aspersions violate the "tolerance" that liberals uphold as the most sacred of all values. We must argue that there's nothing particularly "liberal" about ridiculing people's religious beliefs. And we need to ask whether the current attack on all things Christian would meet with the approval of yesterday's liberal icons—like the Reverend Martin Luther King Jr.

For years I've heard liberals try to win over low-income and minority voters with the vague promise of "hope." Like you, I've heard it all: Jesse Jackson pleading, "Keep hope alive!"; Bill Clinton calling himself "the man from a place called Hope"; and Barack Obama promising "the audacity of hope"—a phrase that seems to mean whatever he decides it means at any given moment.

"Hope" is an easy sell, because anybody can make promises. But hope improves lives only when it is transformed into reality, and that requires action.

As Republicans, our mission today is the same as it was when the Grand Old Party was founded in 1854: to empower people—even the powerless—to bring their hopes into reality. Empty rhetoric won't do it, no matter how catchy and popular. It takes hard work—especially when political leaders show real leadership by doing the right thing when it's not easy to do. We are the party of Abraham Lincoln, and the Great Emancipator took a stand for those whose hands and feet were literally shackled.

Today's Republicans must stand with those who find themselves shackled by new chains: lack of education, lack of opportunity, and most important, lack of knowledge about how they can participate in the American system and make a better life for themselves and their families.

The liberals had their chance and they have failed in tragic, heartless ways. After the civil rights movement of the 1960s, American history should have been a story of triumph and rapid progress for minorities, and especially for African-Americans. Instead, liberals assumed they could simply legislate compassion, mandate acceptance, and everything for black Americans would turn around.

They were wrong.

Human experience teaches that real change must first take root in our hearts, and hearts change by choice, not by force. Law alone is insufficient; it takes the constant and good example of men and women who do the right thing because they want to, not because they have to. The liberals' lack of this basic appreciation for how societies change has led directly to the creation of a perpetual underclass populated by the neediest Americans. Our fellow citizens have been trapped there in part by the refusal of liberals to require even the simplest of moral compasses of themselves and others.

As an African-American man, when I consider how liberals have deigned to excuse ignorance, illegitimacy, and vulgarity as artifacts of black America's "culture"; when I recall how they have made common cause with self-appointed, race-hustling "spokesmen" who make a living by feeding racial conflict, not fighting it; when I see the old "white man's burden" dressed up as liberal *noblesse oblige*—when I see all that against generations of young black men in prison and generations of young black women raising babies all alone, I raise my fists in righteous anger.

People in need deserve to know how America works—that they can get a degree, learn a skill, or start a business and get ahead. Opportunity is not the province of wealth and privilege alone. It is available to everyone, and it is their right as Americans to take advantage of it—but few people show them how.

Instead, they hear over and over that America has made them victims. This starts with what children are taught in public schools: in history class, social studies, and even in ostensibly non-political subjects like math, there is a persistent message—sometimes subtle, other times quite open—that America is little more than an arena for the struggle of oppressed groups. Everyone is a victim—including *you*. And since life's hardships aren't your fault, don't make it your responsibility to overcome them. Find someone to blame, then demand they do the heavy lifting. History is a cast around your legs and a chain around your feet. You are at the mercy of powers beyond your control, and the only reason you have less is that others have more.

We must replace that liberal lie with the truth. Success comes only when we stop feeling sorry for ourselves, stop bellyaching about our circumstances, accept reality for what it is, and use our talents to the best of our abilities.

Is that fair? No. It's not fair that some people are poorer than others, and our society needs to maintain an effective safety net for those who fall through the cracks. But government attempts to *mandate* equality never work—they result in social leveling that degrades the incentive to work hard and start businesses. Under those conditions, a lot of people become poorer, while the poor don't become any wealthier—they only become less free. In fact, the only ones who become better off are members of the governing class.

It is no coincidence that the most economically free countries and territories—America, Hong Kong, Great Britain, Singapore, New Zealand, Switzerland, and Chile, to name a few—tend to have high living standards and high per capita income. At a time when even Communist countries like China and Vietnam are moving toward economic freedom, we should resist exhortations to move in the opposite direction in hopes of achieving some Utopian state of equality.

So life may not be fair, but wallowing in your supposed victimhood is a surefire route to a bitter, unhappy, unsuccessful life. Wait for "fairness" to rescue you from difficulty and you'll be waiting a long, long time. Meanwhile, life is going to pass you by. You'll never get ahead until you start playing the hand you're dealt. The American way—hard work and helping your family and your community—really works. It'll get you ahead.

Pursing the American dream might not make you a millionaire, but most Americans who embrace hard work and self-reliance at least achieve what the vast majority of the world only dreams of: a place to live that they can call their own, some money in the bank, and the satisfaction of making a life for themselves and their family in safety and comfort.

Being an American means you can write your own future. It doesn't matter where you start, as long as you understand that nothing good comes overnight, setbacks are part of moving forward, and there is no substitute for perseverance and self-discipline. It won't be easy—no good thing ever is. But knowledge is a powerful thing, and Republicans are committed to making sure every American knows how to take advantage of the opportunities our system affords.

Liberals see America as an acid stew of bigotry, historic offense, and unchecked individualism. Most Americans—and most people around the world who want to come here—find that bizarre. People know America is not perfect, but most are far more excited at the possibility—the "hope," to put that word in its proper context—that America presents to anyone who reaches out for it. America is where you come when you want tomorrow to be better for your children than today is for you.

Republicans know what America really has to offer, and so do people around the world.

While providing a safety net, the government should seek to elevate those in need to overcome government dependence—yet one of President Obama's first acts was to pay the states to expand their welfare rolls. And that gives you some idea of just what we're up against: the Democrats' idea of success is to make more families dependent on government.

Opportunity and education are critical, but those things alone can't cure the hardest cases. Sometimes we have to reach out and help each other—and the last half-century of history shows that government is too big, too clumsy, and too impersonal to offer real compassion. We have to do it ourselves, as human obligation. When we start caring about each other as neighbors and as fellow members of our communities—something Democrats could learn from the religious conservatives they ridicule—we will improve the life of the most disadvantaged Americans far more powerfully than a government check can.

The light of America is its promise of endless possibilities. She truly is "a shining city on a hill," as President Reagan put it. That city must have a place for everyone, no matter where they come from, and no matter how high they intend to climb.

But what liberals often forget is that it's not the government that makes that city shine. It is the people. What makes the difference for the family on the brink of poverty or prosperity is not government; it is the people. It is the people, not the government, who will raise up those suffering the dehumanizing effects of poverty and addiction—caught in hopelessness that is carried from one generation to the next like an infection across the heart. They deserve the benefits of freedom and free enterprise as much as anyone, and it will be the people of America who will bring that new day, not government.

Like Reagan, I put my faith in people, not government. Like Lincoln, I "declare for liberty." It is morning in America, still, because America *is* morning. America is a place of eternal promise and potential, a place where possibility meets opportunity, a place where the son of a sharecropper's daughter can realize dreams his ancestors never even dared to dream and can help fulfill the promise of a great nation.

27.
STAR PARKER

Star Parker (born 1956) is an African American activist and writer. In 1995 Parker founded CURE, the Center for Urban Renewal Education. It is a not-for-profit organization; the think tank aims to craft strategies to battle poverty, particularly amongst African Americans. Parker, the president of CURE, like other conservatives, advocates personal responsibility and "supply-side" economic policy as a means by which to reform poverty. Parker's activism has gained her notoriety. In fact, she now works as a social policy consultant; she frequently advises Republican legislators and politicians. She has tried her own hand at politics. In 2010 she ran for Congress in California. Although she lost, she has become a dominant voice in modern politics.

Like many African American activists and political leaders, Parker contributes regularly to the press. She has published three books entitled, *Pimps, Whores, and Welfare Brats, Uncle Sam's Plantation*, and *White Ghetto*. According to CURE's website she is working on a new book, *How the Poor Get Rich*. Parker is a syndicated columnist and frequently appears across a wide range of television news programming. She lectures worldwide on conservative principles.

Overview of Ideas

Star Parker, like many African American political thinkers, utilizes her own experiences to shape her political thought. However, in her case, unlike many other conservatives, she spent many years on what she now calls Uncle Sam's Plantation. Parker was on welfare and argues that she has first-hand experience with the program and its noxious effects. For Parker, she overcame poverty through hard work and diligence, not welfare. Many critics argue that conservatives like Parker do not truly understand or care about poor Black people. However, Parker knows what it is to be poor and works hard to craft policies to aid people who are currently in the situation she managed to escape.

Star Parker argues that part of the reason why many African Americans are still trapped in poverty or have not made the progress many hoped for is because civil rights leaders have led the Black community in the wrong direction:

> Unfortunately, after the victories of the 1960s, black leadership, typified by the NAACP, refused to turn from the business of politics to the business of living. The leaders transformed a creative

struggle for liberation into the destructive politics of anger and guilt. By turning their energies to building a new welfare state and culture of litigation, these civil rights leaders of the 1960s created as many problems as they solved.

Leftist Black leaders created a culture of resentment and victimhood. They told Black people that it was the government's responsibility to solve all their problems. Civil rights leaders have encouraged Black people to look to the government for complete support and in turn Black people have returned to the plantation and are once again dependent on "a master." Parkers also posits that many Black leaders do not talk about the expanding Black middle class and all of the Black people since the 1970s who have prospered through hard work and thrift. She has urged powerful Black organizations such as the NAACP to shift its focus from government intervention to promoting self-sufficiency.

Like many other conservatives such as Steele and Keyes, Parker places enormous emphasis on cultural transformation. For example, Parker has written extensively about the impact of HIV/AIDS on the African American community. According to Parker, quagmires such as high rates of HIV infection and teenage pregnancy disproportionately impact the Black community. However, while liberals talk incessantly about structural deficiencies such as poverty, lack of access to healthcare, and adequate education, she says they refuse to discuss individual behavior and individual responsibility. Irresponsible sexual behavior is what causes these problems, not poverty or society. Moreover, this irresponsible behavior cuts across racial lines. Parker warns that our society is in trouble. Many people no longer adhere to values and moral principles that would keep them from contracting sexually transmitted diseases or becoming pregnant before they can afford to care for a child. We need a restoration of traditional family values. This moral and spiritual decay has been caused by the creation of a large-scale welfare state that made many Black people dependent on the government. She argues that many of these social problems develop when you turn control of your life and destiny over to the government.

According to Parker, part of the way we can regain our moral standing is by rekindling our faith. Secularization has had damaging effects on our society. Parker sees the church's role in progress as paramount. For example, she has prescribed that the Republican Party needs to work more formally with Black church leaders and pastors to reach out to Black people. Interestingly, she argues that many Black Americans loved Bill Clinton, not so much because he acted in their interests but because he seemed sincere. After all, Clinton passed incredibly aggressive welfare reform in 1996 and many African Americans still supported him. Many Black people do not dislike conservative policies; they just dislike many conservative leaders. Parker argues that positive relations must be fostered between Republicans and African Americans. The church is a way for the Republican Party to do this.

Golden Chance for the NAACP, 2004

The surprise resignation of Kweise Mfume as president of the NAACP should prompt national leaders to engage in introspection and reevaluation.

The national leadership has lost its way. It sends a message today to its own community that is, at best, irrelevant and, at worst, destructive. Its agenda, the pure politics of victimization, is a caricature of what the NAACP was originally about.

The heads of local NAACP chapters that I meet are out of step with their national leaders and sound much more like local church pastors. Perhaps because these chapter heads live in close proximity to the troubled communities with which they work, they understand that the problems in black communities today reflect the challenges of the business of living and not the business of politics.

As John McWhorter of the Manhattan Institute has aptly put it, today racism is not the main problem of African Americans, but rather "...the mundane tasks of teaching those 'left behind' after the civil rights victory how to succeed in a complex society."

The NAACP has a proud history at the center of the civil rights movement. But, recall the old saying that everything looks like a nail to a man with a hammer. For years, physical, political and legal barriers stood between blacks and freedom. The NAACP and the civil rights movement were born to tear these barriers down and won historic and glorious victories.

Unfortunately, after the victories of the 1960s, black leadership, typified by the NAACP, refused to turn from the business of politics to the business of living. The leaders transformed a creative struggle for liberation into the destructive politics of anger and guilt. By turning their energies to building a new welfare state and culture of litigation, these civil rights leaders of the 1960s created as many problems as they solved.

On the one hand, there have been undeniable gains in the black community. A new black middle class has emerged in which the percentage of black households with a real gross income over $75,000 has quadrupled since 1970. The wage gap percentage between black and white workers is half today of what it was in the 1960s. Blacks now hold top-level positions in government and business that would have been inconceivable 40 years ago.

Yet, a large slice of black life is in sad shape and going backwards. Over the same period since the 1960s, black illegitimacy has almost quadrupled, black families headed by single women have tripled, almost half the number of homicides in the country are among black men, half of our new AIDS cases are among black women, many black kids do not make it through school and those that graduate do so with eighth-grade reading skills, and crime and unemployment are rampant in our inner cities.

According to reports, partisan remarks made by NAACP chairman Julian Bond attacking President Bush have provoked an IRS investigation into the organization's 501c3 tax-free status. This certainly must be contributing to the internal tensions there. However, I think the real shock waves that shook this organization were created by Bill Cosby's remarks at a NAACP gathering in Washington earlier this year.

In those well-publicized observations, Cosby shocked an audience of the black establishment with truth. He attacked the politics of victimization—the very point of existence today of the NAACP. Cosby began a campaign that night, which he continues today, of formulating a message that will foster a new culture of responsibility in the inner cities.

A number of months ago I was invited to address an annual meeting of a local NAACP chapter in a Midwestern city. The invitation came somewhat reluctantly as result of pressure from a local donor who had made a recent major contribution to the chapter. A few board members actually boycotted my speech. Nevertheless, I spoke to a sellout crowd and delivered my usual message that the answer to poverty does not lie in government but in personal responsibility, ownership and faith. The standing ovation I got told me that I had indeed struck a responsive chord.

As the NAACP leadership looks for a new president, I urge them to stop looking in the rear view mirror and start focusing on the road ahead. The organization should use its prestige and $40 million budget to help blacks use the freedom they now have. They should abandon the destructive politics of hate and guilt and start getting out the truth, that life is defined by struggle, and that the principles that form the foundation of freedom transcend race. With this message and real work, we can again move our community forward.

The Answer To Aids Is Values, 2004

A recent Newsweek cover story has helped bring national attention to the HIV/AIDS epidemic among African-American women. Unfortunately, its superficial and biased coverage is itself evidence of the scope of the crisis on which it reports.

Newsweek leaves the impression that traditional values, rather than being part of the solution to this problem, contribute to its cause; that men are helpless victims and responsibility lies exclusively with women; that choice and responsibility play a minimal role in sexual behavior, and that we can think about this problem independently of the general cultural state of affairs of the country.

HIV/AIDS has migrated into the heterosexual community, and women now account for 26 percent of newly diagnosed AIDS cases, quadruple the incidence among women since the 1980s. Black women account for well over 70 percent of these cases. Last October, Gwen Ifill jolted listeners to the debate between Vice President Cheney and John Edwards when she pointed out that "black women between 25 and 44 are 13 times more likely to die of the disease than their counterparts."

AIDS is now the No. 1 cause of death among African-Americans between the ages of 25 and 44.

Joseph Lowery, the former president of the Southern Christian Leadership Conference, once said, "When America gets a cold, black America gets pneumonia."

The "cold" that America has in this case is the ongoing politicization of our society and the breakdown of the traditional values that have been the glue that has held together the American family and our society. The symptoms of this "cold" are obvious: skyrocketing divorce rates and illegitimacy rates, declining test scores that result from a politicized and bureaucratized public-school system and politicization of our legal system that reflects the detachment of law from its moral foundations.

Whether we are talking about breakdown in family, education or law, the symptoms of this cold are more intense and protracted in the black community than in other communities. But it's important to retain perspective that black social problems are symptomatic of a national problem. Irresponsible sexual behavior has no racial boundaries. The rate of out-of-wedlock births among whites today exceeds the rate among blacks 40 years ago.

Health professionals are trying to get a handle on the precise channels through which the HIV virus is being transmitted to black women, and the picture that is emerging is complex. But the themes, drug use and sexual promiscuity, are clear.

It is also clear that in a world of abstinence, monogamy and sex exclusively within the framework of marriage, AIDS and sexually transmitted diseases in general would be rare.

Yet, such a world is such a remote possibility and so irrelevant to the Newsweek reporters that it does not receive a word of mention in the article.

The only attention these reporters give to traditional values is to the claim that they make women submissive and therefore, supposedly, more prone to predatory male behavior. And, according to these reporters, traditional values intimidate men from admitting their homosexual behavior to the women with whom they have sex.

One significant source of the transmission of HIV to black women traces back to the appallingly high percentage of black men who have done time in prison. Prisons are a breeding ground for homosexual behavior and HIV transmission. These men then return home and engage in heterosexual sex.

Yet, the Newsweek reporters never raise the relevance of prison outreach programs such as Chuck Colson's nor do they broach the sensitive area of screening of prisoners for HIV before they are released.

The AIDS epidemic is symptomatic of a society spinning out of control. There is only one answer, and that is to re-establish our mooring rooted in personal responsibility and the traditional sense of right and wrong behavior. What can be the future for a society in which love and personal responsibility are displaced by sexual promiscuity and irresponsibility? What type of society will we be living in when we get to the point where few American adults will have grown up in a traditional family?

Despite what the liberal elite in the media would have us believe, self-esteem programs among black women do not provide the answer to this social crisis. It is these same liberal elite that brought us the welfare state that accelerated the breakdown of the black family.

Our efforts must focus on restoration of values and families in white and black communities. It's not an easy task. But if we lose sight that this is the only solution, we truly will be lost.

How the GOP Can Win the Black Vote, 2004

Black voters joined with the rest of the nation in 2004 to give a vote of confidence to our president.

Getting blacks to vote Republican is no small accomplishment. Yet they did so in sufficient numbers to play an important role in re-electing George Bush. The challenge now for Republicans is to understand what worked and to keep it up. It's essential for African Americans and for the nation.

President Bush got 11 percent of the black vote, up three points from the 8 percent he got in 2000. Given the work we've put in to get the conservative message to blacks, and pre-election polls showing black Republican support upwards, I was disappointed.

But there's more to the story. Black voter turnout surged by 25 percent. So President Bush got 11 percent of a black voter turnout of 13.2 million voters compared to 8 percent that he got of about 10.5 million black voters that turned out in 2000.

The net number of blacks supporting George Bush doubled in 2004.

Black votes for President Bush in key battleground states proved to be crucial. In the pivotal state of Ohio, critical for a Bush victory, the president got 16 percent of the black vote, up 9 percent over what he received in 2000.

Not incidental to the strong black support for the president in Ohio is the fact that Ohio was one of 11 states that had a ballot initiative to ban same-sex marriage. All the initiatives passed, and certainly the initiative in Ohio helped coax out the black vote and helped motivate those black voters to vote Republican.

The same-sex marriage ban has polled strongly all over the nation; however, the issue has been even stronger in the black community than in the white community.

Pundits are writing that this was an election about values. I agree, and the black Republican vote echoes this. However, there remain important differences between the black Christian vote and the white Christian vote. Attention to these differences provides clues to the work that needs to be done to broaden and grow Republican support in the black community.

In particular, the gains that have been made among blacks are almost exclusively on the social agenda. Republicans have made little progress in this community on domestic and economic issues.

Here is my "to do" list for the care, nurturing and growth of black Republican support:

> Continue to focus on the black church. Black Christians still vote overwhelmingly Democratic. Republicans are making gains, as evidenced by this election. But we're not making the gains we should. What does it say when Bill Clinton of Monica Lewinsky fame continues to get the warm welcome he does in black churches? There's a problem here. Black religious leaders need to be engaged to think about what is going on.

Understand that the messenger is as important as the message. One reason Bill Clinton gets the affection he does from blacks, despite the truth that he represents everything destructive to our community, is that blacks sense that he cares. Nothing gets done without trust, and the truth is that there are few Republican leaders who can walk into a black church, even with the best news in the world, and be received with trust. Black religious leaders need to be courted by Republicans they can trust and feel comfortable with.

Really care. Every single black in America should have voted for George Bush. His social agenda and economic agenda are precisely what black America needs. Yet because of the trust issue, the word is not getting through sufficiently. Too many blacks feel that Republicans really don't care about them—that they just want to use them. We need Republicans whose hearts hurt as much as black pastors' hearts hurt about the problems in the inner cities.

Maintain a regular ongoing program of communication. Considering the points above, get the message to black religious leaders that the critical common ground they share with the Republican Party is traditional values.

Educate on the connection between the social agenda and the economic agenda. Ownership and self reliance grow out of faith and family. Black household wealth remains pathetically low compared to white household wealth. Blacks need private social security accounts more than whites. But this community needs education on this and other economic issues.

We have much to do but we can and must do it. Blacks should love George Bush the way they love Bill Clinton. His agenda of traditional values and ownership is the only way out for our community. Fortunately, there are many blacks who are getting the message. But too many still are not.

Moving Back to Uncle Sam's Plantation, 2009

Six years ago, I wrote a book called "Uncle Sam's Plantation." I wrote the book to tell my own story of what I saw living inside the welfare state and my own transformation out of it.

I said in that book that indeed there are two Americas. A poor America on socialism and a wealthy America on capitalism.

I talked about government programs like Temporary Assistance for Needy Families (TANF), Job Opportunities and Basic Skills Training (JOBS), Emergency Assistance to Needy Families with Children (EANF), Section 8 Housing and Food Stamps.

A vast sea of perhaps well-intentioned government programs, all initially set into motion in the 1960s, that were going to lift the nation's poor out of poverty.

A benevolent Uncle Sam welcomed mostly poor black Americans onto the government plantation. Those who accepted the invitation switched mindsets from "How do I take care of myself?" to "What do I have to do to stay on the plantation?"

Instead of solving economic problems, government welfare socialism created monstrous moral and spiritual problems—the kind of problems that are inevitable when individuals turn responsibility for their lives over to others.

The legacy of American socialism is our blighted inner cities, dysfunctional inner city schools and broken black families.

Through God's grace, I found my way out. It was then that I understood what freedom meant and how great this country is.

I had the privilege of working on welfare reform in 1996, passed by a Republican Congress and signed into law by a Democrat president. A few years after enactment, welfare roles were down 50 percent.

I thought we were on the road to moving socialism out of our poor black communities and replacing it with wealth-producing American capitalism.

But, incredibly, we are going in the opposite direction.

Instead of poor America on socialism becoming more like rich American on capitalism, rich America on capitalism is becoming like poor America on socialism.

Uncle Sam has welcomed our banks onto the plantation and they have said, "Thank you, Suh."

Now, instead of thinking about what creative things need to be done to serve customers, they are thinking about what they have to tell Massah in order to get their cash.

There is some kind of irony that this is all happening under our first black president on the 200th anniversary of the birthday of Abraham Lincoln.

Worse, socialism seems to be the element of our new young president. And maybe even more troubling, our corporate executives seem happy to move onto the plantation.

In an op-ed on the opinion page of the Washington Post, Mr. Obama is clear that the goal of his trillion dollar spending plan is much more than short-term economic stimulus.

"This plan is more than a prescription for short-term spending—it's a strategy for America's long-term growth and opportunity in areas such as renewable energy, health care and education."

Perhaps more incredibly, Mr. Obama seems to think that government taking over an economy is a new idea. Or that massive growth in government can take place "with unprecedented transparency and accountability."

Yes, sir, we heard it from Jimmy Carter when he created the Department of Energy, the Synfuels Corporation and the Department of Education.

Or how about the Economic Opportunity Act of 1964—The War on Poverty— which, President Johnson said, "...does not merely expand old programs or improve what is already being done. It charts a new course. It strikes at the causes, not just the consequences of poverty."

Trillions of dollars later, black poverty is the same. But black families are not, with triple the incidence of single-parent homes and out of wedlock births.

It's not complicated. Americans can accept Barack Obama's invitation to move onto the plantation. Or they can choose personal responsibility and freedom.

Does anyone really need to think about what the choice should be?

Dr. King, Religion and Freedom, 2010

Aug. 28 marks the 47th anniversary of Dr. Martin Luther King Jr.'s "I have a dream" speech.

On that steamy summer day in 1963, hundreds of thousands of Americans, black and white, converged on the mall in Washington and heard this black pastor deliver what was essentially a sermon for freedom.

Compared to the unrest then on university campuses, violent outbreaks in urban areas and the protests of the civil-rights movement, today's turmoil seems relatively sedate.

Nevertheless, we do live today in a deeply troubled nation, and it's instructive to think about what has changed since the '60s and what hasn't.

One constant is the turmoil. It's tempting to think that normal is times when things smoothly buzz along—but this is an illusion. The beauty of freedom is the openness for dissent and discussion of life's endless problems and ambiguities.

What changes is what we argue about and how we define our problems. And one notable contrast between today and the '60s is our sense of religion and its relationship to the freedom we so cherish.

To appreciate this, we need look no further than Dr. King's famous speech.

Today, we commonly view freedom as exclusively in the arena of politics, separate and apart from—for some the antithesis of—religion.

Reading Dr. King's words, we can appreciate that for him religion was the handmaiden of freedom, not its adversary.

King said that his dream was "deeply rooted in the American dream," and he quoted Isaiah, saying "...the rough places will be made plain, and the crooked places will be made straight, and the glory of the Lord shall be revealed..."

"This will be a day when all of God's children," he said, "will sing with new meaning, 'My country 'tis of thee, sweet land of liberty'...."

It is reported that when King founded the Southern Christian Leadership Conference, it was suggested to him that he drop the "Christian" label, for fear that it might alienate northern liberals. He refused.

By one report, King said at one point, "In all too many northern communities a sort of quasi-liberalism prevails, so bent on seeing all sides that it fails to become dedicated to any side."

The moral relativism that concerned Dr. King then has come to define civil rights today and has widely captured popular perceptions among Americans about what freedom means.

The sense of freedom as the pursuit of godly ideals has given way to a sense that freedom is about meaninglessness and acceptance and legitimization of all possibilities. The idea that the need for freedom flows from humility that no single man can grasp truth in its totality has given way to a conviction that there is no truth at all.

Just listen to the dialogue in the Ground Zero mosque controversy. For liberals, there is only one American ideal that is relevant—religious freedom. Their love affair with openness as an end in itself dismisses any possibility that Islam, as widely understood and practiced by its own adherents, may promote values in conflict with ours.

It's little wonder that the public is so confused about the religious affiliation and values of our president.

One day he will plead for the rights of women to abort their children, or for legitimization of all imaginable lifestyles, and the next day he'll plead for acceptance of a religion in which people are still stoned for this very same behavior.

The same Pew survey reporting that 43 percent of Americans "don't know" President Obama's religion reports that only 26 percent see the Democratic Party he leads as "friendly" to religion.

When the party in power and its leader, our president, see redemption in government programs and politics, it's no wonder Americans are confused.

At the heart of the turmoil in our country today is a struggle to grasp again what freedom really means, and the place in this struggle for traditional, moral truths that we all accept.

Becoming aware of and coming to grips with the fundamental conflicts tearing at the American soul will help this nation take on more successfully the great challenges we're facing.

PART VI

THE NEW BLACK MODERATE
OBAMA AND BEYOND

28.

BARACK OBAMA

Barack Obama (b. 1961) is the forty-fourth president of the United States and is the first African American to hold this prestigious position. He has been no stranger to "firsts." Obama was the first African American to become the president of the *Harvard Law Review*. He began his political career and public life as a civil rights attorney and activist. In Chicago, as director of Project Vote, he led voter registration drives. He worked diligently with other grassroots activist campaigns aimed at mobilizing the urban poor, particularly Black communities. Obama was passionate about helping poor Black folk on Chicago's South Side. In 1996 he successfully ran for the Illinois State Senate.

While a state senator Obama continued to help poor African Americans. He assisted in the passage of Illinois' first racial profiling law. In addition, he fought to have a law instituted that now requires all homicide interrogations to be videotaped by law enforcement. Police brutality has been an issue that adversely impacts the African American community and Obama, like the Black Nationalists we have read about, has been devoted to protecting African Americans from police brutality and unfair treatment by law enforcement. He initiated legislation to enhance tax credits for the poor. Obama struggled to keep welfare from being cut and was successful in garnering additional childcare subsidies for poor families. He worked to get better access to healthcare for poor and middle class families. After all these successes it is no wonder he was re-elected for this office in both 1998 and 2002. Although, in 2000, he did lose the race for the House of Representatives. However, in 2004 he was elected to the United States Senate. Interestingly, in this election he beat Alan Keyes, whose work we examined in the previous section, in a landslide. This victory made him the only African American in the upper house and the only senator in the Congressional Black Caucus. In February of 2007 the freshman senator announced his candidacy for the president of the United States. Finally, on November 4, 2008, Barack Obama won both the popular vote and the necessary votes in the electoral college and was elected president of the United States of America.

Barack Obama has fought for Black people and other marginalized groups in the United States as president. It is no surprise that the first bill signed by the former civil rights attorney once seated in the Oval Office was the Lilly LedBetter Fair Pay Act 2009. This act was a victory for women's rights and civil rights. The legislation relaxed the statute of limitations originally implemented by the Civil Rights Act, when filing equal pay discrimination lawsuits. In another effort to further his support of women's rights he annulled the Mexico City Policy or the "Mexico City Gag Rule"; this policy made it illegal for any non-governmental organizations (NGOs) that receive any amount of federal funding to utilize any portion of those funds to help perform or assist individuals in the procurement of abortion services.

In 2009 he expanded the Children's Health Insurance Program. In this first strike for healthcare reform, the program appropriated funding for states who would grant access to healthcare for uninsured children who come from homes too poor to afford their own insurance but ostensibly too well-off to qualify for Medicaid. His expansion of the program ensured that at least a further four million children now had health insurance. Certainly, this was a program that benefited many African American families.

In 2009 Obama nominated the first Hispanic to ever sit on the Supreme Court, Sonia Sotomayor. In 2010 he also nominated Elena Kagan to the Supreme Court. Obama's nominations led to another American first. Three women now sit on the high court for the first time in our nation's history. In 2009 Obama signed the Matthew Shepard and James Byrd Jr. Hate Crimes Prevention Act. This landmark victory for civil rights and the LGBTQ community expanded the already existing federal hate crime statute to include gender identity, sexual orientation, and disabilities. In another victory for the LGBTQ community Obama repealed the Don't Ask Don't Tell policy initiated under Bill Clinton.

In probably his most controversial act as president, Obama signed the famous economic stimulus package or the American Recovery and Reinvestment Act, which allocated $787 billion to bailing out the failing economy. Reminiscent of FDR's New Deal, Obama aimed to invest money into the infrastructure of the nation in order to create jobs, improve education, lessen the cost of healthcare for citizens, and stabilize the banking and finance industries. The expansion of social services, unemployment insurance, and aid to failing social institutions such as schools helped Black communities.

In 2010 Obama signed the Fair Sentencing Act, which eliminated the racial disparity in drug sentencing. For example, in such states as New York, under the Rockefeller Drug Laws an individual could be arrested for possession of five grams of crack-cocaine and receive a five-year sentence, while another individual possessing powdered cocaine would need to possess 500 grams to receive the same five-year sentence. These laws were clear examples of the way in which the war on drugs has been shaped by both racism and classism. The cultural imagery associated with powdered cocaine conjures up images of affluent Whites and crack is most associated with poor Blacks. While working within the political system Barack Obama has managed to foster a modicum of change. In both word and deed he has demonstrated a genuine desire to assist Black communities and the American populace.

Overview of Ideas

Barack Obama's ascendancy to the highest political office in the United States may suggest that a new era of Black leadership has emerged. Many African Americans saw this accomplishment as a turning point in American history and as his campaign slogan suggested that the twenty-first century would be filled with hope and change. Readers should reflect on what this watershed in American history actually means for Black people. Barack Obama's major contribution to modern African American political thought has been the astute way he combines conservative, "bootstrap" liberalism with progressive ideas that link social problems with structural deficiencies. He has labored arduously to craft a strategic moderatism that might have hope of uniting an incredibly fragmented United States. Again, the question for scholars and students of African American political thought is whether these efforts will render large-scale change for African Americans. What will this moderatism mean for Black people? In the twenty-first century will Black people and other Black leaders welcome this approach? What predictions can we make for the future of Black leadership?

Obama's critics have not been hopeful about his ability to effectively garner change for African Americans. Malik Miah wrote, "Obama is genuinely concerned about the suffering of the Black community but like all crossover Black elected officials who need the white vote to be in office, he downplays his 'color' and the realities of racism."[1] Miah is accurate; he strategically attempts to make issues long affecting the African American community an American problem. Borrowing from Frederick Douglass, for Obama, the "Negro Problem" is the American problem. "There is not a Black America and a White America and Latino America and Asian America—there's the United States of America." Like previous writers, Douglass, Stewart, Washington, Bethune, King, Chisholm, and others he aims to convince Americans that they will benefit from helping the population's most exploited, impoverished, and marginalized. He argued:

> all Americans [must] realize that your dreams do not have to come at the expense of my dreams; that investing in the health, welfare, and education of black and brown and white children will ultimately help all of America prosper.

While his approach is moderate, as Miah suggested, this does not mean that Obama does not have genuine concern for Black people.

Obama recognizes and is dedicated to resolving problems within the Black community. Education has been a paramount issue in his presidency. Like almost every one of his predecessors he argues that education is paramount for uplifting Black people. Obama acknowledged, "almost 60% of African American fourth graders can't read at even the basic level, and by 8th grade, nearly nine in ten African American and Latino students are not proficient in math." According to Obama, inequality in educational institutions is the primary mechanism by which class inequalities are maintained. Education is a primary force in closing the income gap between Blacks and Whites. In response to this educational epidemic, in 2009, Obama leaned on the Resolute desk and officially signed the American Recovery and Reinvestment Act. The Act allocated $77 billion dollars for reforms to strengthen elementary and secondary education, $30 billion to assist students with the rising costs of higher education and improve overall access to higher education, and $5 billion for early learning programs.

In addition, Obama has been an outspoken critic of our healthcare system. Although his efforts have been met with fierce resistance, like many of the more radical figures in this text he believes in universal healthcare. Like civil rights leaders he continues to fight for the middle class. And although their solutions vary, like Black Nationalists and Black Power activists Obama speaks to the needs of the poor. He acknowledges that unemployment, mass incarceration, new HIV infections, etc. are all problems that disproportionately impact the Black community. To address these issues he has passed the Stimulus Package, extending unemployment insurance, creating healthcare reform, passing programs such as Promise Neighborhoods that has funneled $10 million into fostering local educational programs in poverty-stricken areas. While he recognizes the importance of channeling more funding to remedy structural problems, he also points to problems related to cultural pathologies and in turn emphasizes personal responsibility.

Although conservatives call Obama a radical socialist, when we examine his work closely we often see a much different Obama than the one that is perpetuated by conservative media pundits. He often has more in common with conservatives than either of them acknowledge. In his famous "Race speech," he said:

> Yes, if you're African American, the odds of growing up amid crime and gangs are higher.... But that's not a reason to get bad grades ... that's not a reason to give up on your education and drop out of school. Your destiny is in your hands.

Obama constantly reminds the rabble of the Horatio Alger tale. Like many of his predecessors, particularly his Black conservative contemporaries, he reminds Americans of his own Horatio Alger tale and reinforces the American meritocracy; with hard work and perseverance success is possible for everyone.

Obama has been a huge spokesman against absentee fatherism:

> Too many fathers are M.I.A., too many fathers are AWOL, missing from too many lives and too many homes, they have abandoned their responsibilities, acting like boys instead of men, and the foundations of our families are weaker because of it.

Quagmires plaguing many African American families are the result of long-standing historical racial and structural inequities.

> A lack of economic opportunities among black men ... contributed to the erosion of black families—a problem that welfare policies for many years may have worsened. And the lack of basic services in so many urban black neighborhoods ... all helped create a cycle of violence, blight and neglect that continue to haunt us.

If we read this closely, while Obama argues that the ultimate culprit for the deterioration of the Black family is socio-economic inequality, he also seems to agree with conservatives that welfare has exacerbated this problem and assisted in the reification of a culture of poverty. He acknowledges that more government spending and government-sponsored programs cannot remedy broken families; it cannot fix a large part of the problem impacting many Black people. Without cultural transformation, namely more personal responsibility and emphasis on traditional family values, many African American families are looking into a bleak future in the twenty-first century. This sounds quite similar to ideas presented throughout this text and in the previous section on Black conservatives.

At times, Obama bears a striking similarity to another famous moderate, W.E.B. Du Bois. Reminiscent of the talented tenth, Obama remarked:

> our kids can't all aspire to be the next LeBron or Lil' Wayne. I want them aspiring to be scientists and engineers, doctors and teachers, not just ball players and rappers. I want them aspiring to be a Supreme Court Justice. I want them aspiring to be President of the United States.

Individual motivation is important and disadvantaged African American youth must dream big and harness the American Dream—find the Horatio Alger inside of them.

> Government programs alone won't get our children to the Promised Land. We need a new mindset, a new set of attitudes—because one of the most durable and destructive legacies of discrimination is the way that we have internalized a sense of limitation; how so many in our community have come to expect so little of ourselves.

Obama recognizes the same "Black victimhood" or victim psychology that conservatives discuss. He says that Black people themselves recognize the limitations of politics that solely focus on government intervention. Individuals must take responsibility for their lives, their families, and communities.

> Go into any inner city neighborhood, and folks will tell you that government alone can't teach our kids to learn; they know that parents have to teach, that children can't achieve unless we raise their expectations and turn off the television sets and eradicate the slander that says a black youth with a book is acting white.

According to Obama, good parenting and family stability play a prodigious role in the success of the individual. He posits that this is not a conservative ideal or a liberal ideal. For him this is an issue we can all agree on. Once again, Obama attempts to get liberals and conservatives to see their similarities and common values; this is the mark of a moderate.

21st Century Schools for a 21st Century Economy, 2006

Awhile back, I was reading through Jonathan Kozol's new book, Shame of a Nation. In it, he talks about his recent travels to schools across America, and how fifty years after Brown v. Board of Education, we have an education system in this country that is still visibly separate and painfully unequal.

At one point, Kozol tells about his trip to Fremont High School in Los Angeles, where he meets some children who explain with heart-wrenching honesty what living in this system is like. One girl told him that she'd taken hairdressing twice, because there were actually two different levels offered by the high school. The first was in hair-styling; the other in braiding.

Another girl, Mireya, listened as her friend told this story. And she began to cry. When asked what was wrong, she said, "I don't want to take hairdressing. I did not need sewing either. I knew how to sew. My mother is a seamstress in a factory. I'm trying to go to college. I don't need to sew to go to college. My mother sews. I hoped for something else."

I hoped for something else.

It's a simple dream, but it speaks to us so powerfully because it is our dream—one that exists at the very center of the American experience. One that says if you're willing to work hard and take responsibility, then you'll have the chance to reach for something else; for something better.

The ideal of public education has always been at the heart of this bargain. From the moment we built the first schools in the towns of New England, it was the driving force behind Thomas Jefferson's declaration that "...talent and virtue, needed in a free society, should be educated regardless of wealth, birth or other accidental condition."

It's a bargain our government kept as we moved from a nation of farms to a nation of factories, setting up a system of free public high schools across the country. It's a bargain we expanded after World War II, when we sent over two million returning heroes to college on the GI Bill, creating the largest middle class in history.

And even when our government refused to hold up its end of this bargain and forced Linda Brown to walk miles to a dilapidated Topeka school because she wasn't allowed in the well-off, white-only school; even then, ordinary people stood up and spoke out until the day when the arrival of nine little children at a school in Little Rock made real the decision that in America, separate could never be equal. Because in America, it's the promise of a good education for all that makes it possible for any child to transcend the barriers of race or class or background and achieve their God-given potential.

In this country, it is education that allows our children to hope for something else.

As the twenty-first century unfolds, we are called once again to make real this hope – to meet the new challenges of a global economy by carrying forth the ideals of progress and opportunity through public education in America.

We now live in a world where the most valuable skill you can sell is knowledge. Revolutions in technology and communication have created an entire economy of high-tech, high-wage jobs that can be located anywhere there's an internet connection. And today, a child in Chicago is not only competing for jobs with one in Boston, but thousands more in Bangalore and Beijing who are being educated longer and better than ever before.

America is in danger of losing this competition. We now have one of the highest high school dropout rates of any industrialized country. By 12th grade, our children score lower on their math and science tests than most other kids in the world. And today, countries like China are graduating eight times as many engineers as we do.

And yet, as these fundamental changes are occurring all around us, we still hear about schools that are giving students the choice between hairstyling and braiding.

Today we are failing too many of our children. We're sending them out into a 21st century economy by sending them through the doors of 20th century schools.

Right now, six million middle and high school students are reading at levels significantly below their grade level. Half of all teenagers can't understand basic fractions; half of all nine year olds can't perform basic multiplication or division. For some students, the data is even worse: almost 60% of African-American fourth-graders can't read at even the basic level, and by 8th grade, nearly nine in ten African-American and Latino students are not proficient in math. More students than ever are taking college entrance exams, but these tests are showing that only twenty percent are prepared to take college-level classes in English, math, and science. For African-American students, the figure dips to just ten percent.

What happens to these children? What happens to the one in four eighth graders who never go on to finish high school in five years? What happens to the one in two high school graduates who never go on to college?

Thirty or forty years ago, they may have gone on to find a factory job that could pay the bills and support a family. But we no longer live in that world.

Today, the average salary of a high school graduate is only $33,000 a year. For high school dropouts, it's even closer to the poverty line—just $25,000.

If we do nothing about this, if we accept this kind of economy; this kind of society, we face a future where the ideal of American meritocracy could turn into an American myth. A future that's not only morally unacceptable for our children; but economically untenable for a nation that finds itself in a globalized world, as countries who are out-educating us today out-compete our workers tomorrow.

The President promised that he would change all this with No Child Left Behind Act. Unfortunately, the Administration has failed on the implementation of that law. Not only have they failed to provide billions in adequate funding, they've also failed to design better assessment tests that provide a clearer path for schools to raise achievement.

They've failed to work with states so that they could honor their own commitment to provide every child with a highly qualified teacher. As a result, they've had to exempt numerous states from meeting certain provisions of No Child Left Behind, and now it appears unlikely that they will meet their own goal of getting our children to grade level by the year 2014.

This is unacceptable. If we truly believe in our public schools, then we have a moral responsibility to do better—to break the either-or mentality around the debate over education that asks us to choose between more money or more reform, and embrace a both-and mentality. Because we know that good schools will require both the structural reform and the resources necessary to prepare our kids for the future.

We can learn from innovation taking place all over the country and right here in Chicago. Chicago Public Schools are collaborating on a number of innovations with foundations and groups like New Leaders for New Schools, Teach for America, the New Teacher Project, the Chicago Public Education Fund, The Academy for Urban

School Leadership and the University of Chicago Urban Education Initiative. The Chicago Teachers Union is also now collaborating on the Fresh Start Schools, and we're watching that experiment with great interest. It's not easy, it's not popular with everyone, and, in the end, some of the experiments may be rejected. But we can't stop trying. We have to keep moving ahead for the sake of our children.

Now, the problem on a national level is that we are not applying what we're learning from these reforms to our national education policy. And so we need new vision for education in America—one where we move past ideology to experiment with the latest reforms, measure the results, and make policy decisions based on what works and what doesn't.

Fortunately, educational leaders like the people in this room know what reforms really work: a more challenging and rigorous curriculum with emphasis on math, science, and literacy skills. Longer hours and more days to give kids the time and attention they need to learn. Early childhood education for every child so they're not left behind before they even start school, a measure Governor Blagojevich has recently introduced. Meaningful, performance-based assessments that can give us a fuller picture of how a student is doing. And putting effective teachers and transformative principals in front of our kids.

All of these reforms need to be scaled-up and replicated across the country. But in the time I have remaining, let me use to just talk about a few to point to what's possible, starting with one place where I think we can start making a big difference in education right now.

From the moment our children step into a classroom, new evidence shows that the single most important factor in determining their achievement today is not the color of their skin or where they come from; it's not who their parents are or how much money they have.

It's who their teacher is. It's the person who will brave some of the most difficult schools, the most challenging children, and accept the most meager compensation simply to give someone else the chance to succeed.

One study shows that two groups of students who started third grade at about the same level of math achievement finished fifth grade at vastly different levels. The group with the effective teacher saw their scores rise by nearly 25%. The group with the ineffective teacher actually saw their scores drop by 25%.

But even though we know how much teaching matters, in too many places we've abandoned our teachers and principals, sending them into some of the most impoverished, underperforming schools with little experience or pay; little preparation or support. After a few years of experience, most will leave to pick wealthier, less challenging schools.

The result is that some of our neediest children end up with less-experienced, poorly-paid teachers who are far more likely to be teaching subjects in which they have no training. Minority students are twice as likely to have these teachers. In Illinois, students in high-poverty schools are more than three times as likely to have them.

If we hope to give our children a chance, it's time we start giving our teachers and our principals a chance. We can't change the whole country overnight. But what we can do is give more school districts the chance to revolutionize the way they approach teaching. By helping spark complete reform across an entire school district, we can learn what actually works for our kids and then replicate those policies throughout the country.

So here's the legislation I'm introducing this week—it's the creation of what I call Innovation Districts. School districts from around the country that want to become seedbeds of reform would apply and we'd select the twenty with the best plans to put effective, supported teachers in all classrooms and increase achievement for all students. We'd offer these districts substantial new resources to do this, but in return, we'd ask them to try systemic new reforms. Above all, we'd require results.

In Innovation Districts, we'd begin by working with these districts to strengthen their teaching, and we'd start with recruitment.

Right now we don't have nearly enough effective teachers and principals in the places we need them most: urban and rural schools, and subject areas like math and science. One of the main reasons for this, cited by most teachers who leave the profession, is that no one gives them the necessary training and preparation.

Around the country, organizations like the Academy for Urban School Leadership right here in Chicago are changing this by recruiting and training new, highly-qualified teachers for some of the hardest-to-teach classrooms in the country. We need to expand this by giving districts help in creating new teacher academies that will partner with organizations like this to recruit effective teachers for low-performing, high-poverty schools. Each teacher would undergo an extensive training program before they begin, including classroom observation and participation.

These teacher academies are also showing us that it's not enough to just put outstanding teachers in the classroom—we have to place outstanding principals in the schools as well. In districts across the country, the role of principal is being transformed from bureaucratic manager to instructional leader who can set high standards and recruit great talent. With 230 New Leaders serving more than 100,000 kids annually, New Leaders for New Schools has been at the cutting edge of this process—a process we need to expand nationally.

After we recruit great teachers, we need to pay them better. Right now, teaching is one of the only professions where no matter how well you perform at your job, you're almost never rewarded for success. But with six-figure salaries luring away some of our most talented college graduates from some of our neediest schools, this needs to change.

That's why teachers in these Innovation Districts who are successful in improving student achievement would receive substantial pay increases, as would those who choose to teach in the most troubled schools and the highest-need subject areas, like math and science. The city of Denver is trying pay increases in partnership with the local union, and when Chattanooga, Tennessee offered similar incentives for teachers who taught in high-need schools, student reading scores went up by over 10%.

Of course, teachers don't just need more pay, they need more support. One thing I kept hearing when I visited Dodge Elementary here in Chicago is how much an encouraging principal or the advice of an experienced teacher can make a difference.

That's why teachers would be paired with mentor teachers who've been there before. After a few years of experience, they'd then have the chance to become mentor teachers themselves.

We also know that teachers can't teach and our kids can't learn when there's violence in and around our schools, a problem we've seen right here in Chicago this year in too many tragic incidents. If our kids can't go to school in a safe place, nothing else we do matters. As we move forward with reform, we must make safety a top priority. In the innovation districts, we'd help do this by expanding programs already being used in various states that teach students about positive behavior.

Finally, we would also require Innovation Districts to work with their unions to uncover bureaucratic obstacles that leave poor kids without good teachers, including hiring, funding and transfer policies. Districts would work with unions to tackle these problems so that we can provide every child with an effective teacher.

Beyond policies that help teachers specifically, we'd also ask Innovation Districts to try reforms that create a more effective teaching environment. To give teachers more time with their students and more time to learn from each other, these districts would be asked to restructure their schedules and implement either longer days or summer school.

In December, I also introduced the STEP Up Act that addresses this by providing summer learning opportunities for children at high risk early in their school careers. In addition to more learning, this would provide kids a safe, educational environment while their parents are at work.

To hold schools and teachers accountable for the results of all these reforms, districts that don't improve would be removed from the program. To find out what works and what doesn't, we'd provide them with powerful data and technology, and also give them the option of partnering with local universities to help them improve performance.

These reforms would take an important first step toward fixing our broken system by putting qualified, supported teachers in the schools that need them most. But beyond that, they would show us the progress we can make when money is well spent. And they would allow us to finally break free from the either-or mentality that's put bureaucracy and ideology ahead of what works; ahead of what's best for our kids.

When it comes to education, the time for excuses has passed—for all of us.

During my visit to Dodge Elementary, I was able to speak with a few of the teachers about some of the challenges they're facing in educating their students. And one teacher mentioned to me that one of the biggest obstacles in her view is what she referred to as the "These Kids" syndrome.

She said that when it comes to educating students today, people always seem to find a million excuses for why "these kids" can't learn. That you'll hear how "these kids are nothing but trouble," or "these kids come from tough backgrounds," or "these kids don't want to learn."

And the more people talk about them as "these kids," the easier it is for "these kids" to become somebody else's problem.

But of course, the children in this country—the children in Dodge Elementary, and South Central L.A., and rural Arkansas, and suburban Maryland—they are not "these kids." They are our kids. They want a chance to achieve—and each of us has a responsibility to give them that chance.

In the end, children succeed because somewhere along the way, a parent or teacher instills in them the belief that they can. That they're able to. That they're worth it.

At Earhart Elementary in Chicago, one little girl, raised by a single mom from a poor background, was asked the secret to her academic success.

She said, "I just study hard every night because I like learning. My teacher wants me to be a good student, and so does my mother. I don't want to let them down."

In the months and years to come, it's time for this nation to rededicate itself to the ideal of a world class education for every American child. It's time to let our kids hope for something else. It's time to instill the belief in every child that they can succeed—and then make sure we make good on the promise to never let them down. Thank you.

A More Perfect Union "The Race Speech," 2008

"We the people, in order to form a more perfect union."

Two hundred and twenty one years ago, in a hall that still stands across the street, a group of men gathered and, with these simple words, launched America's improbable experiment in democracy. Farmers and scholars; statesmen and patriots who had traveled across an ocean to escape tyranny and persecution finally made real their declaration of independence at a Philadelphia convention that lasted through the spring of 1787.

The document they produced was eventually signed but ultimately unfinished. It was stained by this nation's original sin of slavery, a question that divided the colonies and brought the convention to a stalemate until the founders chose to allow the slave trade to continue for at least twenty more years, and to leave any final resolution to future generations.

Of course, the answer to the slavery question was already embedded within our Constitution—a Constitution that had at its very core the ideal of equal citizenship under the law; a Constitution that promised its people liberty, and justice, and a union that could be and should be perfected over time.

And yet words on a parchment would not be enough to deliver slaves from bondage, or provide men and women of every color and creed their full rights and obligations as citizens of the United States. What would be needed were Americans in successive generations who were willing to do their part – through protests and struggle, on the streets and in the courts, through a civil war and civil disobedience and always at great risk—to narrow that gap between the promise of our ideals and the reality of their time.

This was one of the tasks we set forth at the beginning of this campaign—to continue the long march of those who came before us, a march for a more just, more equal, more free, more caring and more prosperous America. I chose to run for the presidency at this moment in history because I believe deeply that we cannot solve the challenges of our time unless we solve them together—unless we perfect our union by understanding that we may have different stories, but we hold common hopes; that we may not look the same and we may not have come from the same place, but we all want to move in the same direction—towards a better future for our children and our grandchildren.

This belief comes from my unyielding faith in the decency and generosity of the American people. But it also comes from my own American story.

I am the son of a black man from Kenya and a white woman from Kansas. I was raised with the help of a white grandfather who survived a Depression to serve in Patton's Army during World War II and a white grandmother who worked on a bomber assembly line at Fort Leavenworth while he was overseas. I've gone to some of the best schools in America and lived in one of the world's poorest nations. I am married to a black American who carries within her the blood of slaves and slaveowners—an inheritance we pass on to our two precious daughters. I have brothers, sisters, nieces, nephews, uncles and cousins, of every race and every hue, scattered across three continents, and for as long as I live, I will never forget that in no other country on Earth is my story even possible.

It's a story that hasn't made me the most conventional candidate. But it is a story that has seared into my genetic makeup the idea that this nation is more than the sum of its parts—that out of many, we are truly one.

Throughout the first year of this campaign, against all predictions to the contrary, we saw how hungry the American people were for this message of unity. Despite the temptation to view my candidacy through a purely racial lens, we won commanding victories in states with some of the whitest populations in the country. In South Carolina, where the Confederate Flag still flies, we built a powerful coalition of African Americans and white Americans.

This is not to say that race has not been an issue in the campaign. At various stages in the campaign, some commentators have deemed me either "too black" or "not black enough." We saw racial tensions bubble to the surface during the week before the South Carolina primary. The press has scoured every exit poll for the latest evidence of racial polarization, not just in terms of white and black, but black and brown as well.

And yet, it has only been in the last couple of weeks that the discussion of race in this campaign has taken a particularly divisive turn.

On one end of the spectrum, we've heard the implication that my candidacy is somehow an exercise in affirmative action; that it's based solely on the desire of wide-eyed liberals to purchase racial reconciliation on the cheap. On the other end, we've heard my former pastor, Reverend Jeremiah Wright, use incendiary language to express views that have the potential not only to widen the racial divide, but views that denigrate both the greatness and the goodness of our nation; that rightly offend white and black alike.

I have already condemned, in unequivocal terms, the statements of Reverend Wright that have caused such controversy. For some, nagging questions remain. Did I know him to be an occasionally fierce critic of American domestic and foreign policy? Of course. Did I ever hear him make remarks that could be considered controversial while I sat in church? Yes. Did I strongly disagree with many of his political views?

Absolutely—just as I'm sure many of you have heard remarks from your pastors, priests, or rabbis with which you strongly disagreed.

But the remarks that have caused this recent firestorm weren't simply controversial. They weren't simply a religious leader's effort to speak out against perceived injustice. Instead, they expressed a profoundly distorted view of this country—a view that sees white racism as endemic, and that elevates what is wrong with America above all that we know is right with America; a view that sees the conflicts in the Middle East as rooted primarily in the actions of stalwart allies like Israel, instead of emanating from the perverse and hateful ideologies of radical Islam.

As such, Reverend Wright's comments were not only wrong but divisive, divisive at a time when we need unity; racially charged at a time when we need to come together to solve a set of monumental problems—two wars, a terrorist threat, a falling economy, a chronic health care crisis and potentially devastating climate change; problems that are neither black or white or Latino or Asian, but rather problems that confront us all.

Given my background, my politics, and my professed values and ideals, there will no doubt be those for whom my statements of condemnation are not enough. Why associate myself with Reverend Wright in the first place, they may ask? Why not join another church? And I confess that if all that I knew of Reverend Wright were the snippets of those sermons that have run in an endless loop on the television and You Tube, or if Trinity United Church of Christ conformed to the caricatures being peddled by some commentators, there is no doubt that I would react in much the same way

But the truth is, that isn't all that I know of the man. The man I met more than twenty years ago is a man who helped introduce me to my Christian faith, a man who spoke to me about our obligations to love one another; to care for the sick and lift up the poor. He is a man who served his country as a U.S. Marine; who has studied and lectured at some of the finest universities and seminaries in the country, and who for over thirty years led a church that serves the community by doing God's work here on Earth—by housing the homeless, ministering to the needy, providing day care services and scholarships and prison ministries, and reaching out to those suffering from HIV/AIDS.

In my first book, *Dreams From My Father*, I described the experience of my first service at Trinity:

> "People began to shout, to rise from their seats and clap and cry out, a forceful wind carrying the reverend's voice up into the rafters.... And in that single note—hope!—I heard something else; at the foot of that cross, inside the thousands of churches across the city, I imagined the stories of ordinary black people merging with the stories of David and Goliath, Moses and Pharaoh, the Christians in the lion's den, Ezekiel's field of dry bones. Those stories—of survival, and freedom, and hope—became our story, my story; the blood that had spilled was our blood, the tears our tears; until this black church, on this bright day, seemed once more a vessel carrying the story of a people into future generations and into a larger world. Our trials and triumphs became at once unique and universal, black and more than black; in chronicling our journey, the stories and songs gave us a means to reclaim memories that we didn't need to feel shame about ... memories that all people might study and cherish—and with which we could start to rebuild."

That has been my experience at Trinity. Like other predominantly black churches across the country, Trinity embodies the black community in its entirety—the doctor and the welfare mom, the model student and the former gang-banger. Like other black churches, Trinity's services are full of raucous laughter and sometimes bawdy humor. They are full of dancing, clapping, screaming and shouting that may seem jarring to the untrained ear. The church contains in full the kindness and cruelty, the fierce intelligence and the shocking ignorance, the struggles and successes, the love and yes, the bitterness and bias that make up the black experience in America.

And this helps explain, perhaps, my relationship with Reverend Wright. As imperfect as he may be, he has been like family to me. He strengthened my faith, officiated my wedding, and baptized my children. Not once in my conversations with him have I heard him talk about any ethnic group in derogatory terms, or treat whites with whom he interacted with anything but courtesy and respect. He contains within him the contradictions—the good and the bad—of the community that he has served diligently for so many years.

I can no more disown him than I can disown the black community. I can no more disown him than I can my white grandmother—a woman who helped raise me, a woman who sacrificed again and again for me, a woman who loves me as much as she loves anything in this world, but a woman who once confessed her fear of black men who passed by her on the street, and who on more than one occasion has uttered racial or ethnic stereotypes that made me cringe.

These people are a part of me. And they are a part of America, this country that I love.

Some will see this as an attempt to justify or excuse comments that are simply inexcusable. I can assure you it is not. I suppose the politically safe thing would be to move on from this episode and just hope that it fades into the woodwork. We can dismiss Reverend Wright as a crank or a demagogue, just as some have dismissed Geraldine Ferraro, in the aftermath of her recent statements, as harboring some deep-seated racial bias.

But race is an issue that I believe this nation cannot afford to ignore right now. We would be making the same mistake that Reverend Wright made in his offending sermons about America—to simplify and stereotype and amplify the negative to the point that it distorts reality.

The fact is that the comments that have been made and the issues that have surfaced over the last few weeks reflect the complexities of race in this country that we've never really worked through—a part of our union that we have yet to perfect. And if we walk away now, if we simply retreat into our respective corners, we will never be able to come together and solve challenges like health care, or education, or the need to find good jobs for every American.

Understanding this reality requires a reminder of how we arrived at this point. As William Faulkner once wrote, "The past isn't dead and buried. In fact, it isn't even past." We do not need to recite here the history of racial injustice in this country. But we do need to remind ourselves that so many of the disparities that exist in the African-American community today can be directly traced to inequalities passed on from an earlier generation that suffered under the brutal legacy of slavery and Jim Crow.

Segregated schools were, and are, inferior schools; we still haven't fixed them, fifty years after Brown v. Board of Education, and the inferior education they provided, then and now, helps explain the pervasive achievement gap between today's black and white students.

Legalized discrimination—where blacks were prevented, often through violence, from owning property, or loans were not granted to African-American business owners, or black homeowners could not access FHA mortgages, or blacks were excluded from unions, or the police force, or fire departments—meant that black families could not amass any meaningful wealth to bequeath to future generations. That history helps explain the wealth and income gap between black and white, and the concentrated pockets of poverty that persists in so many of today's urban and rural communities.

A lack of economic opportunity among black men, and the shame and frustration that came from not being able to provide for one's family, contributed to the erosion of black families—a problem that welfare policies for many years may have worsened. And the lack of basic services in so many urban black neighborhoods—parks for kids to play in, police walking the beat, regular garbage pick-up and building code enforcement—all helped create a cycle of violence, blight and neglect that continue to haunt us.

This is the reality in which Reverend Wright and other African-Americans of his generation grew up. They came of age in the late fifties and early sixties, a time when segregation was still the law of the land and opportunity was systematically constricted. What's remarkable is not how many failed in the face of discrimination, but rather how many men and women overcame the odds; how many were able to make a way out of no way for those like me who would come after them.

But for all those who scratched and clawed their way to get a piece of the American Dream, there were many who didn't make it—those who were ultimately defeated, in one way or another, by discrimination. That legacy of defeat was passed on to future generations—those young men and increasingly young women who we see standing on street corners or languishing in our prisons, without hope or prospects for the future. Even for those blacks who did make it, questions of race, and racism, continue to define their worldview in fundamental ways. For the men and women of Reverend Wright's generation, the memories of humiliation and doubt and fear have not gone away; nor has the anger and the bitterness of those years. That anger may not get expressed in public, in front of white co-workers or white friends. But it does find voice in the barbershop or around the kitchen table. At times, that anger is exploited by politicians, to gin up votes along racial lines, or to make up for a politician's own failings.

And occasionally it finds voice in the church on Sunday morning, in the pulpit and in the pews. The fact that so many people are surprised to hear that anger in some of Reverend Wright's sermons simply reminds us of the old truism that the most segregated hour in American life occurs on Sunday morning. That anger is not always productive; indeed, all too often it distracts attention from solving real problems; it keeps us from squarely facing our own complicity in our condition, and prevents the

African-American community from forging the alliances it needs to bring about real change. But the anger is real; it is powerful; and to simply wish it away, to condemn it without understanding its roots, only serves to widen the chasm of misunderstanding that exists between the races.

In fact, a similar anger exists within segments of the white community. Most working- and middle-class white Americans don't feel that they have been particularly privileged by their race. Their experience is the immigrant experience—as far as they're concerned, no one's handed them anything, they've built it from scratch. They've worked hard all their lives, many times only to see their jobs shipped overseas or their pension dumped after a lifetime of labor. They are anxious about their futures, and feel their dreams slipping away; in an era of stagnant wages and global competition, opportunity comes to be seen as a zero sum game, in which your dreams come at my expense. So when they are told to bus their children to a school across town; when they hear that an African American is getting an advantage in landing a good job or a spot in a good college because of an injustice that they themselves never committed; when they're told that their fears about crime in urban neighborhoods are somehow prejudiced, resentment builds over time.

Like the anger within the black community, these resentments aren't always expressed in polite company. But they have helped shape the political landscape for at least a generation. Anger over welfare and affirmative action helped forge the Reagan Coalition. Politicians routinely exploited fears of crime for their own electoral ends. Talk show hosts and conservative commentators built entire careers unmasking bogus claims of racism while dismissing legitimate discussions of racial injustice and inequality as mere political correctness or reverse racism.

Just as black anger often proved counterproductive, so have these white resentments distracted attention from the real culprits of the middle class squeeze—a corporate culture rife with inside dealing, questionable accounting practices, and short-term greed; a Washington dominated by lobbyists and special interests; economic policies that favor the few over the many. And yet, to wish away the resentments of white Americans, to label them as misguided or even racist, without recognizing they are grounded in legitimate concerns—this too widens the racial divide, and blocks the path to understanding.

This is where we are right now. It's a racial stalemate we've been stuck in for years. Contrary to the claims of some of my critics, black and white, I have never been so naïve as to believe that we can get beyond our racial divisions in a single election cycle, or with a single candidacy—particularly a candidacy as imperfect as my own.

But I have asserted a firm conviction—a conviction rooted in my faith in God and my faith in the American people—that working together we can move beyond some of our old racial wounds, and that in fact we have no choice if we are to continue on the path of a more perfect union.

For the African-American community, that path means embracing the burdens of our past without becoming victims of our past. It means continuing to insist on a full measure of justice in every aspect of American life. But it also means binding our particular grievances—for better health care, and better schools, and better jobs—to the larger aspirations of all Americans—the white woman struggling to break the glass ceiling, the white man whose been laid off, the immigrant trying to feed his family. And it means taking full responsibility for own lives—by demanding more from our fathers, and spending more time with our children, and reading to them, and teaching them that while they may face challenges and discrimination in their own lives, they must never succumb to despair or cynicism; they must always believe that they can write their own destiny.

Ironically, this quintessentially American—and yes, conservative—notion of self-help found frequent expression in Reverend Wright's sermons. But what my former pastor too often failed to understand is that embarking on a program of self-help also requires a belief that society can change.

The profound mistake of Reverend Wright's sermons is not that he spoke about racism in our society. It's that he spoke as if our society was static; as if no progress has been made; as if this country—a country that has made it possible for one of his own members to run for the highest office in the land and build a coalition of white and black; Latino and Asian, rich and poor, young and old—is still irrevocably bound to a tragic past. But what we know—what we have seen—is that America can change. That is true genius of this nation. What we have already achieved gives us hope—the audacity to hope—for what we can and must achieve tomorrow.

In the white community, the path to a more perfect union means acknowledging that what ails the African-American community does not just exist in the minds of black people; that the legacy of discrimination—and current incidents of discrimination, while less overt than in the past—are real and must be addressed. Not just with words, but with deeds—by investing in our schools and our communities; by enforcing our civil rights laws and ensuring fairness in our criminal justice system; by providing this generation with ladders of opportunity that were unavailable for previous generations. It requires all Americans to realize that your dreams do not have to come at the expense of my dreams; that investing in the health, welfare, and education of black and brown and white children will ultimately help all of America prosper.

In the end, then, what is called for is nothing more, and nothing less, than what all the world's great religions demand—that we do unto others as we would have them do unto us. Let us be our brother's keeper, Scripture tells us. Let us be our sister's keeper. Let us find that common stake we all have in one another, and let our politics reflect that spirit as well.

For we have a choice in this country. We can accept a politics that breeds division, and conflict, and cynicism. We can tackle race only as spectacle—as we did in the OJ trial—or in the wake of tragedy, as we did in the aftermath of Katrina—or as fodder for the nightly news. We can play Reverend Wright's sermons on every channel, every day and talk about them from now until the election, and make the only question in this campaign whether or not the American people think that I somehow believe or sympathize with his most offensive words. We can pounce on some gaffe by a Hillary supporter as evidence that she's playing the race card, or we can speculate on whether white men will all flock to John McCain in the general election regardless of his policies.

We can do that.

But if we do, I can tell you that in the next election, we'll be talking about some other distraction. And then another one. And then another one. And nothing will change.

That is one option. Or, at this moment, in this election, we can come together and say, "Not this time." This time we want to talk about the crumbling schools that are stealing the future of black children and white children and Asian children and Hispanic children and Native American children. This time we want to reject the cynicism that tells us that these kids can't learn; that those kids who don't look like us are somebody else's problem. The children of America are not those kids, they are our kids, and we will not let them fall behind in a 21st century economy. Not this time.

This time we want to talk about how the lines in the Emergency Room are filled with whites and blacks and Hispanics who do not have health care; who don't have the power on their own to overcome the special interests in Washington, but who can take them on if we do it together.

This time we want to talk about the shuttered mills that once provided a decent life for men and women of every race, and the homes for sale that once belonged to Americans from every religion, every region, every walk of life. This time we want to talk about the fact that the real problem is not that someone who doesn't look like you might take your job; it's that the corporation you work for will ship it overseas for nothing more than a profit.

This time we want to talk about the men and women of every color and creed who serve together, and fight together, and bleed together under the same proud flag. We want to talk about how to bring them home from a war that never should've been authorized and never should've been waged, and we want to talk about how we'll show our patriotism by caring for them, and their families, and giving them the benefits they have earned.

I would not be running for President if I didn't believe with all my heart that this is what the vast majority of Americans want for this country. This union may never be perfect, but generation after generation has shown that it can always be perfected. And today, whenever I find myself feeling doubtful or cynical about this possibility, what gives me the most hope is the next generation—the young people whose attitudes and beliefs and openness to change have already made history in this election.

There is one story in particularly that I'd like to leave you with today—a story I told when I had the great honor of speaking on Dr. King's birthday at his home church, Ebenezer Baptist, in Atlanta.

There is a young, twenty-three year old white woman named Ashley Baia who organized for our campaign in Florence, South Carolina. She had been working to organize a mostly African-American community since the beginning of this campaign, and one day she was at a roundtable discussion where everyone went around telling their story and why they were there.

And Ashley said that when she was nine years old, her mother got cancer. And because she had to miss days of work, she was let go and lost her health care. They had to file for bankruptcy, and that's when Ashley decided that she had to do something to help her mom.

She knew that food was one of their most expensive costs, and so Ashley convinced her mother that what she really liked and really wanted to eat more than anything else was mustard and relish sandwiches. Because that was the cheapest way to eat.

She did this for a year until her mom got better, and she told everyone at the round-table that the reason she joined our campaign was so that she could help the millions of other children in the country who want and need to help their parents too.

Now Ashley might have made a different choice. Perhaps somebody told her along the way that the source of her mother's problems were blacks who were on welfare and too lazy to work, or Hispanics who were coming into the country illegally. But she didn't. She sought out allies in her fight against injustice.

Anyway, Ashley finishes her story and then goes around the room and asks everyone else why they're supporting the campaign. They all have different stories and reasons. Many bring up a specific issue. And finally they come to this elderly black man who's been sitting there quietly the entire time. And Ashley asks him why he's there. And he does not bring up a specific issue. He does not say health care or the economy. He does not say education or the war. He does not say that he was there because of Barack Obama. He simply says to everyone in the room, "I am here because of Ashley."

"I'm here because of Ashley." By itself, that single moment of recognition between that young white girl and that old black man is not enough. It is not enough to give health care to the sick, or jobs to the jobless, or education to our children.

But it is where we start. It is where our union grows stronger. And as so many generations have come to realize over the course of the two-hundred and twenty-one years since a band of patriots signed that document in Philadelphia, that is where the perfection begins.

Fatherhood Speech at the Apostolic Church of God, 2008

Good morning. It's good to be home on this Father's Day with my girls, and it's an honor to spend some time with all of you today in the house of our Lord.

At the end of the Sermon on the Mount, Jesus closes by saying, "Whoever hears these words of mine, and does them, shall be likened to a wise man who built his house upon a rock: and the rain descended, and the floods came, and the winds blew, and beat upon that house, and it fell not, for it was founded upon a rock." [Matthew 7:24–25]

Here at Apostolic, you are blessed to worship in a house that has been founded on the rock of Jesus Christ, our Lord and Savior. But it is also built on another rock, another foundation—and that rock is Bishop Arthur Brazier. In forty-eight years, he has built this congregation from just a few hundred to more than 20,000 strong—a congregation that, because of his leadership, has braved the fierce winds and heavy rains of violence and poverty; joblessness and hopelessness. Because of his work and his ministry, there are more graduates and fewer gang members in the neighborhoods surrounding this church. There are more homes and fewer homeless. There is more community and less chaos because Bishop Brazier continued the march for justice that he began by Dr. King's side all those years ago. He is the reason this house has stood tall for half a century. And on this Father's Day, it must make him proud to know that the man now charged with keeping its foundation strong is his son and your new pastor, Reverend Byron Brazier.

Of all the rocks upon which we build our lives, we are reminded today that family is the most important. And we are called to recognize and honor how critical every father is to that foundation. They are teachers and coaches. They are mentors and role models. They are examples of success and the men who constantly push us toward it.

But if we are honest with ourselves, we'll admit that what too many fathers also are is missing—missing from too many lives and too many homes. They have abandoned their responsibilities, acting like boys instead of men. And the foundations of our families are weaker because of it.

You and I know how true this is in the African-American community. We know that more than half of all black children live in single-parent households, a number that has doubled—doubled—since we were children. We know the statistics—that children who grow up without a father are five times more likely to live in poverty and commit crime; nine times more likely to drop out of school and twenty times more likely to end up in prison. They are more likely to have behavioral problems, or run away from home, or become teenage parents themselves. And the foundations of our community are weaker because of it.

How many times in the last year has this city lost a child at the hands of another child? How many times have our hearts stopped in the middle of the night with the sound of a gunshot or a siren? How many teenagers have we seen hanging around on street corners when they should be sitting in a classroom? How many are sitting in prison when they should be working, or at least looking for a job? How many in this generation are we willing to lose to poverty or violence or addiction? How many?

Yes, we need more cops on the street. Yes, we need fewer guns in the hands of people who shouldn't have them. Yes, we need more money for our schools, and more outstanding teachers in the classroom, and more afterschool programs for our children. Yes, we need more jobs and more job training and more opportunity in our communities.

But we also need families to raise our children. We need fathers to realize that responsibility does not end at conception. We need them to realize that what makes you a man is not the ability to have a child—it's the courage to raise one.

We need to help all the mothers out there who are raising these kids by themselves; the mothers who drop them off at school, go to work, pick them up in the afternoon, work another shift, get dinner, make lunches, pay the bills, fix the house, and all the other things it takes both parents to do. So many of these women are doing a heroic job, but they need support. They need another parent. Their children need another parent. That's what keeps their foundation strong. It's what keeps the foundation of our country strong.

I know what it means to have an absent father, although my circumstances weren't as tough as they are for many young people today. Even though my father left us when I was two years old, and I only knew him from the letters he wrote and the stories that my family told, I was luckier than most. I grew up in Hawaii, and had two wonderful grandparents from Kansas who poured everything they had into helping my mother raise my sister and me—who worked with her to teach us about love and respect and the obligations we have to one another. I screwed up more often than I should've, but I got plenty of second chances. And even though we didn't have a lot of money, scholarships gave me the opportunity to go to some of the best schools in the country. A lot of kids don't get these chances today. There is no margin for error in their lives. So my own story is different in that way.

Still, I know the toll that being a single parent took on my mother—how she struggled at times to the pay bills; to give us the things that other kids had; to play all the roles that both parents are supposed to play. And I know the toll it took on me. So I resolved many years ago that it was my obligation to break the cycle—that if I could be anything in life, I would be a good father to my girls; that if I could give them anything, I would give them that rock—that foundation—on which to build their lives. And that would be the greatest gift I could offer.

I say this knowing that I have been an imperfect father—knowing that I have made mistakes and will continue to make more; wishing that I could be home for my girls and my wife more than I am right now. I say this knowing all of these things because even as we are imperfect, even as we face difficult circumstances, there are still certain lessons we must strive to live and learn as fathers—whether we are black or white; rich or poor; from the South Side or the wealthiest suburb.

The first is setting an example of excellence for our children—because if we want to set high expectations for them, we've got to set high expectations for ourselves. It's great if you have a job; it's even better if you have a college degree. It's a wonderful thing if you are married and living in a home with your children, but don't just sit in the house and watch "SportsCenter" all weekend long. That's why so many children are growing up in front of the television. As fathers and parents, we've got to spend more time with them, and help them with their homework, and replace the video game or the remote control with a book once in awhile. That's how we build that foundation.

We know that education is everything to our children's future. We know that they will no longer just compete for good jobs with children from Indiana, but children from India and China and all over the world. We know the work and the studying and the level of education that requires.

You know, sometimes I'll go to an eighth-grade graduation and there's all that pomp and circumstance and gowns and flowers. And I think to myself, it's just eighth grade. To really compete, they need to graduate high school, and then they need to graduate college, and they probably need a graduate degree too. An eighth-grade education doesn't cut it today. Let's give them a handshake and tell them to get their butts back in the library!

It's up to us—as fathers and parents—to instill this ethic of excellence in our children. It's up to us to say to our daughters, don't ever let images on TV tell you what you are worth, because I expect you to dream without limit and reach for those goals. It's up to us to tell our sons, those songs on the radio may glorify violence, but in my house we live glory to achievement, self respect, and hard work. It's up to us to set these high expectations. And that means meeting those expectations ourselves. That means setting examples of excellence in our own lives.

The second thing we need to do as fathers is pass along the value of empathy to our children. Not sympathy, but empathy—the ability to stand in somebody else's shoes; to look at the world through their eyes. Sometimes it's so easy to get caught up in "us," that we forget about our obligations to one another. There's a culture in our society that says remembering these obligations is somehow soft—that we can't show weakness, and so therefore we can't show kindness.

But our young boys and girls see that. They see when you are ignoring or mistreating your wife. They see when you are inconsiderate at home; or when you are distant; or when you are thinking only of yourself. And so it's no surprise when we see that behavior in our schools or on our streets. That's why we pass on the values of empathy and kindness to our children by living them. We need to show our kids that you're not strong by putting other people down—you're strong by lifting them up. That's our responsibility as fathers.

And by the way—it's a responsibility that also extends to Washington. Because if fathers are doing their part; if they're taking our responsibilities seriously to be there for their children, and set high expectations for them, and instill in them a sense of excellence and empathy, then our government should meet them halfway.

We should be making it easier for fathers who make responsible choices and harder for those who avoid them. We should get rid of the financial penalties we impose on married couples right now, and start making sure that every dime of child support goes directly to helping children instead of some bureaucrat. We should reward fathers who pay that child support with job training and job opportunities and a larger Earned Income Tax Credit that can help them pay the bills. We should expand programs where registered nurses visit expectant and new mothers and help them learn how to care for themselves before the baby is born and what to do after—programs that have helped increase father involvement, women's employment, and children's readiness for school. We should help these new families care for their children by expanding maternity and paternity leave, and we should guarantee every worker more paid sick leave so they can stay home to take care of their child without losing their income.

We should take all of these steps to build a strong foundation for our children. But we should also know that even if we do; even if we meet our obligations as fathers and parents; even if Washington does its part too, we will still face difficult challenges in our lives. There will still be days of struggle and heartache. The rains will still come and the winds will still blow.

And that is why the final lesson we must learn as fathers is also the greatest gift we can pass on to our children—and that is the gift of hope.

I'm not talking about an idle hope that's little more than blind optimism or willful ignorance of the problems we face. I'm talking about hope as that spirit inside us that insists, despite all evidence to the contrary, that something better is waiting for us if we're willing to work for it and fight for it. If we are willing to believe.

I was answering questions at a town hall meeting in Wisconsin the other day and a young man raised his hand, and I figured he'd ask about college tuition or energy or maybe the war in Iraq. But instead he looked at me very seriously and he asked, "What does life mean to you?"

Now, I have to admit that I wasn't quite prepared for that one. I think I stammered for a little bit, but then I stopped and gave it some thought, and I said this:

> When I was a young man, I thought life was all about me—how do I make my way in the world, and how do I become successful and how do I get the things that I want.

But now, my life revolves around my two little girls. And what I think about is what kind of world I'm leaving them. Are they living in a country where there's a huge gap between a few who are wealthy and a whole bunch of people who are struggling every day? Are they living in a country that is still divided by race? A country where, because they're girls, they don't have as much opportunity as boys do? Are they living in a country where we are hated around the world because we don't cooperate effectively with other nations? Are they living a world that is in grave danger because of what we've done to its climate?

And what I've realized is that life doesn't count for much unless you're willing to do your small part to leave our children—all of our children—a better world. Even if it's difficult. Even if the work seems great. Even if we don't get very far in our lifetime.

That is our ultimate responsibility as fathers and parents. We try. We hope. We do what we can to build our house upon the sturdiest rock. And when the winds come, and the rains fall, and they beat upon that house, we keep faith that our Father will be there to guide us, and watch over us, and protect us, and lead His children through the darkest of storms into light of a better day. That is my prayer for all of us on this Father's Day, and that is my hope for this country in the years ahead. May God Bless you and your children. Thank you.

NAACP Speech, 2009

It is an honor to be here, in the city where the NAACP was formed, to mark its centennial. What we celebrate tonight is not simply the journey the NAACP has traveled, but the journey that we, as Americans, have traveled over the past one hundred years.

It is a journey that takes us back to a time before most of us were born, long before the Voting Rights Act, the Civil Rights Act, and Brown v. Board of Education; back to an America just a generation past slavery. It was a time when Jim Crow was a way of life; when lynchings were all too common; and when race riots were shaking cities across a segregated land.

It was in this America where an Atlanta scholar named W.E.B. Du Bois, a man of towering intellect and a fierce passion for justice, sparked what became known as the Niagara movement; where reformers united, not by color but cause; and where an association was born that would, as its charter says, promote equality and eradicate prejudice among citizens of the United States.

From the beginning, Du Bois understood how change would come—just as King and all the civil rights giants did later. They understood that unjust laws needed to be overturned; that legislation needed to be passed; and that Presidents needed to be pressured into action. They knew that the stain of slavery and the sin of segregation had to be lifted in the courtroom and in the legislature.

But they also knew that here, in America, change would have to come from the people. It would come from people protesting lynching, rallying against violence, and walking instead of taking the bus. It would come from men and women—of every age and faith, race and region—taking Greyhounds on Freedom Rides; taking seats at Greensboro lunch counters; and registering voters in rural Mississippi, knowing they would be harassed, knowing they would be beaten, knowing that they might never return.

Because of what they did, we are a more perfect union. Because Jim Crow laws were overturned, black CEOs today run Fortune 500 companies. Because civil rights laws were passed, black mayors, governors, and Members of Congress serve in places where they might once have been unable to vote. And because ordinary people made the civil rights movement their own, I made a trip to Springfield a couple years ago—where Lincoln once lived, and race riots once raged—and began the journey that has led me here tonight as the 44th President of the United States of America.

And yet, even as we celebrate the remarkable achievements of the past one hundred years; even as we inherit extraordinary progress that cannot be denied; even as we marvel at the courage and determination of so many plain folks—we know that too many barriers still remain.

We know that even as our economic crisis batters Americans of all races, African Americans are out of work more than just about anyone else—a gap that's widening here in New York City, as detailed in a report this week by Comptroller Bill Thompson.

We know that even as spiraling health care costs crush families of all races, African Americans are more likely to suffer from a host of diseases but less likely to own health insurance than just about anyone else.

We know that even as we imprison more people of all races than any nation in the world, an African-American child is roughly five times as likely as a white child to see the inside of a jail.

And we know that even as the scourge of HIV/AIDS devastates nations abroad, particularly in Africa, it is devastating the African-American community here at home with disproportionate force.

These are some of the barriers of our time. They're very different from the barriers faced by earlier generations. They're very different from the ones faced when fire hoses and dogs were being turned on young marchers; when Charles Hamilton Houston and a group of young Howard lawyers were dismantling segregation.

But what is required to overcome today's barriers is the same as was needed then. The same commitment. The same sense of urgency. The same sense of sacrifice. The same willingness to do our part for ourselves and one another that has always defined America at its best.

The question, then, is where do we direct our efforts? What steps do we take to overcome these barriers? How do we move forward in the next one hundred years?

The first thing we need to do is make real the words of your charter and eradicate prejudice, bigotry, and discrimination among citizens of the United States. I understand there may be a temptation among some to think that discrimination is no longer a problem in 2009. And I believe that overall, there's probably never been less discrimination in America than there is today.

But make no mistake: the pain of discrimination is still felt in America. By African-American women paid less for doing the same work as colleagues of a different color and gender. By Latinos made to feel unwelcome in their own country. By Muslim Americans viewed with suspicion for simply kneeling down to pray. By our gay brothers and sisters, still taunted, still attacked, still denied their rights.

On the 45th anniversary of the Civil Rights Act, discrimination must not stand. Not on account of color or gender; how you worship or who you love. Prejudice has no place in the United States of America.

But we also know that prejudice and discrimination are not even the steepest barriers to opportunity today. The most difficult barriers include structural inequalities that our nation's legacy of discrimination has left behind; inequalities still plaguing too many communities and too often the object of national neglect.

These are barriers we are beginning to tear down by rewarding work with an expanded tax credit; making housing more affordable; and giving ex-offenders a second chance. These are barriers that we are targeting through our White House Office on Urban Affairs, and through Promise Neighborhoods that build on Geoffrey Canada's success with the Harlem Children's Zone; and that foster a comprehensive approach to ending poverty by putting all children on a pathway to college, and giving them the schooling and support to get there.

But our task of reducing these structural inequalities has been made more difficult by the state, and structure, of the broader economy; an economy fueled by a cycle of boom and bust; an economy built not on a rock, but sand. That is why my administration is working so hard not only to create and save jobs in the short-term, not only to extend unemployment insurance and help for people who have lost their health care, not only to stem this immediate economic crisis, but to lay a new foundation for growth and prosperity that will put opportunity within reach not just for African Americans, but for all Americans.

One pillar of this new foundation is health insurance reform that cuts costs, makes quality health coverage affordable for all, and closes health care disparities in the process. Another pillar is energy reform that makes clean energy profitable, freeing America from the grip of foreign oil, putting people to work upgrading low-income homes, and creating jobs that cannot be outsourced. And another pillar is financial reform with consumer protections to crack down on mortgage fraud and stop predatory lenders from targeting our poor communities.

All these things will make America stronger and more competitive. They will drive innovation, create jobs, and provide families more security. Still, even if we do it all, the African-American community will fall behind in the United States and the United States will fall behind in the world unless we do a far better job than we have been doing of educating our sons and daughters. In the 21st century—when so many jobs will require a bachelor's degree or more, when countries that out-educate us today will outcompete us tomorrow—a world-class education is a prerequisite for success.

You know what I'm talking about. There's a reason the story of the civil rights movement was written in our schools. There's a reason Thurgood Marshall took up the cause of Linda Brown. There's a reason the Little Rock Nine defied a governor and a mob. It's because there is no stronger weapon against inequality and no better path to opportunity than an education that can unlock a child's God-given potential.

Yet, more than a half century after Brown v. Board of Education, the dream of a world-class education is still being deferred all across this country. African-American students are lagging behind white classmates in reading and math—an achievement gap that is growing in states that once led the way on civil rights. Over half of all African-American students are dropping out of school in some places. There are overcrowded classrooms, crumbling schools, and corridors of shame in America filled with poor children—black, brown, and white alike.

The state of our schools is not an African-American problem; it's an American problem. And if Al Sharpton, Mike Bloomberg, and Newt Gingrich can agree that we need to solve it, then all of us can agree on that. All of us can agree that we need to offer every child in this country the best education the world has to offer from the cradle through a career.

That is our responsibility as the United States of America. And we, all of us in government, are working to do our part by not only offering more resources, but demanding more reform.

When it comes to higher education, we are making college and advanced training more affordable, and strengthening community colleges that are a gateway to so many with an initiative that will prepare students not only to earn a degree but find a job when they graduate; an initiative that will help us meet the goal I have set of leading the world in college degrees by 2020.

We are creating a Race to the Top Fund that will reward states and public school districts that adopt 21st century standards and assessments. And we are creating incentives for states to promote excellent teachers and replace bad ones—because the job of a teacher is too important for us to accept anything but the best.

We should also explore innovative approaches being pursued here in New York City; innovations like Bard High School Early College and Medgar Evers College Preparatory School that are challenging students to complete high school and earn a free associate's degree or college credit in just four years.

And we should raise the bar when it comes to early learning programs. Today, some early learning programs are excellent. Some are mediocre. And some are wasting what studies show are—by far—a child's most formative years.

That's why I have issued a challenge to America's governors: if you match the success of states like Pennsylvania and develop an effective model for early learning; if you focus reform on standards and results in early learning programs; if you demonstrate how you will prepare the lowest income children to meet the highest standards of success—you can compete for an Early Learning Challenge Grant that will help prepare all our children to enter kindergarten ready to learn.

So, these are some of the laws we are passing. These are some of the policies we are enacting. These are some of the ways we are doing our part in government to overcome the inequities, injustices, and barriers that exist in our country.

But all these innovative programs and expanded opportunities will not, in and of themselves, make a difference if each of us, as parents and as community leaders, fail to do our part by encouraging excellence in our children. Government programs alone won't get our children to the Promised Land. We need a new mindset, a new set of attitudes—because one of the most durable and destructive legacies of discrimination is the way that we have internalized a sense of limitation; how so many in our community have come to expect so little of ourselves.

We have to say to our children, Yes, if you're African American, the odds of growing up amid crime and gangs are higher. Yes, if you live in a poor neighborhood, you will face challenges that someone in a wealthy suburb does not. But that's not a reason to get bad grades, that's not a reason to cut class, that's not a reason to give up on your education and drop out of school. No one has written your destiny for you. Your destiny is in your hands—and don't you forget that.

To parents, we can't tell our kids to do well in school and fail to support them when they get home. For our kids to excel, we must accept our own responsibilities. That means putting away the Xbox and putting our kids to bed at a reasonable hour. It means attending those parent-teacher conferences, reading to our kids, and helping them with their homework.

And it means we need to be there for our neighbor's son or daughter, and return to the day when we parents let each other know if we saw a child acting up. That's the meaning of community. That's how we can reclaim the strength, the determination, the hopefulness that helped us come as far as we already have.

It also means pushing our kids to set their sights higher. They might think they've got a pretty good jump shot or a pretty good flow, but our kids can't all aspire to be the next LeBron or Lil Wayne. I want them aspiring to be scientists and engineers, doctors and teachers, not just ballers and rappers. I want them aspiring to be a Supreme Court Justice. I want them aspiring to be President of the United States.

So, yes, government must be a force for opportunity. Yes, government must be a force for equality. But ultimately, if we are to be true to our past, then we also have to seize our own destiny, each and every day.

That is what the NAACP is all about. The NAACP was not founded in search of a handout. The NAACP was not founded in search of favors. The NAACP was founded on a firm notion of justice; to cash the promissory note of America that says all our children, all God's children, deserve a fair chance in the race of life.

It is a simple dream, and yet one that has been denied—one still being denied—to so many Americans. It's a painful thing, seeing that dream denied. I remember visiting a Chicago school in a rough neighborhood as a community organizer, and thinking how remarkable it was that all of these children seemed so full of hope, despite being born into poverty, despite being delivered into addiction, despite all the obstacles they were already facing.

And I remember the principal of the school telling me that soon all of that would begin to change; that soon, the laughter in their eyes would begin to fade; that soon, something would shut off inside, as it sunk in that their hopes would not come to pass—not because they weren't smart enough, not because they weren't talented enough, but because, by accident of birth, they didn't have a fair chance in life.

So, I know what can happen to a child who doesn't have that chance. But I also know what can happen to a child who does. I was raised by a single mother. I don't come from a lot of wealth. I got into my share of trouble as a kid. My life could easily have taken a turn for the worse. But that mother of mine gave me love; she pushed me, and cared about my education; she took no lip and taught me right from wrong. Because of her, I had a chance to make the most of my abilities. I had the chance to make the most of my opportunities. I had the chance to make the most of life.

The same story holds for Michelle. The same story holds for so many of you. And I want all the other Barack Obamas out there, and all the other Michelle Obamas out there, to have that same chance—the chance that my mother gave me; that my education gave me; that the United States of America gave me. That is how our union will be perfected and our economy rebuilt. That is how America will move forward in the next one hundred years.

And we will move forward. This I know—for I know how far we have come. Last week, in Ghana, Michelle and I took Malia and Sasha to Cape Coast Castle, where captives were once imprisoned before being auctioned; where, across an ocean, so much of the African-American experience began. There, reflecting on the dungeon beneath the castle church, I was reminded of all the pain and all the hardships, all the injustices and all the indignities on the voyage from slavery to freedom.

But I was also reminded of something else. I was reminded that no matter how bitter the rod or how stony the road, we have persevered. We have not faltered, nor have we grown weary. As Americans, we have demanded, strived for, and shaped a better destiny.

That is what we are called to do once more. It will not be easy. It will take time. Doubts may rise and hopes recede.

But if John Lewis could brave Billy clubs to cross a bridge, then I know young people today can do their part to lift up our communities.

If Emmet Till's uncle Mose Wright could summon the courage to testify against the men who killed his nephew, I know we can be better fathers and brothers, mothers and sisters in our own families.

If three civil rights workers in Mississippi—black and white, Christian and Jew, city-born and country-bred—could lay down their lives in freedom's cause, I know we can come together to face down the challenges of our own time. We can fix our schools, heal our sick, and rescue our youth from violence and despair.

One hundred years from now, on the 100th anniversary of the NAACP, let it be said that this generation did its part; that we too ran the race; that full of the faith that our dark past has taught us, full of the hope that the present has brought us, we faced, in our own lives and all across this nation, the rising sun of a new day begun. Thank you, God bless you, and may God bless the United States of America.

Note

1. Miah, Malik. 2010. "The Black Leaders' Debate: Obama and the Politics of Protest." *Against the Current*, May–June, p. 6.

PERMISSIONS ACKNOWLEDGMENTS

William Monroe Trotter material is republished with permission of the publisher.

For the material from W.E.B. Du Bois, Routledge wishes to thank the Crisis Publishing Co., Inc., the publisher of the magazine of the National Association for the Advancement of Colored People, for the use of the material first published in the April 1915, May 1920, May 1933 and November 1933 issues of Crisis Magazine.

Articles by Bayard Rustin are reprinted with permission from the Estate of Bayard Rustin

Martin Luther King Jr. material is reprinted by arrangement with The Heirs to the Estate of Martin Luther King Jr., c/o Writers House as agent for the proprietor New York, NY.

Malcolm X™ is a trademark of the Family of Malcolm X, licensed by CMG Worldwide. www.MalcolmX.com.

Excerpts from *Stokely Speaks* by Stokely Carmicheal (Kwame Ture) are republished with permission from the *Chicago Review Press*.

Readings from the Black Panthers are republished with permission from the Huey P. Newton Foundation.

Claudia Jones material is republished with permission of the publisher.

Florynce Kennedy material is republished with permission of the publisher.

Angela Y. Davis, "Radical Perspectives on the Empowerment of Afro-American Women: Lessons for the 1980s," Harvard Educational Review, Volume 58:3 (August 1988), pp. 348–353. Copyright © 1988 President and Fellows of Harvard College. All rights reserved. For more information, please visit www.harvardeducationlreview.org.

Material on Clarence Thomas is republished with permission from Transaction Publishers Inc

Articles by Alan Keyes are taken from *Our Character, Our Future* by ALAN KEYES. Copyright ©. Used by permission of Zondervan. www.zondervan.com

Material in the chapter on Michael Steele is taken from the book *Right Now: A 12-Step Program for Defeating the Obama Agenda* by Michael Steele. Copyright © 2009. Published by Regnery Publishing, Inc. All rights reserved. Reprinted by special permission of Regnery Publishing Inc., Washington, D.C.

BIBLIOGRAPHY

Adeleke, Tunde. 2004. *Without Regard to Race: The Other Martin Robison Delany*. Mississippi: University Press of Mississippi.

Angell, Stephen Ward. 1992. *Bishop Henry McNeal Turner and African American Religion in the South*. Knoxville: University of Tennessee Press.

Baxter, Terry. 2004. *Frederick Douglass's Curious Audiences: Ethos in the Age of the Consumable Subject*. New York: Routledge.

Branch, Taylor. 1989. *Parting the Waters: America in the King Years, 1954–63*. New York: Simon & Schuster.

Branch, Taylor. 1999. *Pillar of Fire: America in the King Years 1963–65*. New York: Simon & Schuster.

Breitman, George. Ed. 1965. *Malcolm X Speaks: Selected Speeches and Statements*. New York: Grove Weidenfeld.

Broderick, Francis L. 1970. *W. E. B. Du Bois: Negro Leader in a Time of Crisis*. California: Stanford University Press.

Broderick, Francis L. and August Meier. 1965. *Negro Protest Thought in the Twentieth Century*. New York: Bobbs-Merrill Company.

Brodkin, Karen. 1998. *How the Jews Became White Folks: And What That Says About Race in America*. New Jersey: Rutgers University Press.

Brownmiller, Susan. 1970. *Shirley Chisholm*. Garden City: Doubleday.

Burkett, Randall K. 1978. *Black Redemption: Churchmen Speak for the Garvey Movement*. Philadelphia: Temple University Press.

Carbado, Devon W. and Donald Weise. Eds. 2003. *Time on Two Crosses: The Collected Writings of Bayard Rustin*. San Francisco: Cleis Press.

Carmichael, Stokley/Kwame Toure. 1965. *Stokley Speaks: From Black Power to Pan-Africanism*. Chicago: Chicago Review Press.

Carmichael, Stokley and Ekwueme Michael Thelwell. 2003. *Ready for Revolution: The Life and Struggles of Stokely Carmichael*. New York: Scribner.

Carson, Clayborne. 1991. *The Eyes on the Prize Civil Rights Reader*. New York: Penguin Books.

Chisholm, Shirley. 1970. *Unbought and Unbossed*. Boston: Houghton Mifflin.

Cleaver, Eldridge. 1968. *Soul On Ice*. New York: Delta.

Cooper, Anna Julia. 1969 [1852]. *A Voice From the South*. New York: Negro Universities Press.

Crawford, Vicki, Jacqueline Anne Rouse, and Barbara Woods. 1993. *Women in the Civil Rights Movement: Trailblazers and Torchbearers, 1941–1965*. Indiana: Indiana University Press.

Cronon, Edmund David. 1969. *The Black Moses: The Story of Marcus Garvey and the Universal Negro Improvement Association*. Wisconsin: University of Wisconsin Press.

Crovtiz, L. Gordon. *Clarence Thomas: Confronting the Future*. Washington, DC: Regnery Gateway.

Cruse, Harold. 1967. *The Crisis of the Negro Intellectual: A Historical Analysis of the Failure of Black Leadership*. New York: Quill.

Davies, Carole Boyes. 2008. *Left of Karl Marx: The Political Life of Black Communist Claudia Jones*. Durham, NC: Duke University Press.

Davies, Carole Boyes. 2011. *Claudia Jones: Beyond Containment*. Colorado: Lynne Rienner Publishers.

Davis, Angela Y. 1981. *Women, Race, and Class*. New York: Vintage Books.

Davis, Angela Y. 1984. *Women, Culture, and Politics*. New York: Vintage Books.

Dawson, Michael C. 2001. *Black Visions: the Roots of Contemporary African American Political Ideologies*. Chicago: University of Chicago Press.

DeCaro, Louis A. Jr. 1997. *On the Side of My People: A Religious Life of Malcolm X*. New York: New York University Press.

DeCaro, Louis A. Jr. 1998. *Malcolm and the Cross: The Nation of Islam, Malcolm X, and Christianity*. New York: New York University Press.

Delany, Martin Robinson. [1852] 1993. *The Condition, Elevation, Emigration, and Destiny of the Colored People of the United States*. Baltimore: Black Classic Press.

D'Emilio, John. 2003. *Lost Prophet: the Life and Times of Bayard Rustin*. Chicago: University of Chicago Press.

Douglass, Frederick. 1885. *My Bondage and My Freedom*. New York: Miler, Orton, and Mulligan Publishers.

Douglass, Frederick. [1882] 1962. *Life and Times of Frederick Douglass*. New York: Collier Books.

Du Bois, W.E.B. [1903] 1994. *The Souls of Black Folk*. Chicago: Dover Publishers.

Du Bois, W.E.B. [1920] 1999. *Darkwater: Voices From Within the Veil*. New York: Dover Publishers.

Du Bois, W.E.B. 1968. *The Autobiography of W.E.B. Du Bois: A Soliloquy on Viewing My Life from the Last Decade of Its First Century*. Canada: International Publishers.

Dyson, Michael Eric. 1995. *Making Malcolm: The Myth & Meaning of Malcolm X*. New York: Oxford University Press.

Dyson, Michael Eric. 1996. *Race Rules: Navigating the Color Line*. Massachusetts: Addison-Wesley.

Dyson, Michael Eric. 2000. *I May Not Get There With You: The True Martin Luther King, Jr*. New York: Free Press.

Feagin, Joe R. and Rosalind Chou. 2008. *The Myth of the Model Minority: Asian Americans Facing Racism*. Boulder: Paradigm Books.

Foner, Philip S. 1950. *The Life and Writings of Frederick Douglass, 1817–1849, Vol. 1*. New York: International Publishers.

Foner, Philip S. 1950. *The Life and Writings of Frederick Douglass, 1850–1860, Vol. 2*. New York: International Publishers.

Foner, Philip S. 1950. *The Life and Writings of Frederick Douglass, 1861–1865, Vol. 3*. New York: International Publishers.

Foner, Philip S. Ed. 1970. *The Black Panthers Speak*. Cambridge, MA: De Capo Press.

Fox, Stephen R. 1970. *The Guardian of Boston: William Monroe Trotter*. New York: Atheneum.

Freed, Donald. 1973. *Agony in New Haven: The Trial of Bobby Seale, Ericka Huggins, and the Black Panther Party*. New York: Simon & Schuster.

Gates, Henry Louis Jr. and Kwame Anthony Appiah. Eds. 1994. *Frederick Douglass: Critical Perspectives Past and Present*. New York: Amistad.

Gates, Henry Louis Jr. and Evelyn Brooks Higginbotham. Eds. 2004. *African American Lives*. New York: Oxford University Press.

Giddings, Paula J. 2008. *Ida: A Sword Among Lions: Ida B. Wells and the Campaign Against Lynching*. New York: Amistad.

Grant, Colin. 2008. *Negro with a Hat: The Rise and Fall of Marcus Garvey*. New York: Oxford University Press.

Griffith, Cyril E. 1975. *The African Dream: Martin R. Delany and the Emergence of Pan-African Thought*. Pennsylvania: Pennsylvania State University Press.

Harlan, Louis R. 1972. *Booker T. Washington: The Making of a Black Leader, 1856–1901*. New York: Oxford University Press.

Harlan, Louis R. 1986. *Booker T. Washington: The Wizard of Tuskegee, 1901–1915*. New York: Oxford University Press.

Harris, William Hamilton. 1977. *Keeping the Faith: A. Philip Randolph, Milton P. Webster, and the Brotherhood of Sleeping Car Porters, 1925–37*. Urbana: University of Illinois Press.

Higginbotham, Evelyn Brooks. 1993. *Righteous Discontent: the Women's Movement in the Black Baptist Church*. Massachusetts: Harvard University Press.

Hill, Robert A. Ed. 1987. *Marcus Garvey: Life and Lessons*. Berkeley: University of California Press.

Hilliard, David and Donald Weise. Eds. 2002. *The Huey P. Netwon Reader*. New York: Seven Stories Press.

Hogan, Wesley. 2007. *Many Minds, One Heart: SNCC's Dream for a New America*. Chapel Hill: University of North Carolina Press.

Jackson, David H. 2008. *Booker T. Washington and the Struggle against White Supremacy*. New York: Palgrave Macmillan.

James, Joy. Ed. 1998. *The Angela Y. Davis Reader*. Massachusetts: Blackwell Publishers.

Jeffries, Judson L. 2002. *Huey P. Newton: The Radical Theorist*. Mississippi: University Press of Mississippi.

Jonas, Gilbert. 2004. *Freedom's Sword: The NAACP and the Struggle Against Racism in America, 1909–1969*. New York: Routledge.

Jones, Angela. 2010. "The Niagara Movement 1905–1910: A Revisionist Approach to the Social History of the Civil Rights Movement." *The Journal of Historical Sociology*, Vol. 23, Issue 3, pp. 453–500.

Jones, Angela. 2011. *African American Civil Rights: Early Activism and the Niagara Movement*. Santa Barbara, CA: Praeger.

Joseph, Peniel E. 2001. "Black Liberation Without Apology: Reconceptualizing the Black Power Movement." *Black Scholar*, Vol. 31, Fall/Winter.

Joseph, Peniel E. 2006. *Waiting 'Til the Midnight Hour: a Narrative History of Black Power in America*. New York: Owl Books.

Joseph, Peniel E. 2006. *The Black Power Movement: Rethinking the Civil Rights-Black Power Era*. New York: Routledge.

Joseph, Peniel E. 2010. *Dark Days, Bright Nights: From Black Power to Barack Obama*. New York: Basic Books.

Karim, Benjamin. Ed. 1971. *The End of White World Supremecy: Four Speeches by Malcolm X*. New York: Arcade Publishing.

Kennedy, Flo. *Color Me Flo: My Hard Life and Good Times*. New Jersey: Prentice Hall.

Keyes, Alan. 1996. *Our Character, Our Future: Reclaiming America's Moral Destiny*. Michigan: Zondervan Publishing House.

King Jr., Martin Luther. 1958. *Stride Toward Freedom: The Montgomery Story*. New York: Harper & Row Publishers.

King Jr., Martin Luther. 1963. *Strength to Love*. New York: Harper & Row Publishers.

King Jr., Martin Luther. 1963. *Why We Can't Wait*. New York: Mentor/Penguin Books.

King Jr., Martin Luther. 1967. *Where Do We Go From Here: Chaos or Community?* New York: Harper & Row Publishers.

King Jr., Martin Luther. 1968. *The Trumpet of Conscience*. New York: Harper & Row Publishers.

Kirk, John A. Ed. 2007. *Martin Luther King Jr. and the Civil Rights Movement: Controversies and Debates*. New York: Palgrave Macmillan.

Leader, Edward Roland. 1993. *Understanding Malcolm X: The Controversial Changes in His Political Philosophy*. New York: Vantage Press.

Levine, Daniel. 1999. *Bayard Rustin and the Civil Rights Movement*. New Jersey: Rutgers University Press.

Levine, Robert. S. 1997. *Martin Delany, Frederick Douglass and the Politics of Representative Identity*. North Carolina: University of North Carolina Press.

Levine, Robert S. Ed. 2003. *Martin R. Delany: A Documentary Reader*. Chapel Hill: University of North Carolina Press.

Lewis, Levering David. 1993. *W.E.B. Du Bois: Biography of a Race, 1868–1919*. New York: Henry Holt.

Lewis, Levering David. 2000. *W.E.B. Du Bois: The Fight for Equality and the American Century, 1919–1963*. New York: Henry Holt & Company.

Lincoln, C.E. and L.H. Mamiya. 1990. *The Black Church in the African American Experience*. Durham, NC: Duke University Press.

Lopez, Linda and Adrian D. Pantoja. 2004. "Beyond Black and White: General Support for Race-Conscious Policies among African Americans, Latinos, Asian Americans, and Whites." *Political Research Quarterly*, Vol. 57, No. 4, pp. 633–642.

Malcolm X. 1967. *Malcolm X on Afro-American History*. New York: Pathfinder.

Malcolm X and Alex Haley. 1965. *The Autobiography of Malcolm X*. New York: Grove Press.

Marable, Manning. 1986. *W.E.B. DuBois: Black Radical Democrat*. New York: Twayne Publishers.

Marable, Manning. 2011. *A Life of Reinvention: Malcolm X*. New York: Viking/Penguin Group.

Martin, Waldo E. 1985. *The Mind of Frederick Douglass*. North Carolina: University of North Carolina Press.

McClusky, Audrey Thomas and Elaine M. Smith. Eds. 1999. *Mary McLeod Bethune: Building a Better World*. Indiana: Indiana University Press.

McFeely, William S. 1991. *Frederick Douglass*. New York: W.W. Norton & Co.

McKinney, Richard. 1971. "The Black Church: Its Development and Present Impact." *The Harvard Theological Review*, Vol. 64, No. 4, pp. 452–481.

McMurry, Linda O. 1998. *To Keep the Waters Troubled: The Life of Ida B. Wells*. New York: Oxford University Press.

Miah, Malik. 2010. "The Black Leaders' Debate: Obama and the Politics of Protest." *Against the Current*, May–June.

Moses, Wilson Jeremiah. 1989. *Alexander Crummell: A Study of Civilization and Discontent*. New York: Oxford University Press.

Moses, Wilson Jeremiah. 2004. *Creative Conflict in African American Thought: Frederick Douglass, Alexander Crummell, Booker T. Washington, W. E. B. Du Bois, and Marcus Garvey*. New York: Cambridge University Press.

Newton, Huey P. 1973. *Revolutionary Suicide*. New York: Harcourt Brace Javanovich.

Obama, Barack. 1995. *Dreams From My Father: A Story of Race and Inheritance*. New York: Times Books/Random House.

Obama, Barack. 2008. *The Audacity of Hope: Thoughts on Reclaiming the American Dream*. New York: Vintage Books.

Obama, Barack. 2008. *Change We Can Believe In: Barack Obama's Plan to Renew America's Promise*. New York: Three Rivers Press.

Oldfield, J.R. 1995. *Civilization and Black Progress: Selected Writings of Alexander Crummell on the South*. Charlottesville: University Press of Virginia.

Parenti, Michael. 2010. 9th Edition. *Democracy for the Few*. New York: Wadsworth.

Pfeffer, Paula F. 1990. *A. Philip Randolph: Pioneer of the Civil Rights Movement*. Baton Rouge: Louisiana State University Press.

Redkey, Edwin. 1969. *Black Exodus: Black Nationalist and Back-to-Africa Movements, 1890–1910*. New Haven: Yale University Press.

Redkey, Edwin. Ed. 1971. *Respect Black: The Writings and Speeches of Henry McNeal Turner*. New York: Arno Press.

Reed, Adolph. 1997. *W.E.B. Du Bois and American Political Thought*. New York: Oxford University Press.

Reed, T.V. 2005. *The Art of Protest: Culture and Activism from the Civil Rights Movement to the Streets of Seattle*. Minneapolis: University of Minnesota Press.

Richardson, Marilyn. Ed. 1987. *Maria W. Stewart: America's First Black Woman Political Writer*. Indianapolis: Indiana University Press.

Ritchie, Joy and Kate Ronald. 2001. *Available Means: An Anthology of Women's Rhetoric(s)*. Pittsburgh: University of Pittsburgh Press.

Robinson, Cedric. 1983. *Black Marxism: The Making of the Black Radical Tradition*. London: Zed Books.

Rudwick, Elliot. 1957. "The Niagara Movement." *The Journal of Negro History*, Vol. 42, No. 3, pp. 177–200.

Russell, Thaddeus. 2010. *A Renegade History of the United States*. New York: Free Press.

Seale, Bobby. 1970. *Seize the Time: The Story of The Black Panther Party and Huey P. Newton*. New York: Random House.

Sollors, Werner, Caldwell Titcomb, and Thomas A. Underwood. Eds. 1993. *Blacks at Harvard: A Documentray History of African American Experience at Harvard and Radcliff*. New York: New York University Press.

Steele, Michael. 2009. *Right Now: A 12-Step Program for Defeating the Obama Agenda*. Washington, DC: Regnery Publishing.

Townsend Gilkes, Cheryl. 1998. "Plenty Good Room: Adaptation in a Changing Black Church." *Annals of the American Academy of Political and Social Science*, Vol. 588, pp. 101–121.

Tushnet, Mark V. 2005. *The NAACP'S Legal Strategy Against Segregated Education, 1925–1950*. North Carolina: University of North Carolina Press.

Tyner, James A. 2005. *The Geography of Malcolm X: Black Radicalism and the Remaking of American Space*. New York: Routledge.

Wahle, Kathleen O'Mara. 1968. "Alexander Crummell: Black Evangelist and Pan-Negro Nationalist." *Phylon*, 29, pp. 388–395.

Walker, David. 1965 [1888]. *The Appeal: To the Coloured Citizens of the World, but in particular, and very expressly, to those of THE UNITED STATES OF AMERICA*. New York: Hill and Wang.

Ward, Elijah G. 2005. "Homophobia, Hypermasculinity and the US Black Church." *Culture, Health & Sexuality*, Vol. 7, No. 5, pp. 493–504.

Washington, Booker T. 1900. *Up From Slavery*. New York: Bantam Books.

Washington, James M. Ed. 1986. *The Essential Writings and Speeches of Martin Luther King, Jr.* San Francisco: HarperCollins.

Washington, Mary Helen. 1988. *A Voice from the South: Introduction*. New York: Oxford University Press.

Wells-Barnett, Ida B. 1970. *Crusade for Justice: The Autobiography of Ida B. Wells*. Chicago: University of Chicago Press.

Wintz, Cary D. 1996. *Black Culture and the Harlem Renaissance*. Texas: Texas A& M University Press.

Wintz, Cary D. 1996. *African American Political Thought, 1890–1930: Washington, Du Bois, Garvey, and Randolph*. New York: M.E. Sharpe.

Wolfenstein, Eugene Victor. 1981. *The Victims of Democracy: Malcolm X and the Black Revolution*. Berkeley: University of California Press.

INDEX